SUCCESS! SUCCESS! SUCCESS!

The Book of Inside Secrets

Bottom Line
BOOKS
55 Railroad Avenue, Greenwich, CT 06830

Revised Edition
10 9 8 7 6 5 4 3 2 1

Bottom Line Books are published by Boardroom® Classics.
Boardroom® Classics publishes the advice of expert authorities in many fields. But the use of this material is not a substitute for legal, accounting, health or other professional services. Consult a competent professional for answers to your specific questions.

Library of Congress Cataloging-in-Publication Data
Success! Success! Success! The Book of Inside Secrets
p.cm.
Includes index.
ISBN 0-88723-141-1

55 Railroad Ave., Greenwich, CT 06830

Printed in the United States of America

Contents

21 • FITNESS

22 • BETTER SLEEP

23 • COPING WITH EMERGENCIES

24 • SELF-DEFENSE

25 • BREAKING BAD HABITS

26 • PSYCHOLOGY

27 • VERY PERSONAL

28 • THE SAVVY CONSUMER

29 • FUNTIME

30 • TRAVEL SMARTS

1

Life Lessons

Life Lessons from Ben Franklin

Benjamin Franklin was perhaps the most awesome of our nation's amazing founding fathers.

By his own efforts, he rose from a boyhood of poverty and only two years of formal schooling to become one of America's richest men and a world-renowned author and publisher, scientist and inventor, statesman and diplomat.

But above all, he was a genius at persuasion. Ben Franklin's achievements rested on a foundation of native brilliance and hard work. His incredible success in so many fields, however, was only possible because he was a master salesman. By studying his life and work I discovered his secrets of salesmanship.

I sum up Ben Franklin's formula for sales success by using the acronym *TALKING*... where every letter stands for one of the seven keys for successful persuasion...

•Timing. Franklin was a master of timing. As a printer's apprentice eager to go into business for himself, he decided to become Philadelphia's leading expert in the latest printing techniques in use in London. Unable to afford the trip himself, he made an audacious suggestion to the governor of Pennsylvania—that he should finance Franklin's journey.

Young Ben argued that he would then be able to provide the colony with exceptional printing services...but he was careful to make his case as persuasive as possible by approaching the governor at the most strategic moment —right after he had finished a hearty meal in the colony's best restaurant.

Lesson: For every successful salesman, it's not good enough to have the *right message*...you must also choose the *right moment.*

•Appreciation. Franklin knew the surprising fact of life that people are likely to want to help you with a big favor if they've already done you a small one. He used this psychological knowledge to great effect when he was in France during the Revolutionary War, trying to raise funds for Washington's Continental Army.

The French finance minister, Count Vergennes, refused to see Franklin, who was otherwise an especially popular figure in the royal court. Franklin reasoned that Vergennes was jealous of the attention being showered on Franklin.

Franklin's strategy: He wrote to Vergennes asking to borrow an obscure book from his personal library. Flattered that he had something that Franklin lacked, Vergennes was glad to lend him the book. After this, the two began a useful diplomatic relationship.

Lesson: Anyone who wants someone else to *accommodate* his request should learn to *appreciate* the other one's problems.

• Listening. Franklin was a master at listening closely. This enabled him instantly to take advantage of any opening in the conversation.

Once, at a ball in France, King Louis remarked to Franklin upon a certain lady and the physical features revealed by her low-cut gown. Ben instantly responded: *But you in France can endow our American government, which suffers from the same problem as the lady—an uncovered deficit.*

Lesson: Every good salesman must learn to listen well enough to his customer to find out what he needs and how best to sell it to him—and then to feed back his own words, using *them* to sell him.

• Knowledge. Franklin always realized that knowledge was power. He set up the first library in America and never stopped learning himself. The aged Franklin, universally acknowledged as America's elder statesman, once heard that a town in Massachusetts wanted to erect a bell tower in his honor. He wrote back that he was flattered but suggested that they should use the money instead to set up a library.

Opportunity: Every salesman should take advantage of the knowledge available at libraries—and every other research aid available—to find out where his customers are coming from...and how to get them where he wants them to go.

• Integrity. Franklin was a masterful diplomat—but he never misrepresented his fundamental beliefs. Even as the American minister at the French court, he never sought to disguise his republican beliefs. When playing chess with the French monarch, he began by removing the two kings from the board, joking to the startled Louis XVI that *in America, we have no need of kings.*

Lesson: For salesmen, as for everyone, in the long run honesty is the best policy.

• Need. Franklin realized that the three most persuasive words in the English language are *I need you.* He used their powerful appeal from his youth, when he had to find lodging, to his later prosperity, when he sought to raise funds for public libraries and hospitals.

Lesson: Every persuader should know that when you must ask people for something, the best way to convince them is to show them that they are uniquely qualified to give it to you.

• Giving. Franklin was a master of compromise. He knew that if you want *everything* your own way, you may lose it all. And he was able to exert tremendous influence because he always sought ways to improve his ideas by combining them with those of other people.

Franklin was a strong believer in majority rule. But he was the one who broke a deadlock at the Constitutional Convention by agreeing that the United States should have both a House of Representatives based purely on population and a Senate with just two members from each state, regardless of its population.

Lesson: Every salesman needs to learn the value of giving...nobody ever lost an arm or leg by lending an ear. If you insist on everything, you may wind up with nothing.

Bottom line...

When Thomas Jefferson was sent as the new American minister to France, Count Vergennes asked if he was Franklin's replacement. Jefferson replied, "I have come to succeed Dr. Franklin. No one could ever replace him."

When asked the secret of Franklin's triumph as a diplomat, Jefferson said that it was that he had never heard of Franklin directly contradicting someone else.

The overwhelming lesson of salesmanship taught by Ben Franklin is that the aim of persuasion is not to confront other people, but to appreciate their points of view and try to move them gently in your direction.

Source: James C. Humes, a former legislator and diplomat who wrote and performed a one-man show about Benjamin Franklin. He is the author of *The Ben Franklin Factor: Selling One to One,* William Morrow and Co., 1350 Avenue of the Americas, New York 10019.

Lessons in Life from George Washington

George Washington, the first president of the US, taught Americans what to expect from their leaders. He set an example that has served the nation well for more than 200 years. Washington's personality and behavior can teach us many lessons—in statesmanship and also in life.

Strength...

Washington stood six-feet three-inches tall, head and shoulders above most of his countrymen. At that time, the average American male was five-feet six-inches tall, about three inches shorter than now.

Washington had huge hands and took pride in his physical strength. He put that strength to good use throughout his unusually active life. He was a businessman and farmer, soldier and statesman—often simultaneously. But he recognized the distinction between strength and force.

Example: When Washington campaigned for election to the Virginia State Assembly in 1755, one of his speeches offended a proud man named William Payne. The hot-tempered Payne grabbed a hickory branch and knocked the much bigger Washington to the ground. The next day Washington visited Payne's favorite tavern and demanded to see him. Payne thought he was going to be challenged to a duel. Instead, Washington apologized, retracted his offending comment and asked to shake hands in friendship.

Lesson: The true test of strength is not indulging your natural aggressive instincts but being able to conquer them.

Self-improvement...

As a youth, Washington wanted to become a member of the fashionable Virginia aristocracy and win fame and fortune. He observed very closely the way his high-placed friends and relatives acted and dressed. And he read widely to make up for the deficit in his skimpy formal education.

After he inherited a substantial estate at Mount Vernon, Virginia, from a relative and then came into wealth in 1759 by marrying Martha Custis, the richest woman in Virginia, Washington worked to improve the estate by experimenting with new agricultural techniques and machines, and tested 60 different crops.

As he matured, Washington combined his own ambitions for material advancement with continuous efforts to develop his own character.

Example: Washington had a fierce temper that he struggled his entire life to control. As president, one of his worst moments came when he received news of the fate of an army expedition sent to subdue a group of warring Indian tribes in Ohio. Because of the ineptitude of Major General Arthur St. Clair, who commanded the expedition, two-thirds of the 1,400 men had been killed or wounded.

Washington's immediate reaction was a furious outburst of swearing. But within a few minutes, he controlled his temper and declared that St. Clair would be given a fair hearing.

Lesson: Before you can lead others well, you must learn to lead yourself.

Price of fame...

As president, Washington was probably the most famous man of his time...as a general, his small army of colonials defeated the mightiest army in the world...as a statesman, he was charged with leading a newborn nation based on the unprecedented idea of the freedom of the individual.

Everywhere Washington went, he was met by his countrymen's adulation and foreigners' curiosity. He accepted his historic role but suffered because he was unable to enjoy a private life—outside the one with his closest family members.

Example: Washington's adopted granddaughter, Nelly Custis, described how he would laugh heartily when she described her youthful pranks. But her friends—and even Washington's relatives—were so awed by him that they were afraid to laugh or speak naturally in his presence. When Washington entered a room full of children who were enjoying a lively conversation, they would often be struck dumb. He would stay for a short while and then leave, frustrated and disappointed.

Lesson: Fame is a mixed blessing. A small amount gratifies the ego...but in large doses, it makes life difficult.

Humility...

Washington's military exploits against the French and Indians made him well known when he was still in his 20s.

However, he was acknowledged as the leader of the American cause against the British 20 years later because of the practical economic measures he sponsored...and the judgment he showed as a delegate to the Continental Congress.

After being unanimously chosen as commanding general of the new Continental Army in 1775, Washington left the meeting room, telling Patrick Henry: "From the day I enter upon the command of the American armies, I date my fall and the ruin of my reputation."

Before his first election to the presidency in 1789, he explained his ambition *to live and die on [his] own plantation.* He reluctantly agreed to run for a second term only when it became clear that he was the only person who could hold the country together.

Washington resolutely refused a third term, setting a precedent broken only by Franklin D. Roosevelt and now prohibited by a constitutional amendment.

After he left office in 1797, Washington returned to his beloved Mount Vernon to live the farming life he had always wanted. A constant stream of admirers visited...and each was impressed by the same character traits.

Example: English comedian John Bernard, touring the young United States in 1798, came across an overturned carriage with a woman lying beside it, unconscious, on a rural Virginia road. Bernard saw an elderly man straining to help the woman and free the carriage from the half-ton of luggage burying it.

After they had finished their work, the elderly man invited Bernard to recover at Mount Vernon ...and he realized that the savior was George Washington. Bernard was impressed by Washington's thoughtful remarks—but even more by his behavior, so different from that of most country gentlemen, who would have sent their servants to help. The former president had pitched in himself.

Lesson: Greatness is measured by action, not reputation.

Source: Richard Norton Smith, author of *Patriarch: George Washington and the New American Nation* (Houghton Mifflin, 215 Park Ave. S., New York 10003). He is former director of the Herbert Hoover Presidential Library and now executive director of the Ronald Reagan Center for Public Affairs in Simi Valley, California.

Lessons in Life from John Adams

John Adams, the second president of the United States, was one of the greatest of our nation's founding fathers. Thomas Jefferson and John Adams both died on July 4, 1826—the 50th anniversary of the signing of the Declaration of Independence. And eulogists across the nation saluted both equally as giants in the struggle for American independence.

Most Americans today recognize Jefferson's greatness, but few are aware of Adams's stature. Many people confuse John Adams with his second cousin Samuel Adams, the fiery anti-British orator who organized the Boston Tea Party...or confuse him with his son, John Quincy Adams, the sixth president.

That is unfortunate, because the life of John Adams can show all Americans how to strike a balance between public and private obligations...realism and idealism...and loyalties to friends and personal principles.

Adams in history...

In the Continental Congress, John Adams was a delegate from Massachusetts and the leading advocate of American independence.

As chairman of the committee to draft the Declaration of Independence, he assigned the actual writing task to Thomas Jefferson, Virginia's delegate.

Elected president of the US in 1796, Adams faced the difficult task of following the majestic and revered George Washington. He confronted a major challenge facing the still young United States—to preserve its neutrality between France and Britain, the warring superpowers of the era.

That course required Adams to put the good of the country ahead of his personal ambitions and steer a lonely course with no political allies. His Federalist party was dominated by Alexander Hamilton, who strongly favored the British. The opposition Republicans, led by Vice President Jefferson, favored the French.

Vigorously opposed by both sides, Adams was still able to save the country from war. However, he was not embraced by his own party and did not win a second term in the White House. Although he lost the election, historians today recognize that he led the nation wisely.

• *Lesson:* Resisting pressure from individuals while acting in the best interest of the whole may not be immediately rewarding, but it will be appreciated over the long term.

Realism and self-understanding...

John Adams was never afraid of self-evaluation. He was keenly aware of his own faults. He recognized that he possessed an internal feeling of superiority...tended to be petty and quarrelsome...and was overly ambitious. He thought deeply about how to overcome these flaws.

Assuming that his shortcomings were shared by most men, Adams argued that the new American nation would only flourish if its institutions made allowances for human imperfections...encouraged people to channel their personal ambitions for public good...and contained checks and balances to make change take place at a sensible and slow pace. He favored political *evolution* over *revolution*.

Others—like Jefferson—had a more idealistic and populist attitude. They were thrilled when the French Revolution broke out—assuming that when men were free they would automatically be good. Adams was horrified. He foresaw the bloodshed and social upheaval that followed the revolution.

Over the next 200 years, the disastrous aftereffects of revolutions in France, Russia and China proved Adams right. And today, American society is suffering serious damage because old institutions—including the family—have broken down and there is nothing better to replace them.

• *Lesson:* Enduring change often takes time. Instead of rushing evolution, study and learn from the smaller changes that take place as you move toward your larger goals.

Personal relationships...

Many politicians—today as well as 200 years ago—do not form close personal relationships. They have few true friends...are committed only to their careers...and try to avoid emotional involvement. *Their slogan:* "Don't get mad—get even."

Adams was not like that. He had very strong feelings and was not afraid to show them. But he had a powerful warmth and an intellectual honesty and openness that led to deep and lasting friendships.

Example: After he lost the 1800 election to Jefferson, Adams was so upset that he left Washington, DC before Jefferson was sworn in as his successor. He was the only sitting president who did not attend his successor's inauguration. He spent the next decade vigorously defending his actions and attacking his political opponents.

But after 1812, he reconciled with Jefferson. Despite their continuing political differences, the two began a long and friendly correspondence that lasted for the rest of their long lives.

• *Lesson:* True friendship can transcend political differences. It's possible to disagree without being disagreeable.

Relationships with women...

Adams was no feminist. He opposed allowing women to vote in Massachusetts, and dismissed abstract arguments for women's rights. But he did not look down on women.

He had an extremely close relationship with his wife Abigail, sympathizing with her trials as

First Lady, and formed a strong bond with his daughter-in-law Louisa Catherine. He treated intellectually able women as his equals...and even thought them superior to men. He wrote: *I have a... terror of learned ladies...I can scarcely speak in their presence...I have always come off mortified at the discovery of my inferiority.*

In this respect he was more egalitarian than Jefferson, who believed that all men were created equal, but paid little attention to women. Jefferson restricted his daughters' education to music, art and "womanly" topics, while Adams believed in educating women as seriously as men so they could introduce their children to philosophy, literature and history as taught at his alma mater, Harvard.

• *Lesson:* If you truly respect others, you encourage them to reach their full potential.

Adams and slavery...

Adams strongly opposed slavery all his life. During the struggle for independence he recognized the time was not right to challenge the South to give up slavery, but argued that the issue would eventually have to be dealt with... and predicted it could lead to civil war.

In his old age, Adams vigorously opposed the Missouri Compromise of 1820, which allowed slavery to spread beyond the borders of the South...while Jefferson, the champion of individual liberty and theoretical foe of slavery, remained a slave owner all his life. Later, John Quincy Adams continued his father's anti-slavery tradition as a leading abolitionist in Congress after his term as president.

• *Lesson:* To see what someone really believes, don't just listen to what they say...look at what they do and the legacy they leave.

Source: Joseph J. Ellis, PhD, Ford Foundation Professor of History at Mount Holyoke College in Holyoke, Massachusetts. He is the author of *Passionate Sage: The Character and Legacy of John Adams,* W.W. Norton & Co., 500 Fifth Ave., New York 10110.

Life Lessons from Thomas Jefferson

Author of the Declaration of Independence, founder of the University of Virginia and our nation's third president, Thomas Jefferson was a cerebral politician—a sublime intellect. He was also an exemplar of great pragmatic wisdom, as shown by these anecdotes related by his most famous biographer.

• *Lesson:* Never relinquish your dreams. Jefferson was a young man when he first conceived of founding a university. But not until the eighth decade of his life was he able to realize this ambitious dream. Long after lesser men would have given up, and despite long years of frustration and affliction with heart disease and probably colon cancer, Jefferson pursued his goal with a zeal that belied his old age—and ultimately triumphed.

• *Lesson:* Respect your adversaries. Jefferson endured many fierce political rivalries. Yet no matter how contentious the disagreements, Jefferson always accorded his rivals the utmost respect. When he lost a political battle, he refused to hold a grudge, believing that doing so was simply a waste of time. And when he prevailed, he withstood the temptation to trumpet his victory. Instead, he sought to credit the contributions of his rivals and to help soothe their wounded egos.

When Jefferson became president, Alexander Hamilton—perhaps Jefferson's fiercest rival —wrote to a friend, *While I have not wanted him to become president, I must admit he is an honest man.* Jefferson respected Hamilton as well. At Monticello, two busts face each other across a room. One is of Jefferson, the other of Hamilton.

• *Lesson:* Think rationally, but heed your heart. As a political leader, Jefferson was widely admired for his cool logic and rationality. But he thought that the best decision-makers were those who consulted both their heads and their hearts. Jefferson knew, for instance, that the notion of rebelling against mighty England seemed foolhardy. But the patriots were so eager for revolution that breaking with England seemed not only possible, but inevitable.

• *Lesson:* Be tolerant of others' beliefs. Jefferson today has something of a reputation for being an opponent of religion. In fact, while his beliefs were unorthodox, he himself was deeply religious. He was also extremely tolerant of others' beliefs—so long as these beliefs were truly heartfelt. He was similarly tolerant of differing political beliefs—again, so long as they were heartfelt. Jefferson agreed with Learned Hand, the great judge, who wrote, *The spirit of liberty is the spirit which is not too sure that it is right.* Jefferson was confident enough to fight for his beliefs, yet sufficiently philosophical to know that no one has a monopoly on truth.

• *Lesson:* Be independent, but don't fear conformity. While Jefferson was known as an independent thinker, he was never different just for the sake of being so. For him, avoiding conformity was no less a trap than conformity itself. He refused to join what he called the "herd of independents."

• *Lesson:* Don't give in to self-pity. Upon his wife's death, a grieving Jefferson retired to Monticello, where for two years he allowed himself only minimal social contact. The reclusive life failed to ease his grief. Indeed, he grew so depressed that some family members believed him headed for a breakdown. Only upon the resumption of a busy social life was Jefferson finally able to shake his prolonged sadness. Never again did he allow himself or his daughters to withdraw from the world, no matter how great their difficulties.

• *Lesson:* Be a lifelong student. A gifted linguist, scientist and logician as well as an astute politician, Jefferson was, in the opinion of many, the smartest chief executive in history. While native intelligence accounted for much of his intellectual strength, his appetite for learning played a key role. Jefferson regularly read several books at once, and he insisted upon rereading his favorites. He mastered Latin, Greek, German and French in order to read important works in the original. Most important, he never stopped pursuing his education, tutoring himself wherever and whenever possible. Once, during a six-week European trip, Jefferson not only taught himself Spanish but also read the major Spanish classics.

Jefferson even compiled his own version of the Bible. Yet despite his focus on reading, Jefferson was no bookworm. Throughout his life he made it a point to listen to and learn from those around him, including children and servants as well as distinguished colleagues.

• *Lesson:* Do your share and much more, if necessary. While Jefferson is duly credited with founding the University of Virginia, his actual contribution to the school was far greater. He laid out the curriculum, hired the faculty and selected library books. Once, upon learning that an instructor hired to teach four languages knew only three, Jefferson insisted that the instructor be ready to teach all four languages the following year.

• *Lesson:* Live within your means. Jefferson the President was probably the finest fiscal manager in our nation's history. Yet a handful of unwise decisions kept Jefferson the private citizen on the brink of financial ruin.

He chose to build his beloved Monticello on land that while pretty, was steep and rocky and therefore poorly suited for cultivation. He continued to indulge his appetite for fine food, wine, books and other luxuries long after prudence dictated that he stop. He assumed he would inherit a fortune—yet all his father-in-law left was debts. And, a friend for whom Jefferson reluctantly co-signed a bank note defaulted on the loan. *Result:* Jefferson's heirs lost Monticello.

• *Lesson:* Always help others. Jefferson remained friendly and approachable throughout his long life, even as President. Once, President Jefferson and several companions were fording a deep stream on horseback. A man standing on the bank watched as several of the riders headed across the river, then stopped Jefferson and asked for a ride. Without a moment's hesitation, Jefferson hauled the man onto his horse and carried him across. Later, astonished witnesses asked the man if he had known his benefactor's identity. *No,* replied the man. *Then why did you pick him and not one of the others?* asked one of the witnesses. *Because,* said the man, *he looked like he'd be willing to help.*

• *Lesson:* Be efficient—but take time for important things. Even as President, Jefferson insisted upon answering his own mail. He thought people deserved the courtesy of a personal reply...and knew that writing strengthened both his mind and his connection to friends and constituents. Yet in other areas of his life, Jefferson emphasized efficiency. He organized his days along a very tight schedule. He invented a rotating book holder that let him read several books at once. He even placed his bed in an alcove between his bedroom and his office. When he awoke with an idea, he could jump straight out of bed and into his office.

Source: Alf J. Mapp, Jr., eminent scholar emeritus and Louis I. Jaffe professor of history at Old Dominion University, Norfolk, Virginia. Mapp is the author of two books on Jefferson, including *Thomas Jefferson: Passionate Pilgrim,* Madison Books, 4720 Boston Way, Lanham, Maryland 20706.

Lessons from George Orwell

With the collapse of the Soviet Union, it may seem that the world of the 1990s has at last gone beyond the message of George Orwell's writings, especially his two most famous novels, *1984* and *Animal Farm.*

But even after the fall of communism and the world's largest totalitarian government, Orwell still has something very important to teach us, as we try to create a global future for ourselves different from the past. His core ideas are timeless and account for his lasting popularity and tremendous readership—his books have been translated into 68 different languages. *Animal Farm* and *1984* together have sold more than 60 million copies.

• *Lesson:* Individuals are more important than systems. Orwell's political outlook had a much more personal element than is true of most political thinkers. Orwell's focus was on the human element. He was constantly aware of how the individual's rights and feelings would always rise above any theory, any plan, any system. That brought him under attack from the intellectuals, who also had a stake in the theories. *Their view:* Because Orwell was not theoretical enough, there was somehow a flaw in his thinking.

• *Lesson:* Every system has its flaw. Orwell taught us to be skeptical of theories and systems and of the "isms" that people are constantly trying to sell us—grand solutions to social or political problems.

These systems often fail because of the very thing Orwell pointed out...they don't take into account the individuality of real people. Orwell wanted us always to remember that every human system has its flaw. You can never create any theory or system that can accommodate all the thousands of different ways that people can try to outwit a theory or thwart it in some way. Any system that has no room for differences will be repressive.

• *Lesson:* Take into account the practical realities. Americans have always been pragmatic. That may be the reason why we've accomplished as much as we have. We suffer when we become too obsessed with theory. Certainly during the Cold War, I think we magnified communism. It turned out to be a paper tiger. The Russian economy has collapsed—and yet for years we held them up as great thinkers and warriors. We were wrong.

When Americans are pragmatic, when we roll up our shirtsleeves and look carefully at a situation, not from a theoretical point of view, but just simply asking how we can make something work, we do pretty well.

• *Lesson:* It's important—and possible—to be decent. This is a very old-fashioned concept, which intellectuals scoff at.

Orwell used the word *decent* over and over again.

He talked often about the decency of the common man. By that, he simply meant trying to do the right thing. He didn't mean taking a sanctimonious or self-righteous point of view, telling others that they should do this and shouldn't do that.

Orwell said that at the base of all society, of all civilization, there had to be some concept of what's right and what's wrong—that some things are good for us and some are bad. Our task is to know the difference.

Orwell lived what he preached...

Orwell lived what he preached. Usually people who preach moral values don't follow their own advice—and we are very wary of them.

When Orwell said that he thought it was important to fight for democracy against fascism, he followed through on it. Even before Hitler began to march across Europe, Orwell went to Spain to fight in the Spanish Civil War with the army that was trying to stop the fascist-supported forces of General Franco. He got a bullet through his throat for his troubles and almost died.

Throughout his life, Orwell sacrificed personal comfort and safety in order to stand up for the things that he believed were right.

The message he gives to the rest of us: Make up your own mind as to what you think is right or wrong and stand by it. Don't be afraid of losing or failing—*face failure.* Your life won't last forever that way, but it will be a life you can be proud of.

That's hard for us to follow, because most of us prefer living comfortably, without having to make sacrifices. Orwell believed that you establish in your own mind what you think is decent, and then you practice what you believe with integrity. You don't back down, you don't engage in hypocrisy.

Craftsman...

Anyone who has ever had to pick up a pen or sit down at a keyboard and write could learn something from Orwell. He was a skilled and melodious writer.

Many people who preach democratic values do so in a rather elitist prose style. Orwell tried very hard to make his writing accessible to a wide variety of people.

Trying to be very clear and very straightforward is extremely difficult. When you read Orwell's writing, it's deceptively easy on the surface. If you were to look at his manuscripts, however, you would see how difficult it was for him to achieve that surface simplicity.

He constantly revised. He was trying to get just the right word for just the right state of mind or feeling.

Many writers make the mistake of forgetting that there's someone on the other end who's going to read what they've written. If you're too easy on yourself while you write, you're probably going to make it harder on someone else.

Big Brotherism is still a threat...

Orwell wasn't describing just a Soviet-style system, or even a fascist-style system. He was describing totalitarianism in all its forms. Totalitarian tendencies can exist even in a society that on the surface seems free.

We all know that there are various Big Brothers—maybe also Big Sisters. There are people in our lives—in government, in business—who try to make us do things we don't want to do, to serve them rather than serve the interests of the whole. The methods those people employ on a smaller scale are no different from the ones that Orwell talks about in *1984.*

Big Brother in *1984* was probably American. Orwell divided the world into three huge zones of influence—Oceania, Eurasia and Eastasia. Winston Smith lives in Oceania—whose currency is the dollar. It is North and South America combined. This American empire stretches from the US across the Atlantic to Britain, which has now been renamed Airstrip One. The Americans use the island of Great Britain as a huge aircraft carrier. That isn't far-fetched, because when the Cold War started we established huge air bases in Britain, which are still there. When we struck Libya, the planes took off from outside Oxford, England.

This illustrates how accurate Orwell was in his predictions of what would happen. He said that if the working-class people—the *proles*—ever woke up and realized that there are more of them than there are on the side of the Big Brother types, they would be able to pull the system down. If you think about it, that's exactly what happened. The people went out into the streets and pulled down the Berlin Wall with their hands. They surrounded the tanks in Moscow and protected Yeltsin and Gorbachev.

I don't think we'll ever be able to stop fighting to protect our privacy and individual rights, because someone's always out there trying to take them away from us—for their own interests or those of the larger group. As long as individual freedom and privacy are an issue, *1984* is still relevant.

It illustrates the way people allow—or can allow—those rights to be taken away, and then wake up and realize what they've lost. Orwell believed that with any institution, we need to be constantly vigilant about what we're giving up to authority.

If another relevancy is needed for *1984,* we can't overlook the fact that even though the Soviet Union has fallen there still are totalitarian states around the world.

China remains as bad as any Orwellian state. We've still got those kinds of societies to deal with.

Read Orwell...

Many of his other works, including *Down and Out in Paris and London* and *Homage to Catalonia,* and his other novels and essays, may be ordered through your local bookstore.

Source: Michael Shelden, PhD, professor of English at Indiana State University, and author of *Orwell: The Authorized Biography.* HarperCollins, 10 E. 53 St., New York 10022.

Life Lessons from Eleanor Roosevelt

While it is unclear what sort of national example Hillary Clinton will set, the life of Eleanor Roosevelt argues persuasively that the truly important ingredients for a fulfilling life are compassion, intelligence and grit.

As a beloved First Lady...as an indefatigable champion of the disadvantaged...and as someone who overcame numerous personal struggles, Eleanor Roosevelt has much to teach us...

• *Lesson:* Act upon your convictions and ignore your critics. Eleanor Roosevelt was never afraid to stand up for what she believed in. Over the years, she lent emotional and financial support to a number of unpopular causes, including housing for the poor, relief for Jewish refugees and civil rights for African-Americans. Reporters and political rivals belittled these efforts, arguing that women had no place in political affairs.

Yet no matter what was written or said or drawn about her—for she was a favorite target of political cartoonists—Eleanor Roosevelt never wavered in her commitment to what she believed to be right. "Every woman in public life, she once explained, needs to develop skin as tough as rhinoceros hide." Only one thing about these attacks bothered her—their effect on her friends and family. In 1940, she wrote to a friend, *I am sorry these attacks are causing my friends so much anguish, but I intend to keep on saying what has to be said.* This rare combination of courage and compassion is, I believe, Eleanor Roosevelt's greatest legacy.

• *Lesson:* Transform your misfortunes into compassion for others. Eleanor Roosevelt was born into the kind of family that is now called dysfunctional. When Eleanor was only four, her beautiful but emotionally remote mother told her young daughter, "You have no looks." Four years later, Eleanor's mother died. Eleanor's father— the younger brother of President Theodore Roosevelt—was an alcoholic given to irresponsible and occasionally bizarre behavior. He died when Eleanor was 10.

A child raised under such conditions might easily have grown up to be cold and withholding. But Eleanor matured into an unusually warm and generous woman, full of compassion for those on the margins of life. I was lucky enough to meet her in the late 1950s, and when we were introduced, she smiled, took my hand and looked me straight in the eye. She did the same with everyone she met because she truly loved all people. Wherever she went and whenever she spoke, people knew instantly that her view of the world included them.

• *Lesson:* Overcome your prejudices. Despite their long tradition of philanthropy, the family into which Eleanor Roosevelt was born was marked by intolerance and bigotry. Her early letters reveal her own strong dislike of some groups. Yet unlike other members of her family and her social class, Eleanor Roosevelt retained an open mind...and slowly but surely her attitudes began to change. She cultivated friendships with a large and disparate group of people, including several groups considered "off-limits" by other members of her class.

• *Lesson:* Be steadfast and loyal. The marriage of Eleanor and Franklin Roosevelt was not without its share of problems. Franklin Roosevelt was not always faithful to his wife, and she appears to have had affairs as well.

Yet even after their ardor had cooled, the Roosevelts continued to honor and respect one another. Franklin continually involved Eleanor in his work, and she continued to give full support to his political career. They knew their union was imperfect, but their mutual respect and admiration remained for both of them a source of great emotional strength.

• *Lesson:* Help others as directly as possible. For generations, Eleanor Roosevelt's family had devoted itself to philanthropic and charitable work. Her grandfather helped found both the Children's Aid Society and the Museum of Natural History. So it came as no surprise when, as a young woman, Eleanor Roosevelt took up charity work.

But instead of doing something "safe," such as fund-raising, she chose to lend a hand directly, by working in a settlement house on Manhattan's Lower East Side. This decision horrified her family, who feared she was exposing herself to disease and hardship. But Eleanor continued to work in the settlement house for some time, and she even made it a point to take her suitor Franklin to see the conditions under which poor Americans were forced to live. Eleanor's commitment to the poor touched not only her life and the lives of those she helped, but also helped develop the nascent political policies of a future president.

• *Lesson:* Be proud, but modest. Even after years as a beloved First Lady, Eleanor Roosevelt remained humble and unassuming. Once, upon arriving at an airport, she spied a red carpet and school band...and noted there must be someone important on board, not considering that the display might be for her.

Source: Blanche Wiesen Cook, PhD, professor of history and women's studies at John Jay College and the Graduate Center of the City University of New York. She is vice president for research at the American Historical Association and the author of *Eleanor Roosevelt: Volume One, 1884–1933*. Viking Penguin, 375 Hudson St., New York 10014.

Lessons in Life from Harry Truman

When Harry Truman became President of the United States, few people anywhere in the world expected much of him. But just a few years later, Winston Churchill was calling him the man who saved Western civilization.

Truman's life shows how a seemingly average man was able to change the nation...and the world.

He got to the White House without the help of inherited wealth, personal glamour, influential family connections or higher education. Yet he was the President who...

...put a stop to traditional American isolationism.

...introduced the strategy of containment of the Soviet Union.

...pushed through the Marshall Plan to rebuild Western Europe.

...ended segregation in the US armed forces and the federal Civil Service.

His achievements teach us a series of traditional lessons in life that have been forgotten by many today.

• Hard work. Truman's father, an unsuccessful businessman who eventually returned to farming, taught young Harry how to work hard. And for his whole life, Truman put all he had into everything he did, rising early and working hard well into the night.

When serving in the Senate, he arrived so early that he became the first senator ever issued a key to the building. He learned so much about World War II defense programs that his Committee on War Production inspired major improvements in defense industries, saved millions of taxpayer dollars and gave him a national reputation that helped him become Vice President.

When he suddenly became President, many people didn't think that he could fill Roosevelt's shoes...but when they saw how he tackled the job, they quickly changed their minds.

Lesson: If you really want to move up, be prepared to buckle down.

•Persistence. Before he entered politics, Truman had a long record of failure. As a young man working on the barely profitable family farm, he made unsuccessful efforts to become a speculator in land...in zinc mines... in oil leases ...and he was a 38-year-old bankrupt haberdasher when he first ran for political office. But he never let fear of failure discourage him.

•When Tom Pendergast, the Kansas City Democratic boss and Truman's political mentor, was convicted on corruption charges, Truman faced an almost impossible race for his second Senate term against the man who sent Pendergast to jail. But he persevered...and won an upset victory.

•In the famous 1948 Presidential race against Thomas E. Dewey, Truman's friends...advisers ...all the pundits...were sure he couldn't win. The only man who believed he could was Truman himself. He put on such a gallant fight that millions of people voted for him even though they expected him to lose...and he pulled off the most famous upset victory in US political history.

Lesson: Don't think of yourself as a failure—despite temporary setbacks...you can bounce back to greater heights than before.

•Education. Truman had only a high school education. But he never stopped learning.

•In World War I, he was able to compete successfully in math-intensive artillery school... then was assigned to teach math and engineering to other officers, graduates of top colleges.

•Truman was a voracious reader, and his knowledge of history gave him a perspective on the nation's problems extending beyond the next election. The containment policy introduced by Truman contributed to the eventual collapse of world communism 45 years later.

Lesson: The worth of your education isn't measured by what school you went to or how long you stayed there...it's whether you keep thinking after you leave.

•Loyalty. No "kiss-and-tell" memoirs were written by people close to Truman. Unlike many later Presidents, he inspired lasting loyalty...not fear...in those who worked for him.

•During World War I, Truman commanded 200-odd tough, undisciplined soldiers. He used tough discipline to whip them into a crack artillery battery...but looked after their welfare like a father. Long after the war, many of his "boys" volunteered for his campaigns... and they marched in his inaugural parade.

•When Kansas City political boss Tom Pendergast died in disgrace after serving his jail term, shunned by all, newly inaugurated Vice President Truman flew to Kansas City to honor the memory of his first political supporter.

Lesson: If you want others to be loyal to you, show loyalty to them.

•Family values. Harry Truman really practiced what today's politicians preach when they invoke traditional family values. He relied on his family for emotional support...and his family could rely on him.

•As a 21-year-old in 1905, he left a promising position with a Kansas City bank when his father needed him to work on the family farm. Without complaint, he came immediately and stayed for 12 years. He worked long hours at unpleasant and often menial tasks, until World War I.

•He fell in love with Bess Wallace as a young man in Sunday school, but couldn't persuade her to marry him until he was 33 years old. After their marriage, because Bess was attached to her mother, the couple moved into the Wallace home. And even when he moved to the White House, his mother-in-law came along.

Lesson: Strong family ties not only provide great support...but also require personal sacrifices.

•Self reliance. The famous sign on Truman's desk said "The Buck Stops Here"...and it was true. He dug deeply into every subject that concerned him and was never afraid to take advice, but when the time came to decide, he made the decision himself.

•Before British rule over Palestine ended in 1948, the State Department advised Truman very strongly that the US should not support establishment of a fragile, tiny, new Jewish state surrounded by violently hostile Arab countries. Truman agonized over the issue for months as it was developing. Then he made his decision...and recognized the State of Israel just 11 minutes after it was proclaimed.

•During the Korean War, General Douglas MacArthur carried out a brilliant counterattack, driving the North Koreans back behind their original lines. But MacArthur disregarded orders to change his strategy following massive Chinese involvement in the war...so Truman dismissed him, in spite of the public storm it would provoke because of the General's fame.

•Truman came from a family very sympathetic to the Confederate side in the Civil War, and he was uneasy about social integration between the races. But he knew he was President of all the people, and he fought vigorously in favor of civil rights...seriously splitting the Democratic party in an election year.

Lesson: Always listen to what the experts have to say. But you're the one who must make the decision, so don't be afraid to use your own judgment.

Bottom line...

Harry Truman grew up 100 years ago. He lived by the values he learned then...hard work, persistence, self-reliance, loyalty to family, friends and nation. Those 19th-century values aren't fashionable today. But as the 21st century approaches, they still have much to offer to individuals...and nations.

Source: Irwin Unger, PhD, professor of history at New York University and Pulitzer Prize-winning author of six books on modern American history.

Lessons in Life from Henny Youngman

Internationally famous comedian Henny Youngman is close to 90 and still as funny as ever. Moreover he continues to be as active on the comedy circuit as he's been all his life. *Bottom Line/Personal* found him at his "office"—a VIP table at the Friar's Club in New York, complete with his own telephone—and asked him for the secrets of his long-lived success. *Here's what he had to tell us...*

•Find out what you want to do—and learn all about that business. Few people take the time to find what they are really good at. And ...they're so busy working and paying the family bills that they don't take the time to think and grow.

In my case, none of the adults around me recognized what I was really good at when I was a kid. In fact, I was thrown out of my classes because I was funny—and therefore disruptive to the class.

Now, you may ask yourself—I certainly have—why couldn't the teachers have laughed at me? Why couldn't they have figured out that my being funny was a talent, not a menace? Why didn't they tell my parents, "This kid is funny. Let's develop that." Instead, they sent me out of class because I made everybody laugh.

•Your greatest talent may be something that's right under your nose, but you don't see it. Your real talent may be the very thing everybody complains about. It could also be a talent for something no one around you recognizes as a way to make a living. When I was a kid, I never even dreamed that you could make a living being a comedian. My mother wanted me to be the violinist, Jascha Heifetz—only I couldn't, because Jascha Heifetz was Jascha Heifetz already.

Once, we were both on the *Ed Sullivan Show,* and afterwards I took his violin by mistake. It was a Stradivarius, worth big, big dollars—and all the police were out looking for me. That's the closest I ever came to being Jascha Heifetz. I still play the violin—badly—in all my shows. It's a great prop.

•Get experience. Whatever you're selling, whatever you're doing, you've got to have something to talk about. You've got to have merchandise to put on the shelf.

If you're going to be successful, you have to know what you're doing. You can't blame everything on luck. There's no such thing as luck, all by itself. Luck is where you find it—but you have to find it. Meanwhile, get as much experience as you can, so you'll be ready for luck when you run into it.

I was lucky at certain points along the way. I started out as a musician—I had a band. People came in late—and I made fun of them, and everybody laughed. I was funny.

One night the boss said, "The emcee didn't show up, Henny. I have a big banquet here. Get on and tell your jokes. Save my life." I was so good that I let the band go—and I became a comic.

•Be persistent. If you keep going, you will eventually run into what you really want to do. There's always somebody that needs you somewhere. You can't give up easily.

In my own case, I didn't get discouraged because I didn't have the gift to become a major violinist—or a band leader. My family and friends certainly lived through some difficult times listening to me practice. I used what I had and when a different opportunity came along, I was open to it.

•*Nem de Gelt*—get the money. It has many layers of meaning. The most obvious is, don't believe all the baloney that people tell you when they're describing what they're going to do for you soon. If there's no money that comes with it, it isn't real.

There's a modern version of this that says, *Wait until the check is in your hands.* But, let me tell you, that's not good enough. Back in the 1930s, during the Great Depression, I learned a lot of lessons that are useful to us all today too: A check can bounce...the money counts...you've got to pay the rent...get whatever you can get, with reason...and keep going until somebody finally gives you what you want.

•Don't let your pride get in your way. About half a century ago, I was on the *Kate Smith Show,* earning a thousand dollars a week. In the 1930s, a thousand dollars a week was a small fortune! I did that for two years before I decided to leave. I thought I would be able to ask for the same amount from other clients. I sat around for weeks with no takers.

Finally, one night at Lindy's restaurant, a friend who had heard me moaning and complaining about how tough times were told me I had to decide whether I wanted to keep my pride and starve to death in grand style...or whether I was willing to swallow my pride and work for what people were willing to pay.

It didn't take long to make that decision. I got a job at $350 per week working in a club owned by Billy Rose. And just a short time later I got another job for $750 a week, that I could hold at the same time. So by working for what people were willing to pay, I ended up making what I wanted to after all!

•If you like what you're doing, keep doing it. If you've got something good going—and you enjoy it, and you're in demand, and you're healthy enough to do it—why retire? I'm against the practice of retiring people at the age of 65. I really enjoy what I do—putting on my show...making the deals.

•*Mensh tracht, Gott lacht.* A Yiddish proverb, but it's not a Yiddish lesson—it's a lesson about life. It says: *Man plans, God laughs.*

In other words, life is an accident. Plan ahead as much as you want...plot out your career moves as though it were an arithmetic problem if you enjoy doing that sort of thing. Fate may have something else in mind. It might be great, it might be terrible, but hang on—see how it turns out.

I'm close to 90, and I still don't know why all these wonderful things happened. It's been like a dream. Sometimes I wonder what would have happened if I had done things differently—if I had been a little bit better student, or a better fiddle player. But if I had, I wouldn't have had this fascinating life in show business.

The best I could wish for you is—when you get to be my age—you should be so active... so involved...and so happy.

Source: Henny Youngman, author of *Take My Life, Please!* William Morrow and Company, 1350 Avenue of the Americas, New York 10019.

From David Brown: Lessons in Living Life To its Very Fullest

When David Brown was a young man, the number-one best seller was *Life Begins at Forty,* by Walter B. Pitkin.

Today, that view is outmoded...it's *puberty* that begins at 40. Life doesn't get better until after 50...and it gets even better later on, Brown says in his new book, *The Rest of Your*

Life is the Best of Your Life: David Brown's Guide to Growing Gray (Disgracefully).

The years between 65 and 75 have been the best years of his life...best for work, best for making money, best for making love.

While he admits that he had a lot of fun before 50—as his friend Alan J. Lerner put it, he's glad *he's not young anymore*. Youth is too fragile, too easily intimidated, unsure of itself.

At 75, David Brown likes himself, and now he says and does what he wants—without worrying much about what others may think. The sense of freedom one can have after passing 50 is exhilarating.

Simple rules for staying young...

•Don't retire. Brown intends to work until his death. What keeps him going is his involvement in work. The work is the machine, the motive.

Almost everybody he knows who feels young, vital and sexy—no matter what his/her age—is working. He is certain that if he stopped working and started getting up late, his machine would slow down...and stop.

With his friends Richard and Lili Zanuck, David Brown produced the movie *Cocoon*. They discovered that the older actors they selected to play retirees—Hume Cronyn, Jessica Tandy, Jack Gilford, Maureen Stapleton, Don Ameche, Gwen Verdon—looked too young to play their own ages. They had to be aged with makeup and taught to limp and bend over. They had kept on working and never had time to grow old!

How powerfully retirement can affect your health was shown by a recent study of airline pilots. When they retired at age 55, this group of pilots was in certifiably good health. At the time Brown wrote his book—only a few years later—their mortality rate was higher than that of the general public.

Many people hate their work, he observes, and can't wait for "the machine to stop." But if you retire from one thing, you can always go on and do something you really love.

•Start planning your second career while you're in your first one. Brown believes that when you get a job, you should start looking for the next one—or for the next career—however covertly you do it. If you're 35, prepare to deal with getting fired when you're 55 or 60. If you don't get fired, the planning won't hurt you. But you must start thinking creatively while there's time. Identify what interests you, and what you can develop on the outside as an independent person.

It's very tough for people who work in companies to do this because they've been programmed to depend upon the system. They come to work knowing they'll be required to do certain tasks that have been laid down for them.

But so many companies now are in a desperate state. Those that can't pay their bills pare down their work forces. The economists are saying that most of those who are being let go will not be rehired. What is going on, in Brown's opinion, is not a temporary shrinkage. It's a basic restructuring. So always keep your eye on your options 10 or 20 years down the road.

•Be prepared to start over. What can you do if you are a company man who didn't want to stop working—but got retired?

Brown says he would cut his standard of living, possibly by moving to a much less costly place. Next, he would look around to see what services were needed. Is a messenger service required? Is there something else that isn't being provided in the community?

Then he would go and try to raise money... a modest amount of capital. In other words, he would try to get someone else interested in staking him to a business, after he had done some careful research.

When Brown and Richard Zanuck founded their own movie-production company—after being thrown out of executive posts that they thought they had for life—they decided that never again would they let their lives be controlled by others. But—they weren't certain that they would succeed on their own.

Twice in his fifties, Brown was jobless, a former top executive reduced to collecting unemployment insurance and sending out résumés. What saved him was his refusal to face facts.

If he had held onto his old job, Brown, as an over-65 employee, would have had to retire long ago. Launching out on his own was the best thing that ever happened to him, he feels.

•Worship your body. Even if your body doesn't look as good to you as it did in your twenties, his best advice is to take good care of your body. You won't get far without it. This means paying attention to what you eat and drink, to how much exercise you get, and to the right kind of medical care.

An old friend of his, a gerontologist at Rockefeller University, says that the best recipe for a long, healthy life is to eat half of what you do now...exercise regularly...and make love every day.

Watching your weight is just common sense, and it may have life-extending virtues, too. Experiments at Cornell University and UCLA have shown that underfed mice lived longer than mice who were fed as much as they wanted. Most of the men and women he knows who have reached the age of 80 or more are thin. But don't get too thin, he cautions. There's no advantage to being emaciated. Moderation in all things is a good rule.

The same goes for exercise. There's no medical evidence that hard exercise extends life, and some doctors believe it shortens it. On the other hand, the authors of *Total Fitness in Thirty Minutes a Week* say 10 minutes of peak effort every day gives you 80% of the cardiovascular conditioning benefits of hours of exercise.

About medical care: Remember, doctors aren't gods. If you get a diagnosis that is ominous, or if your doctor wants to do a little fancy tailoring on your interior, get a second opinion. And maybe a third.

One phenomenally successful producer, David Geffen, dropped out of the entertainment business for three years, after being told he was dying of cancer. He wasn't. The diagnosis was wrong.

Actress Peggy Cass came out of surgery to discover that the wrong knee had been operated on.

You can save yourself a lot of worry by being your own medical consultant. Pay attention to how your body feels and what it needs. Make sure you understand and agree with any medical treatment that's suggested.

Finally, there's the question of drinking. As early as your late forties you will notice a decrease in your ability to consume alcohol. Brown has found that even a small amount—a few drinks—can cause his voice to slur and his mind to fog...even though he feels as if he is sharper than ever.

Drinking can also release sudden and inexplicable combativeness, repressed aggressions and paranoia. Brown came closest to wrecking his marriage and friendships while drinking, even drinking moderately. Avoid alcoholic beverages entirely when there is pressure or tension...or when you're tired.

•Keep your friends—including friends of the opposite sex. People who stay young all their lives never stop being interested in the opposite sex. There is hardly a day or an hour when Brown is not aware of the women around him. Whether you're married or single, friends of the opposite sex can be a joy and a rejuvenation.

Brown says his wife, *Cosmopolitan's* pioneering editor, Helen Gurley Brown, cautions older men to beware of women who are too young. Women closer to your own age understand life better—and they are much more interesting than younger women. And Brown agrees.

Source: David Brown, producer of *The Sting, Jaws, Cocoon* and other successful films. He is the author of *The Rest of Your Life is the Best of Your Life: David Brown's Guide to Growing Gray (Disgracefully),* Barricade Books, 1530 Palisade Ave., Fort Lee, New Jersey 07024.

Life Lessons from Daniel Boone

Daniel Boone (1734-1820) was the most famous of the heroic pioneers who led the conquest of the American frontier. He lived in a long-gone era, the time of the birth of the United States, when most of America was still an untamed wilderness. But his life can teach us much about how to approach the challenges we face today.

A long and active life...

Boone lived until age 86 at a time when the average life expectancy was far less than it is now...but he never worried about security. Each time civilization caught up with his family, he moved them further west to settle in a new wilderness, beginning again from scratch.

As a hunter and explorer, he survived the dangers of wild animals and exposure to the elements. As a militia officer in numerous campaigns, he survived battles and sieges...led a daring rescue of his daughter from hostile Indians...for several months during the War of Independence was himself held captive.

He always retained his enthusiasm for an active life. As Boone grew older, he suffered severe rheumatism, the legacy of years spent outdoors in cold and wet conditions...but never stopped hunting, his life-long passion.

Boonestory: When Boone could no longer carry his gun, he went on hunting trips with his wife...she carried the gun. When he became too weak to pursue large animals, he set traps for beaver...at times only able to do that when he was carried.

• *Lesson:* Longevity is tied to limitless enthusiasm and activity.

Between two cultures...

Boone was born to a Quaker family in Pennsylvania. Although he was not a churchgoing man in his adult life, he never lost his attachment to the Quaker values of peace and tolerance.

The Indians taught Boone how to survive in the forest, track animals and live off the land. They taught him enough woodsmanship to make him the premier explorer of his time... the man who marked and laid out the Wilderness Trail to Kentucky, which was later traveled by more than 200,000 emigrants.

Nevertheless, Boone fought alongside his countrymen to wrest control of the land from the Indians...but unlike many Americans, he appreciated the Indian way of life and made friends among them.

Boonestory: During the American Revolution, Shawnee warriors, supported by the British, captured Captain Boone and a group of fellow settlers. Boone's diplomatic skills prevented a massacre of his outnumbered men, and Blackfish, the Shawnee chief, adopted Boone as his own son.

Boone escaped and returned to lead the defense of Boonesborough, the Kentucky settlement he had founded a number of years before. He almost succeeded in forging an equitable peace treaty with Blackfish, but not before the Indians attacked the settlement.

After the war, other men with less tolerant attitudes charged Captain Boone with treason during his captivity, and he was court-martialed by the Kentucky militia. He was not only acquitted...but was promoted to Major.

In his old age, Boone renewed his friendship with his old Indian foes and stated: "I am very sorry to say that I ever killed any Indians, for they have always been kinder to me than the whites."

• *Lesson:* It is possible to accept the worth of other cultures without abandoning your own.

Pioneer women...

The frontier was not settled by men alone... while they were exploring, hunting or warring, their wives had to run the household and often singlehandedly raise their large families.

Daniel Boone and his wife Rebecca were married for 56 years...had 10 children...and brought up six orphaned cousins, too. Boone was away for months...sometimes years...at a time, and Rebecca was left in charge in both times of peace and war.

Boonestory: Once, with the Indians on the warpath and Boone away with the militia, Rebecca and the children left their farm to join others who had taken refuge in a small fort. One day, the women noticed that the men assigned to defend the fort were loafing around outside.

Rebecca, her two oldest daughters and some other wives armed themselves, crept out of the fort, fired a fusillade, ran back inside the fort and bolted the gates. The men locked outside ran around in a state of panic while the women laughed. Later, Boone was put in charge of the fort's defenses, and he improved discipline there.

• *Lesson:* Marriage is an enterprise that succeeds when husbands and wives are equal partners.

Commerce and frontier values...

In his lifetime, Daniel Boone acquired thousands of acres of land...some by purchase, some in exchange for services, and some by government grants. He ended up with almost none of it because his strong ethical values did not fit in the unscrupulous world of commerce that replaced the fair frontier he had known.

As the man who knew the land best, Boone chose and surveyed many tracts of land for others and for himself. But his technical surveying skills did not match the questionable business practices and sharp legal stratagems used by the speculators who followed the pioneers, and he —and those who used his services—lost their lands.

His strong ethical principles compelled him to pay back all his debts...so he lost even more land.

In his old age, he petitioned the federal government to recognize his right to land he had been granted by the Spanish before Louisiana was acquired by the US...and his petition was rejected.

Boonestory: One insolent trickster was Gilbert Imlay, who promised to pay Boone for 10,000 acres of excellent land in Kentucky. After Boone assigned him the rights to the property, Imlay ran off to England without paying...but first signed over the land to a third party. Ironically, Imlay later wrote a book praising Boone and inspired Lord Byron to include a tribute to "General Boone, backwoodsman of Kentucky" in his famous epic poem, *Don Juan.*

• *Lesson:* Encounters with lawyers and speculators can be more brutal than those with wild animals.

Accepting life...

Daniel Boone had a long life, but a hard one. He had financial problems that left him in constant debt...frequent injuries—and also chronic pain from his exposure to the elements...two sons killed by Indians and three daughters who died in their 30s. But he did not despair of life.

Boonestory: A popular folk tale about Boone describes an occasion when he and his brother, Squire, are camped on the riverbank, trapped in a heavy rain and huddling together under a horse blanket. Squire does not understand how Daniel is able to take it without complaining.

When the rain ends, they leave and soon discover nearby a camp recently abandoned by Indians. Daniel tells Squire, "What fretted you so much was really the means of Providence for our salvation. But for the storm, we should have run into the very jaws of our enemies."

• *Lesson:* Don't be quick to complain. Sometimes a new situation can be more trouble than it's worth.

Source: John Mack Faragher, professor of history at Mount Holyoke College. He is the author of *Daniel Boone: The Life and Legend of an American Pioneer,* Henry Holt and Co., 115 W. 18 St., New York 10011.

2 Secrets of Success

How to Avoid the Most Common Obstacles To Success...Love... Happiness

Life is often difficult enough without us standing in our own way, blocking our path to career success, satisfying relationships and the attainment of our personal goals. Yet many of us exhibit particular behaviors and cling to particular beliefs that keep us from getting precisely what we want out of life. *Seven most common obstacles...*

1. Poor time management.

The ineffective time manager doesn't know how to prioritize his/her time. He will often come late for meetings or personal appointments and will hand in things past their deadlines. That's not because he's a procrastinator but because he just doesn't have a realistic feel for how much time things take.

Other possibilities: Job dissatisfaction...or passive-aggressive behavior, which in this case means trying to control events by showing up late and holding up progress. *Solutions...*

- Plan activities the night before so you can prepare for what needs to be done.
- Get a time-and-project organizer to help you anticipate and plan for future activities.
- Look at your watch frequently so you can begin to gauge where your time-management skills are off.
- Build in down time to unwind as well as help you plan future work time better.

2. Disorganization.

People who have a disorganization problem don't know how to control the paper on their desks and can't distinguish between important material and junk.

They feel an irrational discomfort about getting rid of things and have an irrational need to read and know everything. They are forever promising themselves that someday they'll get to those newspapers and magazines, but they never do...and the mess accumulates and swallows them up.

Solution: Stop being a collector. Start prioritizing and acting on everything that comes across your desk or into your home. Toss out all unnecessary papers, and file those you need. The key is to act *immediately*.

3. Unassertiveness.

Unassertive people have trouble saying no to requests...and they don't express annoyance because they fear negative evaluations or being disliked. If they're angry at someone, rather than express their anger directly they will engage in passive-aggressive behavior, such as moodiness or lateness, which is particularly destructive on the job.

Solutions...

•Examine the values with which you were raised. *Example:* Did you grow up believing that being assertive meant being impolite...or that it's wrong to express anger?

•Learn the necessary social and career skills. Do you know the best ways to start a conversation...state your opinions...negotiate a deal?

•Learn to overcome your fear of criticism or rejection. *Helpful:* With a friend, rehearse a difficult situation and deliberately respond differently from the way you naturally would. See how it feels to ask for that raise—while maintaining eye contact and without being apologetic. If a friend isn't available, use a tape recorder and replay your replies.

4. "Awfulizing".

The awfulizer has a fertile catastrophic imagination and always assumes the worst will happen. These anxious, fearful people constantly ask themselves "what if" questions: "What if I don't get the job?"..."What if he/she notices that I'm balding?"

Solutions...

•Shift the degree of intolerability in your mind and recognize that while there may be things in life that are uncomfortable, there's very little that people can't endure.

•Examine the probabilities. In any given situation, ask yourself, "What are the actual chances that the worst will occur?" If you begin to do this regularly, you'll realize the unlikelihood of the horrible outcome you're anticipating.

•Actively challenge your beliefs. If you catch yourself engaging in "what if?" thinking, write down any evidence you have that you won't be able to handle the upcoming situation. This will help you see how silly your fears are.

•Recall past successes. Remind yourself that whatever is coming up is simply a variation on something you've already done.

5. Perfectionism.

Perfectionists can't stand being viewed as wrong or inadequate in any way. And because the perfectionist believes he must do everything perfectly, it can lead to procrastination out of fear of doing an imperfect job.

Solutions...

•Accept the reality that all humans are fallible. We're constantly making mistakes—it's part of our nature.

•Deliberately do some things imperfectly... to prove to yourself that you'll survive.

Example: I have one client who's a perfectionist when it comes to her dressing—she wastes a tremendous amount of time changing clothes, matching accessories and running home from wherever she is if she spots a run in her pantyhose. As an exercise, I've had her deliberately go to work with a run in her pantyhose or with mismatched shoes and purse.

Until you've actually risked being imperfect, you won't make those fundamental philosophical changes crucial to overcoming the problem.

6. Demandingness.

This is the irrational belief that you always deserve to be treated right. Every problem in life is blamed on unfair people or an unfair world. These men and women feel that they're special somehow and entitled to a break because they've always been a good spouse, parent, child, or employee.

Solutions...

•Understand that, in reality, the world operates quite independently from what you want or demand.

Example: A woman discovers that her husband has been philandering. She's devastated because she feels she was such a good, self-sacrificing wife for years. *How could he do this to me?* she asks. That question presupposes that being a good wife will guarantee protection from anything hurtful a husband can do ...but the reality is quite different.

• Look at the big picture. The economy is bad and that's why nobody in your office—not even you—got a raise last year.

• Eliminate the words *should, ought* and *must* from your vocabulary. These are words that set up absolutist thinking. You'll be a lot happier once you start "desiring" and "preferring" things rather than "demanding" and "requiring" them.

7. *Discomfort anxiety.*

These people just can't bear hassles. Anything that disrupts the smooth running of their day is perceived as insurmountable. They can't stand to hear bad news or confront somebody on a difficult issue. So they regularly practice "discomfort dodging"—palming off unpleasant tasks onto others or avoiding the problems altogether in the hope they'll just go away.

Example: An executive flips through her stack of phone messages when she gets to work in the morning and routinely gives all the unpleasant ones to her secretary to handle...or stashes them permanently at the bottom of the pile.

Solution: Try systematic desensitization, the treatment of choice for people who suffer from discomfort anxiety. First, practice relaxing using any common relaxation skill you feel comfortable with—tensing and relaxing the muscles, etc.

Then, while you're completely relaxed, practice "seeing" yourself doing whatever unpleasant activities you regularly avoid. If done often enough, the relaxation will neutralize the anxiety, and in time you should be able to carry out the task in real life.

Source: Psychologist Barry Lubetkin, PhD, director of the Institute for Behavior Therapy in New York. His most recent book is *Why Do I Need You to Love Me in Order to Like Myself?,* Longmeadow Press, 201 High Ridge Rd., Stamford, CT 06904.

Key to Effectiveness: Keep Alert!

In today's 24-hour world, workers are given extensive training, equipped with very reliable automated machinery and provided with comfortable surroundings. But that doesn't guarantee effective performance around the clock.

Bizarre example: In the cockpit of a Boeing 707 en route to Los Angeles, the entire crew fell asleep while the autopilot continued to fly the plane westward...far over the Pacific Ocean. When air traffic controllers on the ground noticed the wayward plane, their verbal inquiries went unanswered. The desperate controllers averted disaster when they managed to wake up the crew by triggering loud chimes in the cockpit.

Alertness is key to effective performance...

That near-disaster was caused by the failure of one critical human factor—*alertness.* Like so many systems today, the airplane was designed to perform so well automatically that it was hard for the pilots to remain alert.

But alertness is vital for people to perform effectively. Only in that state are people fully aware of their surroundings...able to think clearly...consider all options...make sensible decisions.

Physiological basis...

To physiologists, alertness represents a desirable state of balance between two human nervous systems.

One of these nervous systems—*the sympathetic nervous system*—automatically triggers the fight-or-flight response...heart pounding...blood pressure rising...pupils dilating...hair standing on end.

It represents a peak of alertness vital for dealing with emergency situations...but it usually can't be sustained for too long.

Minimum alertness occurs when the body is highly relaxed...under control of the *parasympathetic nervous system.* Consider someone dozing by the fire after a heavy meal...heart beating slowly...blood pressure dropping... pupils constricting. It is essential for the body and mind to rest sometimes...but a state of total relaxation is bad news if you're supposed to be working...studying...even observing.

In a state of alertness, the brain is engaged and ready to react appropriately to evolving situations. But we're often not alert when we need to be because our external environment or our internal state—or a combination of both—work to disengage our brain.

Nine switches of alertness...

Research into the physiology of alertness has shown there are nine switches that control alertness. We can improve our alertness by learning what they are and how to switch them on or off. *They are:*

1. Sense of danger, interest or opportunity. Nothing switches us faster from drowsiness to alertness than awareness of imminent danger. The brain can also be awakened in a less extreme way by other forms of stimulation.

Helpful: If you're in a meeting about a subject that's not too exciting and feel yourself dozing off, try to stimulate yourself. Ask questions...make comments...take notes...bring others into the discussion.

2. Muscular activity. Vigorous exercise can improve alertness for an hour or more. Many people performing tasks where alertness is vital cannot move around—pilots, drivers, nuclear-plant operators. But they can find other types of muscular activity to help keep them alert.

Helpful: Stretch in place...chew gum...take periodic breaks to walk around.

3. Time of day on the biological clock. Humans have their own biological clock that tells when it's time to wake and to sleep. If you're on shift work or traveling between different time zones, it's not easy to adjust your built-in clock to match the environment.

Helpful: If you're running a meeting with people from all over the country or the world, be aware of their biological clocks. Try to schedule a compromise time that helps as many as possible stay awake. Remember that people feel drowsy after lunch and are most alert when their body tells them it's mid-morning or late afternoon.

4. Sleep bank balance. Alertness depends on how long it is since we last slept. It is possible to restore the balance in our sleep bank by a good single night's sleep or by a number of brief naps at strategic intervals.

Interesting: A short nap of 10–15 minutes provides more benefit than one of 30–40 minutes, which leaves you drowsy. Research has shown that people can work 22 hours a day for extended periods if they get a 20-minute nap every four hours.

5. Ingested nutrients and chemicals. Stimulation by food, drink or chemicals can improve our alertness. In moderation, it may be sensible, but it's often a poor way to cope. Two or three cups of coffee are fine to help you stay awake, but any more than that stays in the system and makes it hard to sleep after work, and it makes you more tired the next day. Similarly, people who pop too many stay-awake pills develop insomnia and then become dependent on sleeping pills.

Helpful: A 10-minute coffee break. But if you have the choice, a 10-minute nap is better.

6. Environmental light. Bright light keeps people alert, but to be truly effective, it must be about the level of natural light at dawn—about the level of a hospital operating room, which is twice as bright as a well-lit office. This level of light doesn't just help you see well, it stimulates the brain. Today, exploiting light for alertness is on the technological frontier.

7. Environmental temperature and humidity. We all know that a cold shower wakes us up...a warm bath puts us to sleep...and that when driving on a boring highway, one of the best ways to wake up is to open the window and get a blast of cold air.

8. Environmental sound. The rolling surf at the beach or the smooth rushing of a mountain stream can lull us to sleep. These are examples of "white noise" that is also generated by machines that people use to help them go to sleep...and resembles the background noise produced by much equipment found in industrial control rooms where operators are expected to stay awake at night.

Helpful: In control rooms, try to use irregular sources of sound that vary in pitch and intensity...allow workers to listen to stimulating radio programs when possible.

9. Environmental aroma. Although this switch has not been scientifically investigated as much as the other eight switches, there are intriguing reports that aromas like peppermint may help alertness.

With an awareness of how these nine switches work, you can improve your own alertness. By learning to put them in the "off" position, you can learn how to relax better, as well.

Source: Martin Moore-Ede, MD, PhD, associate professor of physiology at Harvard Medical School, director of the Institute for Circadian Physiology. He is the founder and CEO of Circadian Technologies, consultants to industry worldwide on enhancing alertness in the workplace and author of *The Twenty-Four-Hour Society: Understanding Human Limits in a World that Never Stops*, Addison-Wesley, Jacob Way, Reading, MA 01867.

Positive Reappraisal

Reformulate negative thoughts through positive reappraisal. If you find yourself thinking, "I can't do this," change it to, "This will be a challenge, but I'll go at it—one step at a time." Instead of a negative self-message, this gives you one of being innovative and capable. Instead of "I don't want to get out of bed," say, "I'll feel better after a warm shower." The self-message is that you can help yourself. *Key:* Recognizing negative thoughts so you can rethink them.

Source: *Living with Rheumatoid Arthritis*, by Tammi Shlotzhauer, MD, clinical associate professor of medicine, Rochester Medical Center, Rochester, NY. The Johns Hopkins University Press, 2715 N. Charles St., Baltimore 21218.

Mastery...Quick-Fix Thinking...and Us

We live in a time of instant gratification. We're told to take this pill for fast relief, or go on that quick weight-loss diet or buy a lottery ticket and become a millionaire overnight. Yet our addiction to quick-fix thinking is leading us to social and personal disaster.

George Leonard, a pioneer in work to develop the human potential, is working now to push us all to abandon our continuing search for quick results...and return to a more natural rhythm of life. He is finding more and more that fulfillment comes through what he calls *mastery,* the process of savoring the doing. *We asked him more about his views...*

What do you mean by a natural rhythm of life?

Studies of learning curves show us that in the course of learning anything, your knowledge increases a little...then plateaus for a while, then goes up and down again...and then hits another plateau, but at a higher level.

For people to gain control of their lives they must realize that they're on a path of endless learning and growth. There's no such thing as getting to the top and staying there without further effort.

What is the key to mastering something?

You have to return again and again to the discipline or task...and stick to your work even when you appear to be going nowhere.

Mastery requires doing the best you can to improve—without pushing yourself *too* hard. You have to be willing to stay on the plateau as long as necessary.

Example: I was fortunate in my middle years to have found the practice of aikido, a martial-arts discipline, very difficult and totally resistant to the art of the quick fix.

When I first started with aikido, I assumed that I would steadily improve, but after a year and a half of practice, I was forced to recognize that I was on a plateau of rather formidable proportions. I was shocked and disappointed, but somehow I managed to persevere.

After a few more exhilarating spurts and disappointing plateaus, I found myself thinking, *Oh good, another plateau. I can just stay on it and keep practicing and sooner or later there will be another spurt.* It was one of the warmest moments on my journey toward the black belt I eventually earned.

Most people see practice as a being a burden. What's your approach to it?

Practice is a path. In Chinese, the word is *tao* and in Japanese, *do.* Practice is the road upon which you walk—your path in life.

The great sports figures of our time are masters of their practice—and they love to practice.

Example: Larry Bird, who, without a doubt, was one of the best basketball players, was not all that talented. He owed his success to regular, intense practice—which he loved to do.

We call law and medicine practices, but today that's rarely the case. Modern law today isn't so much a practice as a get-rich-quick vehicle—and you can't call medicine a practice if you hardly know your patients.

In your job, the road to mastery will provide promotions, money and opportunity to excel. But the key is loving your work and being willing to hang in there through the tough times.

Why is mastery so difficult for Americans?

Because of our soured values as a country. We used to learn values from the village elders, rituals, religion and the family. Today we learn values from television and other media, which teach us that the ideal rhythm of life is a series of climactic moments.

Examples: In a cake commercial, you'll see glowing, happy faces around the cake and a child blowing out the candles, but you won't see any of the work that goes into baking. Or you'll see young people relaxing after a bicycle race by drinking diet soda, but you won't see the effort that went into the race. Or on sitcoms, you see complicated social and psychological problems dramatized, then magnificently solved in 22 minutes.

Television has established a rhythm in our culture that values the climax above everything and believes one climax should follow another.

Trying to maintain the rhythm of life as a perpetual high leads to such tragedies as our drug epidemic. Cocaine is the ultimate quick fix.

Quick-fix thinking has pervaded our society at every level. Modern medicine attempts to solve almost every problem with a drug or operation. Modern business sacrifices long-term planning and development to produce quick profits. Education has gone into a sharp decline because no one has the patience to master difficult subjects such as math or foreign languages.

The quick weight loss diet is one of the best examples of the quick fix...and long-term weight control is one of the best examples of mastery. To keep weight off you have to permanently change your lifestyle, not just go on some fad diet for a few months.

What are the most common pitfalls on the road to mastery?

• Obsessive goal orientation. The desire of most people for quick, sure and highly visible results is the deadliest enemy of mastery.

• A conflicting way of life. The traveler whose main path of mastery coincides with career and livelihood is fortunate. Others must find space and time outside of regular working hours for their practice. *Keys:* Be realistic about balancing job, family and path...enlist the support of family and friends. *How to find the time:* Stop watching TV.

• Lack of instruction. For mastering most skills, there's nothing better than being in the hands of a master teacher, either one-on-one, or in a small group. But there are also books, films, tapes and other good instruction available.

• Vanity. To learn something new of any significance, you have to be willing to look foolish. Even after years of practice you may still take pratfalls.

• Inconsistency. Consistency of practice is the mark of the master. *Helpful:* Establish a regular time and place to practice. But if you should happen to miss a few sessions, don't use that as an excuse to quit.

• Perfectionism. We set such high standards for ourselves that neither we, nor anyone else, could ever meet them. We fail to realize that mastery is not about perfection. It's about a process, a journey.

• Dead seriousness. Without laughter, the rough and rocky places on the path might be too painful for us to bear. Humor not only helps to lighten your load, it also broadens your perspective.

Source: George Leonard, author of *Mastery: The Keys to Long-Term Success and Fulfillment*, Penguin USA, 375 Hudson St., New York 10014.

How to Make Your Dreams Work for You

Dreams can help us understand our feelings, attitudes and beliefs—even those hidden from our conscious minds. They can help build intimacy between friends and families... and help us find our way in times of personal crisis... and even warn us of serious illness. *To put your dreams to work for you:*

•Prime yourself for dreaming. All humans dream, but some have trouble recalling their dreams. For best recall, try a period of relaxation before bedtime.

Helpful: Soothing music, bathing or meditating.

Avoid: Alcohol, drugs and caffeine, all of which suppress dreaming.

Next, mentally review the day's events, especially those that elicited strong emotions in you. Focus on the faces of people closest to you. As you drift off, say to yourself that you will recall your dreams in the morning.

Upon waking, lie still for a few minutes. Keep your eyes closed or unfocused and remain in your sleeping posture. Use a regular alarm clock (tone or bell). Music alarms are distracting and can impair dream recall.

•Keep a dream journal. A series of dreams will be more helpful than a single one. A dream journal helps you spot recurring characters, situations and emotional themes that would otherwise remain hidden.

Procedure: After waking and lying still for several minutes, jot down the main points of your dream in your journal. This journal can be a special notebook or a simple pad of paper.

In either case, it must be kept at your bedside.

Don't worry about writing style. The goal is not to write a beautiful story, but to record the key details. Be sure to record all your dreams, even those that seem fragmentary, trivial, illogical or morally repugnant. Do not censor yourself.

Besides the dream's key elements, each journal entry should include your feelings during the dream and upon waking...the insights and hunches you have about your dream...peculiar traits and, if possible, the identities of your dream characters...details about the dream's ending...and a title by which to remember the dream. Conclude by summarizing the dream's main themes and by listing any ideas or strategies for making changes in your life, as suggested by the dream.

•Explore dreams on your own. Find a comfortable place, where you will not be disturbed. Pick a dream from your journal, then close your eyes and pretend you are reliving the dream. Imagine that the events and feelings of the dream were really happening. Then, open your eyes and jot down any feelings, associations or insights that come to mind.

At this point, several exercises often prove productive...

•Automatic writing. Set a timer for five minutes, then jot down as many ideas as you can before the bell sounds. Don't worry about making sense.

•Dream dialogue. Choose two characters or objects from a dream and write a dialogue between them. Write as fast as you can. Do not censor yourself or put down your pen.

•Dreaming the dream onward. "Reenter" your dream in a daydream and continue your dream beyond its original ending. If the original ending is negative or unresolved, imagine a more positive ending. A man troubled by a dream of being chased by a bear might dream the dream onward until the bear was trapped or killed.

•Share your dreams with others. Doing so not only helps you make sense of dreams, it also deepens the emotional bonds between you and those around you.

Helpful: After each daydreaming exercise, relate your dream to a friend or spouse, or even to a dream discussion group. Use the present tense to make the dream as vivid as possible.

Key questions: Are there links between your dream and any personal relationships, events or turning points in your life? Do these links suggest a course of action? Ask your listener for his/her ideas.

Caution: Dream discussion is fruitful only in an emotionally supportive setting, in which participants focus not upon a formal analysis of *dream content,* but upon an *appreciation* of dream imagery. *Bottom line:* View your dreams —and ask others to view your dreams—the same way you would view paintings in an art museum.

• Avoid "cookbook" dream interpretations. Dreams are full of distorted reality and bizarre symbols that defy easy interpretation.

Many people search for a single "correct" interpretation. In fact, dream symbols hold not one correct interpretation, but many...and the best way to understand these symbols is to explore your own associations. A dream about a knife might symbolize one thing to a frustrated housewife, for example, but quite another to a surgeon.

Helpful: The tingle test. Describe your dream to someone else, then ask for his interpretation. If the interpretation evokes no particular emotional response in you, odds are that particular interpretation holds no specific relevance for you. However, an interpretation that elicits a "tingle" in your body is on target. It warrants further exploration.

On rare occasions, people diagnosed with serious illnesses report having had warning (prodromal) dreams. In one instance, a patient discovered that he had throat cancer after dreaming of a feeling of heat in his neck. Usually, however, dreaming of a serious illness or accident does not mean you actually will get sick or hurt. Dreaming of losing your teeth, for example, may suggest you need to visit the dentist...but it's more likely that loose teeth are merely symbolic of a feeling of loss or powerlessness.

• Put your dreams to work. Humans dream more frequently and with greater intensity during times of transition or crisis—marriage, divorce, the death of a loved one, mid-life, etc.

While no one knows precisely why this is so, one plausible explanation is that when strong feelings overwhelm our conscious mind, our unconscious (dreaming) mind begins to work overtime. Even when we try to "paper over" these powerful emotions, our dreams are there to point out strong emotions that need to be "processed" before we can move on with our lives.

Once you have mastered the basics of dream work, you can begin using your dreams to help resolve your problems, whether it's a simple day-to-day aggravation or an emotional crisis.

How it's done: First, spend some time consciously exploring ways to resolve the problem. This process of conscious exploration can be done on your own, or with a therapist or trusted friend. Consider as many options as possible.

Next, write an "incubation question" in your dream journal. This question, designed to encourage dreams that relate to your specific problem, should be open-ended.

Examples: How do I feel about this career change? Why am I still grieving over my husband's death?

Caution: Avoid narrowly focused, yes-or-no questions.

As you fall asleep, focus upon this question. Repeat this "incubation ceremony" each night until a dream that seems to address this problem occurs.

Then, treat this dream as you normally would, using your dream journal, daydreaming exercises...and sharing the dream with others. With a little practice, you will learn to spot clues in your dreams on how best to respond to your problem.

Example I: Just before her wedding, a woman dreamed that she needed a $10,000 heart operation. At first this dream seemed to have no particular significance. The woman was healthy. Then she realized that $10,000 was the cost of the wedding...and that she was, in one sense, going to have a $10,000 "heart procedure." This dream showed her she was nervous about her marriage, and that she needed to discuss her feelings.

Example II: A restaurateur was so unhappy in her work that she had developed an ulcer. Yet she did not know why she was unhappy. Then, a series of dreams in which she screamed at her employees made her realize that she was really angry at them...and suggested that she needed to express this anger and set new performance standards at the restaurant. These changes enabled her to get over her anger—and her ulcer.

Source: Alan B. Siegel, PhD, an adult and child psychologist in private practice in San Francisco. Dr. Siegel, who has led dream workshops for 15 years is the author of *Dreams That Can Change Your Life: Navigating Life's Passages Through Turning Point Dreams,* Jeremy P. Tarcher, 5858 Wilshire Blvd., Los Angeles 90036.

There Are Great Virtues In Stubbornness

Stubbornness is one of those qualities we find terribly annoying in others and are reluctant to admit to in ourselves.

But stubbornness may be underrated as a valuable defense—and coping mechanism. Stubbornness is not only helpful when it comes to dealing with bad times, it's a must for success.

To find out more about the important part this personality trait plays in our lives, we interviewed psychiatrist and admitted stubborn person, Dr. Sue Chance.

Why do people think stubbornness is negative?

It's a matter of degree. They think tenacity is okay, but when it's carried to an extreme, it becomes stubbornness, and that's a negative.

I think there are other ways of looking at stubbornness. What you call it matters less than the purpose it serves. If being stubborn can help us survive some hard knocks, then it's a virtue as far as I'm concerned.

It takes a lot of stubbornness to persist in the face of rejection, to believe in yourself and your own talents despite what others tell you. But that's what it takes to succeed. Stubbornness, not talent, is often the difference between someone who actually achieves his goals and someone who sits around and talks about what he's going to accomplish one day.

In what situations does stubbornness help people survive hard knocks?

In any adverse situation. When you tell yourself that you're going to hold on for dear life until the bad times pass, that's stubbornness.

Stubbornness applies whether the problem is physical or emotional. It's having the courage to say, *I'll be damned if this is going to beat me.* My stubbornness helped me survive my son's suicide. *I just held on*—and assumed if I stayed alive long enough, the worst would pass. It did. I was just too stubborn to give up.

Is that stubbornness or bravery?

To me bravery implies taking action in difficult circumstances. Tenacity and stubbornness is just holding on, battening down the hatches and toughing it out.

If it's such a survival mechanism, why is stubbornness considered a negative trait?

It's a negative trait when you apply it to someone else. We don't think of ourselves, generally, as stubborn. We call other people stubborn if they hold onto something that we think they should let go of.

Stubbornness *can* be a serious problem in interpersonal relationships. If what you're hearing in your relationships is a lot of feedback about how stubborn you are, you need to think about what it is you're doing to elicit that response.

Stubbornness in relationships may be a sign of selfishness and lack of consideration and caring about the other person. It can indicate failure of empathy.

Stubbornness is a positive only when it's you dealing with yourself. It's positive to stubbornly adhere to what you believe, or stick to goals that you think are worthwhile, or just survive the slings and arrows of life.

Doesn't stubbornness make you resistant to change?

My stubborn patients may stubbornly resist change, but when they finally do make changes, they're more likely to maintain them.

I'd rather work with someone who is stubborn at the core because they'll hang on through the hard stuff. They'll be able to tolerate the anxiety of treatment.

I'm very leery of instantaneous changes. The classic example is the alcoholic who says he'll never drink again. You know he's going back —soon. He hasn't done the hard work it takes to change repetitive behavior.

I prefer the person who says he isn't sure, he knows it's going to be difficult but he's willing to give it a try. That person's got a much better chance because that's how we make changes—slowly, with great reluctance and great effort.

Example: Recovering alcoholics who have some sobriety behind them. They were stubborn enough to make a major change in their lives and consequently are able to look at making other major changes.

How should parents handle stubbornness in children?

Use it as an opportunity for communication. If you ask a child who's being stubborn what's going on, he'll often have an explanation that will make sense to you. Don't make it a battle of wills. Ask your child what the underlying problem is.

Example: We moved from Georgia to Texas when my son was starting the third grade. I got a call from his teacher that he wouldn't do anything in class. He wouldn't even take out his books. When I pressed him about what the problem was, it turned out that what looked like stubbornness was actually shame and fear. He couldn't read the books the class was using because there was a drastic difference in the quality of the education from Georgia to Texas. They were way ahead of him. We put him back a half year until he caught up and then everything was fine.

Is stubbornness something you're born with?

Stubbornness seems to be an innate character trait rather than something you learn.

Example: Newborns' hands grip so strongly they can lift their own weight. They're not physically strong, but they do have a strong instinct to survive. That survival instinct is stubbornness.

How can people foster positive stubbornness in themselves?

Most of the time we program ourselves for failure. Our parents and society teach us how to criticize ourselves.

Typical messages: Don't be conceited... What makes you think you can succeed where others have failed?... You're not so special. We get all this negative programming.

Be sure to give equal time to positive programming.

Tell yourself: I'm going to give it my best. If people want to disagree with me, I'll listen to them, and learn if I can, but sometimes there will just be a difference of opinion and I'm going to take mine over theirs.

Don't pay attention to people who think you should only do what's easy. There's no such thing as *instant success.*

Foster your stubbornness and turn it into drive. Stubbornness can even be a substitute for believing in yourself.

Many of us weren't raised to have a very high opinion of ourselves, but we wind up succeeding through sheer stubbornness. Refusal to give up and the desire to prove yourself against all odds is a powerful motivator.

Source: Psychiatrist Sue Chance, MD, who has a private practice in Dallas. Dr. Chance writes a regular column for the *Psychiatric Times.* She is the author of *Stronger Than Death,* which addresses how family and close friends can survive the suicide of a loved one, W.W. Norton, New York.

Championship Factors

Championship factors apply in all life, not just athletics. Self-analysis—know your strengths and weaknesses...self-competition—concentrate on doing your best, not beating others... confidence—set tough but reasonable goals... toughness—accept risk and try to win instead of just trying not to lose...have a game plan—talent alone is not enough.

Source: *Runner's World,* 33 E. Minor St., Emmaus, PA 18098.

Self-Esteem Builder

Talking to yourself helps build self-esteem. *Helpful:* Give yourself a pat on the back for a job well done...compliment yourself...applaud your achievements. *Important:* Speak these positive messages out loud so you think and hear them.

Source: *51 Ways to Save Your Job: Your 30-Minute Guide to Job Security* by Paul Timm, PhD, professor of management at Brigham Young University. Career Press, 180 Fifth Ave., Hawthorne, NJ 07507.

Practical Paths To Personal Success 

The traditional routes to career success don't always work anymore. The time when smart people with impressive academic credentials could link up with big companies and enjoy a non-stop ride to the top is over.

It takes much more to get ahead today. You've got to be shrewd in promoting yourself and your ideas.

Once you choose a company in which to work...

• Get noticed. In many good companies, top executives simply don't have the time to get to know most of the people who work for them. That puts the burden on *you* to make the most of the opportunities. If you have 10 minutes to make a presentation to top management, realize that they may be the most important minutes in the 10 years you've worked for the company.

Example: IBM's Tom Watson, Sr., once promoted a salesman he'd never met to sales manager on the basis of a brief presentation the man made.

When you know key people will be watching, do your homework and prepare for the occasion as though your career depends on it ...because it does.

And if you're offered two positions, take the one with more visibility, unless there's a compelling reason not to.

• Develop your people skills. Learn what motivates people. This applies equally in relations with subordinates, peers and superiors. Learn to *read* people so that you are able to anticipate their actions.

People skills make self-promotion easier. They also enhance your other talents and make up for some you lack.

Example: Ross Johnson, CEO of RJR Nabisco, was no expert at products and marketing. But he knew people and could regularly talk the board of directors into agreeing with his position.

Although there's no magic way to develop these skills, it helps to watch others who have them. *Notice how they...*

• Ask *others* for opinions.

• Make a point to be useful to others.

• Remember special occasions—birthdays, anniversaries, etc.

If you think you need help in developing people skills, look into seminars that focus on these skills.

Identify with a product...

Identifying your career with a hot product can be a fast route to personal success.

Above all, look for products or services that solve problems. They stand the best chance of being winners.

Example: Edwin Land discovered the potential for an instant camera when his young daughter asked why she couldn't see a picture right after she took it.

Read everything you can get your hands on—the major business and financial press, newsletters, journals, consumer magazines, etc. *Aim:* To find out what's going on *beyond* your own company's current product or service line.

Example #1: Lee Iacocca didn't design the Mustang. But he knew enough about people's tastes to know it would sell. In the process, of course, he promoted himself.

Example #2: More recently, smart managers at GM joined the Saturn project. They knew that if the project turned out to be a winner, so would their careers.

It's a myth that once you're past 40 or 50 it's better to stick with your current career path than to change directions. *Reality:* It's hardly ever too late. In fact, a person who changes direction late in life usually has a wealth of experience to help steady the new course.

Classic example: Ray Kroc, a long-time head of McDonald's, didn't sell a hamburger until he was 52.

The power of ideas...

Developing a successful idea can give you a fast ride to the top. Ironically, however, even great ideas aren't always easy to sell.

Example: Ken Olsen, head of Digital Equipment Corp., rejected the idea of making a personal computer until it was too late for the company to enter the lucrative field.

Some basic concepts to keep in mind when selling your ideas...

•Keep ideas simple. Consumers back away from anything complex, regardless of how useful it may be.

Example: Prodigy, the computer database, is marketed with such complex descriptions that relatively few people understand it well enough to subscribe.

•Keep ideas timely. Even great ideas won't work if the market isn't ready.

•Consider taking your idea elsewhere if your own company isn't interested. Ironically, many executives will listen to an outsider's idea with more enthusiasm than they would to one that comes from within. Once your company has rejected an idea, you usually have nothing to lose by taking it elsewhere.

Example: When Al Neuharth couldn't get his company, *The Miami Herald,* interested in the concept for *USA Today,* he took it to Gannett. And even though the paper has struggled, the concept worked well enough to earn him that company's chairmanship.

Source: Jack Trout and Al Ries, authors of *Horse Sense,* McGraw-Hill, 11 W. 19 St., New York 10011.

The Six Thinking Hats

We all think many different kinds of thoughts —from positive to negative and everything in between. One way to become a better thinker is to separate these different kinds of thinking and use each one separately, instead of in a jumper, as we usually do.

How it works...

One of the biggest traps in thinking is that we categorize people according to *type.* This limits people to expressing views that are expected of them.

Example: Someone who is identified as a negative personality is always expected to come up with negative ideas.

By pretending to switch hats, everyone can come up with a wide spectrum of thoughts on the same subject. Wearing the hats also helps overcome ego—another big hangup in thinking.

Example: If a person opposes an idea, he/she usually won't look for any points in favor of it. But if he's wearing a positive thinking hat, it becomes a game to find the positive side.

This gives people the freedom to remove their egos from the thinking process and think in many different ways.

My six hats...

• *White hat:* Objective thinking. *Memory jog:* White...paper...neutral...objective.

While you wear the white hat, you concentrate on the facts. You can also point out any gaps in that information. White-hat thinking does not involve arguments, views or opinions.

• *Red hat:* Feelings. *Memory jog:* Red...fire ...anger (seeing red)...emotions.

While you wear the red hat, you can express hunches and intuitive feelings. You may not be able to explain your feelings...they may be based on experiences you can't put your finger on.

In many discussions—particularly in business—we're not supposed to include our feelings. But we put them in anyway...disguised as logic. The red hat lets us express our feelings openly.

Example: A head of research at DuPont often asks for three minutes of red-hat thinking at the start of a meeting. He wants to know how everyone feels about a project...without having to explain or justify their feelings.

Telling someone, "You've got your red hat on," is a way to let him know he's expressing his feelings when he's trying to be objective.

• *Black hat:* Caution. *Memory jog:* Black... gloomy...negative...the color of a judge's robes.

While wearing the black hat, you can think about logical negatives—why something is illegal, why it won't work, why it won't be profitable, why it doesn't fit the facts or experience.

Although some peole get the impression that black-hat thinking is bad, it's at least as useful as any of the other kinds of thinking.

Black-hat thinking can be used as a way to get people to *stop* being negative. *Good state-*

ment: "That's great black-hat thinking...but now let's try our green hats."

• *Yellow hat:* Logical, positive thoughts. *Memory jog:* Yellow...sunny...positive.

While you wear the yellow hat, you *must* be logical.

Example: A family is considering moving to the country. Yellow-hat thinking involves looking at logical considerations—lowering housing costs, better schools, etc. Just saying that it would be nice to have a change is red-hat thinking.

Note: The black and yellow hats are both judgment hats. *Black says:* Let's look at the difficulties and dangers. *Yellow says:* Let's look at the feasibility, benefits and savings.

• *Green hat:* Creativity. *Memory jogs:* Green ...grass...fertile growth...energy.

While you wear the green hat, you're free to generate new ideas, alternatives and possibilities.

Example: A couple planning a vacation puts on their green hats and brainstorms possibilities—the wilder the better. These aren't ideas they've checked or thought seriously about... they're just ideas.

Normally when we're discussing something, it's very difficult to slip in creative ideas. Wearing the green hat is a way of making off-the-wall ideas acceptable.

• *Blue hat:* Objective overview. *Memory jog:* Blue...cool...the color of a clear sky, which is above everything else.

While you wear the blue hat, you tell yourself or others which of the other five hats to wear. It's like conducting an orchestra.

Blue-hat statement: "We haven't gotten anywhere by being logical. Putting on my blue hat, I suggest we have some red-hat thinking to clear the air."

The blue hat says: Let's look at our objectives and values. It lets you lay out your goals, evaluate how far you've gotten, summarize the results and reach a conclusion.

How to use the hats...

You can use the hat concept to think about any issue. You can use it by yourself, with one other person or in a group. *Good statements:*

• Let's try some green-hat thinking for three minutes to generate some different ideas.

• It seems you're just wearing your black hat...why don't you take it off now?

• That's all red-hat thinking...we need to put on our white hats for a while and consider the facts.

• Putting on my black hat, I want to talk about the difficulties, dangers and problems we might face with this.

• Wearing my red hat, this is how I feel about it.

• Here's a provocative idea I got while wearing my green hat.

To stimulate creativity at a meeting, ask everyone to put on his green hat for three minutes and come up with some creative ideas. This will allow even the most unimaginative member of the group to indulge his creative side. *Note:* Make it a rule that anyone can call for some green-hat time.

Make it feel like a game to get people to play along. If everyone else is wearing a yellow hat, someone who's still expressing black-hat ideas is going to feel very silly. Make sure that every idea that is brought up is analyzed under each hat. Once you've narrowed your options down to three or four, go back and do one more yellow- and black-hat check on each. At the end of this process you will have a well-thought-out plan of what you want to do.

Source: Edward DeBono, PhD, the leading international authority on the teaching of thinking as a skill. He has held faculty appointments at Oxford, Cambridge and Harvard. His Six Thinking Hats program is used by such companies as IBM, Du Pont and Prudential.

Norman Vincent Peale's 10 Rules for Getting Along with People

• Remember their names.

• Be comfortable to be with. Don't cause strain in others.

• Try not to let things bother you. Be easy-going.

•Don't be egotistical or know-it-all.

•Learn to be interesting so that people will get something stimulating from being with you.

•Eliminate the "scratchy" elements in your personality, traits that can irritate others.

•Never miss a chance to offer support or say "Congratulations."

•Work at liking people. Eventually you'll like them naturally.

•Honestly try to heal any misunderstandings and drain off grievances.

•Develop spiritual depth in yourself and share this strength with others.

Source: *Time Talk,* Time Management Center, Grandville, MI.

What's Your Personality Style?

Your personality determines the way you think, feel and behave—all the qualities that make you uniquely you.

Everyone is a combination of many personality styles. But most people have their strongest tendencies in one or two of them. Identifying your styles will help you make the most of your personality.

The 13 personality styles...

•Adventurous. Commonly a male style. Adventurous people are wanderers, real mavericks who will plunge into almost anything. They think every new experience is interesting. Because adventurers are restless, they don't settle down easily. Although many people have elements of this style in their personality, it isn't as common as many of the others as a predominant style.

To be more effective: Try to use your head rather than always being ruled by your appetite for change. Think about what you want out of life five, 10, 20 years from now.

•Aggressive. Take-charge people who are comfortable with power and authority. They are highly disciplined, goal-directed and function well in difficult and dangerous situations. Aggressive people often enjoy competitive sports. *Trap:* Their need to dominate other people can cause problems in intimate relationships.

To be more effective: Even if you're the boss at work, quit trying to be the boss at home. Give people a chance to make their own mistakes. At least once a week, ask those people closest to you what you can do to be helpful to them.

•Conscientious. Hard workers—sometimes even workaholics. They're perfectionists, pragmatic people who love order and detail. *Trap:* Most conscientious people are cerebral and emotionally undemonstrative.

To be more effective: Because conscientious people are susceptible to many stress-related health risks, you should broaden your personal life and learn to relax.

•Devoted. Most often female, the caretakers of the world. They generally put the needs of others before their own. Devoted people feel safe and secure in a relationship with a dominant person who makes life's big decisions for them.

To be more effective: Stop and think about your own needs and assert them more often. Express your anger directly. Practice decision-making.

•Dramatic. A common personality style, particularly among people with careers in film, television and publishing. Dramatic people are *people people.* They're very sociable, emotionally effusive and spontaneous. They like being the center of attention, are interested in clothing and appearance and in seeking sexual pleasure. *Trap:* They may be too impulsive and inattentive to the practical side of life.

To be more effective: Count to 10 before you jump into something exciting. Force yourself to go home and balance your checkbook.

•Idiosyncratic. The world's eccentrics, the individualists who wear and do what they want and don't give a damn what others think. They're interested in fringe ideas—UFOs, ESP, New Age philosophies, etc. Idiosyncratic people are self-directed and independent. They require few close relationships.

To be more effective: Make it easier on yourself to function in the real world—compromise and do the things other people want you to do occasionally. People who insist on setting their own rules often fail in some of life's most important areas.

• Leisurely. What we call the *California types.* They put their personal priorities first. Leisurely people may be willing to work nine to five...but not one minute more. They like to relax and enjoy themselves and jealously guard their personal time.

To be more effective: Expand your priorities to include other people. Helping others is *not* hard work, when you consider the rewards. And stop procrastinating. If you do the things you have to do today you'll have more time to have fun tomorrow.

• Mercurial. Similar in some ways to dramatic people, mercurial people are also impulsive. Extremely intense, they yearn for new experience and will quickly jump into a new love or lifestyle. They are uninhibited, spontaneous, fun-loving and undaunted by risk.

To be more effective: Work on developing some detachment and restraint. It will help you feel more fulfilled and successful.

• Self-confident. The go-getters—ambitious, capable and successful. They have a lot of innate confidence. Donald Trump typifies this style. *Trap:* Many self-confident people are insensitive to the needs of others. They'll climb over anyone in their drive to succeed.

To be more effective: Develop a realistic sense of your own shortcomings. *Ask yourself:* What's *not* so great about me? How would my loved ones answer that question? Stop concentrating on your own goals and focus on the needs of those close to you for a while.

• Self-sacrificing. These people think that to live is to serve...to love is to give. They're generous to a fault, helpful, considerate, accepting, humble, long-suffering and rather naive and innocent. At its best and most noble, this is the selfless style of which saints and good citizens are made. *Trap:* At their worst, self-sacrificers can turn into guilt-pushing martyrs.

To be more effective: Work on establishing a better balance of give and take in your life. Focus more on yourself and less on others.

• Sensitive. Fearful worriers who concentrate on the potential pitfalls before they take any action. They'll pack four suitcases for a weekend trip to make sure they don't forget anything. Sensitive people are very self-conscious and worried about what others think. *Trap:* Although they like other people, they hold back because of their anxiety and lack of self-confidence.

To be more effective: Change one or more of your routines for the sake of change. Doing something you would prefer to avoid will help you overcome your anxiety about the future.

• Solitary. Loners who are perfectly content to be by themselves. Solitary people are usually even-tempered, unsentimental and unflappable. They're not feelers, they're doers and watchers. *Trap:* Because they don't have strong feelings themselves, they often can't understand other people's feelings.

To be more effective: Watch how people express their feelings and accept the fact that feelings are important to most people. Instead of retreating when pressured by people, tolerate your discomfort and stick around a little longer.

• Vigilant. We call this the *New York style*—it's most common in high-powered, competitive, urban areas. Vigilant people are very alert, very watchful and very wary. No one puts anything past them. Perceptive and aware of their environment, they are constantly sizing people up.

To be more effective: Try to remember that others may see your guardedness as a sign that you don't like them. Every time you find yourself wondering about someone's ulterior motives, think about other, better motives that could explain the same action.

Source: John M. Oldham, MD, associate chairman, department of psychiatry, Columbia University College of Physicians and Surgeons and acting director of the New York State Psychiatric Institute. He is coauthor, with Lois B. Morris, of *The Personality Self-Portrait: Why You Think, Work, Love and Act the Way You Do,* Bantam Books, 666 Fifth Ave., New York 10103.

The Perils of Success

There are dangers in being a big success at anything. No matter how good you are at what you do, it eventually becomes second nature.

Trap: People who don't continually update their knowledge—no matter how successful they are—become fearful of new ideas, creativity and risk-taking. *Result:* Their area of success becomes an area of mediocrity.

Problem: Hangers-on...

Some successful people wind up surrounded by people who make their living from winners' ideas. And because these hangers-on fear offending the successful ones, they become a group of yes-men, who insulate the winners from reality.

If that happens, if a successful person stops paying attention to what's really going on in his/ her business and the world, his position is in danger.

Example: In the 1970s, American carmakers, despite massive evidence to the contrary, refused to believe that car buyers wanted high-quality, economical cars, and continued to make low-quality gas-guzzlers.

Problem: Tunnel vision...

Once someone's life is defined by success in a particular field, his focus often gets narrower and narrower. Instead of taking new risks, branching out into new areas, he tackles only projects that repeat what he has already done well...and loses his edge.

Example: Roger Corman, a producer of successful horror films, never wavered from his original low-budget, high-gore formula. Although many of his protégés, film-school grads whom he hired cheaply to act and direct, have gone on to become famous Hollywood stars, Corman is still relatively unknown.

Problem: Continued demand...

Many successful products, ideas, etc., are spawned by the needs of the time and creative, aggressive energy.

Trap: Although the times change, the person who generated the success doesn't change along with them. His next project isn't based on what's needed now...but on what worked for him before.

The difference between doing something because there's an urgency about it and doing something because there's a continued demand for it represents a subtle shift.

Example: Many 1960s rock groups, like the Beach Boys, who were once vibrant and creative, have become caricatures of their former selves. Paunchy and graying, they perform stale renditions of their old hits...to audiences of people who don't want to change, either.

In some instances, a person who is quite successful in his own little corner of a particular field tries to gain recognition from the outside world. But his methods are so outdated he winds up looking ridiculous.

Example: A therapist with a successful practice sent me her manuscript for a book about therapy. I found that the basic theory and assumptions—even the character structures of the people she described—were all 20 years old. There was absolutely nothing new in the book. *What had happened:* Although she had been able to keep a practice going with her outdated methods, she certainly wasn't equipped to write a useful, up-to-date book.

What successful people need to know...

Assume that even if you're doing well... even if your services are in demand...even if you're growing and learning in your specialty, that you're getting out-of-date.

Assume that brilliant new processes and wonderful new people have emerged in your field while you've been busy at your "cobbler's bench."

Keep looking around. Keep seeking opportunities to expand in ways that weren't available when you became successful in the first place.

Example: The therapist mentioned above should have been reading about and attending workshops in the latest techniques. Then, if she still wanted to write a book about her methods, she could have acknowledged that, although the new techniques are good, her old-fashioned approach still works better for certain people.

Ask the people around you if you're resting on your laurels. Ask friends, family and co-workers to tell you things that you may not have noticed about what's going on in your business and in the world.

Helpful: Recognize that it's wise to encourage people to tell you things that may make you uncomfortable. Don't identify with your success. Once you start seeing yourself as Mr. Widget-Maker—rather than Joe who makes widgets, plays tennis and loves his family—you're in danger of losing your identity as a multifaceted individual.

Doing the same thing over and over, no matter how well, leads to disengagement and disinterest. Once you lose interest you start ignoring the changing environment, setting up a vicious cycle.

As soon as you start to feel disinterested, step outside your realm and make a shift in focus. Look for new challenges that may use what you're already good at...but will still get you to try something new.

Source: Martin G. Groder, MD, a psychiatrist and business consultant in Chapel Hill, North Carolina. His book, *Business Games: How to Recognize the Players and Deal With Them*, is available from Boardroom Classics, Greenwich, CT.

Simple System to Help You Operate at Your Highest Level

My *Intensive Journal* process combines one of the oldest methods of self-exploration—keeping a diary—with a new, highly structured format that enables journal-keepers to get to know themselves on ever-deeper levels. The process is designed to help people discover internal resources they didn't know they had.

Simple system...

Putting your day-to-day thoughts in writing automatically forces you to become more introspective. This helps you identify patterns in conscious and unconscious thinking.

As you work in your journal, the experiences of your life—times of exaltation and despair, moments of hope and anger, crises and crossroads, failures and successes—will gradually fit into place. You will discover that your life *has* been going somewhere, however blind you may have been to its direction.

Getting started...

The journal itself is just a large three-ring notebook filled with paper and divided into many sections. Don't think that you have to write something in each section each day. Some sections you'll want to write in quite frequently. Others may be saved for special occasions.

Although you should write in your journal as often as possible, writing should never be a chore. Once you've established a dialogue with your journal, your inner self will tell you when there are things to be written...and you'll naturally turn to your journal as a means of self-expression and discovery.

The major sections...

• Period log. This is where you'll make your first entry each time you write. Write about things that are going on in your life *now*. Now can be a short or a long period of time.

Example: For one person, *now* may reach back three years since he was involved in an automobile accident and was hospitalized. For another person, *now* may be merely a few weeks since he met a new friend, moved to a different city, began a new job or experienced another significant change in circumstances.

Ask yourself: Where am I now in my life? Write in a nonjudgmental way.

• Twilight imagery log. After you complete your basic entry in the period log, try to duplicate the twilight state between sleeping and waking. By working in that intermediate state of consciousness, you can reach consciousness levels that are difficult to contact any other way.

Meditation exercise: Sit quietly in a comfortable position. Relax. Close your eyes. Follow your breathing until you feel a great calm. On your mental screen, picture a deep well. Enter the well and go deeper and deeper. At the bottom of the well is a river. The waters are muddy but they begin to clear.

Examine the images that appear, then allow yourself to become a bit more alert and jot those images down. Then return to the twilight state. Keep moving back and forth jotting down the images.

Ask yourself: Do the images suggest anything?

•Daily log. These entries should focus the emotions you experienced during the day. Include only a minimum of descriptive material. The primary purpose of the daily log is to provide ideas for other sections of the journal.

Example: If you mention your father in the daily log, you might want to talk with him in the upcoming *Dialogue* section.

•Stepping-stones. List the dozen or so key events that have shaped your life. *Include:* Important times in your life from childhood—school, first love, marriage, divorce, parenthood, friendship, relocation. Explore the periods when possibilities were opening for you, when you had alternatives, when critical decisions were made or unmade.

Don't judge yourself. Make neutral observations about your life. *Purpose:* To recreate in the present the exact feelings you had when you were going through a momentous time. Our stepping-stones made us who we are today.

•Life-history log. When you don't want to be sidetracked from the section you're working in, but want to retain a memory that has arisen, record the thought briefly in this section. This will become a grab bag of memories that don't fit anywhere else.

•Intersections: Roads taken and not taken. Record here those experiences that marked an intersection in your life, where some kind of change became inevitable.

The choices you made at those intersections left many potential paths untouched and unexplored. Although those unlived possibilities have never been given their chance, you may still be waiting for an opportunity to do so.

Examples: You got married instead of pursuing an acting career...you took a corporate job instead of starting your own business.

Ask yourself: Can any of these roads still be traveled? How do I feel about doing it now?

•Dialogues. Having begun by recording and exploring much of your life history, it's time to deepen your relationship with the important aspects of your life and let them speak to you.

Create subsections. Start each with a focus statement. Write down what is or was positive or negative about your relationship with that aspect of your life, how it got to where it is and what your hopes are for it.

Next, as best you can, list at least a dozen stepping-stones for that person or part of your life. Do the twilight imagery meditation. Then write a dialogue where you express what you really mean to each other. Listen carefully to what the other party—living or dead, animate or inanimate, spiritual or material—has to say to you. *Subsections:*

• *Person.* Someone who is living or dead, with whom you had an important relationship.

Example: In a dialogue with your deceased father you may ask, *Why didn't you ever really love me?* He may answer, *I did, I was just too busy to express it.*

• *Work.* List the kinds of work you've done in your life. State the situation you find yourself in regarding that kind of work, and listen to what the work has to say.

Example: You may talk to the bills you've been avoiding at the office. They may respond, *You don't want to pay us because you want to be a kid and have Daddy pay the bills.*

• *The body.* List two or three important physical events for each decade of your life, then relax and write a conversation with your body.

Example: An overweight middle-aged woman wrote, *When I was young, I could throw any rag on you and look great. Now I can't find anything big enough to cover you.*

•Now: The open moment. This section is about your future. First, sum up your experiences writing in the journal. Then, focus on your future in the context of your life history.

Write whatever comes to you. It may be a prayer, a poem, a brief focusing phrase that gives you a reminder about the continuity of your life.

Again, although journaling is important, don't feel that you have to write each and every day. What's important is that you *are* writing-...and, in doing so, learning more and more about yourself.

Source: Psychologist Ira Progoff, PhD, who pioneered the Intensive Journal concept, now taught in workshops all over the country. Dr. Progoff is the author of a series of books about keeping an Intensive Journal.

How to Use Fantasy As A Creative Tool

An active fantasy life is as crucial to the mental health of adults as it is to children. We tend to think that as we grow up we must leave our fantasies behind. But without fantasy, we would never dare to push or grow psychologically. We would become bland and constricted half-people. Fantasy has many useful functions in our lives. Here are some of them:

•Fantasy lets us "try out" new roles. For example, anyone who contemplates a job or career change first fantasizes what it would be like to do other kinds of work.

•Fantasy is a way of testing concepts and ideas, from new products to financial systems.

•Fantasy helps us master negative emotions and events. If we're very depressed over a loss or other unhappy event, we can allow ourselves to feel better by imagining something that makes us feel good.

•Fantasy can relieve boredom or an unpleasant experience. We've all fantasized through a traffic jam.

•Fantasizing can mean the difference between life and death in truly traumatic situations—war, solitary confinement, etc. Diaries of concentration camp survivors and prisoners of war attest to this.

•In sex, fantasy has been touted as an enhancer of pleasure, and shared sexual fantasies can indeed do this. But unshared fantasy during sex can be one way of tuning out and avoiding intimacy with the other person.

•Love relationships are predicated on fantasy. We project onto the loved one our fantasy of the ideal lover. This is an obstruction in one way because it keeps us from seeing the real person, but if we didn't do it we wouldn't fall in love at all.

•Fantasy displaces fear. We displace frightening things through fantasy as adults, just as we did as children. Thus, we imagine that harmful things will happen elsewhere—that someone else will have a car accident or get cancer.

While fantasy has many benefits, it's important to temper fantasy with reality. When we retreat into a fantasy world untempered by reality, there is the real danger of becoming nonfunctional—not getting out of bed in the morning or not taking care of the routine matters that ensure our daily existence.

Source: Dr. Simone F. Sternberg, a psychotherapist and psychoanalyst in private practice in New York.

To Develop Genius

Geniuses are made by sheer hard work more often than by simple inborn talent. *Steps toward developing genius:*

•"Falling in love" with a particular subject.

•Sharpening skills with time and effort.

•Mastering a personal style, with the goal being excellence rather than praise.

Source: Study by education specialist Benjamin Bloom, University of Chicago, cited in *Success!*

Pushing Toward Peak Performance

You have undoubtedly had the experience at one time or another of finding yourself in a high-pressure situation and performing way above your usual level.

A few people—you could call them peak performers—seem able to turn on the superchargers almost at will. Studies reveal that to be a peak performer you must be:

•Deeply and unambiguously committed to your goals.

•Confident of your ability to perform well.

•In control of your actions.

The commitment connection is fundamental...

•If you're not doing what you really want to do, it's not likely that you will give your best attention and energy to what you do.

•True commitment requires that you be in touch with your true desires.

•Pay attention to your most unguarded daydreams. Take note of these with an open mind and, in a tranquil moment, reflect on what they're telling you about you innermost desires. Give them credence. Don't edit. As you begin to act in accordance with those desires, you should find your performance improving.

Build or enhance confidence by controlling fear...

•When you feel fear taking hold, extricate yourself immediately from the bog of undefined apprehension and get a firm grasp on the concrete realities of the situation.

•Measure the difficulty of the problem. Make a mental or written profile of exactly what has to be accomplished. It is almost invariably much less than your undefined fears projected.

•Rate the problem on a scale of one to 10. This further serves to put the problem into realistic perspective, making it concrete rather than abstract.

•Compare your problem with others you have handled successfully in the past. Reflect on past instances in which you have performed well on similar or even more difficult problems.

•Imagine the worst. Define as objectively as you can the worst possible consequences that could result from completely "blowing it."

•A reality check won't alter the reality, but it will help to interrupt the self-perpetuating cycle of fear that keeps you from doing your very best. It will help you to act.

The importance of control in high-pressure performance is largely a matter of momentum and efficient use of energy:

•Distinguish between elements you can control and those you can't, and focus on what you can do.

•Choose an action (a can-do) that is concrete, that can be embarked on immediately, and that is in your power to carry out. As one can-do follows another, the task will be rapidly completed and the problem solved.

Source: Robert Kriegel, PhD, coauthor with Marilyn Harris Kriegel, PhD of *The C Zone: Peak Performance under Stress,* Anchor Press/Doubleday, Garden City, NY.

Dangers in Perfectionism

Emotional perfectionists believe they should always be happy and in control of their feelings.

They believe they should never:

•Feel insecure...so they worry about shyness, thus adding to their anxiety.

•Feel ambivalent about a commitment... so they're unable to make a decision in the first place and then feel miserable about their vacillation.

•*More reasonable goal:* To have general control of emotions and accept emotional flaws as part of our humanity.

Source: Dr. David D. Burns, cognitive therapist, Presbyterian-University of Pennsylvania Medical Center, Philadelphia.

How to Change Type A Behavior

Here are some ways to modify dangerous Type A behavior:

•Walk and talk more slowly.

•Reduce deadline pressure by pacing your days more evenly.

•Stop trying to do more than one thing at a time.

•Don't interrupt other people in mid-speech.

•Begin driving in the slow lane.

•Simply sit and listen to music you like while doing nothing else.

Developing Your Own Image of Success

•Recognize that you have talents and skills that are ingredients of success. Focus on these and forget your bad points entirely.

•Concentrate your energy. *One way to focus energy:* Split up your day into the smallest possible segments of time. Treat each segment as independent and get each task done one at a time. This will give you the feeling of accomplishment and will fuel your energy.

•Take responsibility. Be willing to accept personal responsibility for the success of your assignments, for the actions of people who work for you, and for the goals you have accepted. Seize responsibility if it is not handed over easily. There are always company problems that are difficult to solve and that nobody has been assigned to—take them for starters.

•Take action instead of waiting to be told. Listen to other people's problems and link their ambitions to your goals. Then deliver what you promise.

•Nurture self-control. Don't speak or move hastily. Don't let personal emotions color decisions that must be hard and analytical. Before taking a major action, ask yourself, "What's the worst that can happen?" Let that guide your next step.

•Display loyalty. No matter how disloyal you feel, never show it. Show loyalty to your boss, your company, your employees. Be positive about yourself and about others. Never run anybody down.

•Convey a successful image. Move decisively—walk fast and purposefully, with good posture. Look as if you are on the way to something rather than moping along.

•When you sit, don't slump. Sit upright and convey alertness. Choose a chair of modest dimensions. A large chair makes you look small and trapped. The chair should have a neutral color and be of a material that doesn't squeak or stick to your body.

•Avoid large lunches—they deprive you of energy. Successful people tend to eat rather sparingly.

Source: Michael Korda, author of *Success! How Every Man and Woman Can Achieve It,* Random House, New York.

Are You Really as Ambitious as You Think You Are?

To test your ambition quotient, rate the following statements on a scale of 1 to 5 to indicate how much the statement applies to you. A rating of 1 means it doesn't apply at all, and 5 means it applies very much.

•I truly enjoy working.

•Given free time, I would rather be out socializing with people than sitting home watching television.

•My first response to a problem is to attempt to figure out the most practical solution.

•One of the things I like best about work is the challenge of it.

•I believe very strongly in the work ethic.

•I have a strong desire to get things done.

•When there's a difficult situation, I enjoy assuming the responsibility for correcting it.

•I frequently come up with ideas—day and night.

•I'm not satisfied with the success I already enjoy.

•I rarely miss a day of work because of illness.

•I enjoy vacations, but after four to five days I look forward to getting back to work.

•I can usually get along with six hours of sleep.

•I'm interested in meeting people and developing contacts.

•I set high standards for myself in almost everything I do.

•All in all, I consider myself a lucky person.

•I'm not afraid to rely on my instincts when I have to make an important decision.

•I can think of very few situations in which I don't have a great deal of control.

•I recover from setbacks pretty quickly. I don't dwell on them.

•I'm not afraid to admit it when I make a big mistake.

•Achieving success is very important to me.

Scoring: 85-100 indicates very high ambition. With the right skills, you're almost certain to achieve your goals. 70-84 means higher-than-average ambition, and chances of achieving goals are very good. 55-69 is about an average score. If you achieve your goal, it won't be on ambition alone. A score below 55 indicates that success isn't an important goal for you.

Source: Robert Half, author of *Success Guide for Accountants,* McGraw-Hill, New York.

Setting Goals for Success

The lack of a clear goal is the most common obstacle to success, even for people with large amounts of drive and ambition. Typically, they focus on the rewards of success, not on the route they must take to achieve it. *Remedy:*

•Whenever possible, write down your goals, forcing yourself to be specific.

•Periodically make a self-assessment. Take into account your education, age, appearance, background, skills, talents, weaknesses, preferences, willingness to take risks and languages spoken.

•Ask for feedback from others.

•Don't try to succeed at something for which you have no talent.

•Try out your goal part-time. If you dream of owning a restaurant, work in one for a while.

Targeting Success

•Visualize the results you intend to achieve and write them down. *Example:* I will increase output 10%.

•List the personal benefits that reaching the goal will confer.

•Jot down at least 10 obstacles and try to find three possible solutions for each.

•Set a target date.

•Start tackling the problems, beginning with the easiest.

Source: Audrey Cripps, Cripps Institute for the Development of Human Relations, Toronto.

Climbing to Success Without Stumbling

The behavior our parents reinforce in us when we are children always encourages us to strive for bigger and better things. We gain approval for achievement and disapproval for failure. As adults, we keep striving because our developmental makeup says "You've got to have more."

To avoid rising to your level of incompetence:

•Take your life and your job seriously. But don't take yourself seriously.

•Don't spend your life climbing and acquiring. Instead, combine accomplishment and satisfaction.

•Climb to a level that you find fulfilling, stay there for a long period, and then move forward.

•Approach promotion avoidance indirectly. One successful ploy is to display some charming eccentricities that in no way effect your work performance, but which might discourage a promotion.

Source: Dr. Laurence J. Peter, whose latest book is *Why Things Go Wrong,* or *The Peter Principle Revisited,* William Morrow & Co., New York.

Overcoming Obstacles To Success

Personality traits can be a straightaway or a dead-end on the road to success.

Don't be caught in the following common traps:

•Inability to let go. People often stick with a dead-end job out of pride, stubbornness or unwillingness to admit that they made a mistake. Sometimes the comfort of the familiar is just too seductive. *To start letting go:* Take small, safe steps at first. Start talking to friends and associates about possible new jobs. See what's available during your vacation. Shake things up at the office by suggesting some changes in your current job. Take some courses and learn new skills.

•Lack of self-esteem. This is an enormous stumbling block. But, in fact, you may be judging yourself by excessively high standards.

•Procrastination. Like alcoholism, procrastination is a subtle, insidious disease that numbs the consciousness and destroys self-esteem. *Remedy:* Catch it early, but not in a harsh, punitive, self-blaming way. Look at what you're afraid of, and examine your motives.

•Shyness. If you're shy, the obvious remedy is to choose an occupation that doesn't require a lot of public contact. But even shy salespeople have been known to succeed. As long as they're talking about product lines and business, a familiar spiel can see them through. Concentrate on getting ahead by doing a terrific job rather than by being Mr. or Ms. Charming. Or take a Dale Carnegie course. They are helpful.

•Unwillingness to look at yourself. If you're not willing to assess yourself honestly, success will probably forever elude you. People tend to avoid self-assessment because they feel they must be really hard on themselves. Realize you've probably taken the enemy into your own head—you've internalized that harsh, critical parent or teacher from your childhood. Instead, evaluate yourself as you would someone you love, like a good friend whom you'd be inclined to forgive almost anything.

Source: Tom Greening, PhD, clinical supervisor of psychology at the University of California at Los Angeles and a partner in Psychological Service Associates, Los Angeles.

Secrets of Success

Top performers in all fields have these qualities in common:

•They transcend their previous performances.

•They never get too comfortable.

•They enjoy their work as an art.

•They rehearse things mentally beforehand.

•They don't bother too much about placing blame.

•They are able to withstand uncertainty.

Source: David A. Thomas, Dean of Cornell University, Graduate School of Business.

What Successful Men Think Makes Them Successful

•Bill Blass: "I guess it is my ability to concentrate and a dedication to the best in design —first fashion, and then the best in design for other things."

•David Klein, Dav-El Limousines, New York: "Even when I was a kid in New Rochelle, New York, I had more paper routes than the rest of the kids. Then I began to run parking lots at the local country club, graduated to being a chauffeur and continued to work, work and work more. I really do love to work."

•Tom Margittai, co-owner, Four Seasons restaurant, New York: "Determined professionalism combined with high standards of quality. Also, a lot of hard work. We try to understand the psychology of our market and to be first in everything."

•Mickey Rooney: "Through the years, it has been my great faith in God, and lots and lots of energy. At last I have it all together. I guess my good health is also a factor. I've been luckier than a lot, and I have always taken a positive outlook."

•Carl Spielvogel, Backer Spielvogel Bates Worldwide: "I think getting in early and staying late and not taking the 5:15 to Greenwich is one reason [for my success]. Also, being where the business is. As Lyndon Johnson once said, "You have to press the flesh." People you do business with want to know you and to be with you socially."

•Ted Turner, head of Cable News Network and sportsman: "Every day I try to do my very best. When you wish upon a star, your dreams really do come true."

How to Be Known As an Expert

Improve your chances for promotion and attract outside job offers by displaying expertise and calling attention to yourself.

Some ways to do it:

- Write an article for a key trade journal.
- Join an association of peer professionals. Get to know your counterparts and their superiors in other companies. Run for office in the association.
- Develop a speech about your work and offer to talk to local groups and service clubs.
- Teach a course at a community college.
- Write letters to the editors of trade journals, commenting on or criticizing articles that they publish in your field.
- Have lunch with your company's public relations people. Let them know what your department is doing, and see if they know of some good speaking platforms for you.
- Use vacation time to attend conferences and seminars.
- Write to experts, complimenting them (when appropriate) on their work and their articles. Whether or not they reply, they'll be flattered and they'll probably remember your name.

Source: Errol D. Alexander, president, Profiles, Inc., Vernon, CT.

Lessons in Judgment

Good judgment is important for a successful career and personal life. But how does one develop it? There are virtually no books written on judgment and our researcher couldn't find any great articles on the subject. So—we asked six people known for their good judgment to define it and suggest strategies most people can use to improve their own judgment.

Alexandra Armstrong, financial planner...

I base logical judgments on past experiences. Whatever happened in the past is likely to repeat. What worked before is likely to work again.

Though all decisions are affected by intuition to some degree, I follow the principle *If it's logical and recurrent, go with it.* I ground my professional advice by reviewing financial trends of the past.

Example: In the summer of 1987, the price/earnings ratio of stocks was at historically high levels. In the past, this has signaled a stock market downturn. Thus our clients were prepared for the subsequent decline, although the enormity and brevity of the crash were a surprise to all of us.

Dr. Herbert Benson, cardiologist...

Judgment can't really be defined in any exact way. There has been some philosophical emphasis on decision theory, but that's very different from practical decision-making skills. Those can only be developed over time through trial and error, learning from your own experiences as well as those of others.

Good judgment really boils down to being able to weigh the relevant risks and benefits involved in a given situation and, as a result of this process, making an accurate assessment of what you should do.

When both the risks and benefits are substantial, it's important to look for ways to modify the risks without losing too many of the benefits.

One of the best ways to clarify the risks and benefits is to list them in two columns. This will help you be specific about each point and look at the decision more objectively. Before making that list, however, you've got to understand the implications of the decision.

Once I have looked at the problem objectively, I find it useful to back off and go on to something else—for a while. In our increasingly stressful world, the pace and anxiety that we live with hamper our decision-making abilities.

Being able to relax and let things rearrange in your mind is crucial to good judgment. Sometimes it just takes one night's sleep for the new perspectives—the sound perspectives—to fall into place.

Norma Kamali, clothing designer and entrepreneur...

As a designer my goal is always to create something new. I live by inspiration. What I *feel* is more important to the process than what I *think*, and a great deal of my judgment is governed by this.

Everything in my life is a totality—blending every experience and creating a spiritual connection between the outside and my inside world. I *sense* keenly everything that is going on in the world and filter it through my emotions and experiences. Then I create pictures in my head and visualize them by sketching, drawing or doodling.

I trust my intuition when making judgment calls, but I'm constantly open to improvement since I believe there is always another way to do it. I make quick decisions but then have to edit myself. Fortunately, another side of me likes to pay attention to detail. Keeping "to do" lists helps me stay disciplined and focused. I don't do this on a computer, which is too impersonal, but with pen and paper.

Bouncing back and forth from the concept to the details, zooming my mental lens in and out, is key to staying flexible, having perspective and exercising good judgment.

Dr. James Masterson, psychiatrist...

There are several important capacities that contribute to good judgment:

- The ability to perceive reality rather than living in your fantasies.
- The ability to control your impulses to act until you have figured something out.
- Having the imagination to see beyond the present to what the future holds.

But the sum of these capacities doesn't necessarily make for good judgment in all areas of life. The capacity for judgment in one arena is not always evident in another arena.

Example: Many people are very successful at work but have enormous problems in relationships because their judgment becomes severely inhibited when their emotions are involved. They act mostly on the basis of their own fantasies. The more objective they can be, the freer they are to use this capacity for judgment.

Often, bad judgment is just part of a pathological defense mechanism, as when people make self-defeating or self-destructive decisions about their lives.

Example: There are people who, because of their own fears and anxieties, pick unavailable mates to act out their fantasies. You could say their judgment is poor, but it isn't really their judgment that is operating. It's reality being denied. They never have the data to make the right judgment.

You can develop finely tuned judgment as long as you can see reality as it is—that's number one. Next—comes being able to figure out the meanings and consequences of the reality you are seeing...articulating the choices...and choosing the one that works out best.

In my profession, we tend to think that everybody who is healthy has good judgment, but I'm sure that's not true.

There is definitely an element of intuition to good judgment. We all operate on it, sometimes consciously and maybe more often subconsciously. You can hone your intuition through experimentation. Learn from what you judged —well and poorly—and put it back in the "computer" to decide how you're going to deal with the next problem. Remember where you went wrong, so that next time you will have a sense of when to back off from a course of action and reconsider what you should do.

Dr. Dagmar O'Connor, psychologist...

We use judgment in two different ways. First —when we're asked to make decisions for others. Second—when we must make decisions that directly involve ourselves.

Most of us have good judgment about an issue that involves someone else. That's because we're emotionally detached and therefore free to reason more clearly. That is also why it's smart to seek the advice of others...and why no one should serve as his/her own lawyer.

Judgment is steered by motivation to do well or badly for ourselves—to succeed or fail. Such motivations are usually formed in childhood by parental permission.

When we turn *inward* for advice or assistance, unconsciously we are searching our pasts for reference points to help us solve the problems. When we are unable to reach rational decisions, it is often because memories from our pasts are holding us back or distorting our reasoning.

This helps to explain why it is possible for someone to excel in judgment for others—but fail miserably for himself. Every day there are examples of judges—financial planners, bus drivers and parents—who consistently make wise decisions on behalf of society, clients and children but do not exercise the same good judgment for themselves. *Examples of how unresolved childhood issues can impair your judgment:*

•Personal relationships. You've ended a relationship with someone who is nice and supportive because you feel he/she is boring. You clearly want some passionate excitement with someone who is not so available. *Reason:* You probably had parents who were not emotionally available.

When you continually find yourself in abusive or dysfunctional relationships, it could mean that you were raised by parents who didn't act toward you in respectful and loving ways...and, therefore, you have learned to be attracted to people who are not respectful or loving.

If, when you were a child, your parents gave you the feeling that you didn't deserve much, you will make judgments that reaffirm that treatment. If parents teach children that they are worth a lot and will be successful, the children will then grow up to realize that in their own judgments.

Going forward, you need to present a role model of success, self-esteem and happiness for your children, because good judgment originates out of that confidence.

•Business relationships. You pick a bad business partner and confide too much in him. Everyone tells you the person isn't quite right for your needs, and the evidence confirms this, too. Yet you persist, simply because you want to be different and believe that you know better than anybody else.

You have a need to not listen to anybody's advice. This may mean that as a child you could not trust your parents—perhaps for good reason. Your parents may have been too controlling, and you are still fighting that perceived parental control in your adult life. If you consistently pick bad business partners, you should look for deeper reasons for why you want to hurt yourself. You may be reliving a parental relationship rather than succeeding at your business.

Dr. Clifford Sager, psychiatrist...

Good judgment helps you make the right decision at the right time. It can be a very small —or very important—matter. It can also be something you have time to mull over or something that must be done in a split second, such as when a car is coming toward you in the wrong lane. Some business decisions must be made almost as quickly.

Judgment is partly instinctual and partly developed through experience. As children, we learn to judge when the stove is hot. Later we must make judgments between or among a variety of alternatives, including complex decisions about other people.

The higher you go professionally, the more difficult it is to make these judgments. No matter how much information you have, you reach a point at which you must consult your instinctive judgment to make the right decision.

Often your reasons may be subliminal. Over time, you learn to discern which instincts are solid and which are based on your own associations and preconceptions.

When it comes to personal relationships, it can be more difficult to judge from instinct because we're not aware of what we're reacting to. We are often attracted to people because we want to become like them. Or we may heartily dislike someone without recognizing that it is because they share our faults—faults that we don't like and can't confront in ourselves. Part of developing good judgment is knowing your limitations—and that is important. It's best not to make judgments regarding things about which you know little.

Sources: Alexandra Armstrong, a certified financial planner and chairman, Armstrong, Welch and MacIntyre, financial advisers, 1155 Connecticut Ave. NW, Washington, DC 20036.

Herbert Benson, MD, Mind/Body Medical Institute, associate professor of medicine, Harvard Medical School and chief of the division of behavioral medicine, Deaconess Hospital, Boston.

Norma Kamali, owner and president, Norma Kamali, Inc., 11 W. 56 St,. New York 10019.

James Masterson, MD, a psychiatrist in private practice in New York, and author of *The Search for the Real Self: Unmaking the Personality Disorders of Our Age.* The Free Press, 866 Third Ave., New York 10022.

Dagmar O'Connor, PhD, psychotherapist and sex therapist in private practice in New York. She is the author of *How to Make Love to the Same Person for the Rest of Your Life and Still Love It.* Bantam Books, 1540 Broadway, New York 10036.

Clifford Sager, MD, psychiatrist and psychotherapist, 65 E. 76 St., New York 10021.

Check Your Premise

Many times we are stumped by a problem, even though what we're doing seems to be consistent and logical.

The problem in such cases is often with us —we often have the wrong premise or make faulty assumptions and fail to consider the possibility that these errors are the source of our problems.

Even in mathematics, which we consider an exact science, certain premises for a given set of assumptions are arbitrary. This means that they may as well be picked out of a hat—there's no way of proving them. People choose premises from their experiences, observations and firm beliefs, and these premises are sometimes faulty.

Example I: Euclid said the world was flat because, as far as the eye could see, it was. Since his geometry was based on a flat world, no matter how logically and consistently he worked it out, it had to be flawed.

Example II: Gorbachev believed Communism would work better if it was reformed. He believed that central planning could satisfy people's needs as well as individual free choice. And he mistakenly assumed that loosening repression would allow a slow change in Soviet society rather than the rapid dissolution of Communist rule that actually occurred. His faulty premises led to results that were the opposite of those he intended.

Premises governing human relationships are equally arbitrary. It was once assumed that women couldn't be economically independent. This was one of the premises that all social arrangements were based on. In fact, because that was assumed to be true, it made sense not to give a woman the vote because she was a dependent part of a single household and the household was thought of as having one vote, which should be cast by the breadwinner. When that premise fell away, many other things that seemed logical also changed, such as women always deferring to men in relationships.

Problems in business...

The same arbitrariness has governed many major business decisions.

Example: For many years, Detroit operated under the assumption that Americans wanted big, fast cars that could—and had to—be traded in regularly.

Faulty premise: Quality control wasn't important. The Japanese realized that quality was important and became major competitors in the American market. That false premise resulted in a huge shift of assets from one country to the other.

How false premises affect your life...

The first few times you fail with something, it may be because your technique is wrong... you haven't practiced enough...you need to clean up your act. If you fail persistently, however, you need to check your premises.

Example: The woman who is involved with her third alcoholic because she believes this one is going to go to AA as he promises.

False premise: Alcoholics need her, or someone like her, to save them. She's not seeing how dependent she is on having to take care of someone so she doesn't have to face her own problems.

People often fail when they go into business for themselves because they never check their premises.

False premise: If you invent a better mousetrap, you'll be a success. Many of the currently available great ideas have already been invented and either failed because of inherent flaws, because they're not marketable or because the skills of the business owner were poor. The process of taking a great idea and turning it into a successful business is very complex. Just having the idea is only one of the multitude of elements needed for success.

We have a strong resistance to checking our premises because life would be unbearable if we didn't come to some firm conclusions about what various commonplace things mean —clothing, certain manners, types of speech. We've learned that it's too expensive or time-consuming to check our premises, and 99% of the time things do mean what they seem to mean.

Con men take advantage of this aspect of human nature. A con man sets up a scene that conforms to your premises. He knows your reactions will not lead you to check your premises until *after* he has fleeced you.

When you should check your premise...

You should check your premises whenever things are going wrong. Even in a con situation, people usually have an intuitive feeling that something is a little off. If your intuition tells you something is fishy, check your premise. It's always worth the effort.

Helpful: Take time to think for a while if you're asked to do something that doesn't seem right. Don't let embarrassment keep you from checking someone out thoroughly.

Listen to feedback. Whenever someone criticizes you, presume he's right and your defenses are wrong. This is a tremendous learning experience. If you listen to critiques carefully, you'll find there is some truth, no matter how far-fetched. You don't have to agree with what's said, but you do have to understand where it's coming from.

Example: Someone tells you he likes your suit, but it's the wrong color for you. Instead of getting defensive, ask questions about what's wrong with the color. As a result, you might find out about color analysis and decide to see a color consultant.

False premise: If it is a well-manufactured garment and fits well, the color doesn't matter.

Important: You need to analyze not just the criticism, but the premises on which it is based. You must understand the difference between the premises of the person giving you feedback and your own.

Example: Lionel is not getting what he wants from his employees. He asks Joe, one of his workers, what the problem is and is told that he's too pushy and demanding. When Lionel takes Joe's advice, and demands less and listens more, productivity improves enormously.

False premise: The harder you push, the more you get.

Source: Martin G. Groder, MD, a Chapel Hill, North Carolina psychiatrist and business consultant. His book, *Business Games*, is available from Boardroom Classics, Greenwich, CT.

Secrets of Appreciating Life

Despite the ever-growing amount of information we have about human nature, the soul is still impossible to define in pragmatic terms and still remains an enigma.

Unlike the brain, the soul has no physical or material reality. Yet it governs our values, relatedness and personal substance. Lose touch with your soul and the effects can be debilitating...even devastating.

For example, many people who are in perfect physical health and have attained wealth and fame feel a deep sense of unease when they neglect their souls.

Not knowing how to care for your soul leaves you at a serious disadvantage, since painful experiences are unavoidable. Confronting them and learning from them are the ways to nurture the soul.

Most of us recognize that some of the more simple aspects of life are particularly satisfying.

That is why we refer to them as "food for the soul" and "music that is good for the soul."

But every aspect of life—family, love, work ...even dark aspects like jealousy, depression, and illness—can provide spiritual food for the soul if we approach them in a receptive way.

Family and the soul...

Many people today who regard themselves as self-sufficient have lost the important truth, which was taught by traditional societies, that we must honor our families.

Honoring the family helps the soul because the family is a source of religious awareness. A family forces you to realize that you did not create yourself...that you have a unique place in the world. Within your family, you can be who you really are and learn to appreciate the individuality of others.

To help family appreciation: Don't expect too much from your family. Try to appreciate each member's unique qualities. If you are miserable and feel it's because of the way you were treated by your family when you were young, try a different perspective. Ask yourself, "Where did my good qualities come from?" It's highly likely that your family had a great deal to do with them.

Love and the soul...

Many people have unrealistic expectations of love—within the family, with spouses, with friends. Love isn't perfect and eternal. It passes through different stages...and often ends.

To satisfy your soul, a loving relationship must honor the other person's soul as well. That means recognizing who the other person really is...and allowing that person to change. You must pay attention and allow the relationship to develop.

For soul-satisfying relationships: Spend time together...write letters to each other...visit friends together. When you talk to each other, don't just talk about work—talk about what's in your heart.

Work and the soul...

Work is a major part of life. Few things satisfy the soul more than a fulfilling vocation. But if the work you do conflicts with your soul—because of your sense of ethics or aesthetics—it may make you very unhappy, no matter how much you earn.

If you are in that position, look into a career change. If a change isn't immediately feasible, don't despair. Look around...for years, if necessary. And meanwhile, even though you are unhappy in your current work situation, practice other ways to care for your soul.

To help your soul if you are unhappy at work: First, acknowledge your situation. Then, make the best of it by putting more effort into areas that do satisfy your soul...family, friendships, hobbies, sports, travel, etc.

Soul and the darker side of life...

Anyone who thinks that life's only goal is happiness will be troubled. The less-pleasant parts of life cannot be avoided.

If you reflect on your unhappy experiences, you will find that they offer their own gifts... and contribute to the development of your soul. *These experiences include...*

- Jealousy, which comes with intense relationships. It teaches that relationships are demanding...and deepens your understanding of both the self and the relationship.
- Depression, which deepens the personality, leaving you better able to cope with future problems. People who have only seen the sunny side of life may be overwhelmed when something bad happens...those who have gone through depression look at the world in a more realistic, accepting way.
- Illness, which forces you to reflect on your own mortality and teaches that you are not as strong or as independent as you thought.

To benefit from troubles: When you suffer physical, social or economic setbacks, see what you can learn from the experiences. Acknowledge your human frailties...don't be afraid to ask others for help. You will gain a richer perspective on friendship and the meaning of life.

The art of life...

Modern society pursues functionality and efficiency at all costs, but the human soul craves beauty. Much of the unhappiness in today's world comes from a neglect of the beauty of life in favor of acquiring things and getting results quickly.

Since schools don't often teach the arts, your soul is starved of the imaginative diet it needs. You can make up this deficiency by striving to bring beauty into your life.

To feed your soul in everyday life: Even if you don't consider yourself artistic, you can use your imagination to enrich the way you live.

When you decorate your home, for example, don't settle for someone else's taste... even if it's advice from a high-priced interior decorator. Your home should express your feelings and imagination. Think about the location, the furnishings, and the decorations, so they satisfy you emotionally and express your soul's individuality.

By living in a way that cares for your soul faithfully every day, you can let your individual genius emerge and discover in full measure who you really are.

Source: Psychotherapist Thomas Moore, PhD, a former monk with academic degrees in theology, music and philosophy, and author of the best-seller *Care of the Soul: A Guide for Cultivating Depth and Sacredness in Everyday Life,* HarperCollins, 10 E. 53 St., New York 10022.

Key to Self-Confidence

No one is born competent. We develop competence through repeated exposure, study and practice. This requires willingness to take some risks without knowing what the outcome will be. *Also important:* Accepting the possibility of failure. Ironically, fear of failure actually creates failure. If you do not test your dreams or try to do something important to you, you are sure to fail.

Source: *On Target: Enhance Your Life and Ensure Your Success* by Jeri Sedlar, president, Sedlar Communications, New York marketing and productivity consultants. MasterMedia Limited, 17 E. 89 St., New York 10128.

The Importance of Self-Esteem

Healthy self-esteem is a basic human need. It is indispensable to psychological development...to resilience in the face of life's adversities...to our feeling of belonging in the world ...to our ability to express joy. As the world becomes more complex, competitive and challenging, self-esteem is more important than ever.

The shift from a manufacturing-based society to one based on information, and the emergence of a global economy characterized by rapid change have created growing demands on our psychological resources. Recently, the focus of my work has been to show how self-esteem principles and technology can be used to improve performance in the work place.

Self-esteem defined...

Despite the abundance of books, studies, workshops and committees devoted to the subject of self-esteem, there is little agreement about what it means. I think self-esteem has two essential components:

- Self-efficacy. Confidence in the ability to cope with life's challenges. Self-efficacy leads to a sense of control over one's life.
- Self-respect. Experiencing oneself as deserving of happiness, achievement and love. Self-respect makes possible a sense of community with others.

Self-esteem is a self-reinforcing characteristic. When we have confidence in our ability to think and act effectively, we can persevere when faced with difficult challenges. *Result:* We succeed more often than we fail. We form more nourishing relationships. We expect more of life and of ourselves.

If we lack confidence, we give up easily, fail more often and aspire to less. *Result:* We get less of what we want.

What self-esteem is not...

Self-esteem is a necessary condition of well-being. But it's not the only one. Its presence doesn't make life problem-free. Even people with high self-esteem may experience anxiety, depression or fear when overwhelmed by issues they don't know how to cope with.

I think of self-esteem as the *immune system* of consciousness. A healthy immune system doesn't guarantee you'll never become ill, but it does reduce your susceptibility to illness and can improve your odds for a speedy recovery if you do get sick.

The same is true psychologically. Those with strong self-esteem are resilient in the face of life's difficulties.

It's impossible to have too much self-esteem. People who are arrogant or boastful actually show a lack of self-esteem. Those who are truly comfortable with themselves and their achievements take pleasure in being who they are... they don't need to tell the world about it.

Becoming successful, powerful or well-liked does not automatically confer good self-esteem. In fact, talented and powerful people who doubt their own core value are usually unable to find joy in their achievements, no matter how great their external success.

Important: Self-esteem has to do with what I think of me, not what anyone else thinks of me.

The highly touted use of affirmations is also ineffective, or at best of marginal value, in raising self-esteem. Telling yourself you're capable and lovable accomplishes little if you are operating irresponsibly in key areas of your life.

Roots of self-regard...

Genetic inheritance may have a role in a person's self-esteem—it's conceivable, anyway. Parental upbringing can also play a powerful role.

Parents with strong self-esteem lay the foundation for that quality in their children. They raise them with plenty of love and acceptance, believing in their competence and setting reasonable rules and expectations.

Yet there are exceptions that we still don't understand. Some people who have these positive factors in their backgrounds become self-doubting adults, while others who survive seemingly destructive childhoods grow up with a strong sense of self-worth.

Strengthening self-esteem is not a quick or easy process. We can't do it directly. Self-esteem is a consequence of following fundamental internal practices that require an ongoing commitment to self-examination. I call these practices the *Six Pillars of Self-Esteem:*

- Living consciously. Paying attention to information and feedback about needs and goals ...facing facts that might be uncomfortable or threatening...refusing to wander through life in a self-induced mental fog.
- Self-acceptance. Being willing to experience whatever we truly think, feel or do, even if we don't always like it...facing our mistakes and learning from them.
- Self-responsibility. Establishing a sense of control over our lives by realizing we are responsible for our choices and actions at every level...the achievement of our goals...our happiness...our values.
- Self-assertiveness. The willingness to express appropriately our thoughts, values and feelings...to stand up for ourselves...to speak and act from our deepest convictions.
- Living purposefully. Setting goals and working to achieve them, rather than living at the mercy of chance and outside forces... developing self-discipline.
- Integrity. The integration of our behavior with our ideals, convictions, standards and beliefs...acting in congruence with what we believe is right.

Most of us are taught from an early age to pay far more attention to signals coming from other people than from within. We are encouraged to ignore our own needs and wants and to concentrate on living up to others' expectations.

Self-esteem requires us to listen to and respect our own sensations, insights, intuition and perspective. For some people, learning to do this may require the help of a competent therapist. For all of us, developing the pillars of self-esteem is a lifelong—and worthy—challenge.

Source: Nathaniel Branden, PhD, a clinical psychologist in private practice and founder of the Branden Institute for Self-Esteem in Los Angeles. He is the author of 11 books, including *How to Raise Your Self-Esteem,* Bantam Books, 666 Fifth Ave., New York 10103.

Unexpressed Feelings

Beware of unexpressed feelings—especially negative ones. People who do not express feelings get sick more often...stay sick longer...and die sooner than expressive people. *Example:* Nonexpression of emotion and denial of hostility or anger are two of the factors most related to unfavorable prognosis in cancer patients. Unexpressed negative feelings feed on themselves—for instance, anger can turn against the self and emerge as depression or severe anxiety.

Source: *Lethal Lovers and Poisonous People: How to Protect Your Health from Relationships That Make You Sick* by Los Angeles psychologist Harriet Braiker, PhD. Pocket Books, 1230 Avenue of the Americas, New York 10020.

Use It or Lose It... Physically...Mentally

Part of the brain is devoted to learning, striving to meet challenges and dealing with frustration, while another part takes care of establishing habits and routines. Let one part atrophy, and its functions are taken over by the areas that are used more. When you stop challenging yourself and expanding your skills, that part of your brain goes quiet and brain activity shifts to its humdrum mode. The more you let yourself become stodgy and fail to challenge yourself, the harder it is to reactivate that part of your brain.

Motivation is often a major victim of this process. Once you let your skills decay, it's harder to feel excited.

A little practice...

Practicing many of your skills just a little bit is more important than concentrating on just one or two.

How much practice is enough? There's no universal rule, but when it comes to physical exercise, a workout every other day for 20 to 40 minutes appears to be enough to keep you in shape...and healthy.

In music, too, it appears that a half-hour to one hour of practice every other day will maintain a significant level of skill.

So—using what you don't want to lose at least two to three times a week for a half-hour to an hour is a good minimum for which to strive.

Make practice count...

- Use the right equipment. If you're walking to maintain fitness, get good walking shoes. Want to hone your piano-playing skills? Get the piano tuned. It will make the experience more rewarding and increase the odds you'll keep doing it.
- Make practice enjoyable. Some people like to walk, run or bike alone...while others need to feel the support of fellow strivers in a gym or health club. Ask yourself what works best for you.
- Find your level of practice and stick with it. Some people want to keep their skills sharp in a relaxed way, without strain, as an enjoyable leisure pursuit. Others prize the exhilaration of feeling themselves tested and stretched. Let your personal preference guide you in choosing whether you practice your skills for fun or find opponents who will force you to stretch.
- Know your limits. A big mistake many people make when practicing is falling into the "pro" trap. They don't bother practicing their skills because they know they won't ever become the champions they so admire. Admire those who have achieved excellence, but don't model yourself after them. Realize your limitations, and remind yourself that the goal is to keep your abilities alive, not to conquer the world.

Be kind to yourself...

Attitude plays a big role in how well you perform and whether you stick to your practice regimen. A positive outlook fuels your determination to keep your capacities sharp, while negativity kills motivation. *Helpful...*

- Be generous and accepting toward yourself, particularly if you're trying to retain or regain competence in an area where you were once highly skilled.
- Accept the role of a student, even if your endeavor is something at which you once excelled.
- Don't match your performance against memories of a younger self at the peak of your powers...at a time when lots of practice had honed your skills.
- Be a kindly, patient teacher or coach to yourself, the kind who throws the ball to a kid a thousand times before the child learns to catch it properly. Summon up thoughts of past mentors. Enlist patient, supportive companions who will encourage you.

Source: Martin Groder, MD, a Chapel Hill, North Carolina, psychiatrist and business consultant. His book, *Business Games: How to Recognize the Players and Deal with Them*, is available from Boardroom Classics, Box 11401, Des Moines 50336.

3

Putting Your Best Foot Forward

Top 10 Etiquette Rules For Adults

•Return calls and answer letters promptly. Calls should be returned within 48 hours and letters within two weeks. If you cannot respond yourself within that time, have someone else do it for you.

Telephone etiquette: When you call someone and your call-waiting signals, ignore it. You made the call, so you should give it priority. Be respectful of a person's schedule and obligations when choosing a time to call.

•RSVP within one week to all invitations. Go to an event when you have accepted...call ahead if you can't make it. If you accept an invitation and then fail to attend, call or write to apologize.

•Introduce people properly and in a flattering way. State the person's name clearly and correctly, as well as his/her title, occupation, and city of residence if somewhere other than where you are. Also give their hobbies or interests especially when they are similar to those of the person to whom you're making the introduction. And always introduce the less important or younger person to the more important or older.

•Take care to use people's titles properly. Doctors, judges, people of military rank, and elected officials should always be addressed with their titles or "the honorable." Too few of us are doing this today, and it's very bad manners.

•Be sensitive to the culture, religious laws, and diet of international friends and colleagues. Brief yourself on their country before you see them. Know their country's leading politicians, the names of their country's great museums, their universities, and what types of foods they can and cannot eat.

•Watch your table manners. This can never be stressed enough. Don't stuff food in your mouth or talk while eating. Do not leave your dirty napkin on the table when you excuse yourself during a meal. Leave it on your chair instead. Wipe your mouth frequently. When finished, move your fork and knife to the right-hand rim of the plate—and sit up straight. Ignoring these things makes you appear rather uncouth.

•Don't monopolize the guest of honor. Give equal time to every guest, regardless of how important or unimportant his/her position. This is an act of kindness as well as good manners.

•Teach your children to respect their elders. Have them stand up when your friends enter the room...say, "How do you do?"...and shake hands. Parents seem to be failing in this, perhaps because they are not around their children as much these days. But making the effort will make your children's lives much easier as adults.

•Know how and when to apologize. Always make your apology as soon as possible after the event. Some acts require only a spoken apology, others require a spoken and written apology...and some require much more.

Example: About 10 years ago, I accepted an invitation to be the guest of honor at a dinner party, and then completely forgot about it. I called several times to apologize, wrote two letters of apology, and finally sent a dozen roses. To this day, I am still apologizing for that incident.

•Write thank-you notes for gifts, favors, meals, or any act of kindness. Also write notes to encourage, congratulate, and commiserate.

Source: Letitia Baldrige, renowned expert on manners and author of 14 books, including *Letitia Baldrige's New Complete Guide to Executive Manners,* Rawson Associates, 866 Third Ave., New York 10022. The book draws upon her experiences in the business world, diplomatic life, and the Kennedy White House.

Clothing Language

To psychiatrists, grooming, clothes, makeup, and all-around physical appearance are important clues to personality and mental health. Those clues can be useful, too, to people making hiring decisions or who otherwise want to be able to size people up.

Key: Appropriateness. Clothes and appearance have to be viewed in the context of a person's position and the milieu in which he operates.

Appearance clues:

•Overly meticulous. Constricted neat, not elegant neat. (*Example:* Very narrow, tight ties. Jackets always buttoned. People who arrange trouser creases each time they sit down.) Usually good indicators of an obsessive personality. Obsessiveness may be fine for employers seeking industrious, dependable types concerned with detail. It is not for those who want someone with creative capacity.

•Careless, torn, stained clothing and lack of attention to detail. These are signs of depression. *Another trouble sign:* Somber colors such as black or maroon, worn much or most of the time.

•Incongruous clothes that seem markedly inappropriate to the age of the person wearing them. This usually indicates a lack of friends and associates through whom he would have learned what to wear.

•Clothes that are too young: Short skirts or a "little girl" look on an older woman or the "preppie" look on a man obviously too old for the style generally indicates an image problem. Such a choice of clothes suggests an inability to tune into reality.

•Identification. People who go in for prestige symbols generally are using them as a means to inflate their self-esteem and for virtually no other reason.

•Focus. Attention-getting attire, particularly on men. *Example:* Going to the office (where such dress isn't expected) in jeans and work-shirt. This is usually a sign of a narcissistic personality, a type that sees the world as revolving around him and what he wants.

•Very manly styles on women. Increasingly evident in women who have left their roles as homemakers and gone back to the business world, it may well indicate discomfort about leaving home and reversing women's traditional roles. Overdoing anything in a dramatic way, whether it's "looking businesslike" or some other posture is always a sign of conflict.

•Button wearers. Whatever the message of their buttons, they have a shaky sense of self-esteem (which they try to bolster by identifying publicly with a group).

• Wearing sunglasses unnecessarily. People trust others more when they can see their eyes.

Source: Dr. Michael Levy, psychiatrist, New York.

Dressing for Success

Businesspeople's concern isn't with fashion but with function—the impact their clothes have on people. Let's face it, clothes are a power tool. Wear the right clothes and you can "sell" yourself successfully.

• Successful dress is really no more than achieving good taste and the look of the upper-middle class. The traditional styling of Savile Row dominates the world of businessmen's clothing—the understated elegance of English tailoring.

• Designers have been responsible for many positive changes in men's clothing in recent years, and some liberalization of styles, patterns and colors has taken place, but this trend is basically confined to leisure wear. Designers have had little influence on the mainstream of American business dress.

• Business styles change with glacier-like slowness, and there's no point in risking career, income and social position by gambling on fads.

• The most important element in establishing a man's authority is his physical size. Large men tend to be extremely authoritative. But they can frighten people. The large man should avoid all dark suits. *He should wear very soft colors:* Medium-range gray suits, beige suits and very light suits in the summer. The small man has the reverse problem. *The smaller man should wear high-authority clothing:* Pinstriped suits, pinstriped shirts and vests.

• Expensive ties give authority to the young. Buy the kind of tie which would obviously not be bought by a boy.

Source: John T. Molloy, corporate image researcher and consultant and author of *Dress for Success* and *The Woman's Dress for Success Book,* Warner Books, New York.

Male Body Type: A Factor in Executive Dressing

• For short men. The pinstripe contributes to an illusion of height. The vertical line formed by the classic three-button jacket will enhance the illusion, as will pockets that point inward and upward. No cuffs on trousers.

• For heavy men. Dark suits impart a lighter look. Best for men of ordinary height is a single-breasted jacket with a center vent. A double-breasted jacket is suitable for taller men—of any weight. Avoid pleats in trousers, as they add bulk. Darts are better for comfort and a well-tailored look.

• For thin men. Use pale, heavier-gauge fabrics to create a sense of bulk. Straight-legged trousers will give the legs a fuller appearance. Avoid tapered trousers, which conform to the shape of the leg.

For Men: What to Wear At the Office

Successful men dress very carefully for the office:

• Dress conservatively, in a style as similar to the style of those around you—and above you—as you can.

• Always wear a suit.

• To convey a stronger impression of authority, wear a darker suit—with a vest.

• To emphasize a financial aura, wear dark gray or blue pinstripes.

• Wear solid-color cotton shirts or conservative stripes. Avoid elaborate patterns and anything flashy, sharp or gaudy.

• The best ties are striped ("rep"), solid, dotted, "club," and "Ivy League" patterns. No flowers, foulards, or paisleys for office wear.

Source: John T. Molloy, author of *Dress for Success* and *The Woman's Dress for Success,* Warner Books, New York.

How to Dress for Success At Your Company

The key is to emulate your boss, but don't be obvious about it. *General rules:*

•Conservative-looking suit, white shirt (pale pastels if your boss and other senior managers wear them), matching tie.

•Muted colors connote trust, upper-middle-class status.

•Black, navy, pinstripe, and chalk-striped suits exude power, competence, and authority.

•Beware of loud pastels (gaudy); shades of pink (effeminate); gold or green-gray (unflattering); light blues, gray-beige (you're more likely to be liked than respected).

•*Also out:* European cuts, turtlenecks, clashing colors that hint of sloppiness or academia, sports clothes (save them for sports).

•Avoid styles or colors that threaten to become overpopular.

How to Buy Clothes that Make You Look Good

•Choosing color to "go with" your hair and eyes is a mistake. It's your skin tone that determines how a particular color looks on you.

•The more intense and dark your clothing, the larger you'll appear and the less likely to blend into the environment.

•White tends to wash out the face and yellow the teeth. Soft ivory tones are somewhat better.

•Don't rule out whole color groups—all blues or all greens. Most people can wear certain shades of most color groups. *Exceptions:* A few colors, such as orange and purple, are really not good for many people in any shade.

•Pay attention to pattern or weave. People who are short or small-boned should not wear big prints or checks. They can wear small true tweeds. Slender, smallish men and women are overwhelmed by heavy fabrics. Light wools are better for them than heavy worsteds.

•Consider aging skin in choosing colors. Wrinkled skin is minimized by softer shades. Hard, dark, intense colors maximize the evidence of aging.

•The colors surrounding you in your home or office determine the way in which the eye perceives your skin and even your features. Some colors will produce deep shadows, enlarge certain features or produce deep facial lines because of the way they interact with your skin tone.

•Don't change makeup to "go with" clothes. Makeup should be chosen according to skin tone only. Using the wrong color makeup is worse than wearing the wrong color clothing.

•Most men can't wear madras or bold plaids. When men choose sports clothes, they go wild in the other direction from the conservative clothes they wear to work. Most have had little practice in choosing dramatic colors that are suitable.

•A tan does make you look healthier, but it doesn't change the basic effect of certain colors on your skin. With a tan, wearing colors you normally look good in is important, because that's when those colors look better than ever.

Source: Adrienne Gold and Anne Herman, partners in Colorconscious, Inc., Larchmont, NY.

Dressing for Special Occasions

Unusual circumstances may call for a thoughtful adaptation of basic dress rules. Learn as much as possible about the geographical, educational and socioeconomic background of the people you'll be dealing with and tailor your wardrobe to their expectations. *Examples:*

•Appearing in court. The main problem here is establishing credibility, and the best way to appear credible is to surprise no one. For maximum effectiveness, look just as others expect you to look.

If you are appearing as a high-ranking financial officer, you'll dress differently than if you're appearing as a technical expert—even though you may be both. The higher up the management pyramid you wish to represent yourself, the more quietly opulent your dress should be.

• Keep regional/local considerations in mind. A New Yorker, for example, testifying in Texas would be well advised to tone down his dress, keeping it low-key.

• Appearing at an IRS audit. The right image for this situation combines authority with humility—respectable and respectful, but not too prosperous. *Keep it simple and conservative:* Wear one of your older suits (a well-worn Brooks Brothers would be excellent), preferably two-piece, with a plain white shirt and a conservative striped tie. Avoid jewelry and other signs of affluence.

• Television appearances. The dress standards of a TV show host are a reasonable guide. Dress less conservatively. Wear lighter colors. Leave the three-piece suit and other power symbols at home. Keep accessories simple and understated. Wear solid colors. Avoid small patterns.

• Public speaking. If you know in advance what color the background will be (or if you can choose it), wear a suit (preferably dark) that will stand out. Wear a contrasting shirt (preferably light-colored) and a solid tie.

• Job interviews. Dress for the interview, not for the job. Even if you will be a field engineer, come to the interview in a three-piece suit.

Tailor the quality of your dress to the level of the position you seek. A recent college graduate will be forgiven a $200 suit. A candidate for an $80,000 management position will not.

Source: John T. Molloy, author of *Dress for Success* and *The Woman's Dress for Success,* Warner Books, New York.

How to Prolong the Life of Your Clothes

• Hang jackets on wooden or plastic hangers that are curved to the approximate shape of the human back.

• Remove all objects from pockets.

• Leave jackets unbuttoned.

• Keep some space between garments to avoid wrinkling.

• Allow at least 24 hours between wearings.

• Use pants hangers that clamp onto trouser bottoms.

• Remove belt before hanging up pants.

Hair Care Hints

• Baby shampoos are not as mild as special-formula shampoos for dry or damaged hair. Detergents and pH levels put baby shampoos into the middle range of hair cleansers, which makes them right for normal hair.

• People with oily hair need a stronger shampoo especially made for that condition.

• Wet hair should be combed, not brushed. Hair is weakest when wet and can be easily damaged then. Use a wide-tooth comb to reduce the chance of breaking your hair.

• Twenty-five brush strokes a day is optimal for best distribution of natural oils in the hair. More brushing can cause damage.

Men's Hairstyles: The Trend isn't Trendy

Men's hairstyles today are short and genuine. Men want to look natural, not as though they just left the barbershop.

• The best stylist is nature. If we cut and comb our hair the way it wants to be cut and combed, it always looks good. If we try to imitate someone else's hairstyle, we always end up getting into trouble.

• A good barber makes the hair fit the customer's facial structure. He cuts the hair so the customer can take care of it himself. When the customer goes back to the office, his colleagues shouldn't realize that he just had a haircut. They should notice only that he looks better.

•A banker or Wall Street executive wants a conservative look. His hair doesn't come down over the tops of his ears. You shouldn't see a circle around the ear, either—just a perfect, neat haircut that tapers cleanly above the ear.

•Men in advertising can be a little more daring, with fuller, longer hair.

•The cosmetics company executive, who is in the business of making people look good, wants a little flair.

•Years ago, men who could afford it would get a toupee to cover bald spots. No more. If they do anything, they go for a transplant. But more and more, men want to look natural. They feel that if they have hair, good—if not, that's okay. As long as whatever they have is cut properly, they'll look fine. Hollywood reflects the change. Attractive middle-aged and younger stars are frankly balding: Jack Nicholson, Robert Duvall or John Malkovich.

•Eighty percent of men in their early forties cover the gray. By that time a man may have a good executive position, but he's aware that if he loses his job or wants to change jobs there's still a stigma attached to looking old.

•The man who is 50 or 60 doesn't care anymore about gray. He's been around, and he's confident about who he is. It's important to color the hair discreetly, so it looks natural. Regular touch-ups are important. Even the most professional hair-coloring jobs start to fade quickly and must be touched up.

•Beware of the former barbershop that suddenly changed its name from Joe's Barbershop to Joe's Hairstylist. The change may be in name only. The best method is to ask someone whose haircut you consistently like where he got it done.

Source: Peppe Baldo, a New York City hairstylist for bankers, brokers, lawyers, advertising executives, and other corporate and media executives.

The Secrets of A Great Shave

Treat your face to the most up-to-date equipment. It is false economy to buy anything less than the best, since the entire annual cost of shaving seldom exceeds $100. Also, blades and shaving creams are constantly being improved.

•*Shaving cream:* All types of cream (lather, brushless and aerosol in either lather or gel form) are equally efficient. Brushless shaving cream is recommended for dry skin. Buy three or four different kinds of shaving cream. Use different ones for different moods.

•*Blades:* Modern technology makes the current stainless-steel blades a real pleasure to use. *The best type:* The double-track blade.

•Proper preparation. Wash your face with soap at least twice before shaving. This helps soften the skin, saturate the beard and remove facial oils. *Best:* Shave after a warm shower.

•Shaving cream is more effective if left on the face for a few minutes prior to actual shaving. This saturation causes the facial hairs to expand by about one-third, which enhances the cutting ability of the blade.

•Except on the warmest days, preheat lather in the can or tube by immersion in hot water.

•The manufacturing process leaves a slight oil residue on the edge of the new blade. This can catch and pull the tender facial skin during the first couple of strokes. So start by trimming the sideburns, a painless way of breaking in the new blade. Always shave the upper lip and chin last. *Why:* The coarsest hairs grow here. Your skin will benefit from the extra minutes of saturation and wetness.

•When you have finished shaving, rinse the blade and shake the razor dry. Never wipe-dry a blade; this dulls the edge. When rinsing the blade, hold it low in the water stream for quicker results.

•After shaving: Save money by skipping the highly advertised aftershave lotions. Use witch hazel instead. It is odorless, less astringent, leaves no residue and is better for your skin than most of the aftershave lotions.

Clean Up

Best face-washing technique:

•Fill a sink with the hottest water your face can stand.

•Take a hard-milled soap, such as Grey Flannel (for men) or Old English Lavender (for women), and work up a rich lather.

•Work the lather into your face and throat with the tips of your fingers.

•Rinse by splashing with the sink's water, not running water. Never rinse with clear or cold water, which can dry skin or break capillaries. Hot water helps to both moisten dry skin by stimulating oil glands and dissolve excess surface oil if your face is oily.

•Blot gently (don't rub) with a towel, and let remaining moisture evaporate from your skin.

Source: James Wagenvoord, *Personal Style,* Holt, Rinehart and Winston, New York.

Messies Don't Have to Be Messy Forever

Messies are people who live with stacks of things they'll never need again—old books, last year's Christmas cards, worn-out clothes, etc. They're perfectionists who avoid making decisions for fear of making the *wrong* decision.

But so much clutter makes them inefficient. Messies save so much, they can never find the things they really *do* need.

The terrible truth: In one way or another, we're all Messies. Even people with the neatest-looking houses usually have a secret spot that has been taken over by things that really should be thrown away.

The first step in getting over the problem is to understand what makes you tick. *People hold on to things...*

...for sentimental reasons. They want to keep memories alive, and think that this means holding on to the objects associated with the memories.

...for future use. Messies keep things they think they might need one day.

...to define themselves. Many Messies surround themselves with objects from a life they think they *should* be living.

How to recover...

Once you understand *why* you're a Messie you can take control of your life by taking control of your environment.

The best way to start is by giving your house a thorough cleaning...and throwing out everything that you really don't need. *To succeed...*

•Break your cleaning project into small, manageable portions. The best strategy is now being used by the housekeeping staff at George Washington's home, Mount Vernon. *How it works:* They clean one room completely...then the next...and the next, moving in one direction around the house in a circle. When the last room is finished, the cycle starts again.

Some Messies become stalled just worrying about where to begin. *Solution:* Start at the front door. After cleaning that area, move to the first piece of furniture to the left, and so on until the whole house has been cleaned. *Exception:* Save the kitchen until the end. It's much too tough for a rookie.

Don't try to do the whole house in one day. Set a goal—an hour a day or a room a week... and stick to it. *Helpful:* Reward yourself for getting over rough spots (that awful closet, etc.) with a dinner out...or some other treat.

•Sort as you go. Get three boxes. Label them...

•Give away. Messies are frugal—they'd rather give something away than throw it out. The contents of this box must be given away within one week. *Reason:* Without a deadline, Messies will agonize over who to give things to. Do not wait to write cousin Enid to ask if her son wants the catcher's mitt.

•Throw away. Some things can't even be given away. The contents must be disposed of the same day.

•Store elsewhere. Messies are easily distracted. If they try to put something away in another room, they may turn on the TV or pick up a book...and the cleaning will end.

•Decide which items go in which box. *Ask...*

•*Does this have any monetary or sentimental value?* Messies see potential value in things. A broken toaster could be fixed, a stack of National Geographics might be worth a lot of money one day. But if there is no immediate value, the item belongs in the throw-away or give-away box.

•*Have I used it in the past year?* If the answer is *no*, get rid of it.

•*Might I find some use for this in the future?* If you have to ask this question about an item ...get rid of it. This is the sort of reasoning that got you into this mess in the first place.

How to live with a Messie...

It's not easy to live with a spouse or a child who balks at the thought of letting go of things.

Solution: Put his/her old magazines, toys and other things that you think should be thrown away into a box and write the date on it. Tell the person that the box will sit in X place (the garage, the basement, etc.) for six weeks...and that he may retrieve what he wants. At the end of six weeks, throw the box away.

If you treat the person with respect, he'll realize that you're trying to help him. And, chances are, he'll take little out of the box.

Source: Sandra Felton, a member of the National Association of Professional Organizers and founder of Messies Anonymous (MA).

Common Sense Business And Social Manners

A common error today is the failure to realize that there are at least two sets of manners—one for the business world and another for the social world. In the business world, it is not vulgar to talk about money or to brag. But the social world is just the opposite.

•In business, manners are based on rank and position, not on gender. The business lunch or dinner check, for instance, belongs to the person who initiated the invitation or the superior in the office. The gender of the person does not alter this tradition.

•Never worry about what service people (waiters, maitre d's, hotel clerks) think of you. If you use the wrong fork, it is up to the waiter or busboy to supply you with another. Don't worry about what he thinks of you.

•If you are critical of someone while at a dinner party, only to discover that the person you are belittling is the father (or close relative or friend) of the person with whom you are speaking, make a quick and complete U-turn. Add to the defamatory statement, "Of course, that's the basis of my admiration for him." Remember dinner table conversation doesn't have to be logical.

•The notion that it is unhealthy to disguise your feelings has helped lead to a decline in manners and social health. *One advantage of a little disguise:* You will have more feelings to share with intimates.

Source: Judith Martin, otherwise known as Miss Manners.

4

Communication Secrets

How to Develop the Fine Art of Negotiation

Too often we walk into a negotiation unprepared—and consequently uncertain. Whether we are going to be talking about a raise, a job, a house, the rent, summer plans, or where the kids go to school, it's unrealistic to expect to get everything we want.

That's because each person involved in a negotiation has different interests. Being well-prepared will help you understand the different interests. There is always the prospect that each side would do better by working out an agreement. The basic question is how to pursue that possibility—as a form of warfare or as joint problem solving.

Traditional haggling, in which each side argues a position and either makes concessions to reach a compromise or refuses to budge, is not the most efficient and amicable way to reach a wise agreement.

Better: Principled negotiation, or negotiation based on the merits of what's at stake, which is a straightforward negotiation method that can be used under almost any circumstances.

Checklist for principled negotiations...

Separate the people from the substantive problem. Think of preserving the relationship. Attack the problem, not the person. If the other side attacks you, as often happens, call him/her on it and ask him to return to the problem.

Focus on interests, not positions. Negotiating positions often obscure what people really want. Try to determine the true interests on both sides—usually you can find some common ground.

Generate a range of options before deciding upon one. Having a lot at stake inhibits creativity. Do not try to determine a single, correct solution. Instead, think of a wide range of possibilities that could please both sides. Look for a solution that benefits everybody.

Insist on using some legitimate standard of fairness. By choosing some objective standard

—market value, the going rate, expert opinion, precedent, what a court would decide—neither party loses face by conceding. He is merely deferring to relevant standards. Never yield to pressure, only to principle.

Develop your best alternative to a negotiated agreement. If you haven't thought through what you will do if you fail to reach an agreement, you are negotiating with your eyes closed. You may be too optimistic about your other options—other houses for sale, buyers for your used car, plumbers, jobs, etc.

The reality is that if you fail to reach an agreement, you will probably have to choose just one option.

An even greater danger lies in being too anxious to reach an agreement because you haven't considered your other options. It may be better to walk away.

Consider what kind of commitment you want. It's a mistake to think that every meeting has to result in a final decision. It's much smarter to view a meeting as an exploratory session. You can draw out what interests motivate the other side and draft promises without nailing anything down. This gives you a chance to sleep on the alternatives or consult others. If the other side comes back with new demands, you have the right to renegotiate as well.

Communicate. Without communication, there is no negotiation. But whatever you say, expect the other side to hear something different.

Solutions: Listen actively, paying close attention and occasionally interrupting to make sure you understand what is meant. Ask that ideas be repeated if there is any ambiguity or uncertainty. It's very important to understand perceptions, needs, and negotiating constraints.

Understanding is not agreeing. You can understand the other side's position—and still disagree with it. But the better you understand the other side's position, the more persuasively you can refute it.

Negotiating strategies...

• Marital roles. Learn to disagree without being disagreeable. You can disapprove of someone's behavior but still love that person. Discuss problems in a caring way. Make a joint list of issues that need to be addressed. Be firm but reasonable. Don't try to decide right away ...mull things over for a few days.

• Requesting a raise. As with all negotiations, prepare beforehand. Find out what others at your level are earning, both inside and outside your company. Be ready to explain why you deserve more—you've been coming in every Saturday to help with the workload...you've been training newcomers...you're dealing with the company's toughest customers...or you've been offered more elsewhere. Your boss needs a rationale that he can use with his boss or other employees who also want raises.

• Buying a house. Often, by exploring various options and payment schedules, an agreement can be reached that provides maximum tax advantage and financial satisfaction for both the buyer and the seller.

Example: If you want to move in before the current owners want to move out, you might allow them to store their furniture in the garage. Flexibility might be enough to make your offer more acceptable than a higher one from someone else.

• Divorce negotiation. Suppose you are a wife who doesn't trust your husband to make his agreed child-support payments. Fearing that you will have to keep going back to court to get payment, you ask your lawyer to negotiate for equity in the house instead. Your husband's lawyer says that's ridiculous. He's certain that your husband will meet his obligations. "OK," says your lawyer, "then the husband won't object to signing a contingent agreement—if he misses two payments for any reason, his ex-wife will automatically get the equity in the house and he will be off the hook for future child-support payments."

• Resisting early retirement. Your company is having financial difficulties and has to lay off thousands of people. Early retirement packages are being offered, but you really can't afford to retire yet. Instead, see what you can negotiate—offer to take part of your pay in promissory notes...if you don't need the medical coverage, offer to give it up...if health benefits kick in at 20 hours per week, offer to work only 19 hours...become a freelance contract worker.

If you can dodge the bullet for six months or a year, the company may be on track again.

Source: Roger Fisher, director of The Harvard Negotiation Project and Williston Professor of Law Emeritus, Harvard Law School, 1563 Massachusetts Ave., Cambridge 02138. He is coauthor of *Getting to Yes,* Viking Penguin, 375 Hudson St., New York 10014.

Writing it Out

Write down everything you do for one day. Be as specific as possible. *Example:* Woke up ...lay awake in bed a few minutes planning my day...went to the bathroom...took a shower ...dressed in blue sweat suit...reviewed notes for today's meeting.

Making changes in your life begins by knowing what your life already is. By recording the many things that take up your time, you can view your life clearly, without illusion or distortion.

Source: *How To Be Happier Day by Day: A Year of Mindful Actions* by Alan Epstein, PhD, co-founder, True Partners, a Marin County, California relationship counseling service. Viking, 375 Hudson St., New York 10014.

How to Read People

Much of people-reading involves making elementary, commonsense observations and then acting on them.

Observation tips:

• Don't generalize. Conventional wisdom says that if someone slumps in his chair, he's not very commanding, or if he leans forward, he's ready to make a deal. However, I've seen a lot of erect, attentive types who hung on my every word but never made a move. Any useful observation must be considered in the context of the particular situation.

• Learn the difference between posture and posturing. Look out for people who lean in toward you, who push things back on the desk at you, who sit back and strike poses, who dress pretentiously, who do strange things with lighting, or who have your chair placed lower than theirs. All those things are keys that you're dealing with a phony, someone who's more concerned with appearance than with accomplishment.

• Look at the eyes. People communicate with their eyes in situations where silence is called for. The next time you're in a meeting with people you don't know, notice the eye contact of the participants. It will tell you who's allied with whom, who is most influential, and, if you're the speaker, whether you're boring everyone to death.

• Use ego to your advantage. Most successful people are one giant ego with a couple of arms and legs attached. But a giant ego isn't necessarily a strong ego. It may be compensating for low self-esteem. Or someone who seems to have a weak ego may simply be low-key. When you know these things, you can work with them or around them.

• Make inferences from coworkers and subordinates. For example, if someone seems unwilling to commit himself to even minor details, it may be that his boss is a person whose ego demands that he make all the decisions.

• Take the fish out of water. People tend to reveal themselves in unexpected ways when outside their usual settings. For this reason I favor breakfast, lunch and dinner meetings. Even the way someone treats a waiter can be very revealing.

Source: Mark H. McCormack, author of *What They Don't Teach You at Harvard Business School: Notes From a Street-Smart Executive.*

How to Complain... Successfully

Complaining is a normal part of human life, especially among people who live together. Without complaining, our resentments fester into permanent barriers to communication. But even though they are essential, complaints have two strikes against them...

• They convey that there is something wrong with the other person's behavior, which no one likes to hear.

•They contain a command or a request—which is an indirect command—that the other person's behavior be changed.

Most adults have knee-jerk negative reactions to commands from other adults. *Result:* Rather than considering the content of the complaint, they respond with denials, defensiveness, and counteraccusations.

To complain more effectively, it's important to define the goal of your complaint. If you're simply venting your anger, it doesn't matter what you say. But if you want the other person to change his/her behavior, you should use a different technique.

The three-part message...

I use a verbal tool for complaining that works so well it seems almost magical. I call it the "three-part message": When you X...I feel Y...because Z.

The point of the three-part message is to avoid triggering the listener's resentment. It succeeds by targeting a specific, verifiable behavior and then linking that behavior to the speaker's feelings and a real-world consequence.

Example I: "When you forget to water the tomato plants, I feel angry, because the plants die."

Example II: "When you overdraw our checking account, I feel embarrassed, because our checks bounce."

Example III: "When you bring the car home with no gas, I feel anxious, because I might run out on the way to work the next morning."

The three-part message works only when you absolutely stick to the pattern. *Ground rules...*

•Part One/When you X: Cite one—and only one—specific behavior, which must be verifiable and beyond dispute. *Useful:* "When you yell at the children...." *Not useful:* "When you act like some tyrant...."

•Part Two/I feel Y: The emotion should be stated simply and without any exaggeration. *Useful:* "I feel distressed...." *Not useful:* "I feel like a second-class citizen...."

Pitfall: Drawing conclusions about your partner's feelings. *Not useful:* "I feel as if you don't respect me...."

•Part Three/because Z: Complainers must prove their right to complain...by describing a nondebatable consequence that reasonable people would want to avoid. *Useful:* "When you leave all the lights on, I feel frustrated, because our utility bills get so high." *Not useful:* "...because it means you don't care about how hard I work for my money."

The three-part message is not suited for intimate or complex issues. But if you use this to-the-point tool for your everyday problems, your partner may become more receptive to longer discussions as the need arises.

Source: Suzette Haden Elgin, PhD, founder of the Ozark Center for Language Studies in Forum, Arkansas (501-559-2273). She is the author of 23 books. Her latest book is *Genderspeak: Men, Women, and the Gentle Art of Verbal Self-Defense,* John Wiley & Sons, 605 Third Ave., New York 10158.

How to Say No to Anyone

Many of us say *yes* more often than we'd like. Whatever the reason, if you find yourself saying yes because you feel too guilty about saying *no,* here are some practical measures to help you protect yourself.

•Stall. This gives you precious time to work up an honest rationale for a total refusal. *Simply say:* "I don't know. I need time to think about it—give me an hour" (or a day, or whatever seems reasonable).

•Use humor.

•Try flattery.

•Tell white lies, if necessary.

Source: Barry Lubetkin, PhD, Institute for Behavior Therapy, New York.

How to Spot a Liar

Less than 5% of the population are natural liars...performers who lie flawlessly and make no mistakes. But research shows that the majority of people are fooled by liars. *Clues to look for:*

•The single biggest giveaway is a series of inconsistencies in the lie.

•Watch for changes in patterns of speech, especially when a person has to pause and think more often than usual to answer a simple question.

•Look for signs that the person is deviating from a usual pattern of behavior. Liars may use a monotonous tone of voice or change inflection less frequently when they lie. They may also use fewer hand and body motions than usual.

•A smile is the most common mask of a person's true feelings.

•Liars sometimes lie just for the thrill of telling a successful lie. *Giveaways:* Widening of the eyes and a trace of a smile.

•Ask questions when inconsistencies start to pop up in a story. Most people become willing prey to liars because they don't want to act suspicious or don't think they have the right to ask questions.

Source: Dr. Paul Ekman, professor of psychology, University of California, San Francisco, and author of *Telling Lies,* W.W. Norton & Co., New York.

To Rescue Yourself from Embarrassing Situations

What to do:

•Simply and quickly apologize. That gives you time to think, if nothing else. But don't overdo it. Apologizing profusely just makes the other person uncomfortable.

•Don't put yourself down by saying "I'm so clumsy" or "I can't seem to do anything right." If you go overboard, you might wind up convincing the other person that there really is something wrong with you.

•If you're habitually tactless, ask yourself if you felt enmity or anger toward the person you insulted...if something about him made you uncomfortable or envious.

•How to apologize: Don't play innocent by insisting your remark was unintentional. The other person knows you meant to hurt because that was the result. If you apologize honestly, telling the other person about your angry feelings, you're much more likely to be forgiven.

•Make a joke about your mistake. It relieves the tension of the moment and shows you're a good sport. The other person also feels less embarrassed. Sharing a good laugh about something that could have created a rift can even improve rapport.

When you get in a tough, embarrassing spot:

•If you have personality traits that make you feel awkward in certain situations, ask a friend for feedback about how you're really coming across. You might be very self-conscious about some traits, such as your shyness or a tendency to talk too much. But others most likely won't even notice.

•Change the subject when it seems that you've put your foot in your mouth.

•Agree to disagree. One of the most awkward moments for people is disagreement, especially about personal matters. Acknowledge that you have differences, but make it clear that you still like and respect that person.

•Don't relive the embarrassing moment, wishing you'd done it differently. Forget it. Don't spend the rest of the day telling everyone what a fool you made of yourself, and don't keep bringing up the incident whenever you see the person it happened with.

Source: Dr. Judith Meyerowitz, PhD, a psychotherapist in private practice in New York.

How to Start a Conversation with A Stranger

•Pay attention to the person's name when introduced. Repeat it. If it's unusual, ask about its origins.

•Look directly at the person. Lean forward a bit.

•Ask the person something about her/himself in a flattering way.

•Ask encouraging questions as the person talks about himself.

•Don't interrupt. If you have an interest in keeping the conversation going, let the other person talk about himself and his interests. Don't immediately begin talking about yourself. Be patient.

Source: James Van Fleet, author of *A Lifetime Guide to Conversation,* Prentice-Hall, Inc., Englewood Cliffs, NJ.

•Bombarding the other person with questions.

•Being too quick to give advice.

•Giving too many personal details.

Sources: *Better Communication* and Gerald Goodman, associate professor of psychology, UCLA, quoted in *US News and World Report.*

How to Say "No"

Say *yes* quickly. Say *no* slowly. When a letter or conversation begins with a rejection, the other person usually ignores the rest of the discussion, including the reasons for the negative decision.

The pattern to follow when saying no:

•Review the facts and reasons for the decision without revealing it.

•Build an argument in a step-by-step, fact-by-fact manner.

•Provide information to support the decision. (The goal is to have the other person acknowledge the validity of the rejection.)

•Say no politely.

Always say something good about the rejected idea, organization or person. Acknowledge the problem and the difficulty of its solution.

Source: William C. Paxson, *The Business Writing Handbook,* Bantam Books, New York.

Conversation Basics

Here are some ways to keep good conversation flowing:

•When talking with someone from a field you either don't know or don't care anything about, steer the conversation toward feelings rather than facts or details. By focusing on emotions that everyone shares, you can feel secure discussing anything.

•Make sure both people have equal power to bring up topics, change the subject and demand attention. *Avoid common conversational mistakes:*

Conversation Killers

Intimate talks will be more pleasant and productive if you avoid the following:

•Sentences that start with the accusatory *You* or the inclusive *Let's* or *We.* (Instead, try to begin more sentences with *I,* to make your honest feelings known.)

•Absolute statements. *Example:* "That was a stupid movie."

•"I don't know." (You probably have some inkling of an answer, even if it's only to add, "Let me think about it.")

•"I don't care." (Even a weak preference should be voiced.)

•*Ought, should, must, have to.* Instead, try *I might, I would like to* or *I want to.*

•Questions beginning with *Why,* such as "Why are you feeling that way?" *Better:* Begin with a *What,* as in "What is bothering you?"

•*Always* and *never.* More flexible phrases are *up to now* and *in the past.*

Source: Dr. Theresa Larsen Crenshaw, author of *Bedside Manners,* Pinnacle Books, New York.

How to Be a Better Conversationalist

•Don't start with your name. A name exchange gives a conversation nowhere to go. Instead, mention something in the environment that you can both talk about, such as "How's the cheesecake in this restaurant?" Then pay attention to the cues to find out whether the other person wants to talk with you. Consider tone of voice, facial expression and body language.

•Develop your descriptive power. The well-told anecdote or story will express your personality and convey warmth and charm. Many people are afraid to express their feelings when it comes to description. They stick to a dry recitation of facts instead.

•Be sensitive to the other person. Pick up on messages about how that person is feeling. Watch body language as well as listening to what's being said. Don't be one of those insensitive, endless talkers who fear that if they stop, their partner will get bored and want to leave.

•Don't use boredom as a defense. People who always claim to be bored are usually just erecting a defense against rejection. If you're at a party and don't talk to anyone because you tell yourself they're all boring, you've just insulated yourself against failure. If you feel you're boring to others, that's just another excuse for not trying and therefore not failing.

•Don't keep asking questions. Constant queries to keep a conversation going can be a crutch. The other person will finally realize that you're not really listening but are thinking up the next question. People dislike feeling interrogated and resent answering questions under those circumstances. Ask a question only when something genuinely sparks your curiosity.

Source: Arthur Reel, who teaches the art of conversation at New York City's Learning Annex and at Corporate Communications Skills, Inc., an executive training center in New York.

Learning to Listen

Here are some simple techniques to help you improve your listening ability:

•Relax and help the speaker relax, too. Give your full attention to what's being said. Stop everything else you're doing. Maintain eye contact.

•Don't let the speaker's tone of voice or manner turn you off. Nervousness or misplaced emotions often cloud the message the speaker is trying to get across.

•Prepare beforehand for the conversation. Take a few minutes to consult information pertinent to the discussion. That also helps you to quickly evaluate the speaker and the subject.

•Allow for unusual circumstances (extreme pressure or disturbing interruptions). Judge only what the speaker says, given the conditions he's faced with.

•Avoid getting sidetracked.

•Listen very closely to points you disagree with. (Poor listeners shut out or distort them.)

•Mentally collect the main points of the conversation. Occasionally, ask for clarification of one of the speaker's statements.

Bad Listening Habits

If you want to be a better listener, try to avoid:

•Thinking about something else while waiting for the speaker's next word or sentence. The mind races ahead four times faster than the normal rate of conversation.

•Listening primarily for facts rather than ideas.

•Tuning out when the talk seems to be getting too difficult.

•Prejudging, from appearance or speaking manner, that the person has nothing interesting to say.

•Paying attention to outside sights and sounds when talking with someone.

•Interrupting with a question whenever a speaker says something puzzling or unclear.

Source: John T. Samaras, University of Oklahoma.

How to Listen to A Complaint

Many people don't hear anything that doesn't fit their own assumptions. If someone comes to you with a complaint or claim, listen —just listen.

• Don't answer or explain.

• Take notes on exactly what's said.

• Try to imagine that the person is right, or at least justified.

• Put yourself in the other's place and imagine how you would feel in the same situation.

• Give yourself time to think the matter over before making any decision.

• Nobody can see all sides of an issue immediately. New facts or ideas take time to sink in.

Source: *Levinson Letter,* Cambridge, MA.

How to Get Information From Others

• Speak softly. This encourages others to take center stage where they should be if you want to learn something from them.

• Look responsive. Most people don't use nearly enough facial expression. Raising one eyebrow a little and smiling slightly makes you seem receptive. Eye contact and a calculated pause will invite the person you're talking with to elaborate.

• Give reinforcement. Comments such as "Very impressive!" or "Excellent!" can be dropped into the discussion without interrupting the flow.

• Follow up and probe. If someone fails to explain the reasons for an action that you're curious about, try a casual follow-up question.

Source: Richard A. Fear, author of *The Evaluation Interview,* published by McGraw-Hill, New York.

Hidden Meanings In What People Say

Key words tell what people are really trying to communicate. These words and phrases may be spoken repeatedly or hidden in the middle of complex sentences. But they relay the true message being delivered through all the chatter of conversations, negotiations and interviews.

What to watch out for:

• Words that jump out at you. The speaker may be mumbling, but suddenly a word (or proper name) is emphasized or spoken loudly.

• Slips of the tongue, especially when denied by the person who made them. *Example:* "We won't leave this room until we have reached a derision" (instead of decision). The speaker is mocking either you or the subject under discussion.

• Embedding. The repetitive use of words or slogans manipulated to reshape your thinking. Embedding can be insidious. *Example:* At a meeting of parties with irreconcilable differences, one side keeps repeating the word "consensus." "After we reach a consensus, we'll break for lunch." This one concept is repeated relentlessly by the speakers and members of their team until it dominates the meeting. This is a mini-version of the Big Lie.

• Hostile words and phrases. Any statement that hurts or sounds hostile is an affront, even when pawned off as a joke.

• Unstated words. These key words are those not spoken. *Prime example:* The husband or wife who can never say "I love you" to the mate.

• Metaphors. The turns of expression people choose often signal their inner thoughts. *Example:* A metaphor such as "We'll cut the opposition up into little pieces" takes healthy competition into the realm of aggression.

Source: Martin G. Groder, MD, psychiatrist and business consultant, Durham, NC.

How People Say "Yes" But Mean "No"

Here are some apparently acquiescent verbal expressions that really mean "no":

• "Yes, but..."

• "I don't know why, but..."

• "I tried that, and it doesn't help."

• "Well, to be perfectly honest with you..."

• "But it's not easy..."

- "I know, but..."
- "I don't remember."

Spot the Unspoken Thought Behind The Poker Face

Watching people's actions can bring you a lot closer to the truth than merely listening to what they say.

Here are some typical feelings and mental machinations—and their common outward expressions:

- Openness: Open hands, unbuttoned coat.
- Defensiveness: Arms crossed on chest, crossing legs, fistlike gestures, pointing index finger, "karate" chops.
- Evaluations: Hand to face, head tilted, stroking chin, peering over or playing with glasses, cleaning glasses, cleaning or filling a pipe, hand to nose.
- Suspicion: Arms crossed, sideways glance, touching/rubbing nose, rubbing eyes, buttoned coat, drawing away.
- Insecurity: Pinching flesh, chewing pen, thumb over thumb, biting fingernail, hands in pockets.
- Cooperation: Upper body in sprinter's position, open hands, sitting on edge of chair, hand-to-face gestures, unbuttoning coat.
- Confidence: Steepled hands, hands behind back, back stiffened, hands in coat pockets with thumbs out, hands on lapels of coat.
- Nervousness: Clearing throat, "whew" sound, whistling, smoking, pinching flesh, fidgeting, covering mouth, jiggling money or keys, tugging ears, wringing hands.
- Frustration: Short breaths, "tsk" sound, tightly clenched hands, wringing hands, fistlike gestures, pointing index finger, rubbing hand through hair, rubbing back of neck.
- SOS: Uneven intonation of voice, wringing of hands, poor body posture, or failure to make eye contact.

How Not to be Put On the Defensive

Criticism from fellow workers or superiors on the job can escalate if you react defensively. How to avoid this instinctive reaction:

- Paraphrase an accusation as a way of slowing down reaction time and giving the accuser a chance to retreat. *Accuser:* "How come that report isn't ready? Can't you ever get your work done on time?" *Response:* "Do you really think that I never get my work done on time?"
- Describe in a tentative fashion what appears to be the other person's psychological state. In response to a scowling superior, say: "I'm uncomfortable. I don't understand what your frown means."
- Ask for clarification. *Accuser:* "This proposal isn't what I asked you to design at all." *Response:* "Is nothing in the proposal acceptable?"
- Use a personal response to assume responsibility. *Accuser:* "This is entirely wrong." *Response:* "I guess I didn't understand. Can I review the instructions again?"

Source: Gary P. Cross, management consultant, Cross Names & Beck, Eugene, OR.

Arguments: Keeping Your Cool

- Don't fear to negotiate, even when the difference with the other person is so huge that agreement seems impossible.
- If the issue is important, you probably cannot accurately predict when and how a resolution will finally be made. The outcome may become apparent only after extensive discussions.
- Avoid the temptation to start off in a hostile manner out of anger at the other person's extreme stance.

Source: Dr. Chester L. Karrass, Karrass Seminars, Santa Monica, CA.

When to Offer a Solution To a Dispute

Let the two sides clear the air by exchanging accusations and expressing pent-up resentments over extraneous issues, not just the one now on the table. Any trained mediator waits for this venting of feelings and buildup of frustrations before exercising influence.

• The best (often the only) time to recommend an innovative solution comes when desperation peaks. Both sides know they have a problem. And both know they can't settle it without third-party help.

• To be a hero, deliver a solution where mutual goals are not being met and where all parties already recognize that there is a gap between expectations and performance.

Build Trust During A Discussion

• Begin with a positive statement, for example, "I've been looking forward to talking with you. Joe Smith said if anyone could help us, it's you."

• Avoid pulling rank.

• Don't make veiled threats.

• Don't offer a reward.

• Show yourself to be an expert.

• Associate yourself with someone the other person respects.

• Restate the other person's opinions or feelings periodically. But do not preface the restatement with "you said" or "you think." The other person may quibble over what is attributed directly.

• Share something personal about yourself if the other person is wary.

• Point out ways the information you need will help you.

• Indicate ways you can help the other person.

• Make a commitment to action, and then ask for a commitment in return.

Source: Pamela Cumming, author of *The Power Handbook,* CBI Publishing, Boston.

Choose Your Words Carefully

Avoid:

• Using popular but vague modifiers, such as "exceptional" or "efficient," without defining precisely what is meant. For example, an exceptional record can be either exceptionally good or bad. Describing something as efficiently designed does not say enough. It's better to use facts, numbers, details.

• Exaggerating. Overstating a fact is acceptable (and common) in conversation, but it destroys credibility in writing because readers take it literally.

• Generalizing. Do not use absolutes, such as: All, right, wrong, true, false, always, never. Instead, say "this is true under such-and-such conditions."

Source: William C. Paxson, author of *The Business Writing Handbook,* Bantam Books, New York.

Write as Clearly As You Think

Concentrate on simplifying your sentence structure. It's the easiest way to say what is meant and to make sure the message gets across. *Three basic rules:*

• Keep sentences short. They should be no more than 17 to 20 words. If an idea has multiple parts, use multiple sentences.

• Vary the length of sentences. The 17-20 word rule is the average. When sentences drone on at unvarying lengths, the reader's attention begins to wander.

• Vary the punctuation. Include plenty of commas, as well as a sprinkling of semicolons, to go with the necessary periods. Well-placed punctuation is a road map, leading the reader comfortably and accurately through the message.

Source: Paul Richards, author of *Sentence Control: Solving an Old Problem,* Supervisory Management, New York.

How to Measure the Clarity of Your Writing

Use the "Fog Index" to measure how clearly you write letters, memos, and reports.

- Count off a 100-word section.
- Count the number of sentences and divide 100 by that number, which gives average words per sentence.
- Count the words with more than two syllables. Add this figure to the average words per sentence.
- Multiply the total by 0.4 to get the Fog Index (indicating minimum school grade level a reader needs to comprehend it).

The lower the index, the better. A score of 11 to 12 is passable for most business writing. (The Fog Index for this item: 7.6)

Source: *Time Talk,* Grandville, MI.

How to Write A Persuasive Letter

- Grab your reader's attention by fitting in with his interests, either personal or in business. Tell him how he is going to benefit by doing as you ask.
- Give proof of what you say. The best proof is to suggest that the reader get in touch with others who have benefited from your suggestion. (Of course, you must make sure that you have people who will back you up.)
- In the next-to-last paragraph, tell the reader exactly what he must do to take advantage of the benefits you're offering.
- Close with a hook. Encourage the reader to take action by telling him about a loss of money, prestige or opportunity if he does not act at once. (A time penalty is one of the best ways to get the action you want.)

Source: James Van Fleet, author of *A Lifetime Guide to Conversation,* Prentice Hall, Inc., Englewood Cliffs, NJ.

Help Readers Understand Your Report

Readers understand a report better when they are carefully led through it. Use the right words or phrases to signal a shift of subject or emphasis:

- To get your reader to stop and consider alternatives. *Use:* However, but, by contrast, nevertheless, on the other hand, still, despite, notwithstanding.
- To expand the idea. *Use:* Actually, realistically, at the same time, unexpectedly, perhaps.
- To concede to a limitation. *Use:* Sometimes, to be sure, possibly, to some extent, conceivably.
- To make an aside. *Use:* Incidentally, digressing for a moment.
- To move ahead in the same direction. *Use:* Additionally, also, besides, moreover, furthermore.
- To make a comparison. *Use:* Similarly, in the same way.
- To strengthen an assertion. *Use:* Indeed, in fact, certainly.
- To signal importance. *Use:* Significantly, notably, remarkably.

Source: A. Weiss, author of *Write What You Mean,* AMACOM, New York.

Speeches with Impact

Only rarely is it possible to change your audience's deep-seated attitudes or beliefs. Aim no higher than getting the listeners to question their attitudes.

- Avoid alienating an audience by pressing points too hard.
- State conclusions.
- Call for action.

•When you have to speak extemporaneously, develop a theme early and stick to it.

•Use silence to underline a point.

•End a speech with a short, emotional, conviction-filled summary of the main points.

Source: Michael Klezaras Jr., director of research and planning, Roger Ailes & Associates, Inc., New York.

Public Speaking: Secrets of Success

Contrary to a lot of advice about making a speech, there is no need to memorize, rehearse, rely on extensive notes or spend weeks getting ready. The key is to keep the presentation spontaneous.

The only requirements for spontaneous speaking:

•Thorough knowledge of the subject.

•Self-confidence.

•An assured manner of delivery.

To make sure the speech does not sound rehearsed or canned:

•Don't use notes because you'll have no more than two seconds to look down, find the place in the notes and speak to the audience. You'll end up looking, reading, memorizing and reciting, but not communicating.

•Instead of notes, use one- to three-word "triggers" instead of notes. Triggers are facts or concepts designed to spark off the next train of thought. Using triggers allows you to deal easily with what is to be said. The result is that you'll gesture more, be more animated and vary your tone of voice.

•As a structure for the speech, adopt the same format that people use to communicate every day: State the purpose, support it with details, then recommend what should be done.

•Start with a 15- to 30-second grabber. The grabber explains the purpose and stimulates the audience. Work through the details by using the triggers. About five of these should suffice.

•End by telling the group something specific to do. If questions follow the talk, restate the recommended action at the conclusion.

•Stand in front of the lectern and as close to the audience as possible. This makes the talk seem more like a conversation. In a big auditorium, use a lapel microphone to avoid getting stuck at the lectern. Establish eye contact with people one at a time. Don't look at the wall.

Delivering An Important Speech

•Find out what common bonds unite the audience so that the speech can be directed to meaningful subjects.

•Remember that your audience is interested first in people, then in things, finally in ideas.

•Start by tape-recording a spontaneous flow of ideas. Don't attempt to be logical or to follow an outline. This initial tape is the raw material to prepare the final speech.

•Avoid opening with a joke. Most jokes backfire. The best grabbers are a question, personal story, famous quote, vital statistic, comparison, or contrast.

•Use questions throughout.

•Avoid unnecessary phrases such as "Now let me explain...." Or: "The point I want to make is..."

Audience attention drops off sharply after 20 to 30 minutes, so no presentation should run beyond that. If it's necessary to fill more time:

•Use slides when appropriate.

•Have a question and answer session after the speech.

Talking Effectively to Small Groups

•Meet personally as many people as possible beforehand.

•Get right to the point. The first 15 seconds is what grabs the listener. Don't start with "Thank you" and "I'm very happy to be here."

•Make eye contact with everyone in the audience at some time very early in the presentation.

•Support main points with factual information and examples.

•Repeat the main points to be sure the listeners have gotten them.

•Look for a creative conclusion—a provocative thought or action-suggesting statement.

•Never let a talk end with an answer to a question from the audience. After answering questions, always return to the main point of the presentation. The last word is important. It shouldn't be yielded to a questioner.

•Never ask the audience, "Any questions?" If there aren't any, the silence will be embarrassing. Instead, suggest, "There may be some questions." It makes a difference.

•Limit use of notes because it inhibits spontaneity. Write out key words or short phrases to jog thoughts. Alternate lines with different color ink to facilitate quick focusing on material.

•Rehearsing is usually not recommended. Unrehearsed presentations have the advantage of freshness and spontaneity which only come from thoughts uttered for the first time.

Source: Dr. Roger Flax, communications training consultant, Motivational Systems, South Orange, NJ.

Using Humor Successfully

•Avoid humor when speaking outdoors. The laughter tends to get lost, leaving people with the feeling it wasn't funny at all.

•Avoid puns, even though they may go over well in a parlor. They almost always cause the audience to groan more than laugh.

•Leave enough time for the laugh before proceeding. Audiences sometimes react slowly, especially if the humor was unexpected. To a nervous speaker, a second's delay seems like an hour.

•Be prepared to carry on smoothly and self-confidently if the audience doesn't laugh. The audience will quickly forget that the speaker laid an egg if he remains calm.

Source: Paul Preston, *Communication for Managers,* Prentice-Hall, Englewood Cliffs, NJ.

Lines to Live By

Wit surprises...*humor* illuminates. Wit is often aristocratic in its clever superiority...while humor is usually popular.

Here are just a few examples of true wit...

•*Mark Twain on his father:* "When I was a boy of 14, my father was so ignorant I could hardly stand to have him around. But when I got to be 21, I was astonished at how much he had learned in seven years."

•*Oscar Wilde:* At a dinner party, Oscar Wilde bet that he could produce a witticism about any subject that was offered.

"Queen Victoria," suggested another guest.

"Ah," said Wilde, "but she is not a subject."

One time, when James McNeill Whistler, the painter, uttered a bon mot, Oscar Wilde remarked, "I wish I'd said that."

Whistler replied, "You will, Oscar, you will."

•*George Bernard Shaw:* The actress Pat Campbell sighed to Bernard Shaw, "What a wonderful child we would have with my looks and your brains."

"But suppose," mused Shaw, "it had my looks and your brains!"

Once, when a heckler booed him after a performance, Shaw stepped to the edge of the stage, peered up at the balcony, and said, "My dear sir, I quite agree with you. But who are we among so many?"

Shaw's *Candida* opened in New York with Cornelia Otis Skinner in the title role. The critics were enraptured, and Shaw cabled the actress: "Excellent. Greatest." G. B. S.

Miss Skinner replied: "Undeserving such praise."

Shaw cabled: "I meant the play."

To which she smartly answered: "So did I."

•*Winston Churchill:* Lady Astor once hissed at Winston Churchill, "If you were my husband, I'd put poison in your coffee."

"If I were your husband, I would drink it," Churchill blandly replied.

• *Ronald Reagan:* "The Soviet Union would remain a one-party nation even if an opposition party were permitted," said Ronald Reagan, "because everyone would join that party."

• *J.B.S. Haldane:* The British scientist J. B. S. Haldane was asked what his studies had revealed to him about the nature of God. "An inordinate fondness for beetles," Haldane replied.

Source: John Train, chairman of Montrose Advisors, an investment firm, and author of *The Craft of Investing,* HarperCollins, 10 E. 53 St., New York 10022. He writes a column for the *Financial Times* and has published several books of humor.

The Fine Art of Verbal Self-Defense

The most important thing to remember is that verbal abuse is almost never done out of cruelty...the true purpose is to get *attention* and elicit a reaction. The attacker is like a little child who would rather be spanked than ignored.

Verbal abuse requires *two* participants. Without a partner who supplies the emotional response, the attacker is disappointed, disarmed and unable to continue.

Most people react to verbal attacks by fighting back, pleading or trying to engage the attacker in rational debate. These strategies don't work...they just encourage more abusive behavior by giving the attacker the attention he/she craves.

What *does* work is a strategy that follows this basic rule: *Don't do anything that feeds the attacker's need for attention.*

The goal in verbal self-defense isn't to get even or inflict pain in return...but simply to stop the abuse.

Strategies that work...

It's not always easy to recognize a verbal attack, and *too* easy to feel that you're being overly sensitive. One giveaway is the "tune" rather than just the words. *Verbal attacks have extra emphases:*

• "If you *really* cared about your *health*, you wouldn't *eat* all that *junk food.*"

• "*You're* not the *only* person with *problems*, you know."

• "*Why* don't you *ever* think about others?"

Instead of becoming defensive or going on the counterattack, give a neutral, *boring* response. Talk in the third person—in generalities, in a calm, flat, informational tone.

• "People have different tastes in food."

• "It's true that everyone has problems."

• "It's important to think about others."

Boring Baroque Response...

Another effective technique is the Boring Baroque Response. *Take the attack at face value, and answer it at impossible length:*

"*Why* are you *always* so *selfish*?" "That's a good question. It's because of what happened when I was 10 years old. Or was it 11? We were living in Minneapolis, and Aunt Sadie came to visit. No...I think it was in St. Louis, and we were visiting Aunt Ethel. She had two dogs...or was it cats?..." And on and on.

Whichever approach you use, the effect is the same—the attacker realizes there's no fun in attacking you. You're not going to play, and it's impossible to go on with the abuse. Because you're giving the attacker the opportunity to desist without losing face, the cycle is broken.

Always/Never...

"Always/Never" attacks are so common that you may want to try a special strategy to deflect them—especially if the attacker is someone whose friendship or love you value.

Instead of getting angry or defensive, make an offer, on the spot, that invalidates the accusation.

Source: Suzette Haden Elgin, PhD, founder of the Ozark Center for Language Studies. She is author of 24 books on verbal self-defense, including *Staying Well with the Gentle Art of Verbal Self-Defense* (Prentice Hall) and *You Can't Say That to Me! Stopping the Pain of Verbal Abuse* (John Wiley & Sons).

5

Self Improvement

All About Selficide

Many people do not find satisfaction in today's world. They find life to be a flat, unreal experience. They cannot enjoy intimate relationships with others. They are not in touch with their own selves. I use the word *selficide* to describe this state of being unable to learn and grow from life's experiences.

As we age, we increasingly need to understand who we are and how to behave as responsible, caring adults. Important questions to ask yourself to see if you are on the right track...or on the road to *selficide*...

•Do you control your own behavior...or are your actions governed by a need to rebel or comply with other's rules? My patient Denise was anorexic. She ate sensibly—but whenever she reached a healthy weight, she stopped eating and lost weight again.

Her eating problem was the symptom of an internal struggle between her perception of the voice of her parents, which told her she must eat to be loved, and her desire to be herself.

She was able to solve her problem when, with encouragement, she disciplined herself not to control her eating habits. Instead she focused on doing something that she really *wanted* to do...*not* what she felt she *should* do.

•Are your thoughts, feelings and actions consistent with each other? We all know the old joke about the Boy Scout who took an hour to help an old lady across the street... because she didn't want to go. His behavior was inconsistent with his goal—to do good.

•Do you truly play a meaningful part in your own activities and dealings with others ...or are you often just there physically? Some people are so involved in regret over the past that they can't think about what they should be doing now. Others are so busy daydreaming about the future that they aren't acting now to make their dreams possible.

•Do you willingly surrender yourself to reality...or do you begrudge it? Can you ever leave a discussion without having the last word?

• Are you able to give and take...or do you insist on only one direction? Do you feel like a martyr...and let everyone know it?

• Do you accept others as they are...or do you always feel the need to judge them?

• Do you act naturally, without pretension... or are you dishonest or phony?

• Do you take joy in your experiences... not just look at life as a series of tasks to accomplish?

Example: Ned, a patient of mine, wondered why his business was always outperformed by a small rival company, so he went to check on it. He noticed that the owner of the company was an exceedingly enthusiastic individual. When Ned asked him, "You really enjoy what you do, don't you?" he replied, "Yeah, it sure beats the hell out of working!"

• Do you have an inner aesthetic sense of morality that makes it seem repellent to you to do something wrong?

• Are you willing to take risks—to try something new to satisfy your real inner desires... or are you afraid of doing anything that people don't expect of you?

• Do you exercise your creativity—the willingness to dismiss old ways or experience to be free to grow in new directions...or are you afraid to lose the security provided by always repeating the same pattern—even when you find it to be unsatisfactory?

How to avoid selficide...

People who cannot give positive answers to any of the questions are well on their way to selficide. But selficide is not the same as suicide...life always contains the possibility of growth.

If you are willing to look into yourself as you confront the issues of everyday living and examine your inner feelings, you can find new responses that better satisfy your needs and those of the people close to you.

Those new responses will develop as you embrace new experiences and adopt less fearful ways of dealing with the world. That joyful approach is not really alien to anyone's nature, because it represents a return to the way everybody starts out life.

Babies explore the world fearlessly and joyfully...they accept bumps and falls as the price of growth. They learn to walk and talk at their own pace...nobody else can make it happen faster or slower. Before babies learn to walk, they crawl...but when they learn to walk they stop crawling.

As long as they are able to act naturally, children continue to learn and grow because they are *open to new experiences*...willing to *acknowledge their true feelings*...able to *react in new ways.*

Many adults have forgotten those natural instincts.

As analyst Erich Fromm said, "We listen to every voice and to everybody but not ourselves. We are constantly exposed to the noise of opinions and ideas hammering at us from everywhere...motion pictures, newspapers, radio, idle chatter. If we had planned intentionally to prevent ourselves from ever listening to ourselves, we could have done no better."

But if we pause as we go about our daily activities and look carefully at the world around us...at the people we are with...and most of all deep into ourselves...we can find what we want from life and we can achieve it.

Source: Patrick Thomas Malone, MD, medical director of Mental Health Services at Northside Hospital in Atlanta, and a psychotherapist at the Atlanta Psychiatric Clinic. With his father, Thomas Patrick Malone, MD, PhD, he wrote *The Windows of Experience: Moving Beyond Recovery to Wholeness,* Simon & Schuster, 1230 Avenue of the Americas, New York 10020.

All About Civility

The great lack of civility in America is the major factor behind the breakdown in family life, unethical practices in business, selfishness, and dishonesty in politics.

Civility means much more than politeness. Civility is all-embracing—a general awareness by people that personal well-being cannot be separated from the well-being of the groups to which we belong...our families, our businesses, and our nation.

Lack of civility is tied to unreasonable expectations in recent decades of constant happiness and constant comfort. When real life presents us with painful experiences...when something hurts us...when we feel unfulfilled—we feel cheated. And too many of us—too often—reach for instant happiness by illegitimate means that disregard the interests of other people.

Consciousness and civility...

The route to improved civility begins with greater awareness of our shortcomings and our tendencies to manipulate others.

Greater awareness leads to a willingness to accept pain in the short term, recognizing that it is an unavoidable part of any growth process, leading to significant personal growth. Learning how to handle pain realistically is a prerequisite for warmer, more meaningful relationships over the long term. Civility does not happen automatically. You have to train yourself to be aware of your true motives, to be honest with yourself and others, and to judge yourself first.

Civility in the family...

The first training ground for civility is the family. Children learn how they are expected to behave by observing their parents' behavior, not just by listening to their words. So if you want your children to demonstrate civility now and later in life, you have to practice it yourself.

Example: Your two kids are having a disagreement and your six-year-old son slugs his little sister. Then you tell him, "Don't ever hit your sister!" and hit him.

That will deliver quite a different message than you want to give: "It's OK to hit someone else...but don't hit your sister when your mother or father is around."

With that kind of discrepancy prevalent between parental educational words and actions, it's not surprising that so many people grow up with an internal moral code that tells them, "You can do whatever you want as long as you don't get caught doing it."

Civility in business...

Successful businesses are built on cooperation. Businesses have a right to both demand and expect cooperation from their employees, because the main purpose of any business is to make a profit. But companies also have a responsibility to treat their workers fairly and honestly in the process.

Example: Some companies that vest workers with pension benefits only after a long period of employment save money by laying the workers off only a short time before they become vested.

This is uncivil. It is obviously unfair to the workers and may also hurt the company by encouraging the best employees to leave.

Better way: Set up a system that recognizes both the company's interest in dedicated, hard-working employees and the employees' interest in security and fair compensation. This will only work when both sides honestly keep their parts of the bargain.

Honest communication...

Companies, families, and all types of organizations become more civil when they encourage honest, two-way communication—straight talk and listening. That is not easy, but it can be done if you follow these principles:

- Don't expect perfection...just do your best and learn from your mistakes.
- Set aside time for communication.
- Clear your mind and listen to the other person.
- Be honest...with yourself and others.
- Judge yourself first. Look into your real motives.
- Take time to respond and think. Don't be afraid of silence.
- Be willing to be hurt—and to risk hurting others by speaking honestly. If someone is too fragile to respect your point of view, he/she cannot be a part of your community.
- Try to be as gentle as possible. Don't make any unnecessary, painful statements...yet don't be so subtle that the point is completely missed.
- Speak personally and specifically. Don't talk about "the system" or some impersonal authority. Don't generalize. Document what you say.
- Don't analyze other people's motives. Don't play psychologist.

• Speak when you are moved to speak. Don't cop out.

Bottom line: It takes hard work to get an organization to operate in a mode of civility. But those who have made the transition do not want to go back.

Source: M. Scott Peck, MD, a founder of the Foundation for Community Encouragement. He is the author of *The Road Less Traveled* and *A World Waiting to be Born*, Bantam Books, 1540 Broadway, New York 10036.

Whatever Happened To Loyalty

Loyalty is out of fashion these days. People would sooner switch than fight...not only in the marketplace, where customers rapidly switch to suppliers who offer better deals...but also in their personal, social, and political lives.

As soon as they think they might do better elsewhere, baseball players change teams ...professors leave their colleges...voters desert their parties...husbands abandon their wives, and vice versa.

Rather than trying to build better relationships where they are, people abandon their old associations and enter into new ones... which are likely to be temporary, too.

What happened to loyalty?

The breakdown of loyalty is not only a result of selfishness—it also has ideological roots.

For the past 200 years, giants of philosophy, particularly Immanuel Kant and Jeremy Bentham, have argued that people should not make decisions based on what is best for themselves but instead based on an impersonal calculation of what would be best for the entire society.

These ideas have had a powerful effect on the way many educated people think, but they certainly have not produced a society in which people act better...or even feel better. That is because the world is too complicated for people—even philosophers—to figure out what is best for humanity at large.

Result: Many people reject the old-fashioned belief that we owe loyalty to those who are close to us and helped to make us what we are. They also do not believe we owe loyalty to the nation whose benefits we enjoy. In the short run, this disregard of loyalty hurts some people. In the long run, this attitude hurts everyone.

Advantages of loyalty...

Loyalty in marriage, family life, social interactions, and politics strengthens bonds between people. It assumes that the relationships we are born into—or choose voluntarily—should continue. It encourages us to accept the other party's good faith and so includes a willingness to accept mistakes.

Under these conditions, with time to correct mistakes and a healthy degree of flexibility, relationships can become stronger. Each partner is willing to allow the other to change previous patterns of behavior without fear of immediate abandonment, so each can help the other to grow.

A one-sided, individualistic approach to life may work as long as things are going well, but it is likely to fail when problems arise. Loyalty builds strong, long-lasting mutual relationships that can help overcome temporary setbacks... it leaves both sides better off in the long term.

Loyalty in families...

Successful families are built on a web of loyalty between father, mother, and children. Today's emphasis on personal happiness over loyalty to others is a major cause of family breakdown.

The same emphasis on self that leads to divorce also corrodes the relationship between parents and children.

Example: A huge number of divorced fathers who have remarried simply abandon the children from their first marriage...therefore, a new generation fails to learn how to practice loyalty and enjoy the satisfaction it provides.

How to build loyalty...

Loyalty stands us in good stead when times are tough...but it should be established when things are still going well. *Five steps to loyalty:*

• Affirmation. Think about the good things others are doing for you. Show them how much you appreciate them...in both word and deed.

•Confrontation. Show that the relationship is important to you by pointing out how it can be improved. When you disapprove of your partner's behavior, don't be afraid to say so... but always constructively.

•Complicity. I use this term, which is translated from the French, to mean the sense that you and your partner(s) are separate from the rest of the world. You possess something nobody else has. Feel very happy about it.

•Ritual. Find ways to do things for the special people in your circle.

Example: When loved ones are coming to visit, meet them at the airport.

•Privacy. Keep the details of your shared relationship away from outsiders. How you make decisions is nobody else's business. Never complain to outsiders about your partner.

The tendency today is to think of intimate relationships in political terms. Both men and women are excessively concerned about whether their private conduct meets the standards of behavior set by their friends. Traditional men are concerned about whether they look like they are "wearing the pants in the family." Liberated women worry about whether their sisters would approve of their cooking and washing dishes. This manner of looking over one's shoulder reflects a conflict of loyalties. Loyalty to one's spouse comes into tension with loyalties to those outside the relationship. This conflict undermines trust and destroys intimacy.

Conclusion: Be loyal to your spouse and forget how your private way of doing things may look to outsiders.

The toughest challenge of personal loyalty is to stand by another when the going gets tough. Loyalty becomes important only when we are tempted to "jump ship." Fair-weather loyalty is but convenience. The next time you are tempted to leave, think, "This is the time to show my loyalty."

Source: George P. Fletcher, Beekman Professor of Law at Columbia University and author of *Loyalty: An Essay on the Morality of Relationships,* Oxford University Press, 200 Madison Ave., New York 10016.

The Importance Of Solitude

Many Americans admire the rugged individualists in novels and films who take on the system or overcome adversity single-handedly.

Yet, we don't feel comfortable with those who keep to themselves. We tend to distrust contemplation and view solitary people and pursuits with suspicion.

Opportunity: We would be better off if we engaged in positive solitude—time alone that is used thoughtfully to benefit mind and soul. Positive solitude is an important element of self-discovery and growth.

Solitude provides the opportunity to identify your most cherished goals and develop ways of achieving them. Regular reflection contributes to a sense of inner peace...and makes you feel more in control of your life.

The problems of being alone...

Positive solitude takes conscious effort, whether you live with others or alone.

•People who live with others are often so caught up in the demands of family life that they don't take time for self-reflection. Time alone feels like an expendable luxury to them. Thus, they're in danger of defining themselves through others.

These people need to make private time a priority and be creative about ways of finding it.

Examples: Evaluate work and community responsibilities, and determine which are essential—and which can be cut back. Join a babysitting co-op so someone else can look after your children one or two days a week. Plan a solitary retreat to a quiet place for a few days to reflect on what's really important to you.

People who live alone may feel left out in a world of couples and families. They may fight solitude by compulsively seeking company, filling their days with "busy-ness" that isn't very satisfying...and missing a wonderful opportunity for self-discovery and growth.

They need to challenge the belief that having a family is the only way to be happy...look for ways to nurture themselves instead of waiting for a partner to make life satisfying...and take advantage of the chance to learn more about their own values and perceptions.

I believe that living alone doesn't have to be lonely—nor should it be viewed as a way station on the path to "coupledom." Living alone can be a deeply rewarding lifestyle in its own right.

Positive solitude actually enhances relationships when people do come together. People who are not afraid of solitude can meet as strong wholes instead of incomplete halves that are desperate for fulfillment.

Turn off the TV...

One of the biggest threats to positive solitude is television. It's the easiest, but possibly least-satisfying, way to fill up your time.

Watching television does not put you in contact with other people or yourself. Instead, it bombards you with the agenda and values of the TV programmers and advertisers.

Spending a lot of time in front of the TV feeds loneliness. It encourages us to let someone else decide what's interesting, discourages us from looking inward and takes up time that could be spent developing original ideas or actively challenging or supporting the ideas of others.

Ways to use private time...

In solitude, we can explore what's most meaningful to us—free from other people's expectations. We can begin to develop a personal philosophy or life plan.

This isn't an easy task, but it's an exciting one. *Key:* Ask yourself the kinds of questions that don't have simple answers...and be prepared to return to them again and again. *Examples...*

What contribution do I want to make to the world? Focus on what's significant to you—not to your parents, spouse or boss. *Possibilities:* Create a new variety of rose...raise healthy, loving children...comfort people in distress... make music...gather and analyze information about nature or politics.

What are the gaps in my life? Are there things you'd like to understand better or have more control over? Goals you've abandoned out of fear—but still wonder about? What are some ways to address these gaps?

Tools that can help in your exploration include a journal...walking...meditation...quiet time in a natural environment. *Exercises:*

- Write for 15 minutes about a topic of your choice, without stopping or censoring yourself. You'll be surprised at the ideas that come up.
- Write about a dream you had recently, the emotions it stirred and the messages it might have. Dreams often introduce important themes we haven't yet faced consciously.

Moving outward...

Quietly thinking and writing aren't the only ways to discover meaning. In fact, planning and taking part in challenging activities can be an outgrowth of positive solitude. We can try activities that reveal new aspects of ourselves—physical, intellectual and spiritual. The key is to identify and follow those pursuits that engage you—not to please friends or family or because you've always done them. *Exercises:*

- Write down 10 or 20 activities that you used to love but haven't done for a long time. What did you most enjoy as a child or adolescent? Try some of these activities again.
- Make a list of activities you always wanted to try but never got around to. Pick one—and do it.

Planning is essential for this stage. If we don't plan, then the easiest things will happen, not the most fulfilling. We'll come home and switch on the TV instead of going to a concert or arranging a kayaking trip.

Make activity dates for yourself...pencil them into your calendar...and make sure you keep them.

Be patient...

Don't be surprised if this self-analysis feels uncomfortable at first—or if you don't make dramatic discoveries right away.

Getting to know yourself takes some time. Challenging and reexamining your assumptions do not happen in a day. But the effort will bring satisfying rewards...including a deeper understanding of your values and needs...increased confidence in your capabilities...a richer enjoyment of life...and a greater receptivity to others.

Source: Rae André, PhD, associate professor of management psychology at Northeastern University. A consultant, lecturer and workshop leader, she is the author of *Positive Solitude: A Practical Program for Mastering Loneliness and Achieving Self-Fulfillment.* HarperCollins, 10 E. 53 St., New York 10022.

To Break a Bad Habit

Make a 21-day agreement with yourself to change your behavior. It takes 21 days to form a new habit or break an old one. If you come up with excuses to break your 21-day deal with yourself, remind yourself that you only have less than 21 days to go. *Key:* If you skip one day, the whole 21-day cycle starts over again.

Source: *Choose to Live Peacefully* by Susan Smith Jones, PhD, founder, Health Unlimited, Los Angeles human potential consultants. Celestial Arts, Box 7327, Berkeley, California 94707.

Easier Learning

Make learning easier by not expecting to be perfect right away. Accept your mistakes until you learn to do things well. *Benefits:* You'll develop a solid foundation on which to build ...you'll wipe out fear of failure...the more you learn about a subject, the easier it is to learn even more.

Source: *The Secret of Getting Straight A's: Learn More in Less Time with Little Effort* by aerospace engineer Brian Marshall. Hathaway International Publications, Box 6543, Buena Park, California 90622.

Learn While You Drive

The average person drives from 12,500 to 25,000 miles each year. Translated into hours, that's one to two college semesters. *Helpful:* Use time spent behind the wheel listening to creative or self-help tapes or your favorite music. Avoid radio shows that cause you to think negatively.

Source: *101 Simple Ways to Be Good to Yourself: How to Discover Peace and Joy in Your Life* by Oklahoma City stress consultant Donna Watson, PhD. Energy Press, 5275 McCormick Mountain, Austin, Texas 78734.

Auditing Classes

You can still attend college even if you don't want a degree. Even the most prestigious, competitive colleges and universities will allow you to take two or three courses without actually applying to the school. Some let you "audit," or sit in on, classes. You pay a fee but do not have to complete exams or written assignments and, of course, you get no college credit. But auditing a course is a good way to see if you like a particular school, major or course.

Source: *College After 30: It's Never Too Late to Get the Degree You Need!* by college and university consultants Sunny and Kim Baker. Bob Adams, Inc., 260 Center St., Holbrook, Massachusetts 02343.

College Success

Students do much better in college when they form alliances with fellow students, faculty members and student advisers. *Helpful:* Enrollment in at least one small class every semester. The frequent interaction among students and between students and teacher helps counter the anonymity of large lecture classes.

Source: Five-year study by Harvard University professors, led by Richard J. Light, professor of education, reported in *The New York Times.*

Chutzpah Lessons

Probably no one knows more about chutzpah than the undefeated grand master of the art, Alan Dershowitz. His reputation as Chutzpah champion of the American legal system has been spread by his spirited defenses in famous cases like Claus von Bulow, Leona Helmsley, Rabbi Meir Kahane, Jonathan Pollard and Jim Bakker.

We asked Dershowitz, author of the best-selling book *Chutzpah,* to share his expertise...

What is chutzpah?

A polite word for it would be nerve. Chutzpah is not something you're born with...it's an acquired characteristic.

Chutzpah is a survival technique. Its goal is to level the playing field—when you are confronting someone who is more powerful than you in a situation.

Where does the word come from?

Nobody knows for sure. It's neither Yiddish nor Hebrew in origin, but is probably Aramaic, going back thousands of years. Today, its Yiddish and Hebrew meanings are different. In Yiddish it's more positive—a kind of assertiveness, a boldness, an aggressiveness. In Hebrew the meaning is more negative—arrogance and pushiness. The word has always had both positive and negative connotations, but I use it in the positive sense.

What is the value of chutzpah?

Chutzpah helps underdogs fight against bullies—people who have more power. It should never be used in a bullying way.

I believe that the reason chutzpah is considered a Jewish quality is that Jews, for centuries, have always been on the bottom, trying to fight their way up.

Is chutzpah just for Jews?

Absolutely not! You don't have to be Jewish to have chutzpah. In fact, today, in America, chutzpah is needed, and used, by several less-advantaged groups—women, Asian-Americans, African-Americans, Hispanic-Americans, etc.

You mean that any American can aspire to have chutzpah?

I have the sense that chutzpah is now the quintessential American characteristic. If you ask a native French person what Americans are like, they say we are too pushy—too aggressive...although they don't use the word chutzpah.

Mark Twain, who was able to put everybody down using his incredible wit, was one of the great *chutzapahniks* in history.

What's a chutzpahnik?

A chutzpahnik is one who possesses the quality of chutzpah.

Judge Wapner from TV's *People's Court* is the epitome of lack of chutzpah—quiet and soft-spoken. He told me that he was raised believing that chutzpah was negative and shouldn't be used. After reading my book, he realized that there was a positive meaning for it, and now he would be happy to call himself a chutzpahnik.

How do I develop chutzpah if I haven't got it?

The first rule of chutzpah is to constructively challenge authority. You have to think of yourself as equal to anybody else. You have to say over and over again in your head, *I'm just as good as they are.*

Also important: Understanding that everybody has different talents, techniques and weapons in this contest of life...and knowing where your special strengths lie. The next time someone looks at you with an aloof, smug look—because he's a foot taller than you, a million dollars richer than you, etc.—you can break through that veneer using your superior talent. That's chutzpah. That's what you have to practice.

To use chutzpah, you have to go against character. If someone is expecting you to raise your voice, for example, lower your voice.

One of the greatest acts of chutzpah of all time was author/Holocaust survivor Elie Wiesel, telling President Reagan not to go to Bitberg. He whispered to the point where Reagan had to lean over so he could hear what he was saying. Wiesel, a powerless little man, without an army, without a constituency, without a bank account, lectured the President of the United States on the immorality of the Bitberg and of going to a cemetery where the victims of the Storm Troopers were buried.

Can chutzpah be misused?

Definitely. It's often misused. I think people use it promiscuously, as a way of dealing with everything.

You shouldn't use it with working-class people—taxi drivers, waiters, etc.

And it should never, *ever,* be used in your personal life. It's too potent a weapon to be used against a loved one. It's a contest. There's a winner and a loser. In love, there should always be a tie.

I have a friend who was married to a woman whom he loved very much for many, many years. But he dealt with everything by using his chutzpah—by putting her down, by being funnier than she. My friend was a wonderful date, but a terrible husband. He had all the clever put-downs and the wonderful things that would have kept his wife laughing all the time—*on a date.* But you can't laugh 24 hours a day. There comes a time you have to have serious, direct discussions.

Can you be shy and still develop chutzpah?

Absolutely. You can develop a public personality that is very aggressive. I'm very shy at parties. I find it hard to begin a conversation with someone unless I'm spoken to first. But I am very successful using my chutzpah in my professional life.

Where did you learn chutzpah?

From my mother. But I never, never use it in relation to my mother! I learned it from watching my mother use it on other people.

My mother is a brilliant woman. I've always said, had my mother lived 30 years later, she probably would have been the first woman on the Supreme Court. She is almost 80 years old, and to this day, she's the quickest repartee of anybody I know. She could beat Jackie Mason and Alan King to the punch line every time.

Do you think that chutzpah has a future?

Without any question. My book has been very successful. I've been getting letters from people all over the country. It was even reviewed by the *Korean Times!* The sky's the limit.

Source: Renowned attorney Alan Dershowitz, Harvard Law School professor and author of *Chutzpah,* Little, Brown and Company, 205 Lexington Ave., New York 10016.

Mind Power Opportunities

There is increasing evidence that the mind has many more resources than the experts once thought.

There are hundreds of studies now that show how to use the mind more effectively—if we take the time to understand what is there for us.

Part of my interest in this area comes from the work of my grandfather, Edgar Cayce. Known as *The Sleeping Prophet,* he had an unusual mental talent: He could enter a sleep-like trance in which he accurately diagnosed the illnesses of thousands of people—whether they were in the same room or thousands of miles away.

You can train your mind to work more powerfully for you in these areas...

Healing...

The mind has a great deal of control over the immune system. Harvard psychologist Mary Jaznowski took 30 healthy students and divided them into three groups...

- One worked crossword puzzles.
- One was given relaxation training.
- One received relaxation training and visual imagery training—imagining their powerful and strong immune systems attacking weak flu and cold viruses.

Group One showed no increase in immune cells. Group Two showed a slight increase. Group Three showed a *significant* increase in immune system activity after only one hour of training.

We, too, can use the mind to teach ourselves to relax, to visualize changes in the body and to increase the probability of those changes actually occurring.

Problem-solving and creativity...

Our program teaches that if we simply pay more attention—more time and energy—to becoming aware of our mental processes, we will be much more effective. One simple way of doing this is to work with your dreams. We all dream every night. If you aren't aware of your dreams, you are missing important messages from your inner mind.

Valuable habit: Put a pencil and paper by your bed and when you wake up, write down immediately what you recall from dreams during the night. If you do this consistently, you will find answers to problems from everyday life popping up in the dream state—how to deal with a situation at work, handle specific relationships, etc.

The *pre-sleep* state is also valuable. Both Einstein and Thomas Edison got important insights while in the pre-sleep period, and both found that the mind can function more creatively then—as opposed to when it is fully awake. Suggestions made during the pre-sleep period can help you to reshape your behavior.

Example: One of my students was trying to stop smoking. He worked with pre-sleep suggestion and visualization. He made a tape for himself, describing a number of situations in which he usually enjoyed smoking—but described them without the cigarettes. Every night for four months, he played this tape just before going to sleep. Then one weekend he threw away all his cigarettes and told himself that on Monday morning he would stop smoking. It worked. Months have passed...and he hasn't resumed smoking. He had tried other techniques, but none had ever worked before.

Stress reduction...

Meditation is one of the most vital tools used in reducing mental and physical stress. But recent research suggests that beyond these effects, the regular practice of meditation can enhance creativity and increase your attention span as well.

In meditation, you quiet the body and mind, and then place the mind on a single focus for a period of minutes. Harvard psychologist Herbert Benson found that the word "one," or even a nonsense syllable, worked just as well as a mantra.

Benson showed that the body begins to change as we work with the meditation process—there is a decrease in oxygen consumption...the muscles relax and the general level of stress is reduced. In addition, I have found meditation helps to discipline and control the mind, which helps us focus our attention wherever we need to.

Intuition and ESP...

Intuitive ability is probably distributed normally in the population, just the way any other ability is—playing the piano or throwing a baseball accurately or running fast.

There are a few people who have a tremendous amount of many abilities, and a few who have almost none. Most of us are in the big bump in the middle on the bell curve. If we practice, we begin to see improvement, but we can't just sit down at the piano and play a sonata without training, as Mozart did.

Intuition can be very useful in your business life, your personal life and your health. Meditation, pre-sleep suggestion, dreams and visualization can all enhance your ability to focus the mind in an intuitive way.

Helpful: Start now asking your inner self questions...*Can I trust this person? Where did I leave my keys?* Over time, the answers will get better and more frequent.

Developing our mind's capacity doesn't take much time. People generally begin to recognize results from these exercises after a month or so.

Remember: In the Jaznowski study, results showed after only one hour of training!

Source: Charles Thomas Cayce, PhD, president of the organization founded by his grandfather, Edgar Cayce—the Association for Research and Enlightenment, Box 95, Virginia Beach, Virginia 23451.

The Secrets of Effective Thinking

The world is filled with success stories—very limited success stories...but few of us ever achieve success in even two of the following three *life dimensions...*

- Successful careers
- Satisfying work
- Rich personal lives

...and genuine "three-dimensional" success is extremely rare.

To learn more about three-dimensional success, I studied 1,200 people—lawyers, artists, blue-collar workers, teachers and students. All had successful careers, and so had achieved at least *one-dimensional* success.

My psychological tests gauged their success in the other two dimensions—job satisfaction and personal life satisfaction. *Results:*

•Fifteen percent enjoyed their work but not their personal lives—and thus had achieved two-dimensional success. *Sad:* Most thought their successful, enjoyable careers resulted from a willingness to sacrifice their personal lives. One executive I asked to rate his personal life, responded, "Personal life? What personal life?"

•Four percent enjoyed both their work and their personal lives. These people had achieved three-dimensional success. They were good at their jobs...*and* they enjoyed their work... *and* they had fulfilling personal lives. I call these people *Uncommonly Successful People* (USPs).

To learn more about three-dimensional success, I subjected these USPs to additional psychological testing. *I found that all USPs share three important traits...*

•*Inner calm* that helps them to stay focused.

•*Clear goals* and a sense of purpose that guide their lives.

•*Adventurousness* that lets them laugh at themselves and gives them the courage to take necessary risks.

Effective thinking...

That wasn't all they shared. All USPs also share an uncommon way of thinking—what I call *effective thinking*.

Effective thinking is not the same as positive thinking, although positive thinking can sometimes be effective. Effective thinking is any thought pattern that leads, directly or indirectly, to personal and professional success...to a rich and satisfying life.

Effective thinking is always result-oriented. There is an effective thought for every situation we encounter.

Note: Most USPs weren't born effective thinkers. They learned to think effectively, just as all of us can. *What's needed:*

•Finding out exactly what you want in each dimension of your life.

•Committing yourself to achieving these goals.

•Using this standard approach to effective thinking...

•*Step one:* Take notice. As you hurry through life, pause five or six times a day to take stock of your life.

Am I doing well? Am I moving toward my goal of three-dimensional success? If you can honestly answer these questions in the affirmative, no additional action is needed. Go back to what you were doing. But if the answer is no, you must pause to get back on track.

Uncommon success does not mean vast riches, nor does it mean you must enjoy every moment of your life.

Example: A meeting might not be fun, but enduring it might help land you that next promotion. Viewing such experiences as important steps along your way to uncommon success makes them easier to bear. What you *think* is entirely under your control. Don't blow minor or temporary annoyances out of proportion.

•*Step two:* Pause. If while taking notice you discover that you are not heading toward uncommon success, you must pause. This pause may last from just a few seconds to several months, while all other aspects of your life continue as before. Whatever the duration of the pause, its purpose remains the same—to break your self-defeating mind-set.

Background: All humans approach life using certain mind-sets that have been programmed into our brains by parents, friends and teachers. At times these mind-sets are helpful...but at other times they make life needlessly difficult, interfering with our journey toward uncommon success.

Example: In my seminars, I ask participants if they're familiar with Ivan Pavlov, the Russian scientist who first demonstrated the conditioned response in which an animal's assumptions begin to control his behavior—a dog fed at the ring of a bell begins to salivate as soon as the bell is rung. Invariably, several participants raise their hands. When they do, I ask who told them to do so. Of course, no one did. They assumed they should raise their hands because they had in the past. Life works the same way. We behave in certain ways and think certain thoughts because we've been trained to do so. By pausing, we learn to break old habits and view life in fresh, creative terms.

• *Step three:* Identify effective thoughts. USPs always take responsibility for their life situation, shifting away from the external to the internal.

Example: A non-USP might think, *Pressures on my job make me nervous.* But a USP in the same situation thinks, *Pressures on my job do not make me nervous. My thoughts about these pressures make me nervous.*

In this way, USPs pinpoint defective thoughts and then identify—or create—effective thoughts with which to replace them. *Aids to effective thinking:*

• Understanding anger. All anger stems from fear. Eliminate the fear, and you eliminate the anger. If you become angry, ask yourself what you fear. In most cases, fears are not justified. If you encounter an angry person, don't think, *What a terrible person!* Instead, ask yourself, *What is he/she afraid of?*

• Understanding depression. All of us experience depression at some time or another. Depression helps us cope with sadness and then provides the impetus to get us back on track. Avoiding sadness or depression actually has a negative effect. The trick is not to spend too much time being depressed.

• Understanding intimacy. No matter how many friends you have, no matter how big and loving your family, each of us, alone, is responsible for ourself. This is especially true for uncommonly successful people, who operate at the upper echelons of business and society. Accepting the inevitability of occasional loneliness makes life more pleasant.

• Understanding neediness. People prefer to have all sorts of things—love, a nice house and car, a high-paying job, etc. In reality, they need only the basics—food, shelter, and clothing. Realizing that you can make do without all your preferences helps you appreciate what you already have.

Paradox: In many cases, realizing that you don't need something makes it easier to get that something.

• Understanding resentment. Life is not always fair. Rotten people sometimes thrive, and naive people occasionally suffer. But being indignant about this unfortunate fact is useless.

Better way: Try to set right an unfairness when you can. When you cannot, mourn briefly, then get on with your life.

Once you have identified effective thoughts, all that remains is to implement them—by choosing to do so.

• *Step four:* Choose. The brain is capable of enormous tasks. Unfortunately, most people believe they have little control over their thoughts, and so are enslaved by them. As USPs already know, humans are unique among animals in that they can choose their thoughts.

In many cases, it's possible simply to choose to think of a particular effective thought to focus upon. If conscious choosing fails, however, there is an alternative...

Reverse psychology: Exaggerate whatever effective thought you are thinking until you grow weary of it. Then use this newfound sense of control to choose the effective thought. If you have insomnia, for example, try thinking thoughts that will wake you up. Once you tire of doing this, choose to think sleep-promoting thoughts.

Source: Gerald Kushel, EdD, Professor Emeritus of mental health counseling at Long Island University and president of the Institute for Effective Thinking. Lecturer and seminar leader, Dr. Kushel is the author of several books, including his most recent, *Effective Thinking for Uncommon Success,* Amacom, 135 W. 50 St., New York 10020.

New Year's Resolutions— Effective any Time Of the Year

For most people, New Year's resolutions are forgotten or abandoned soon into the year. What to do? *Stop blaming yourself.* And begin fresh with *effective* resolutions.

The problem with most New Year's resolutions is that people don't know how to make good ones.

Sworn in a haze of champagne bubbles and high expectations, New Year's resolutions sound more like a *wish* list than a *to do* list.

For more effectiveness...

• Be realistic. A *wish* has nothing to do with committing yourself to an idea and developing and following a plan. A good resolution is a goal with a starting point, a plan and a deadline.

Example: When you take a plane trip, your goal is to be on the plane before takeoff. Days before your flight, you make plans to get there on time—you calculate the travel time to the airport, pack, arrange child-care, etc. You create a *reverse calendar,* starting at your goal (the plane ride) and working back to a starting point.

Resolutions work the same way. You start with a goal...then figure out what steps you must take to accomplish it.

• Know what to do. Most resolutions involve don'ts—*Don't smoke, don't eat, don't be late.* You never get a clear picture of what it is you're supposed to *do.* By asking yourself, *What's wrong with me?* instead of, *What can I do better?* you set yourself up to fail.

Successful resolutions focus on things you can do that will build your self-esteem or make you a better person.

Examples: Breathe fresh air, eat more vegetables, leave the house earlier.

• Think small. Great expectations lead to great disappointments. *Better:* Take small steps that are easily attainable and build the momentum you need to succeed. Start with just 15 minutes a day—go for a walk, clear your desk, etc. *Key:* Be patient.

• Daydream. Think about your ideal condition one year from now—imagine that you've already achieved your goal.

Examples: If your goal is to lose weight, feel what it will be like to be thinking, eating and exercising as a thin person. If you want to stop smoking, *feel* what it will be like to breathe freely, not relying on a cigarette.

Trap: Telling yourself, *I haven't reached my goal yet, I wish I had*...or *I should be*...Such statements lead to frustration and depression.

It's also important to think about long-term goals—three to five years from now. This will let you see how accomplishing your one-year resolution—changing a bad habit or learning a new skill—will bring you one step closer to attaining your long-term goals. *Result:* You will be motivated to see each resolution through to the end because you can see how it fits into your big picture.

Alternate plan...

If you're tired of making resolutions year after year, give yourself a break. Don't make any now. Keep the same job. Don't work on the relationship with your mate. Don't change your habits. Take time to discover who you really are and how it feels.

Then...if you can't bear to stay where you are, you will be more motivated to make a big change later.

When to resolve and re-resolve...

There are many turning points in the year during which you can examine what you've been doing and define goals to which you're willing to commit yourself.

Best times: In addition to January 1, there's also your birthday, or the day after you've filed your tax return, the end of summer, etc.

About once a month, examine your progress and reevaluate your resolutions. As time goes by, your resolution may no longer be useful.

Example: You may find that running 40 miles per week is not satisfying your goal to run a marathon, or is in conflict with other important goals—like being able to spend more time with your family.

Key: Use your goals to help you become wiser. As you learn more, your goals may change. Apply your new knowledge to making your resolutions more realistic.

Resolutions and others...

It's usually a good idea to tell someone else about the resolutions you've made. This creates a subtle social pressure that will help you to persevere when sticking to your goals gets tough.

If you don't want to disclose your entire resolutions to anyone else, it is often useful to at least tell someone about your short-term plans. Telling your spouse that you plan to walk for 15 minutes every day, for example, will help you reach that goal.

Important: Even if you share your resolutions with others, they are still *your* resolutions. Keep them under your control and be sure they are devised for your own personal improvement.

Example: You can't resolve that your spouse will stop smoking—that decision must come from your spouse. But you can resolve to support his/her efforts to kick the habit.

Resolutions needn't all be serious. Often, we get so wrapped up in *doing* resolutions that we forget about *being* resolutions.

Resolve to give yourself plenty of guilt-free time to relax, exercise, socialize and regenerate yourself. Only when you are at peace with yourself can you be truly in control of your life.

Source: Neil Fiore, PhD, a psychologist in private practice in Berkeley, California, and author of *The Now Habit: A Strategic Program for Overcoming Procrastination and Enjoying Guilt-Free Play,* Jeremy P. Tarcher, Inc., 5850 Wilshire Blvd., Suite 200, Los Angeles 90036. His most recent book is *The Road Back to Health: Coping with the Emotional Aspects of Cancer,* Celestial Arts, Box 7327, Berkeley, California 94701.

What They Don't Teach In Even the Best Schools

Our high school and our college teachers meant well, but they drilled into us huge quantities of information that we promptly forgot...and neglected to teach us some of the most fundamental skills for living well. *Key things that they left out:*

- The purpose of life.
- The importance of forgiveness.
- The need for balance.
- How to figure out what we want.
- The usefulness of mistakes.
- How to love ourselves.

Fortunately, our education doesn't end just because we leave school. Life itself is a classroom, and our teachers are everything that happens to us—both positive and negative.

In addition, each of us has our own *Master Teacher*—that voice inside us that seems to be making calm, sure comments in the midst of mental chaos. In a sense, it's life that teaches us how to live.

Why are we here?

We can't know for sure if there's meaning to life. But it makes great practical sense to at least *assume* that there is. I believe that life's purpose has three parts:

- Doing. Human beings are busy creatures. We do far more than simple survival would require. This suggests that we thrive on doing. *All this doing leads to...*
- Learning. The more we do, the more we learn...and the more we learn, the more we do. It's a continuing cycle. *But it would quickly become tedious without the third element...*
- Enjoying. Some people complain about being on a treadmill. Others pay hundreds of dollars for the privilege of going into a gym and running on one.

Joy can exist no matter what else is going on in your life. There are lessons to be learned even from confusion and pain...and learning is enjoyable, even if the events themselves aren't.

The attitude of gratitude...

The human brain evolved to take familiar things for granted, allowing our ancestors to sit up and take notice when a saber-toothed tiger approached. That means we need to be *consciously* grateful for the good in our lives, or we may not notice it at all.

You choose your attitude at any given moment. *Ask yourself:* Do I focus on the good things in my life or the bad things?

We all have plenty of both, and the mind can only concentrate on a narrow spectrum at any one time.

It's a simple formula. If you focus on the good stuff, life is enjoyable. If you focus on the bad, life is miserable.

That doesn't mean we should never feel bad. Pain and loss happen to everyone from time to time, and sometimes feeling bad is precisely the appropriate response to a situation.

But it's more often the little, day-to-day occurrences that make or break our happiness. You can focus on the guy who cut you off in traffic on the way to work this morning...or the one who kept the store open a few minutes late just to accommodate you.

Think about all the little miracles in life. Oxygen, for example—we've never been without it.

You can have anything you want...

The Puritan ethic tells us, *It's wrong to want things. Life is nothing but sacrifice and duty, and people who have what they want are wicked.* That belief leads to frustration.

In recent decades, the popular philosophy shifted to *I want it all!* But that philosophy also leads to frustration. If you have it all, you don't have enough time to learn how to use it, much less enjoy it.

The truth: You can have *anything*...but not *everything* you want.

Sure, there are limitations, but not as many as most of us believe. It's just that you may have to give up some things you want less for things you want more.

Don't be ashamed of your desires. It's great to want noble things (world peace, good health for all), but it's okay to want mundane or *self-focused* things, too—a red sports car, great sex, etc.

Respect the whole range of your aspirations. You can't get what you want unless you know what it is. And you won't figure out what it is unless you're willing to accept it.

Love your mistakes...

One of the most destructive things we learned in school is that mistakes are bad and should be punished.

It you avoid mistakes, you avoid accomplishing anything.

Without failure there's no experimentation ...no learning...and no growth.

It's by finding out what *doesn't* work that we learn what *does*. James Joyce wrote, *Mistakes are the portals of discovery*. Make excellence, not perfection, your goal.

Forgiving is for giving...

Nursing a grievance may make us feel righteous...but it doesn't make us feel happy. Forgiving and forgetting makes you available *for giving* and *for getting*.

When you forgive someone, you give not only to that person, but to yourself. Instead of focusing on hurt, anger and betrayal, you open yourself up to love, joy and adventure.

When we judge others, we also judge ourselves for being judgmental. Deep down, we know that we're inhibiting our happiness.

Say to yourself, *I forgive (name of person) for (perceived offense). I forgive myself for judging (person) for (offense).*

It's simple. Try it.

Life is a balancing act...

Another incorrect thing that school taught: *There's always a right answer.* Life is one contradiction after another...and most contradictions are valid.

We need to be vigilant to sense when we should rest and when we should act...when we should be flexible and when we should stand firm...what we should accept and what we should change.

When in doubt, consult your Master Teacher —that quietly confident and sensitive inner voice. *Ask:* What would a Master do? Then do it.

Source: Peter McWilliams, coauthor (with educator John-Roger) of *Life 101: Everything We Wish We Had Learned About Life in School—But Didn't* and *DO IT!: Let's Get Off Our Butts,* Prelude Press, Los Angeles.

The Importance of Self-Discipline

Without discipline, we can't improve ourselves, or solve problems, or be competent, or delay gratification or assume responsibility.

Without discipline we cannot find reality and truth...we never evolve from children into productive adults.

Yet discipline is a trait that's in short supply these days, especially among young people.

M. Scott Peck, best-selling author of *The Road Less Traveled*, tells us why this is so—and what we can do about it.

Why is discipline so powerful?

Most people think that the point of life is to be happy. But life is really about self-improvement. We're not born perfect. It's our job to make ourselves as good as we can be.

As Benjamin Franklin once said, "Those things that hurt, instruct." Yet the concept that life can be difficult is alien to most people.

The only way we can improve ourselves is through discipline. Without it, we can't solve any problems. With some discipline, we can solve some problems. But with total discipline, we can solve all of our problems. Discipline makes us competent.

I used to tell my patients that psychotherapy is not about happiness, it's about personal power and competence. If you get hooked into therapy and go the whole route, I can't guarantee you'll leave one bit happier. But you will leave more competent.

The problem with competence is that there's a vacuum of it in the world. So as soon as people become more competent, either God or life gives them bigger problems to deal with.

There is, however, a certain kind of joy that comes with knowing you're worrying about the big problems and that you're no longer getting bent out of shape about the little ones.

How can people determine which problems are truly important?

Think about them. Most people don't.

I spend the first hour of each day sitting in my bedroom thinking about my priorities. *What should I be working on now? What can be put off until later?*

Important problems are ones that affect all of us.

Example: I work with many organizations, businesses and agencies on how to better integrate psychiatry, religion and spirituality. That's a big problem.

It's impossible to think about big problems if you're spending your time worrying about what you're going to watch on TV or what you're going to say to someone. Spending time on that kind of problem is a waste of energy.

Isn't it true that some people think about the little problems to put off working on the important ones?

This relates to one of the main issues of discipline—delayed gratification.

This means doing the things in life that are *un*pleasant before those that are enjoyable. If you do what you have to do first, you'll be free to enjoy yourself later.

Most people—and I'm not just talking about children—dash to what they want to do, and then feel terrible trying to get around to what they have to do.

Why do so many people, especially young people, have so much trouble delaying gratification?

Gratification is something that must be learned. We rejoice in the spontaneity of small children. But, in truth, children are all born liars, cheats, thieves and manipulators who don't know how to delay gratification.

It's hardly remarkable that many of them grow up to be adult liars, cheats, thieves and manipulators.

What's even harder to explain—but what life is all about—is that some children grow up to be disciplined, God-fearing and honest.

There are many reasons why people grow up undisciplined. Most importantly, many children lack good parenting. Parents are role models. And kids with undisciplined parents have a much harder time growing up to be disciplined.

Discipline also suffers from an image problem in our culture. We think of discipline as something that's imposed by someone else rather than as a form of self-love.

Learning discipline requires real effort. But this is what it takes for people to find the most joy and lead the most productive lives. Delaying gratification means, ultimately, enjoying things *more.*

Does a person have to be completely unselfish to be able to accept discipline?

There's no such thing as an unselfish person. I myself am totally selfish. Strictly speaking, I've never done a thing for anyone else.

When I water my flowers I don't say, *Look, flowers, what I'm doing for you...you ought to be grateful.* I do it because I like pretty flowers.

When I extend myself for my children, it's because I want to have an image of myself as a good father.

You could look at monks and nuns and think how unselfish they are. But they've decided that this is the best way to personal joy.

We need to distinguish between the path of smart selfishness and that of stupid selfishness.

Stupid selfishness is trying to avoid all pain and all problems, while smart selfishness is learning the difference between unnecessary pain and that which is an inherent part of life.

Get rid of the unnecessary pain, but meet the necessary pain head on. Work it through and learn from it.

In what ways do people fail to accept discipline?

People often look to someone else to solve their problems. This is a natural tendency. Being disciplined requires assuming responsibility. And that means saying, *This is my problem.* You can't solve a problem until you admit that you own it.

Example: Three years ago, I had a sharp disagreement with my 18-year-old son. I raked him over the coals. The next morning I found an angry letter from him outside my door. I thought about it and decided he was right. So I apologized. It wasn't easy for me, but it was very healing for my son to have his father apologize.

Lesson: You can't apologize unless you accept responsibility for being at fault.

To take responsibility, you have to value yourself. And you have to have role models. Kids who won't assume responsibility undoubtedly have parents who won't, either.

In the example with my son, one of the beauties of my apology was not just that it made peace between us and increased his self-esteem, but that it gave him a model of taking responsibility.

How do we get the discipline to accomplish what we set out to do?

It requires dedication to reality...the truth. The more clearly we see the world, the better equipped we are to make wise decisions.

But reality and truth are only things we can approach. We can't get them tied in a nice little package and put it in our briefcase.

What else does it take for people to be disciplined?

People need deadlines.

When I used to work with groups and they weren't getting anywhere, I'd impose a six-month deadline. It's amazing how a group of people who had been acting as if they had all the time in the world could get moving once they had a concrete deadline.

Death is the ultimate deadline. None of us has forever to accomplish what we want to.

Is it possible to be over-disciplined?

Yes, it certainly is.

Our parents and our culture teach us that certain things must be done in certain ways.

Result: We can become so disciplined that we're not able to stop and smell the flowers.

Example: I used to think that if I went into a fancy restaurant I had to order an appetizer, entree and dessert. But sometimes I'd be attracted to two or three appetizers. Only now that I'm in my 50s can I order two appetizers and forget the entree. It's more constructive for me to eat what I want than to please the waiter.

Lesson: You can fiddle around with discipline ...as long as you're not doing anything that's harmful.

Source: Psychiatrist M. Scott Peck, MD, author of *A Bed By the Window, A Novel of Mystery and Redemption,* Bantam Books, 666 Fifth Ave., New York 10103. His big best-seller is, of course, *The Road Less Traveled.* Much of Dr. Peck's time is spent now in management consulting. His office: Bliss Rd., New Preston, Connecticut 06777.

Secrets of Much Better Problem Solving

We run into problems every day—at home and at work, with our families and our associates. And we spend tremendous time and energy trying to solve them.

Yet at the end of the day (or the week, or the quarter), we often find ourselves no further than when we began.

Better: Breakthrough Thinking...an approach to planning and problem solving that is based on both scientific theories and years of research with effective managers and professionals.

What is Breakthrough Thinking?

Breakthrough Thinking combines Oriental vision with Western pragmatism. Rather than focusing on what's wrong with a situation, it begins by defining our *purpose* in solving it.

Breakthrough Thinking asks more than just *how* we can get something done, it also asks *what* we want to accomplish...and *why* we want to accomplish it. In the process, it saves us from wasting time and energy on the wrong problem.

Breakthrough Thinking assumes that the world is always in flux. Each solution begets a new problem. No one solution can work all the time or for all things, no matter how similar the problems may appear on the surface.

To take advantage of ever-changing conditions, Breakthrough Thinking always seeks out the *solution-after-next.* As a result, it represents a process rather than a fixed goal—a flexible plan to achieve what matters most to us.

Although there is no magic formula to Breakthrough Thinking, it rests on these basics:

•The Uniqueness Principle. Each problem is unique and requires an approach that dwells on its own contextual needs. Although no two situations are alike, most people rely on impulsive idea-borrowing to solve their problems.

Problem-solvers who accept *differences* are much more likely to be successful than those who see only similarities, and who try to shoehorn borrowed solutions into situations where they are not appropriate.

Breakthrough Thinkers don't strive to *keep up with the Jones's*...they understand that the Jones's needs are different from their own. The childless couple next door may be deliriously happy with their sporty little Mazda Miata. But if you have a large family, a Volvo station wagon will solve *your* transportation problem far better.

•The Purposes Principle. Focusing on purposes helps strip away nonessential aspects to avoid working on the wrong problem.

Example: After years of struggle to keep your lawn alive, your sprinkler breaks. The obvious solution is to buy a new sprinkler—if your exclusive goal is to have a lush, green lawn. But if you expand your own context and examine your bigger purpose first, a more satisfying range of options will present itself...

•*Broader purpose:* To maintain an attractive outdoor environment in your current location. *Possible solution:* Replace the grass with drought-resistant shrubs and ground cover.

•*Even broader:* To have a beautiful view. *Possible solution:* Move to a home (in the mountains or on the beach, for instance) where lawns and landscaping are not an issue.

•The Solution-After-Next Principle. Innovation can be stimulated and solutions made more effective by working backward from an ideal target solution.

In applying this principle, a job seeker might accept a lower salary at a growing firm with strong opportunities for advancement, rather than a higher salary in a dead-end job at a small family firm. The key question is not *What is best for me next week?* but, *What do I want to be doing five years from now?*

•The Systems Principle. Every problem is part of a larger system. Nothing exists by itself. Successful problem-solving (and problem prevention) takes into account these interrelationships between many elements and dimensions.

Example: Many people rush into a divorce because their immediate goal is to detach themselves from their spouse. They may neglect the related *outcomes* they desire from the divorce, at heavy cost later on. Without advance consideration of the property settlement, child support and social ramifications, a divorce can create more problems than it solves.

Using Breakthrough Thinking, a woman who plans to get custody of her children may decide against staying in the family's home in an isolated suburb. *Reason:* As a single mother, she may need the social support and services she can find in the city. *Possible solution:* A liquidation of the family property.

•The Limited Information Collection Principle. Knowing too much about a problem initially can prevent you from seeing some excellent alternative solutions.

Information junkies think that facts are the keys to problem-solving—and that the more facts you have, the better your solution will be. They fail to realize that facts are only *representations* of the real world, not the real world itself. And representations can be distorted, poorly interpreted, irrelevant (the wrong problem) or just plain wrong.

Even if they are accurate, a flurry of facts will obscure the primary factor in any good solution—the purpose for it.

Example: I recently bought a new car. I might have immersed myself in data about suspension systems and engine design—and gotten progressively more confused. Instead, I asked myself what I wanted from my car—Prestige? Power? The latest features? The answer, each time, was *no*. The truth is that I hate to drive, so I do as little of it as I can. My top priority is reliability, followed by economy. *My solution:* I bought an inexpensive, no-frills car.

•The People Design Principle. The people who will carry out and use a solution must work together to develop the solution.

Too many meetings are searches for blame. Because they focus on the particulars of a problem, participants take turns in pointing fingers at someone else.

Breakthrough alternative: At the beginning of the meeting, ask everyone to discuss the *purpose* of your getting together. When individuals feel free to express their needs, they become more useful (and less defensive) contributors.

•The Betterment Timeline Principle. A sequence of purpose-directed solutions will lead to a better future.

Breakthroughs often occur over a period of time, not just at one point. The easy, *foolproof* solution is usually a patch job—and it's almost always wrong. Since solutions are changes that include the seeds of *later* changes, Breakthrough Thinking demands *continual* improvement in the area of concern.

Traditional thinkers say, "If it isn't broken, don't fix it." But Breakthrough Thinkers say, "Fix it *before* it breaks."

Source: Gerald Nadler, IBM Professor of Engineering Management at the University of Southern California and a consultant to some of North America's top corporations. He is coauthor of *Breakthrough Thinking*, Prima Publishing, Box 1260GN, Rocklin, California 95677.

Everyone Can Be More Creative

One of the world's biggest myths is that there is such a thing as *creative people*.

The truth: Everyone is creative. It's just that some people know how to use their creativity, while others do not. You can experience creativity more often by using four tools...

If at first you don't succeed...

Surrender. This doesn't mean giving up. It actually means surrendering to the answer already in you, but that you're not recognizing. This is the first tool—*having faith in your own creativity.*

What's going on: Something is blocking your thought processes. It may be anxiety, concern for your self-image or your need to impress others. *Exercises:*

•Recognize that apprehension, anxiety, tension, competition and anticipation all stifle your creativity. *Helpful:* Picture yourself full of intuition, will, strength and joy.

•Apply yourself to a task. Doing something for the sheer joy of it enables you to experience your inner creativity.

Example: One of my students, a lawyer, came up with an idea for an especially difficult legal issue. After racking his brain with various lines of reasoning, he just gave in and started with the easiest section of the legal brief, hoping the rest would follow. The ideas popped up as he worked.

•Acknowledge that you don't know how things will turn out. Instead of worrying about what could happen, just go ahead and see what develops.

Destroy judgment...

The second tool is an *absence of judgment.* It's hard to pay attention to your own creativity when a little voice inside your head keeps telling you that only special people—geniuses or great artists—can create...so you can't possibly be creative.

That voice comes from our parents who said things like, *Who do you think you are?* when we tried to do something original.

To get rid of that little voice—we call it the *Voice of Judgment*, or *VOJ*—you have to pay attention to it. Watch how many times it pops up during the day and stops you from doing something you want to do.

Example: When you arrive at work, you see someone you'd like to talk to, but she's talking to someone else. You turn away because your VOJ is saying, *She'd rather talk to Tom.*

As you monitor your Voice of Judgment, you'll start to notice that the voice isn't really you at all. It comes from outside.

At that point, you'll be able to make a conscious decision not to be affected by it. You'll start to get mad at the voice for stopping you from doing what you want to do and from being all that you could be.

To get rid of your VOJ: Shout at it. Tell it to get out of your life. Make it look ridiculous by exaggerating it beyond belief. Every time you attack the VOJ you weaken it more and more.

Pay attention...

By paying attention to what's going on around you, you develop the third tool for creativity—*precise observation.* An essential part of creativity is the ability to see things *very* clearly.

If you concentrate on what you're doing, even if it's something like washing the dishes, you slow down internally. This feeds your sense of deep appreciation and lets you focus without distraction on the task at hand, a valuable tool that most of us lost in childhood.

Example: A child building a sand castle is entirely absorbed in what he's doing. He's not thinking about it, he's just creating.

There are several ways you can teach yourself to concentrate. *Exercises:*

- Set your watch to go off on the hour to remind yourself to pay attention.
- Go to the ocean and sit there for an hour and soak in the tranquility...or the powerful turbulence.
- Listen carefully to what people say.
- Make lists of things you always wanted to pay attention to but never had the time.

To be creative, you have to pay attention to your own creativity.

Exercise: Sit quietly with your eyes closed. Pay attention to your breathing until you're calm. Then remember when you had a great idea, something that solved a problem or dealt with a situation. Get absorbed in it. Think of what happened before you got the idea, how long that took, how you felt, what you sensed, what you thought. Then think about what happened afterwards, what you did about it.

The more you pay attention to your own perfect performance—the times you were creative—the greater the probability that you'll be creative in future situations. *Helpful:* Start small. Think of the many little ways in which you're creative every day.

Example: The alternate route you chose to avoid a traffic jam getting to work.

Ask dumb questions...

Creativity starts with a question, which is the basis for the fourth and final tool of creativity—*asking penetrating questions.* A creative approach to living means making your entire life a questioning process.

When you ask creative questions, you don't care what you find. You ask for the fun of it, without expectation.

Examples: Columbus asked, *Is there a sea route to India?* and discovered the new world. Picasso asked, *Is it possible to depict the human form another way?* and found Cubism. Freud asked, *Do mistakes have meaning?* and founded psychoanalysis.

Preschool children ask dumb questions about everything. And sooner or later parents and teachers give them the message that such questions aren't welcome. Their VOJ begins to build a defense against questions. Pretty soon cynicism sets in.

Exercises: Ask a dumb question or question of wonder every day to develop your curiosity naturally. Start by asking yourself, then work up to asking other people. Start small. Don't frighten yourself with, *Is there a God?* Ask, *What's a preposition?* or, *Why are you digging that hole?*

Source: Social psychologist Michael Ray, PhD, professor of creativity at Stanford Business School. He is coauthor of *Creativity in Business*, Doubleday, 666 Fifth Ave., New York 10103.

Expanding Your Thinking Power

Over the past few years, there have been important developments in our understanding of effective thinking and how to teach it.

You can improve your reasoning skills by:

• Using analogies and metaphors. Deliberately ask yourself, *What am I assuming? If art is creative, for example, does that mean business is noncreative?* This will lead you to think about the real meaning of creativity.

• Not getting bogged down in a particular line of reasoning. Deliberately step outside it. *Suggestion:* Take 10 minutes to think of the problem in a completely different way. If that doesn't work, you've lost only a little time.

• Paying more attention to the aesthetic aspects of the problem than to the pragmatic ones. If you're designing an inventory system, for example, it shouldn't only be functional but should also solve certain difficulties in keeping track of things in an easy, elegant way.

• Looking at how you're being conventional. Break that conventional set. Watch out for cliches. Avoid timeworn and obvious answers.

• Being self-conscious. It's a myth that self-consciousness is a barrier to effective thinking. Be aware of the way you do things. Do you brush aside problems, or do you take them seriously? Do you look for opportunities to think about something a little longer, or do you pass them by?

• Opening up to ideas. Don't dismiss suggestions with *That's just common sense* or *I already do that.* Common sense isn't always common practice, and if you think you already do it, you probably don't. Research on actual behavior tells us that people don't accurately perceive whether or not they follow their own advice. Typically, they don't.

• Taking a course in thinking. Look for one that requires a lot of small-group work over a 6-to-20-week period. Investigate the course carefully, including the teacher's credentials, before taking it.

Source: David N. Perkins, Ph.D., senior research associate in education, Graduate School of Education, Harvard University, author of *The Mind's Best Work,* Harvard University Press, Cambridge, MA.

Scheduling Time To Concentrate

• Time budget should include "quiet hours" when you have a chance to think without interruptions. Best time in the office is early morning before official hours begin.

• If possible, work during noon hour when interruptions are rare because most others have gone to lunch. Go out to eat at 1 p.m. or later.

• When scheduling your day, schedule the interruptions, as well. Try to restrict all calls on routine matters to a certain time of the day. If calls come in at other hours, have your secretary say you'll call them back. (Even VIPs will accept this if you establish a reputation for returning calls when promised.)

• Spend a few "office hours" at home. Use an answering machine to cover telephone calls so you won't be interrupted.

Use Your Intuition to Improve Your Thinking

Intuition, the spontaneous generation of fresh ideas for solving problems, can help you in your work and personal life. Here are some ways to use intuition and evaluate its effectiveness relative to other methods of making decisions:

Keeping a journal will enable you to discover successful intuitions. For each intuition, record at the moment it happens:

• The date and time.

• Content.

- Type (future prediction, creative insight, problem solution, etc.).
- Description (verbal, visual, a faint idea, etc.).
- Vividness.
- What you were doing and how you felt immediately before and after having it.
- Your initial reaction (skepticism, belief, etc.).

Later, add the following to your journal:

- Was the intuition a departure from custom, authority or logic?
- Was it something you wanted or didn't want to hear?
- Did it return at various times?
- Did you analyze it, try to verify it, seek other opinions?
- Were you under pressure to come up with a decision?
- Did it represent a high risk?
- How did it work out in the end?
- If you went with an intuition that was wrong, do you understand why?
- Leave room in your journal for random thoughts and observations.
- Note any patterns that you may come across.

Source: Philip Goldberg, author of *The Intuitive Edge,* Jeremy P. Tarcher, Inc., Los Angeles.

Real Problem Solving

Management's job isn't simply to predict the problems—many of them can't be predicted, no matter how well the project is planned. *What is critical:* The way managers respond to inevitable problems.

- Seeking a victim and assigning blame is the most common response to a problem—and the least effective way to solve it. *Inevitable result:* Everyone avoids blame and argues if others had done what they should have, the problem wouldn't have come up.
- Not putting the emphasis on blame creates the atmosphere for making rolling adjustments and changes in plans and specifications in any new venture. This will not take place if individuals feel that concessions will be held against them or are an admission of guilt for originating the problem.
- Don't gloss over problems and figure mistakes can be fixed up later. Solve problems when they first surface.

Source: Dr. Leonard R. Sayles, Center for Creative Leadership, Greensboro, NC.

Finding Solutions To Problems

We all have a tendency to underestimate our most serious problems and to overestimate less serious ones. Often there are serious problems that we simply refuse to face by denying that they exist.

One big mistake is waiting for a problem to solve itself. To wait is to waste time and opportunity.

- If the solution to a problem lies in getting help from some other source, don't hesitate to ask for that help.
- Insulate yourself from the negative forces and negative personalities that constantly surround you. How many times has a positive idea been slaughtered, strangled, or sunk with the words *No way?*
- Attack your problem with courage...and the possibilities with enthusiasm.
- Ask your mind and heart what your real motives are and what price you're willing to pay.
- Add up your strengths. You're stronger than you think you are.
- Adjust your mind to change.
- Accept the irrevocable negative realities.

Source: Robert H. Schuller, founding pastor of Crystal Cathedral, Garden Grove, CA, and author of 15 books, the most recent of which is *Tough Times Never Last, But Tough People Do!,* Thomas Nelson Publishers, Nashville.

Problem Solving: Some Traits that Get in the Way

Would-be problem solvers often run into trouble because they:

- Cannot tolerate the ambiguity associated with a complex problem and believe all problems must be clear-cut.
- Stick to a preconceived belief and reinterpret inconsistent data to fit it.
- Hesitate to ask questions for fear of appearing ignorant.
- Give in to unrealistic anxiety about failing without systematically doing worst-case scenarios.

Roadblocks to Creativity

- Assuming that creative means new. Borrowing and modifying the ideas of others is just as useful.
- Relying too heavily on experts or self-styled creative types, who often are blinded by traditional approaches.
- Believing that only a few gifted people can be creative.
- Confusing creativity with emotional instability. What is needed instead is the ability to let the mind wander without fear of losing control.
- Failing to promote ideas voluntarily. Not pointing out achievements to superiors (a common failing of fired executives).
- Waiting for inspiration. Concentration and fact-finding are the most solid bases for innovation.
- Getting bogged down in technology. Look for solutions that can be accomplished with existing hardware and systems.

Source: M. LeBoeuf, *Imagineering: How to Profit from Your Creative Powers,* McGraw-Hill, New York.

Fears that Stifle Creativity

- Making mistakes.
- Being seen as a fool.
- Being criticized.
- Being misused.
- Standing alone.
- Disturbing traditions.
- Breaking taboos.
- Not having the security of habit.
- Losing the love of the group.
- Truly being an individual.

Learning How To Remember

Contrary to the conventional wisdom, memory doesn't work like a muscle. You can't exercise your way to a perfect memory. But you can learn tricks and techniques that can give you a far better memory than you'd believe. *Here are the best ones:*

- *Chunking:* That's the basic technique for short-term memory improvement. *How it works:* Grouping apparently isolated facts, numbers, letters, etc., into chunks. Thus, the series 255789356892365 turns into 255 789 356 892 365.
- *Sleep and remembering:* There is some evidence to indicate that things learned just before sleep are retained better.
- *Spacing:* Don't try to memorize by swallowing the whole thing down in one gulp. Instead of a three-hour study marathon, try two 1½ hour spans. Experiment to see what time period is best for you.
- *Reciting:* Vocalizing provides a kind of feedback as you literally hear (in addition to seeing) the words. It also forces you to organize the material in a way that is natural for memory improvement.
- *Story system:* A very effective way to remember some obviously unrelated objects. Just make up a silly story, using each of the objects

in the story. Thus, if you want to remember the words *paper, tire, doctor, rose, ball,* try this story:

The paper rolled a tire down the sidewalk, and it hit the doctor, knocking him into a rose bush, where he found a ball.

Source: Kenneth L. Higbee, author of *Your Memory: How It Works and How to Improve It,* Prentice-Hall, Englewood Cliffs, NJ.

Improving Your Short-Term Memory

Memory exercises are most useful for those who face special short-term tasks such as the memorization of facts for a presentation. These tasks can be accomplished through the application of a few simple techniques.

Basic steps:

•Before resorting to memorization, use such aids as shopping lists, memos, or charts.

•When you do need to memorize, do so in the kind of environment in which you function best. Learn whether you concentrate better in total silence, with background music, etc.

•Arrange for short, frequent periods of study. Memory wanes during long sessions.

•Outline what you need to learn, and carry your notes with you in a small notebook.

•Refer to your notes at every empty interval during the day—waiting in line, riding the bus, etc.

How to Remember People's Names

To remember the names of people to whom you have just been introduced, the classic system is best:

•Take an interest in the person.

•Concentrate by looking directly at him or her. Notice appearance and dress.

•If you forget the name right after hearing it, ask immediately for it to be repeated.

•Repeat the name to yourself every few minutes. Over the next few days, keep calling the name to mind.

•Gradually decrease the frequency of repetition.

Source: Alan Baddeley, author of *Your Memory: A User's Guide,* Macmillan, New York.

How to Develop Intuition

We all have intuition, though we may not be aware of it and tend to devalue it as irrational. But many of the greatest scientific and creative people in history, including Einstein and Mozart, relied heavily on intuition.

To develop intuition, the first step is to accept that it isn't a gimmick. Intuition is spontaneous. It can't be contrived or programmed. However, you can create the conditions under which it's most likely to occur:

•Promote inner calm. An agitated, tense mind creates too much mental noise for intuition to operate. Stress-management techniques help people to be more intuitive, though this isn't their stated aim.

•Relax your mind by allowing it to wander. Take a walk on the beach, watch fish swim in a fishtank, take long baths, go away for the weekend. Some people have had their best intuitions while shaving or washing the dishes.

•Don't keep working harder and harder, struggling desperately for an answer to a problem. Like having a word on the tip of your tongue, the answer will come of its own accord when you're thinking of something else. The old saw, *Sleep on it,* really works.

•Approach problems in a flexible way. Many people acquire such rigid thought patterns that they effectively inhibit intuition. Loosen up. Be prepared to go with your feelings. Improvise. Get started before you know where an idea is going.

•Avoid outlining a project before you begin. This method can extinguish the spontaneity crucial to intuition.

• Don't feel you have to defend every idea rationally. Suspend judgment long enough to keep the idea as a possibility, to let it take concrete form. No idea is too bizarre to consider.

• Try brainstorming. Do for yourself what is generally done in groups. Sit quietly and let ideas pass without evaluating them. You can analyze and evaluate them later.

Source: Philip Goldberg, author of *The Intuitive Edge,* Jeremy P. Tarcher, Inc., Los Angeles.

Remembering Faces And Names Better

There are no special gimmicks to remembering important names and faces. You need only apply a few simple techniques:

• Take every opportunity to study lists of names that are important to you. It takes time, but it's worth it.

• Look through the names carefully, taking time to study each one and recollect when, and if, you ever met the person.

• If a name looks familiar, try to recall something about the person.

• Jot a friendly note to the person thanking him for the donation or order. The act of writing the note reinforces your memory of the person.

Source: Joseph F. Anderson, vice president for communications and development, Hamilton College, Clinton, NY.

Words of Wisdom

Here are the mottoes and proverbs that helped the following celebrities get to—and stay at—the top:

Isaac Asimov, writer:

"Laugh, and the world laughs with you; Weep, and you weep alone; For the sad old earth must borrow its mirth, but has trouble enough of its own."

Helen Gurley Brown, editor, *Cosmopolitan*:

"I don't remember any motto or saying that was valuable to me when I was 'getting there,' but there is one I like now (not that it helps, but it just happens to be true.) 'There is no free lunch.'"

Midge Decter, former director, Committee for the Free World:

"The perfect is the enemy of the good."

Jean Louis Dumas-Hermes, chairman, Hermes:

"Patience and time do more than force and anger."

The late Rose Kennedy, matriarch of the Kennedy clan:

"To whom much is given, much will be required." (St. Jude)

Edward Koch, former mayor of New York City:

"Be not afraid."

Jack La Lanne, pioneer physical fitness expert:

"Pride and discipline. If you use those two words, you can't fail."

Leonard A. Lauder, president, Estee Lauder, Inc.:

"Anything can be done as long as everybody gets the credit."

Willard Scott, weatherman on NBC's "Today" show:

"If a job is once begun, do not leave 'til it is done. Be it great or be it small, do it well or not at all."

Carl Spielvogel, chairman, Backer Spielvogel Bates Worldwide:

"Do unto others as you would have others do unto you."

Gloria Steinem, founder of *Ms.* magazine and author of *Outrageous Acts and Everyday Rebellions:*

"If there's no dancing, it's not my revolution!"

Some Tough Questions

Before you can make the right decision about more job responsibility, a new venture, travel, or a big move or change, you must identify your own strengths, interests, goals, needs and priorities. *Ask:*

• To whom do I owe what? How do job-related responsibilities (to stockholders, employees, customers) rank in priority with family responsibilities? Most big jobs preclude giving equal rank to both.

•Do I feel good about my work, the people in my life, myself?

•Do I waste valuable time and energy on things that don't really matter?

•When is the last time I ___ (fill in two or three activities you enjoy for pure fun)? If it's been too long, something's wrong.

•Is the desire for "bigger, better, more" causing me to work harder without joy?

•What should I be doing differently in my work to be happier, more productive, less frustrated or bored? The answers will be an adventure in self-discovery.

Rules of Thumb

Rules of thumb are useful because they cut down on the time needed to get information and figure things out ourselves. *Some especially helpful and little-known ones:*

•Extracurricular. Don't expect any more than one third of any professional-club members to attend a meeting. Build up a large membership so enough members are around to make up for those away.

•*Horses:* To get the best price on a riding horse, the best time of year to buy is Fall.

•Walking. Without a pack, you should be able to walk 25 miles a day without serious strain. With a pack one-fourth your weight or less, 15 miles a day is reasonable on an average trail.

•Dieting. Most overeating happens at night. If you can't diet all the time, diet after dark.

•Most for your money. You can mail five sheets of average paper for 29¢.

•Holiday time. To find out how many lights a Christmas tree needs, first multiply the tree height by the tree width measured in feet. Then multiply this figure by three.

•Determining your frame size. You can determine your body frame by wrapping your thumb and index finger around your wrist. *Small frame:* Thumb extends past the index finger. *Average frame:* Thumb and index finger just meet. *Large frame:* Thumb and index finger don't meet.

•Fixing up. It takes the average person one hour to paint 1,000 square feet plus one hour for each window or door.

•Bad weather. Second gear is best for driving on ice and snow.

Source: *Rules of Thumb* by Tom Parker, Houghton Mifflin Co., Boston.

While Standing in Line

•Do isometric exercises.

•Listen to instructional tapes.

•Read a paperback.

•Watch your miniature TV set.

•Meditate.

•Meet your neighbors in line.

•Plan the week's schedule.

•Plan an upcoming trip.

•Bring along a dictionary to expand your vocabulary.

•Make a list of people you want to meet to improve your business or social life.

How to Prevent Mistakes In Decision Making

•Never make unnecessary decisions. All decisions involve risk. It can occasionally be wiser to leave well enough alone.

•Identify recurring problems. Resolve them once and for all.

•Don't develop grandiose schemes to solve simple problems. Evaluate solutions in terms of costs.

•Don't delay the decision. Moving quickly allows more time to correct the decision if it turns out wrong. And it frees you to tackle other problems.

Source: Don Caruth and Bill Middlebrook, Caruth Management Consultants, Carrollton, TX, authors of *Supervisory Management,* Saranac Lake, NY.

6

Getting Organized

Priorities

The classic crisis between work and home life for busy people with children is the school play, recital or Little League game that conflicts with an important business meeting.

Trap: Making spur-of-the-moment decisions about priorities when these conflicts arise. That almost always results in hurt feelings, poor productivity, or your own disappointment in having accomplished too little.

Solution: Longer-term time management. Budget specific amounts of time each day for certain activities—and consistently hold to the schedule you set. *Examples:*

- No business calls after 7 p.m.
- Four hours of take-home work over the weekend, and no more.
- An hour or half-hour alone with your spouse when you both get in from work—no interruptions from children, work, or neighbors.

Make those times inviolate—something that others can count on.

Helpful: Make a public announcement to family and key coworkers of the times you've scheduled. That helps "trap" you into keeping to the plan.

When you establish a record of setting and sticking to priorities, the occasional missed Little League game or dinner out won't be seen as such a catastrophe—either for family members or for yourself.

First: Choose the right priorities.

For most families, life is too full of opportunities and responsibilities to be able to do everything. To accomplish as much as possible, some low-priority activities must be eliminated. *Challenge:* Choosing *which* activities to drop. Start by asking yourself: "What must I accomplish this week...or this day, this month, this year...even if I accomplish nothing else?"

Example: For daily priorities, set aside a time each evening to list what you must do the next day. Review that list in your head in the morning as you get ready to start the new day.

Key question: "What must I absolutely get done today?" If it's a phone call or a meeting with someone that you know will be difficult but which must be done that day—don't make excuses for not following through.

Caution: Don't fall into the trap of dutifully making a long "To Do" list every day—only to end up completing less than half of it each day. "To Do" lists are useless unless you score at least a B grade every day—getting at least seven out of 10 tasks accomplished. C—five out of 10 tasks—isn't good enough. And, three out of 10 is an F.

Important: Don't get so caught up in daily schedules that your weekly, monthly and yearly priorities go unattended.

For longer-term priorities, keep a file for updating your progress weekly or monthly.

More than just getting it done...

Even a good record of task completion, however, doesn't mean you're setting priorities most effectively. For that, you must track the quality of your progress.

Key: Take time at the end of the day to analyze whether you devoted significant attention to each project you handled. Are you sure that the time and effort you spent on each task succeeded in moving it closer to completion?

General rule: To improve the quality of your work, tackle the complicated tasks first. It's too easy to persuade yourself that it makes sense to get rid of the least demanding tasks to free yourself to take on the big jobs. But it rarely works that way. This is simply a classic delaying tactic. Avoidance takes more energy than it's really worth—energy that you can direct better elsewhere.

Executives have another set of priority traps...

- Spending more and more time on big strategic decisions that are removed from the day-to-day realities of keeping the business running smoothly.
- Avoiding big decisions by spending more time on minutiae.

There's no magical way to achieve the proper balance. The most successful managers, though, are constantly aware that they are in danger of veering toward one side or the other.

They keep developing a kind of dual vision that allows them to set the short-term, day-to-day priorities that keep the company moving and improving...and to continually set longer-range, strategic priorities that steer the company toward important goals.

As you struggle to work out these priorities, explain to your staff what the priorities are and why you have set them that way.

Encourage discussion. The more those who work with you buy into your goals for improvement and positive change, the more cohesively they work and the more productive the results of their efforts.

Source: Mortimer R. Feinberg, PhD, chairman, BFS Psychological Associates, Inc., 666 Fifth Ave., New York 10103.

The Great Alan Lakein On Time Management... 20 Years Later

Those who achieve the most in this world are not those with the highest IQs...the greatest natural skills...the hardest workers...but those who make the best use of their time.

The search for better ways to use your time every day is not a recent phenomenon. Americans were grappling with the same issue back in 1973, when Alan Lakein, a leading expert on personal time management, wrote *How to Get Control of Your Time and Your Life.* This book is still a rich resource when you're looking for ways to create more time and make better use of the time you have...when you want help in deciding what you really want to do and making time for it. *His advice today...*

Time planning...

The key to using your time wisely has not changed during the past 20 years—learn how to improve your efficiency and effectiveness.

Doing things as quickly as possible—mechanical efficiency—is certainly valuable. Choosing the best task to do—and doing it the right way—that's effectiveness.

Since I wrote my book, technology has helped us boost our efficiency, but I haven't noticed a comparable improvement in effectiveness.

The mechanics of time planning have improved, thanks to a proliferation of planning books and forms that are now available from every office-supply house.

Using these aids and, more recently, computer scheduling software, we are able to account for nearly every free minute and coordinate our schedules with those of other people so that mutually acceptable meetings can be arranged.

We have become more efficient at using our time...but not necessarily more effective at doing the right thing. That depends on how you set priorities.

Setting priorities...

Setting priorities requires determination and clear thinking. To do it right, you need to make firm decisions about what you want to achieve in your lifetime as well as during the next few years, months, days...and, ultimately, right now.

As I explain in my book, only when you have a firm grasp on your priorities can you classify the tasks facing you as As, Bs and Cs. Then you have to discipline yourself to tackle the most important first—the As...and only after they are accomplished should you turn to the Bs and the Cs.

Setting priorities is more critical and more difficult than ever. In today's harried environment, you probably don't even have enough time to complete all your As.

Time management and groups...

Back in 1973, I emphasized the importance of setting your own individual priorities...making private time for yourself...avoiding pointless meetings, etc. Your personal needs are still important, but if I were writing the book for today's more complex world, I would pay more attention to the importance of teamwork.

Today, businesses—and families—realize that success depends on groups working together. The watchwords of current management philosophy are total quality management and reengineering continuous improvement. These concepts can be implemented only by group commitment to common goals and priorities.

The whole group will be able to follow priorities successfully—and the priorities will be realistic—only if they are set in a way that allows and encourages every member to participate.

That same principle is necessary to make everyone agree on the priorities shared by the whole group and the individual members.

Complexity and time pressure...

Everywhere we turn today, growing complexity is increasing the pressure on our time. Businesses are faced with new complexities... increased competition...workforce diversity. Working husbands and wives must juggle their work, homes, and families.

How can you choose priorities when you are faced with so many alternatives and they all seem to be As?

There is no simple solution. You just have to work at it. Think it through from all sides... listen to different opinions...and make a decision.

Example: You are a successful advertising copywriter who has always dreamed of writing a book. Thanks to your spouse's income, you might be able to take off some time to work on it...but your spouse wants to start working part-time in order to spend more time at home with your young child.

The only way you can arrive at a reasonable set of priorities is to discuss all sides of the question...how the decision will affect you, your spouse, and your child...and your respective employers.

Important aspects: What is most important to each of the parties...economic well-being, personal fulfillment, parental attention? How is the situation likely to change in a year or two ...or five or ten?

You are likely to come up with the best solution if everyone gives it his best try. While you are unlikely to come up with a completely consistent and mutually satisfactory set of priorities right away, don't be afraid to try out whatever seems reasonable.

If it doesn't work, you can try something else. With your hard-earned knowledge of what didn't work for you—and some thinking about why it didn't work—your next approach should do better.

Bottom line...

Setting priorities with others is more important today than ever. Investing time and effort today is the key to saving time further down the road.

Source: Alan Lakein, author of the classic time-management book, *How to Get Control of Your Time and Your Life*—more than 3,000,000 copies sold. Signet, 375 Hudson St., New York 10014.

How to Make the Most of Your Time... Without Driving Yourself Crazy

People have less free time than they did a generation ago—37% less than in 1973, according to a recent Harris survey. There is, though, more time available than you think. *Three general rules...*

• Eliminate slave-of-habit routines. *Example:* Spending 45 minutes each morning with the daily paper...when you can get the news you need with a quick scan of the front page or 10 minutes with an all-news radio station.

• Change your schedule so that you're at your best for your most important and challenging tasks. Many executives waste the start of their work day—when they may be freshest—by going through their mail. They'd do better by plunging into a tough report and saving the mail for later in the day, when they're slowing down.

• Learn to do two or three things at the same time. When you go to the bank, always bring something you need to read on the inevitable line. When you make a call and are placed on hold, switch to your speaker phone and take care of some paperwork. When your party comes on the line switch back.

Most time-saving ideas are small in scale—but those minutes add up. In most cases, a newly efficient person can save an hour a day—and that is a significant amount of time.

The morning routine...

• Pop out of bed as soon as you wake up, rather than lingering under the covers. *Incentive:* Think of the most pleasant activity on your schedule that day.

• Plan a pre-breakfast work segment—30 to 60 minutes of uninterrupted concentration in some quiet part of your home.

• Write a "to-do" list in your daily organizer book—a schedule of the high-priority tasks you need to address. Do it the night before. Less urgent tasks should be listed under "Things to Be Done This Week" and "Things for Following Weeks."

• Schedule tasks that require others' actions for early in the day. By reaching people early, you're more likely to get them to do what you need that day.

Organizing your office...

• Angle your desk away from open doorways, busy corridors or windows—all sources of distraction.

• Keep your desk neat. Clear away everything unrelated to the project at hand. *To dispose of clutter:* Eliminate dispensable items, including photos, gadgets and magazines. Put in a few inexpensive bookshelves you can get to without rising.

• Install the largest wastebasket your office can gracefully contain.

Communications...

• Use a dictation device, rather than a secretary's shorthand. *Advantages:* More speed and flexibility...simpler changes...enhanced concentration.

• Computerized electronic mail eliminates much time-wasting telephone tag. *For maximum efficiency:* Note when you'll be available for a return phone call.

• Rely on your answering machine to screen incoming calls. Your highest priority should always be the most important item on your schedule...which is rarely attending to the telephone.

The media...

Read selectively. Concentrate on one general newspaper. *Before you start reading:* Examine the general and business news indexes for stories of interest.

•If you find an item of interest in a newspaper or magazine, rip it out and read it when appropriate—and throw the rest of the publication away.

•Read for 15 to 30 minutes before bedtime. This is a good time for books that inspire or entertain.

Source: Ray Josephs, public-relations pioneer and author of the newly revised *How to Gain an Extra Hour Every Day.* Penguin USA, 375 Hudson St., New York 10014.

How to Set Your Life Goals and Attain Them Too

Everyone has dreams, but not many people know how to take the steps necessary to turn dreams into reality.

Key: Setting goals. Goals are simply changes you want to make in your life. They can be large (going to law school)...or small (making a phone call to keep up a friendship)...external (I'd like to double my salary in five years) ...or internal (I'd like to feel more comfortable with myself).

Common mistake: Confusing dreams with goals. Dreams remain in the realm of fantasy. Goals are the building blocks that make fantasies come true.

Goal-setting and life satisfaction...

Goals are necessary to give direction to our lives...but reaching them doesn't automatically make us happy.

Example: It's tempting—but unrealistic—to think, *If I lose 10 pounds, my marriage will improve, my boss will respect me, I'll communicate better and make more friends.*

Reaching goals, then setting new ones, improves the quality of our lives. But if we expect the process to make our lives perfect or problem-free, we'll be frustrated.

Trap: Focusing intently on one particular goal at the expense of other aspects of your life.

Example: If you throw all your energy into your job, you may get the promotion you want—but your health and family relationships may suffer. The overall quality of your life will not have improved.

To really make goal-setting work, you must pay attention to goals in all the major areas of life, not just one or two.

That's not as overwhelming as it sounds. We routinely juggle the many aspects of life on a daily basis—we just don't step back and think about it methodically.

Realistic approach: Set simple, easily reachable goals in some areas and tougher, longer-term goals in others...always keeping sight of the overall quality of your life.

The major life areas...

1. Self-esteem: How you feel about yourself.

Example: I'll write down three different things that I like about myself every day for a week.

2. Health and fitness: How well you take care of yourself physically.

Example: I'm going to cut back to one cup of coffee per day.

3. Communication: How clearly you express in words your identity, wants and needs.

Example: I'm going to take a workshop in assertiveness training to help me learn to say no.

4. Relationships: How you interact with the people in your life, whether family, friends or coworkers. *Included:* Developing key qualities—trust, honesty, retaining a healthy sense of individuality in the presence of others.

Example: I'll initiate a talk with my partner about where our relationship is headed.

5. Career/lifework: Experiencing challenge, satisfaction and fulfillment from the work you have chosen, be it paid or unpaid. *Included:* Job, raising children, volunteer activities.

Example: I'm going to look into training programs that can help me upgrade my job skills.

6. Finances/personal wealth: Managing your money to enrich your life.

Example: For one month, I will write down everything I buy so I'll know where my money goes.

7. Life crisis: Overcoming personal trauma through a process of healing and recovery. A *life crisis* is any event or circumstance—such as the end of a relationship, a chronic health

problem or a job loss—that interrupts the flow of your life for a period of time.

It's difficult to think about goals during a crisis, but goal-setting is an important part of recovery. Too many people grit their teeth and try to tough it out, but if they don't go through the healing and recovery process, buried emotions will come back to haunt them later. A man who is devastated by the breakup of a romance may try to cope by immediately starting to date again...but he may find that unresolved feelings of pain and betrayal make it hard for him to be open to a new relationship.

Examples: I'll find out about support groups for people with my health problem. Or...I'll read a book about coping with grief.

8. Your spiritual self: Connecting the physical and emotional aspects of your nature with spiritual awareness. Spiritual understanding has four components...

- Appreciation of nature.
- Faith or belief in a power greater than yourself.
- Faith or belief in an overall structure that gives purpose to life.
- Intuition, or sensitive perception of the world around you, that helps you feel connected to the rest of the world.

Examples: I'm going to buy a book on meditation. Or...Each day for the next two weeks, I'm going to take a walk in the woods.

Goal-setting steps...

Key elements of the most effective, achievable goals:

- Role model: An image of the person you'd like to be—or the life you'd like to have—once you achieve your goal. Your role model might be a famous person, a character in a novel or a mental vision of yourself with the qualities you hope to achieve.
- Mission: A simple statement of what you want—your motivating desire.

Example: I want to live in a house by the ocean.

- Emotional core: What the goal means to you.

Example: Having my own house would give me a sense of rootedness. Being by the ocean makes me feel centered and at peace.

- Commitment: The element that helps you distinguish between goals you set for yourself —and goals you set to please others. Ask yourself two questions:
  - *How badly do I want to achieve my goal?*
  - *Am I willing to work for it?* If you're not willing to work at a goal, you don't want it as badly as you think—and you'll be fighting yourself at every step.
- Guidelines: The action plan that will help you reach your goal. Be as specific as possible.

Example: If your goal is to lose weight, specify how much weight you will strive to lose, by what date and how you plan to lose it—the foods you'll cut back on, where and how often you'll exercise.

- Focus: Gathering information and resources.

Example: If you want to take a trip to Europe next summer, this step would include calling travel agents, pricing airfares, reading guidebooks and talking to people who have recently visited the countries that interest you.

- Timetable: A realistic and flexible target date for accomplishing each goal.
- Assessment/achievement: A review of your progress. Simple and immediate goals give you immediate feedback. For longer-term goals, assess your game plan every few weeks or months.
- Flexibility: Being able to change on a set goal. There's nothing wrong with changing a goal 30 seconds after you set it or even three years later. You may find that the steps you've been taking are ineffective and you need to adopt a new strategy. Your time frame may be too ambitious and require revision. Or changes in yourself or your life circumstances may have made the goal less valid—perhaps you need to drop it and set a new one.
- Reward: Taking time to pat yourself on the back whenever you achieve a goal, no matter how small. This will help you keep up your motivation and take pleasure in your accomplishments.

Source: Amy E. Dean, a speaker on self-help and recovery topics and the author of *Lifegoals,* Hay House, Inc., 1154 E. Dominguez St., California 90749.

Secrets of Getting Organized

•Does it often take you more than 10 minutes to unearth a particular letter, bill or other paper from your files?

•Are there papers on your desk, other than reference materials, that you haven't looked through for a week or more?

•Have you forgotten an appointment or a specific date in the past two months?

•Do your newspapers and magazines pile up unread?

•Do you frequently lose or misplace things?

•Do things pile up in corners of closets or on the floor because you can't decide where to put them?

•When you go shopping, do you find yourself running all over town, only to come home and find you have forgotten something?

•In case of a tragedy, would your spouse be able to find your valuable papers and records?

•Do you want to get organized but everything is in such a mess you don't know where to start?

If you answered "yes" to any of the above questions, you're making one or more of these mistakes...

•*Mistake:* Failure to divide a complex problem into manageable segments. *Better:* Forget about straightening up your life as a whole. Just work on the six elements in your life that need to be put in order.

Examples: Being late to work because you can't seem to get ready in the morning...losing things because you can't figure out where to put them so you can find them.

Helpful: Divide the problems on your list into smaller units. If the problem is a physical one —a disorganized wall unit or a messy closet— stand in the doorway, visually check out the entire room and list elements to work on.

If the problem is a system or process, mentally run through it and break it down.

Example: Getting up in the morning. *Breakdown:* The alarm rings too softly...you can't move quickly in the morning...you don't have time to decide what to wear.

Then, rank the problems on a list on a scale of one to 10—according to how much they irritate you.

A problem that creates serious tension is a #1...one that could wait until next year is #10. Tackle the #1s first...and so on.

Important: Work on solving only one small problem at a time.

Example: Not being able to get to work on time. *Solution:* Arrange for a wake-up service instead of depending on the alarm...lay out your clothes the night before...get up a half-hour earlier so you don't have to move so fast.

•*Mistake:* Failure to make time to organize. Set a specific time for tackling your organization problems. Write it in your appointment book as if it were a doctor's appointment.

•*Mistake:* Failure to deal with paper. There are only four things you can do with a piece of paper. I call it the TRAF system...

•*Toss it.*

•*Refer it (pass it along to someone else).*

•*Act on it.*

•*File it.*

Each piece of paper requires its own small decision. The worst mistake is picking up a piece of paper, staring at it and putting it down again because you don't know how to handle it.

To sort the papers you need: A wastebasket— and file folders marked: *Things to Do...To File ...Home...Financial.* Divide the mail according to what has interest to you and what doesn't. Toss the "no interest" pile.

Divide what you're saving into reference piles—papers you may need to refer to later— and action piles. Put the reference pile into the "To file" box or folder.

Divide the action pile into things having to do with money—bank statements, bills, financial statements—which go in the financial folder.

Anything you need to discuss with your spouse put into your home folder. Otherwise all action materials go in the "Things to do" folder.

•*Mistake:* Failure to follow up. Don't assume you'll remember what you have to do in the future. Even if you could remember, why would you want to clutter up your mind?

Simplest system: The calendar/holding file system. On your regular calendar write down what you have to do on what date. Keep a file folder labeled "holding," and if there's a document needed for a particular day, drop it in that file. That way nothing gets lost and you're always in control.

•*Mistake:* Failing to set priorities.

Use the Two-List Master List/Daily List system. *Needed:* A day-to-day appointment calendar and a notebook.

Master list: In your notebook write down every single future task that arises as it arises. Don't organize the tasks or set priorities initially.

Examples: An assignment from your boss. A reminder to call a friend.

Daily list: Each morning or evening list 10 things to do that day, compiled for the most part from items in your List notebook, follow-ups from your calendar, and one or two items from your "Things to do" file folder. *Include:* Fun things like a bike ride or a trip to the museum.

Then, rank each item on the Daily List in terms of its importance.

Mark each item #1 for high priority, #2 for medium or #3 for least urgent.

#1: Deadline items.

#2: Basic tasks.

#3: Routine tasks.

Cross each item off when you finish it. Transfer unfinished items to the next day's list.

•*Mistake:* Failure to plan ahead. If you're working on a complex project, it is extremely important to pace yourself over the weeks or months you have to complete it.

Helpful: On a single sheet, list the starting and deadline dates for *each* component. Then enter each starting and deadline date on your daily calendar. When you reach that date you can then put that job or its components on your daily list.

On a simple project, list the components and then enter each of them in your daily calendar on the appropriate date. On that date enter it on your daily list.

•*Mistake:* Failure to make use of services. Many of us were raised to feel that it's wrong to hire others to do menial tasks for us. *Necessary attitude change:* My time is worth too much to waste it doing things I loathe.

Helpful: Pickup and delivery services offered by merchants...a taxi service or private driver to take children to appointments...exercise teachers, hairstylists and others who make house calls...messenger services to deliver packages...a student to run errands...a cleaning person who'll also do the laundry.

•*Mistake:* Failure to consolidate. Return all phone calls during a specific time period rather than responding to each one as you get it.

Combine errands. When you're out grocery shopping also get your shoes and the broken lamp fixed.

Consolidate movement.

Example: Pull up the sheets, blanket and spread on one side of the bed before moving to the other.

Source: Stephanie Winston, founder and director of The Organizing Principle, a New York City-based consulting firm. The information here and more can be found in her books, *The Organized Executive* and, most recently published, *Getting Organized: The Easy Way to Put Your Life in Order,* both published by Warner Books, 666 Fifth Ave., New York 10103.

The Master List

I am a *very* organized person. As a result, I get more things done with less effort. And I make fewer mistakes.

When I work on a project, I start early and do it well. When I've finished, I never say to myself, "I could have done it better if I'd had more time." I know it's the best I was able to do...and I move on to the next project.

My secret: The Master List...

We're overwhelmed with so much information, our circuits are overloaded. We're overstimulated. Everybody is screaming for our immediate attention. Everything has become urgent.

Our projects are hanging in limbo, half done, and we can't decide what to do first. Most mistakes are self-inflicted, the result of negligence, improper planning or procedure.

To avoid these pitfalls that erode your precious time, write down all your unfinished work on a Master List.

You make lists all the time—grocery lists, lists of party guests, etc. If you make a Master List of all your current and pending projects, you'll find that it's the engine that makes your day run.

People jot down their chores, their projects, phone calls they have to return on little slips of paper. *Result:* They have 25 notes tacked to their office walls or sitting in piles on their desks.

Consolidate those notes onto one page, one that you can scan from top to bottom.

With that Master List, you know what you have to do and the time frame in which you have to do it. Without it, you're frantically trying to remember what needs to be done next.

The Master List is an inventory of all your unfinished work and ongoing projects. Go through all your papers. Ask yourself: *Is there any work that must be done by me—a phone call...a letter or report?* Write it on your Master List.

If it concerns someone else, send it on.

If it's not important, get rid of it.

The simple act of writing things down on your Master List gives you freedom—nothing will slip through the cracks, nothing will sneak up behind you and hit you on the back of the head. The more you write down, the less you have to remember.

Make a file folder for each project, and as soon as you make a note on that project, or get an idea concerning it, file it with the rest so that every folder is current and contains everything you need to know—every scrap of information—about that project.

Make an appointment with yourself...

Use your calendar to schedule appointments with yourself to complete work.

If you need to meet with a person face-to-face, you schedule an appointment. If you have work to do for that same person, why not block out an hour on your calendar and treat it just like that face-to-face meeting? Hold all calls. Close the door. Allow absolutely no interruptions.

Plan for interruptions...

I anticipate emergencies. I don't know what they'll be, but I expect them. I do this by being ahead in my work, not behind.

There are two ways you can go through life. One is by figuring that everything will go as expected. When something unexpected happens, it takes you by surprise. The other is by figuring that anything that can go wrong will go wrong.

Expect unexpected detours and distractions, so you're not thrown for a loop when they do pop up.

Deal with the disorganized...

Many of the people I work with are disorganized. Therefore, I have to be even more organized in my dealings with them—otherwise I'll never get anything done.

If you give an assignment to someone, you must assume that they are not going to do it on time. You have to take it upon yourself to follow up with them.

I try to maintain control and don't let the deadline slip through my fingers. That's where the Master List comes in again. Note the deadline on your Master List, since it's your responsibility to make sure the assigned work gets done.

When you're dealing with people who are chronically late to meetings and appointments, allow 50% more time and call to confirm how late they are running. Don't schedule appointments back-to-back. Give yourself a cushion between meetings...otherwise you're asking for trouble.

As a general rule, projects will take more time than you expect them to. If you need an hour, schedule an hour and a half.

Stay on top of your work. Expect and anticipate disorganization and lateness from others and you will take the nasty surprises out of your business day. *Result:* You'll complete twice as much work, in half the time.

Source: Jeffrey J. Mayer, one of the country's leading authorities on time-management and founder of the consulting firm Mayer Enterprises, 50 E. Bellevue Place, Suite 305, Chicago 60611. Its clients include Ameritech, Commonwealth Edison, Encyclopedia Brittanica, Sears Roebuck, Navistar and First National Bank of Chicago. He is the author of *If You Haven't Got the Time to Do it Right, When Will You Find the Time to Do it Over?* Fireside Books, 1230 Ave. of the Americas, New York 10020.

How to Conquer Clutter

Sooner or later, clutter invades nearly everyone's life. A key to clutter control is to have a place for everything. *To figure out what belongs where...*

•Organize the clutter in one complete area without stopping. Set aside a minimum of a half day—or tell yourself you won't stop until "two closets, the bathrooms or the garage" are clutter-free. *Important:* Avoid distractions.

Example: While cleaning her bedroom closet, Mary found something that belonged in the kitchen. But when she opened the kitchen cupboard she decided it needed to be organized as well—and never made it back to the bedroom closet.

Other distractions: Phone calls (take the phone off the hook)...old magazines, high school yearbooks, college term papers (do not stop to read anything)...errands (put them off until your task is complete).

•Set up large cardboard cartons. *Recommended:* One each for—elsewhere, charity and toss.

•Elsewhere. For anything that goes in another room. Do not put away items from this box until the end of the day.

•Charity. For usable items you no longer want. Do not put junk (torn clothing, broken toys that cannot be fixed, etc.) in this box—it will only tax the resources of the charity you're trying to help. Put this box into the car immediately and drop it off the next time you go out.

•Toss. For the true junk. *Suggestion:* If you're the type of person who has a problem throwing things away, have another member of the family come by once every hour and empty this box in the trash.

•Empty the target area of clutter. Sort it into the three boxes as you go. Anything not sorted into a box should be temporarily put elsewhere—the hall or on top of the bed.

What doesn't go into a box goes back to where it came from—but stored neatly. *Hint:* Group like items together and keep in "clutter containers."

Examples: Underwear goes in the same drawer with drawer dividers to keep it separated...bobby pins and hair clips are stored in a covered container, etc.

•Reward yourself for a job well done. Have a nice dinner out, take in a movie...or spend a quiet evening in your newly clutter-free home.

To help keep your clutter from getting out of control in the future...

•Take 20 minutes a day to tidy up by putting everything in the right room. Toys go in the kid's room, papers and magazines go into a reading stack, etc. Later, when you have more time, you can put things away more specifically.

Examples: Toys in the toy chest, last week's unread newspapers in the trash, etc.

•Find effective clutter storage containers. Games can be stored in a trunk that doubles as a table on top of which children can play the games.

•Make an ongoing effort to get rid of things you never use. Keep a *charity box* on hand for useable items that you no longer want. The minute the box gets full, put the items in bags and take them to your favorite charity.

Source: Stephanie Culp, founder of The Organization, a company dedicated to helping people and businesses get organized and stay organized, and author of *How to Conquer Clutter,* Writer's Digest Books, 1507 Dana Ave., Cincinnati 45207.

How to Get Your Paper Flow Under Control

Though many office workers don't agree that it's necessary to have a clean desk, few would dispute the importance of being able to quickly put their hands on information when they need it.

My principle: If you don't know you have it —or you can't find it—it's of no value to you.

Clients often tell me sob stories of missing important meetings because they misplaced the notice. Others bemoan their failure to meet loan payments or other deadlines. One entrepreneur even lost out on a promising business opportunity because he couldn't locate his passport.

Reality: Even with computers playing a bigger part in everyone's lives, there will always be plenty of paper to manage. The same principles that guide this paper management system can be applied to computers.

First—centralize...

Offices are dedicated to handling a flow of paper. But everyone needs a similar central location at home. If possible, this should be a permanent spot, available to you at all times. Avoid desks that look pretty but aren't functional.

Effective: A large butcher block top or a piece of plywood placed across two good-quality file cabinets. Since filing is a major factor in managing paper, it's ideal to have the filing system located close by.

Install adequate lighting and a comfortable chair. You want to make doing paperwork as pleasant as possible.

Key supplies: A "To Sort" tray (better to think of it this way than as an "In Box"), a large wastebasket, a nearby telephone, a rotary telephone file and a calendar.

Where to start...

Paper clutter indicates a pattern of postponed decisions. You've let those papers pile up because you failed to make an immediate decision about what to do with them. Begin now by putting today's mail, or whatever pile of papers you wish to organize, into your "To Sort" tray.

Use this spot consistently, bringing papers from everywhere to this base location. But think of it as only a temporary stopover. For most people, the goal of handling a piece of paper just once is too ambitious. But you should decide on its final resting place when it comes out of the "To Sort" tray. Sort out the tray on a regular basis.

The duty to discard...

Learning to throw out unneeded paper is the next step toward effective paper management.

People never use 80% of the paper they collect.

Your stress level will decrease as your use of the large wastebasket increases. Before the wastebasket, however, think about how to avoid even *seeing* unnecessary paper. *Examples:*

• *Get rid of 40% of your promotional mail* by writing to Mail Preference Service, Direct Marketing Association, 11 W. 42 St., Box 3861, New York 10036, and asking them to remove your name from direct mail lists. Every chance you get, instruct companies not to sell or rent your name and address.

• *Don't send for magazines you won't read.* Uncontrolled information is not a resource—*it's a burden.* Piles of old magazines or clippings—no matter how interesting or informative they may be—soon turn into dust collectors that depress you and make you feel guilty.

Better: Play a game with yourself to see how much you can throw away or recycle. *Questions to ask yourself:*

• Did I request this?

• Is this the only place this information is available?

• Is it recent enough to be useful?

• When, exactly, might I need this information? "Just in case" is not an acceptable answer.

• Are there any tax or legal reasons to keep it?

• What's the worst possible thing that could happen if I threw this away? (Most things can be reordered, found at the library, etc.)

Keep a calendar...

Using a calendar can eliminate lots of paper from your desks (home and office), dressers, mirrors, bulletin boards, and wallets.

Key: Get into the habit of extrapolating the needed information, entering it on your calendar, and then throwing away the paper—or filing it if you really must.

The most effective paper managers I know keep a master calendar that records all business and personal commitments for every member of the family. You can keep it either at home (the refrigerator door is accessible to everyone) or the office. Or, you can carry it with you.

In addition, you may need separate calendars for specific functions—a travel schedule, a meeting schedule, etc. But don't fall into the trap of having too many calendars. Coordination is an ongoing problem, especially when dates are changed. Keep key players informed.

The calendar is a tool that helps you to be realistic about time management. People who are most successful in accomplishing their goals make appointments with themselves to complete specific tasks by a certain date or to at least check on things.

I've developed some abbreviated symbols that remind me what I need to do: C (call), D (discuss), H (hold in file), LM (left message), WC (they will call me).

Note: I keep a corresponding WC file near the phone so that when people do call back I'll remember what I wanted to talk about.

If you're comfortable with a computer, you may want to use one of the many software scheduling programs now on the market. They're especially helpful when more than one person schedules your time.

Names and numbers...

Many of the little scraps of paper floating around our homes and offices contain important telephone numbers or ones that we think might become important.

Solution: Think of the one word that would prompt you to call this person—such as Atlanta...or kitchen...or speechwriter.

Then record or file the information that way and throw away the paper. I use my rotary phone file for all kinds of names and numbers, even for listing family Social Security numbers and the numbers of combination locks. Rotary phone-file cards now come in a variety of colors that you can use to flag different categories.

Action vs. reference files...

After you've eliminated as much paper as possible by using your wastebasket, calendar, a daily "To Do" list, and telephone listing, what remains will go into action files or reference files.

Action files: For papers that need immediate attention.

Reference files: For papers you know you will need at some point in the future.

Reference files can become action files or vice versa.

Example: A reference file on Europe can become an action file if you're planning a trip to Paris.

You can also have reference files and action files with the same or nearly the same heading —*Community Association* and *Community Association–1993 Dues Campaign.*

Potential action categories: Based on the next action needed, here are some of the action file categories I find useful...

- Call
- Computer entry
- Discuss
- File
- Pay
- Photocopy
- Read
- Sign
- Take to office/home
- Write

The key to reference files is not only to put papers away but to be able to find them again. File information according to *how you will use it,* not where you got it.

Ask yourself: Under what circumstances would I want this information? What word would first enter my mind?

Example: If you will need the information when you sell your house, then set up a *House—Main Street* file.

Put all papers in their most general category first—such as *Warranties and Instructions.* If that file becomes too bulky, you can break it down into *Warranties and Instructions–Kitchen Appliances, Warranties and Instructions–Autos.*

Organize your files logically—such as *Medical—Anne, Medical–John.* Group like files together.

Example: Instead of filing *Biking* under B and *Skiing* under S, you could have files named *Recreation–Biking* and *Recreation–Skiing.*

The very important master file: To remind yourself of how you filed information, keep an alphabetical master file index, with cross-references to related files. Keep the master file index right up front so when you file something, you can tell whether to put it under *Auto, Car, Chrysler,* or *Vehicle,* and you won't end up with all four.

If there's a particular piece of paper you're afraid of losing, you can list it in the index—*"Divorce decree,* see *Legal Information."*

Source: Barbara Hemphill, Hemphill & Associates, Inc., 1464 Garner Station Blvd., Raleigh, North Carolina 27603. She is president of the National Association for Professional Organizers and author of *Taming the Paper Tiger,* Kiplinger Books, 1729 H St. NW, Washington, DC 20006.

10 Ways to Get More Time in Your Life

•Slow down. Take the time to do things right...and enjoy the time you saved by not having to do them over.

•Say *no.* Just because someone requests that their concerns become important to you does not mean you must agree.

•Define your mission. Clarity comes from knowing where you are going and why you are on that path. From clarity comes vigor. From vigor comes the energy to accomplish what you want.

•Delegate. Accept that things will be done a little differently than you might have done them. Be willing to let others bring their own vision, process and reasonable autonomy to the project.

•Eliminate. Find time to address the small yet important tasks that come up each day. Otherwise they will add up, and you'll have to deal with them all at once.

•Simplify. Don't make your life more complex than it has to be. Organize your desk before you leave work or choose your clothes before going to bed, so you won't be sidetracked by these decisions the next day.

•Know when to hire help. Not every task you do yourself is a savings. Think about the do-it-yourself projects you're working on and whether they're actually the best use of your valuable time.

•Exercise/energize. Exercise gives you energy, vitality, alertness, stamina—and a longer life.

•Relax/savor. Recharge your mind and soul by closing your eyes, breathing deeply, drifting away and thinking soothing thoughts.

•Design your perfect vision. Draw a circle representing a 24-hour clock, and chart the way you now spend your time. Then, draw a second circle representing the way you would like to spend your time. This exercise will help you prioritize your time...and plan your future.

Source: Maggie Bedrosian, director, Bedrosian Communications Inc., a company that helps executives operate more effectively, 4509 Great Oak Rd., Rockville, Maryland 20853. She is the author of *Delights, Dilemmas, and Decisions: The Gift of Living Lightly.* The Positive Publisher, 1131-0 Tolland Tpke., Suite 175, Manchester, Connecticut 06040. 800-826-0529.

How to Stay Focused

We all have things in our lives that we wish would go away—marital conflicts, work stress, financial woes, problem in-laws, misbehaving kids, aging parents.

The conventional way we deal with the anxiety caused by these problems is by distracting ourselves with ordinary activities— exercising, reading the paper, watching TV, shopping, talking on the phone, socializing, doing volunteer work, visiting family members.

Although there's nothing wrong with any of these pursuits, by carrying them to extremes we turn them into dangerously addictive distractions. And we often do this without even noticing.

Why we distract ourselves...

Facing real problems by talking things out with the people involved or taking definitive action is scary. It's human nature to try to delay doing anything at all when a really painful problem arises.

Example: A dual-career couple is having marital problems, but neither partner ever talks about them. They structure their evenings at home so that while one is on the phone, the other reads the paper. They alternate using the computer. Then they go to bed, too tired to talk. *Trap:* They use their activities as an excuse for not confronting their problems.

People can fool themselves into thinking that their distractions are useful because so many of them are socially acceptable. Exercising, reading, socializing, etc., are all worthwhile...until they're overdone.

It can sometimes be hard to distinguish between a helpful activity and an addictive distraction.

Example: JoAnn talks incessantly about her romantic problems. She has fooled herself into thinking that she's doing something about them because she's constantly thinking about them. But talking to her friends on the telephone, complaining and listening to their advice only helps her *avoid* confronting the growing differences with her boyfriend.

Some distractions masquerade as very positive activities.

Example: Doing volunteer work. Although a little is great, if you start doing more than eight hours a week, it interferes with your personal life.

How it starts...

People are attracted to distractions because they're enjoyable and they relieve anxiety.

But as the time spent on a particular distraction increases, it changes from being a pleasant, anxiety-reducing, intrinsically positive experience into one that's addictive.

Example: Although following the news keeps you informed about world events, some people are so obsessed with all the bad news that they spend hours of free time reading the paper, listening to the radio and watching for more bad news on TV. It becomes their major topic of conversation.

In addition to all the time spent actually pursuing the activity, there are often many hours spent preparing for it, thinking about it, telling people about it and so on. All this helps people avoid their real problems.

Self-defense...

One way I get people to deal with their problems is to ask them to eliminate distractions. I put them on a *distraction diet.* The first step in getting rid of distractions is to find out what you're avoiding. *Ask yourself:* Is there anything I don't want to talk about?

If you're stymied and can't figure out what's bothering you, ask someone close to you what problems he/she thinks you may be hiding from.

Then look for your distractions. *Important:* Don't just look for one or two activities. Some people fill their lives with many different distractions.

If you think you don't have any problems, try giving up your distractions for a week and see what happens. It may be very illuminating.

Don't watch TV, don't read the papers, don't make unnecessary phone calls and don't exercise more than you need to keep fit. If you feel comfortable, then your distractions aren't addictive. But if you find yourself getting anxious, you'll know you're using your distractions to hide from something.

The journaling secret...

The best way to get rid of your distractions and confront your problems is through journal-writing. Write about the anxiety-provoking conflict—or situation—that you're trying to avoid.

To keep a journal, get a notebook and a soft-tipped pen, pick a quiet place and set aside some time each day when you're going to write.

Write about things that are hard for you to face, things that scare you, things that make you mad. Know that what you write is for your eyes only.

Instead of trying to express a single point of view, let each side of your personality have a full say. *Helpful:* Use multicolored pens to express the different parts of your personality.

When you've finished writing, sit quietly for a while or take a long walk by yourself. Open yourself to the babble of voices that are inside you. Let your thoughts flow. Just listen. Don't try to make judgments or come up with resolutions.

Example: If you're angry at your spouse, let yourself feel the anger without assigning blame or trying to decide what to do about your marriage.

The next step is to share your problem with someone—either a good friend or therapist. *Gained:* When you explain a problem to someone else, you clarify your own feelings and see things from a fresh point of view.

Source: Martin G. Groder, MD, a psychiatrist and business consultant, 104 S. Estes Dr., Chapel Hill, North Carolina 27514. His book, *Business Games: How to Recognize the Players and Deal With Them,* is available from Boardroom Classics, Greenwich, CT.

How to Make the Most of The Time In Your Life

Write a game plan for the rest of your life. It should include answers to the following questions:

•What things are really important in your life?

•What practical considerations have to be taken into account (earning a living, raising children, lifestyle)?

•What are your greatest personal strengths? Rank them.

•What are your most limiting shortcomings? Rank them, too.

•What are the activities you most enjoy and most dislike?

With these lists as a guide, make three sets of goals:

•Long-term—assume normal retirement age, plus 20 years.

•Mid-term—from today until retirement.

•Short-term—the next one to five years.

Long-term goals tend to be general (they should be), and short-term goals tend to be overly ambitious. A typical long-term goal is "Happiness." A typical short-term goal is "To get out of this rat race and open my own business."

Source: *Overcoming Executive Mid-Life Crisis,* John Wiley, New York.

Easy Ways to Get Organized

The most efficient people usually use systems that have two things in common—they're easy to set up, and they can be used consistently.

•Part-time employees are the key. Intelligent and motivated students will work for relatively low wages. Young mothers, too, are often looking for part-time work, and a note posted in pediatricians' waiting rooms will help them find you. Use them to prepare your tax returns, match paint swatches, address invitations to a party, collect the RSVPs, deliver collection envelopes for your favorite charity and wait in your home for the appliance repair service to arrive.

•As soon as you can each morning, make two lists of things you want to accomplish that day. The first list is activities that absolutely must get done. Reserve the second list for the wouldn't-it-be-nice-if jobs. You'll probably accomplish everything on the priority list. Consider yourself lucky if you make even a dent in the wish list.

•Find ways to get something done, no matter where you are. Carry notebooks to jot down ideas as they occur to you, or keep required reading material close at hand to review whenever a spare moment crops up.

•Don't force the issue if you're working on one thing but really want to be doing something else. Work on what you feel like doing.

•Create a master list—one place to write everything of importance that you need to remember. Include things to do, important names and phone numbers, good ideas. Use a spiral notebook instead of a pad so pages won't fall off.

Sources: Dr. Marilyn Machlowitz, author of *Workaholics: Living with Them, Working with Them,* The New American Library, New York, and Gerard R. Roche, executive recruiter.

How to Develop Good Time-Use Habits

All of us can make more of ourselves if we take the trouble to cultivate good time-use habits until they are second nature. Habits automatically steer our lives. When habits become time-thrifty, people get better use of their time for the rest of their lives, automatically.

To develop better time-use habits:

•Pick those habits that are good and drop bad ones. Make a list of times and places to substitute a new habit for an old one. It takes a month or more until a new habit is second nature.

•Concentrate on using the new technique as often as possible. Every time you use a new habit, give yourself a mental pat on the back. Otherwise, a mental kick is in order.

•Put weekly reminders to change habits on a calendar. When the reminders come up, evaluate your progress. Then list additional times and places to apply the new habit.

• Announce your intentions to develop new habits to other people. This strengthens your motivation to finish the job.

Source: Robert Moskowitz, time-management consultant, Canoga Park, CA.

Hard-Nosed Ways To Manage Time

• Concentrate on the best ways to spend time, instead of worrying about saving it.

• Keep an accurate log of activities to identify and define work patterns.

• Have only one chair (besides yours) in your office. Keeping people standing saves time.

• Each meeting should have an announced time limit.

• Have all calls screened. Make a list of who should be put through immediately.

• Arrange your office with your back to the door.

• If someone asks, "Do you have a minute?" say, "No."

• List tomorrow's priorities before leaving the office today.

• Don't rush needlessly. It takes longer to correct a mistake than to avoid making one.

Source: Merrill E. Douglass, director, Time Management Center, New York.

Avoiding the Obligation Overload

The prime cause of the overload syndrome is outside pressure to accept too many work or volunteer obligations. Another factor is the initial receptiveness of certain personality types to taking on tasks. Those people are particularly prone to guilt feelings.

Overload symptoms:

• Fear that the additional responsibilities (which suddenly seem overwhelming) won't be met.

• Inability to make decisions.

• Difficulty in communicating with family. The usual excuse is exhaustion.

• Isolation. Discarding the usual recreational outlets and exercise habits on grounds that there is no time.

What it takes to say *no:*

• A clear awareness of priorities. It's easier for a responsible person to say no if it's clear what's at stake: Obligations to family and personal health.

• The strength to accept temporary feelings of guilt.

Dealing with Details

When your mind is cluttered with details, use one of these techniques to redirect energy and improve organization:

• Take a mini-break. A short walk or a minute of relaxation and a drink of water. Or, simply breathe deeply for 30 seconds with your eyes closed (this can help concentration when you shift from one subject to another).

• Keep your schedule on paper. Resist the temptation to keep it in your head.

• Avoid interruptions. Work away from the office and keep your distance from the telephone.

• Delegate details. Rely more heavily on your secretary. Let subordinates handle routine jobs. Let them attend most of the less important meetings.

• Set time limits. If a task isn't completed within an allotted time limit, come back to it later.

Source: *International Management,* New York.

7

Finding a Job

How to Make Networking Work for You

Networking is not just for executives who have fallen off the success track and need powerful contacts to help them find new jobs, assist in closing deals, etc.

Aside from helping in a career crisis, networking—continuously building contacts with people with information, expertise, and ideas from a wide spectrum of business, politics, and philosophy—is invaluable for day-to-day productivity, efficiency, and achievement.

Executives from unrelated companies face many common concerns. Sharing experiences—good and bad—on questions of compensation, incentives, labor negotiations, regulatory and legislative activities, and other topics is very helpful.

A peer outside the company may provide new information, suggest a consultant or expert, or provide an entirely fresh way for you to evaluate recommendations from your own corporate staff.

Organizing your network...

Important networking rule: Make a continuous investment of time in assessing the strengths of your own network—to identify where you are already strong and where you need to build. You can't delegate this task...you're the only one who can do it.

Tools for managing your network: A three-ring binder with loose-leaf, lined paper. *It should contain:*

- Address book.
- Business card file.
- Professional directories.
- Alumni associations and class reunion publications.
- Christmas card list.
- Membership rosters of organizations you belong to and contribute to—including groups such as the Little League, health and recreation club members.

Some people prefer to use a computer and personal organization software instead of paper and binder. There are many such programs available.

Identify your base of contacts...

Take several sheets of loose-leaf paper and give each sheet a heading from the following list:

- People in position to influence.
- People who know others.
- Coworkers and former coworkers.
- Clients and former clients.
- Suppliers.
- Colleagues and competitors.
- Family.
- Ex-family.
- Extended family.
- Neighbors/former neighbors.
- Classmates and alumni.
- Associates from organizations, charities, religious affiliations.
- Special interest groups (health, sports, bridge, etc.).

List names, addresses, and phone/fax numbers from your input sources under each category. Continue to add names and numbers as you build your network.

Once you've organized your contacts, identify gaps...and ways to fill them. Identify areas where the network can be significantly strengthened. *Key questions to ask yourself:*

- What kind of advice or information is most difficult to get?
- What group could I join that might help?
- Do I know enough senior executives in my own industry...among suppliers to my industry...in related businesses...in other areas?

Using the network...

Some of the best networkers find it difficult to use their contacts when they most need them. They're never reluctant to call a person if they have a useful piece of information or a new contact to offer. But it's hard for many successful executives to ask for help from network contacts when they really need the help and have nothing to offer in return.

It's important to remember that if you have been a giver in the past, people will respond when you need them. Call in your chips... that's part of the value of strong networks.

Example: A successful real-estate developer fell on hard times when commercial real-estate values collapsed in the late 1980s. When times were good, he had been very generous with his help to others. Now he was about to declare personal bankruptcy—and for the first time in years was looking for a job. He confided his situation to a colleague and asked him to keep his ears open for any openings. Before the day was over, the business friend's son called, explaining that his father-in-law was in a business that might be able to use the man's skills. He invited the developer to his child's christening party that weekend so that the two of them could meet. It worked. The developer was able to join the father-in-law's firm and stave off financial disaster.

Reciprocity is the glue that keeps networks together. And it's not only a career-building skill...it can be a career-saving skill. Giving without expectation works. In fact, giving is what builds your standing with a network.

Not giving back usually backfires. The network has a way of knowing when you owe too much.

Caution: A critical but frequently overlooked part of giving involves simply acknowledging advice, time, referrals, leads, or gifts from others. Gestures of appreciation are a powerful tool in the networking game.

Source: Susan RoAne, The RoAne Group, 14 Wilder St., San Francisco 94131. She is the author of the best-selling *How to Work a Room* and *The Secrets of Savvy Networking.* Both books are published by Warner Books, 1271 Ave. of the Americas, New York 10020.

First Person Interviewed Rarely Gets the Job

It shouldn't make any difference in hiring whether the candidate was interviewed first or last. But it does.

One of the major reasons that the first person interviewed is frequently not hired is that after many interviews, the interviewer tends to forget the first person. *How to avoid this trap...*

•Pay attention to your choice of interview options. You may be offered an interview on Monday, Tuesday, or Wednesday. Pick Wednesday. Or, you may be offered a choice of 9 a.m., 10 a.m., 11 a.m. or 4 p.m. If possible, opt for the last appointment.

•Don't make the mistake of deferring any interview too long. By the time you're ready to pick a mutually convenient time, the job may be filled.

•Follow up the interview by calling the hiring executive to thank him/her for his time, and if possible, add something that was not discussed at the interview.

Example: It didn't come across in our interview that I have excellent writing ability.

•Then, in a few days, mail a letter to the interviewer to serve as another reminder. It would be nice to include a newspaper or magazine clipping that you think the executive would appreciate. Polite persistence pays off.

Source: Robert Half is founder of Robert Half International, Menlo Park, California 94025, and author of *How to Get a Better Job in this Crazy World,* Plume, 375 Hudson St., New York 10014.

Businesses You Can Start for Under $500

Starting a business is not as hard as you think. You don't even need a great deal of money to launch one. Here are seven businesses that you can run out of your home with an investment of $500 or less...

•Credit-repair service. Customers usually seek this service after being rejected for a home or car loan. You would resolve their credit disputes, set up payment schedules with credit-card companies, etc.

Key: Screen potential clients. You want those you can actually help. To be eligible for your services, problem accounts must have been paid off for at least one year, preferably three or four. Guarantee clients an overall improvement in their credit.

Cost: $500 for office expenses, placement of ads in area newspapers, research of credit record-keeping and reporting laws. *Earning potential:* $100,000 a year.

•Drop shipper. You publicize, take orders for, and accept payment in full for a small manufacturer that produces consumer products such as books, garden tools, gourmet foods, etc. In effect, you are acting as a middleman.

First you negotiate a reduced price for the product with the manufacturer. When the orders come in, you forward them to the company along with half the negotiated price plus postage. The company then ships the orders with your mailing labels. You pay the balance of what you owe the company after your customers pay up.

Don't compete with established direct-mail businesses. Find a niche and work with specialized manufacturers.

Cost: $50 to $250 to publicize a product, process orders, and print labels. *Earning potential:* $3,000+ a year, part-time.

•Estate sales. Visit estate sales and study the business before soliciting clients of your own. You will need to learn how to price antiques and how to draw up a contract with clients.

Key: Letting clients know that you will take care of everything.

Cost: $200 to $300 to advertise your service in daily and shoppers' newspapers. The clients pay to advertise sales. *Earning potential:* 25% of sales.

•Mapmaker. Create colorful, informal community maps featuring advertisements for local businesses. Market each as a "community promotional piece."

Calculate costs of hiring an artist and printing. Charge businesses to appear on the map, plus $35–$40 in production costs. When the maps are printed, deliver 35 to 40 maps to each business, which they can sell for $1, recouping this cost.

Cost: $500 or less to solicit businesses. *Earning potential:* $11,000 or more per project.

•Meeting planner. Put together events, meetings, and conventions for clients.

Key: Pay attention to details. Thoroughly research hotels, restaurants, meeting facilities, and travel arrangements you make for clients. Your business will grow through word-of-mouth referrals.

Cost: $500 for office expenses, yellow pages ad. *Earning potential:* $30,000+ a year.

• Self-publisher of booklets. Research, write, and have printed—either at a copy shop or on a desktop system—informative booklets on specialty topics.

Your writing must be accurate, authoritative, and clear. *Most popular:* "How-to" booklets on money, self-help, self-improvement, special skills.

Cost: $200 to $500 for first printing, classified ads. *Earning potential:* $5,000+ a year.

• Tradespeoples' referral agency. Screen and schedule top-notch painters, carpenters, plumbers, and electricians to do everything from small repairs to major remodeling. Solicit tradespeople to list with you for free. Take 10% of the jobs you book.

Key: Familiarity with construction basics, reliability, commitment to quality.

Cost: $500 for a phone line, answering service, classified ads, flyers. *Earning potential:* $65,000 to $100,000 a year.

Source: Stephen Wagner, associate publisher and editor of *Income Opportunities* magazine and author of *Mind Your Own Business: The Best Businesses You Can Start Today for Under $500,* Bob Adams, Inc., 260 Center St., Holbrook, Massachusetts 02343.

Working the Room

The more people you know, the greater your chances for career advancement.

When you go to trade-association meetings, alumni get-togethers, or social occasions, try to have a little conversation with a number of people—mostly those you don't know.

• Introduce yourself...start with a bit of idle chatter: "This is a nice party. How long have you known the host?"

• Drop a hint about what you do: "I'm with one of the Big Six CPA firms." Then add, "What do you do?"

• If you consider it appropriate, give the person your business card. You might very well get one in exchange. If you had an interesting conversation, offer to send him/her something such as a clipping of a news item that you had just discussed. Now you have an address and perhaps a phone number, too.

Do's and don'ts...

• Don't be a leech. As soon as it appears the person you're talking to is getting restless, excuse yourself and move on.

• If you suspect that someone may be a good contact but you don't think it is appropriate to ask for an address and phone number, write down his/her full name—but not until after you walk away. You can get other information from the host.

• Don't give a sales pitch while working the room. That may be offensive to your host ...and others.

• A good way to start off is with social talk. Talk about family, friends—or play the geography game: "Oh, you're from Detroit. Do you know Charlie Smith? I think he's with one of your competitors."

• If you have unusual credentials, casually and quickly let them be known.

• Discuss interesting things—even humorous ones—that happened at work.

• If you have unusual education and business qualifications, let them be known—but keep it short.

A long time ago, I met a lawyer at a small gathering in London. We exchanged business cards. His practice was in Louisville, Kentucky, and at least once a year for 10 years, I received announcements of partnership changes, etc., from him. I thought that he was wasting his time since I would never need a lawyer in Louisville—and I was right.

But...a friend of mine, who knew our company had offices almost everywhere, asked me if I knew a lawyer in Kentucky. Guess what?

Source: Robert Half, founder of Robert Half International Inc. and Accountemps Worldwide, 2884 Sand Hill Rd., Menlo Park, California 94250.

Should You Take That New Job?

Key questions to ask your interviewer...

• What's the most common reason that people leave the company?

• What are your personal satisfactions and disappointments since you've been with the firm?

• What are the firm's overall strengths?

• When it comes to dealing with people, what are the firm's strengths—and weaknesses?

• Have you had—or do you expect—any big staff cutbacks?

• Do you generally fill openings from the outside or from within?

• What are the particular qualities my prospective boss is looking for?

Also, consider asking to meet a few current employees.

Source: Harvey B. Mackay, chairman and CEO of Mackay Envelope Corp., Minneapolis and author of *Sharkproof: Get the Job You Want, Keep the Job You Love...In Today's Frenzied Job Market.* HarperBusiness, 10 E. 53 St., New York 10022. 800-242-7737.

Landing a Job Through the Classifieds

To better your odds of landing a job through the classifieds, underline any words or phrases in the ad that relate to your qualifications. Then use similar terms to emphasize your attributes in a brief cover letter.

Source: *Careering and Re-Careering for the 1990s* by Ronald L. Krannich, PhD, Manassas, Virginia-based author of more than 20 career books. Impact Publications, 9104-N Manassas Dr., Manassas Park, Virginia 22111.

Résumé Smarts

Put your address at the bottom of a résumé for out-of-town jobs, not at the top. *Aim:* To get prospective employers to focus on you, not your location. You may fit perfectly a job that is 1,000 miles away—and be very willing to relocate at your own expense. But if your address is at the top, the company may read no further—wanting to avoid a costly relocation. *Bottom line:* For a better shot at a job, sell your credentials first, before the firm sees where you live.

Source: *The Right Job: How to Get the Job That's Right for You* by Robert Snelling, Sr., chairman, Snelling and Snelling, a Dallas-based worldwide network of franchised employment services. Penguin Books, 375 Hudson St., New York 10014.

Making the Most Of College Career Counselors

To make better use of college career counselors: Visit their facilities regularly. Get to know them while they get to know you. Find out their backgrounds, schooling, first jobs out of college. Be polite and courteous. Tell the counselor you know job hunts take time and do not expect miracles. *Best demeanor:* Serious, respectful, realistic.

Source: *How to Survive Without Your Parents' Money: Making it from College to the Real World* by Geoff Martz, author of four books for college students and recent graduates. Villard Books, 201 E. 50 St., New York 10022.

How to Turn Around Bad First Impressions

Bad first impressions aren't cast in stone. They can be neutralized. Many situations heal themselves naturally. As people get to know you, other more positive attributes will overcome the initial problem.

Or, if you don't want to leave it up to chance, there are things you can do to counteract a bad first impression:

Stop and take stock...

Before you try to correct a bad first impression that you've made, decide how serious it really is.

Most people overreact to what they perceive as a bad performance on a date, on a job interview, at a cocktail party, etc. *Ask yourself:*

•Do I have a history of tearing myself down?

•Do I analyze every little detail of my performance over and over again?

•Do I obsess about what I did wrong?

If you answer "yes" to any of these questions, you are probably being much too hard on yourself. Chances are, you did not make as bad an impression as you think you did. Try to forget about the incident.

Three types of bad impressions...

If you answer "no" to the above questions, and you think you really did make a bad impression, there are steps you can take to correct the situation. *What to do:*

•*Bad impression #1. You did something physically wrong.* Dressed inappropriately for the occasion...forgot to shave...or felt too fat, too tall, too short, etc. *Remedies:*

•Get feedback on how you look. Ask a friend for advice. Take suggestions seriously.

•Review how you prepared for the occasion. People who usually look good sometimes lose their sense of appropriateness when it comes to special occasions.

Example: Loretta, a lawyer who went to work in conservative suits, overcompensated by wearing tight, low-cut dresses on dates...and then got upset when men made passes.

•Groom yourself better. Some people consistently make bad impressions because they think others should like them no matter how they look. Recognize that the world plays by certain rules and if you want to win at the game you have to play it well.

•Feel good about yourself. Recognize that the more comfortable you are with yourself, the more likely it is that others will overlook your physical flaws.

Example: Sally blamed her nonexistent social life on her excess weight. Once she decided to accept herself the way she was, she became more relaxed and friendly...and men started to ask her out.

•*Bad impression #2. You gave inaccurate information.* Went to a meeting unprepared... pretended to know the facts when you didn't ...or made a stupid mistake. *Remedies:*

•Recognize that most people welcome the chance to correct someone. Making that mistake may not have been so terrible...some people actually do it deliberately, as a strategy to get others to open up.

•Recognize that no one condemns you for one mistake. There has to be a build-up of evidence for a really bad impression to sink in. If you make just one mistake, most people are more than willing to overlook it. Even if they don't say so...that's usually what they're thinking.

•*Bad impression #3. You said something wrong.* Came across as nasty...syrupy sweet... angry...tactless...or inappropriate in one way or another. *Remedies:*

•Give yourself credit. Recognize that if you've gotten this far in life without major trouble, your personality is probably okay.

•Ask for feedback from a friend. And review any feedback you've received from other people at other times.

•Analyze why you messed up. Maybe you need to relax, prepare better or increase your self-confidence. Perhaps you were anxious.

Example: Bobby was nervous around new people. But they often thought he didn't like them. Once he realized that a certain amount of nervousness and awkwardness was appealing, he was able to drop his aloof behavior and let others see his vulnerable side.

People are turned off by anger, belligerence or too much compliance. Nervousness is fine.

Other techniques...

Several techniques will work in any situation where you've made a bad first impression. *Included:*

•Call to explain your mistake, or do so the next time you see the person. Be appropriately self-effacing without being totally self-denigrating.

Studies have shown that unconcealed flaws evoke compassion. Embarrassment is endearing. *Especially likeable:* People who acknowledge that they made a mistake.

•Don't mention your gaffe at the time, but the next time you see the person, make a determined effort to correct it.

Assume that people will judge you not on one particular flaw but on the whole package you present over time.

Warning: Don't overcompensate.

Example: If someone gave you feedback that you were nasty, the next time you see that person watch out for acting too sweet. Or, if you gave them incorrect information the first time, don't overwhelm them with data the next.

•Use imagery to try out new ways to make a good impression.

Example: If you're anxious about a business lunch, imagine yourself at the table being confident, calm and relaxed.

•Tell yourself you don't have to be perfect. Just do the best you can.

Source: Barry Lubetkin, PhD, director of the Institute for Behavior Therapy, 137 E. 36 St., New York 10016. He is coauthor of *Bailing Out,* Prentice Hall, 15 Columbus Circle, New York 10023.

Common Mistakes That Job Hunters Make

With more people chasing fewer jobs, you can help your job hunting friends increase their odds of finding work by helping them avoid some of the most common mistakes. *Included:*

•*Mistake.* Jumping into a job search too quickly. Most executives are action-oriented people. If they find themselves out of work, their first instinct is to get on the phone and start looking for a new position. But it's never a good idea to act when emotions are in turmoil.

Better: Take at least a few days to sit back, assess the situation and analyze the options. Inform family, friends and close business associates about the situation, but limit contact with others for the time being.

•*Mistake.* Hanging out in the old office. Companies often give workers the option of remaining in their old office for a period of time after they've been dismissed. *Reason:* They can use the facilities while they look for a new position. Some people actually think that if they remain in the office their ex-boss will come to his/her senses, realize how invaluable they are and rehire them. *Reality:* Once everyone in the office learns a person has been fired, communications start to become embarrassing and awkward.

Although it's not necessary to pack up and leave by the end of the work day (unless asked to), the sooner the psychological break is made, the better.

•*Mistake.* Relying on a résumé as a door-opener. Many job-hunters spend days crafting their résumés. Then they're shocked when a mass mailing produces nothing.

Reality: People are busy. An unsolicited résumé is just a rung or two above advertising mail. A résumé is most effective when it's passed on by someone the person respects.

Think of a résumé as a short note left behind after a meeting that summarizes the qualifications already discussed in detail. Or, include one with the follow-up thank-you note that's always sent after a meeting.

•*Mistake:* Relying on recruiters. On the managerial level, employment agencies fill, at best, 10% of all available positions. Informal networking is the best way to land a new job.

This doesn't mean you shouldn't register with several agencies. But remember that finding a job depends primarily on the steps you take yourself.

•*Mistake.* Networking incorrectly. Some people think networking means calling friends and business acquaintances and asking them for a job. But the chance is remote that they'll have an appropriate position open when they get the call.

Networking is like building a spider web. Contacts are made piece by piece until a job is caught. Contacts should be used to offer ideas, suggestions and names of other executives with whom you can speak. Get in touch with them, ask for an appointment and pick their brains for ideas and additional contacts. Eventually, a solid job lead will appear.

Rule of thumb: To reach enough people, schedule an average of two networking meetings per day.

•*Mistake:* Getting in to see someone for an informal chat...and then asking for a job. This puts the person in an awkward position and lessens the odds that he'll be willing to help.

• *Mistake:* Not keeping in touch with people you've already networked with. Maintaining contact keeps the job hunter's name fresh in the person's mind.

Example: A man with a very common last name had a networking meeting with me. Several weeks later, after his name had begun to grow fuzzy in my memory, he sent a note just to say hello. That night, I came across a job lead that was perfect for him. If he hadn't written, I might not have thought of him.

Use any excuse you can think of to stay in touch.

Example: I know a woman who loves to read business magazines. While looking for a job, if she saw an article that related to a contact's company, industry or just something the two had discussed, she'd clip it and send it along with a short note.

• *Mistake:* Winging the interview. When they finally do get a job interview, many candidates go in unprepared. Learn as much as possible about the industry, the company and, if possible, the person conducting the interview.

Sources: The library, other executives in the company or industry, the business editor of the local newspaper.

Have an agenda. Know the half-dozen or so points that should be made during the meeting.

Examples: How past experience fits in with the company's needs, ideas for improving a particular division's profitability, etc.

Don't be embarrassed to go into an interview with a written list. This shows the interviewer that you've taken the time to be prepared.

• *Mistake:* Not dealing with the emotional fallout of a job hunt. No one likes to be rejected. And during the average six-month executive job search, everyone is going to be rejected more than once.

It's important to maintain a positive attitude. *Helpful:* Stay physically active. And don't keep things bottled up inside...and share your feelings with family and friends.

When to start...

The best time to start preparing for a job hunt is while you still have a job. Make it a point to make as many professional contacts as possible...and keep in touch with them. These contacts will prove invaluable if you ever find yourself out of work.

Small world: Never refuse to meet with someone who is networking. That person may one day turn out to be *very* helpful.

Source: Karl Gimber, senior vice president, Right Associates, outplacement specialists, 640 Fifth Ave., New York 10019.

Triumphing in a Job Interview

Job seekers often don't like the interviewer. But usually, they won't be working for the person who does the first interview or even some of the subsequent ones. *The goal:* To be successful enough in each interview to finally reach the person you will be working for—the one you're going to have to relate to.

But first, even if there is no "chemistry," you have to win over the lower-echelon people.

• Practice by going to as many interviews as possible.

• Practice at home. Sit before a mirror and answer stock questions ("Tell me something about yourself") into a tape recorder. Gradually, you will improve and be more at ease during real interviews, even if the stock questions don't come up.

• Be pleasant, polite and friendly—but not too friendly. Remember, you have something to sell.

• Don't eliminate the job on the basis of lower-level interviews. You might not know enough to make a choice until you move up to the next level.

• Tailor your résumé for the job you're going after and make it easier for the interviewer to pick out the highlights that apply to that particular opportunity.

• If the interviewer steers you into an area where you are weak, take charge, and steer the conversation in another direction—toward a strength.

•Make yourself as comfortable as possible at an interview. If the sun is in your eyes ask permission to move your chair or to sit somewhere else.

•Arrive on time. If it's a hard-to-reach place, do a dry run in advance. It's better to come early. You will be more relaxed that way.

•Try to avoid being the first person interviewed. Studies show that the first person has much less of a chance of getting the job. Although you can't always control this, avoid Mondays, in any case. Mondays and Fridays, the most disorganized days in an office, are also the worst for an interview.

•Don't smoke. It can't do you any good—and it can do you harm.

•Try to learn something about the interviewer, especially as you move to higher levels. You will be able to make more meaningful comments and you will be more relaxed.

•If the interviewer is getting a lot of phone calls, suggest coming back another day. He will either refuse further calls or accept your offer. Many on-the-spot decisions like these are a matter of being considerate, as you would be with a friend.

•If the interviewer stops talking, ask a specific question, such as, "Is there anything else you'd like to know about me?" Don't ramble your way into trouble.

•Somewhere near the end of the interview, tell the interviewer that you like the job, that you like the company and that you'd like to work for him/her. *Also:* Impress the interviewer with your confidence. Say, "I know I can do the job. I won't let you down. You can count on me."

•Follow up by sending a note to the interviewer. Send a note of thanks to that person's secretary, too. The secretary might mention it to the boss.

•After the interview, analyze what went wrong. Work on the assumption that something did. We're all amateurs at job interviews. If you can honestly figure out your mistakes, you won't make them again at the next interview.

Source: Robert Half, founder, Robert Half International, Inc., executive recruiters, San Francisco.

How to Handle the Silent Treatment At an Interview

A popular technique in interviewing a candidate is to clam up somewhere in the middle of the interview. This takes candidates off guard, and they sometimes get into trouble with too much loose talk and lots of nonsense.

How to keep from being derailed by the silent treatment:

•Be prepared with interesting and pertinent ideas.

•Shift the conversation to your strengths. In the event of the silent treatment, talk about these strengths as they apply to the company and to the function for which you're being interviewed.

•Sell your abilities. Instead of feeling ill at ease, consider a pause a benefit. Pick your own subject.

•Don't talk too long. After a few minutes, ask the interviewer if he wants you to continue or would like to ask you a question. If you are told to go on, do that for another several minutes and then ask again if you should continue.

•Remember, the interviewing process is a game. It's to your advantage to play it skillfully.

Source: Robert Half, founder, Robert Half International, Inc., executive recruiters, San Francisco.

Being Prepared (But Appearing Casual) At a Job Interview

•You should do about 85% of the talking in the interview. If an unskilled interviewer is doing too much talking, gracefully try to make your points. Otherwise, the interviewer will discover after you left that he knows very little about you.

•Study up on the company but don't appear too prepared. A skilled interviewer will be cautious that you are keying your replies to what you know the company wants.

•Try to find out what happened to the last person who had the job without asking a direct question. Encourage the interviewer to tell you about the job, what the best people did right and what mistakes others made, etc. The information may come out anyway.

•Don't prepare long, rehearsed answers to questions such as "Why didn't you make better grades in college?" Answer briefly and with confidence.

Source: Richard Fear.

How to Check Out Your Job Interviewer

•Find out in advance the name of your interviewer.

•Dig into his background for education, former jobs and outside interests.

•If you know his coworkers, quiz them about his personality and reputation in the company.

•Armed with this information, you may be able to maneuver the interview to your advantage. At least you'll have an idea about his priorities and interests.

Eleven Most Common Reasons Job Applicants Aren't Hired

•Too many jobs. Employers are suspicious of changes without career advancement.

•Reluctance of applicant or spouse to relocate if necessary.

•Wrong personality for the employer.

•Unrealistic salary requirements.

•Inadequate background.

•Poor employment record.

•Unresponsive, uninterested or unprepared during the interview. (Being "too aggressive" is not a serious handicap.)

•Negotiations with employer handled improperly.

•Little apparent growth potential.

•Long period of unemployment.

•Judged to be an ineffective supervisor.

Source: National Personnel Associates.

Negotiating Salary In a Job Interview

Negotiating salary is often the hardest part in a job interview.

Here are some suggestions:

•Avoid discussing salary in detail until you're close to getting an offer. If the first interviewer asks what salary you want, respond, "Salary is important, but it's not the most important thing. Why don't we develop an interest in each other and then we'll see."

•If the interviewer insists, mention your current salary and suggest using that as a guideline.

•When you are actually offered the job, you are in a much stronger bargaining position. That is the time to negotiate.

•Do not demand more than the market will bear. It's a mistake to lie about what you have been earning, especially if you're unemployed. The higher the salary, the fewer the jobs.

Source: Robert Half, founder, Robert Half International, Inc., executive recruiters, San Francisco.

How to Evaluate A Job Offer

Questions you must ask (yourself and the recruiter) to increase the chance that you land in a job that offers opportunity for promotion, mobility, power, personal growth:

•Who's in the job now?

•What is the average length of time people have stayed in the job?

•Where do they go?

•Ask to talk to people holding the same or similar jobs. Find out what other people in the company think about the job. If they think the job is dead-end, don't consider taking it. You may think you can overcome and be the "pleasant surprise." But chances are excellent that you will fail.

• Will the job give me a chance to know other people in the organization doing lots of different jobs?

• Will I represent the department (or group or section, etc.) at meetings with people from other parts of the organization?

• If the job is in the field, do I get much chance to meet with managers from headquarters? Does the job have too much autonomy? (Working on your own too much can be the kiss of death for upward movement if no one else gets to know you and your abilities.)

• Is this job in an area that solves problems for the company? The best jobs for getting power (and promotions) fast always have a sense of danger. Jobs in safe areas where everything is going well offer a slower track to promotion.

Best Days to Job Hunt

Most job seekers think Monday is the best day to look for a job because there are more jobs advertised in the papers on Sunday. But jobs advertised on Sunday actually become available the previous Wednesday.

Helpful:

• Look every day of the week.

• If you have to skip one day, Monday is the best choice. You will not be slowed down by the same hordes of competition on other days.

• The best job hunting may be when the weather is bad. Again, there are fewer competitors. Management may well believe that the bad-weather candidate is more interested in employment and will work harder with less absenteeism. However, interviewers may be depressed and executives busy filling in for absent staff when the weather is poor.

Source: Robert Half, founder, Robert Half International, Inc., executive recruiters, San Francisco.

Most Common Job Search Mistakes

• Failure to look within before looking outside. Self-assessment is the key to a successful job search. Before you begin, take the time to look inside and ask, "What have I to offer?"

• Failure to approach the job search as a multifaceted process. A good campaign mixes at least three of the following methods: Personal networking, using employment search firms, answering classified ads, doing research, conducting a direct-mail campaign and targeting (the thorough analysis of one or two companies). Do some of each, but be sure that you spend at least half of your time on personal networking. Studies show that about 70% of all jobs are filled through personal contacts. Most people know 200-500 people, though they seldom realize it. Some can be valuable to you.

• Failure to plan and organize a campaign. Map out each week ahead of time.

• Failure to keep careful records of everything you do and everyone you speak to. A month from now, you may be talking to someone whom you've spoken to before, and you might not remember what was said in the initial meeting. Information is the job seeker's most powerful tool.

• Failure to maintain the ideal job seeker's attitude: Nonjudgmental. Treat everyone with warmth and courtesy. Realize that in a job search you get back what you put in. If you're putting out positive energy, you will connect with people much more easily.

• Failure to spend enough time on the telephone. Productivity in any campaign is directly related to the number of calls you make. It is easy to fall into a campaign of sending résumés and writing letters. Spend 50% of your time on the telephone. That's the way everything happens. It's more personal. It also forces you to call people whom you know—essentially doing the networking that you might otherwise neglect. If you have a goal of meeting 10 people a week, the only way that you can do it is by using the telephone.

• Failure to maintain your vitality during a campaign. Work to keep mentally and physically fit. A good campaign is a combination of work, rest, exercise and good diet. Some people think that if six hours a day of job searching is good, 10 hours will get the job that much faster. But such people usually burn themselves out.

•Failure to prepare ahead of time for interviews. Simply go to the library and get an annual report. *Find out:* The size of the company, its products or services, and any problems in the company or in its industry. You'll be ahead of 90% of the other applicants if you know something about the company before the interview.

•Failure to maintain good grooming and personal appearance. Take care of your appearance, even when dressed informally for networking. First impressions are hard to change.

•Failure to send thank-you notes to people in the network who have helped you—and to people who have interviewed you.

•Failure to follow up...and follow up...and follow up.

Getting a job is a social process. The interaction among people is what makes jobs happen.

Source: William Ellermeyer, president of Career Management Services, Irvine, CA.

How to Win the Temp-Work Game

Temporary work has become a credible permanent career choice as the market for competent, specialized part-time help expands. Whether one views temporary work as an interim measure or enjoys the flexible lifestyle of a "professional temporary," more can be gained from the experience if the disadvantages are offset.

Here are the worst problems most temps face and how to minimize them...

•The *just-a-temp* attitude. Although temps are called in as skilled, fast-learning pinch hitters, many complain of being treated as unintelligent or unimportant. This attitude is rapidly receding as the old image of the unskilled and disinterested temp disappears.

Self-defense: Don't assume an *I'm just a temp* attitude. Temps must prove their abilities before they're taken seriously.

•Lack of benefits. Temps generally have to buy their own insurance and save toward vacations, sick leave and retirement. If the government passes a national health plan this year, some of this problem may be partially eased.

In the meantime: Shop carefully for a temporary service. Many services have begun to offer medical insurance to their regular temps, and some offer accrued vacation and sick time—but temp services with benefits are likely to pay lower wages.

•Social isolation. Those who depend on the workplace for close, long-term friendships should probably not work as temps. Temps are not treated as "one of the gang."

Self-defense: Those who want the best of both worlds can ask to be reassigned to the same companies regularly. On new assignments, seek out other temps with whom you might have lunch. Personalize your work area with flowers, or bring cookies for coworkers.

•Work isn't always available. To improve the frequency, temps can let the service know when they want to work or if they are willing to take lower-paying jobs just to be working. Call in twice a day to check on new assignments. Ask the service if it uses standbys—temps who report to the service to be available for emergency replacement calls and are paid for a minimum number of hours, whether or not they are sent out.

•Getting dumped on. Many temps find themselves the *office scapegoat*—either for piles of work no one else wants to do or for blame when regular employees make errors.

Self-defense: Don't be bullied by regular employees. Clarify your priorities with a supervisor when more than one person needs to have work done.

•Boredom. Some companies hire temps even when they have little need for them. As a result, temps may not have much to do for long periods of time.

Self-defense: Become familiar with the office equipment. Ask for more work, which always surprises and impresses employers. As a last resort, bring letters to write and other personal work so that you always look busy.

•Adaptability anxiety. Many temps experience *first-day-at-a-new-job* stress almost every week.

Self-defense: Don't become stressed. Companies that call for temps do not expect miracle workers. Be prepared to ask questions and do a professional job. If the work or workload is unreasonable, be honest. Call the temp service and say so.

•Acceptance of limited influence. Temps often see potential improvements because they are objective and have worked for many companies. But a clever temp may be resented or be seen as a threat by permanent employees.

Self-defense: Make your suggestions tactfully.

Example: Write a memo to the supervisor on the *last* day of the assignment, crediting the employees who were helpful. Add suggestions as a way of saying *thank you* for the assignment.

•Lack of growth and no clear career path. Temping tends to be a series of similar assignments that allow you limited improvement in your skills and earnings.

Self-defense: Be realistic about what can be achieved by temping.

Exception: Many temp services now function as outsourcing firms for companies with seasonal, by-the-project or right-sizing needs. They employ temps who are *already* professionals—doctors, lawyers, plant managers, executives. Many temps choose a service that promises glamorous assignments with the hope that they will be offered permanent positions.

Temporary jobs are generally *not* trial positions. But temping *is* a great way to tap into the "hidden job market"—job postings that are not advertised or sent to an employment service.

•Temp work is not accepted as work experience on résumés.

Self-defense: Temps should create résumés that detail the positions they have filled, the companies for which they have worked and their responsibilities. Prepare a positive answer in advance to the job-interview question *Why were you a temp?*

Example: "I wanted exposure to various communications industries. I've worked in publishing, advertising, public relations and television production companies. I now know I'm happiest in an advertising environment."

Source: William Lewis, president of Career Blazers, Inc., an employment and training service, 590 Fifth Ave., New York 10036. He is coauthor, with Nancy Schuman, a vice president at Career Blazers, of *The Temp Worker's Handbook.* American Management Association, 135 W. 50 St., New York 10020.

Why Job Interviewees Are So Poorly Prepared For Their Interviews

Very few people who go on a job interview are prepared because they are *afraid* to confront their weaknesses—and/or to present their strengths.

Rather than spend time taking a hard look at themselves and their careers to identify and address the flaws, they assume their personalities and enthusiasm will be sufficient.

They also assume that an interviewer has carefully read their résumés—so they don't review all of their strengths.

Result: Interviewees are surprised by interviewers' tough questions and are often unable to answer them skillfully.

Strategies for doing well in any job interview...

•Do your homework about the company. Failing to sufficiently research the company, its top executives and its business is perhaps one of the biggest mistakes job candidates make.

While many things that happen at job interviews are out of your control, you can get a clear understanding of what the company does and where it stands in its industry before your interview.

Strategies: Call the company's switchboard for the name of the person who heads the department in which you might be working. Ask your friends or business contacts about his/her reputation.

Read the trade publications that cover the company and the key people there. Find magazines and newsletters that are published weekly for cutting-edge news.

Even if they don't make reference to the key people at the company, they will give you enough information about the business so you can carry on an informed conversation. Such research will help you stand out from others interviewing for the same position.

If the publications are not at your local library, call the publishers and pay to have a half-dozen issues of each publication sent to you by overnight mail. And consider subscribing so you can stay informed.

•Rehearse your interview script. Great trial lawyers avoid asking witnesses questions to which they don't already know the answers. Such preparation keeps these lawyers from being thrown off guard by the answers. Likewise, during an interview, you should not hear a question you have not already anticipated. Of course, it's important that you not answer in a rapid-fire, know-it-all manner.

Strategy: List the obvious questions, such as *Tell me about yourself...why are you leaving your current position...why do you want to work here...what are your long-term ambitions?* Using a tape recorder, practice interviews and play them back. Keep answering the questions until you sound convincing.

•Describe your previous business relationships cautiously and creatively—especially if you had a problem boss. Attribute problems to differences in expectations or structural changes rather than personalities. Above all, don't demean anyone. Your last supervisor, for example, wasn't a *paranoid fault finder who drove you crazy*...he was a *micromanager*.

Solution: If you feel defensive about some episode in your job history, it is especially important to practice your response on tape—until you sound perfectly at ease.

•Think about the job-related questions an interviewer might throw at you. Some will ask questions to see how you perform under pressure—*what if you had to fire your best friend... what if your boss asked you to reveal inside information?* Be honest. Don't get flustered while you explain how you would handle the dilemma.

•Make it clear that you really want the job. Strangely enough, many job candidates fail to say explicitly that they want a position. People I know who do a lot of hiring say they often give the job to the person demonstrating enthusiasm for it.

Strategy: Before the interview, ask yourself if you really want the job. Spend a few minutes going over the reasons why you want it.

Then, at some point during the interview, tell the interviewer, *The job seems like a wonderful opportunity...I know I can contribute a great deal*—or words to that effect.

The key is to strike a balance between being eager and sounding desperate. After the interview, write a thank-you note to the interviewer saying you enjoyed your meeting and indicating that you hope there will be a fit for you at the company.

Important: If you make it to the final stages but don't get the job, write another gracious thank-you note stating again how much you would like to work for the company and then call to suggest the interviewer pass your name along to others in the company looking for an excellent employee. You should also drop a friendly note from time to time, praising an accomplishment or to pass along an important article. You never know where a lead or a job will come from.

Source: Adele Scheele, PhD, career strategist for organizations and individuals, 440 E. 79 St., New York 10021. She is author of several books, including *Skills for Success* (Ballantine, 201 E. 50 St., New York 10022) and, most recently, *Career Strategies for the Working Woman* (Simon & Schuster, 1230 Avenue of the Americas, New York 10020).

8

Getting Ahead On the Job

The Secrets of Career Success

After more than two decades of research on the subject of career success, I have concluded that people on the "fast track"* are made—not born.

As a group, fast-trackers are not any brighter than their slow-track colleagues. They didn't attend better colleges. And, biggest surprise of all, they don't work any harder.

The main difference: Fast-trackers advance within their companies because they know how to tap into critical resources. Slow-trackers often aren't even aware that these resources exist.

Companies don't inform people about critical resources in their orientation materials. In fact, more than 90% of what you need to know to succeed is not published anywhere.

*A career path of highly enriched professional growth opportunities.

If you want to thrive in today's competitive corporate environment, you cannot simply play by the rules and keep your nose clean. Horatio Alger is dead, and he has been replaced by a fast-track breed that has mastered the hidden code for success.

The foundation...

In virtually every case, fast-trackers are launched by bosses who invest in their subordinates' future careers.

This goes beyond training a person to do the present job well. When a boss invests in a worker, the goal is to help the person outgrow the present job and move on to increasingly responsible positions within the company.

Are you on the fast track?...

On average, the bosses studied engaged in these critical actions with 64% of their fast-trackers, but with only 27% of their slow-trackers.

You can be confident you're on the fast track if your boss...

•Provides you with special information that allows you to learn how the company really operates.

•Warns you about changes to be made within the organization.

•Assigns you challenging tasks.

•Advertises your strengths to higher management.

•Prepares you to handle more difficult assignments.

•Helps plan your long-range career.

•Gives you enough authority to complete important assignments.

•Notifies you about any promotion opportunities.

•Warns you in advance—and in confidence—about your career problems.

•Asks for your input in decisions for which only the boss is responsible.

Getting your boss to believe in you...

In deciding which of their subordinates to select for the fast track, bosses seek several qualities above all others:

•Decision-making similarity. Given the same complex problems, the boss and subordinate will make the same decision. They view the company, its markets and its constituents from similar perspectives.

•Dependability. In an emergency, the boss can count on the subordinate to complete an assignment the boss started. The subordinate rises to the occasion in times of crisis.

•Positive collaboration. The boss and subordinate have an effective working relationship. They communicate well and coordinate their efforts efficiently.

Beyond excelling in these critical areas, potential fast-trackers can boost their chances of selection and investment by:

•Learning about their organization beyond their job requirements.

•Telling their boss they want extra work.

•Making their boss look good.

•Giving their boss credit in the presence of other people.

How fast-trackers advance...

Fast-trackers engage in several activities more often than their slow-track colleagues. *To get (or stay) on the fast track:*

•Demonstrate initiative. Show the boss that you're eager to outgrow your job. Identify problem areas and act to correct them.

•Exercise leadership. Help coworkers perform their jobs more efficiently, and provide direction when necessary. Offer to take charge of special projects, such as interdepartmental task forces.

•Take risks. Let your boss know about problems in the work unit. Take stands you think are correct, even if you're bucking the tide. Admit your mistakes—and show what you've learned from them.

•Add value to your work. Go beyond your job description. Write unsolicited reports that can help your boss make improvements in your unit.

•Persist on a project. If an assignment appears to be going nowhere, try to view it in a new way.

•Seek opportunities for self-improvement. Request special training, or take on assignments that require the use of new skills. Ask your managers to define your strengths and weaknesses so that you can improve.

•Build *competence networks*. Find out who is responsible for getting things done in the organization. Then initiate relationships with these people by offering favors or providing information. *Result:* You'll compile credits with these people that can translate into critical resources down the road.

•Influence others. When coworkers come to you for help or advice, deal carefully with each person's problems.

•Resolve ambiguity. When a boss makes an ambiguous request, gather as much information as possible from other sources. Make educated assumptions (when necessary), and approach the boss for *brief* feedback regularly throughout the assignment.

•Seek wider exposure. Learn more about the company by associating with managers outside your department.

•Build up—and build on—existing skills. Keep up with technical advances in your field.

•Develop a close working relationship with the boss. This cannot be overemphasized. Volunteer favors and information. Take an interest in the boss's family and career. *To avoid being obvious or causing resentment:* Show an interest in your coworkers as well.

• Help the boss. When you help make your boss look good, the boss will be more likely to take you along as he/she advances through the organization.

Source: George B. Graen, director of the Center for International Competitiveness Studies at the University of Cincinnati. He is the author of *Unwritten Rules for Your Career,* John Wiley, Dept. 0-1006, Box 6793, Somerset, New Jersey 08875.

Behaving Like a Top Professional

You can reap a great deal of self-esteem and a wide variety of other rewards by learning how to behave like a real professional.

Essentials:

• Sense of responsibility for clients (or customers). People who are cynical about their work, who despise the people they have to deal with, demoralize themselves and generally perform badly in the long run.

• Avoid rules of thumb, quick answers and rigid thinking. Be on the lookout for exceptions—incidents where theories don't seem to fit the facts. This is an opportunity to perform creatively.

• Stay current. Take additional training and/or coursework. Force yourself to work on tough problems, do heavy business-related reading.

• Be thoughtful about trade-offs in making difficult decisions that often involve several contradictory factors.

• Approach complex problems with a general strategy plus the readiness to change as the situation unfolds or new factors develop.

• Think more about task accomplishment than about hours spent accomplishing it. Professionals aren't clock watchers. They're driven by goals that they've set for themselves. And because these are, in large part, their own goals, they're motivated to attain them.

• Be responsible for developing subordinates. You'll end up with better people, increase loyalty and motivation, and experience the pride of seeing someone you've trained advance from neophyte to polished performer.

• Understand that excellence isn't an end state. It's a process of continuously striving to meet more challenging goals, learn new things and become more adept at solving difficult problems. Suppress the temptation to take destructive shortcuts or gain selfish advantage.

Source: Dr. Leonard Sayles, Center for Creative Leadership, Greensboro, NC.

Who Gets Promoted First?

The four most important factors in determining how fast you are promoted:

• How top management feels about the person who recommended your promotion.

• Your exposure and visibility to those in higher management.

• Your background, education, work experience.

• How well you perform in your present job.

Why Managers Fail... And Succeed

People who fail in business usually have no trouble finding external reasons for their failure—economic conditions, discrimination, politics, uncooperative employees.

Although these play a part, internal factors are frequently as important.

In my psychiatric practice, I have observed that powerful unconscious issues affect work just as they do other areas of life. Our interactions are guided by a whole spectrum of beliefs and behavior styles developed over many years.

What we learned growing up influences the way we react to challenges in adulthood. Understanding and grappling with these issues can make a significant difference in job performance.

Personality style is one of the major internal factors in managerial performance. *Three lead-*

ership styles are responsible for the most serious managerial problems...

The narcissistic leader...

Characteristics: Narcissists are drawn to leadership positions by a deep need for power and prestige. They are often highly talented, hard-working and charismatic. But feelings of inferiority lead to self-aggrandizement and the need for constant, unconditional affirmation and positive feedback from others. Narcissists also tend to have a low tolerance for frustration.

Consequences: The narcissist inspires people to action, but can't always follow through. By surrounding himself/herself with yes-men —people who idealize him and reflect back exactly what he wants to hear—he is unlikely to anticipate and prepare for potential trouble spots as his ideas are executed. The narcissist's need to be in the spotlight makes it hard for him to build an effective team. He may resent and even sabotage employees whose creativity threatens to overshadow his own.

Most dangerous, the narcissist fails to encourage balance and diversity of opinion. The result can be disastrous, both to him and the company, as he inspires others to pour resources into implementing his brilliant—but unworkable—ideas.

Issues: The narcissist is likely to have grown up in an environment where nothing he did was ever quite good enough. He never developed a strong sense of self-esteem. To mask this sense of inferiority, he learned to rely on self-aggrandizement and seeks out only those people who will reassure him that he's wonderful.

The narcissist needs to develop a more complete sense of self—one that is not dependent on others' perceptions or on always being the best. He needs to recognize the value of clear, attainable goals that are reached step by gradual step. *Skills to develop...*

- Share credit. Use the words *we* and *us* rather than *I* and *me.*
- Be generous in giving praise instead of always expecting to receive it.
- Rather than relying on coworkers for affirmation, explore ways to meet that need outside work. Put time into developing family relationships and satisfying hobbies.

The authoritarian leader...

Characteristics: The authoritarian personality has an obsession with order, with being right and in control. This type of manager is poorly attuned to the emotional needs of employees. He relies on a competitive, rather than affiliative, model of work relationships.

Consequences: Though corporations and departments do need an authority figure in order to function efficiently, the authoritarian's excessive need for control can lead to numbing bureaucracy and a rule-bound, by-the-book decision-making style.

Autonomy and creativity are stifled—which can spell disaster when a crisis arises that requires quick, effective decisions.

The authoritarian manager is unlikely to build loyalty or team spirit among staff. He may appear petty and defensive...employees respond with feelings of dislike and by doing the bare minimum required of them.

Issues: Authoritarians learn this style by growing up in families where control and rules are valued...and emotions are ignored or denied. The authoritarian leader must work to become more aware of how he feels, not just what he does...and recognize that intellect and emotion can work together. Skills to develop...

- Learn to listen carefully, without interrupting or becoming defensive.
- Practice seeing things from a subordinate's point of view. You may come across more harshly than you mean to.
- Welcome criticism instead of rejecting or punishing it. Invite feedback from others.
- Share credit for positive results.

The emotionally isolated leader...

Characteristics: The emotionally isolated manager is so uncomfortable with social interaction that he becomes almost invisible—business is carried out via subordinates, other managers or committees.

This type of leader is so afraid of making a mistake that he'll avoid taking action or making a commitment—which could turn out to be the greatest mistake of all.

Consequences: Subordinates may form small groups or pairings, seeking the direction and support that is lacking from above. Since each group is likely to have its own agenda, the organization may become fragmented. This is not an environment that fosters lively, productive collaboration and interchange.

In some cases, a more socially skilled peer or subordinate will act as a kind of buffer between the manager and the rest of the organization, helping to create a responsive climate for employees. Having a gifted coworker interpret and carry out the leader's ideas may be enough. But the leader risks being left behind as the department or company grows beyond him.

Issues: Emotionally isolated leaders lack confidence in their ability to lead or even communicate with others. They are uncomfortable with the concept and enactment of power. Some dislike people and prefer the world of ideas... others are simply shy.

Many of them have been high intellectual achievers all their lives—but received little modeling or encouragement from their parents in getting along with peers. Skills to develop...

- Read about and take courses in assertiveness training to become more comfortable with collaboration, leadership and basic social skills.
- Learn to see mistakes as a way of finding out what is and isn't effective. Errors can be corrected.
- Fight inaction by recognizing that there's always more information to be gathered—but that's no reason to postpone action indefinitely. *Helpful:* Set deadlines. Resolve to stop research and to make decisions based on data gathered by that date.

Source: David W. Krueger, MD, clinical professor of psychiatry at Baylor College of Medicine and author of *Emotional Business: The Meaning and Mastery of Work, Money, and Success,* Avant Books, Slawson Communications, Inc., 165 Vallecitos de Oro, San Marcos, California 92069.

How to Turn Your Ideas Into Successful Realities

Generating significant ideas and nurturing them to reality requires stretching the mind and following six essential steps that I call the STRIKE process...

Before taking the first step toward mind expansion, loosen up your thinking power by breaking old routines and trying something new.

Change helps unleash creativity by stimulating the right side of your brain—the side that controls intuition and imagination. *Possibilities:*

- Rearrange your day's routine. Start with a bath instead of a shower. Watch a different TV program.
- Eat food you've never tasted before. Then describe the flavor in 10 words. It's harder to do than you might think.
- Try writing with your other hand for a while.
- Take movies with a camcorder as you crawl through your house on your stomach. This snake's eye view will show you a home you've never seen before.

Once the brain's right side is loose and agile, you're ready to start the STRIKE process.

"S" is for stew...

Start by thinking almost aimlessly about things you'd like to do...improvements you'd like to make...problems to solve...goals to achieve, etc.

Whether it takes two hours or two months, don't be concerned about how long you stew over the possibilities. Give your mind time to explore each area.

Helpful: Write down the main subjects and tape that list to your bathroom mirror. Seeing them next to each other helps you to evaluate them.

You'll know that the stewing phase is over when one objective begins to dominate and you're eager to go on the next step in the process.

"T" is for target...

As soon as a single objective emerges, write it down in no more than 10 words. Make sure that the statement clearly embodies the idea you want to pursue.

Example: You may have started the stewing phase with a dozen or more thoughts on how to advance your career and lifestyle. Next you may have pared these down to the desirability of a transfer to the West Coast. From that, your *target* emerges—*I want to transfer to Portland.*

You can be virtually certain that you have the right target when seeing it written down begins to generate stirrings of excitement.

"R" is for research...

You can't afford to skimp on research. Go to libraries, computer databases and public sources of information. If the goal is moving to Portland, investigate home prices, school quality, tax rates, opportunities for hobbies and other outside activities, etc.

Most overlooked source of information: People. Talk to friends with areas of expertise that you lack. Use your network to find other knowledgeable people. If Portland is the goal, don't just try to find *any* people who have lived there, but people who have moved there from *your* city.

If you have a mentor or an especially wise confidante, this is the time to ask for his/her advice. This friend might be able to see a flaw in your reasoning that you have overlooked.

There's no absolute rule for knowing how much research to do, but when a file folder is one inch thick, you've usually done enough... and are ready to go to the next step.

"I" is for ideas...

The object here is to generate ideas that will let you achieve your target goal. Start by keeping the target in mind while you conjure up words and pictures that show you how to get from where you are to where you want to be. Jot down ideas as they come to mind. Try to visualize them on paper as they unfold.

This is the point at which you'll see a big payoff from the exercises you did to loosen your mind.

"K" is for key idea...

From the ideas that you generate, pick the one you consider to be the best and the most practical. If you have new doubts, go back and do more research or consult again with your confidante. *Five essential questions...*

1. Is the idea simple?
2. Will it truly get me to my target?
3. Is it practical?
4. Can I visualize myself making the idea happen?
5. Am I passionate about it?

If you can't answer with an emphatic yes to each question, go back and mull the ideas over further.

Never choose more than one idea to act on. *Reason:* A good idea requires all your energy. Choosing more than one spreads your energy too thin.

"E" is for execute...

Now act on your idea. From your research and visualization, you'll know exactly what to do. But since it's impossible to envision every obstacle, you may indeed run into stumbling blocks. When that happens, go back and create ideas that can get around the obstacle.

Example: Mickey Schulhof, vice chairman of Sony USA in the 1970s, helped develop the idea of compact discs. But his idea initially ran into a stumbling block when he couldn't sell it to industry executives who were more interested in protecting their investment in LP (long-playing) record technology than in sound quality.

Schulhof went back to the idea phase and realized that there was another route—selling recording stars on the technology. Once top musicians became enthusiastic about CD sound, the industry took another look at the idea. The payoff for Sony and Schulhof was immense and historic.

Source: John Emmerling, chairman of the advertising agency John Emmerling Inc., 135 E. 55 St., New York 10022. He is the author of *It Only Takes One: How to Create the Right Idea and Then Make It Happen,* Simon & Schuster, 1230 Ave. of the Americas, New York 10020.

Personal File Power

All companies keep a file on each employee. It contains the employee's résumé, application form, memos for doing things above and beyond the call of duty—and memos on what the employee may have done wrong.

You should keep a personal personnel file to keep a record of your achievements—little ones and big ones—along with a copy of your latest résumé. Every time you accomplish something worthwhile, scribble a note on a piece of paper, date it, and insert it into your file. *Why this is valuable:*

•If you want to ask your boss for a raise or promotion: The best way to get the raise you want is to remind your supervisor of your achievements. If you don't write them down, you'll forget them. And if you forget, you can be sure your boss will, too.

•If you need to work up an effective résumé in a hurry: Take your old résumé and plug in your current data and significant achievements.

Source: Robert Half is the founder of Robert Half International Inc., and Accountemps Worldwide, 2884 Sand Hill Rd., Menlo Park, California 94250.

How to Read Body Language

Reading other people depends very much on developing your ability to decipher non-verbal messages. In every exchange between people, messages are sent, through words and through the underlying dynamics of the non-verbal information—what you could call *subtext*...

Subtext can reinforce and strengthen the spoken text, or it may contradict the text, canceling out any verbal promises or agreements. It is a mixture of many different elements, including...

•Each person's body language—posture, hand movements, eye contact, etc.

•How a person handles space.

•How a person uses touch.

•Tone of voice.

•How a person dresses and his/her overall appearance.

•What a person does outside a conversation that confirms or contradicts what is said during the conversation.

Identifying honesty...

What is there in the subtext of a person that tells you he's not being honest about who he really is? Or...what he really thinks? Or...what he feels? There can be any number of elements.

Most important:

•Facial expression. Maybe he smiles at inappropriate times. A real, genuinely felt emotion causes a quick smile. If someone wants to fake an emotion, he'll hold the expression too long.

A genuine smile goes up into the eyes, and involves the top of the face.

A false smile just involves the bottom of the face and is usually not as wide as a real smile.

•Physiological responses. There is no one gesture that gives away a lie. But there are a lot of little physiological responses that go with a lie—certain gestures that are used consistently by many people.

Example: When a politician is about to tell a whopper, he'll usually rub the side of his nose with his finger. In the presidential debate between Carter and Reagan, both men did this at various points—Reagan, when he said he'd accomplish all his proposals without raising taxes! We don't know why this gesture is so consistent, but it is.

It's easiest to detect these bits of non-verbal information if you know the person well and you can identify abnormal or atypical behavior. Or, if you can observe his interactions with other people and compare them to his interactions with you.

•Look for discrepancies. *Examples:* Again, a smile that appears only on the lips, not on the rest of the face...smooth words backed by nervous mannerisms.

•Know your situation. If a business deal is a bad one, you're not going to find the flaws in the way the associate is behaving. You have to examine the deal itself. Abnormal behavior is really just a tip-off that you need to look at the situation more closely. You're not going to know that this person is putting over a phony deal unless you know what a good deal is and understand the whole situation.

In the same way, you're not going to become powerful by wearing power clothes. If you're a lawyer, you're not going to become competent by wearing an expensive gray suit.

You become competent by knowing your job. Then the gray suit may help a little.

Intuition...

One term we use for this ability to read cues is *intuition*—but it's not really that magical—it's a computer in our brains adding up all the little things that are wrong in a situation, judging the subtext of the whole.

I don't believe in mysticism. And I don't believe that intuition is a leap into uncharted realms, through some telepathic power. It is the summing up of all the little things that you know about a situation, and drawing a conclusion.

Example: If your intuition tells you that you shouldn't trust your company's management team and their promises for the future, then start job hunting immediately. Chances are you're picking up lots of tiny signals that your conscious mind doesn't even see, but your inner "computer"—the brain—does.

In general, women in our society are much more intuitive than men. *Reason:* Women are raised to be more nurturing than men. As a result, they take more time to learn about other people and to really understand what motivates them.

But anyone can cultivate their intuition. *First step:* Look for the subtexts in your interactions with other people—acquaintances and strangers. When you have a funny feeling about an individual or a situation, pay attention to it. Try and figure out exactly what bothers you and why. Often you can make an intuitive leap from there.

To improve your subtext...

It is possible to learn to cultivate your appearance and manage the impression you give to other people. This is why, for example, business people and politicians hire image consultants. Or why Donald Trump works so hard for publicity. If he didn't have that aura, I don't think that the banks would have given him the leeway to get himself into such financial trouble.

But while appearance is important, giving excessive importance to appearance doesn't make sense. There are people who aren't handsome who are really wonderful, lovely people. And a fancy exterior can't make up for an inner lack of ability or talent.

Although your appearance and subtext can help you communicate who you really are to others, the best message you can send in the world is that you're someone who knows what he's talking about. Understand your talents... and learn to use them at their highest levels. The self-confidence it gives you will be the best addition to your subtext that you can possibly make.

Source: Julius Fast, author of more than 30 books on the subjects of business and psychological communication. He is most famous for his best-selling book *Body Language*. His latest book is *Subtext: Making Body Language Work in the Workplace,* Viking Penguin, 365 Hudson St., New York 10014.

Modesty Traps

Being overly modest is as bad as unabashed bragging. In either case, the people who should be aware of your accomplishments either won't learn about them (if you're too modest) or won't believe you (if you brag). *Best:* Share your accomplishments matter-of-factly, in casual conversation. For example, tell how a customer was satisfied, a crisis averted, or a problem solved. And when someone compliments you, express your appreciation.

Source: Ted Pollack, management consultant, Old Tappan, New Jersey, writing in *Production*, 6600 Clough Pike, Cincinnati 45224.

What Leaders Do Best

Leaders make the people who follow them feel secure and give them a sense of harmony.

A leader should be able to:

- Handle social occasions well.
- Use stress constructively.
- Be smooth and unruffled in tense situations.
- Rally a group to a common goal.
- Feel comfortable when faced with diverse points of view.
- Make decisions that support independent behavior by members of the group within organizational limits.

•Learn more about individuals in the group to better match their tasks to their goals and abilities.

•Review recent decisions objectively. If too many were risk-free, it could be a danger sign that the leader is failing to lead.

Power Lunching

Power lunching tactics can turn a restaurant meal into an occasion to impress your lunch partner.

Power lunching aims to impress without letting the luncheon become a tasteless display of ego and one-upmanship.

Here are some tips:

•Patronize restaurants that have a reputation for business lunches and where you're known. Select restaurants with excellent service and plenty of space between tables. Eat in restaurants that important people frequent.

•Avoid luncheon invitations to other people's private dining rooms. You lose power on their turf.

•Call the maitre d' personally to make reservations. Tell him where you want to sit and how long you expect to stay. The more details you give the maitre d', the more his staff will be in tune with your needs.

•Don't order drinks served with a paper umbrella or a lot of vegetables or fruit. Draft beer is appropriate, but bottles look tacky. The "fancy waters" are wimpy now...club soda is a power drink.

•Order food that's easy to handle. *Example:* Steak instead of lobster so that you can do a lot of talking without fumbling. *Power foods:* Black bean soup, fresh oysters and clams, brook trout, calves' liver, London broil, paella, venison and gumbo. *Wimp foods:* French onion soup, fried oysters and clams, corned beef, coquilles St. Jacques, chicken a la King, lasagna, shrimp de jonghe.

•Pay the bill with cash, if possible. Next best is a house charge. You don't have to wait for a credit card to be processed. You can quickly sign the check and leave before your guest becomes anxious to get back to the office.

•Tip 20%.

Source: *Power Lunching* by E. Melvin Pinsel and Ligita Dienhart, Turnbull & Willoughby, Chicago.

If a Rival Beats You to A Promotion By a Hair

Assuming that you and your rival are very much alike in experience, education and service with the firm, you need to find out why you lost. The reasons can affect your future with the company. *Areas to explore:*

•Your rival appeared more committed to the company. Management judged you ready to bolt for a better opportunity.

•Your rival had a sponsor higher up in the company of whom you were unaware.

•Your boss personally prefers your rival's company.

•Your boss saw your rival as less of a threat to his job.

•You are being saved for something bigger down the road, but no one thought to tell you.

•You failed at an assignment that you thought was insignificant, but your boss judged you likely to fail again.

•You have been too active politically within the company outside your department.

•You are perceived as untrustworthy by some, or they question your loyalty to your boss.

Source: Marilyn Moats Kennedy, author of *Career Knockouts: How to Battle Back,* Follett Publishing Co.

Career Booster

Volunteer to serve at a charity fund-raiser. It's the quickest way to get to know the movers and shakers in your community.

Source: *The Sir Winston Method: The Five Secrets of Speaking the Language of Leadership* by communications consultant James C. Humes, William Morrow & Co., 1350 Avenue of the Americas, New York 10019.

Better Memo Writing

Good memos use lots of white space to make points more effectively. Instead of using long sentences, indent individual items. Place bullet symbols in front of each one. Do not use numbers, which indicate priority, unless you *intend* to prioritize. *Also useful:* Subheads for dealing with multiple topics. And insert dashes within an item to highlight it. Avoid parentheses—they break up the flow.

Source: *The Perfect Memo! Write Your Way to Career Success* by Patricia H. Westheimer, corporate writing trainer, La Jolla, California. Park Avenue Publications, 720 N. Park Ave., Indianapolis 46202.

Delegation Secrets

The first step in delegating is figuring out what you should give away. *Helpful:* Delegate tasks that do not require your expertise or judgment. When in doubt, ask yourself whether an activity will get you closer to your goal...if someone else could do it just as well...if your boss would mind if you give it to someone else...if anything really bad could happen if that person could not handle the work. Always package the delegated task so it looks like an opportunity. *Important:* Delegating work does not mean abandoning responsibility. You still should supervise work you have delegated to be sure it is done properly.

Source: *Why Good Girls Don't Get Ahead...But Gutsy Girls Do* by Kate White, editor-in-chief, *Redbook*. Warner Books, 1271 Avenue of the Americas, New York 10020.

Persuading Others... What It Takes

Virtually all successful people owe their success at least in part to their exceptional powers of persuasion. In fact, the ability to persuade is the single most common trait among successful people. *To build your power of persuasion...*

• Know the history of the idea you are presenting. Do thorough research before making the presentation so you know what decisions have been made in the past about alternative ideas, solutions, etc. Know what objections are likely to be raised—and prepare to answer them.

• Be clear about how your idea will help. This includes all of those directly and indirectly affected by your proposal. Find out what criteria are important in the area of work affected by your idea. Then present your option in a way that gives it a high rank among alternative options, given those criteria.

• Provide alternatives or "safety" actions as part of the proposal. This will minimize risks that may be perceived by your listener.

Example: Describe the checkpoints at which progress could be reevaluated—and where the project could be stopped, if necessary.

• Use concrete examples. Anecdotes are an extremely useful tool to help your audience understand your proposal.

• Dress appropriately. Avoid distracting attention from your message by your attire. When in doubt, go conservative.

• Be confident. Your audience will sense uncertainty if it is there. Look directly into the eyes of as many people as you can for about four or five seconds each. And be yourself. Most people who try to adopt a style that's not their own come across as artificial.

Source: Guy Hale, chairman, Alamo Learning Systems, a management training company based in San Ramon, California.

About Self-Control

Instead of blowing up when an employee does something that bothers you, stop...take a deep breath...and get your gut reaction under control. *Key:* If you fail to control your emotions, the people you work with will withhold information and offer suggestions only when they know that you are in a good mood.

Gain control by asking yourself: *Am I angry because I expected something different?...Does that matter?...What lies at the core of my feeling of anger, frustration, disappointment or bitterness?...Does it really bear on the specific situation or is it related to something else entirely?*

Source: William Hendricks, PhD, editor, *Coaching, Mentoring and Managing*. Career Press.

9

Developing Good Work Habits

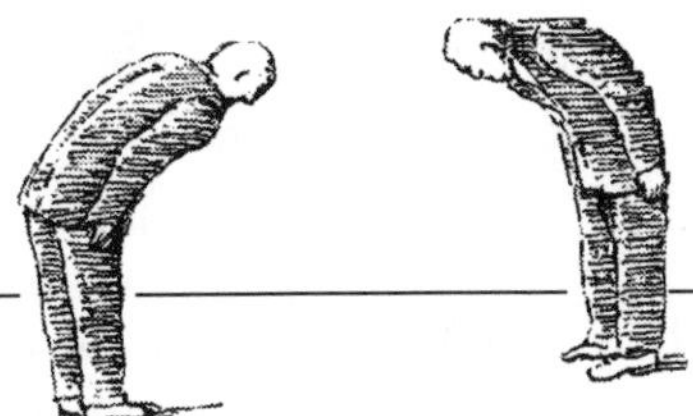

Meeting Mistake

Don't feel obligated to say something in a meeting because silence will be interpreted as ignorance. *Better:* Choose statements very carefully at the first few meetings. If what you say is well thought out and insightful, you will carry far more weight at future meetings. *Caution:* Do not use meetings to say uncomplimentary things about subordinates. This can undermine the department—and you, as its manager.

Source: *The First-Time Manager* by Loren Belker, a management trainer based in Escondido, California. Amacom, 135 W. 50 St., New York 10020.

Work and Self-Esteem

The "who/where/what we do" connection has created difficult problems for a growing number of people today who feel trapped in unsatisfying jobs. These people are afraid they won't be able to find another one...or they can't afford to lose seniority and pension rights...or they can't face the difficulty of relocating their families.

Problem: If you feel unappreciated or taken for granted or inadequately rewarded at work, it has an adverse effect on your work, your relationships with your boss and colleagues... and your own psychological and emotional well-being.

The unresolved anger that you feel in your job may spill over into your private life, with family and friends its innocent victims as you scream at the kids, kick the dog, knock down two fast martinis, etc.

Getting back on track...

Doing nothing only adds to feelings of anger, frustration and exploitation, and victimization will probably continue.

Helpful: Realize that because you have control over yourself, you have control over the situation. Then figure out what you can do to improve the situation. *Questions to ask...*

•*Am I appreciated?* The very fact that you have a job is an important sign that you are valued by your employer. If you're being paid more than people doing similar work elsewhere, that's another good sign.

•*Should I be appreciated?* If your work is marginal or if your achievement level is lower than colleagues in your unit, then it's not realistic to expect compliments and reassurances about the quality of your work.

Try to appraise your real contributions to your employer...and look for ways to bring those to management's attention.

In addition to self-appraisal, it's imperative to get frequent feedback from your boss. If your company doesn't have formal evaluations, request a meeting to discuss your job effectiveness. Work review sessions—in one form or another—should happen much more than once or twice a year, for they give you a good sense of whether you're on the right track.

Try to communicate with your boss about signs of appreciation. If he/she seems to be piling work on you or always giving you the tough tasks, you might interpret it as punishment, while your boss meant to show confidence in your ability. *It helps to talk these things out.*

Also ask colleagues what they think of your work. Assure them that you're not fishing for a compliment, but that you really need an objective appraisal.

You may find that you are far more respected than you realize—perhaps for talents or skills you didn't know you had. Team support is a two-way street. Remember to thank and congratulate coworkers when they have done something well, too.

Customers can also be a valuable source of recognition and job satisfaction. When they thank you for your promptness or effectiveness or thoughtfulness, accept the compliments graciously and tell them how much you appreciate the kind words.

But if someone *withholds* praise that you believe you deserve, do not let it cause you to lose confidence in yourself. There's nothing wrong with giving yourself a pat on the back—or a special reward.

Boredom—the bane of self-esteem...

We read frequently about the financial costs of smoking or substance abuse in the workplace, but we rarely hear about the costs of boredom.

Some of boredom's many manifestations: Indifference, anger, disillusionment, procrastination, gossiping, tardiness, absenteeism, and physical aches and pains—like headaches.

Bored individuals are not stimulated to go to work, to get there on time, to do the job promptly or well, or to remain loyal to the company. People who are bored because they feel their skills or talents aren't being adequately used often become resentful toward their employers.

Boredom is also a classic cause of stress. It is stressful to spend an eight-hour day in an unstimulating environment. It is stressful not to have the opportunity to work on challenging problems.

And, it is stressful to realize that you are not growing or developing or reaching the goals you set for yourself. We become spiritless, listless zombies whose minds are on hold.

Solutions to job boredom...

First admit that job boredom does exist and then take personal responsibility for overcoming your boredom.

Some suggestions:

•Create a log. Chart the activities that you find stimulating and those that are deadly dull. Include contextual information that might help identify whether you're truly bored or simply tired or depressed.

•Analyze your activities and look for patterns. After several weeks of keeping a log, analyze the data to see what patterns emerge. If meetings bore you but you feel stimulated while preparing for and delivering a sales presentation, it may be that you need to perform, to persuade, to be creative. Ask yourself how you can do more of this in your job.

•Reenergize your job. Balance routine, repetitive tasks with work that you find more stimulating. Wherever possible, shuffle the order, break boring patterns, and change locations. If you have a morning full of mind-deadening tasks, reward yourself by going out to lunch instead of brown-bagging it. Question whether all routine tasks are really necessary. Take occasional work breaks. Try to rotate jobs or swap responsibilities with a colleague to vary the monotony.

• Stretch—reach beyond your grasp. If you have mastered your job so that it no longer uses your full talents and abilities, ask for a new assignment or see if your job description could be broadened. *Alternative:* Transfer to a different job in another department.

• Welcome positive problems at work. Confronting and solving problems adds spice to a job. Finding solutions keeps us emotionally and intellectually alive.

• Shake it up—avoid complacency. If you've become too comfortable in your job, take a new look at it. Look for ways to improve cooperation. Set additional goals. *Bonus:* The fresh excitement new accomplishments generate.

• Do something new. Read new, relevant books. Attend a seminar, a workshop, a professional meeting, or an educational course. Create or design a new product, a new production process, a new marketing strategy, or a new information system and then try to "sell" it to management. Study Continuous Quality Improvement (CQI) to stimulate yourself by planning to do all that you do better—each time you do it.

• Develop a life outside of your job. Thoughts of how you will spend your free time away from the job can provide a mental escape from work that is boring. Pleasurable activities in private life can also provide the excitement and fulfillment that may be missing in your career—and maybe even add to it.

Coaching, reading, working on a political campaign, listening to music, volunteer work, sports and hobbies give balance and verve to your life and put you in control of your emotional well-being. Spend time with people who are energetic and enthusiastic, vital and vibrant ...and thoughtful about their life and work. *Learn from them.*

If it's impossible to eliminate boredom and reenergize your enthusiasm for the job, face the fact that it's time to move on. You've grown and changed and are now ready for new challenges...new beginnings...new dreams.

Source: John Sena, PhD, professor of English, and Stephen Strasser, PhD, associate professor, division of hospital and health services administration, both at Ohio State University. They are authors of *Work is Not a Four Letter Word*, Business One Irwin, 1818 Ridge Rd., Homewood, Illinois 60430.

How to Overcome Teamwork Blues

Teams and teamwork have become terms of worship in American business. Amazingly, though, neither works very well in most US companies. In fact, only 17% of managers and team members surveyed by Wilson Learning in 1992 said that teamwork was working well for their companies. The rest of the respondents said teamwork was mostly talk and little substance.

Probing further, Wilson Learning discovered what the companies that have succeeded in team-building have in common...

• They evaluate individuals on their effectiveness as team members. The vast majority of company performance appraisal systems still concentrate entirely on individual accomplishments—with no measures of team performance.

• They compensate managers and team members for their performance as members of teams—and for meeting defined goals.

• They reduce barriers to the free flow of important business information across functional lines in the company. Getting people to give up their urge to withhold information to bolster their status within the firm is a key factor in getting teams to function efficiently.

• They give teams clear goals and ensure that team members understand and are focused on those goals. *Too typical:* Management responds to pressure from consultants or managers who read about teams or go to seminars explaining how teams work by asserting how important it is for the company to adopt teamwork. But they fail to realize that teams are not an end in themselves. The most important factor in generating a team's effectiveness is the clarity of its objective and focus.

Mechanics of effective collaboration...

Once the company has clarified a team's goals, the team's effectiveness in meeting those goals depends on how well members work together.

Trap: Managers often stall team performance by getting too involved in working out team processes and techniques of team leadership. Instead, right from the start, management should focus on coaching team members to...

• Support themselves as individuals. This means encouraging them to advocate their own ideas and training them in ways to persuade others of their points of view. Too often, emphasis on not making waves and cooperating inhibits this essential training.

• Support others in the team. Valuing other people's styles for solving problems is essential to working well on a team. *Managing* conflict does not mean *reducing* conflict. On a team, efficiency often requires creating tension while at the same time effectively resolving conflict. Politeness alone won't suffice. Team members must learn how to air differences, tell hard truths, and ask hard questions of one another. When a team is not facing the core issues that prevent it from reaching its goal, its work will not move forward and creative solutions will not unfold.

• Support the team. Keep the goal in focus. Commit team members' energy to getting the team to work. Discourage those who try to undermine the team—or who simply refuse to "buy in" to the team spirit.

Bottom line...

Teams represent a valuable way for organizations to structure work processes. However, the key to success is getting people to work together toward common goals. Creating this collaborative environment is the challenge businesses face.

Source: Michael Leimbach, PhD, research director, Wilson Learning Corporation, developer and implementer of business training in management, quality, customer service and sales for companies around the world, 7500 Flying Cloud Dr., Eden Prairie, Minnesota 55344.

How to Increase Your Productivity

At an almost breathtaking pace, medical science is discovering new insights into human biology.

Used the right way, much of this new knowledge can help managers heighten workers' job satisfaction and increase their own productivity. *Major discoveries...*

Light and color secrets...

Researchers have found that light has a profound effect on our bodies. Though not completely understood, the reason is probably linked to the effect light has on two vital areas of the brain—the hypothalamus and the pineal gland.

Our moods, even those of color-blind people, are affected by the intensity and color of the light around us.

Examples: People brainstorm better when surrounded by bright colors. Subdued shades are usually best for negotiating. Red cars command higher prices.

Helpful: Use a consultant to help you decorate your office...and choose your wardrobe. The right color and lighting can raise output and make work more enjoyable. Wearing the right colors can also boost a sales rep's closing rate.

Where to find an expert: Most large management consulting firms can make recommendations. For color, try the Pantone Color Institute, 201-935-5501.

Also, bring more natural light into the workplace. Tests show that it has a positive impact on performance. There are lights available now that simulate natural light. For advice, consult a lighting engineer.

Sound secrets...

Women are far more sensitive to sound than men. They can also hear higher-pitch sounds. Some research suggests that women may even be subliminally sensitive to sounds beyond the conscious hearing range.

Example: Some scientists believe high-frequency tones given off by computer terminals can cause stress in women who use them. Harm may occur even though users aren't actually aware of the sound.

If your company has complaints from VDT users, consider hiring an acoustical engineer. The problem may be with the sound, not the light source.

Other research has discovered how we screen background noise from conversation that we want to hear.

Helpful: If you want someone's attention, don't talk more loudly, just move closer. Halving the distance quadruples the sound.

Smell secrets...

This may be the most exciting area of research. Science has discovered that odors have a profound effect on our moods and performance.

Examples: Exposure to apple-cinnamon may improve editing skills...fruit scents may induce women to make certain purchases...clove has a calming effect...and peppermint elevates mood and may relieve headaches.

Try scenting your office with various fragrances to find the ones that have the effect you want.

Helpful: Contact the Fragrance Foundation (212-725-2755). This organization tracks the latest research in the field and can put companies in touch with consultants.

Biorhythm secrets...

Each individual has a natural rhythm to his/her activities, but in a typical business environment we're all expected to arrive, work and eat at more or less the same times.

Helpful: Give yourself (and employees) more schedule flexibility. Experiment with having several snacks instead of one long meal. Take a midday nap if it helps rejuvenate you in the afternoon.

As far as possible within the demands of the business world, tell employees you're more interested in results than in when they're achieved.

Biorhythms are also affected by sunlight. If you must start work before sunup, take an outdoor break as early in the day as possible. It can boost your mood and productivity.

Keep a chart of your own cycles of high and low energy levels. Try to schedule meetings and other tasks accordingly.

Gender secrets...

The latest tests confirm again that women are biologically equipped to process a wider range of sensory information than men.

Women are less obsessed with beating out rivals and getting super-rich than men are. They want to succeed for the sake of personal emotional fulfillment.

Men are more prone to tunnel vision—aiming at destroying their enemies quickly. Women, by contrast, see the broader picture and strategize better for long-term success.

Despite these differences between the sexes, managers don't have to plan one set of tasks for women and another for men. Instead, be attuned to using the assets of each to the best advantage.

Example: When assembling a project team, try to include a balance of men and women. If you don't, chances are greater that the team will overlook an important strategy, side-effect, market, or other opportunity.

Age secrets...

As people grow older, their gender-hormone levels decline. In women, declining estrogen during menopause can bring on irritability and forgetfulness. In men, declining testosterone levels can cause low energy levels and loss of concentration.

If you manage people who show these symptoms, help them find support. And do the same for yourself if you're nearing 50.

Helpful: To increase productivity and job satisfaction among older workers, offer to redesign offices for them—provide softer colors, comfortably built chairs, equipment with large enough displays to be seen by someone with less than great vision.

Brain secrets...

Science is rapidly discovering that while the brain has many similarities to a computer—which stores and processes information—the brain also *interprets* information.

Not appreciating this difference has led many companies to rely too heavily on computers.

The brain works in a way that usually makes it easier to remember what we read in a book than what we see on computer screens.

Example: You probably have a good idea of where in this issue of *Facts of Life* the chapter entitled "Very Personal" appears. But you would have much less of an idea if you had scrolled through the chapters on a computer.

Recommended: Ask for advice from a neuropsychologist or neurobiologist at a local university whenever the company is developing or revising training programs. Their expertise about how people learn can be valuable in making training techniques much more effective.

Source: Edith Weiner, president, Weiner, Edrich, Brown, Inc., futurists and strategic planning consultants, 200 E. 33 St., New York 10016. She is also coauthor of the very useful and insightful new book, *Office Biology,* MasterMedia Ltd., 17 E. 89 St., New York 10128.

Business/Career Resolutions... Just in Time

Today, knowing the right way to behave in business is more than polite. It's a vital strategy for keeping clients and customers and for getting ahead.

Based on interviews with top executives, as well as an analysis of 108 surveys by human-resource professionals, here are 12 fundamental business protocol rules you should follow...

1. Cultivate new business...and maintain contact with old clients/customers...and fulfill current work assignments. Keep up with your customers throughout the year—and remember them during the holidays. Interest in others goes a long way to promote business success.

• Stanley Heilbronn, first vice president at Merrill Lynch, makes it his business to keep in touch with his clients: "If there's an article in a magazine or newspaper that I think would be of interest to them, I scribble a note right on the top—and keep the information flow to clients constant."

2. Be courteous, positive, and upbeat regardless of how you or your company is doing. Especially in these challenging economic times, customers and associates want to be around those who work even harder because times are tough. They avoid pessimists and complainers. For similar reasons, if things are going well, be humble—don't brag.

3. Accept criticism graciously. Give it carefully, preceding and following it with something positive.

• J. Douglas Phillips, senior director of corporate planning at Merck & Co.: "Look for the positive within the negative situation."

4. Sexist/racist/ethnic slurs/jokes and actions are unacceptable.

5. Say "thank you." Drop a note or send flowers, fruit, or another appropriate gift to someone who sends business your way.

• Nella Barkley, president of Crystal-Barkley Corporation, a career-consulting firm: "Make thank-you's timely and very appropriate to the occasion and the person—never pro forma. A warm, personal note or follow-up phone call with news about what happened as a result of a referral will mean much more to the recipient than a standard gift ordered by your secretary."

6. Be discreet about company business or secrets—and the intimate details of your personal life.

• Mitchell P. Davis, editor at Broadcast Interview Source, an information publisher: "People don't want to hear about your problems. They want to hear about opportunities. That's why they're in business."

7. Cultivate friendships at work and with customers. It helps to create a very pleasant workplace. It also enhances productivity, since work friends provide emotional support and comradery and network with each other. But exercise discretion in work-based friendships.

• Marsha Londe, director of corporate accounts, Shadco Advertising Specialities: "You don't have to spill your guts to make a friend."

8. Dress appropriately. Even at companies with new "dress down" codes of more casual dress, it's still important to dress to impress.

• Irene Cohen, chairman, Corporate Staffing Alternatives, Inc., a human-resource management company: "If you're in a business where letting down your guard in terms of dress code for even one day, for one hour, could make a difference with a customer, client, or applicant, don't do it. Business is too important in this economy to take this kind of risk."

9. Use proper written and spoken language. Scrutinize your memos, proposals, reports, and letters. Are you proud of the way your correspondence and written communications look and read? Are your letters too long? Show concern for others, who are also very busy, and keep written communications as brief and clear as possible. While it's usually harder to write a short, lucid letter, it's easier on the person receiving it. For the same reasons, keep your phone conversations succinct. However, include enough appropriate "chitchat" so you continue to build your business relationships. Most importantly, avoid foul language.

10. Be on time. Arriving at work on time in the morning, or turning in a report when it's due, shows you're a good time manager, a necessary trait in today's competitive workplace. It also shows you put others before yourself—another attribute of the successful businessperson—since lateness usually involves inconveniencing others.

•Lucy Hedrick, time-management consultant: "By being on time, you're saying that the person you have an appointment with is important to you."

Return phone calls within 24 hours, if possible. Try to answer letters immediately, but definitely within a week.

11. Start planning now, so next year's holiday cards, gifts, and parties are extra special.

•Mary Kent, photographer, likes to design a holiday card that can serve as a mailing piece throughout the year: "In these hard economic times, we have to think in those terms."

•Nona Aguilar, director of a money-management service for women, has figured out a special gift for her clients with substantial net worth: "They receive a letter saying that I'm paying to send an inner-city kid to the country for two weeks *in their names.*"

12. Be concerned with others. Concern for others should include customers, coworkers, superiors, and subordinates.

•Dorothy Paleologos, director, strategic planning for information technology for Aetna Insurance: "What we are selling are promises and the trust relationship that underlies those promises, and that the company is going to look after a client's best interest when it makes good on those commitments."

Source: Jan Yager, PhD, is a Stamford, Connecticut-based business-protocol and executive-communication consultant and speaker. She is the author of 10 books, most recently *Business Protocol: How to Survive & Succeed in Business,* John Wiley & Sons, 605 Third Ave., New York 10158.

How to Safeguard Your Job

When employees read about the millions of Americans who have lost their jobs in the current economy, they wonder how secure their own positions are.

They're right to wonder. If a company is concerned about financial survival, the first area to be cut is jobs.

While I believe that the worst of the employment crisis is over—that we're headed for a positive turnaround within one to two years—large and mid-sized companies are still spooked ...and still trying to cut back to "fighting weight" after the wild expansion of the 1980s.

In this climate, your job becomes more than the duties you were hired to do. It's now imperative to safeguard your job.

Even though you may be operating with smaller support staff and be busier than ever, you must take the steps now that will make you invaluable to your company—someone it can't afford to let go.

Warning signs...

When jobs in your company are in danger, you can see it...if you look. Many people close their eyes to the signals and deny reality. But denial is not a good survival skill. *Signals that your job may be on the line:*

•You or your department has been losing accounts...you're now just holding steady—rather than gaining back lost business.

•You're being left out of the communications loop. Your supervisors may have stopped including you in meetings. Or you may sense that you no longer have access to the grapevine...that informal sources of information are drying up.

•An outsider is called in—someone who looks grim and doesn't socialize. Since no company likes to fire its own people, a large organization is likely to turn over the dirty work to a consultant from outside the company...or someone from the head office, if the company is a subsidiary.

The best time to put survival strategies in place is before your job is in imminent danger. By the time you notice the warning signs, the decision to fire may already have been made.

No matter how late you develop them, the following strategies will help you build alliances with others in the industry. And if you should lose your job, these skills will help you get—and keep—a new one.

Guiding principles for job survival...

•Strengthen your relationship with your boss...and your boss's boss. Imagine that the fate of the company depends on your activities during the next few months. What would you do? Do those things now.

•Think creatively about ways to generate business. Examine past successes and build on them. Look for old projects that you can expand on or old clients you can call.

•Actively gather information. Read journal articles and conference reports. Discuss developments with others in your company—and industry. Brainstorm. Share what you're doing with your superiors.

Example: "I'd like to look into projects we've done in the last few years and see how we can piggyback on them." Or, "Here's what I've been thinking. We could have a focus group with our suppliers"..."We could continue with the project, part two"..."We could talk about a different kind of extended credit."

Bonus: If you do fall victim to "downsizing," your research will keep you up-to-date on where the opportunities are in your industry.

•Analyze the past. Examine projects that lost money, and find out where errors occurred. Look for ways to protect the company next time.

•Build morale. If you're naturally sociable, capitalize on that by organizing low-cost celebrations to boost your department's spirits.

Examples: A Labor Day picnic...a free concert in the park...a trip to a ball game to celebrate the end of a project.

•Treat your boss like a human being. For fear of appearing too eager or desperate, some employees practically ignore their bosses, except to follow orders. But at work, as in every other situation, people are your best resource. You should put as much energy into developing work relationships as you put into the technical aspects of your job.

Bosses, like everyone else, need to be appreciated. When your boss handles something difficult in a way you admire, say so. Bosses also need to be heard. So develop your listening skills.

Example: Look for an opportunity to say, "As you look ahead to the next few months, what do you see?" Ask how you can help your boss get there. Then let him/her talk for 10 minutes or so—without telling your own story or offering advice.

•Expand your network. Make sure your boss is not the only superior with whom you have a relationship. Pay attention to company reports and newsletters to find out who's doing what. Riding in the elevator or passing someone in the hall can be an opportunity to discuss what's going on.

•Improve yourself. What do you need to know in order to do your job even better? Don't wait—learn it now. If your company is exploring overseas markets, take a course in one of those country's languages. If your public speaking needs work, join Toastmasters or give presentations for your professional association. If you're dissatisfied with your appearance, get someone to go shopping with you...or use an image consultant.

•Enrich your personal life. The more stressful your job, the more you need nonprofessional, creative outlets—to lift your mood, give you a feeling of achievement, and keep your job in perspective.

Examples: Start a woodworking project...sew a quilt...join a community choir.

If the job is lost...

It's not the end of the world. Many, many people find that once they get past the initial shock, a job loss leads to opportunities they never imagined.

Make the most of the contacts and information you have been gathering. Even if every company in your industry is laying off people in your type of position, employers must still get these skills somewhere—you may be valuable to them as a consultant.

This may also be your chance to evaluate whether you'd like to change careers—or make a renewed commitment to your current career.

Source: Adele Scheele, PhD, career consultant, 225 W. 83 St., New York 10024. She is the author of *Skills for Success,* Ballantine Books, 201 E. 50 St., New York 10022.

Avoid Sabotaging Your Own Success...or Else

Why do some seemingly sensible people act in ways that harm their own interests?

They set out to succeed but somewhere along the way they either misjudge how to achieve their goals...do not want to face criticism and failure...or defeat themselves with the intention of hurting someone else. The most common types of self-defeating behavior and how to avoid them...

Deliberate miscalculation...

Most of us go through life trying to overcome the hurdles set in our way. We avoid doing things that slow us down or increase the odds of failure. Those who exhibit self-defeating behavior choose strategies that will backfire.

Poor decisions are made either because of overconfidence or because the desire for a short-term gain is stronger than the appeal of a long-term goal.

Example I: Jane wanted to study clinical psychology in graduate school. After her initial application was rejected, she decided to show the school she was really a desirable prospect by taking a few courses as a nondegree student at her own expense...a good strategy if carried out correctly. But instead of demonstrating her prowess by taking subjects in which she could easily get A's, she took the hardest courses she could find and scored only C's...dooming her graduate school hopes.

Jane miscalculated because she was overconfident. Had she estimated her strengths and weaknesses more realistically, her chance of success would have been much greater.

Example II: Gary was happily married and prosperous. For many years, he indulged his hearty appetite for eating, drinking and smoking but avoided exercise. Not surprisingly, he suffered a heart attack while only in his early 50s. When the doctor told him he had to change his lifestyle, he did so...for a time.

But after just three months, Gary decided he couldn't do without his vices. Two years later, he had another heart attack...this one fatal.

While it doesn't always lead to such unfortunate results, the same kind of poor trade-off between present benefits and future costs is found in many kinds of self-destructive behaviors—drug addiction...excessive sun exposure...overdependence on credit cards...even procrastination.

To avoid miscalculation mistakes: Evaluate your strengths and weaknesses and the long-term costs and benefits of your actions as realistically as you possibly can...and try to consider all the alternatives.

Trying to avoid the truth...

Many forms of self-defeating behavior occur because people don't want to admit their limitations. They sabotage their own success in ways like these:

- Self-handicapping. This occurs when successful people deliberately construct obstacles for themselves so they will have an excuse for failure.

Example: Whenever French chess champion Deschapelles played, he insisted on giving his opponent the advantage of removing one of Deschapelles' pawns and taking the first move.

Result: Deschapelles increased his chance of losing...but always had a good excuse if he lost.

- Substance abuse. Alcohol and/or drug abuse serves two purposes for self-destructive people. It helps them blot out their own faults and inadequacies...and gives them an external excuse for failure.

Example: A well-known musician won a coveted competition to become a national hero. But within a few years, his reputation sank as he turned to drugs and was eventually arrested after breaking into a hotel room.

Reason: Great fame at an early age creates great expectations in audiences...and great stress in performers. Drugs eased the stress Fodor felt and provided an excuse for his failure to perform adequately—but allowed him to believe in his musical ability.

To face the truth: Develop a sense of perspective on yourself, recognize your imperfections and learn to accept criticism.

The quest for revenge...

Sometimes self-defeating behavior is a misguided attempt to redress emotional wounds inflicted in childhood.

Example: Despite obvious talent, Stuart, aged 36, would break rules...steal...drink on the job...in an obvious manner that was sure to be detected. Then his supervisor would reprimand him and threaten his job.

This replicated a pattern from Stuart's childhood, when his father would beat him. After the beating, while Stuart was sobbing, his alarmed mother would scream at his father until his father withdrew into a state of depression. Thus Stuart would enjoy the sweet taste of victory over his father...even though he was in physical agony himself.

I call this self-defeating strategy "Pyrrhic revenge," after the famous "victory" of the Greek king Pyrrhus, who won a battle against the Romans but almost wiped out his whole army in the process.

Pyrrhic revenge is typically found in marriages in which one spouse suffered abuse as a child...often from an alcoholic parent. He seeks out a partner who has the same problem his parent had. He tries to correct the problem and, in doing so, cure his own childhood wounds. This usually doesn't work, so instead he ends up venting the long-repressed anger against the parent...and doesn't mind destroying himself as long as his spouse goes down, too.

To avoid self-destruction via revenge: Realize your own interests...judge whether you are acting to help yourself or to hurt someone else.

Choking under pressure...

Choking is a self-defeating behavior that occurs when people under pressure, striving to do their best, fail because they try too hard to succeed and do not perform as well as they can.

Example: Beth, an outstanding student, had to recite a speech from Shakespeare in front of her high-school class. After memorizing it perfectly, she stood up to speak...and nothing came out.

Reason: Smoothly speaking memorized lines is an automatic process. Beth wanted so intensely to succeed that her self-consciousness prevented her memory from working naturally.

The same phenomenon causes sports champions to falter in important matches and winning teams to lose championship games.

To avoid choking under pressure: Develop perspective. Remind yourself that success in life doesn't depend on just one event.

Example: If it's the last minutes of an important event or presentation, and victory or defeat depends on your next move, remember that just being there shows that you already are a success.

Source: Steven Berglas, PhD, clinical psychologist and management consultant, Harvard Medical School, Boston. He is coauthor with Roy F. Baumeister, PhD, of *Your Own Worst Enemy: Understanding the Paradox of Self-Defeating Behavior,* Basic Books, New York.

How to Win at Telephone Tag

Telephone tag, the seemingly endless cycle of calls and returned calls that are missed, is one of the more time-consuming frustrations of executive life. Beat the frustration by organizing your telephone tactics.

If the person you want to talk with isn't in, and you do want him to call you back:

• Leave a detailed message of the subject of the call.

• Note a time span when you'll definitely be available.

• Make a phone appointment—a specific time when the party can reach you.

• Tell the secretary that no reply will be an assumed consent or agreement.

If you don't want the other party to call back:

• Ask for a specific time when he/she will be available, so you can try again.

• Find out if the person can be paged.

• Request that the secretary relay the information to your secretary, keeping the bosses out of the phone process.

Source: *Execu-Time,* Box 631, Lake Forest, IL 60045.

Simple Ways to Reduce Job Stress

Job-related psychological stress takes an enormous toll on Americans. It affects one of every five workers in this country...and costs our economy billions and billions of dollars a year in absenteeism, lost productivity, and medical expenses—including expenses caused by accidents and alcoholism, both of which often originate in stress. Stress produces a remarkable variety of emotional and psychological symptoms.

Typical: Rapid heart rate and/or breathing... stammering...a sense of isolation from colleagues...headaches, stomachaches and chest pain...reduced sex drive...stomach upset, diarrhea, and other gastrointestinal problems ...chronic fatigue and insomnia...sweating... proneness to accidents...ulcers...and even drug addiction.

If you suffer from one or more of these symptoms—or if a coworker or family member remarks that you seem irritable or ill—it's time to evaluate the stress in your work life... and, if necessary, take steps to alleviate it.

The costs of chronic stress...

Untreated chronic stress leads not only to burnout, but also to heart attack, stroke, and other deadly health problems.

Workers often try to control their job stress via nonpsychological approaches—exercise, hobbies, vitamin pills, special diets, vacations, etc. While these approaches are healthful and might afford temporary relief, they eventually fail. In fact, such approaches often wind up increasing stress levels.

Example: A man who jogs every day to reduce stress feels even more anxious than usual if for some reason he must forgo jogging even for a day.

Bottom line: Stress is a psychological problem, and it can be fully controlled only by a psychological approach. I believe that the best way to do this is to recognize the 12 types of myths that cause job stress...and to systematically replace these myths with attitudes that are healthy and more realistic.

Stress-causing myths...

Myth 1. Something awful will happen if I make a mistake. *Reality:* Mistakes in the workplace may be a source of embarrassment and frustration, but rarely do they lead to anything more dire than a reprimand. The lesson sounds trite, but it's wise—don't fear mistakes, learn from them.

Myth 2. There's a right way and a wrong way to do everything. *Reality:* What's right for one person or situation is often not right for another. Mistakes are common in business, and they seldom result in tragedy. In fact, many excellent business decisions appear at first blush to be enormous blunders.

Myth 3. Being criticized is awful. *Reality:* Criticism—of oneself and of others—is central to personal growth. Being criticized is not tantamount to failing, and the process should never be viewed as something to be endured. Instead, workers should welcome criticism as a learning opportunity. *Note:* Do not accept criticism that is abusive or disrespectful.

Myth 4. I need approval from those around me. *Reality:* While you might welcome praise for a job well done, you don't really need "positive strokes" to be an effective, fulfilled worker. Expecting praise in a work environment where it is rarely forthcoming can lead to disappointment and frustration.

Myth 5. I must always be viewed as competent. *Reality:* No one is good at everything. Even if you were perfect, there is no guarantee that your coworkers would admire you. How others view you lies entirely within their control. Worrying about your image only sets the stage for anxiety and more frustration.

Myth 6. People in authority must not be challenged. *Reality:* Most superiors are willing to listen to their subordinates' complaints and criticisms—if these are presented fairly and constructively. In fact, many bosses welcome complaints because they suggest better ways to do things. If you're inclined to confront your superior, do so. Even if you don't get all you want, the act of speaking out releases emotions that might otherwise lead to anger and resentment.

Myth 7. The workplace is essentially fair and just. *Reality:* Hoping for total fairness at work is not only unrealistic, it's not even desirable. Some of the best and most productive business solutions result from controversy and argumentation, which may seem unfair at the time.

Myth 8. I must always be in control. *Reality:* The notion that you can easily meet every deadline and fill every quota is appealing, but it only sets you up for frustration and stress. Even the best routines and systems break down occasionally. Rather than worrying about control, focus upon what you're doing...and what you want out of life.

Myth 9. I must anticipate everything. *Reality:* Surprises are inevitable on the job as in other parts of life. Sensing things before they happen and gauging colleagues' "vibrations" certainly makes good sense—but remember, you are dealing with probabilities, not foregone conclusions.

Myth 10. I must have my way. *Reality:* Good salaries, beautiful offices, and prestigious positions don't come easily—in fact, they may never come. No doubt there will be setbacks along the way. Effective workers do their work conscientiously without insisting upon immediate realization of their goals. Certainly you can strive toward such goals. Just don't demand them as conditions of continued employment.

Myth 11. Workers who make mistakes must be punished. *Reality:* An effective workplace calls for effective teamwork...and teamwork is impossible when employees are continually trying to assign or escape blame.

Essential for workers: Acceptance, tolerance, patience, allowance for imperfections—in yourself as well as in others.

Myth 12. I need a shoulder to cry on. *Reality:* A compassionate coworker is often helpful in difficult times—but not essential. Workers who resent not having one only cultivate their own self-pity and dampen the morale of themselves and of people around them.

Source: Samuel H. Klarreich, PhD, vice president of Mainstream Access Corp., a Toronto-based consulting firm. He is the author of several books on stress, including *Work Without Stress: A Practical Guide to Emotional and Physical Well-Being on the Job*, Brunner Mazel Inc., 19 Union Square West, New York 10003.

Secrets of Working Much More Effectively

Being ineffective at work can lead to a downhill spiral...especially these days.

We derive a lot of our self-esteem from doing a good job and being rewarded for it. An unhappy work situation diminishes our self-esteem...and decreases our ability to work effectively.

The best way to stay effective—or become more effective—is to learn to spot the reasons for the problem.

Ineffectiveness traps...

• *Trap:* Stale technical know-how. People who haven't kept up with their basic field—whether it's engineering or sales—know less and less every year. They wind up living off their intellectual capital and eventually go bankrupt.

Fifty years ago, increased wisdom, maturity and judgment would have compensated. But today, the actual basic knowledge—the theory, practice and machinery in any field—becomes obsolete quite quickly.

Remedy: Read the latest books on relevant subjects in your field. Take refresher and training courses. Visit competitors. Read the key journals and trade magazines. Talk to the bright young stars in the company about the weird ideas that they're into...some of those ideas will become the tools of your trade in five years.

• *Trap:* Failure to maintain a network. When most people start a job, they put a lot of effort into networking. They look for mentors and take challenging and highly visible assignments.

But after many years at the same firm, their networks begin to deteriorate. Some people become so isolated that new people in the firm wonder who they are...and why anyone wants to have them around. The worst offenders are introverts, especially technical types, who don't like socializing.

Remedy: Keep up your contacts. Schedule at least one useful contact into each day. Consider this part of your work.

You can't create a network the instant that you need one. In times of reorganization or retrenchment, your network can make all the difference between whether or not you survive.

The bigger your network, the better. You never know who can help you.

• *Trap:* Inappropriate transfer. People often become ineffective after they're moved from a job that matches their talents to one that doesn't.

Example: Joette, a people person, managed a large department of a big company. After the firm reorganized, she was assigned to a technical job that she hated. Although she tried to do the new job, she became more and more frustrated and unhappy, until she was finally fired.

This is a big problem for people who are passive. They may have gotten along by going along. But that only works as long as good choices are made for them.

Remedy: Assume a tough renegotiation stance. Most companies won't force you to do an inappropriate job...but you have to stick up for yourself. *Exception:* Companies that are shy on firing may pressure people to quit by giving them jobs that they hate. Tough renegotiation makes it more likely that employees will at least get good severance and leave feeling good about themselves.

• *Trap:* Change of boss. Doing a good job under one boss doesn't mean you can work effectively with a new one.

Remedy: If the new boss is flawed—but redeemable, be a good lieutenant and work to help him/her succeed. It could give your career a big boost.

During this process however, look into lateral transfer opportunities. And think about your options outside the company.

More steps to take...

Make a careful analysis of what is going on in your job. *Ask yourself:*

• In what areas am I ineffective?

• Are my expectations too high?

• Is there enough challenge and opportunity for advancement?

• Do I have too much or too little work?

• What kind of relationship do I have with my boss and coworkers?

• Why does this job contrast so bleakly with other, more positive experiences?

• What are the ways in which this job doesn't meet my needs or that I don't measure up to it?

Once you've analyzed where the problem is, think through a strategy to increase your effectiveness.

Speak with coworkers and your boss about the dilemma. Get feedback. Your analysis of the problem may be wrong.

If you can't be open with anyone in your company, speak to people in comparable positions at other companies. Find out how they deal with the issues you're facing.

Give yourself a time limit to experiment with your strategy. *Suggested:* Six months. After the time runs out, don't sit around and get more depressed. Start looking aggressively for something else.

Source: Martin G. Groder, MD, a psychiatrist and business consultant in Chapel Hill, North Carolina. His book, *Business Games: How to Recognize the Players and Deal with Them,* is available from Boardroom Classics, 55 Railroad Ave., Greenwich, CT 06830.

Office Gift-Giving Etiquette

Giving the wrong gift can be worse than giving no gift at all—so here's how to give the right one...

•Avoid inappropriate gifts. Humor can backfire, so beware of giving a gag gift. Cash is only appropriate for tipping garage attendants, hairdressers and others in service positions—not for coworkers. Some gifts are always in poor taste —liquor...perfume and other intimate items... jewelry, neckties and other items that impose your taste.

•Don't be extravagant. While there's nothing wrong with generosity, going overboard on a gift will only make the recipient feel uncomfortable. For peers and subordinates, I recommend spending no more than $25. If you and the recipient have a special relationship or if you've worked together for many years, then it's fine to spend more.

Caution: Giving your boss a fancy gift can be interpreted as inappropriate by peers and by the boss. If you want to give him/her something, stick to a small, tasteful gift, such as well-chosen and well-presented flowers or even a simple handwritten note.

•Wrap the gift beautifully. Pretty wrapping paper makes even a modest gift seem truly special. Be sure to enclose a thoughtful note, written in ink on personal stationery. Avoid platitudes like "Thanks for your support last year." Be more specific—and creative, too.

•Present the gift in person. Mailing the gift, leaving it on a doorstep or having someone else deliver it suggests a lack of sincerity on your part. Magazine subscriptions and other items that cannot be delivered in person should be announced via a card that you hand deliver. Gifts that you receive should be acknowledged with a written thank-you note within one week.

•Keep a permanent gift record. It will help you avoid the embarrassment of presenting two coworkers with the same gift or giving the same gift twice to the same coworker. *Remember:* The gift you select today sets a precedent for future gifts. If you give your secretary an expensive gift this year, for example, don't expect him/her to be satisfied with an inexpensive trinket next year.

Source: Mary Monica Mitchell, president of *Uncommon Courtesies,* a Philadelphia-based consulting firm that teaches etiquette and international protocol to business executives. Box 40186, Philadelphia 19106.

Better Business Relationships

Good intentions don't count in a business relationship. Neither do feelings or attitudes... *unless they are reflected in overt action.* Relationships are defined by *behavior*—what each party does for and to the other.

Source: *Overcoming Resistance: A Practical Guide to Producing Change in the Workplace* by management consultant Jerald M. Jellison, PhD, based in Los Angeles. Simon & Schuster, 1230 Avenue of the Americas, New York 10020.

Leaving the Office At the Office

It's important to learn to separate your professional from your private life. Particularly today, when the business world seems more fast-paced than ever, this can be hard to do. In the now famous quote of a hard-driving executive: "Nobody ever said on his deathbed, 'I wish I had spent more time at the office.'" Bear in mind that work has its busy seasons and its peak periods. Then, and during ambitious times such as a business start-up, it may not be appropriate to think of leaving the office behind every day. But that shouldn't always be the case. Balance is the goal to work toward.

•Make a conscious effort to change your mind-set when you are not at work. Clues that your head is still at the office: You chafe because the host is slow in moving you and other guests to the dining table...You make an agenda before going out to spend the afternoon with your child and stick to the agenda even when something more interesting intrudes. These are business mind-sets inappropriate to nonoffice activities.

•Give yourself a steady stream of physical cues to help you separate your office from your private world. Don't wear a watch on weekends. If you feel time pressures even when you're at home, don't use digital clocks in the car or home. They pace off the seconds and minutes too relentlessly for many people.

•Change your clothes as soon as you get home. And if you feel naked without your dictating machine or your briefcase with you at home, experiment with feeling naked!

•Use your physical setting to help you keep work in its place. Tell yourself that you can work only at a particular place at home if you must work. Don't take papers to bed with you. Don't spread them out over the couch, the dining table and the floor.

•Relax before plunging into housework or domestic activities. Working women especially have trouble giving themselves a 10-minute break when they get home because they're inclined to feel anxious about talking with the children or starting dinner. Take the break. It can make all the difference between experiencing the rest of the evening as a pleasure or as yet another pressure.

•Rituals are a useful device for making the switch. Secretaries do this by tidying up the desk or covering the typewriter. Lyndon Johnson symbolically turned off the lights in the Oval Office when he left. For managers, some useful rituals are loosening ties or other constricting clothing, turning a calendar page or making a list of things to do for the next day. They all help make the break. The to-do list also helps curb the desire to catch up on tomorrow's tasks while you're at home.

•Resist the growing tendency to abuse the whole winding-down process by taking up activities that create problems of their own...compulsive sex...addictive exercise...overeating or overdrinking...recreational drugs. *Better:* Use the transition time as a period of discovery. Walk or drive home along a different route. Pick up something new at the newsstand instead of the usual evening paper.

...The other side of leaving the office at the office is to leave home at home. It may be productive to use lunchtimes to buy paint, but that's not helpful in keeping the two worlds separate.

Source: Dr. Marilyn Machlowitz, Machlowitz Associates, a management development firm, New York.

How to Give Productive Criticism

Although criticism is destructive if it is used to hurt, belittle, shame, insult or embarrass another person or if it is used to make someone look good or feel powerful, it can be used as a tool for positive change.

Needed: The ability to give criticism in a positive, productive manner.

To criticize constructively...

•Think strategically. Plan your criticism in advance. Take responsibility for how and what you communicate. Avoid sarcasm, blame or accusation.

Plan exactly what you want to change, and ask yourself *why?* How can you best say this so the person you're criticizing will be receptive? What solutions and goals can you offer? How can you help? What is a realistic time frame in which to expect change?

Example: A woman who works for you delivers a proposal at a meeting. But it's too long, detailed and dry.

Ineffective: "I thought you'd never finish...I almost fell asleep."

Better: "Nice job." *Then, the next day, say:* "I've been thinking...your research was so exhaustive, you may have lost a few of us early on. Next time, you might find it more effective to come to the point right away—grab our attention. Then just summarize the statistics."

•Time the criticism properly. Pay attention to the time, place and emotional state of the person you need to criticize. *Very important:* Don't criticize when other people are present.

Ineffective: "Skip the statistics and just get on with it."

Better: "I see you've done excellent research. But would you mind summarizing your statistics for those of us with limited time? Please distribute copies to the marketing people after the meeting."

•Concentrate on how the person can improve. People naturally feel more confident if it's clear that they will have a chance to improve.

Ineffective: "Your proposal was a disaster. You'll never get anywhere."

Better: "Your research gives us a firm base to build on, and your conclusions are sound. Let's develop a strategy from here."

•Protect the person's self-esteem. You want to help, not attack.

Ineffective: "You took forever to get to the point."

Better: "It's hard to cover such thorough research in a staff meeting. Next time, provide the tables in a hand-out so we can study the numbers in detail later."

•Be interactive. Allow the person you are criticizing to respond.

Ineffective: "You spent so much time on the statistics, you lost sight of the big picture. You'll never get ahead that way."

Better: "Next time, I'd like you to concentrate more on the big picture and less on the details. How else could you tighten your presentation and make it more lively?"

•Be flexible. Communicate from an advisory, teaching stance, rather than from an authoritative one, which provokes resistance. Avoid rigid *should* statements that imply your way is the only right way.

Ineffective: "You should only describe the highlights of your research."

Better: "If you think it's important to back up your conclusions in detail, let's find a way to help you do it more quickly."

•Communicate the helping spirit. Criticism is much easier to accept if the recipient thinks the critic is concerned with his/her welfare and growth.

Ineffective: "You made our whole department look silly."

Better: "Next time, I'll ask Jack in graphics to design an attractive cover for your research report, and you can distribute it before the meeting."

•Identify your criteria. Blanket criticisms do not work.

Ineffective: "No one liked your report."

Better: "Your data was useful to the marketing staff. But the sales staff gets bored in meetings that don't apply to them."

•Offer specific solutions or direction for improvement. Show the person you want to help.

Ineffective: "You need to cut your material in half."

Better: "Open with your project description and highlight the benefits. Then summarize the research."

•Come up with an incentive. What's in it for the person you're criticizing?

Ineffective: "Do it...or else."

Better: "You'll be in line for a promotion if you improve your meeting skills."

•Include the positives. Give the person something to feel good about.

Ineffective: "You didn't do anything right."

Better: "Your attention to detail has always been one of your great strengths. We know we can trust you if you tell us the research backs up your conclusions."

•Get a commitment for action. A timetable will motivate the person to act.

Ineffective: "You've simply got to improve."

Better: "When can I see a revised report?"

•Follow up. If you notice improvement, acknowledge it.

Ineffective: "Who's next?"

Better: "Thank you, that was an excellent report."

Source: Psychologist Hendrie Weisinger, PhD, a specialist in anger management and criticism. Dr. Weisinger teaches at UCLA's Anderson Graduate School of Management and conducts seminars. He is the author of *The Critical Edge*, HarperCollins, 10 E. 53 St., New York 10022.

How to Reduce Stress At Your Desk

You'll get more work done and feel better if you make your working environment comfortable. *Try these techniques:*

•Make certain that your chair is comfortable.

•Quiet your telephone's ring.

•Alter the lighting to reduce glare...or increase brightness.

•Personalize your work space with photos, prints, etc.

•Adopt at least a partial closed-door policy for your office. (If you have no way to be alone in your office, find a place elsewhere in the building where you can take breathers.)

•Avoid tight collars...they can cut blood flow to the brain and result in light-headedness and even panic attacks. Tight belts are troublesome, too.

• Establish a regular time for meals, especially lunch.

Source: Stephen Cohen, author of *The Termination Trap,* Williamson Publishing, Charlotte, VT.

Smoking Restrictions At Work

Companies can legally discriminate against smokers. More companies are doing so because it may actually head off trouble in the form of lawsuits brought by nonsmokers who demand a healthful, smoke-free work environment.

Here are some measures companies have taken:

• Total ban. Employees may smoke only in the company parking lot, and then only during work breaks and on lunch hours. And it applies to everyone, including top management, visitors and customers.

• Work station ban. Smoking is prohibited in working areas but allowed during work breaks in specified areas.

• Softer policies such as dividing the work area between smokers and nonsmokers. However, these rarely work well.

Source: Dr. William L. Weis, Albers School of Business, Seattle University, writing in *Personnel Journal.*

Recognizing Fatigue For What it is

Fighting fatigue is a concept of success-oriented people that actually makes them fatigue-prone. Fatigue is a symptom—the purpose of which is to get your attention—to tell you there's something wrong with the way you live. The main cause of fatigue is a monolithic lifestyle, in which the rational sense is used to the exclusion of the other senses, movement, and the emotions. To beat fatigue, you have to get your life back in balance.

What is fatigue?

The tiredness we feel after jogging for instance, is not fatigue. Fatigue is an absence of energy, joie de vivre, interest...It's a blunting of sensation, a shutting out of stimuli.

Behavioral clues:

• Difficulty in getting going or persevering.

• Not having the energy to do things you know you enjoy.

• Having trouble waking up or getting to sleep.

• Taking too many naps.

Most vulnerable...

People who:

• Do virtually the same thing all day, every day. The classic case is the executive who spends his work hours hunched over a desk, grabs a sandwich at lunch, takes a break only to talk to coworkers about business, and goes home to a set routine with his family each evening.

• Have lifestyles contrary to their natural inclinations. Each of us has a rhythm of activity with which we are most comfortable. If a natural doer is forced to lie on a beach in the Bahamas for two weeks, he'll come back exhausted.

Source: Mary E. Wheat, MD, an internist and counselor on fatigue at Mt. Zion Hospital and Medical Center, San Francisco.

Are You a Workaholic?

People who love their work passionately and spend long hours at it are not necessarily work-addicted. True workaholics cannot stop working even in non-work situations. They make all other activities and relationships secondary to work. While the reasons differ widely, almost all work addicts share these traits:

• Oriented to activities involving skills and skill development. Averse to activities where skill is not a factor.

• Strongly analytic. Focus on precise definitions, goals, policies, facts, lists, measurements and strategies.

• Aggressive and unable to leave things alone. An urge to manipulate and control their environment to gain a sense of satisfaction.

•Goal-oriented, product-oriented. Uninterested in the sensations of the present unless they yield products or contribute to their creation.

•Concerned with efficiency and effectiveness. Severely upset by waste and loss. Ironically, many work addicts are inefficient because they are perfectionists and refuse to delegate authority.

Source: Jay B. Rohrlick, MD, *Work and Love: The Crucial Balance,* Summit Books, New York.

Good Business Communication

•"What happened?" is the question to ask when something's gone wrong. Don't try to blame someone for the mistake right at the start. Asking "What happened?" focuses on the mistake itself, not on the person who did it, and is much more likely to lead to useful information. *Contrast:* "Who did it?" is a phrase that can turn off information flow.

•Oral orders are usually all that's needed to correct a basic mistake. If the oral order changes an existing policy, though, confirm it in writing as soon as possible to prevent future confusion.

•Tuesday is the best day for having a serious heart-to-heart discussion with an employee concerning job performance. *Friday risk:* Person broods all weekend about the conversation and comes back embittered on Monday. After the Tuesday talk, find a way by Wednesday to indicate that there's no ill will.

•Discuss serious problems with a subordinate in your office where your authority is evident. Minor matters can be handled in the subordinate's office as long as there's privacy and quiet.

•Value of a dumb question or a simple and honest "I don't know" is that you'll probably learn something you don't know now...and that you couldn't find out any other way. "It's what you learn after you know it all that really counts," said President Harry S. Truman, an expert at turning seeming modesty into great strength.

Source: James Van Fleet, former US Army officer, manager with Sears, Roebuck & Co. and US Gypsum, and consultant on the psychology of management, writing in *Lifetime Conversation Guide,* Prentice-Hall, Inc., Englewood Cliffs, NJ.

Dealing with Political Infighting

•Don't decide that one of the infighters is "right" and the other is "wrong." That encourages the winner to pick more political fights in the future, while it leaves the loser spoiling for revenge. On the other hand, deciding that neither is right and that they must compromise leaves both parties unhappy and convinced that the boss wasn't fair.

•Look for a third choice that both parties can live with, without each one feeling that he's lost or that the other one has won. The ideal "third way" incorporates all the important points of both sides. Only the irritants are omitted.

•The person who leads the way to a solution comes out stronger.

Source: *The Effective Manager,* Warren, Gorham & Lamont, Boston.

High-Level Incompetence

High-level incompetence has many faces and lurks in some heretofore unsuspected areas:

•Physical incompetence. A person who is professionally or technically competent may develop such anxiety over his work that he gets ulcers or high blood pressure. And that results in a poor attendance record. His boss and coworkers assume he's really very competent but just has health problems. In reality, he is physically incompetent to handle the strain of the job.

•Mental incompetence. This occurs when a person is moved to a level where he can no longer deal with the intellectual requirements of the job.

•Social incompetence. A person who is technically competent may be unable to get along with others. Or, problems may arise if he is promoted in an organization where a different class of social behavior is required when moving up the ladder.

•Emotional incompetence. A technically competent person may be too unstable emotionally to deal with a particular job. Creative types, who tend to be insecure, are particularly prone to this type of incompetence when promoted to administrative positions.

•Ethical incompetence. Richard Nixon is a good example. Only when the White House tapes revealed his dishonesty beyond a doubt was it clear that, in office, he had reached his level of ethical incompetence. His brand of manipulative persuasiveness, an asset in local politics, became a liability in the highest office in the land.

Source: Dr. Lawrence J. Peter, author of *The Peter Principle.*

Sexual Harassment On the Job

Sexual harassment on the job is unlawful and a violation of fair employment practices. Supervisors who allow it to occur in their offices, even though they themselves don't commit any offensive acts, can be charged.

If you think someone is sexually harassing you at work:

•Keep a diary and write a brief description of each event right after it happens. Note the time and the place, the people involved, the names of any witnesses.

•Confront the offender. Tell the person that you think the remark or action is harassment.

•Write a letter to the offender, describing the event and noting that you consider it sexual harassment. Send the letter "personal receipt requested," which means the Post Office will only deliver it to the person to whom it is addressed and give you a receipt that the person signs. Or, hand the letter to the person in the presence of a witness you can trust.

•Report the event to management and explain the actions you have taken.

As a supervisor:

•Take every complaint about sexual harassment seriously. Document the actions taken in response to a complaint.

•Write a policy statement against sexual harassment which defines it, condemns it and provides a way in which employees can bring events to management's attention.

•Don't condone a regular practice of sexually-oriented conversations and jokes in the work place. And certainly don't make such remarks to the people you supervise.

•Don't permit employees to post sexually-oriented pictures or cartoons in the workplace.

•Never tie sexual favors to job performance—not even in jest.

•Never touch an employee in a sexually-oriented manner.

Source: Howard Pardue, director of human resources, Summit Communications, Inc.

Avoid Unnecessary Overtime

Many experts feel that regular late hours at work signal inefficient, disorganized work habits, not ambition. *Ways to accomplish your work during office hours:*

•Do not linger over an office breakfast or a long lunch.

•Keep visits and phone calls to a minimum.

•Establish times when your door is shut so that you can concentrate on your work without interruptions.

•Before a late afternoon meeting, make it clear that you have to leave at a specified time. Most meetings will proceed more quickly.

•Before taking on a new job, find out if any overtime is required, aside from normal emergencies. Weigh this against the rewards of the job.

Source: *Bottom Line,* Boardroom, Inc., Greenwich, CT.

How to Reduce Work Related Stress

•Recognize the aggravating aspects of your job. Stop fighting them.

•Identify your emotional needs and accept them. Most executives are competitive, need to be liked, need to vent anger. They should have outlets for each of these needs.

•Practice listening. Listening is more relaxing than talking, and it can help you know what's really going on in the organization.

•Be sensitive to change. Recognize when it's occurring on the job and figure out what adjustments are necessary. By consciously recognizing change, you make it manageable.

•Keep alcohol consumption under control. Excessive drinking creates the illusion of dealing with stress, while in fact adding to it.

Source: Rosalind Forbes, author of *Corporate Stress,* Doubleday, Garden City, NY.

New Projects: Keep Them Exciting

New ideas have a way of exciting people, then fading away. *To maintain interest:*

•Pump in emotion and excitement by remaining personally involved.

•Organize schedules so that people working together have a sense of directed action.

•Remind everyone of the target. Make it stand out clearly as the common goal.

•Show respect for all participants by continuing to listen to their comments and ideas to improve ongoing projects.

Source: Craig S. Rice, author of *Secrets of Managing People,* Prentice-Hall, Englewood Cliffs, NJ.

What Makes Committed Employees

Committed people get a great deal of personal satisfaction from their accomplishments. They totally immerse themselves in a project and often need a brief break to recover emotionally before a new assignment.

In addition, they:

•Assess the feasibility of a task and speak up when they think the odds are bad. Uncommitted people take on anything without caring whether it is possible.

•Back up and cover for coworkers and supervisors without concern for who is responsible.

•Understand the underlying plans and objectives of a project. Know how to proceed without checking with supervisors at every point.

•Feel apprehension and anxiety at the possibility of failure. Unhesitatingly ask for help from supervisors when it seems necessary.

Source: W.C. Waddell, author of *Overcoming Murphy's Law,* AMACOM, New York.

Characteristics of A Good Helper

•Works well with colleagues.

•Is systematic. Sets priorities well.

•Gives a stable and predictable work performance.

•Accepts direction well.

•Shows up regularly and punctually.

•Detects problems in advance and refers to them when necessary.

10

Relationships

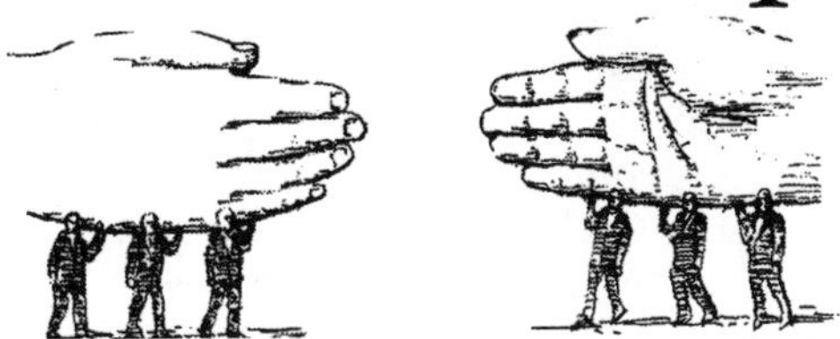

How to Get the Love that You Want

There is hope: A deep and long-lasting love and companionship in marriage *is* possible...

The secret: Couples must change from an *unconscious* marriage to a *conscious* marriage.

Almost all couples start their relationship as an unconscious marriage just by falling in love. In this state of romantic love, infatuation or "love at first sight," you feel your union is "magical"—and that your beloved is "the perfect one"... "the answer to your dreams."

What you do not realize is that this "person of your dreams" has qualities—voice tone, posture, facial expression, mood and character traits—that match an "image" in your unconscious mind of important people from your past (parents, other childhood caretakers). You actually fall in love with someone similar to those childhood caretakers.

More often we unconsciously choose mates who have similar negative rather than positive traits, that become obvious and disturbing after the "glow" of romance fades. They also have positive traits but the negative traits are more apparent.

Examples: Picking a husband who ignores you like your father, or a wife who nags like your mother.

The marriage becomes "unconscious" because both people try to recreate—in order to repair—their childhood.

They feel more or less in love depending on their unconscious anticipation of getting early needs met in the marriage.

Problems emerge when the partner, similar to the past figure, does not repair the initial hurt or give them the love they never got from their parents, leading to disillusionment, distrust or divorce.

Instead of love notes, back rubs, avid listening and time together, now each "escapes" into separate interests, friends, activities.

This unconscious repetition of the past to satisfy unmet needs—wanting from your spouse what you did not get from your parents—explains why spouses sometimes get more furious at their partners than the situation warrants.

Example: If your husband isn't at the office when you call, you panic, fearing he's having an affair or will leave you, triggering old feelings of abandonment when mother left you with a baby-sitter, or was sick and unavailable—or worse—died.

Another common problem emerging from the unconscious marriage is the power struggle, where spouses react like children toward each other or as their parents reacted toward them.

While couples may panic over such conflicts, there is a hidden gain: The end of romantic love and being numb to each other's negative traits can be the beginning of more realistic reappraisals and growing up.

This is where "Imago Relationship Therapy" comes in (imago means image). This is a synthesis and expansion of ideas and techniques from other schools—including psychoanalysis, social learning theory, transactional analysis, gestalt and systems theory—to help couples move from repetitions in an *unconscious marriage* to a constructively *conscious marriage.*

The conscious marriage brings an end to romantic attachment and power struggles. The couple makes a commitment to uncover the unconscious needs that ignited their initial attraction, to heal their wounds, and to move to a more evolved relationship based on personal wholeness and accepting and appreciating each other as separate beings. The spouse goes from being a surrogate parent to a passionate friend.

The steps to create a conscious marriage can be done alone—or with the professional help of a therapist. *Important:*

• Learn the dialogue—an essential communications skill that enables couples to heal each other's emotional wounds by...

Mirroring—repeating back what each other says about needs.

Validating—telling your partner you understand the logic of his/her needs given his/her childhood frustrations.

Empathy—experiencing your partner's feelings.

• Use the dialogue process, mutually identifying unmet needs and the corresponding specific request underlying a complaint.

Example: "You come home late" reveals "I need to feel loved" and the resulting request, "I would like you to come home by 7 p.m. on Tuesday nights."

• Identify the unmet agenda, the one from childhood that repeats in the marriage (attention, praise, comfort, independence) and how it sabotages the current relationship.

Example: "Isolators" need *"space"* out of fear of being smothered by a spouse as they were by a parent. *"Fusers,"* abandoned as children, want to merge with a spouse.

Helpful: Imagine addressing each important person in your childhood home, noting their positive and negative traits, what you liked and didn't like, wanted but didn't get. Ask then for what you want—and imagine them giving it. And—to separate yourself and your partner from parents, compare positive and negative traits, what you enjoy most, what you want and don't get.

• Develop personal wholeness—instead of seeking a mate to fill in your "holes." Find your "lost self."

Example: Because your father drank, you learned to ignore feelings of shame and sadness.

Drop the facade or "false self" that protects you from hurt. Reclaim your "disowned self" that was criticized and denied.

Example: Your mother always said you're not as smart as your brother so you don't act smart even if you are.

Change your own negative traits without projecting them onto a partner (complaining "He's bitter, not me" when *you* are really bitter) or acting them out.

• Validate and support each other's efforts.

• Communicate your needs instead of clinging to the childhood belief that your partner instinctively knows your needs. Fulfill some needs on your own.

• Meet your partner's needs more often than putting yourself first—in healing his/her wounds, you heal your own.

Example: When an emotionally unavailable man marries a woman with a similar type father, the husband heals her wound and his own by becoming more sensitive to her needs.

Stretching exercise: Do something that your partner wants that is difficult for you to do.

Make a verbal or written commitment to stop "exits"—escapes from intimacy like overworking, over-involvement with children, shopping, drinking, lying, picking fights—and to work together for a defined time. Set aside an hour of uninterrupted time together for a defined time.

Write a personal and joint relationship vision —"we are affectionate with each other," "we are loving parents," "we have fun."

Communicate better by taking turns as deliverer—who describes a thought, feeling, anger or complaint, starting with "I" ("I felt anxious today at work")—and as receiver—who paraphrases the message and asks for clarification. ("This morning you woke up wanting to stay home. Did I understand you right?").

"Re-romanticize" by sharing what pleases you now—("I feel loved when you call me from work...and when you massage my back...and when you listen when I'm upset"—what once pleased you—"I used to feel loved when you held my hand, wrote love notes, whispered sexy things in my ear.").

What would please you—("I would feel loved if you took a shower with me...watched my favorite TV show...slept in the nude.").

Do two each day for the next two months—and keep adding to the list.

Surprise each other with one new pleasure each week and one fun activity—walking, tennis, dancing, showering.

Visualize your love healing your partner—visualize your partner's love healing you.

This new conscious love will create a stable and passionate bond between the two of you, and improve physical and emotional health. This new conscious love will also help you strengthen your immune system. It will flower into broader concern for others and the environment and a spiritual union with the universe.

Source: Harville Hendrix, PhD, educator and therapist who is the founder and director of the Institute for Relationship Therapy in New York. He is the author of the best-selling book *Getting the Love You Want: A Guide for Couples*, Harper/Perennial, 10 E. 53 St., New York 10022, and *Keeping the Love You Find: A Guide for Singles*, Pocket Books, 1230 Avenue of the Americas, New York 10020.

Are You Ready for Love?

Love résumé...

Here is a way to consider—and maybe rethink—what you really want in a loving relationship and what you respond to. Think of this as a love résumé. Sometimes just the act of writing can change your thinking. Like a work résumé, it may show a tendency toward instability. Or it may show a logical progression from one "job" to the next. You can discover your own patterns in relationships.

Write a detailed report* about your three (or more) most serious relationships, including:

- A description of the person and what you did and didn't like.
- What worked and what didn't work.
- How it ended and how you got over it.
- What you think you should have done differently.
- What your partner would say worked or didn't work, and why it ended.
- Would you be attracted to such a person today?

Write a description of the person you would like to meet now, including:

- Is this person like the ones in past relationships? If not, why not?
- What sort of relationship you want (marriage, a companion for weekends, an escort, etc.)
- Characteristics you would avoid.
- Your three highest priorities.

Scoring...

Scale 1: Use a red pencil to underline the times you have written *I* or *me*. Count them, and put the score in a box.

Use a blue pencil to underline the times you have written *he, she, we, us* or *both*. Count them. Put this score in another box.

Add the numbers in both boxes. Divide the total into the number of red underlines. If the percentage is anywhere up to 35%, you're available for a relationship. From 36% to 50% means you are borderline (okay on short-term dating but unable to sustain long-term relationships). Over 50% indicates a counterfeit lover. Your concern for yourself and lack of empathy for others almost guarantee that nothing will work, no matter who the partner is.

Source: Abby Hirsch, founder and director of *The Godmothers,* a dating service.

Beyond Self

We all need to pay more attention to our roles as members of society rather than focusing on our individual rights and personal interests.

If more of us were willing to tackle our community responsibilities, we could correct many of the social ills that afflict us today.

Example: A recent study found that young Americans vigorously uphold their right to be tried before a jury of their peers...but are reluctant to serve on juries themselves.

If every citizen accepted jury duty as an opportunity to fulfill an obligation to society, it would demonstrate that our nation really wants to attack crime...not just deplore high crime rates while accepting them as an inevitable condition of modern life. Within a relatively short time, that signal would be transmitted to the entire society.

In the same way, a renewed commitment to community by more people can help improve our public schools...repair family ties...fight corruption in government...and restore faith in a political system that too often responds to special interest groups but neglects the general welfare.

The importance of strong families...

The foundations of a healthy society are adults committed to building lasting marriages, stable families and strong communities. Today, that is too often *not* the case.

Men and women show inadequate long-term commitments to their partners, children and neighbors. The whole community suffers the consequences.

In the worst cases, neglected children become juvenile delinquents who wreak havoc on themselves and society through drug addiction and violent crime. Those troubled ones who manage to survive adolescence become undesirable workers or lifelong dependents on government assistance. And even many parents who provide their children with physical care and education fail to set an example of community concern and instead raise a new generation of self-centered adults. But we can —and should—do better.

How to strengthen marriages...

• Encourage couples contemplating marriage to attend classes in conflict resolution. Every marriage has disagreements, but they are far less likely to end in divorce if the couple knows how to resolve them amicably. Premarriage programs give couples the opportunity to thrash out basic issues—how to make decisions, how to budget, etc.—before actually being faced with such problems.

Better: Require all high school students to study the subject of marriage. It will help them in all areas of adult life.

• Popularize the idea of premarital super-commitments, such as agreeing to get counseling if you have marital problems.

• Maintain open communication in your marriage. Talk about problems as they arise instead of letting them simmer. Consider renewing your vows on your anniversary to renew your commitment.

Developing children's character...

Parents need to make some tough choices that involve trading time and possibly income and job advancement for the sake of a better next generation. *Specific examples:*

• Never leave children at home alone for an inappropriate amount of time (depending on the ages of the children).

• Rearrange work schedules so at least one parent is home when the children are there.

• Look for jobs that offer some type of flextime...consider the possibility of working at home via computer.

• Before sending your young child to a day care center, investigate it carefully...pay surprise visits to see what it is really like.

As children grow older and spend more time in school, do things they may not appreciate today but will thank you for later...

• Provide a quiet setting for homework... strictly ration TV watching.

• Set a curfew on school nights.

•Don't allow children to work at a job more than 10 hours a week.

•Don't let them squander all their earnings. Require them to save for college.

Ways to improve education...

While home schooling is growing, you can only do so much...but by taking an interest in community activities, you can help your children and other people's children.

•Make the quality of schools a major factor when you decide where to live.

•Don't choose schools on hearsay...see for yourself by making surprise visits.

•Attend PTA meetings...take an active interest in school board elections.

Strengthening your community...

We don't have to live in isolation from our neighbors. We will have a better society if we take active steps to strengthen community bonds. *First steps...*

•Get to know your neighbors—join block associations...support activities that get people interacting in positive ways.

•Take an interest in local politics—support developments that encourage people to become more community-minded.

Example: Zoning changes allow people to work at home, giving them more time to devote to their families and community activities.

•Devote 5% of your time and your money to community projects you favor. Make your voice heard.

Source: Amitai Etzioni, PhD, a professor at George Washington University in Washington, DC. He is author of *The Spirit of Community: Rights, Responsibilities, and the Communitarian Agenda*, Crown Publishers, New York.

Tactful Flirting

Matchmaking is a thing of the past, so if you hope to find that special someone, you have to know how to go about it. Luckily the art of flirting can be learned.

To initiate contact with a stranger you think you would like to know better:

•Don't come on with obvious lines or a standard act. You'll be seen as crude or a phony.

•Don't get too personal. Make your conversational opener about something neutral, or you may be seen as pushy.

•Do pick up on an innocuous topic and comment on it. *Good:* "That's a lovely ring you're wearing. Is it Art Deco?" *Poor:* "You have the most beautiful hair."

•Do make eye contact—but not for too long. According to a psychological study, three seconds is optimal to indicate interest without seeming to stare.

•Don't touch the person right away. Women especially are very put off by men they consider "grabby." You might even move away to create allure.

•Do show vulnerability. People love it when you're not Mr. or Ms. Self-Confidence. If you're nervous, say so. Your candor will be appealing. *Also:* Your admission will allow the other person to admit that he or she is nervous, too. This breaks the ice, and then you both can relax.

•Do ask for help as a good conversation opener. *Example:* "I don't know this area well. Could you recommend a good restaurant around here?"

•Don't feel you have to be extraordinarily good-looking. If you have confidence in yourself as a person, the rest will follow. Whatever your type may be, it is certain to appeal to someone.

•Do be flexible. The same approach won't work with everyone. If you're sensitive and alert, you can pick up verbal and nonverbal cues and respond appropriately.

•Don't oversell yourself or feel compelled to give all your credits. Make the other person feel like the most important person in the world to you at that moment. Being interested is just as important as being interesting (if not more so). Really listen. Don't just wait until the other person finishes a sentence so you can jump in with your own opinion.

•Don't let your confidence be shattered by a rejection. It may not have anything to do with you. You may have approached someone who is married, neurotic, recovering from a devastating love affair, in a bad mood, or averse to your eye color. *The best remedy:* Try again as soon as possible.

Source: Wendy Leigh, author of *What Makes a Woman Good in Bed, What Makes a Man Good in Bed,* and *Infidelity: An American Epidemic,* William Morrow, New York.

Subjects that were least liked:

- Sports such as baseball, football, and boxing.
- Politics.
- Religion.

Source: James Van Fleet, author of *A Lifetime Guide to Conversation,* Prentice-Hall, Inc., Englewood Cliffs, NJ.

What Men Like In Women

- Brunettes come in first with 36% of the men surveyed.
- Blondes come in second at 29%.
- Hair color is unimportant to 32% of the men surveyed.
- *Favorite eye color:* 44% select blue, 21% like brown and 20% prefer green.
- By two to one, men choose curly hair over straight.
- *The trait men first associate with a beautiful woman:* 42% say personality, 23% think of the smile, 13% say eyes and only 6% zero in on the body.
- *Favorite look:* Striking and sophisticated is first, with 32%.
- *Biggest turnoffs:* Heavy makeup, 26%; excess weight, 15%; arrogance, 14%.

Source: *Glamour.*

Talking to Women

A survey of 1,000 women revealed that they liked most to talk about (in this order):

- Family and home, including children and grandchildren.
- Good health.
- Work or job (if a working woman).
- Promotion and advancement (if employed).
- Personal growth.
- Clothes and shopping.
- Recreation.
- Travel.
- Men (especially single women).

How to Talk with Men If You're a Woman

The topics men most like to talk about are strikingly similar to those women like:

- Family and home, including children and grandchildren.
- Good health.
- Work or job.
- Promotion and advancement.
- Personal growth.
- Recreation.
- Travel.
- The opposite sex (especially young single men).
- Sports.
- Politics.

Men generally dislike to talk about:

- Religion.
- Clothes, fashion, or shopping.

Source: James Van Fleet, author of *A Lifetime Guide to Conversation,* Prentice-Hall, Inc., Englewood Cliffs, NJ.

Personal Ads: A Woman's View

The personal classified ads in *The New York Review of Books, New York* magazine and *The Village Voice* are becoming an increasingly useful social medium.

Here are some tips on answering and placing ads:

- Don't lie. Even white lies do damage. Don't say you're a college professor if you really teach occasional courses in night school at several local colleges. Stretching the truth sets up unrealistic expectations, and your "date" is certain to be disappointed. Important omissions also count. If you weigh 300 pounds, it's better to say so.

•Look in the mirror. Don't say you're handsome, beautiful or very attractive if you're not. You have a better chance being honest because different people want different things.

•Don't ask for photos. When it comes to wallet-size portraits, they lie at worst. At best, they say nothing. When you like someone, that person becomes better-looking to you. And when you don't like someone, it doesn't matter how good-looking he is. Besides, some very attractive people photograph badly…and vice versa. You'll get the best sense of a person from the letter, not from the picture.

•Try humor. It always gets a better response.

•Avoid attractiveness requirements. Just on general principles don't answer any ad by a man who asks for a "very beautiful" woman or a woman with a "fabulous figure." If he's preoccupied with looks, he's superficial.

•Don't limit yourself with age requirements. Why do men in their fifties consistently ask for women in their twenties and thirties? Unless you want children, don't limit your possibilities.

•Don't brag. This unpleasant trait breeds skepticism and distaste in the reader.

•Be sincere. Nothing catches a woman's attention more surely than a sincere, straightforward, informative letter. When you answer an ad that looks inviting, let the person know why. Respond to the particulars in the ad in a warm and personal way. Talk honestly about yourself, your likes and dislikes, favorite vacations, funny anecdotes, etc. And never, never, never send a photocopy response.

•If you really liked a woman's ad but she hasn't answered your response, write again. Persistence is a virtue.

•Don't be discouraged. Chances are you won't be attracted to 99.9% of the people you meet this way. But that will also be true of singles you meet other ways. This is more efficient, however, since people are already preselected. They're singles who want to meet someone—just like you.

What You Need to Know Before Getting Married

When deciding to marry, people expect their feelings to be *completely* clear, *completely* unambiguous. *I don't really love him/her enough to marry him/her,* is a common statement.

Dagmar O'Connor, a well-known psychologist and sex therapist, dispels some of the confusion about how much you should love in order to marry.

What is the biggest mistake that people make in choosing a marriage partner?

The choice of a mate is usually based on early parental influences. *Problem:* Many of us grew up in dysfunctional homes where parents impeded rather than enhanced children's emotional growth, or treated each other with such disrespect and unkindness that they created a negative role model for adult love relationships. People raised in such environments often develop feelings of sexual attraction toward people who resemble their parents.

Example: A woman whose father verbally or physically abused her may only be attracted to abusive men. In a room full of wonderful men, she will have an attraction for the "wrong" man.

Lesson: Whom we love and how much we love them is determined by our early experiences of love interactions with our parents and siblings. If you don't love someone enough to want to marry them, listen to your feelings. If you *never* feel like committing to anybody, it may be useful to investigate your childhood through therapy.

One common reason for rejecting marriage is not feeling turned on by a partner. Yet physical attraction can also be a sign of these old dysfunctional influences and you must therefore evaluate its importance carefully.

Sexual attraction should only be a part of the package along with friendship. If the attraction isn't strong in the beginning, but the other elements are there, sexual feelings may develop as the emotional intimacy deepens, unless you have learned in childhood to separate love from sex.

Some couples who hate each other and wind up divorced have good sex all the way through their marriage—and even after the divorce. Their problem is that sex becomes a substitute for emotional intimacy.

What should you look for in a marriage partner?

A companion. Not a parent figure to fill needs that were not met in childhood. Use friends or therapists to meet those needs. For the emotionally mature person, the criteria for love are that you enjoy being with the person...you feel comfortable with him/her...and you can totally trust him. Look for qualities you'd want in a friend: Honesty, generosity, integrity, sense of humor, similar values, sensitivity and similar interests.

Why is companionship so difficult to maintain in a marriage?

Because 90% of being "in love" is the feeling that you've finally found the parent you didn't have as a child. Then if your mate refuses to act like your parental fantasy, you get furious.

Companions accept each other as separate individuals with often conflicting needs. They don't demand unconditional love or approval.

Example: When Mary has a hard day at work, she expects her husband, Joe, to be comforting and sympathetic. But sometimes Joe is too exhausted from his own day and just wants to be left alone. Mary goes into a rage and accuses him of not caring about her. If she viewed Joe as a companion rather than as a parent, she would back off, recognizing his need to be alone, and take care of her own needs by calling a friend.

It's important for couples to listen to each other, instead of each partner defending his own innocence so vehemently that the other partner's message is drowned out.

What are good reasons for rejecting someone you might marry?

If you have any reason to believe that you cannot trust this person...or if you suspect the person has destructive habits he's not willing to change.

Examples: Someone who has a problem with drugs or alcohol, is unfaithful, lies to you or has hit you a few times—even though he has promised never to do it again.

Also: Don't marry someone because of "potential." You need to accept someone the way he is. If you marry someone with potential, the person is a fantasy in your own head and the reality is bound to disappoint you.

A prospective mate might be a perfectly nice person, but have a quality you just don't think you can live with.

Example: A successful female executive dates a sweet, generous fellow who totally lacks ambition. But, she doesn't think she could accept that over the long run.

What should people who are considering a serious commitment look at in themselves?

Background patterns. Is this the first person you feel you don't love enough to commit to, or have there been several others? If so, delve deeper and investigate your difficulty loving or committing to anybody.

Trap: If you have a pattern of getting into uncomfortable or abusive relationships and you're with someone who is loving, you may find this person boring. It's important to work out your own attraction to "excitement." Excitement can at times be a way to avoid your underlying feelings.

Helpful: Ask yourself, *Who in my family does this person resemble? How does that make me feel?*

Bottom line: Any time that you feel like rejecting someone or protecting yourself, it's because your unconscious computer is talking to you. No matter what the underlying reasons are, it's important to respect that.

I don't believe that you should go against your instincts. But discovering where they are coming from can help you to make healthier decisions about your love relationships.

The most important component of a healthy love relationship is self-knowledge. Before you can decide wisely about marriage, you must learn about yourself as an individual and strive to understand your feelings.

How do you learn to trust your judgment about the opposite sex?

You make mistakes and learn from them. People who are too afraid of making mistakes don't learn much about life.

Nowadays, divorce, premarital sex and living together are permitted, so we're allowed to learn and profit from mistakes about love relationships.

Many people, unfortunately, do not learn. As a therapist, I see people who have had three or four marriages and they marry the same type of person each time—making exactly the same mistakes. They don't realize that they can only change themselves—not their partner.

What should you do if you're unsure of your decision?

I think premarital counseling is an excellent idea.

Source: Dagmar O'Connor, PhD, author of *How to Make Love to the Same Person for the Rest of Your Life and Still Love It,* Bantam Books, 666 Fifth Ave., New York 10103. She is in private practice in New York City.

Secrets of Much, Much Better Male/Female Communications

During a conversation in their car, a woman asked her husband, *Would you like to stop for ice cream?* Her husband answered, truthfully, *No,* and they kept on driving.

Later on, the man was frustrated when he realized his wife was annoyed...because she had wanted to stop. *Why didn't you say what you wanted?* he asked. *Why do you play these games with me?*

In fact, each spouse had misread the other. The wife had incorrectly taken the husband's *no* as a non-negotiable position. The husband had misconstrued his wife's questions as a request for information, rather than the start of a discussion about what *both* would like.

What's going on...

This kind of misunderstanding stems from the fundamentally different ways in which men and women speak.

Men generally engage the world as individual competitors within hierarchies of power and accomplishment. They are either one-up or one-down. Their conversations are aimed at achieving status and keeping the upper hand, as part of their struggle to preserve independence and avoid failure.

Women approach the world as individuals within a network of connections. In this world, conversations are negotiations for closeness—tools to preserve intimacy and avoid isolation.

Note: I'm not suggesting that women care nothing about status, or that men are indifferent to intimacy, but they are focused on different goals.

Both approaches are equally valid. The problems enter when we pretend that men and women express their thoughts and feelings in the same way. When we don't see the differences, we run into major misunderstanding.

Men and women who understand each other's conversational styles are better able to express themselves...and understand what others are saying.

Differences...

Men and women differ in how they express almost everything. *Examples:*

• Surviving conflict. Childhood studies show that girls attempt to reduce verbal conflict and preserve harmony among peers by compromise and consensus. Boys use appeals to rules and threats of physical violence. Boys' conflicts also tend to be more prolonged—and are often devices to create greater closeness after the argument is over.

• Coping with problems. Women often talk about problems not as a way of finding solutions, but to seek understanding and sympathy. Since men don't talk about problems unless they want advice, they're likely to frustrate women by offering advice instead of understanding.

• Asking questions. Women show concern by responding to a friend's troubles with pertinent questions. Men are more likely to change the subject out of respect for the other's need for independence. *Male assumption:* Extended discussion of a problem would make it seem more serious—and make the other man feel worse.

• Making confessions. Women are more willing to reveal emotional secrets and weaknesses, because the payoff in intimacy is worth the risk of vulnerability. Men are less likely to take the risk—particularly with other men—out of fear of landing one-down. They are more inclined to barter impersonal news about politics or sports.

• Giving feedback. Women are more inclined to ask questions when listening to someone talk.

They offer small cues like *uh-huh*. A woman who says *yeah* may mean *I'm with you...I follow,* but most men will say *yeah* only if they agree.

Men give fewer signals overall, and are more likely to respond with statements and challenges. Men also listen to women less frequently than women listen to men. *Reason:* Many men are uncomfortable listening because they don't like being passive.

•Making apologies. When women say, *I'm sorry,* it is often to establish a *connection* with the other person, as in *I'm sorry you feel bad about this—I do too.* To many men, *I'm sorry* denotes an apology, an admission of fault. To accept the apology places the accepter as one-up.

•Joking. Men are more likely to store away a set of jokes, which they can use to seize center stage in a group. *Point:* Making others laugh gives you a fleeting power over them. Women are less likely to remember jokes, but are quicker to laugh at them.

•Using body language. When women talk, they look at one another directly, with a steady gaze that supports their connection. Men normally look away from each other. *Reason:* To look directly at another man might suggest hostility—a barrier to friendly connection. A man who looks directly at a woman may imply a different kind of threat—*a flirtation.*

Source: Deborah Tannen, professor of linguistics at Georgetown University. She is the author of *You Just Don't Understand: Women and Men in Conversation,* William Morrow & Co., 105 Madison Ave., New York 10016.

Secrets of Happy Couples

The high rate of divorce, combined with the skyrocketing number of dysfunctional families, suggests that there is no such thing as a truly happy marriage...*but my interviews with couples across the country show otherwise.*

The couples I talked to had been married between seven and 55 years. More than half described themselves as very happily married. Only two or three were actually miserable.

The remaining 35 couples are hanging in there and doing all right.

The happiest couples share a number of characteristics—qualities from which we can learn. And they dispelled several popular misconceptions...

Myth: Be realistic, not idealistic.

Reality: In fact, the most happily married people idealize their spouses. Many of them say they think their husbands or wives are the greatest people in the world. That belief certainly helps bring out the best in their partners. Research has shown that people live up—or down—to our expectations.

Even after the "crazy-in-love" phase has long passed, the happy partners continue to see each other through rose-colored glasses—often more positively than others might see them.

Myth: Happy couples rarely fight.

Reality: Of course, happy couples fight—some more often than others. But happy couples fight by the rules and are able to keep conflicts from escalating.

The rules differ depending on the temperaments of the people involved. Some couples say, "We never go to bed angry." They insist on resolving issues rather than walking away from them.

Happy couples have impulse control. They are willing and able to censor themselves, even in the midst of rage, so as not to say or do the thing that would be "fatal" to the relationship.

Myth: There's no such thing as love at first sight.

Reality: Some romances blossomed slowly. But there were also many who remembered feeling a powerful attraction at their first meeting...and who are still in love with each other years later. There were also cases in which one partner fell in love immediately, while the other partner took longer to come around.

Myth: Friendship, not sex, is the key to a long-lasting relationship.

Reality: Both sex and friendship are important.

While the happiest husbands and wives say they are each other's best friends, they also have very strong sexual bonds. True, the intense infatuation—being ready to jump into bed at any opportunity—fades after a few years. But the sexual chemistry remains, even during periods when a couple isn't making love.

Example: One wife was so exhausted after having a baby that she temporarily lost interest in sex. Nevertheless, she continued to have vivid sexual dreams about her husband.

Myth: Happy couples have independent lives.

Reality: Even if they don't share all the same interests, happy couples spend a lot of time together.

This is another characteristic that has to do with temperament—some couples require less togetherness than others. But the idea that separate identities are essential is completely untrue. These couples have definitely found a shared identity. Over time, they stopped feeling *single at heart* and came to be *married at heart.* If that process doesn't happen, the marriage is in trouble.

Myth: The happiest couples raise children together.

Reality: The few childless couples I interviewed are quite happy. What seemed to be important is not whether or not a couple has children, but whether they agree that children should or should not be part of their lives together.

In fact, children are the subject couples fight about most often—more than sex, money or in-laws. Children can disrupt the unity of a couple, introducing an element of separation and continuous potential conflict.

That doesn't mean that children damage a relationship—far from it. But raising children is very difficult, with a lot to disagree about. Happy couples who are parents face and grapple with these conflicts and learn from each other.

Example: One husband was a severe disciplinarian, while his wife was very gentle with the children. This difference caused an ongoing disagreement between them. Eventually, he realized that she was able to get exactly the response she wanted from the children *without* screaming or yelling...and he began to temper his own approach.

Why couples get along...

"For a marriage to be happy, the partners need to be identical in background but opposite in personality,"one woman said.

I saw this truth borne out over and over again. If a couple shares the same background (age, religion, ethnicity, economic status), they are more likely to agree on many of the day-to-day decisions, such as how to raise the children, what vacations to take, what colors to use when decorating the house, etc.

Having opposite personalities is what provides the spark. I saw many couples in which one partner was somewhat depressive and pessimistic and the other was optimistic. They seemed to balance or compensate for each other.

I'm not suggesting that people with different backgrounds can't have good marriages. But shared reference points do make marriages work better.

Source: Catherine Johnson, PhD, author of *Lucky in Love: The Secrets of Happy Couples and How Their Marriages Thrive.* Viking Penguin, New York.

How to Improve the Quality of Time You Spend with Your Mate

Married couples today spend so much time apart that the little time spent together loses the richness it once had. They forget that the quality of time spent together is just as important as the quality in everything else.

Traps that can lower the quality of time together and what to do about them:

- Limiting conversation to terse exchanges of information. *Instead:* Speak in a way that conveys interest, involvement, a sense of love.
- Displaying affection only during full-fledged sexual interludes. *Instead:* Learn to appreciate a little physical contact, especially during very hectic or stressful periods. Don't be hesitant to touch...while shopping together,for instance, or while you're working around the house. It's important to let one another know you like each other.
- Choosing recreational activities that might prove stressful or draining, especially when work demands are heavy. *Instead:* Choose less taxing forms of entertainment at these times.

For example, watch a football game on television instead of going to a crowded, cold, noisy stadium. Talk about the game and how you feel while watching it. Take advantage of the relaxed and familiar home environment. Fix a small drink...put your arm around your spouse.

•Looking on nonwork time as a void that must be filled with more work. *Instead:* Plan and share activities from which both can benefit...redecorate a room, take tennis lessons, cook a meal together, work in the garden.

•Being afraid to talk about your deepest desires and feelings. *Instead:* Verbalize aspects of your personality that aren't apparent in daily living. Sharing sexual fantasies, for example, can be both a means of communication and a way of revitalizing a relationship.

Source: Anthony Pietropinto, MD, supervising psychiatrist, Manhattan Psychiatric Center, New York.

Successful Marrying And Remarrying

Today, with the statistical probability that two out of every three marriages will end in divorce, couples who marry or remarry need all the help they can get.

Here is some advice for a good start:

•Choose the right person for the right reasons. Too often, people make the wrong choice because they have needs they don't admit even to themselves. They know what they want, but even though the person they plan to marry doesn't fill the bill, they think he/she will change.

•Have realistic expectations about the marriage. Another person can do only so much for you. No one person can fill every need. It is important for both partners to develop their own lives and interests and not depend solely on each other.

•Learn to communicate. Get issues out on the table and talk about them. Try to reach conclusions regarding conflicts rather than let them stay unresolved.

•Respect the other person's style of communication. People express affection in different ways. Instead of expecting a spouse to react as you do, try to be sensitive to what he or she is telling you in his/her own way.

•Respect the other person's feelings about space and distance. Many people have difficulty understanding someone else's needs for privacy and time alone. Conflicts about space needs can be resolved by trial and error—and patience.

•Create a new lifestyle. Each partner comes with different concepts about customs, handling money, vacations, etc. One may be used to making a big thing about celebrating holidays and birthdays, the other, not. Combine the best elements to get a richer blend that is distinctly your own.

Source: Barbara C. Freedman, CSW, director of the Divorce and Remarriage Counseling Center, New York.

The Fine Art of Touching

Touching and being touched can solve many of our problems. You can increase your sense of general well-being and rejuvenate your relationship by learning the language of touch. *Here's how a couple should get started:*

•Have sessions in which they alternate touching each other without sexual intercourse.

•Each partner gets to initiate sessions...and to be both passive and active.

•Learn to be selfish and communicate what you like—eventually developing a nonverbal language of touch.

Helpful suggestions...

•Don't insist on separating sex and affection. Women complain that when they just want to be affectionate the man will turn it into foreplay. *Problem:* We fail to see affection and sex as a continuum. We're too used to turning ourselves off during affectionate moments because we had to as children when we kissed and hugged our parents. And now we have to as parents with our own children. But you should remember that the affectionate hug or kiss with your spouse is exactly the same physical act that turns you on during sex.

•Communicate with your body. If you can't say "I love you" with your body, there's a whole dimension lacking in your relationship. How you express yourself is an individual matter.

•Sleep in the nude to create a sense of intimacy.

•Be flexible...in terms of touch, body contacts, positions...and where you touch each other in the house.

•Don't make it a power struggle. People who have trouble touching each other often toss accusations back and forth, such as "I always touch you—how come you never touch me?" The one who's having trouble gets more resistant because he or she feels forced. *Solution:* Take it in small steps. Keep touching your partner for your own gratification, no matter what the response. Eventually your partner will stop feeling threatened and reciprocate of his or her own accord.

•Don't forget about usually untouched areas. If I don't tell my clients to touch heads and feet, they'll forget about them. Licking toes and massaging feet can be very sensual.

Source: Dagmar O'Connor, author of *How to Make Love to the Same Person for the Rest of Your Life—and Still Love It,* Doubleday & Co., Garden City, NY. Ms. O'Connor is director of the sexual therapy program at St. Luke's-Roosevelt Hospital Center in New York City.

Therapeutic Separation

Living apart temporarily can help couples on the verge of divorce resolve their differences. Most couples who try living apart temporarily remain married—and eventually resume cohabitation.

How to do it:

•Both spouses must be committed to using the time apart to work through their differences.

•During separation, keep a diary of experiences and insights.

Source: Dr. Norman Paul, psychiatrist, Lexington, MA.

Will This Marriage Survive?

Five premarital indicators that marriage will last:

•Economic stability. Neither spouse should feel they are making a great financial sacrifice or will have to overwork to maintain an unrealistically high standard of living.

•Maturity. Spouses should be able to minimize selfishness and practice selflessness comfortably.

•Commitment. A committed pair will be more able to compromise.

•Compatibility. A couple must like to do things together, enjoying each other's company.

•Parent success. Spouses who come from happy families with stable marriages have a better shot.

Source: Dr. John Curtis, Valdosta State College.

All About Adultery

Although many species of animals are monogamous...just like many human beings, they also cheat on the side—according to the latest studies from all over the US.

Helen Fisher, PhD, a leading anthropologist and expert on human sexual behavior, tells us more about why adultery is so common in so much of the animal world...

What exactly is monogamy?

It basically means one person has one spouse ...but it doesn't mean that the person has just one sex partner.

Forming pair bonds and raising children as man and wife is a hallmark of the human species, as much as language is. But we also follow the laws of nature. And the conflicting drives to form pair bonds and be adulterous is built into both animal and human nature.

Example: A male and female beaver form a pair bond and build their dam and lodge and create their territory, just the way we create our home and maintain our lawn. But naturalists have seen male beavers slip out of their lodges at night and into a neighboring female's lodge. It's the same among some birds, like chickadees, ducks and other creatures.

Is polygamy an answer?

Polygamy has been a custom in many societies...but that arrangement doesn't work, either. Co-wives fight, husbands show favoritism and the divorce rate is extremely high.

There are polygamous animals, such as horses, where one male travels with a harem of females. I would suspect that there's no jealousy in a harem-building species. But we're not a harem-building species. For the past four million years we've been monogamous.

This is why open marriages and communes have never worked. Within a few months after joining the commune, a man and a woman fall in love and want to be exclusive. It's natural.

Are men more likely to commit adultery than women?

No. In societies without a double standard, women avail themselves of extramarital sex just as often as men do.

We believe that men are more sexual than women, so our polls bear out that belief. Men like to brag about sex, women deny it. But in fact, the most recent polls show that women are just as adulterous as men are.

I wouldn't be surprised to see that in a society where women controlled the money and the power they were more adulterous than men. It's the sex that needs the other sex more that puts all its eggs in one basket.

Is adultery more acceptable now than at other times in history?

Polls say no, but the consequences today are nowhere near as harsh as they used to be. We haven't changed our negative opinion about adultery, but you're not put to death for it anymore or forced to wear the letter "A" branded on your head. Women today don't lose alimony or custody of their kids because of adultery.

We're much more relaxed about it and will probably become even more relaxed as women become less and less dependent on men economically.

Why do some people have a drive to cheat?

There are all kinds of psychological reasons—a desire for more attention, excitement, intimacy or sex—but none of those is the underlying reason.

The real reason dates back to the grasslands of Africa four million years ago where male and female hunter-gatherers formed pair bonds to raise their young.

A man who formed a pair bond with one woman and occasionally had sex with another was likely to have more children. Since the more children a man had the more likely it was that his genes would live on, by being adulterous he increased the number of genes he put into the gene pool. An adulterous ancestral man survived and passed to modern man whatever it is in the male spirit that makes men pursue extramarital affairs.

A woman, on the other hand, can't have more than one child every nine months. So it might seem as if she wouldn't have a motive for adultery. But adulterous women also had a slight reproductive edge.

If an ancestral woman took a husband and sneaked around on the side, she got extra food and extra protection. If her husband died or was injured, her lover could step in and help her raise her children. Or if she ended up with a husband with, say, lousy eyesight, she could have a child by a lover who had better genes.

Even though having children is the last thing people have in mind today when they commit adultery, from a Darwinian perspective, what occurs in an adulterer's brain is an old, unconscious pattern that drives us to look for variety.

Does adultery have to cause tremendous social upheaval?

No. That depends mostly on the individual culture.

Examples: According to Eskimo tradition, a woman is at liberty to offer sex to her mate's hunting partner or to a guest in the igloo in order to extend kinship and hospitality. And among the Kurkuru, a group of Amazon Indians, everyone in the village has between four and 12 lovers.

Americans are exquisitely prudish compared with world cultures. In a study of 139 cultures, 39% permit adultery at certain times of the year with certain relatives.

In some cultures, a man is permitted to have sex with his wife's sister, because if his wife ever dies she could legitimately become his wife. Some societies have puberty rituals with nights of sexual license.

If adultery is genetically ingrained, do we really have a choice about committing it?

Absolutely. There is something called the triumph of culture over the human spirit. Since 50% of all people are adulterous, that means 50% are not.

The most important thing the human animal does is reproduce, but we also have thousands of years of people believing in and practicing celibacy. We're genetically programmed for survival, but we will sacrifice ourselves for our country or a cause we believe in. Culture regularly triumphs over biology.

People can decide to be faithful and stick to it. But not always without a struggle. One has to appreciate that struggle and not think it's going to be easy.

Source: Helen Fisher, PhD, research associate, department of anthropology, American Museum of Natural History, New York. She is the author of *The Sex Contract: The Evolution of Human Behavior,* William Morrow, 105 Madison Ave., New York 10016.

Adultery—His and Hers

Men tend to justify their extramarital affairs by citing sexual grounds. More than half consider "sexual deprivation" a good enough reason to stray. *Gender contrast:* Women are more influenced by emotional justifications for a fling ...and 77% said they were swayed by "falling in love."

Source: Shirley Glass, PhD, a psychologist in private practice in Owings Mills, Maryland. Dr. Glass's study of more than 300 married people was published in *Journal of Sex Research,* Box 208, Mount Vernon, Iowa 52314. Quarterly.

Dividing Chores in The Two-Income Family

Family ties are strongest when both husband and wife share household responsibilities as well as contribute to economic needs. According to an ad agency survey of married men:

- 32% of the men shop for food.
- 47% cook for the family.
- 80% take care of children under 12.
- The majority said they directly influence the decisions about which brands of disposable diapers, pet food, bar soap, and toothpaste to buy.

When both spouses work, a fair division of household tasks is crucial. *One good approach:*

- Select the mutually most-hated tasks and hire someone to do as many of them as possible.
- Negotiate the remaining disliked jobs.
- Don't alternate jobs. That only leads to arguments about whose turn it is.
- Schedule quarterly or semiannual review for adjustments and tradeoffs.

Source: Nancy Lee, author of *Targeting the Top,* Doubleday & Co., New York.

How Not to Bring Up Babies

Babies may not be as delicate as many first-time parents think...but they are vulnerable to certain mistakes—some less obvious than others. *Mistakes to avoid:*

- *Mistake:* Being overly fearful of making mistakes. Conscientious adults try to avoid mistakes when interacting with children. But adults should keep this caution from turning into worry. *Reason:* It drains away the joy children bring.

Mistakes in interacting with children are inevitable—but seldom serious.

Examples: Some babies don't get enough to eat because the feeding process is rushed. Other babies get cranky because the process is prolonged. Savvy mothers minimize frustration at feeding time by paying close attention to the child's responses.

Bottom line: Even good parents make mistakes...but they learn from them.

- *Mistake:* Underestimating a baby's mind. Adults often treat babies as if they were more digestive tracts than human beings. But even at a very early age, babies feel and think. They have a very good sense of what's going on from day one.

The big difference is that babies cannot verbalize their thoughts and feelings.

For effective communication: Try to imagine what the baby thinks and how the baby feels, then act accordingly. Not all your assumptions will be on target, of course, but mistakes of this type seldom are harmful.

• *Mistake:* Exposing a baby to danger. Any activity that places a baby at risk of injury should be strictly forbidden. Even minor lapses in judgment—like leaving a baby unattended to answer the phone—can be dangerous.

• *Mistake:* Avoiding baby talk. Many adults intuitively use baby talk when addressing infants and small children. They raise the pitch of their voice, slow the rhythm, adopt a singsong melody and soften consonant sounds.

Example: "Pretty rabbit" becomes "pwitty wabbit."

Such changes are appropriate. *Reason:* Babies respond more enthusiastically to baby talk than to conventional speech.

Using baby talk does not retard the process by which a child learns to talk. Babies learn to talk by imitating speech overheard from adult conversations, not by speaking directly with adults.

• *Mistake:* Going too far when playing games. Adults who love children often go to great lengths just to elicit a smile or a laugh. Bouncing a child on your knee, playing peekaboo, hide-and-seek and games like *I'm going to get you* are great fun for adult and child.

But adults sometimes go too far. Babies—especially young ones—cannot tolerate as much intensity as adults. *Result:* Overstimulation.

Because babies cannot tell adults to tone it down a little, they resort to the only options open to them—turning away from the source of stimulation or wailing.

If a baby bursts out crying or turns away from you, take a breather. Try again later if you like, but at a lower intensity.

• *Mistake:* Feeding inappropriate foods. A toddler who can eat a cracker with no trouble can choke on a peanut. And even small quantities of alcohol can be fatal. It's shocking that so many parents allow children to sip an alcoholic drink.

• *Mistake:* Being too rigid in scheduling eating and sleeping. During the first two months of a child's life, parents should concentrate on getting the baby to eat and gain weight and to establish a regular sleep schedule.

Child-care experts often recommend feedings every four hours. Such a guideline makes sense in general terms, but individual babies are highly variable—it does not pay to be too rigid.

If a baby seems to prefer a three-hour schedule, stick to that. If a baby thrives with only one feeding every five or six hours, that's fine, too.

Similarly, experts often say that children should be able to go to sleep on their own by the age of six months. But if your six-month-old needs to be stroked or sung to sleep, so be it.

• *Mistake:* Misreading motives. Adults occasionally cause needless trouble by ascribing to children incorrect motives or emotions.

Example: Babies and young children (especially two-year-olds) are remarkably curious about their environments. They explore everything around them, including eyes, ears, noses and hair. Adults sometimes perceive such explorations as aggression and presume that the child is hostile. They may yell at or slap the child. But odds are, the child is just being curious.

Be careful when ascribing hostility or any other negative emotions to a small child—you're probably missing the mark.

• *Mistake:* Being inconsistent. The goal of discipline is to set limits to a child's behavior. Parents do this in different ways.

Some set absolute limits and mete out harsh punishment for even minor transgressions. Others adopt a relaxed approach, in which most constraints on behavior are subject to negotiation.

Children can flourish under either system, but only if parents are consistent.

Example: Spanking a child for one acting out episode and then simply discussing another similar episode only confuses the child.

Children need to know the rules.

•*Mistake:* Forcing eye contact. Adults should respect a baby's desire not only to establish, but also to break eye contact.

Breaking eye contact is the baby's way of saying, "I am overstimulated or bored." Trying to force eye contact on a child who does not want it is inappropriate.

•*Mistake:* Not keeping up with a baby's development. Babies outgrow activities and shift their interests very rapidly. Games and other modes of interaction that work well at one stage in the baby's development are inappropriate as little as one week later.

Bottom line: Always be flexible in your dealings with babies and small children.

Source: Daniel N. Stern, MD, professor of psychology at the University of Geneva and adjunct professor of psychiatry at Cornell University Medical Center, 525 E. 68 St., New York 10021. He is the author of several books on infants, most recently, *Diary of a Baby,* Basic Books, 10 E. 53 St., New York 10022.

New Parent Trap

New parents often lose support from friends and coworkers—simply because those new parents are too exhausted to maintain social ties. Mothers, who often have more friends than fathers, find it difficult to stay in touch—especially with friends from work, whom they do not see if they stay home with a baby. Fathers often work longer hours or take on extra jobs to make ends meet—and therefore have less time for friends. *Helpful:* Some investment outward —as well as inward on the new baby.

Source: *When Partners Become Parents* by University of California at Berkeley psychologists Carolyn Pape Cowan, PhD, and Philip Cowan, PhD. Basic Books, 10 E. 53 St., New York 10022.

Family Disagreements Don't Have to Be Disagreeable

Although friends, lovers—even spouses—all come and go, the families we grew up with are always with us. There is no escaping them.

Even if they live thousands of miles away or are all dead, our families are part of who we are, how we live and how we view ourselves.

Our families can be a source of extreme stress. Just because we're related doesn't mean we'll automatically get along. Unfortunately, the opposite usually applies.

Keys to family harmony...

•Plan your communications. Many people drop verbal bombs on their families, and then let their spontaneous reactions get out of hand.

Better: Make announcements at carefully chosen times. And avoid making generalizations such as *You always*...or *You never.* Stay in touch by letter and phone.

•Adjust your expectations. We expect more from family members than from others in our lives. Many people try to get their families to live up to an unrealistic TV image of domestic bliss.

Better: Instead of hoping family members will change, change the way *you* relate to them.

•Tolerate...but don't endorse. It's not necessary to like or approve of everything your relatives do. You can love them anyway.

Better: Grit your teeth and tell yourself, *Their behavior is no reflection on me.*

•Adopt a surrogate family. No matter how much we'd like them to, family members can't satisfy all our needs. Developing relationships with friends to fill the gaps will make family conflicts less important.

Examples: If your mother keeps trying to run your life, make friends with an older woman who accepts your choices. If your siblings belittle your success at work, find friends who cheer you on.

•Laugh. Much of the family chaos that drives you crazy would actually seem funny if it were happening to someone else.

Better: Pretend the incident is happening in a different family and laugh about it. You'll be more relaxed in the midst of tension—and better able to appreciate your relatives' diversity.

Cast of characters...

In all families, different members play certain roles. When you understand what those roles are, you can start to change the way they affect you...and assume some control over your reactions.

Roles aren't static—they often alternate, depending on which branch or member of the family you're dealing with. *Common family roles:*

• Dictator. Usually a parent or grandparent, this person needs to be in charge and tries to call the shots in everyone's life. Other family members live in fear of the dictator and walk on eggshells trying to please.

Most dictators are highly competent and like to see things done right. They also don't know of any other way to relate to people. They get away with their behavior because the rest of the family is too scared to stand up to them.

To deal with a dictator: Stop being a victim. Remember that you're no longer dependent on this person for survival, and set boundaries. Say *no* when necessary—politely but firmly. You'll hit major resistance at first, but if you hold your ground, eventually you'll be treated with more respect.

• Pot-stirrer. Like the dictator, the pot-stirrer loves to be at the center of attention. But unlike the dictator, he/she won't admit it.

Pot-stirrers call themselves *good communicators,* when what they're really doing is making trouble between family members by carrying gossip and inciting conflicts.

To deal with a pot-stirrer: Identify the person who's always the bringer of bad tidings. Recognize the behavior for what it is—a bid for power, not an attempt at bridge-building. Refuse to play along. Without losing your temper, say, *I don't think that's any of my business, and I don't think you should be passing this information around.* Then back off.

• Butterfly. Charming but irresponsible, the butterfly makes promises and never keeps them ...offers help but fails to deliver...disappears whenever a crisis arises.

Butterflies can't cope with real life. They want to be liked, so they agree to everything, but can't follow through because of their fears.

To deal with a butterfly: Admit to yourself that you can't count on this person. Enjoy the butterfly for what he can offer and stop expecting things he'll never be able to give.

• Free spirit. Operating under a very solid sense of values, free spirits are very secure in themselves and are not subject to feeling guilt. They balance loyalty to the family with loyalty to themselves.

To deal with a free spirit: Understand that this person is not going to change and fit into your mold. You may envy the free spirit for having the courage to do what he wants to do—and things that you may want to do as well. Reexamine your expectations for this person—you may have to lower them.

• Diplomat. This person mediates disputes instead of causing them. Always even-tempered, diplomats do the communicating that other family members should be doing themselves.

The payoff is power—the diplomat's skills are very valuable to the family. *Cost:* Burnout. Unlike the first four family types, diplomats don't cause stress to other family members—but are a danger to themselves.

If you're a diplomat: Let others fight their own battles. As hard as it may be to relinquish power, learn to say, *I'll give you my opinion, but you'll have to work it out for yourselves.*

• Scapegoat. In dysfunctional families, this unfortunate member is blamed for everyone else's problems—problems the others aren't willing to deal with themselves.

It's easier to say, *We're poor because it costs so much to send Tommy to school* than, *We're poor because Dad drinks and can't hold a job.*

Scapegoats believe the rap—whenever anything's wrong, they assume it's their fault. Like diplomats, scapegoats are more a danger to themselves than to others.

If you're a scapegoat: Build a surrogate family that accepts you as you are and gives you a lot of positive reinforcement...consider seeing a therapist...get whatever outside help you need to build your self-esteem to the point where you can say, *You're wrong—it's not my fault.*

Proceed with caution...

Change is difficult, and family members will not be happy about your efforts to disrupt old patterns. It's a good idea to warn them—lovingly—that you're going to be handling things differently from now on.

Expect some turmoil, but don't give up—eventually, your family will get used to it. In the meantime, the strength, sanity and self-esteem you regain will be worth the trouble.

Source: Denise Lang, author of *Family Harmony: Coping With Your Challenging Relatives,* Prentice Hall, 15 Columbus Circle, New York 10023.

Rules for Family Fights

Essential: Fighting fair. Every couple must develop its own rules of combat, but the following are generally sound:

- Never go for the jugular. Everyone has at least one soft, defenseless spot. A fair spouse attacks elsewhere.
- Focus on a specific topic. Don't destroy your spouse with a scorched-earth campaign. *Fair:* "I'm angry because you don't make breakfast before I go to the office." *Unfair:* "I'm angry because you're useless, and my mother was right—you're not tall enough, either."
- Don't criticize things that probably can't be changed. A physical blemish or a spouse's limited earning power is not a fair target. On the other hand, it's dangerous to stew in silence if your partner drops dirty socks on the floor or chews with mouth agape. Minor irritations fester.
- Don't leave the house during a fight. You'll be talking to yourself—your own best supporter. *Result:* A self-serving reconstruction of what happened, rather than an objective view of the situation.
- Argue only when sober. Alcohol is fuel for the irrational. Disagreements are beneficial only if you use reason.
- Keep your fights strictly verbal. A fight that turns physical intimidates rather than resolves.
- Don't discuss volatile subjects late at night. It's tempting to sum up your day at 11 o'clock. But everything seems worse when you are tired. And if you start arguing at 11, you'll be still more exhausted the next morning. *Better:* Make a date to go at it when both sides are fresh.
- Always sleep in the same room, no matter how bitter the fight. The bed is a symbol of the marital bond, and it's more difficult to stay angry with a spouse there.
- If you're getting nowhere after a long stretch of quarreling, simply stop. Don't say a word. Your spouse will have great difficulty arguing solo. You can always resume the next day.
- Don't sulk after the real fighting is over. Pride has no place here. The winner of the fight should be the one to initiate the reconciliation.
- Consider outside help. If you never seem to resolve an issue despite both parties' best efforts, use other resources...not necessarily a 10-week course or a formal session with a counselor. You might simply cultivate a couple whose marriage you admire and try to profit by their example.
- Don't give up too easily on either the fight or the relationship. A strong marriage demands risk-taking, including the risk of feeling and showing extreme anger. The intimacy of marriage is won through pain and friction as well as through pleasure.

Source: Kevin and Marilyn Ryan, coauthors of *Making a Marriage,* St. Martin's Press, New York.

How to Pick the Right School for Your Young Child

- Visit each school you're considering. Be wary of schools that try to sell themselves to you over the phone. The good ones will insist you judge their curriculum firsthand.
- Talk with the director and the staff members who will be involved with your child.

• Ask to see the school's license, insurance contract, and health and fire department inspection forms.

• Be sure the school allows only approved persons to pick up your child at the end of the school day. The school should have a strict rule that if someone who is not on the list comes for the child, the parent should be called immediately.

• Check cleanliness and hygiene.

• Review the school's educational goals. The program should be designed to develop social, emotional, intellectual, and physical skills. See the teacher's lesson plans.

• Ask how students are disciplined.

• Observe the other children. Will they be compatible with yours?

• *Ask yourself:* "Could I spend a few years of my life here?"

• If possible, make surprise visits to the school at different times of the day after your child has been enrolled. If you're denied admission to areas you wish to see, be suspicious.

When You Have to Refuse A Family Member

This is the hardest kind of refusal to deal with. You not only need the interpersonal skills to say no gracefully but you also have to rethink your real obligations to your family, so you can say no without guilt. *Suggestions:*

• Resist the hidden-bargain syndrome. Parents often operate under the assumption that since they've done all these wonderful things for their children to bring them up, the offspring owe them everything. Both young and grown children can be manipulated by this assumption. *Remedy:* Recognize that parents do nice things at least as much for their own benefit as for their children's sake.

• Recognize that a family member who acts hurt at a turndown—when it's for a legitimate reason—is torturing himself. You're not responsible for other people's reactions.

• Don't sit on guilt. As soon as you feel it, share it. Guilt pushers know better than anyone how awful it is to feel guilty. Frequently, just pointing out a guilt manipulation makes the other person back off. Once that's done, you're free to sit down and honestly discuss how making another person feel guilty hurts a relationship.

• Learn to say no to your children. Parents, more than anything, want their children to like them. But children need structure and limits in order to learn self-discipline and independence. Remind yourself that you are teaching him how to grow up rather than remain a perennial emotional infant.

Source: Barry Lubetkin, PhD, Institute for Behavior Therapy, New York.

What Makes So Many Siblings So Very Different

Any parent of more than one child—or anyone who has brothers and sisters—knows how different siblings can be.

Sometimes it's hard to believe that they come from the same family. Yet they share most of the same genes, as well as the same homes...and, of course, parents.

Judy Dunn, PhD, an expert who has studied the interactions between family members, tells us what accounts for the differences...

How is your view of child development different from the traditional approach?

Most theories about how families work assume that parents' behavior affects everybody in the family the same way. If this were true, you'd expect siblings from the same family to turn out quite similar to each other.

Yet our data show that for most psychological characteristics, the differences between siblings far exceed the similarities—and any parent will tell you the same thing.

Since Freud's day, psychologists looking at the effects of parental attitudes on children have made their comparisons *between* families. We're saying it's much more relevant to compare experiences of children within the same family.

What are some of the differences?

Kids from the same family vary widely in personality and emotional adjustment—their self-esteem, their tendency to be anxious or easygoing, the way they deal with crises.

Some children sail through unexpected events that hit the whole family, such as unemployment or their parents' divorcing, while others are badly thrown by the same events.

We do find similarities in moral, political and religious beliefs among people who have grown up together. I'm not sure why—it may be that those issues are more intellectual and less influenced by emotional dynamics.

How do kids experience the same family environment differently?

Despite our good intentions, parents tend to treat different children in different ways...in the degree of warmth and affection they show their kids, in their responsiveness, in the disciplinary measures they use.

That in itself is not so surprising when you consider not only children's inborn personality differences but also their ages—you wouldn't expect a mother to behave toward a two-year-old the same way she behaves toward a six-year-old.

In fact, parents' behavior toward children *based on age* is fairly consistent—a mother is likely to behave similarly toward a younger child at two as she did when the older child was that same age.

Some mothers absolutely love babies, and by the time the first child has turned into a contrary preschooler she'll be irritable with the child ...but very affectionate toward the new baby.

Another mother may find babies a bore and become much more responsive when her child is learning to talk.

What hasn't been acknowledged is that children as young as a year old are monitoring these differences, with extraordinary sensitivity.

Children are particularly sensitive to differences in how they're treated by their fathers. Fathers are seen as very special because the amount of time and attention they have for kids is often small. When daddy comes home from work, the children really notice who it is he relates to.

Key: We're learning that what matters to children isn't so much how well they're loved in a general sense, but how loved they are in relation to their brothers and sisters.

Couldn't some of the differences be explained by heredity?

That's one of the intriguing questions. Some personality differences appear very early in children and probably have a great deal to do with heredity.

At the same time, inborn traits may elicit different treatment from parents—a mother may find it easier to relate to an outgoing child than a shy one, or to a docile child rather than one who's always getting into trouble. We almost always find that any variation explained by heredity is magnified by the different family experience of each child.

Is this only true of early childhood?

I think it's a continuing story. The oldest children we've studied have reached early adolescence, and the findings still hold true for them.

The *kinds* of differences that matter to children may change with age.

It's also possible that peer relationships gradually become more important to adolescents than sibling relationships.

How do the interactions between the children in a family affect their development?

Siblings, of course, do have an effect on each other.

For instance, although more research needs to be done, in some families children appear more likely to develop especially well in those areas in which a sibling does *not* shine.

And if two very smart kids are growing up together, the one who thinks he is less intelligent will have lower self-esteem—even though he is very bright compared with children in other families.

What about the influence of birth order?

There's a great deal of folk wisdom about birth order.

Most people believe very strongly that firstborns are more neurotic, responsible, eager to succeed, dependent on parental approval...that

*Do this before going on to read the scoring section that follows.

youngest children are easygoing...that middle children are mediators.

Over the past five years, however, researchers have examined this issue extremely carefully, using very large samples. And they've found that birth order doesn't explain *any* of the personality differences previously thought.

Differences that used to be attributed to birth order may actually have more to do with family size, and the fact that larger families tend to be from lower educational and socio-economic levels.

What can parents do?

Unfortunately, there's no cut-and-dried rule for parents. You want to treat each child equally, yet kids of different ages have different needs.

It's important to keep an eye open for the vulnerable child—the one more likely to be shattered by a family crisis—so you can help to buffer the blow.

Key: Be aware of how closely children are picking up on any kind of competition, and try to avoid preferential treatment, while also appreciating the differences between your kids.

Making sure each child feels loved is more important than trying to figure out the rules of parenting.

Source: Judy Dunn, PhD, distinguished professor of human development at Pennsylvania State University in State College. She is the coauthor of *Separate Lives: Why Siblings are So Different,* Basic Books, 10 E. 53 St., New York 10022.

When Siblings Fight

Squabbles between siblings are inevitable. Parents can't prevent them, but they can play a constructive role.

• Ignore normal bickering. Your children will become more ingenious about settling their own disagreements.

• Avoid acting as a referee any more than you absolutely have to.

• Don't try to get to the bottom of things to affix blame. In most cases you'll never reach the unbiased "truth," anyway.

• Don't dwell on past misbehavior.

• Don't allow children to play you against your spouse. Back up each other.

• Avoid situations that are bound to cause problems. *Example:* A competitive game between a demanding eight-year-old and a six-year-old who can't stand losing.

• Help your children find varied outlets for emotions.

• Encourage children to work out their own solutions...unless the two in question are ill-matched to do so.

Source: *Raising Good Kids: A Developmental Approach to Discipline* by Louise Bates Ames, PhD, a founding member of the Gesell Institute of Human Development.

Dealing with Sibling Rivalry

• Don't blame yourself. Much sibling rivalry is unavoidable. There's no way you can blame a mother for an intense relationship with her firstborn child.

• Try to minimize a drop in attention to the first child. This change in attention is dramatic —not just because the mother is occupied with the new baby, but because she is often too tired to give the older child the kind of sensitive, playful focus he or she received in the past. (A month after a new baby was born, half the mothers in a recent study were still getting less than five hours' sleep a night.) *Helpful:* Get as much help as possible from the father, grandparents and other relatives and friends.

• Quarreling between siblings increases when the parents are under stress. Anything that alleviates marital stress will also quiet sibling rivalries.

• Keep things stable. A child's life is turned upside down when a new baby arrives. Toddlers of around two and three appreciate a stable, predictable world in which the daily schedule of events—meals, naps, outings—can be counted on. In families where the mother tries to keep the older child's life as unchanged as possible, there is less disturbance.

• Involve the older child in caring for the baby. In families where the mother draws the older child in as a helper for the new baby, there is less hostility a year later.

•Offer distractions to the older child. An older child gets demanding the moment the mother starts caring exclusively for the baby. Mothers who are prepared with projects and helping tasks head off confrontations.

•Recognize and avoid favoritism. Studies show that mothers intervene three times as much on behalf of a second child, although the second is equally likely to have been the cause of the quarrel. The first child's feeling that parents favor the second is often well-founded. Older siblings tend to hold back because they know their aggression is disapproved of, while younger ones often physically attack brothers and sisters because they feel they can get away with it.

•Be firm in consistently prohibiting physical violence. In the context of a warm, affectionate relationship, this is the most effective way to minimize sibling rivalry and to keep jealousies in check.

•Try to keep your sense of humor and your perspective when a new baby is born. Things will get better sooner than you think.

Source: Judy Dunn, author, *Siblings: Love, Envy & Understanding,* Harvard University Press, Cambridge, MA.

Understanding Sibling Rivalry

There are patterns in families that may help parents better understand how sibling rivalry is triggered.

•Where there is an intense, close relationship between the mother and a first-born daughter, the girl is usually hostile to a new baby. A year later, the children are likely to be hostile to each other.

•Firstborn boys are more likely than girls to become withdrawn after a new baby's birth. Children who withdraw (both boys and girls) are less likely to show positive interest in, and affection for, the baby.

•In families where there is a high level of confrontation between the mother and the first child before the birth of a sibling, the first child is more likely to behave in an irritating or interfering way toward the new baby.

•Where the first child has a close relationship with the father, there seems to be less hostility toward the new baby.

•A child whose parents prepare him for the birth of a new baby with explanations and reassurances does not necessarily react any better than a child who wasn't prepared. *More important:* How the parents act after the new baby is born.

•Inside the family, girls are just as physically aggressive as boys.

•Physical punishment of children by parents leads to an increase in violence between children.

•Breastfeeding the new baby can have a beneficial effect on firstborns. *Reason:* Mothers who breastfeed tend to find distractions for the older child during feeding. This turns a potentially provocative time into a loving situation where the first child is also cuddled up with the mother, getting special attention while the baby is being fed.

Source: Judy Dunn, author, *Siblings: Love, Envy & Understanding,* Harvard University Press, Cambridge, MA.

How to Build a Personal Support System

Individuals need not only a few intimate friends but also a network of friendly relationships that make anyone more effective. *To build a support system:*

•Join groups: Participate in self-help groups —not so much for the help as for the support, to get a sense of community and belonging.

•Pursue with other people some of the activities you like. A runner can join a running club, a photographer can take a photography course. This way, you weave your interests into a friendship network.

•Reciprocate acts of friendship. If someone waters your plants, you'd better be prepared to do the same for him. Reciprocity—both giving and accepting—is part of keeping any kind of friendship. People who have problems with accepting favors should remember that other people feel good doing things for them.

•Mentor friends. The younger person ordinarily seeks out the older one. However, the older person might do well to encourage such a relationship because there's something in it for him or her, too—a revitalization that comes from dealing with a younger person with ambition, enthusiasm, and a fresh education.

What Nourishes And What Poisons A Friendship

Key nourishing qualities:

•Authenticity. Inauthentic behavior is contrived and false. Authentic behavior is spontaneous and unpremeditated. Being freely and deeply oneself is important to friendship.

•Acceptance. A sound friendship permits the expression of anger, childishness and silliness. It allows us to express the various facets of our personality without fear of harsh judgment. A feeling of being valued promotes our fullest functioning with other people.

•Direct expression. Coaxing, cajoling, dropping "cute" hints, manipulating and beating around the bush are all barriers to clear communications. When people know what they want from each other, they establish clear communication and contact. They're in a position to attempt an agreement regarding their desires. They may also realize they're too different to get along and that they may be less frustrated if their relationship is more casual.

•Empathy. This involves an effort to understand another's beliefs, practices and feelings (not necessarily agreeing with them). Empathy means listening, trying to understand, and communicating this understanding to the speaker.

What poisons friendships:

•Blame. Blame shifts responsibility and also can be a way of avoiding self-examination. The antithesis of blame and defensiveness is to assume responsibility for one's own feelings. If a person is honest enough to admit his mistakes and finds he's forgiven, he can then be tolerant of his friends' foibles.

•Excess dependency. Some people have lost touch with their values and their strength and need other people to lean on. This kind of person feels unable to be alone. In the dependent friendship, growth and development are stifled rather than enhanced.

Source: Dr. Joel D. Block, clinical psychologist and author of *Friendship: How to Give it, How to Get It,* Macmillan, New York.

Making Friendships Stronger

Even the best of friendships can have their ups and downs. *How to minimize this type of stress:*

•To move closer to a friend, take him or her into your confidence. Share your thoughts and feelings. There's no guarantee that this approach will produce positive results, but the probabilities increase dramatically when you give what you want to get.

•Use compromise to resolve differences. The only other alternatives are domination by one and the consequent resentment on the part of the other or withdrawal. Compromise restores the reciprocity needed in friendship.

•Avoid a mismatch. It's foolish to pursue a friendship with someone who isn't interested in you. Friendship involves mutual feelings.

•Observe the Golden Rule. Most of us want the same things in our friendships—honesty, a sharing of good feelings and thoughts, empathy, support, fun. If you're not getting these, ask: *Do I offer the same things to others that I want for myself?*

Source: Dr. Joel D. Block, a clinical psychologist, and author of *Friendship: How to Give It, How to Get It,* Macmillan, New York.

How to Help a Friend Who Has Been A Crime Victim

The *emotional* harm caused by a crime—from a rape to a burglary—is frequently much worse than any physical damage.

Crime victims are 10 times more likely than the average person to become severely depressed—even after a decade or more.

The quality of a crime victim's support system makes a big difference in his/her recovery. *Trap:* Many well-meaning people unknowingly treat crime victims in callous or hurtful ways.

To be truly helpful, friends and family members need to understand what the person is going through.

Emotional aftereffects...

Almost every crime victim experiences rage, anger, fear, anxiety, helplessness, hopelessness, guilt, shame and humiliation—although not necessarily in this order.

Victims deal first with the emotion they can handle best. That's why some people are initially angry while others are fearful and still others are ashamed.

Crime victims feel shame because, as adults, we're supposed to be in control. When something happens that's beyond our control, it makes us feel weak and childlike. This is especially true for men. *Also common:*

- A sense of being permanently damaged. Many rape victims, for instance, may think they'll never be able to enjoy sex again.
- Inability to trust others.
- Loss of belief that the world is just.
- Intrusive, distressing recollections, dreams and flashbacks.
- Distress at exposure to events or places that symbolize or resemble an aspect of the crime.
- Denial. Avoidance of thoughts or feelings connected with the crime.
- Inability to recall an important aspect of the crime. People block out what is painful.
- Diminished ability to enjoy life.
- A sense that he is not going to live very long.
- Being overly cautious and easily startled.

Secondary victimization...

After the crime, most victims go through a *secondary victimization*—often worse than the crime itself—when they have to deal with insensitive family members, police officers, courts, hospitals, insurance agencies, etc.

Sometimes a victim will think he has recovered...only to walk into a situation that reminds him of the crime, and all the terrible memories flood back. If the crime happened in the person's home, office or a place he visits regularly, he may relive it over and over again. The aftereffects can last for years.

Although rapes and other personal attacks are particularly devastating, burglaries, auto thefts and other property crimes frequently cause emotional problems also.

Reason: We have two major barriers in our lives—the walls of our home and our skin. When either is breached we feel violated.

Others make it worse...

Crime victims need to talk about the crime. But after a week or two, friends and family often tune out. *Why:* They feel subconsciously threatened by the idea that this crime could have happened to them.

This leaves the victims isolated and their feelings unresolved. Some think that there is something wrong with them because they can't forget.

Many well-meaning friends and family members inadvertently give victims the message that they were dumb to get victimized. *Typical statements:* "What were you doing out so late at night?" "Why don't you live in a building with a doorman?"

People who do this are trying to reassure themselves that a similar crime could not happen to them—they would never walk down that street or open the door under the same circumstances.

But the victims, reliving the crime, feel ashamed. They try to figure out what they should have done differently.

How to know when victims need help...

Because most victims want to put the crimes behind them as soon as possible, emotional problems may lie dormant for months before they emerge. *Signs of trouble lying dormant:*

• Inability to concentrate. The victim finds it hard to hold a conversation, read, do paperwork ...anything. He feels like he's losing his mind.

• Behavioral changes. These can include avoiding the scene of the crime—work, school, the subway...even being out-of-doors anywhere after dark.

• Increase or decrease in oral habits. These include talking, drinking, smoking, taking drugs, having sex and eating.

• Trouble sleeping. Repeated nightmares or nightsweats are common, as are frequent wakenings.

How to help...

Encourage crime victims to get help *immediately* from a therapist or counselor trained in emotional trauma.* *Warning:* Tremendous damage can be caused by therapists who are not trained in post-traumatic stress disorder—from which crime victims suffer.

Don't tell victims to forget about the crime. Be supportive. Listen. And keep listening. *Helpful response:* "I'm sorry this happened. What can I do for you?"

Try to help in a concrete way. Offer to do the kind of things you would do if someone had a physical injury—take out the garbage, make dinner or stay overnight.

Treat victims as if they were ill or wounded, even if there's no *physical* injury. This is especially important for rape victims. Although you can't see emotional wounds, they're there just the same.

Be willing to confront your own past. Deal with any victimizations you may have encountered.

Example: Many people who have been raped in the past don't want to be with recent rape victims—it brings up bad memories.

People also shy away from victims because they remind them of traumas they've suppressed, like having been abused as a child.

Don't blame crime victims. Help them to stop blaming themselves for being responsible in any way. *Helpful questions:* "Did you mug yourself?" "Did you beat yourself up?" "Did you rob your own home?" "If you could have done it differently, you would have."

**For a referral in your area call:* National Organization for Victim Assistance, 202-232-6682...Crime Victims' Counseling Services, Inc., 718-875-5862...National Victims' Center, 817-877-3355.

Source: Psychotherapist Shelley Neiderbach, PhD, executive director of Crime Victims' Counseling Services, Box 023003, Brooklyn, New York 11202. She is the author of *Invisible Wounds: Crime Victims Speak*, Haworth Publishing Co., 10 Alice St., Binghamton, New York 13904.

What to Do When You Are Caught in the Middle Of Feuding Friends

Being in the middle of arguing friends or spouses is a very difficult position in which to find yourself.

Too often your loyalties are tested, and you're called upon to play the intermediary, act as a sounding board or perform other tough duties that you'd rather avoid.

Consolation: Being in the middle is actually a sign that you're living an interesting life filled with passionate people. *You just have to know how to deal with them.*

Roles to avoid...

• *Don't* play intermediary. Carrying information back and forth makes people feel special. But the message often gets distorted in the translation. And you may wind up the target of both parties' anger.

Just as some ancient Romans killed the bearers of bad news, intermediaries too often wind up being symbolically "killed" by one or both parties who end the friendship.

Example: Janet told Carole that Carole's husband was having an affair. Carole and her husband patched things up and saved their marriage, but Carole no longer speaks to Janet.

• *Don't* offer opinions. Even people who ask what you think don't actually want to know the truth. What they really want is to hear that you support their position.

Better way: When friends ask for your opinion, ask them what they *want* to hear—what do they wish you'd say. Once that's out in the open you can be honest.

• *Don't* be a secret-keeper. Arguing friends often tell a third party things they don't want passed on to the other person. *Purpose:* To win you over to their side. People who tell other people secrets are attempting to control them.

Self-defense: Say you don't want to hear secrets —that it would put you in a compromising position.

Sometimes, however, people get drawn into secret disclosures whether or not they want to hear them. In that case, listen...but keep it to yourself. Although it's tempting to reveal to one side what the other side thinks, *don't do it.* You may wind up losing both friends.

• *Don't* openly take sides. Even people who ask you to take sides secretly want you to remain impartial. *Reason:* If you openly take sides, you strengthen one person's position. This increases the possibility of a breakup—which neither really wants.

Trap: They may hold you responsible if their relationship collapses.

How to be truly helpful if you can't get out of the way...

Help each person reinterpret and relabel what the other's anger is all about.

Example: Lorraine and JoAnn were estranged because JoAnn thought Lorraine expected too much of her. Hurt by the rejection, Lorraine was ready to write the friendship off. Susan helped by telling JoAnn that Lorraine was a needy person who was afraid of being abandoned by her friends. And she helpfully told Lorraine that JoAnn was sensitive about her privacy and didn't want to feel smothered. *Result:* Once they saw how the other felt, the two women were able to save their friendship.

Sometimes a friend who's involved in a long, ongoing argument will insist that you're being disloyal if you don't openly take sides. *What to do:* Take the time—it may stretch on for hours —to have an honest talk about your friendship. *What to discuss:* How and why you became friends...the common elements that keep you together...why your friendship is important.

Such a straight-from-the-heart talk will show your friend that your taking sides in the argument is not crucial to your relationship and that what you have is based on a long history of caring and honesty.

Also convey that if you do take sides, it will only prolong the argument. *Reason:* The more allies they have, the longer people are willing to argue.

It also helps to counsel your friends *how* to argue. You don't need to be a therapist to teach people that it's wrong to *kitchen sink* (throw in every grievance that they've stored up for years) or *zap* (go for someone's weak spots).

What is important: Teaching people how to listen when they argue. *Best:* Encourage them to paraphrase—restate in different words—what the other person has said.

Example: If Elaine is obviously angry, rather than counterattacking, the person she's angry at could say, "I understand that you're angry at me because you think I haven't returned any invitations after you've put yourself out for me...but I'd like you to allow me to explain the reasons for my behavior."

Sometimes a friend in the middle can use a long-standing friendship with each person to remind them that they're letting their emotions run ahead of their intellect. *Also helpful:* Point out to them that most arguments aren't about important issues, they're really about ego and pride, about not wanting to lose face.

Bottom line: Even though it may feel unpleasant at the time, being in the middle of arguing friends can bring out the best in you. It gives you a chance to demonstrate your compassion and loyalty as well as negotiating and mediating skills that you may not even know you have.

And reuniting two people you care about can be quite gratifying.

Source: Psychologist Barry Lubetkin, PhD, director of the Institute for Behavior Therapy, 137 E. 36 St., New York 10016.

How to Enjoy Relationships

• Accept people as they are. Nothing kills a relationship faster than the expectation that you can change someone. It's impossible. The best you can do is to become more tolerant and flexible yourself, encourage an atmosphere for change, and then hope for the best.

•When you give, give freely. If you expect people to give the same back, measured by the cup, you'll always be disappointed. If they respond, that's great. And if they don't, that's all right, too.

•Be honest with the people you care about. Get rid of petty irritants. Don't suffer in silence until you finally explode.

•Honesty needn't be cruel. *Good rule:* Be as tactful with your spouse and children as you are with friends and distant relatives. Most people are wonderful in courtship but later get careless. Love is not a license for rudeness.

•Don't use your family as an alibi when you fall short of goals. Stop underestimating these people. They're much more flexible than most people assume. You can make your dreams real if you want them enough—and share them with the people you love. But if you never say, "Let's go to Nepal!" you'll never get there.

•It's a gamble to be vulnerable. But you never really lose because the risk itself reminds you how richly you are living.

Source: Leo Buscaglia, author of *Loving Each Other*, Holt, Rinehart and Winston, New York.

Terminating a Relationship

In terminating either a business or personal relationship, those who initiate the termination have the upper hand. They also have the bulk of the responsibility.

To walk away from the termination with a sense of moral clarity, it is essential to have made a genuine attempt to come to some degree of accommodation with the other party, whether employee or spouse. Terminators should meet with those terminated to share their dissatisfaction when they are still open to finding a solution.

Terminators should answer these questions:

•What do they need from the other party to continue the relationship?

•What support are they prepared to give the other party?

•What is an acceptable time frame for the changes to be made? A reasonable period should be allowed for making changes and adjustments. Announcing requirements for change on Friday, and then deciding on Monday that the relationship won't work, is unfair.

•What don't the terminators want?

•What aren't they prepared to give?

•How would they describe the consequences if satisfactory changes aren't made? People often resist making major changes not because they fear what's ahead but because they are unwilling to give up what they have. The same fear hinders organizational change as well as change in personal life.

Source: Gisele Richardson, president, Richardson Management Associates, management consultants, Montreal.

Changing an Enemy Into an Ally

If there's someone in your business with whom you're always at odds:

•Think of this person as someone you like, someone who can work with you.

•Create in your mind an image of the relationship restored.

•Treat this person as a valued friend and associate.

•You won't see immediate results, but over time, you'll find that this person is responding to you in a more positive way.

•*The lesson:* Be aware of your expectations of others. People are likely to deliver what you expect them to deliver.

Source: The late Dr. Norman Vincent Peale, author and lecturer, New York.

Better One-on-One Conversations

It's been said before, but the surest way to improve your one-to-one conversations is…to become a better listener. Listening skills may seem simple enough, but many people (particularly men) need to work on them.

•Live in the present moment. Resist distractions. Don't let your mind wander to your bank balance or to after-dinner plans.

•Stay alert and concentrate on what your "partner" is saying—not only the words, but the emotions behind them. Rephrase what you've heard in your own words (mentally or verbally).

•Maintain consistent eye contact.

•Lean toward the person if seated.

•Nod or smile in response.

•*To handle a long-winded anecdote or complaint:* Steer the conversation to a mutually interesting subject. Or...approach the old subject from a new angle.

•When it's your turn to talk, think about the point you want to make before you start speaking.

•Get to the point in as few steps as possible.

•Consider your audience. Make what you're saying relevant to the particular person you're addressing.

•Don't be afraid to ask a "dumb" question about a subject that's new to you.

•If your conversations seem bland, maybe you're suppressing honest disagreements. A dispute shouldn't hurt an exchange (or a friendship), as long as a certain etiquette is respected.

•Give the other person credit for something before you disagree. Never say, "How can you think something like that?" *Better:* "That's a good point, but I see it differently..." or, first point out areas of similarity: "We agree that world peace is vital—therefore..."

Sources: Mark Sherman, associate professor of psychology, and Adelaide Haas, associate professor of communications, State University of New York, New Paltz.

All About Nerds

Nerds get attention by being obnoxious. They don't pay attention to the signals other people send them.

How not to be a nerd:

•Let people finish what they are saying.

•Don't always insist that you know more than other people about the subject under discussion.

•Slow down on advice-giving.

•Open up to new ideas.

•Let yourself change your mind once in a while.

When a nerd starts to realize that much of his behavior stems from anxiety about being accepted and loved, he is well on his way to being a nerd no longer.

Source: Doe Lang, author of *The Secret of Charisma,* Wideview Books, New York.

Three A's for a Lasting Marriage

Attention—listen to your spouse and help him/her when that help is least expected. *Acknowledgment*—do not take your partner for granted. Recognize him for the little things he does to make your life easier. *Appreciation*—thank your spouse for working to make your marriage a success and say you love him for helping make you happy.

Source: Lawrence Grossman, PhD, professor of clinical psychology, Adelphi University, Garden City, New York.

Men, Women and Sex

Men and women want sex for different reasons at different points in their lives. In order to establish his own identity, a young boy separates emotionally from his mother—thus, his early relationships keep women distant. The maturing process enables men to have more loving and connected sex. Young girls are always connected with mother, and therefore, the maturing process for a woman is to learn more "separate," freer sexuality. *As teenagers:* Boys have sex for pure pleasure, while girls often are motivated by affection. *Ages 21 to 35:* Men still yearn for physical pleasure, while love remains the prime motivation for women.

After age 35: Women are now free to seek sexual pleasure, while men are more open to the love and intimacy that comes with sex.

Source: Dagmar O'Connor, PhD, psychologist and sex therapist in private practice in New York. She is author of *How to Make Love to the Same Person for the Rest of Your Life and Still Love It,* a book and video set from Dag Media Corporation, 57 W. 58 St., New York 10019.

Try on Your Partner's Life

Switch roles with your partner for a weekend—each of you takes on the responsibilities of the other. This can be a real eye-opener—a chance to see yourself as your partner sees you and to develop more empathy in the future.

Source: *100 Ways to Make Sex Sensational and 100% Safe: Enjoy Monogramy Without Monotony* by Rachel Copelan, PhD, marriage counselor and sex therapist, Beverly Hills, California. Lifetime Books.

Kids and Apologies

Apologize to your child—it's important—if you make a mistake or say something you did not mean. Keep the apology simple—*I'm sorry ...I was feeling cranky.* Kids need to know that adults, including their parents, do get angry... but that anger is not the end of the world.

Source: Nancy Samalin, founder of Parent Guidance Workshops in New York, and author of *Love and Anger: The Parental Dilemma,* Penguin Books, 375 Hudson St., New York 10014.

Children and Stress

Help children handle stress by encouraging comforting habits—a blanket or toy for young children...then exercise, deep breathing, guided imagery, music and other stress-reduction techniques as they get older. Show kids a lot of affection. If you are divorcing, let your children discuss their feelings about the breakup (remember that young children often blame themselves for their parents' divorce). If necessary, get professional help to resolve your anger. Seek professional help for kids if they seem to be overwhelmed by stressful experiences.

Source: Lawrence Kutner, PhD, clinical psychologist in Lafayette, California, and author of *Your School-Age Child.* William Morrow & Co.

Children and Frustration

To understand kids' frustrations when learning something new, make it a point to learn something new yourself every month. The experience will help you empathize with your children, who are learning so many new things all the time.

Source: *Little Lessons for Teachers* by Mary Kay Shanley, member of the Board of the Iowa Talented and Gifted Association in W. Des Moines. Sta-Kris, Inc.

Negotiate with Your Kids

Negotiate with your children instead of seeking to impose your will on them. Fair negotiation helps avoid fights by averting power struggles. Consider negotiating any situation that does not pose a health or safety risk to the child and does not go against your personal, religious or spiritual beliefs. *Useful:* Negotiate compromises. *Example:* If a child hates doing the dishes, offer to do them all the time in return for the child being responsible for taking out all of the trash.

Source: *The Challenging Child* by Mitch Golant, PhD, clinical psychologist, Bel Air, California. Berkley Books.

Children and Hand Preference

Trying to change a child's hand preference can interfere with his/her learning—and self-esteem. Several studies have shown that left-handed children are twice as likely to have allergies and asthma...and are at greater risk of heart disease and dying in an accident. So some parents try to change left-handed children into right-handed ones. *Better:* Let your child use his natural hand. Parents should instead focus on disease prevention—such as allergy testing if your child wheezes...and accident prevention—such as teaching your child to be especially cautious when using right-handed tools and utensils.

Source: *The Left-Hander Syndrome* by Stanley Coren, PhD, professor of psychology, University of British Columbia, Vancouver. Vintage Books.

11

Your Home

Checklist for Move To a New House

•Arrange for the utilities (gas, electric, water, etc.) to be turned on in the new house or apartment a few days before you move in.

•Install the telephone a month before you move (or as early as is feasible).

•Enroll your child in the new local school.

•Open savings and checking accounts promptly at a bank in the new neighborhood.

•Notify companies of change of address (insurance, credit card, magazines, etc.).

•If you are moving to a new state, check to see if your auto coverage is applicable.

•Notify the IRS of the move, both at the time of the move and again when you file your income tax.

•Have pharmaceutical prescriptions renewed before moving so that adequate amounts of medication will be on hand.

•Ask the previous occupant for a list of reliable local service people (electricians, plumbers, carpenters, etc.) and good nearby stores.

•*Moving outdoor plants to a new home:* For a long move, place them in a plastic bag and cover with wet straw or weeds. If you know in autumn you'll be leaving in the spring, use a spade to cut a deep circle around a shrub or young tree to sever the roots and outline the root ball.

Cutting Utility Costs at Home

Most of us turn out the lights when we want to save energy, but there are even smarter ways to reduce your bills...

Refrigerators...

The refrigerator represents about 30% of most electric bills. To find out how well yours operates, open the door and place a dollar bill against the seal. Then close the door. If you can remove the bill easily, the seal needs replacing. Vacuuming the coils behind or below the unit can improve efficiency as well, but be sure to first unplug the refrigerator.

Insulation...

Up to 40% of home heating escapes outdoors unnecessarily because of inadequate insulation. A free energy audit by your local power company will show you how to improve insulation. *Opportunities:* Install more insulation under the roof and behind walls, and weather strip the windows or replace them entirely.

Lighting...

Compact fluorescent bulbs last at least 10 times longer than regular bulbs and use one-fourth of the electricity while producing the same amount of light. Unlike the long fluorescent bulbs found in offices, these screw into ordinary sockets. Some utilities offer compact fluorescents at a discount. Some even give them away.

Water...

Once all leaks are fixed, the largest water-waster is the toilet. At about six gallons per flush, a lot of good water—and dollars—go down the drain. Low-flush toilets only use about 1.6 gallons, but there are other ways to save water without replacing the fixture. *Simple way:* Fill two or three slim plastic bottles with dirt or gravel and place them in the toilet's water tank. This will displace the tank water so that less is used with each flush. Flow-restricters for shower heads save water, too.

Source: Susan Jaffe, a writer who has been specializing in environmental issues for well over a decade.

Environmentally Friendly Household Cleansers

Your favorite household cleansers may do a great job, but their contents are often toxic to breathe, hard on the hands and surfaces—and hazardous to the environment. In addition to being expensive, the containers in which they're sold add up to mountains of waste.

How to make environmentally friendly versions that are just as effective, but cost much less...

• Air freshener. Place a few slices of lemon, orange or grapefruit in a pot of water. Let simmer gently for an hour or more. Your house will be filled with a citrus scent.

• All-purpose liquid cleanser. Cuts grease and cleans countertops, baseboards, refrigerators and other appliances.

Combine in a plastic spray bottle: One teaspoon borax, one-half teaspoon washing soda (a stronger form of baking soda—available in supermarkets), two tablespoons white vinegar or lemon juice, one-half teaspoon vegetable-based detergent (i.e., Murphy's Oil Soap), two cups very hot water.

• Floor cleaner. Use on wood, tile or linoleum for a long-lasting shine.

Mix one-eighth cup vegetable-based detergent, one-half cup white vinegar and two gallons warm water in a plastic pail.

• Oven cleaner. Sprinkle water on the grimy spots, then cover with baking soda. Repeat the process, and let sit overnight. The grease will wipe off the next day. Use liquid soap and water to sponge away any residue.

• Overnight toilet-bowl cleaner. Pour one cup borax into the toilet bowl. Let sit overnight. Flush in the morning. Stains and rings are lifted away.

• Nonabrasive cleanser. Scours sinks and bathtubs, and leaves no gritty residue.

Combine one-quarter cup baking soda and enough vegetable-based detergent to make a creamy paste.

• Window cleaner. Combine in a plastic spray bottle...one-half teaspoon vegetable-based detergent, three tablespoons white vinegar, two cups water.

• Wood-furniture dusting and cleaning cloth. Mix one-half teaspoon olive oil and one-quarter cup white vinegar or lemon juice in a bowl. Apply to a cotton cloth. Reapply as needed.

Source: Annie Berthold-Bond, editor of *Green Alternatives,* a magazine on environmentally friendly products and services, 38 Montgomery St., Rhinebeck, New York 12572. She is the author of *Clean and Green: The Complete Guide to Nontoxic and Environmentally Safe Housekeeping,* Ceres Press, Box 87, Woodstock, New York 12498.

Smoke Detector Disposal Challenge

Most smoke detectors contain radioactive material that could, if the unit become damaged, be dangerous. *Helpful:* Pick the smoke detector up with your hand in a plastic bag. Then turn the bag inside out around the unit and seal the bag. Don't throw the detector in the trash. Don't take it to a hazardous-waste collection site—they don't accept radioactive materials. *Best:* Return the unit to the manufacturer or retailer.

Source: *Complete Trash: The Best Way to Get Rid of Practically Everything Around the House* by Norm Crampton, secretary, Institute for Solid Wastes of the American Public Works Association, M. Evans and Co., 216 E. 49 St., New York 10017.

Dust Allergy Self-Defense

House dust is the most common irritant for allergy sufferers and asthmatics. *Self-defense:*

•Dust and vacuum your home at least twice a week. Conventional vacuum cleaners can blow dust back into the room. Use a vacuum fitted with a HEPA (High-Efficiency Particulate Actuation) filter, such as Nilfisk Model GS90. *Note:* The allergic person shouldn't perform these tasks. If no one else can do the cleaning, the allergic person should wear a face mask while doing the work.

•Keep floors bare. Dust mites, the main allergen in dust, thrive in carpets.

•Cover pillows, mattresses, box springs, and furniture with plastic encasings. Mites breed in furniture and bedding, but can't get through plastic encasings. The plastic should be vacuumed once a week when the linens are changed.

•Wash linens in hot water. Warm or cold water doesn't kill mites.

•Keep the windows in your house shut. This helps to keep outdoor allergens outside. *Note:* Many trees pollinate between 2 a.m. and 4 a.m., so keep windows closed at night.

•Don't use a humidifier. It increases the mold content in the air. Use a dehumidifier for damp spaces.

•Avoid heaters that release irritating particles, such as wood-burning stoves, fireplaces.

•Use the air conditioner in warm weather. It filters out a lot of troublesome particles from the air. Clean or change the filter once a week.

•Get an air filter. Use it when it's too cool for the air conditioner. *Best:* A HEPA filter, which can remove particles that other filters can't. *Important:* When the filter is on, keep room doors and windows closed. *Cost:* About $150 and up.

•Ask your allergist about injections.

Source: Gerald L. Klein, MD, Allergy and Immunology Medical Group, 2067 W. Vista Way, Vista, California 92083. Dr. Klein is an associate clinical professor at the University of California and a member of the Board of Regents of the American College of Allergy and Immunology.

Closing Costs Vary Widely

Closing costs vary widely, from 3% to 10% of a home's purchase price. *Biggest variable:* The number of points charged. *Bottom line:* Shopping around for a no-point or low-point mortgage is an important way to keep closing costs down.

Source: *The Mortgage Book* by John Dorfman, *The Wall Street Journal* reporter and author of seven books on personal finance. Consumer Reports Books, 101 Truman Ave., Yonkers, New York 10703.

Energy Saver

Save energy by adjusting the humidity level in your home. Use a *humidifier* to add moisture to the air in winter to make your home feel warmer without turning up the heat. Use a *dehumidifier* in summer to remove moisture and make your house feel cooler without pumping up the air-conditioning.

Source: *Common Sense,* Box 215, Morrisville, Pennsylvania 19067.

Do-It-Yourself Cookbook

Use standard photo albums (the kind with clear plastic pages) to file newspapers and magazine clippings, as well as recipes written on index cards.

Source: *The Kitchen Survival Guide: A Hand-Holding Kitchen Primer with 130 Recipes to Get You Started* by cookbook author Lora Brody. William Morrow & Co., 1350 Avenue of the Americas, New York 10019.

Better Countertop Cleaning

Laminate countertops should *not* be cleaned with abrasive or chemical cleansers. They strip the high-gloss finish. Then, the only way to restore the finish is to have the countertops professionally resurfaced—at about $9 per linear foot. *Better:* Clean laminate countertops with a mild dishwashing detergent and warm water.

Source: *The Family Handyman,* 7900 International Dr., Suite 950, Minneapolis 55425.

Scratch Preventer

Prevent scratches on the kitchen floor by waxing the floor and the bottom of chair legs.

Source: *Skinflint News,* 1460 Noell Blvd., Palm Harbor, Florida 34683.

Separating Eggs

Easy way to separate eggs: Break the egg into a funnel. The white will run through, and the yolk will remain.

Source: *The Non-Consumers Digest,* Box 403, King Hill, Idaho 83633.

Better Housecleaning

Establish a halfway house for those items (clothing, books, papers, etc.) that you haven't used in years but can't bear to part with. *How it works:* Pack everything into cartons, marking the boxes with a date two years from now, and store it all away. After two years, review contents.

House Sitting Checklist

To decide what kind of sitter you need (to live in or to visit regularly, long term or short term), determine your requirements. *Typically, sitters should:*

- Make the house look lived in, so it won't be burglarized.
- Care for plants, pets and grounds.
- Make sure the pipes won't freeze.
- Guard the house and its possessions against natural disasters.

Where to find help:

- Some communities have sitting services or employment agencies that can fill the job.
- *Better:* Someone you know—the teenage child of a friend, a cleaning woman, a retired neighbor.
- Placement services at colleges.
- When interviewing, test the resourcefulness and intelligence of the candidate.
- Check references.
- If you find a writer looking for a place to stay or a person from the place you are heading to who would like to exchange houses, you might make a deal without any money changing hands.

Before you leave:

• Walk through every sequence of duties with the sitter.

• Put all duties in writing.

• List repair, supply and emergency telephone numbers and your own telephone number or instructions on how to reach you.

• Make clear that no one is to be admitted to the house or given a key without your prior consent.

Air Conditioning Secrets

Room air conditioners mounted in a window or through the wall are ideal for keeping small, comfortable havens against the worst of summer's hot spells. They can be more economical than central air conditioning because they are flexible—you cool only the rooms you are using. But even a single unit can be expensive.

To keep a room cool with minimum use of the air conditioner:

• Limit the use of the air conditioner in the "open vent" setting—it brings in hot outside air that the machine must work hard to keep cooling.

• Protect the room from the direct heat of the sun with awnings, drapes or blinds.

• Close off rooms that you are air-conditioning.

• Turn off unnecessary lights. They add extra heat (fluorescent lights are coolest).

• Turn off the unit if you will be out of the room more than 30 minutes.

• Service room air conditioners annually to keep them efficient. Replace filters, keep condensers clean and lubricate the moving parts.

• Supplement central air conditioning with a room air conditioner in the most-used room.

Source: John A. Constance, licensed engineer specializing in industrial ventilation, Newtown, PA.

Using Fans to Save on Air Conditioning

Ventilating fans can cool a whole house—or a single room—at a fraction (about 10%) of the cost of air conditioning. The trick is knowing how to use them to move in cooler air and to move hotter air out.

• Control the source of the cooler air by manipulating windows. During the day, for example, downstairs windows on the shady northern or eastern side of the house are most likely to provide cool air. All other windows should be closed and shaded from direct sun with blinds and drapes.

• At night, shut lower-floor windows for security while upstairs windows provide cool air.

• Attic fans are permanent installations above the upper floor. They are powerful enough to cool a whole house. The opening to the outside must be as large as the fan-blade frame in order to handle the air flow properly.

• Louvers, bird screening and (particularly) insect screening all reduce the exhaust capacity of a fan.

• A doorway or other opening must allow the fan to pull cool air directly up from the rest of the house.

• Direct-connected fans are quieter than belt-driven fans.

• Some attic fans have thermometers that automatically turn them off and on when the attic temperature reaches a certain degree of heat.

• Window fans have adjustable screw-on panels to fit different window sizes. Less powerful than attic fans, they serve more limited spaces.

• Box fans are portable and can be moved from room to room to cool smaller areas.

• Ventilating fans are rated by the cubic feet per minute (CFM) of air that they can exhaust. For effective cooling, engineers recommend an air-change rate of 20 per hour (the entire volume of air in the area to be cooled is changed 20 times every 60 minutes).

• To calculate the required CFM rating for a particular room, calculate its volume in cubic feet. Then multiply this figure by 20/60 (⅓). *Example:* A room 20 feet by 15 feet with an eight-foot ceiling contains 2,400 cubic feet of air.

This, multiplied by ⅓, gives a CFM rating of 800 for a proper-size fan.

•The CFM rating of an attic fan is done the same way. Total the cubic feet of the rooms and hallways you want cooled before multiplying by one third.

Source: John A. Constance, licensed engineer specializing in industrial ventilation, Newtown, PA.

How to Save Water

Whether you live in an area plagued by periodic droughts or simply want to save money on rising water bills:

•Install flow restricters in your showers and take shorter showers. (A normal showerhead sprays up to eight gallons per minute, so even a short, five-minute shower uses up to 40 gallons.)

•Get in the habit of turning off the water while shaving, brushing teeth and washing hands, except when you need to rinse.

•Put a weighted plastic container into the toilet tank to cut the normal amount of water used in flushing (approximately six gallons per flush) by as much as half. Some people use bricks to displace water in the tank, but this may damage the tank.

•Wash only full loads in your dishwasher and clothes washer. Running these machines half empty is a big water waster.

•Fix all leaks. Dripping water, even if slow, can cost you a lot of money over the course of several months.

•Use buckets of water to do outside chores like washing the car and cleaning the driveway. If you must use a hose, turn it off between rinsings—don't just let it run.

Home Energy Savers

After you've insulated your home, here are some smaller steps that can trim added amounts from your heating and electricity bills:

•Air conditioner covers. Outdoor covers not only block drafts, they also protect the machine from weather damage during the winter. Check the caulking around the outside of the machine, too. Indoor covers can be even more effective draft stoppers than outdoor ones. You can make your own from heavy plastic or buy Styrofoam-insulated ones.

•Door and window draft guards. Sand-filled fabric tubes effectively prevent uncomfortable drafts from entering around doors and windows. Easy to install and to remove.

•Light dimmers. The newest solid-state dimmers consume little energy themselves but allow reduced lighting levels and lower energy consumption. Some dimmers are installed in the wall in place of conventional switches. Others simply plug into existing sockets or are inserted into lamp cords. A dimmer can save you approximately 50% a year on a single light fixture if you dim it halfway.

•Air deflectors. Used in homes heated by forced air, these direct air from the vents away from walls and into the room. Depending on the location of your registers, significant savings can result.

•Heat reflectors. Reflectors direct radiator heat into the rooms to save energy. Very inexpensive ones can be made by covering a sheet of plywood or foam board with aluminum foil and placing it between the radiator and the wall.

•Storm window kits. You can make your own storm windows with sheets of plastic and tape. Kits are available to install them either inside or outside your existing windows. The cost ranges from as low as 85¢ to $35 per window. Removable rigid plastic storm windows in permanently installed frames are also big energy savers. Some companies will cut them to fit any window at a cost of $4–$5 per square foot. For city dwellers, they also reduce noise levels significantly. Storm windows reduce heat loss by as much as 30%, so an investment in permanent storm windows may pay off in the long run.

•Energy audits. Your local utility may offer free home energy audits. For absolutely no cost or obligation, it will inspect your home and suggest ways you can reduce your energy costs. Also, more and more utilities are acting as general contractors in making energy-efficiency changes on houses, ensuring that the work is done properly and on time.

Source: *Bottom Line/Personal,* Greenwich, CT.

Keeping Street Noise Out of Your Home

Noise intrusion is a constant and nagging problem in many buildings because of thin walls and badly insulated floors and ceilings.

How to noise-proof walls:

• Hang sound-absorbing materials, such as quilts, decorative rugs, carpets or blankets. *Note:* Cork board and heavy window draperies absorb sound within a room but do not help much with noise from outside.

• If you don't want to hang heavy materials directly on your walls, consider a frame that attaches to the wall. Insulation goes on the wall within the frame, and then a fabric is affixed to the frame.

How to noise-proof ceilings:

• Apply acoustical tile directly to the ceiling with adhesive for a quick and inexpensive fix.

• If you can undertake more extensive work, put in a dropped ceiling of acoustical tile with about six inches of insulation between the new and existing ceiling.

How to noise-proof floors:

• Install a thick plush carpet over a dense sponge rubber padding.

• *Key:* The padding must be dense, at least three-eighths of an inch thick. Your foot should not press down to the floor when you step on the padding.

When You Need an Exterminator and When You Don't

Bug problems can usually be solved without an exterminator. *Keys:* Careful prevention techniques, basic supermarket products and apartment-building cooperation.

Roaches...

Roaches are persistent pests that are the bane of apartment dwellers. The problem is not that roaches are so difficult to kill but that the effort has to be made collectively, by every tenant in a particular building. Roaches cannot be exterminated effectively from an individual apartment. If one apartment has them, they'll quickly spread throughout the building.

Most landlords hire exterminating services that visit during daytime hours when most tenants are at work. They wind up spraying just a few apartments, which is totally ineffective.

Better:

• Apartment dwellers have to get together, contact their landlord and arrange for all apartments to be exterminated at the same time. If the landlord is uncooperative, the Board of Health should be notified. If you live in a co-op, the co-op board should make arrangements for building extermination. *Best:* A superintendent or member of the building staff should perform regular exterminations, since he can get into apartments at odd hours when the tenants are not home. A professional exterminator should be called only as a backup, in case of a severe problem in a particular apartment.

• Incinerators that no longer burn garbage are a major infestation source in large buildings. Many cities, to cut down on air pollution, have ordered the compacting rather than the burning of garbage. Garbage is still thrown down the old brick chutes, which have been cracked from heat, to be compacted in the basement. Roaches breed in these cracks, fed by the wet garbage that comes down the chute, and travel to tenants' apartments. *Remedy:* Replacement of the brick chutes with smooth metal chutes which don't provide breeding places. *Also:* Compactors must be cleaned at least once a week.

• Rout roaches without poisoning your kitchen. Boric acid or crumbled bay leaves will keep your cupboards pest-free. *Another benign repellent:* Chopped cucumbers.

• Homeowners do not need regular extermination for roaches. Since a house is a separate unit, a one-time extermination should do the job.

Food stores are the major source of roach infestation in private homes. People bring roaches home with the groceries. Check your paper grocery bags for roaches before you store them.

•Ants and silverfish can be controlled by the homeowner himself, unless there is a major infestation. Don't call the exterminator for a half-dozen ants or silverfish. Try a store-bought spray first. *Exception:* Carpenter ants and grease-eating ants must be exterminated professionally.

•Clover mites come from cutting the grass. They look like little red dots. The mites land on windowsills after the lawn is mowed and then travel into the house. *Remedy:* Spray your grass with miticide before cutting.

•Spiders don't require an exterminator. Any aerosol will get rid of them.

•Termite control is a major job that needs specialized chemicals and equipment. Call an exterminator.

•Bees, wasps and hornets should be dealt with professionally. Their nests must be located and attacked after dusk, when the insects have returned to them. If the nest is not destroyed properly, damage to your home could result. *Also:* Many people are allergic to stings and don't know it until they are stung.

•Clothes moths can be eliminated by hanging a no-pest strip in your closet and keeping the door tightly closed.

•Flies can be minimized with an aerosol or sticky strip. An exterminator is of no help getting rid of flies. *Best:* Screens on all the windows and doors.

•Weevils and meal moths can be prevented by storing cereals, rice and grains in sealed containers. *Also:* Cereals are treated with bromides to repel infestation. The bromides eventually break down. Throw out old cereals.

•Wood storage and insects. Firewood kept in the house becomes a refuge and breeding ground for insects. *Risky solution:* Spraying the logs with insecticides. (When the sprayed wood burns, dangerous fumes could be emitted.) *Better:* Stack the wood (under plastic) outside and carry in only the amount needed.

Mice...

There is no 100% effective solution for exterminating mice. *Try these alternatives:*

•Trapping is effective unless you have small children or pets.

•Poison should be placed behind the stove or refrigerator where children and pets can't get at it.

•Glue boards (available in supermarkets) placed along the walls can be very effective. Mice tend to run along the walls due to poor eyesight.

Pesticides and prevention...

Many of the residual (long-lasting) sprays have been outlawed because they don't break down and disappear in the environment. The old favorites, DDT and Chlordane, are generally no longer permitted. *What to use:*

•Baygon, Diazanon and Dursban are general-purpose, toxic organo-phosphates meant for residual use in wet areas. They're recommended for all indoor insects, including roaches.

•Drione is a nontoxic silica gel, which dries up the membranes in insects. Recommended for indoor use in dry areas only, it is especially effective on roaches.

•Malathion is helpful in gardens, but it should not be used indoors.

•Pyrethrin is highly recommended, since it is made from flowers and is nontoxic. It has no residual effect, but is good for on-contact spraying of roaches and other insects. If there is a baby in the house, Pyrethrin is especially useful, since children under three months should never be exposed to toxic chemicals. Don't use it around hay-fever or asthma sufferers.

•When buying products in the store, look at the label to determine the percentage of active ingredients. Solutions vary from 5% to 15%. The stronger the solution, the better the results.

•Prevention is synonymous with sanitation. If you are not scrupulous about cleanliness, you will be wasting your money on sprays or exterminators.

•Moisture is the main attractor of insects. If you live in a moist climate, you must be especially vigilant. Coffee spills, plumbing leaks, fish tanks, pet litter and pet food all attract bugs. Clean up after your pets, and take care of leaks and spills immediately. If puddles tend to collect around your house after it rains, improve the drainage.

•Word of mouth is the best way to choose a good exterminator. Don't rely on the Yellow Pages.

•Contracts for regular service, which many exterminators try to promote, are not recommended for private homes. A one-time extermination should do the trick, but apartment dwellers must exterminate buildingwide on a regular basis.

•To remove a bat from your house at night, confine it to a single room, open the window and leave the bat alone. Chances are it will fly right out. Otherwise, during the day when the bat is torpid, flick it into a coffee can or other container. (Use gloves if you are squeamish.) Release it outdoors. Bats are really very valuable. A single brown bat can eat 3,000 mosquitoes a night. *Note:* Bats, like other mammals, can carry rabies. If you find a downed bat or you are scratched or bitten by one, call your local animal control agency and keep the animal for testing. However, very few people have contracted rabies directly from bats. *More likely source:* Skunks.

Source: Tom Heffernan, president of the Ozane Exterminating Co., Bayside, NY, and Clifton Meloan, chemist, Kansas.

Painting Trouble Areas

Often, paint peels in one section of a wall or ceiling. *Causes:*

•A leak making its way through the walls from a plumbing break or an opening to the outside.

•The plaster is giving out in that area due to age or wear and tear.

•The layers of paint may be so thick that the force of gravity, plus vibrations from outside, make the paint pop and peel in the weakest spots.

How to fix the problem:

•If it's a leak, find and correct it first.

•Otherwise, remove as much of the existing paint as you can.

•Scrape away any loose, damp or crumbling plaster.

•Spackle and smooth the area.

•Prime and paint it.

For real problem areas:

•Spackle, then paste on a thin layer of canvas. Apply it as though it were wallpaper.

•Smooth it out so it becomes part of the surface.

•Then prime and paint it.

Wrapping a Package The Right Way

•Seal a sturdy carton with six strips of two-inch-wide plastic tape (not masking or cellophane tape, which tears easily): A strip across the center of top and bottom and across each open edge on flap ends. Don't just go to the ends. Go a few inches around.

•Put an address label inside so that if the outside label is lost or defaced, the package can be opened and sent with the second label.

•Don't use brown paper or string; they only increase chance of loss if paper tears and label rips off or the string unties and gets caught in a sorting machine.

Things You Never Thought of Doing With Plastic Bags

Use plastic bags:

•As gloves when greasing a cookie sheet, cleaning the oven or changing oil in the car.

•To help preserve a plant when you are going away. Spray the leaves with water, then cover the pot with a bag secured at the top with a rubber band.

•To protect your camera, film and lenses from moisture.

•As storage bags for woolens. Add a few mothballs.

•Put meat to be tenderized inside a bag before pounding.

Cleaning Jewelry

•Gold and platinum: Use a soft brush with a mild, warm water/detergent solution.

•Turquoise, ivory, lapis and other porous gems: Mild soap and water only.

•Opals: Use barely cool distilled water (they're sensitive to cold).

•Pearls: Roll them in a soft cloth moistened with water and soap (not detergent). *To rinse:* Roll them in a cloth dipped in warm water.

•Most other gems: Add a tablespoonful of baking soda to a cup of warm water. Swish the jewelry through or rub it with a soft toothbrush. Rinse well.

Source: *Woman's Day,* New York.

Home Remedies For Plant Pests

•Red spider mites. Four tablespoons of dishwashing liquid or one-half cake of yellow soap dissolved in one gallon of water. Spray weekly until mites are gone, then monthly.

•Hardshell scale. One-fourth teaspoon olive oil, two tablespoons baking soda, one teaspoon Dove liquid soap in two gallons of water. Spray or wipe on once a week for three weeks; repeat if necessary.

•Mold on soil. One tablespoon of vinegar in two quarts of water. Water weekly with solution until mold disappears.

•Mealybugs. Wipe with cotton swabs dipped in alcohol. Spray larger plants weekly with a solution of one part alcohol to three parts water until bugs no longer hatch.

Source: Decora Interior Plantscapes, Greenwich, CT.

How to Make Flowers Last Longer

•Cut off the stems half an inch from the bottom. Make the cut at an angle so that the stem will not press against the bottom of the vase, closing off the flow of water.

•To slow water buildup (which makes petals droop), make a tiny incision at the base of the bloom.

•Fill an absolutely clean vase with fresh water.

•Add floral preservative. *One recipe:* Two squeezes of lemon juice, a quarter teaspoonful of sugar and a few drops of club soda.

•Change the water and preservative daily.

•Display the flowers out of the sun, and keep them cool at night.

•Remove leaves below the water line.

Source: T. Augello and G. Yanker, coauthors, *Shortcuts,* Bantam Books, New York.

Ten Foolproof Houseplants

These hardy species will survive almost anywhere and are a good choice for timid beginners without a lot of sunny windows.

•Aspidistra (cast-iron plant). This Victorian favorite, known as "The Spittoon Plant," survived the implied indignity in many a tavern.

•Rubber plant. Likes a dim, cool interior (like a hallway). If given sun, it grows like crazy.

•Century (Kentia) palm. A long-lived, slow-growing plant that needs uniform moisture. Give it an occasional shower.

•Philodendrons. They like medium to low light and even moisture, but will tolerate dryness and poor light.

•Dumb cane. Tolerates a dry interior and low light, but responds to better conditions. Don't let your pet chew the foliage or its tongue will swell.

•Bromeliads. Exotic and slow-growing, they like frequent misting, but are practically immune to neglect and will flower even in subdued light.

•Corn plant (dracaena). Good for hot, dry apartments.

•Snake plant. Will survive almost anything.

•Spider plant. A tough, low-light plant that makes a great trailer and endures neglect.

•Nephthytis. Will flourish in poor light and survive the forgetful waterer.

Source: Edmond O. Moulin, director of horticulture, Brooklyn Botanical Garden, Brooklyn, NY.

Poison Plants

Plant poisoning among adults has increased alarmingly in the last decade. For children under five, plants are second only to medicines as a cause of poisoning. *Prime sources:* Common houseplants, garden flowers and shrubs, as well as wild mushrooms, weeds and berries.

Among the most common poisonous plants:

•Garden flowers: Bleeding heart, daffodils, delphinium, foxglove, hens and chickens, lantana, lily of the valley, lupine, sweet pea.

•Houseplants: Caladium, dieffenbachia, philodendron.

•Garden shrubs: Azalea, mountain laurel, oleander, privet, rhododendron, yew.

•Wildflowers: Autumn crocus, buttercups, jimson weed, mayapple, moonseed berries, poison hemlock, water hemlock, wild mushrooms.

Flowers that Are Good to Eat

Many common flowers also make gourmet dishes. *Here are some suggestions:*

•Calendula (pot marigold): Add minced petals to rice, omelets, chicken soup, clam chowder or stew.

•Nasturtium: Serve leaves like watercress on sandwiches, or stuff flowers with basil- and tarragon-seasoned rice, then simmer in chicken stock and sherry.

•Squash blossom: Pick blossoms as they are opening, dip in a flour-and-egg mixture seasoned with salt, pepper and tarragon, then deep-fry until golden brown.

•Camomile: Dry the flowers on a screen in a dark place to make tea.

•Borage: Toss with salad for a cucumberlike taste, or use fresh for tea.

Source: *House & Garden*, New York.

All You Need to Know About Bird Feeders

The main thing is to mix your own seed. You can create a mix that will attract a wide variety of birds. *What birds like most:*

•Niger seed (Thistledown).

•Sunflower seeds (particularly the thin-shelled oilseed).

•White proso millet.

•Finely cracked corn.

Avoid:

•Milo and red millet, which are used as filler in commercial mixes and are not attractive to birds.

•Peanut hearts attract starlings, which you may want to avoid.

Requirements of a good feeder:

•It should keep the seed dry (mold by-products are toxic to birds).

•Be squirrel resistant (baffles above and below are good protection).

•For winter feeding of insect-eating birds (woodpeckers, chickadees, titmice and nuthatches), string up chunks of beef suet.

Source: Aelred D. Geis, Patuxent Wildlife Research Center of the US Fish and Wildlife Service, Laurel, MD.

When to Trade in Your Old Furnace

If your fuel bills seem higher than they should be, it may be time to replace your old furnace with a new one.

•Calculate whether your old oil furnace is costing you more than the price of a new one:

(1) Estimate your annual fuel bill.

(2) Divide your present furnace's efficiency rating by the efficiency rating of the new model

you're considering. (Your local utility will rate your system for a small fee or for free.)

(3) Multiply the result by your annual fuel bill to estimate the savings. A new furnace should pay back its costs in about five to seven years.

Source: *Home,* Des Moines, IA.

Painting Guidelines

Follow these simple suggestions for the effect you are looking for:

- To make a room look larger, use the same color on walls, floor and ceiling.
- Dark colors don't always make a room look smaller, though they can make a large room more intimate.
- Dark colors on all surrounding surfaces can highlight furniture and give an illusion of spaciousness.
- Cool wall colors make a room seem bigger.
- Warm colors make a room seem smaller.
- A long, narrow room can be visually widened by painting the long sides a lighter color than those at the ends.
- A ceiling slightly lighter in color than the walls appears higher...a darker one, lower.

Source: *Woman's Day,* New York.

Fiber Danger

Some organically grown fibers can be bad for the environment. *Example:* Cotton grown in some areas of the desert. Water to grow it is diverted by man-made channels. The diversion threatens dozens of species.

Source: Jason Makansi, editor, *Common Sense on Energy and Our Environment,* Box 215, Morrisville, PA 19067.

Rug Care Regimen

To keep rugs in good shape, vacuum the *underside* at least twice a year. Rotate rugs to prevent fading and limit their attraction to insects. The insects that are attracted to rugs prefer quiet, static situations.

If you rotate rugs, you disturb insects and you also have the opportunity to examine the rugs for problems. If you have a rug with chemical dyes, use window treatments and screens or shades to keep the sun away from it or it will probably fade.

Do not mothproof—the chemicals can damage rug dyes. If a rug becomes damaged, have it repaired quickly—when damaged areas expand, they can be costly to fix.

Source: Sara Wolf, director of conservation and collections management, The Textile Museum, Washington, DC.

One Way to Test for Termites

Poke a screwdriver or an awl into exposed wood near areas where termites might enter—especially where wood is near soil. If you can poke into the wood easily, termites may be present. *Self-defense:* Contact a licensed pest-control expert for an inspection. *New type of treatment:* Termite baiting systems—monitoring stations in the soil around the house, containing wood as termite bait. The stations are monitored until termites appear—then replaced with a slow-acting poison. *Cost:* Approximately $1,100 to $1,600.

Source: Greg Baumann, president, New York National Pest Control Association, Dunn Loring, Virginia.

Natural Mosquito Repellant

Mix two cups of witch hazel with one-and-a-half teaspoons of citronella and one tablespoon of apple-cider vinegar. Pour the mixture into a spray bottle, and shake to mix thoroughly. Apply it to your exposed skin as needed, being careful to avoid eyes, nose and mouth as you would with any insect repellent.

Source: *Feel Great, Be Beautiful Over 40!* by Lillian Müller, European film star and former model. General Publishing Group.

12

Buying/Renting a Home

Money for First-Time Homeowners

First-time home buyers in need of extra cash for a down payment can borrow from their 401(k) plans—without paying penalties to the IRS. You can pay back the loan over several years as long as you make equal loan repayments on at least a quarterly basis. *Drawback:* The money you use to pay the interest on the loan will be taxed twice—once as you pay interest in after-tax dollars and again when you begin withdrawing the money —including the interest you paid to yourself—after age 59½.

Source: Jonathan Pond, president of Financial Planning Information Inc., 9 Galen St., Watertown, MA 02172.

How to Buy Property with Little...or No Money Down

As hard as it is to believe, it's not only possible to buy property with no money down, it's not even that hard to do—provided you have the right fundamental information.

Note: No money down means the seller receives no down payment. It means the down payment doesn't come from your pocket.

Success strategies...

• Paying the real estate agent. If a seller uses a real estate agent on the sale, he's obligated to pay the agent's commission. *Strategy:* You, the buyer, pay the commission, but not up front. You approach the agent and offer a deal. Instead of immediate payment, suggest that the agent lend you part of the commission. In return, you offer a personal note guaranteeing to pay the money at some future date, with interest. If you make it clear that the sale depends on such an arrangement, the agent will probably go along with the plan. If he balks, be flexible. Negotiate a small monthly amount, perhaps with a balloon payment at the end. You then subtract the agent's commission from the expected down payment.

•Assuming the seller's debts. Let's say, as so often happens, that the seller is under financial pressure. *Strategy:* With the seller's cooperation, contact all his creditors and explain that you, not the seller, are going to make good on the outstanding debts. In some cases, the relieved creditors will either extend the due dates, or, if you can come up with some cash, they'll likely agree to a discount. Deduct the face amount of the debts you'll be assuming, pocketing any discounts, from the down payment.

•Prepaid rent. Sometimes you, the buyer, are in no rush to move in and the seller would like more time to find a new place to live—but you'd both like to close as soon as possible. *Strategy:* Offer to let the seller remain in the house or apartment, setting a fixed date for vacating. Then, instead of the seller paying the buyer a monthly rent, you subtract from the down payment the full amount of the rent for the entire time the seller will be living there.

•Satisfying the seller's needs. During conversations with the seller, you learn that he must buy some appliances and furniture for a home he's moving into. *Strategy:* Offer to buy those things—using credit cards or store credit to delay payment—and deduct the lump sum from the down payment.

Source: Robert G. Allen, a real estate insider and author of the bestseller *Nothing Down.* He's also publisher of the monthly newsletter *The Real Estate Advisor,* Provo, UT.

Figures to Check at Real Estate Closing

•Monthly payments.

•Per diem figures for utilities, taxes, and/or interest.

•The broker's commission.

•The rents, security deposits, and/or interest on deposits that have not as yet been transferred.

•A charge for utility bills already paid.

•A charge for loan fees already paid.

•A contractor, attorney, appraiser, or some other party to the contract who has not been paid.

Protect Mortgage Point Deduction

"Points" paid to get a mortgage loan may not be immediately tax-deductible.

Interest must actually be paid to be deductible by cash-basis taxpayers, which most individuals are. In one case, the Tax Court held that, since the points were deducted from the loan proceeds, they weren't actually paid, thus no deduction could be claimed that year. The deduction would have to be taken pro rata as the mortgage was repaid.

Problem: The typical real estate closing statement mixes up credits to the buyer and amounts actually paid.

Solution: Pay the points by single check to the lender. Don't lump the payment in with other payments.

Questions to Ask Before Signing Mortgage Papers

Because it is such a long-term contract, conditions that may seem minor when signing a mortgage loan contract can end up costing a lot of money during the life of the agreement. Some typical mortgage clauses to negotiate before signing:

•Payment of "points": Percentage of the amount of the loan paid to the lender at the start of the loan. Banks and thrift institutions have no statutory right to charge points. Their presence may reflect competitive local market conditions. And when interest rates are high, points are common. They're inevitable when rate ceilings exist. *Helpful:* Try to negotiate on points.

•Prepayment penalties: Sometimes as much as six months' interest or a percentage of the balance due on the principal at the time the loan is paid off. With mortgages running for 25 or 30 years, the chances of paying them off early are relatively high.

•"Due on encumbrance" clause: Makes the first mortgage immediately due in full if property is pledged as security on any other loan, including second mortgages. Not legal in some places and usually not enforced when it is legal. Request its deletion.

• "Due on sale" clauses: Requiring full payment of loan when property is sold.

• Escrow payment: The popular practice of requiring a prorated share of local taxes and insurance premiums with each monthly mortgage payment. The bank earns interest on the escrow funds throughout the year and only pays it out when taxes and premiums are due. Amounts to forced savings with no interest.

Have your lawyer check your state's law to see if interest on escrow-account money is required. (It is, in several states.) If not, try to eliminate escrow —pay taxes and insurance on your own.

Other alternatives to escrow...

Capitalization plan, in which monthly tax and insurance payments are credited against outstanding mortgage principal until they are paid out to the government or insurer, thus lowering amount of mortgage interest.

Lender may agree to waive escrow if borrower opens an interest-bearing savings account in the amount of the annual tax bill.

Option of closing out the withheld escrow payments when the borrower's equity reaches 40%. At that point, the bank figures, equity interest will be a powerful incentive to keep up tax payments.

Source: *The Consumer's Guide to Banks,* by Gordon L. Well, Stein & Day, Briarcliff Manor, NY.

Suggestions for Condominium Hunters

Look for a building about to undergo conversion. If you sublet an apartment in it, you get first crack at buying the apartment.

If you have trouble getting a mortgage, look for a condominium developer who has a mortgage commitment from a lender.

Rent a portion of the condominium apartment to a friend. This helps meet the monthly payments.

When Buying a New Condominium

Buying a condominium is more complicated than buying a house. *Reason:* The purchase is really for two separate pieces of property—your unit and the property held in common. Before signing any contract for a new condominium, which is harder to check out than an established condominium, buyers should study the prospectus for any of these pitfalls:

• The prospectus includes a plan of the unit you are buying, showing rooms of specific dimensions. But the plan omits closet space. *Result:* The living space you are buying is probably smaller than you think.

• The prospectus includes this clause: "The interior design shall be substantially similar." *Result:* The developer can alter both the size and design of your unit.

• The common charges set forth in the prospectus are unrealistically low. Buyers should never rely on a developer's estimate of common charges. *Instead:* They should find out the charges at similarly functioning condominiums.

• *Common charges include:* Electricity for hallways and outside areas, water, cleaning, garbage disposal, insurance for common areas, pool maintenance, groundskeeping, legal and accounting fees, reserves for future repairs.

Variation on the common-charge trap: The developer is paying common charges on unsold units. But these charges are unrealistically low. *Reason:* The developer has either underinsured or underestimated the taxes due, omitted security expenses, or failed to set up a reserve fund.

• The prospectus includes this clause: "The seller will not be obligated to pay monthly charges for unsold units." *Result:* The owners of a partially occupied condominium have to pay for all operating expenses.

• The prospectus warns about the seller's limited liability. But an unsuspecting buyer may still purchase a condominium unit on which back monthly charges are due, or even on which there's a lien for failure to pay back carrying charges.

•The prospectus makes no mention of parking spaces. *Result:* You must lease from the developer.

•The prospectus is imprecise about the total number of units to be built. *Result:* Facilities are inadequate for the number of residents.

•The prospectus includes this clause: "Transfer of ownership (of the common property from the developer to the homeowners' association) will take place 60 days after the last unit is sold." *Trap:* The developer deliberately does not sell one unit, keeps on managing the condominium, and awards sweetheart maintenance and operating contracts to his subcontractors.

•The prospectus specifies that the developer will become the property manager of the functioning condominium. But the language spelling out monthly common charges and management fees is imprecise. *Result:* The owners cannot control monthly charges and fees.

Source: Dorothy Tymon, author, *The Condominium: A Guide for the Alert Buyer*, Golden-Lee Books, Brooklyn, NY.

Condominium Emergency Reserves

Make sure the board of directors sets up a contingency reserve for emergencies. It should be at least 3% of the annual operating budget for newer buildings and 5% for older ones. *Danger:* A major assessment on very little notice when an emergency arises if no reserve is set aside.

Source: *The Condominium Community*, The Institute of Real Estate Management of the National Association of Realtors, Chicago.

Condos vs. Co-ops

When you purchase a condominium, you own real property, just like when you buy a house. You arrange for your own mortgage with the bank, pay real estate taxes directly to the local government, pay water bills individually, and have an individual deed.

When you buy a cooperative apartment, you are participating in a syndication. A corporation is formed, shares are issued, and people subscribe to the shares. The corporation raises money, takes out a mortgage, and owns the building.

Maintenance charges for a condominium are likely to cost 50% of a cooperative's charges for an equivalent building. *The reason:* The maintenance on a condominium covers only the common area upkeep. *That includes:* Labor, heating oil, repairs, and maintenance of the playground, swimming pool, and other community areas. Co-op maintenance fees cover those same items plus mortgage payments, local real estate taxes, utility and water bills.

Capital improvements: If an extensive, major repair needs to be made (such as the replacement of a roof or boiler), the board of managers of a condo cannot borrow funds from a bank, unless it receives the unanimous consent of the condo owners. *Problem:* If a dozen owners are content to live in a dilapidated building, improvements must be funded through maintenance cash flow, which may be very expensive. In a co-op, the board of directors can take out a second mortgage to fix a roof, plumbing, or other major problem. Individual co-op shareholders cannot easily obstruct the board.

Delinquency in paying maintenance fees can be handled more expediently in a co-op than in a condo. In a co-op, an owner who doesn't pay maintenance fees can be evicted almost immediately. The person is served with a dispossess and can be evicted within days. In a condominium, a lien must be placed on the apartment and then a foreclosure proceeding is brought. It could take two years to get the money, and it is a difficult legal proceeding.

Exclusionary rights: Since a co-op is considered personal property, not real property, prospective tenants may be rejected by the co-op's board of directors for any reason whatsoever except race, creed, color, or national origin. *Reality:* As long as the co-op board members don't state the reason, anyone can be excluded for any prejudice. *Problem:* A tenant may have trouble subletting a co-op if the co-op board members don't approve of the new tenant. In a condominium, each owner has the right to sell or sublet to anyone the person wants, subject only to the condo's right of first refusal, which is rarely exercised.

From the entrepreneur's point of view, a co-op can be more advantageous if the building at the time of the conversion date has a low-interest mortgage. *Reason:* When a building is converted into a condominium, it must be free and clear of all liens. In a co-op, the former financing can be kept intact.

Source: David Goldstick, senior partner, Goldstick, Weinberger, Feldman, Alperstein, Rotenberg, Grossman & Barr, Inc., 261 Madison Ave., New York 10016.

Before You Renovate An Old House

The positive aspects of renovating an old house are enticing: A sense of accomplishment, an outlet for creativity, and the possibility that it will be a good investment. However, the experience of returning a house to its former glory can be frustrating and overwhelming to anyone who attempts it for the first time without proper understanding.

The worst aspects, according to old-home buffs:

- Not knowing what you are getting into.
- Living amid the chaos of reconstruction for very long periods.

Some things to consider when buying an old home to renovate...

- Choosing the right neighborhood is the most important element on the investment side. If many homes are being renovated in your neighborhood, chances are good that your choice will be expensive. *Best:* Find a neighborhood where one or two homes have been renovated on your block and several more a few blocks away. There is a strong possibility that the neighborhood will blossom and values will rise.
- Speak to owners of similar homes in your area before you purchase. Concentrate on the steps they took.
- Get a good engineer's report about the home, and focus on foundation, plumbing, electrical, and mechanical systems. These are the most difficult to restore. Choose an engineer with considerable experience in old homes.
- If you want a modern interior and expect to gut most of the house and substitute modern fixtures, find a house that's just a shell. *Reason:* Old homes with fine architectural details such as marble mantels and restorable wainscotting cost more.
- Don't put your last penny into a down payment and take a big mortgage. The fixing-up process can be extraordinarily expensive, even if you expect to do much of the work yourself. Expenses vary nationwide, correlating most closely with labor costs in your area.
- Don't get an architect to draw up a master plan for your house immediately. It usually takes a while to know what you want out of a house. Unless you have lived in it at least six months to a year, you will probably make expensive mistakes.
- Learn how to deal with contractors. You can't do everything yourself. You must hire experienced people. Read the contract. Make sure the contractor is bonded. *Possibility:* If you are fairly handy, call in a professional to do a small portion. Watch carefully. You may be able to finish the job yourself.
- Gutting an interior can be done easily by anyone. All you need is a crowbar, sledge hammer, old clothes, and elbow grease. Most homes can be gutted in a weekend. *Keys:* Hire neighborhood teenagers to help. Find a dumpster for the plaster.
- Don't be discouraged by broken beams, crumbling interior plaster, or even a leaking roof. As long as the exterior walls and the foundation are solid, shabby interiors are secondary.
- Study local zoning laws before you make major changes. *Reason:* Removing a pipe or a wall frequently requires a building permit. However, after you get the permit, your tax assessment will be raised, probably by as much as the value of the renovation. *Important:* Be prepared to try negotiating with the tax assessor.

Most expensive changes: Changing the location of the kitchen or bathrooms. *Why:* Plumbing. Don't do it if you can possibly live with things where they are.

Way to boost resale value: Organize a walking tour of restored homes in your area. These walking tours are great sales tools.

Source: Benita Korn and Patricia Cole, directors of the Brownstone Revival Committee, Inc., 200 Madison Ave., New York 10016.

Getting a Higher Price For an Old House

An old house (built between 1920 and 1950) can be sold as easily as a new one. The right strategy and a few improvements can raise the selling price significantly.

- Invest in a complete cleaning, repainting, or wallpapering. Recarpet or have the rugs and carpets professionally cleaned.
- Get rid of cat and dog odors that you may be used to but potential buyers will notice.
- With the trend to smaller families and working couples, it may be desirable to convert and advertise a four-bedroom house as two bedrooms, library and den.
- The exterior of the house is crucial. It's the first thing a buyer sees. Clean and repair porch and remove clutter. Repaint porch furniture.
- Landscaping makes a great difference and can sell (or unsell) a house. Get expert advice on improving it.
- Good real estate agents are vital to a quick sale. There are one or two top people in every agency who will work hard to show houses and even arrange financing. Multiple listings lets these super salespeople from different agencies work for the seller.

Law When Trespassing Children are Injured

A property owner or contractor may be liable for damages if a child is hurt on the property (or by unguarded machinery), even though the child trespassed. A "No Trespassing" sign isn't enough.

Example: A swimming pool should be surrounded by an adequate fence and a locked gate.

General rule: The attractive nuisance doctrine in the law makes the property owner responsible for trespassing children who are too young to understand the dangers.

Special problem: Protection while construction work is being done or when machinery is left unguarded in a residential area (or near heavily traveled streets).

Liability for Injuries to Uninvited Guests

Courts in many states are more likely than ever to hold an owner responsible for injuries to a visitor. That's so even though the person was on the property without an invitation. The old distinction between an invitee (someone asked onto the property) and licensee (someone on the property without an invitation) is breaking down. Traditionally, invitees would be awarded higher settlements for damages.

Now courts in about one-third of the states ignore the distinction between an invitee and licensee and hold the property owner responsible for keeping the property safe for both invitees and the self-invited.

Now: Salespeople, whether they contacted the customer before their visit or not, are generally treated (by courts recognizing the distinction) as invitees.

Forming a Tenants' Organization

The most effective method of confronting a landlord about problems with rented apartments is through a tenant organization. If you are having problems with your landlord, the other tenants in your building probably are, too. If you approach the problem as a group, your chances of success improve immeasurably.

How to go about it:

•Speak with the tenants in your building and distribute flyers calling a meeting. At the meeting, elect a committee of tenants to lead the group.

•Pass out questionnaires to all tenants, asking them to list needed repairs in their apartments.

•After the questionnaires have been collected and reviewed, call the landlord and suggest a meeting with him to negotiate complaints. Many landlords will comply with this request, since the specter of all their tenants withholding rent can be a frightening prospect. Negotiation is always preferable to litigation.

•If negotiation fails, organize a rent strike. That's a procedure whereby tenants withhold rent collectively, depositing the money each month in an escrow fund or with the court until repairs are made. If your tenant organization is forced to go this route, you will need a good lawyer. Be prepared for a long court battle.

Tenant vs. Tenant

If a tenant in your building is involved in a crime or drugs or is excessively noisy, you have a number of ways to deal with the problem.

•Take out a summons, claiming harassment or assault. *Probable result:* The court will admonish the tenant to stop causing a disturbance (which may or may not have any effect).

•Sue for damages in civil court. You may win (although collecting the judgment is another story).

•Try to persuade your landlord to evict the undesirable tenant. *Best way:* Put pressure on him through your tenant organization. A landlord can't be forced to evict anyone. He has the right to rent to whomever he chooses. But if your association has a decent relationship with the landlord, he might comply, especially if the tenant is causing a dangerous condition or destroying property.

•You have the right to break your lease if you're being harassed by another tenant, but this may not be much comfort if apartments are scarce in your area.

Five Easy Ways to Cut Heating Costs

1. Clean furnaces. Home heating bills can be cut 10% or more by having the furnace cleaned and adjusted properly. If you have an oil burner, an annual inspection by a qualified technician is important.

2. Replace furnace burners. Find out if your oil burner is a *conventional* or a *retention head* burner. The latter is much more efficient. These use smaller fuel nozzles and save as much as 15% on your fuel bill.

3. Clean filters. Forced warm-air furnaces need to have their air filters cleaned and replaced at least twice each winter. A clogged filter chokes off the necessary breathing of the furnace and makes it work harder.

4. Unblock registers. When you are rearranging furniture, be sure that radiators, warm-air registers or heating units aren't blocked from proper functioning. If you prefer an arrangement that blocks heat flow, let it wait until summer when it won't affect heating efficiency.

5. Add humidity. A little extra humidity permits a lower thermostat setting without discomfort. Some furnaces will accept a humidifying system easily and inexpensively. If yours won't, use pans of water on radiators or heat registers to put a little moisture into the air.

Source: *547 Tips for Saving Energy in Your Home*, Storey Communications, Box 445, Schoolhouse Rd., Pownal, Vermont 05261.

The Biggest Mistakes Renters Make—and How to Avoid Them

Some of the toughest battles renters face with landlords could have been avoided. *Here's how to make sure they don't happen to you...*

• *Trap:* Not signing a formal lease. In most states, a written document is required if the lease term is one year or more.

Most people avoid such documents when they rent from a friend or relative. They go with an oral agreement because a lease seems like a cold, formal document.

But without a written lease, neither party knows where it stands on subjects such as repairs, lease termination and security deposit.

Helpful: Use a standard lease form from an office-supply store or legal-document book. That's better than trying to draw one up from scratch.

The lease should say that the landlord is responsible for keeping the water, gas, electricity, heat and major appliances in working order.

• *Trap:* Not taking the security deposit seriously. One common misconception is that a security deposit is a prepayment of the last month's rent.

Reality: The security deposit is for reimbursing the landlord for any damage that may be done to the apartment.

Legally, such damage must be beyond normal wear and tear. It is expected that carpets will get dirty and appliances will break down or wear out.

It is not assumed, however, that you will accidentally slice a rug in two or smash a hole in a wall.

Strategy: To protect yourself, walk through the residence *with the landlord* before signing the lease. Take notes about cracks in the walls and other defects. Make a list of all defects, and have the landlord sign it.

Legally, it doesn't matter if this list is formally incorporated into the lease or not.

If an existing problem seems serious, take a picture of it for your files.

• *Trap:* Not being able to get out of the lease when you need to. A tenant who is abruptly transferred to a new city may regret not having this flexibility.

Self-defense: If a transfer is a possibility, try to find a lease—or add a clause—that says you can terminate on short notice if you are transferred to a new position more than 50 miles away.

In addition, retain the right to sublet or assign the remainder of the lease to another person, subject to the landlord's written approval of the subtenant. This is a standard clause in most leases. If the landlord won't grant it, consider walking away from the deal.

• *Trap:* Not informing the landlord about important changes. This isn't exactly asking for trouble, but it's close. Just because a lease doesn't explicitly prohibit you from making significant structural changes, it doesn't mean you should do so without consulting the landlord. Not informing the landlord can generate ill will —and even a future lawsuit.

Example: Don't put in an elaborate rack system for a closet without seeking the landlord's blessing. What you may consider an expensive improvement may be regarded by the landlord as a destructive eyesore—or a threat to the building's electrical system or structural integrity.

Strategy: Get written acknowledgment from the landlord that an improvement is acceptable.

• *Trap:* Not knowing the rules when renting a condo. With so many condos now being rented out by their owners, this is very important. Generally, the responsibility for repairs is divided this way:

- If you have a problem with something inside the dwelling, and the cause does not come from outside, as it would in the case of a leak, you must deal with the person who rented you the condo. Before signing a lease, make sure the condo's owner is a reasonable person who can be easily reached in the event of a problem.
- If the problem comes from outside the dwelling, then you as a tenant will usually have the right to deal directly with the homeowner's association to get the problem resolved. Before leasing, find out if you have permission to do so—or if it is the landlord's responsibility. The association bylaws will contain the answer.

Strategy: Before renting, review a copy of the condo's bylaws. When everybody's responsibility is spelled out in advance, future finger-pointing and yelling become much less likely.

• *Trap:* Not buying renter's insurance. Your possessions are not covered by the owner's or landlord's insurance policy, which only protects the structure. Renter's insurance is cheap. Make sure it guarantees the replacement value of your goods in the event of a fire, flood or other calamity.

Source: Brent Terry, a Chicago-area attorney specializing in personal and family law. Mr. Terry is author of *The Complete Idiot's Guide to Protecting Yourself from Everyday Legal Hassles.* Alpha Books.

13

Smart Money Management

Get Control of Your Finances...Now

All too many people today are wondering where all their hard-earned money is going. They feel like they're working harder than ever ...yet have nothing to show for it.

Researchers recently determined that it takes $60,000 to live the American dream. But people making $60,000 said they needed $75,000 ...people making $75,000 said they needed $100,000...people making $100,000 said they needed $150,000...and so on.

The truth is, most of us already have *enough* —we just need to shape up our spending and saving habits to what we really want and need. And that takes introspection.

What to do...

• Act now. Don't make the mistake of thinking that the future will take care of itself. Your financial future is a direct result of the decisions you make today.

Just as someone with a heart problem can avoid trouble by making lifestyle changes, changing spending habits can avert financial crises in the years ahead.

• Set goals. Every family needs goals that are tied to their values. Write them down and put a price tag on them—if necessary, get the help of your accountant or financial planner.

It's only when you spell out your goals—retiring at a certain age or income level, putting your children through college, maintaining a certain standard of living, etc.— that you can face up to the trade-offs that will have to be made.

• Analyze your spending. First identify your major spending categories.

Included: Housing, child care, groceries, debts, medical/dental treatments, transportation, insurance, work- and investment-related expenses, clothing, gifts, personal needs and entertainment.

Then gather all your cancelled checks, credit-card bills and cash-withdrawal records for the past year.

Divide the checks and credit-card receipts among the various categories. Then figure out how you spent your cash withdrawals. Don't worry about being precise. Put items you can't account for in the *personal needs* pile. Knowing where your money went will lead to better spending decisions.

•Figure out what you really need. Determine whether you spend more on *experiences*—travel, education, entertainment, etc...or on *things*—clothing, toys, collectibles, electronic gadgets, etc.

Ask yourself: Which of these provide more lasting value in my life? What could be eliminated?

Then take the money you would have spent and start saving it.

•Save at least 10% of your income. It's amazing how quickly even a small amount will grow, if you invest regularly.

Example: A 25-year-old who saves $1,000 a year and earns 8% on it will have $15,650 after 10 years. Even if he then stopped making contributions—which we don't recommend—that modest amount would grow to $157,440 by the time the investor was 65. If the 25-year-old waited until the age of 35 to start, he would never catch up with the 25-year-old, even if he made 30 years of contributions to 10 years of the 25-year-old. So act now! It's never too early to start.

•Maximize pre-tax savings. Use 401(k) plans, IRAs and Keoghs. This year you can make pre-tax 401(k) contributions of up to 16% of your pay to a maximum of $8,475. If your employer contributes, this is the opportunity of a lifetime.

Trap: Too many employees put all of their 401(k) savings into Guaranteed Investment Contracts (GICs). GICs guarantee the rate of interest and the principal.

Problem: GICs are written mostly by insurance companies...a few of which are in very shaky financial condition. The guarantee comes from the insurance companies...not your company. They also don't offer inflation protection. *Self-defense:* All long-term investors need some common stocks in their portfolios.

In deciding how much to invest in fixed-income versus equity-type investment, use your age as the maximum percentage to invest in fixed-income investments. Sometimes more should be invested in stocks or real estate, but typically not less. *Examples:*

•Forty-year-olds should put 40% of their money into fixed-income investments and 60% into stocks.

•Sixty-year olds should put 60% of their money into fixed-income investments and 40% into stocks.

•Dollar-cost average. When you invest in stocks, you can expect substantial swings in value—often 30% or more a year. But over the long term, stocks, especially small stocks, appreciate much more than bonds or Treasury bills.

You can reduce the risk of volatility and market swings by dollar-cost averaging—investing the same amount of money at regular intervals over time.

Example: If you invest $100 per month in a fund valued at $10 in the first month, $5 in the second month and $10 in the third month, you would get 10 shares the first month, 20 shares the second month and 10 shares the third month for a total of 40 shares, worth $400. But you would only pay $300...for a total return of 33% on your investment.

Dollar-cost averaging has been an effective way to reduce risk through all types of economic periods, including the Great Depression.

Example: If, starting in January 1929, a person had invested $100 a month in the Dow Jones Industrials for 64 months, he would have watched the Dow Jones Industrial Average drop 73%... yet his $6,4000 investment would have increased to $7,157 during one of the worst economic periods in history.

The key is to make regular contributions. No matter how much you save, it should be automatic. *Best:* Have the money taken out of your paycheck or bank account before you can spend it.

Increase your savings contribution as your income rises. The day you get a raise is a good time to increase your savings allotment.

Source: Glenn Pape, CPA, APFS, JD, vice president, financial-related services. The AYCO Corp., a subsidiary of American Express Co., One Wall St., Albany, New York 12205. AYCO is an independent fee-based financial counseling firm that works with corporations and individuals.

How to Cut Credit Card Costs

The effective cost of carrying a credit card balance can hit 30% annually. While various charges are almost always disclosed in fine print, credit-card terms are now so complex that they're commonly confused.

Here's a plain-English summary and advice on how to cut costs...

• Interest on unpaid balance. This has come down in recent years, to an average annual rate of 18.5%, but most consumers are effectively paying more than 20%. Those who regularly carry a balance should shop around for the lowest rate.

• Interest calculations. Banks can use several different methods to calculate interest charges. The most common is the average daily balance method including new purchases: If you start the month with a $1,000 balance and make a payment of $990, you will be charged interest on $1,000—not the $10 you still owe. The cheapest method for calculating interest is the average daily balance method, excluding new purchases, which does not include new purchases when figuring your finance charge. Only a few banks use this method.

A few issuers use the two-cycle average daily balance method, which in certain cases calculates interest on last month's and this month's balances and adds them together. This method can be very expensive for consumers who sometimes pay in full and sometimes carry a balance.

Some banks now charge interest from the date an item is purchased, rather than the date a charge is posted to one's account. This adds several days' worth of interest per month.

• Grace period. With most cards, holders have 25 days to pay a bill before interest is assessed. However, for the roughly 70% of holders who make a partial payment, and thereby have an unpaid balance each month, the grace period doesn't apply. To cut costs, send your payment as soon as you get your bill. If you pay off your balance each month, look for a card offering a full grace period.

• Cash advances. Fees range from 2% to 2.5% of a cash advance. Usually there's a minimum fee such as $2 and a maximum fee as high as $20. Few credit cards extend grace periods to cash advances. Because of these terms, cash advances are often the most costly way for consumers to borrow money.

• Additional fees. When shopping around, don't overlook additional fees that can add to the effective interest charges. For instance, fees for exceeding one's credit limit commonly run about $11 per month. Late payments entail additional fees of around $8 per month.

• Minimum payments. Many banks have low minimum payments, encouraging more people to maintain larger balances. The result, of course, has been higher credit-card costs.

Example: If you owe $2,500 and make a minimum payment of 2% per month, it would take you more than 30 years to pay off the balance and would cost $6,500 in interest charges. *Best:* Pay off your balance as fast as you can. Even paying $25 per month beyond the required minimum will help make an appreciable dent in credit-card costs.

Source: Gerri Detweiler, director, BankCard Holders of America, Suite 120, Herndon, Virginia 22070.

How Two-Paycheck Couples Can Make Their Money Work as Hard As They Do

Most working couples fail to exploit their financial clout. It gets lost in the hassle of everyday living.

A two-earner couple can raise capital much more easily than a one-earner...and capitalize on that additional borrowing power—even gamble on one of them starting a business.

What you can do...

• Take your joint earning power seriously. If you are jointly bringing home $100,000 (or $50,000), you are more than mere wage earners. Managing your money is a business.

•Start now. Two-earner couples typically talk themselves into a "tomorrow" attitude about starting to save and invest. Few take the time to compute the enormous sums they will need to buy a home, rear children, have a comfortable retirement, etc.

Guideline: Newlyweds should save at least 5% of their joint income and gradually increase the amount to 20% during peak earning years.

•Set goals. But make them flexible enough to enable you to deal with new situations—the arrival of a baby, the purchase of a home, a promotion, etc.

•Keep the lines of communication open about how to handle money. That way you can resolve differences and negotiate changes necessary to meet changed conditions. No matter how in love you are, no two people are going to agree completely about money.

Make time for making money...

Juggling job, home and family doesn't leave much time for financial management. *Helpful:* Transfer your combined knowledge of the business world to family finances. Modify the reports, forms, controls and filing systems you use at work to serve your needs at home.

•Get organized. Until you hack through the jumble, you can't tackle the real business of money management—investing.

•Set up a portion of your home as an office—with enough work space for each of you.

•Buy a filing cabinet for investment publications, articles and prospectuses, and for your bookkeeping records.

•Use in and out baskets. Pay bills when received and balance checkbooks monthly.

•Set up a "tickler" file to alert you to matters requiring action. Start with 12 file folders, one for each month, with the current month in front. Behind the current month's file, add 31-day files. File documents or projects according to the day you must start work on them, not by the deadline. At the end of each week, transfer the now-empty day files to the next month and start over.

•Open a single joint bank account. It cuts down on paperwork and administrative fees. The fewer accounts of any kind, in fact, the better...cuts down opportunities for errors.

Keep enough money in the checking account for day-to-day expenses and avoid bank charges.

Automatically transfer any excess funds to a joint money-market account with a higher interest rate. Use your money market account to pay large bills and hold savings while you decide where to invest them.

If you want to have some money separate from your spouse, pool the bulk of your incomes and put the rest in separate accounts. Do not use these accounts to pay for tax-deductible expenses unless you intend to file separate returns. You would have too many trails to follow at tax time.

•Cut back on credit cards. Carry only a few credit cards in your *individual* names. One spouse should be the "primary" cardholder on Mastercard, for instance, and the other spouse the "primary" Visa cardholder. You will save time, checks, postage and membership fees as a result.

•Keep good records. The driving force behind record keeping is taxes. You cannot intelligently spend, invest or plan without being aware of tax implications.

Sort your income and expenses in folders labeled by categories behind subject dividers. Each of you will file cancelled checks written on your separate accounts. One of you will be responsible for filing the joint accounts.

Keep current on filing. This way, you will always know where you stand. And tax time will be a snap.

At regular intervals, summarize these records, preferably on a computer. Financial software packages save time in tracking your assets and help in controlling spending—essential for successful investing.

•Staple cancelled checks and their related receipts together. Don't pay cash for tax-deductible expenses but if you must, get a receipt. Use a separate credit card for business travel and/or entertaining. There's no reason to spend time separating business from personal expenses. The monthly total will be the amount deductible.

•Delegate and rotate responsibility so that you both gain experience in all aspects of finance. In the event of disability, death, overtime or out-of-town meetings, either partner should be able to carry on. This also prevents one person from getting stuck with boring chores or losing sight of the overall financial picture.

You can divide tasks equally, then switch jobs every six months. Or one spouse can take charge completely for six months at a stretch. This latter arrangement may be the best approach if one of you is in a seasonal business or travels extensively at certain times of the year.

Consider a tradeoff if one of you is constantly traveling. The wandering spouse can assume three or four big tasks, such as preparing the tax return or studying investment prospectuses—perfect hotel reading.

Splitting authority is a great time-saver. You don't have to do everything in tandem. After a joint initial visit with an attorney, accountant or stockbroker, only one of you need go thereafter except in matters of great importance.

• Discuss financial goals and share decisions. Schedule periodic meetings to assess your financial status, confer about problems and review plans for the future. Make an appointment if you have to. Reserve a table at your favorite quiet restaurant, bring your documents and go over the scheduled topics as you would at any business dinner.

• Form an investment club with your spouse. Decide what types of investments are needed to meet your goals, then divide the work.

Example: One spouse can research and select stock funds while the other does the same for bond funds. Or you might each agree to pick one stock and one bond fund.

Compare results. Analyze why one outperformed the other and learn together.

As you get your financial affairs under control you can branch out from easy, no-fuss investments like CDs and money-market funds into more diverse and potentially more profitable ventures.

Work efficiently...

It's not enough to carve out time. You must also use it effectively.

• Batch related activities. Write all your checks on the first Sunday of the month, for example, then drop them into your tickler file by mailing date.

• Make a list of tasks that need to be done. Then work through the list, crossing off each job as it is completed. Update the list daily or weekly.

• Be decisive. Plan the research...carry it out ...see if more research is desirable...move ahead. Don't procrastinate.

Source: Mary L. Sprouse. She is the author of *Sprouse's Two-Earner Money Book,* Viking Penguin, 375 Hudson St., New York 10014.

Money Moves to Help You Get Ready for The Next Century

A tougher job market...higher taxes...an end to traditional company pensions...more litigation...bloodbaths on Wall Street. These are among the awful things in store for us as we approach the 21st century.

Are you ready? If not, here are 10 ways to prepare yourself financially for the year 2000 and beyond...

• Get ready for job insecurity. There's a growing probability of unemployment at some point in your career. And once unemployed, chances are you will stay unemployed for a longer period than you would have in the past.

Ask yourself, *What would happen if I lost my job tomorrow?* If you are prepared, you may be more assertive in demanding a better severance package. The time to demand better severance pay is when you're getting the ax, not 24 hours later.

Also consider how to survive financially if you become unemployed. There's nothing like money in the bank to prepare for unemployment.

• Pay off your debts. If you lose your job, you will be in better shape if your debts are under control. Paying off debt is also a better use for your money than leaving the cash in low-yielding bonds or certificates of deposit. How come? Being indebted has virtually no tax advantages, unless the debt is a mortgage. And the cost of borrowing money, when compared with the inflation rate, is much higher now than it has been historically.

•Get "umbrella" liability insurance. That will protect you in case you get sued. Our society is becoming more litigious. One out of 17 people gets sued each year. Umbrella liability insurance doesn't just buy you protection if you lose a suit—it also pays your legal defense costs. For $1 million of extra protection, you will pay only $100 to $200 a year.

Warning: Umbrella liability does not cover job-related lawsuits.

•Live beneath your means. There are two reasons for this:

•It gives you the latitude to pay for unexpected expenses without going into debt.

•You will free up money that can be saved for retirement. The amount you need to save for retirement is exploding—as prices rise, people live longer and company pensions are eliminated.

•Become a long-term investor. Otherwise, you could face dire consequences when it comes time to retire. Traditional company pension plans are fast disappearing. Social Security will provide only a small amount of the money needed to retire.

If you are going to live well after you leave the workforce, you need to commit a large portion of your investment portfolio to the stock market today so that you can build wealth by tapping into the handsome long-run gains generated by stocks.

But remember, those gains have a price. You must learn to live with wild swings in share prices during the short term.

•Invest internationally. In the years ahead, there will always be a bull market going on somewhere in the world, and more often than not it won't be in the US. To invest in foreign markets, buy mutual funds instead of individual stocks.

My favorite no-loads...

•*T. Rowe Price International Stock Fund* (800-638-5660) and...

•*Scudder International Fund* (800-225-2470).

•Load up on tax-advantaged investments. Taxes aren't going down, and they may well go up, so you need to protect yourself from Uncle Sam.

Consider tax-free municipal bonds, which provide better after-tax returns than corporate or government bonds, presuming you are in the 28% or higher tax bracket.

Also take full advantage of retirement savings vehicles, such as 401(k) plans, 403(b) plans and individual retirement accounts. Your money will grow tax-deferred, and your investments each year may also be tax-deductible.

•Actively manage your stock portfolio. Our parents could buy and hold good-quality stocks. That doesn't work anymore. In 1993, hardly a day went by without a sound company getting bashed on Wall Street for no good reason. The next stock to be bashed could be sitting in your portfolio. As a result, you must take a more active approach to managing your stock portfolio.

Strategy: Use mutual funds to get active management. Funds offer professional money management at a relatively low cost. They are a particularly good way to invest in foreign stocks as well as aggressive small-company stocks in the US.

•Consider sophisticated estate-planning strategies. More people are going to become subject to estate taxes. If you are married and have an estate worth more than $600,000, at a minimum you'll need a trust that will allow both husband and wife to make use of the $600,000 unified credit. In addition, people with estates that are likely to be subject to estate taxes should talk to their attorneys about putting their life insurance into irrevocable life insurance trusts.

•Learn to do it yourself. With company pensions on the wane and Social Security under attack, you can't blindly rely on a financial planner or an investment adviser for financial security. Even if you use an adviser, you still have to teach yourself about financial matters, or your finances could be mismanaged for years without your realizing what's happening.

Best of all, do it yourself. That way, you will have true control over your finances—and you will also save yourself a bundle on brokerage commissions and investment advisory fees.

Source: Jonathan D. Pond, president, Financial Planning Information Inc., 9 Galen St., Watertown, Massachusetts 02172. He is the author of *The New Century Family Money Book*, Dell Publishing, 1540 Broadway, New York 10036.

How to Stay in Control Of Your Money...Now

What should individuals expect to be charged when they retain an adviser to help them make investment decisions?

The annual fee that a financial adviser charges should not be more than 1.5% of the value of your stock investments under management. For a bond portfolio, a fair annual fee is closer to 0.75%.

Annual fees should be on a sliding scale that declines as your investment assets increase. International investing is more complex, however, and it is the only category of investments for which a higher annual fee is justified.

In addition, most money managers charge a minimum fee of about $1,000 a year. That is warranted, in my view, since a substantial amount of time goes into setting up accounts, reviewing and reporting on performance, managing paperwork and counseling clients.

Most brokerage firms offer *wrap accounts*, which combine financial planning and trading services. The money-management and brokerage commissions are grouped into a flat, annual fee of about 3%. Over time, that can be pretty steep if you don't do much trading. I think those fees will eventually come down.

What services can clients expect for these money-management fees?

At the very least, you should receive a report each quarter on how your investments are doing. Each quarter, your adviser should also give you his/her opinion about what's going on in the economy and suggest changes in your investments—if applicable—based on that outlook.

When looking for a money manager, what information can an individual get on his/her past performance...or that of a brokerage firm's wrap account?

The performance of money managers, like that of mutual funds, is monitored by independent analysts. When you're considering a money manager for equity investments, ask to be shown his/her CDA performance rating* and review it on the basis of total return—*capital gains plus reinvested dividends.* Compare it to the total return of a market index, such as the S&P 500.

If you're considering a wrap account offered by a brokerage firm, you'll be able to choose a money manager based on your financial objectives from among a group that the firm selected.

Keep in mind that how well the manager has beaten the market in the past shouldn't necessarily be the primary reason for selecting him. Equally important might be how well the manager conserves capital in bear markets or the volatility of his performance.

After you've chosen a money manager, is it unusual for him to insist on managing only a cash deposit?

Not at all. A money manager is justified in thinking that he can perform better for you if you hand over a sum of cash to manage rather than a portfolio of stocks and bonds—from, say, an inheritance. In fact, some managers will take on a new account only if it's in cash.

Reason: Since money managers report their performance to independent analysts, they don't want their records hampered by investments in a portfolio that they would not have recommended.

This means you'll either have to liquidate some of your portfolio or authorize the manager to sell securities so that he has cash to invest for you.

If someone is paying a manager to monitor an account, should any of the money be in an index fund, whose portfolio matches that of a broad-based index such as the S&P 500?

I don't think so. You're already paying the money manager to do as well—and better—than the market or an index over time.

Should investors be concerned if they don't receive a stock or bond certificate?

No. Money managers don't actually have custody of the certificates. The brokerage or bank with which they do business does.

In the near future, stock and bond certificates will probably be phased out and your holdings will increasingly appear only as computer entries. You'll just get a confirmation from the firm that handles the transaction, not a certificate.

Mutual funds do this now—sending you a regular statement showing how many shares you own, whether dividends or capital gains were reinvested, etc. Individual investors are resisting this trend, but it's inevitable.

How, then, is an investor protected when all he/she has is a statement from the broker to acknowledge what he owns?

Well, there's the brokerage industry's own insurance program, which covers up to $400,000 in securities and $100,000 in cash in each customer's account. Most firms buy additional insurance to protect their customers in case the company fails.

What kind of personal bookkeeping works best once you own a variety of investments rather than just a few bank CDs?

There are several computer software programs available that can help you keep track of your funds. I find, however, that the simplest, most effective system is a three-hole binder, loose-leaf paper, a set of tabbed dividers and a three-hole punch. You should use a tab divider for every investment account—brokerage account, trust fund, mutual funds, bank CDs, IRAs and so on.

Then, each time you receive paperwork in the mail—the original confirmation of a transaction, a dividend statement, notice of stock split, etc.—punch the holes if they aren't there already and slip it into the rings at the front of the specific section.

Mutual fund statements are cumulative, of course, so you can just take out the previous notice and put in the new one. The whole record will be right there when you do your taxes. Set it up right now for this year if you've had a lot of trouble getting your records together for last year.

Source: Alexandra Armstrong, chairman, Armstrong, Welch, MacIntyre, Inc., 1155 Connecticut Ave. NW, Washington, DC 20036.

Ten of the Most Common Mistakes in Financial Planning

Mistake: Not knowing what is enough for your financial objectives. Too many investors are caught up in the cultural bias for *more*... more for more's sake. This is akin to putting the cart before the horse and then killing the horse. Too often, in investing, the push to make more requires overreaching—taking risks that can result, in the end, in *less* rather than more. Since more is by definition never enough, financial planners are driven to accomplish the impossible. This creates anxiety for both you and your planner.

What I advocate in my professional planning practice is a radically different school of thought that I call *Enough*.

This approach puts the client into personal financial planning. It recognizes the essential truth that financial resources are only a means to achieve personal objectives. The goal is to look inward and identify your life goals and then align those goals with your personal resources.

If your retirement income needs can be met, after adjusting for inflation and tax increases, with an investment that is safely earning 6%, why take a big risk to earn 20%?

When you have *enough* you can relax and be satisfied, or you can start a new fund. But you don't have to push for more.

Mistake: Abdicating responsibility. Too many people work for 40 years (that's about 80,000 hours of making money)—but don't spend the relatively few hours needed to protect their life's earnings.

You can't abdicate that responsibility. It's OK to let a planner help you row the boat, but *you* must steer.

Once you have determined your objectives, you can use a personal financial planner to provide technical advice. Avoid planners who are transaction-oriented, such as brokers and life insurance salespersons. They're working for themselves, not you. *Fee-only* planners are a better choice, *though they're not guaranteed to be competent.*

Beware: There are 250,000 people in the US who call themselves personal financial planners but have virtually no expertise and are subject to no industry or government regulations.

Mistake: Wanting results *now.* Remember, anything worth doing is worth doing slowly. This is particularly true of investments. Going for a quick kill is a sure way to get burned. Don't convey a sense of impatience to your planner. Be satisfied to make steady progress.

Mistake: Piecemeal planning. By doing piecemeal planning you may solve one problem, but you can create two others. Planners are now pushing what's called modular planning—e.g., how to finance your child's education. But you can't plan that in isolation. What if you need to put aside $10,000 a year and you become disabled? Comprehensive planning is the only answer.

Mistake: Concentrating on finances instead of on personal goals. Much too much financial planning is based strictly on managing assets instead of on aligning your personal finances with your personal goals. Life planning must come before financial planning, not the other way around. *Enough* is a very personal thing.

Mistake: Not asking what could go wrong. Before making any investment, you should know about the downside. What could go wrong? What would be the cause of trouble? What's the probability? The seriousness? How can you prevent or minimize risk? The best surprise is no surprise.

Mistake: Neglecting to ask to see the planner's own financial plan. This should not be a secret. If he/she is going to see your personal finances, you should be able to see his. If he doesn't have a plan or won't show you, go elsewhere. People who can't plan for their own lives certainly can't help you plan for yours.

Mistake: Not distinguishing the "closer" from the "doer." There are a lot of charming professionals out there who are very good at making the sale but don't actually do the work. It may be the partner of the CPA firm who signs you up, but your account is really handled by some clerk in a position that turns over every two years, meaning that you have to keep re-educating new people. Don't pay partner fees for a partner you never see. By the same token, an hour spent with a very good (but expensive) planner may be worth more than a month of someone else's time.

Mistake: Not getting an estimate of fees and commissions up front. Don't accept an answer of, *"We won't know until we see how your account works out."* Any professional planner knows how to qualify prospects. At the very least, the planner can tell you what other investors of your general description are paying in average fees and commissions.

Note: Although there are only about 1,000 fee-only planners, you may be able to negotiate a fee-only relationship with a normally commissioned planner who's willing to strike a deal.

Mistake: Believing that the specific investment is more important than asset allocation. The term "financial planning" is used by insurance companies, brokers, investment companies, banks, partnership syndicators and others who are trying to put an independent-looking mask on what is really just a delivery system for the sale of a product. Fully 93% of portfolio value is based on investment classifications (how assets are allocated between different types of investments), *not* on the specific investment or the timing of the purchase. If you tell a planner you have, say, $100,000 to invest and the planner tells you where it should go *before* finding out about your plans, goals, other assets, etc., the planner has failed.

Source: James D. Schwartz, a fee-only personal financial planner and president of ENOUGH, Inc., Englewood, Colorado. He is the author of *ENOUGH, A Guide to Reclaiming Your American Dream,* Re/Max International, Inc., Creative Ad Fund, Box 3363, Englewood, Colorado 80155.

Better 401(k) Investing

It pays to know your options for investing your 401(k). Most company plans offer three to five choices. *Examples:* Company stock, equity mutual funds, money-market funds, and/or guaranteed investment contracts issued by insurance companies. *Helpful:* Request a prospectus from each company that manages one of these investment options and read it very carefully—with your accountant, if necessary. Contact your employer's retirement-plan manager for the name and address of each of these companies.

Source: Legg Mason, president, Legg Mason Wood Walker, Inc., investment advisers and stockbrokers, 99 Summer St., Box 1, Boston 02101.

Savings Bond Savvy

US savings bonds now pay higher annual yields than any other low-risk, liquid investment. Currently, savings bonds pay 4%, compared to tax-free money funds (3.3%), one-year CDs (3%), three-month Treasury bills (2.91%), money funds (2.6%) and money-market accounts (2.4%). *Catch:* Savings bonds must be held for at least six months before being redeemed.

Source: Norman Fosback, editor of *Income & Safety,* 3471 N. Federal Hwy., Fort Lauderdale 33306. 800-442-9000.

Student Loan Repayment Plans

Student loan repayment plans can ease the burdens of recent graduates who have low-paying jobs or none at all. *Trap:* Those who ignore lenders' collection notices can seriously damage their credit ratings. *Self-defense:* Loan holders should talk to their lenders as soon as possible if they cannot meet loan terms. Lenders contacted before payments fall behind are more likely to consider other repayment options. Possibilities include deferment—postponing repayment and perhaps stopping interest from accruing...forbearance—postponing repayment of principal while interest still accrues...consolidation—combining many loans into one...graduated repayment—smaller payments in early years, larger ones later...or some other special arrangement.

Source: Patricia McWade, dean of financial aid, Georgetown University, Washington, DC.

What to Ask a Financial Planner

The probing questions to ask:

• What's your specialty? If the planner lists specialties—say, hard assets or insurance or stocks or tax shelters—scratch him/her from your list. *What you should be looking for:* A generalist with a professional staff.

• What percentage of your income comes from fees and how much from commissions? If much of the income is generated by commissions, also scratch him.

• What are your educational background and professional experience? If he passes the background test, call his references.

• Are you affiliated with any other firm? Some planners are affiliated with an insurance company, a stockbroker, or even a marketer of tax shelters. You should eliminate them.

• Can you quantify what you can do for me? Eliminate planners who jump to that bait and start reeling off numbers.

• How much will it cost? If he immediately quotes you a package price, go on the next candidate.

Source: Connie S.P. Chen, a former financial consultant at Merrill Lynch's Personal Financial Planning Group and, for the last seven years, head of Chen Planning Consultants, New York.

No-Haggle Hassle

Car buyers who shop at one-price "no-haggle" dealerships to avoid the discomfort of negotiating may pay as much as $1,000 more for the convenience.

Reason: Prices at no-haggle dealerships are inflexible and typically higher than those that consumers could negotiate for themselves at traditional showrooms.

Source: W. James Bragg, author of *In the Driver's Seat: The New Car Buyer's Negotiating Bible.* Random House, 201 E. 50 St., New York 10022.

How to Make Your Money Work

- Earn up to 21% risk-free by paying off charge-card balances early. You may not realize that carrying a $500 balance on a bank card can cost as much as $105 per year.
- Make contributions to your IRA or Keogh Plan as early in the year as possible.
- Borrow money from your corporate profit-sharing or pension plan rather than from a bank. You may still claim the interest expense as a deduction.
- Shift income to your children with trusts or custodial accounts. The money will be taxed at their low rate.
- Increase your insurance deductibles.
- Don't rely on your accountant to find the best possible tax deductions for you. Invest in a good self-help manual.
- Prepay your mortgage. An extra $100 a month will dramatically shorten your term and total interest expenses.

Source: Dr. Paul A. Randle, professor of finance, Utah State University, writing in *Physicians Management,* New York.

Quick and Easy Ways To Save Money

- Comparison shop by phone, not by car.
- Make your own gift wrap and greeting cards.
- Use heavy-duty brown bags from the supermarket for garbage.
- Make your own liquid dishwashing soap out of leftover soap slivers (put them in a jar, cover with water and stir occasionally).
- Use toll-free numbers (call the toll-free information operator at 800-555-1212).
- Rent a room in your home to a local college student.

Source: *Parents* magazine, New York.

Stretching Due Dates On Bills

Due dates on bills can be stretched—but not far—without risk. *Typical grace periods:* Telephone companies, eight days. Gas and electric utilities, 10 days. Banks and finance companies, 10 days. Even after a late charge is imposed on an unpaid bill your credit rating should be safe for 30 days.

Source: Terry Blaney, president of Consumer Credit Counseling Service of Houston and the Gulf Coast Area.

How to Find Money You Didn't Know You Had

Few people take full advantage of the capital at their disposal. *There are a myriad of simple ways to optimize your personal financial resources:*

- Convert passbook savings accounts, savings bonds, etc. into better investments. Americans still have $300 billion sitting in low-interest passbook savings accounts when they could be so easily transferred to CDs at nearly double the yield! Review your portfolio now, particularly bonds that have recently registered nice gains. Should you still be owning what you do? People often hold investments long after they've forgotten why they originally made them.
- Borrow on life insurance (such low interest rates aren't being offered today). Many folks who bought life insurance back in the 1960s and 1970s (term insurance is more prevalent today) could borrow back the money at 3% to 6% and reinvest it in insured CDs at a higher rate.

• Pay real estate taxes directly instead of through the bank. Most banks withhold an amount on monthly mortgage payments for paying the homeowner's real estate taxes. Yet, in most towns, real estate tax bills are sent annually. The bank is earning interest on your money. *Caution:* You must make the payments on time. Banks can call in your mortgage if the taxes are delinquent, and they'd just love to do it if you are fortunate enough to have a low-interest mortgage.

• Prepay mortgage principal. Making a monthly $25 prepayment of principal from day one on a $75,000, 30-year, 13% mortgage would save $59,372, and the mortgage would be paid off in 23 years and four months. (Most mortgages allow prepayment.)

• Conduct a garage sale. Turn unwanted items into cash. (Sotheby's or another auction house will appraise a possible collectible for free.)

If you are self-employed:

• Keep good records of travel and entertainment expenses and of the business use of cars, computers and other property used for both business and personal purposes. Taxpayers who can't back up their deductions with good records will lose the deductions and may be charged negligence penalties.

• Reward yourself first. Plan for your future by putting money into your tax-deferred retirement plan now. Too many entrepreneurs wait until they're successful before taking money out of the business and risk receiving nothing.

• Park company cash in the highest yielding CDs. It's easy to compare CDs. Look at the table called Highest Money-Market Yields, now published in 23 major newspapers. The highest-yielding CDs in the country are paying 2% to 3% above the average yield. That translates into $200 to $300 a year with a $10,000 CD.

Source: William E. Donoghue, publisher of several investment newsletters, including *Donoghue's Moneyletter,* Holliston, MA.

Smart Borrowing

Even many super-successful business people find themselves short of cash at times, whether in paying a child's college tuition or in taking advantage of an irresistible investment.

Once you have decided on a sound reason and a sound plan for borrowing, you naturally want to find the best possible interest rate. There are a variety of ways to avoid the high unsecured loan rates being offered at most banks and thrifts across the country:

• Insurance policy loan: Particularly attractive if you have an old policy that provides for low interest rate loans. It is especially good if the policy has been in effect for more than seven years. *Reason:* There is a legal provision that policyholders must have paid four out of the first seven payments to get a tax-deductible loan. If the policy has been in effect for seven years, there is no question about tax deductibility. *Safety valve:* Many people fear borrowing on their life insurance policies because this reduces the coverage in case of death. *Solution:* You can use the dividends on the policy to buy additional term insurance to keep the insurance level at face value. That permits you to borrow and to maintain the death value.

• Qualified savings plan: Many corporate savings plans, including 401(k) plans, permit employees to borrow the savings that they (and their employer) have put into the plan. Typically, the borrowing rate on savings plans is lower than bank rates, although each company has its own rules. Ask your personnel office about your company's policies. *Caution:* Do not confuse this with IRAs or Keoghs. You cannot borrow against them. And although some firms permit employees to borrow against their pension funds, it isn't advisable.

• Brokerage house loan: The current big thing in the brokerage houses is cash management accounts (in their various guises)—and home equity accounts. Cash management accounts let you borrow against stocks and bonds. Home equity accounts include the value of your home as collateral against loans. Brokerage houses have the resources to appraise your home, and they permit you to borrow at a fairly good rate—the broker loan rate. *Problem:* Margin loans against stock can be called if the stock market goes down sharply and the collateral loses value.

•Second mortgage: Exercise extreme caution when using this technique. You are giving someone a lien on your home. You might lose your job, or your business might falter. It is a dangerous way to get into a bind—and you could end up losing your home.

Source: Thomas Lynch, senior vice president, Ayco/American Express, a financial consulting group that advises corporate personnel about financial and tax matters.

The Best Places to Borrow Money

There are now more ways to borrow money than ever before. By carefully shopping around, you may be able to save big dollars while establishing valuable new credit lines.

•Interest-free loans from the company have been a favored perk for key executives for years. The bookkeeping is now more complicated, but both the company and the executive may be left in the same position they were in before the new tax laws went into effect, owing little or no tax as a result of the loan.

•Preferred financing terms are often provided by banks to the employees of major commercial accounts. *Typical benefit:* Home mortgages at a half point to a full point lower than the standard mortgage rate.

•Company pension plans frequently contain provisions that allow employees to borrow against their plan accounts. Many plans allow loans to be made at a reasonable interest rate in order to help finance the purchase of a new primary residence or to meet specified emergencies. Employees can typically borrow as much as half the value of their non-forfeitable retirement benefits, up to a maximum of $50,000.

•Credit unions are usually a cheap source of funds for their members. Because they have less overhead than banks and are looking to break even rather than to make a profit, they lend at rates lower than commercial rates. *Typical:* Personal loans of up to half your salary. Many credit unions also have insurance programs.

•Home equity loans. When the original mortgage on a house has been largely paid off, and the house has gone up in value, a borrower may be able to get a loan at about two points over the prime rate. *Caution:* There are drawbacks to using your house as collateral. First, you're establishing a lien against your home. Second, there are charges involved—often a one-time fee of 2% on the credit line, plus an annual maintenance fee of $25 to $100, and perhaps a mortgage recording tax.

•Bank loans. It's important to shop around for the best terms. Remember that as a borrower you don't have to worry about the bank's solvency. You can safely take advantage of unusual terms offered by a bank that's desperate for business.

•Credit and debit cards may be the most expensive form of financing (typically charging interest rates of 18% to 20%), but they also offer the most convenient source of cash around. *Danger:* Letting charges pile up. *Rule of thumb:* Monthly loan payments, exclusive of the home mortgage, should total no more than 10% to 15% of net income.

•Merchant financing may represent a better deal than the average bank loan. *Typical case:* An auto purchase. While a local bank may offer auto loans at 12% to 13%, many auto dealers, helped out by funds from the major manufacturers, can extend credit at 8% to 9%.

Sources: David S. Rhine, partner, BDO Seidman, New York, and Israel A. Press, partner and director of personal financial management, Touche Ross Financial Services Center, New York.

Lending Money to A Friend

•No matter how friendly a loan, draw up a note stating terms and conditions.

•Be businesslike. Include a provision for reasonable interest.

•Be prepared to document the loan, so that you can take a tax deduction on any loss.

Filing a Claim for Bodily Injury

Claims against insurance companies for bodily injury can be the most complicated and negotiable type of claim, especially when based upon pain and suffering. *Be aware:*

• In a no-fault state, you are limited to out-of-pocket expenses in a nonserious injury. This includes lost wages. In a fault-governed state, you can negotiate for more.

• Don't miss damages. Start at the top of your head and go down to your toes, to include every part that's been hurt.

• Photograph your injury. In addition to medical reports, photos are the best documentation of suffering.

• Consider every aspect of your life affected by your injury. Include your career, sports, hobbies, future interests and family relationships.

• Ask the insurance company what a lawyer would ask—at least twice the actual expenses when there has been no permanent disability. Where liability is clear, the insurance company will be likely to give you what you ask, if it believes that you really had difficulties and were out of work for a few weeks. However, where there has been permanent disability, multiples of expenses do not apply. *Example:* Your medical bills for a lost eye might have been only $3,000, but a jury might award you 50 times that amount.

Source: Dan Brecher, a New York City attorney.

Before You Sign A Contract with A Health Club

• Inspect the club at the time of day you'd be most likely to attend. Check on how crowded the pool, sauna and exercise rooms are.

• Make certain all facilities that are promised are available.

• Avoid clubs that require long-term contracts.

• Once you sign a contract, if you wish to terminate, it's usually possible to avoid liability for the full term of the contract by notifying the club by registered mail, paying for services already rendered and a small cancellation fee. Check your local consumer protection agency for rules.

• *Most important:* Don't be pushed into a hasty decision by a low-price offer. Specials are usually repeated.

Financial Aid for the Mugging Victim

Financial compensation programs for mugging victims exist in more than 30 states. Compensation can cover both medical expenses and lost earnings. However, most of these programs utilize a means test that effectively eliminates all but lower-income victims. Additionally, the victim's own medical and unemployment insurance must be fully depleted before state compensation is granted.

If you are mugged, check the following:

• Workers compensation may cover you if you were mugged on the job or on your way to or from company business during your workday. It will not cover you while commuting.

• Homeowners' policies may cover financial losses suffered during a mugging.

• Federal crime insurance insures up to $10,000 against financial losses from a mugging. This program is for people who have had difficulty purchasing homeowners' insurance privately.

• Mugging insurance is now available in New York. It covers property loss, medical care and mental anguish. If successful, it may spread rapidly to other states.

• A lawsuit may be successful if you can prove that the mugging was the result of negligence.

Source: Lucy N. Friedman, executive director, Victim Services Agency, New York.

If the Dry Cleaner Loses Or Ruins a Garment

• You should be reimbursed or given a credit. Most dry cleaners are neighborhood businesses where reputation is vital. You can hurt a cleaner's reputation by giving the cleaner bad word-of-mouth. You might remind the store of this fact if there is resistance to satisfying your complaint.

• If your cleaner fails to remove a stain you were told could be removed, you still have to pay for the cleaning job.

• If your cleaner dry cleans a garment with a "do not dry clean" label, the store is responsible for ruining the garment.

• If your cleaner ruins a garment that should not be dry cleaned but lacks the "do not dry clean" label, responsibility is a matter of opinion. The cleaner may reimburse you to keep your goodwill, or you may have to complain to an outside agency.

• The amount you will be reimbursed is always up for bargaining. You will have to consider original value and depreciation, and whether you have a receipt.

• If you cannot get satisfaction from your cleaner voluntarily, most states have dry cleaners associations to arbitrate complaints. These associations go under various names in different states, so check with your local Department of Consumer Affairs. Make sure to keep all dry cleaning receipts and other relevant information to substantiate your complaint.

Social Security Number Secret

Few people know it, but the first three digits of a Social Security number are a code for the state in which the card was issued. This code, which can be used to confirm a place of birth or an employment history, is not public knowledge. However, many private detectives have the key to the code and will crack the Social Security number for a fee.

Source: Milo Speriglio, director and chief of Nick Harris Detectives, Inc., Van Nuys, CA, the second-oldest private detective agency in the US, and administrator of Nick Harris' Detective Academy.

When to Use Small Claims Court

Suing in small claims court can bring both spiritual and material satisfaction when you feel that you have been wronged. Although the monetary stakes are low—most states limit small claims settlements to no more than $1,000—the rewards can be high.

Take a case to small claims court when you:

• Have the time. Usually it takes a month for a case to be called and you'll have to spend at least a few hours in court during the hearing.

• Value justice over a monetary settlement.

• Want a public hearing of your grievance.

• Feel the money involved represents a significant sum to you.

Savings and College Financial Aid

Some people fear that if they save to finance college, they will be penalized—with more financial aid going to someone who did not save at all. *Reality:* Financial aid formulas weigh *income* more heavily than *assets.* If you have good income but no savings, you will still be expected to make a substantial contribution to college costs. *Also:* A significant amount of aid is in the form of loans—which have to be repaid. The more cash you save before college, the less debt you and your children will have afterward.

Source: Kalman A. Chany, president of Campus Consultants, Inc., a fee-based firm that assists families in maximizing financial aid eligibility, and author of *The Princeton Review Student Access Guide to Paying for College.* Random House, 201 E. 50 St., New York 10022.

Pension-Plan Savvy

Monitor your company pension plan for possible mistakes that could prove costly when you retire. First, get a summary plan description from your employer that tells how retirement benefits are calculated. It's a good idea to see the description of a prospective new employer's plan before quitting your old job and letting your old pension plan go.

Key questions: Do bonuses, overtime and commissions—or just salary—count toward retirement benefits? Are benefits at retirement based on your top-earning years...or on all years of service? How are years of service calculated if you take a pregnancy break or some other leave of absence?

Source: *Baby Boomer Retirement: 65 Simple Ways to Protect Your Future* by Don Silver, an estate-planning lawyer in Los Angeles. Adams-Hall Publishing, Box 491002-BR3, Los Angeles 90049.

Fees and Performance

There is no correlation between what a mutual fund charges as management fees and how well that fund performs. But funds often assert that higher fees translate into greater shareholder value. *Reality:* In index funds, like those whose portfolios mirror the S&P 500 Index, fee differences account for almost all the difference in returns to investors. Now, about 14% of funds have management fees of 0.5% of assets or less...24% charge 1% or more ...the rest fall in between.

Source: Ken Gregory, editor, *No-Load Fund Analyst,* 4 Orinda Way, Orinda, California 94563.

Top-Yielding Fund Alert

Many top-yielding money-market funds quickly lose their top rankings. *Reason:* Their high yields come from waiving some—or even all—of the fund's expenses. When high yields bring in enough money so the fund reaches its desired size, it starts to phase in expense payments—and yields drop. *Self-defense:* Check your money-market fund yield regularly. Compare it with yields of other funds—and consider switching if your yield starts to slip. Selling money-market fund shares is not a taxable event, since the net asset value of each share is constant at one dollar.

Source: Walter Frank, chief investment officer, *Moneyletter,* which tracks mutual funds, 1217 St. Paul St., Baltimore 21202.

Brokerage Account Form Self-Defense

Brokerage account forms provide information about you that can be used against you if you ever face some sort of dispute. Many forms required to open a brokerage account ask for information on your investment goals, finances and personal background. If you lose money and believe you were unfairly treated, the brokerage can and will use whatever you said on the forms to prepare its case against you. *Self-defense:* Read the forms very carefully. Be sure you understand them. Decline to respond to questions you do not wish to answer. Write a letter to your broker confirming your understanding of your investment goals.

Source: John McKeegan, partner, Shockman & McKeegan, a law firm in Scottsdale, Arizona, that represents investors in brokerage disputes.

14

Your Car

What to Look for When You Test Drive a Car

Before you buy a new car, take full advantage of your test drive. Make sure the dealer lets you drive the vehicle where you can give it a thorough workout...on bumpy roads...in stop-and-go traffic...and on highways, especially the entrance and exit ramps. Pay special attention to how the car matches up to your expectations for comfort, drivability, interior layout and power.

Comfort...

- Engineers call the science of fitting the car to the person "ergonomics." You'll soon see how well they did when you climb in behind the driver's seat.
- You probably won't be the only one driving the new car regularly. Don't forget that the "feel" of the car should suit your co-drivers and frequent passengers.
- *Clearance:* Can you get in and out without hitting your head?
- *Headroom:* Your hair shouldn't touch the ceiling. If it does, and you love the vehicle, consider ordering it with a sunroof. This will give you another inch or two.
- *Seat height:* Does it give you good road visibility?
- *Headrest:* Will your head, neck and back be comfortable after driving for a while?
- *Leg room:* Does the seat move far enough forward and back not only for you but for all drivers?

Drivability...

- Test drive the car at night to make sure that the headlights are powerful enough for your comfort.
- *Power:* Does the car run smoothly and accelerate adequately? *Hint:* Make sure the car you test has the engine size, transmission type, or gear ratios that you want.
- *Rear visibility:* Can you see adequately with the exterior rear-view mirrors? If they're too small, be aware that replacements don't exist.

• *Noise:* Does engine exhaust or wind noise bother you?

• *Fuel type:* Does the car need expensive high-test gas? High-performance, multi-valve, super- and turbo-charged models all do.

Interior...

• *Instrumentation:* Can you read the gauges easily?

• *Controls:* Do you hit the wiper switch and put the radio on?

• *Door handles:* Can you find them in the dark?

Bottom line...

• If you're satisfied with your test drive, don't assume the car that the dealer delivers to you will be as good.

• Check out the finish of the car you want to buy to make sure you haven't been sold a vehicle that already has been driven...or damaged in transit. Look for tell-tale signs of repainting ...like paint traces on the rubber stripping or trim, mismatched colors and misfit panels. And take a good look at the undercoating. It should look slightly weathered—not sparkling clean and still soft.

• Insist on a test drive of your new car before you accept delivery. *Also:* Never take delivery at night. You want to examine your car carefully in broad daylight. You may also want to have the car looked over by a good mechanic.

Source: David Solomon, editor, *Nutz and Boltz®,* Box 123, Butler, Maryland 21023.

Understanding Car Terms

• *Rack-and-pinion steering:* This compact system has fewer moving parts than older systems and therefore is cheaper to make. But it is not necessarily better than the standard system.

• *Unibody construction:* Everything fastens onto the body, reducing the car's weight and increasing mileage. But a minor fender-bender can create hidden damage in another part of the structure.

• *Automatic overdrive transmission:* This is a fuel-economy measure. An extra high gear slows the engine when the car is cruising at a constant speed. *Disadvantage:* The car has reduced acceleration and hill-climbing ability when in this gear.

• *Overhead camshaft engine:* This slightly improves efficiency at high speeds, which is why some race cars use it. But this difference is not significant in normal driving.

Source: Automobile Club of New York.

Making the Right Choice of Options On a New Car

The value of an optional feature depends on how, when, and where most of the driving will be done.

Important for everyone: Options that make the car safer.

• Air bags.

• Steel-belted radial tires. They hold the road better, provide better fuel economy and longer life.

• Buy accessories that relate to the character of the automobile. A very lightweight car does not require power steering or power brakes.

Important but not essential:

• Cruise control. This is a great advantage for driving long distances on a regular basis. It sets the pace and helps the driver avoid speeding tickets.

• Air conditioning. This is very important for comfort and for the subsequent resale value of the car.

• Heavy-duty suspension system. It makes the car feel taut and firm and hold the road better. There is little initial cost and little value on resale. It is important for car owners who are either going to carry heavy loads or who love to drive and are extra sensitive to the performance of the car. It's not an important feature for those whose car use is limited mainly to trips to the supermarket.

• Power seats. Extremely useful feature for drivers who go long distances regularly. Permits moving the seat back. Allows arm position to be manipulated and fine-tuned in relation to steering wheel. In some ways a safety factor because it helps ward off driver fatigue. Power seats are quite expensive.

• Adjustable seat back. Some form of this is highly recommended and should be considered because it wards off driver fatigue and thus is a safety element.

• Tilt steering wheel. This is another aid in fine-tuning the driver's relation to the car and is therefore recommended as a safety factor. It is an important feature especially for large or short people.

• Electric door locks. Key unlocks all doors simultaneously. Button locks all doors at once, including the trunk lid. It is a convenience because it makes it unnecessary to open each door from the outside in bad weather. When driving through dangerous neighborhoods, the electric lock provides immediate security with the touch of a button.

Some options have disadvantages:

• Sunroof. Redundant if the car has air conditioning. Noise and the problem of water leakage are constant irritations.

• Power windows. They are recommended for drivers who use toll highways on a regular basis. Power windows can be dangerous to both small children and pets.

Fixing your present car vs. buying a new one:

Most older cars can be refurbished—and in fact be made as good as new—for far less than the cost of a brand new car. *The key:* The break-even point of the deal.

To figure fix-up costs: Have a competent mechanic give you a detailed list of everything that's wrong and costs to fix it up. With that kind of renovation, a car should be good for another five years with no major repair expenses.

• Even if the car needed a completely new engine, it would still be cheaper to repair the old car than to buy a brand new one.

• Gas mileage is not a key consideration. Assume that a new car would get 50% better gas mileage than the older car. It would still take at least 10 years to break even on mileage alone. *Example:* Your present car gets 15 MPG, and a new car would get 30 MPG. You buy 1,000 gallons of fuel per year (15,000 miles of driving) and it costs $1.40 per gallon. Your present gas bill is $1,400 per year. The 30 MPG car would cost you $700 per year. At that rate, disregarding all the other expenses of the new car, it would take 14 years for a payback on the improved mileage.

• On the other hand, if your car is worth less than $1,000 and is rusting, rebuilding is not recommended. Severe rusting can't be fixed.

Source: Tony Assenza, former editor of *Motor Trend.*

Shopping for a Used Car

Before looking for a used car, decide the exact make, model and price you want (just as you would if you were buying a new car).

• Determine whether you want to use the car for extensive traveling, for weekends and summer travel, or just for getting to the train station and back. This helps you decide whether you want a 3- to 5-year-old car (extensive travel) or one 5 to 7 years old (suitable for weekend use and summer travel). For trips to the train station in the morning, or for equivalent use, a car that is 7 to 10 years old will do.

• Choose a popular make in its most successful and long-lasting model. Repair parts are also easier to find.

• Get the local paper with the most advertising for used merchandise. Privately owned cars are often very well maintained and are generally available at prices much lower than those being offered by dealers.

• Look for the deluxe model of the popular make you've chosen. Since it cost a lot more when it was new, there's a better chance it was well cared for.

• Establish (by shopping) the going price of your desired make and model. Then select only those cars offered at above the average price. Owners of the better-cared-for cars usually demand a premium, and it's usually worth it.

How to Check Out A Used Car

You don't have to be an expert to decide whether a used car is worth paying a mechanic to check out. *The key steps:*

•Get the name and telephone number of the previous owner if you buy the car from a dealer. If the dealer won't give you this information from the title, pass up the car. (It could be stolen.)

•Call the former owner and ask what the car's major problems were (not if it had any problems). Also, get the mileage on the car when it was sold. If the odometer now reads less, it has been tampered with. Go elsewhere.

•Inspect the car yourself. Even a superficial look can reveal some signs that will warn you off or will be worth getting repair estimates for before you settle on a price.

•Check the car for signs of fresh undercoating. There is only one incentive for a dealer to undercoat an old car—to hide rust. Check this with a knife or screwdriver (with the dealer's permission). If you find rust, forget the car.

•Rub your finger inside the tailpipe. If it comes out oily, the car is burning oil. Your mechanic should find out why.

•Kneel down by each front fender and look down the length of the car. Ripples in the metal or patches of slightly mismatched paint can indicate bodywork. If a rippled or unmatched area is more than a foot square, ask the mechanic to look at the frame carefully. (Ask the former owner how bad the wreck was.)

•Open and close all the doors. A door that has to be forced is another sign of a possible wreck.

•Check for rust around moldings, under the bumper, at the bottom of doors, in the trunk, under floor mats, and around windows. Lumps in vinyl tops are usually a sign of rust. Rust and corrosion on the radiator mean leaks.

•Check the tires. Are they all the same type? Does the spare match? If there is excessive wear on the edges of any single tire, the car is probably out of alignment.

•Check the brakes by applying strong pressure to the pedal and holding it for 30 seconds. If it continues to the floor, it needs work.

•Test drive the car, and note anything that doesn't work, from the air conditioner to the windshield wipers. Listen for knocks in the engine and grinding or humming in the gears. Check the brakes and the steering. Drive over bumpy terrain to check the shock absorbers.

Source: Remar Sutton, author of *Don't Get Taken Every Time: The Insider's Guide to Buying Your Next Car,* Penguin Books, New York.

Sensible Car Maintenance

•Average life expectancy for some vital parts of your car. *Suspension system:* 15,000 miles. *Ignition wires:* 25,000 miles. *Water pump:* 30,000 miles. *Starter:* 40,000 miles. *Brake master cylinder, carburetor and steering mechanism (ball joints):* 50,000 miles. *Fuel pump:* 75,000 miles. *Clutch, timing gear chain/belt, universal joints:* Up to 100,000 miles.

•Replace brake fluid at least once a year. This isn't a common practice, and few owner's manuals mention it, but brake fluid attracts water (from condensation and humidity in the air), often causing corrosion in the master and wheel cylinders, shortening their lives. Replacing brake fluid regularly saves the more costly replacement of cylinders.

•Cold weather probably means your tires need more air. A tire which may have lost a few pounds of pressure during the summer and fall driving season could easily become 8–10 pounds underinflated on a freezing day. This is enough to cut tire life by 25%. *Rule of thumb:* For every 10-degree drop in the ambient temperature, the air pressure in a tire decreases by one-half to one pound.

•The oil-pressure warning light on the dashboard is not a foolproof system. By the time the light flashes, the engine has been without oil long enough to harm the machinery.

•Car-scratch repair. *When the scratch hasn't penetrated to the metal:* Sand with fine sandpaper (400–600 grit) until the scratch disappears. Wipe the area clean with a soft cloth. Paint it carefully, and let the paint dry for a few days. Then apply rubbing compound according to the directions in the package. *When the scratch has penetrated to the metal:* After sanding with fine paper, apply a primer. After the primer dries, sand again with 320–400 grit sandpaper. Paint and let dry. Apply rubbing compound. Buy materials at an auto-supply store.

• Use vinegar to clean dirt from chipped exterior car surfaces. Then, when the spot is dry, restore with touch-up paint.

• Essential warmup. Idling the car doesn't warm up all the car's systems, such as lubricants, steering fluid or even all the drive train. *Better:* Keep speeds under 30 mph for the first quarter mile and not much over that for the next several miles.

• Replace radials whenever the tread is worn down to 1/16 inch from the bottom of the tire groove. At that point, the grooves are too shallow to take water away, and hydroplaning may occur at higher speeds.

• Do not "cross-switch" radials. Always exchange the left front with the left rear and right front with the right rear. Radials should never be remounted in a manner that will change the direction of rotation.

• If your car is shaking and vibrating, wheels may need aligning. Improper alignment causes excessive tire wear and increases fuel consumption.

• Wax your car at least twice a year...more often if it is exposed to salt air, road salt or industrial air or if it's parked outside. *Clue:* If water doesn't bead up on the car's surface after rain, waxing is needed.

Sources: *National Association of Fleet Administrators' Bulletin* and *The Durability Factor,* edited by Roger B. Yepsen, Jr., Rodale Press, Emmaus, PA.

Auto Service Intervals

Average recommended service intervals (in miles) under both normal and severe driving conditions, from a survey of mechanics:

• Oil & oil filter change. *Normal:* 4,155, *Severe:* 2,880.

• Replace air filter. *Normal:* 10,363, *Severe:* 5,927.

• Replace fuel filter. *Normal:* 11,597, *Severe:* 8,591.

• Replace spark plugs. *Normal:* 14,185, *Severe:* 11,298.

• Tune-up. *Normal:* 14,254, *Severe:* 11,245.

• Replace PCV valve. *Normal:* 16,202, *Severe:* 14,288.

• Flush & change coolant. *Normal:* 22,848, *Severe:* 18,049.

• Replace V-belts. *Normal:* 24,853 or when necessary, *Severe:* 20,610 or when necessary.

• Replace radiator and heater hoses. *Normal:* 29,031 or when necessary. *Severe:* 24,679 or when necessary.

• Change auto-transmission fluid. *Normal:* 25,862, *Severe:* 18,994.

• Adjust auto-transmission bands. *Normal:* 26,591, *Severe:* 19,141.

• Chassis lubrication. *Normal:* 5,550, *Severe:* 4,701.

• Repack wheel bearings. *Normal:* 21,580, *Severe:* 16,414.

• Rotate tires. *Normal:* 9,003, *Severe:* 7,929.

• Replace windshield wiper blades. *Normal:* 15,534 or when necessary, *Severe:* 11,750 or when necessary.

Source: *National Association of Fleet Administrators' Bulletin.*

Car Battery Rules

Car batteries give off explosive hydrogen gas and contain sulfuric acid. *When cleaning or working around a battery, take the following precautions:*

• Never smoke or light a match.

• Remove rings and other jewelry. The metal could cause a spark if it touches a battery terminal.

• Wear goggles to prevent acid from splashing into your eyes.

• If acid spills on your skin or on the car, flush the area with water immediately.

• Work in a well-ventilated area.

Source: *The Family Handyman,* New York.

Buying the Right Size Tire

With the exception of high-performance sports cars, the tires manufacturers install as original equipment are too narrow and too small. While they're perfectly adequate for the kind of day-to-day driving most people do, they don't offer the same performance offered by aftermarket tires. Finding the right tire depends on your needs.

•If you're a very aggressive driver, you'll want a wider, low-profile tire that puts more rubber on the road.

•If you're an average driver, who makes modest demands on his car, switching the original tires may not be a worthwhile expense. However, even an average, non-high-performance driver can gain some safety advantages in braking and wet weather adhesion by investing in uprated (wider, lower) tires.

• *The key to determining tire size for any car:* The ratio of the width of the tire to its height (called "aspect ratio").

•Most compacts these days are fitted with a 14-inch wheel and a 70 series (aspect ratio) tire.

•Some small cars still come equipped with a 13-inch wheel.

•To increase performance and traction, a driver with a 14-inch wheel and 70 series tire could move up to a 60 series tire with little or no compromise in ride.

Rule of thumb: Virtually any original equipment tire could be replaced by one size larger.

Source: Tony Assenza, former editor of *Motor Trend.*

Small Car Trap

Smaller cars are twice as deadly as larger cars. In 1991, the death rate in passenger cars with wheelbases shorter than 95 inches was 2.4 per 100,000 registered vehicles, compared to only 1.1 deaths per 100,000 in cars with wheelbases longer than 114 inches.

Source: *Fatality Facts 1993,* Insurance Institute for Highway Safety, 1005 N. Glebe Rd., Suite 800, Arlington, Virginia 22201.

Gas Trap

Taxes make up one-third the cost of a gallon of gasoline. *State with the highest taxes:* New York—45.8 cents a gallon, including 14.1 cents in federal taxes and 31.7 cents in state levies. *Lowest-tax states:* Alabama, Arizona, Kansas, Mississippi, New Hampshire and South Dakota—18 cents a gallon, including the federal portion.

Source: *Consumer's Research Magazine,* 800 Maryland Ave. NE, Washington, DC 20002.

Latest Car-Repair Scam

Beware of freon theft. Freon, used in car cooling systems, is now so expensive—between $12 and $20 per pound, with three to five pounds per car—that shady car-repair companies are stealing it while they service your car. *Tip-off:* Your car's cooling system doesn't work as well or stops working following other car repairs. *Important:* Be sure to have your car serviced by someone you trust.

Source: David Solomon, editor of *Nutz & Boltz®,* Box 123, Butler, Maryland 21023.

Highway Fatalities Down

39,235 people died in 1992 on US highways. This was the lowest number in 30 years. The fatality rate of 1.8 deaths per 100 million miles driven was the lowest number ever recorded. *Possible reasons for improvement:* Airbags...increased use of seat belts...fewer alcohol-related deaths.

Source: Statistics from the US Department of Transportation, reported in *Automotive News,* 1400 Woodbridge Ave., Detroit 48207.

Best Car Burglar Alarms

Most insurance companies will give you a discount if your car is equipped with a burglar alarm system. Generally it's 10% off the premium—each year.

Don't put stickers in the car window announcing to the world what type of burglar alarm system you have. Most experts feel that this removes the element of surprise and can even help the thief.

Cheap alarms provide little more than a false sense of security for a car owner. A good thief can foil them easily. *The features of a good alarm system:*

• Passively armed. That is, it should require nothing more of the driver than shutting off the motor and removing the ignition key, without complicated setup procedures.

• Instant "on" at all openings. That means the alarm should trigger as soon as any door, the hood, or the trunk is opened.

• Remotely disarmed by a code, instead of by means of a switch or a key. A lock can be picked. A code is impossible to break.

• Hood lock. Denying a thief access to your engine, battery, and siren is a major deterrent.

• Backup battery to prevent a thief from crawling under your car, cutting the car's main battery and killing the entire electrical system, and, therefore the alarm system.

• Motion detector. The best kinds are the electronic motion detectors that sense a car's spatial attitude at the time the alarm is armed whether it's on a hill, on uneven ground, etc. (Also least prone to false alarms.)

• *Extras:* Pressure-sensitive pads in the seats and under carpeting. Glass-breakage detectors. Paging systems and air horns.

• Wheel locks if you own expensive optional wheels.

Make Your Car Hard to Steal

• Lock your car.

• Take your keys.

• Park in well-lighted areas.

• Park in attended lots. Leave ignition key only (not trunk key) with attendant.

• Install a burglar alarm.

• Activate burglar alarm or antitheft device when parking.

• Don't put the alarm decal on your car.

• Install a secondary ignition switch.

• Park with wheels turned toward the curb.

• Remove rotor from distributor.

• Install a fuel shut-off device.

• Remove coil wire from distributor cap. (Especially useful for long-term parking at airports.)

• Close car windows when parking.

• Replace T-shaped window locks with straight ones.

• Install a steering-wheel lock, and use it.

• Install an armored collar around the steering column to cover the ignition.

• Don't hide a second set of keys in car.

• Never leave your car running when no one is in it.

• Don't let a potential buyer "test drive" alone.

• For front-wheel-drive cars, put on emergency brake and put in park.

• Back your car into your driveway. A potential thief will then be forced to tinker with ignition system in full view of neighbors.

• Lock your garage door.

• Lock your car in your garage.

• Be sure inspection sticker and license tag are current and were issued by the same state.

Source: Aetna Life and Casualty.

Flat Tire Do's and Don'ts

• Avoid use of instant tire sealants. They camouflage the slow loss of air that signals a punctured tire.

Repair a tire (rather than replace it) only when the puncture in the tread area is 1/4 inch in diameter or smaller. This puncture must be at least 15 inches away from a prior one, and tire tread depth must be more than 1/16 inch.

• Remove the tire from the wheel. A permanent repair can be made only from inside the tire. An internal inspection is a must. Driving on a flat (even a short distance at low speeds) can damage the crucial inner surface.

• After repair, have the tire and wheel assembly rebalanced. This will more than pay for itself in a smoother ride and longer tire life.

Coping with Car Trouble On the Highway

Unexpected breakdowns on the open road are frustrating and can be very dangerous.

How to avoid them:

• Practice preventive maintenance. Have your car checked before you set out on a long trip.

• *Likeliest sources of trouble:* Battery, tires, belts and engine hoses.

• Be sure you have emergency supplies, such as flashlights, flares and basic tools, and that your spare tire is inflated.

• At the first hint of trouble, move off the road, activate your emergency flashers and only then assess the problem.

• Fix the things you can yourself.

• If your car is overheating, you may be able to let it cool down and then proceed slowly to a gas station if you know one is nearby.

• If you are really stuck, wait for help. Major highways are regularly patrolled by troopers. Less traveled roads may require a Good Samaritan.

• Don't leave your car. An abandoned car is vulnerable to theft and vandalism. And in winter, you are vulnerable to the elements.

• To signal for help, raise your hood or your trunk lid as a distress signal. Hang a white handkerchief or colored scarf from it. If you have flares or reflectors, set them out (in those states where they are legal).

• Run the motor (and heater or air conditioner) only 15 minutes out of every hour, keeping a window slightly open to guard against carbon monoxide poisoning.

• If you are a woman alone, keep the car doors locked and the windows rolled up while waiting. This gives you a protected vantage point for sizing up strangers who approach the car.

• When help arrives, describe your car problem clearly so a service station can send the proper equipment. Beware of helpful strangers who are not mechanically inclined. Using battery jump cables incorrectly can cause an explosion or ruin your alternator. Improperly hitched tows can ruin your automatic transmission.

• You must stay calm and be patient. If this is too upsetting a proposition for you, consider investing in a car phone or CB radio so that you can get help sooner.

Source: Francis C. Kenel, PhD, director of traffic safety, American Automobile Association, Falls Church, VA.

Driving Small Cars Safely

In a severe crash between a large car and a small one, those in the small car are eight times more likely to be killed. *Defensive strategies:*

• Wear seat belts. A belted occupant of a small car has the same chance of surviving as the unbelted occupant of a big car in a crash between the two.

• Keep your lights on at low beam full time to increase visibility.

• Be aware that light poles and signs along the road may not break away as designed when hit by a lightweight compact car.

• Respect the inability of larger vehicles to maneuver or stop as quickly to escape a collision.

Dealing with Trucks On a Highway

To pass a truck:

• Blow your horn or blink the headlights to indicate your intentions.

• If it's raining, pass as quickly as possible to reduce road spray.

• After passing, speed up to avoid tailgating.

When following:

• Maintain a distance of 20–25 feet so the truck driver has a complete view of your vehicle.

• Be prepared for a possible truck shift to the left (even when it's signaling a right turn) as the driver makes sure he clears the right curb.

• Stay at least one or two car lengths back so as to remain in the truck driver's line of vision. This is especially important on an upgrade, where the truck may roll back a few feet.

Source: *Canadian Vehicle Leasing's Safe Driving Bulletin,* as reported in the *National Association Fleet Administrators Bulletin,* 295 Madison Ave., New York.

Driving in Hot Weather

• Inspect the auto radiator for leaks, and check the fluid level.

• Check all hoses for possible cracks or sponginess. Make sure all connections are tight and leak free.

• Test the thermostat for proper operation. If it does not operate at the proper temperature, overheating could occur.

• Inspect the fan belt for cracks and proper tension. Belt slippage is a common cause of boil overs. It also drains electrical power.

• If loss of coolant has been a problem, check for water seepage on the water pump around the engine block.

• Don't turn off the engine when the temperature warning light goes on. If stuck in traffic, shift to neutral, and race the engine moderately for 30 seconds at two-minute intervals.

• Shut off the air conditioner to avoid further overtaxing of the cooling system.

• Turn on the heater for a few minutes. It may help.

• If the radiator continues to overheat, drive the car off the road, turn off the engine and raise the hood.

• Wait at least half an hour before removing the radiator cap. Then do it very slowly and carefully, with the help of a towel or thick rag. Keep your face turned away from the radiator.

• If your car has the see-through overflow catch tank, replace any loss of coolant. Don't touch the radiator.

• If the fluid level is low, restart the engine while adding cool or warm water as the engine idles.

Source: Automobile Association of America.

Preparing for Cold Weather Driving

• *Radiator coolant:* Read the label on your antifreeze to be sure you make the right blend of water and antifreeze. The antifreeze keeps your radiator from freezing and cracking; the water, even in winter, keeps your car from overheating.

• *Battery condition:* Your car needs three to four times more starting power in winter than in summer. Have a mechanic do a complete battery draw and load test. If your battery fails, a recharge may save it for another year. Otherwise, invest in a new one.

• *Windshield washer fluid:* Frozen fluid in the washer tank is dangerous. Use a premixed commercial fluid. Check that the hoses are clear, and clean the washer nozzles out with a thin piece of wire.

• *Electrical system:* Make sure the distributor cap, points, condenser, ignition coil, spark plugs, and spark plug cables are in good shape. Borderline components that still function in summer will give out in cold weather.

• *Hoses and belts:* If they are cracking or fraying, replace them.

• *Tires:* If you have all-season tires, be sure the tread is still good enough to give you traction on slippery roads. Otherwise, put on snow tires. *Important:* If you have a front-wheel drive car, the snow tires go on the front. Store summer tires on their sides, not on the tread. (Storing on the tread causes a flat spot and an unbalanced tire.) Inflate stored tires to only 50% of their operating pressure.

• *Windshield:* Apply antifogging compound to the inside.

• *Cleaning:* Clear dead bugs off the radiator by hosing it from the inside of the engine compartment. Pick out dead leaves and debris from the fresh-air intake box of the ventilation system.

• *Stock up:* Buy flares, an aerosol wire-drying agent, a scraper and brush, chains and a military-style collapsible trench tool for emergencies. Keep a lock de-icer at home and/or at the office.

How to Brake on Ice

• Start early.

• Squeeze the brakes with a steady pressure until just before you feel them begin to lock.

• Ease up, and slowly repeat the pressure.

• Disk brakes do not respond well to pumping (the old recommendation for drum brakes). They will lock, causing you to lose control of the car.

Source: National Safety Council, Chicago, IL.

How to Get Out Of a Snow Drift

To get unstuck:

• Turn your wheels from side to side to push away the snow.

• Check to be sure that your tailpipe is clear (so carbon monoxide won't be forced into the car).

• Start the motor.

• Put the car in gear, and apply slow, steady pressure to the accelerator to allow the tires to get a grip.

• Don't spin the wheels (this just digs you in further).

• Let the car pull out straight ahead if possible.

• *Extra help:* Sprinkle kitty litter in front of the wheels for traction.

Source: National Safety Council, Chicago, IL.

Auto Dealer Ripoff

• *Car purchase padding:* A prep fee of $100 or more (whatever the dealership thinks it can get away with). The cost of preparing your car for delivery is already included in the manufacturer's sticker price.

Source: *Consumer Guide to Successful Car Shopping* by Peter Sessler, TAB Books, Blue Ridge Summit, PA.

Accidents with Aggressive Drivers

Violent and aggressive drivers are dangerous when they get into an accident. If you're in an accident with one, stay calm.

• Don't escalate any argument.

• Copy down the other driver's license number immediately.

• If you are threatened, leave at once.

• Call the police so that you won't be charged with leaving the scene of an accident...but do it from a safe distance.

• If your car is disabled, lock the doors and wait for the police to arrive.

All About Speeding Tickets

The best way to avoid speeding tickets is, of course, to avoid speeding. But all of us drive over the limit occasionally.

Here are some suggestions to help you avoid tickets:

• Know the limits. It's no illusion that police officers generally ignore cars driving just slightly over the posted speed. In fact, many departments set threshold speeds (six miles an hour above the limit in one state, for example) at which officers are to take no action. You might be able to slip by at 65 mph in a 55 mph zone, but you're unlikely to do the same at 70 mph.

• Be selective. Most speeding tickets are written during the morning and evening rush hours, when there are more motorists and more police officers on the road. Late night and very early morning are not watched nearly as carefully.

•Drive unobtrusively. Flashy cars attract attention, something to keep in mind if you drive a red Maserati. The same applies to flashy driving styles. Don't tailgate slower cars to force them aside. Don't weave in and out of traffic.

•Be vigilant. The likeliest spot to get nabbed on the highway is just beyond a blind curve or the crest of a hill, the best hiding places for patrol cars. Learn to recognize likely traps, and reduce your speed whenever appropriate.

•Remember that police officers can nab speeders from virtually any position—the rear, the front, the side, or even from aircraft. Be on the lookout at all times. An unmarked car on the side of the road with its trunk open is especially suspect. (A radar device may be inside.)

•Fight back. Radar guns can be foiled occasionally. *What to do:* Position your car close to other cars whenever possible. Police officers generally cannot match you with the speed indicated on their guns unless they have an unobstructed view of your car. In most states, motorists also can make use of radar detectors, devices designed to alert drivers to radar early enough to slow down before police officers can get a good reading. If you do a lot of driving, a detector is a sensible investment if it is legal in your area.

•Use psychology. All is not lost even if you are pulled over. Police officers feel vulnerable when stopping speeders—you could be speeding away from a murder for all they know, and consequently they are usually nervous. Put them at ease. Sit still, keep your hands in plain view (on the steering wheel is a good place). Be courteous and respectful. Above all, be honest. If you have a good excuse for going over the limit, state it. Otherwise, admit guilt and apologize. Police officers can be surprisingly lenient if you're cordial.

How to Ease Long-Distance Driving

For a safe, healthy trip when you're driving a long distance:

•Do most of your driving during daytime hours. Visual acuity is lessened at night.

•Be particularly careful to check out your car's exhaust system before leaving—a leak can send odorless but deadly gases into the car.

•To insure sufficient fresh air inside the car, leave both a front and a back window open. Tailgate windows should be kept closed. Use your air conditioner. It provides fresh air and quiet inside the car. Although it reduces gas mileage, the loss is not much more than the loss from open windows' drag.

•Use seat belts and shoulder harnesses to relieve fatigue, as well as to boost safety.

•Take 20- to 30-minute rest breaks after every one-and-a-half or two hours of driving.

•Exercise during your breaks.

•Eat frequent high-protein snacks for improved driving performance.

•Don't stare straight ahead, even if you're the only car on the road. Keep your eyes moving.

Eating on the Road

•Don't simply follow the truck drivers. Their first priority is a huge parking lot, not the best food.

•Avoid restaurants on or very near major highways and shopping centers. You're likely to do better downtown. *Good bets:* College or university towns.

•*Best authorities:* Bookstore managers, fancy kitchenware and gourmet food store's personnel. *Worst:* Tollbooth or gas-station attendants.

•Beware of large signs and quaint spellings.

•Check out the parking lot. Too many out-of-state license plates suggest a tourist trap. *Good sign:* A high proportion of foreign cars (especially European ones).

Source: *Travel & Leisure.*

How Never to Get Lost On Interstate Highways

The system to the numbering:

•One- or two-digit even-numbered highways: Major East-West routes.

•One- or two-digit odd-numbered highways: Major North-South routes.

•Three-digit figure starting with an even number: Loop route around a city.

•Three-digit figure starting with an odd number: Road that is heading to or from center city.

Safest Car Colors

Greenish-yellow is best...then cream, yellow and white. *Least-safe colors:* Red and black. *General rule:* Light-colored, single-tone cars are safer. They have significantly fewer accidents than dark cars because it is easier for other drivers to distinguish them from the surroundings.

Source: *Lemon Book: Auto Rights for New & Used Cars* by Ralph Nader and Clarence Ditlow, Moyer Bell, Ltd., Colonial Hill, Mt. Kisco, New York 10549.

Safety Tests are Misleading

Car-crash safety tests by the government give misleading results. *Why:* All cars are run into a wall at 35 mph. Lighter cars hit the wall with less momentum than heavy cars, so less damage results. But in real life, heavier cars have better safety records, especially in collisions with lighter vehicles. *Examples:* Although government tests panned the Ford Taurus, insurance records show it to be among the safest vehicles. And the Ford Escort scored well in tests, but has a poor record with insurers.

Source: *The Wall Street Journal.*

Car Engine Death Trap

Teflon engine oil additives—advertised as engine protection agents—can actually *destroy* your engine. Depending on driving conditions, these additives can either cause engine oil pressure to drop to zero, cause the engine to freeze—or have no effect at all. Safest strategy is to stay away from the Teflon products altogether.

Source: David Solomon, editor, *Nutz & Boltz®*, Box 123, Butler, Maryland 21023.

Gasoline Cancer Trap

Gas and gas fumes contain toxic chemicals that can cause cancer. *Unsettling:* Gas-station attendants have a significantly elevated risk of death from leukemia. *Consumer self-defense:* Carry old gloves in the car—wear them when you fill up at a self-service station to keep gasoline off your skin.

Keep windows closed so fumes won't accumulate in the car. Be sure to stand upwind from the pump. Choose stations equipped with vapor-recovery lines. These accordion-like bellows on the nozzles return gas vapors to an underground tank.

Source: Peter Infante, Occupational Safety and Health Administration, quoted in *Good Housekeeping,* 959 Eighth Ave., New York 10019.

Airbag Self-Defense

Airbags in cars have their own safety risks. Cars equipped with airbags require different driving techniques. Don't drape your hand or arm inside the steering wheel—you could get a broken wrist or arm if the airbag fires and traps your hand.

Airbag units are meant to be most effective for drivers sitting with their arms extended—any closer and you could suffer facial abrasions if the airbag is activated.

If you frequently rent cars with airbags, be sure you know where the horn button is on any model you drive—they're all in different locations.

Added risk for smokers: It is dangerous to have a lit cigar or cigarette in your mouth when the airbag goes off. *Important:* Even if the car you drive is airbag-equipped, always buckle up.

Source: David Solomon, editor, *Nutz & Boltz®*, Box 123, Butler, Maryland 21023.

Get More for Your Old Car

Get 25% more for your old car—on average—by selling it yourself. But beware of keeping your old car after you buy a new one—even if the dealer will not give you what you think it is worth. *Reason:* It is usually more important to lower the amount borrowed on the new car than to get the most possible for the old one. Use the trade-in value—or cash—to reduce the new car loan.

Source: *Life After Debt: How to Repair Your Credit and Get Out of Debt Once and For All* by Bob Hammond, credit consultant based in Redlands, California. Career Press, 180 Fifth Ave., Hawthorne, New Jersey 07507.28

When Buying A New Car...

If you're shopping for a new car, research the make's current national sales performance and inventory before you begin negotiating price. *Reason:* Dealers are more likely to drop a model's price dramatically when its sales are down or flat and inventory is high. This data can be found in the weekly trade publication *Automotive News*—available at most libraries.

Source: W. James Bragg, author of *In the Driver's Seat: The New-Car Buyer's Negotiating Bible.* Random House, 201 E. 50 St., New York 10022.

Look at Total Car Costs

Look at total car costs, not just the purchase price, when selecting the best car for your budget. The cost of such items as fuel, oil, tires, maintenance, insurance, financing, depreciation, licenses and registration fees, and taxes have a big impact on the total price of owning a car.

The typical total car ownership costs for different classes of cars, assuming a three-year 60,000-mile trade-in cycle:

	Cents per Mile	Monthly Fixed Cost ($)	Annual Cost ($)
Subcompact	8.65	383	6,330
Compact	8.70	425	6,834
Intermediate	9.95	458	7,480
Full-size	10.95	523	8,462
Luxury	12.25	870	12,884

Source: Larry Snyder, executive vice president, Transportation Division, Runzheimer International, management consultants, Runzheimer Park, Rochester, Wisconsin 53167.

How to Win the Car Buying Game

Car salesmen thrive on confusion. They bombard you with questions and numbers to divert your attention from simple issues.

Tactics:

• Go shopping armed with specific information. Remember that you're not there to fall in love with a car or to make a friend of the salesman. Get answers you can understand.

• Buy the latest edition of *Edmund's New Car Prices.* It lists the base costs of each car and accessories, such as air conditioning and automatic transmission.

• When you find the car you like, copy down all pricing information from the manufacturer's sticker on the window. Compare the sticker prices with those in *Edmund's* to determine the dealer's profit. This gives you real bargaining ammunition.

• Be indecisive. The salesman will think there's a car you like better down the road. That means he must give you his best shot.

• *Best times to shop:* The last day of the month, when dealers close their books and want good sales figures, and very late in the day, when the sales staff is exhausted.

• Beware of red tag sales. Dealers' profits are higher than at any other time. Customers mistakenly assume they will save money during special sales. Really, they are fantasies that draw you away from reality. Stay with black-and-white issues you can control.

•Stick with what you can afford. *This is determined by two things:* How much cash your trade-in gives you towards the down payment and how much you can pay each month.

•Tell dealers you are interested in selling your car for cash. Their figures will give you a better idea of what your car is worth than a blue book. It's best to sell your car privately.

Source: Remar Sutton, car dealer and author of *Don't Get Taken Every Time: The Insider's Guide to Buying Your Next Car,* Penguin Books, New York.

Buy a Car at Police Auction

Big-city police departments, in the course of their work, collect abandoned cars, evidence vehicles (those used in crimes) and towed-away cars that haven't been picked up. Buying a car at auctions of these vehicles can be a good deal, especially for a teenager who can do repair work.

Rules to follow:

•Inspect the autos the day before the auction. Each is listed by its make and year and is given an auction number that also appears on the windshield of the car. (You can make notes on the list of the cars that interest you and then check prevailing prices for such cars in the local newspaper want ads or in publications at the library.)

•Usually there is no ignition key, and in most cities you're not allowed to hotwire a start, either. *What you can do:* Inspect the car by opening the doors and hood and working the windows. Inspect the engine compartment for quality of maintenance and check the wires, hoses, motor oil level, transmission and brake fluid levels. Find out the mileage and determine the condition of the interior and tires.

•At the auction, fill out a form with your name and address to get a bidding number. All transactions are cash. You must pay the full price, plus tax, during the auction, not afterward. All sales are final.

•Set limits to your bidding and stick to them. No more than one-half the *Blue Book* value is recommended, and no more than one-third is safer. This way you'll come out ahead even if major repairs prove necessary.

•Collect a bill of sale acceptable to the local state motor vehicle department for registering the car when you pay. If you live out of state, check with your state automotive agency to see what other documents might be necessary to register the car in your state.

•Arrange to have the car towed away within a day or two of the auction. Even if you replace the ignition or jump-start it, the car has no license plate or insurance. It also may not run.

Auto Lemonaid

If that new car you just bought has been in the shop more than on the road, don't despair. Under state "lemon laws" you may be able to get most of your money back, or at least a more reliable car...and without the risk of heavy court costs.

• *The law:* The car is usually covered for one year or the written warranty period, whichever is shorter.

•If a defect isn't repaired in four tries, the manufacturer must replace the car or give a refund (less depreciation). The same goes if the car is out of commission for 30 days or more for any combination of defects.

•If the manufacturer has a federally approved arbitration program, you must first submit your complaint to the arbitrators. But if you aren't satisfied with their decision, you can still take the company to court.

Strategy:

•Check the state attorney general's office for details of the law. *Key point:* Whether the manufacturer (as well as the dealer) must be given a chance to solve the problem.

•Submit a list of repairs to the dealer each time you bring the car in. Keep a copy for yourself.

•Keep a detailed record of car repair dates and of periods when the car was unavailable to you.

•If the company agrees to settle but offers too little money or a car with too many miles, don't be afraid to dicker. The company doesn't want to go to court any more than you do.

Source: *Medical Economics,* Oradell, NJ.

New-Tire Do's and Don'ts

• First check your owner's manual for the correct tire size. It may also list an optional size, but tires must be the same size and construction on each axle.

• If you must mix tire constructions, the radial pair should be on the rear axle.

• If you're buying only a pair of replacement tires, put the new ones on the rear wheels for better handling.

• Buy tires according to your needs. If you are planning to sell your car soon, don't buy long-lasting radials—get a shorter-term tire, such as a bias ply or bias belted.

• Consider the new all-season tires, especially if you live in a colder climate. These radial tires combine the traction of snow tires with the quiet ride and longer tread wear of a highway tire. And twice-a-year changing is not necessary, as it is for conventional snow tires.

• Radial tires are expected to last for 40,000 miles; bias-belted tires for 30,000; and bias-ply tires for 20,000.

• Spring and fall are best for good discounts on tire prices.

• All tires sold in the US must meet Department of Transportation standards. You should always look for the DOT symbol on the sidewall of any tire sold in the US, whether foreign or domestic.

• Any tires, old or new, must be properly inflated if you expect good performance and long wear.

Source: Ed Lewis, deputy director, Tire Industry Safety Council, Washington, DC.

Cutting Down on Gas Usage

• Tuning. Poor engine tuning adds 5%–20% to fuel usage.

• Acceleration. The best mileage is at cruising speed (usually 35–45 mph). *Recommended:* A brisk, smooth acceleration to the highest gear.

• Stopping. A red light ahead? Slow down. If you can avoid stopping altogether, you will save gas. Don't follow others closely, or you'll pay for their stops in your fuel bill.

• Luggage. Every 100 pounds of needless weight costs up to .5 mpg.

• Remove ski or luggage racks (which create wind drag) when not in use.

• Speed. Driving an eight-mile commute each day at 70 mph instead of 55 mph will add more than $100 a year to fuel costs.

• Tire pressure. Inflate to the maximum listed on the sidewall.

• Radials. Cut 3–4% off the average gasoline bill.

• Hill driving. A 3% grade will add 33% to fuel usage. On the downward slope, build up momentum to carry you through the base of the next hill. Let up on the accelerator as you climb.

• Gas usage increases 2%–6% with automatic transmission: 1%–2% for each 10°F drop in temperature, 10% with heavy rain or head winds.

Source: California Energy Commission.

How to Winterize Your Car

To make your winter driving easier:

• Put snow tires on all four wheels for maximum traction. If this isn't possible, make sure to put them on the drive wheels.

• Drain and flush the cooling system on any car more than two years old. On newer cars, add antifreeze if necessary.

• *Use a concentrated windshield-washing solution:* One quart rubbing alcohol, one cup water and one tablespoonful of liquid dishwashing detergent.

• Keep your gas tank at least half full to prevent condensation that might freeze and block the fuel line.

• For better traction on rear-wheel-drive cars, place sandbags in the forward part of the trunk.

• *Keep these winter supplies where you can get at them easily:* A scraper/brush, a shovel, and a bag of sand or kitty litter.

Source: *Parents,* New York.

Your Car Radio

• Don't turn on your car stereo during the first five minutes of your drive. Use that time to listen for noises that could signal car trouble.

• Organize your stereo tapes before you leave, so you can pick them out without taking your eyes off the road.

• Keep all tapes within easy reach.

• Don't wear headphones while you drive. A safe driver must be able to hear the traffic as well as watch it.

• Wait for a straight patch of road before glancing at the stereo to adjust it.

• Read your tape cassette titles at eye level so you can see the road at the same time.

Source: *High Fidelity,* New York

Top-of-the-Line Car Stereos

For the serious music lover who spends a lot of time in a car, first-rate radio and tape systems are available—at a price. Although most factory-installed stereos are mediocre, a number of audio companies make good sound systems for cars.

Like home stereo systems, car stereos are bought in components:

• *Radio/tape decks:* Alpine, Kenwood, and Sony.

• *Speakers:* Sound to rival home units...B and W and ADS.

• *Amplifiers:* High-powered units with low distortion and good reliability are made by ADS and Alpine.

• *Essential:* Professional installation with a warranty. Proper mounting and wiring of the components affects not only the sound but also the system's longevity.

For the Best Deal Now On a Rented Car

• Don't rely on travel agents. Travel agents usually won't get you the best price—but it's not their fault. Prices quoted in computer-reservation systems are typically higher than the best deals offered through the car rental firms' 800 numbers. So, before renting, call *all* of the major companies serving the market you'll be visiting. *Note:* Don't assume that a particular rental company is always cheapest—or never cheapest.

• Keep checking. After booking your best deal, keep calling to see if other companies' rates have dropped. They often do, and there's seldom a penalty for canceling—unless you've reserved a special vehicle. *One more time:* When you pick up your car, ask again if a new, lower rate is in effect.

• Use newspaper ads properly. Ads can guide you to great rates, but seeing the ad isn't enough. When you call to reserve, cite the code numbers or letters at the bottom of the ad or you might not get the advertised rate.

• Look for special deals. Seek a corporate rate, club membership discount or room-and-car package.

• Get the right package for you. A weekend or weeklong package will always be cheaper on a per-day basis than the standard midweek day rate. In many cases, you'll have to keep a car for at least five days to qualify for the weekly rate.

Warning: If you book a weeklong rate and return the car after four days you'll end up paying the higher daily rate. *Note:* If you get a multiple-day rate, ask about the "minimum keep"—the minimum number of days you must keep the car for the rate to apply.

• Save by renting *away* from the airport. Special airport charges can add as much as 15% to 20% to your rental bill. So you could save big by renting the car downtown instead.

• Consider a mileage cap. Unlimited mileage is now a standard feature, and it's a good deal for most renters. But if you'll be doing little driving, ask for a deal with a mileage limit. It is often a money-saver.

Source: Ed Perkins, editor of *Consumer Reports Travel Letter,* Box 27337, San Francisco 94127.

15

Insurance and Banking Savvy

How to Protect Your Money from the People Who Protect the Places That Protect Your Money

Most of us who have accounts at banks or savings and loan institutions know little about Federal Deposit Insurance Corporation (FDIC) protection.

This lack of knowledge can be costly if your bank or savings and loan goes under—for part of your money may not be insured. Answers to the most common questions about FDIC coverage...

Are all banks and savings and loans protected by the FDIC? Most banks are protected, but some private banks are not. Be sure to look for the FDIC label on your bank's door or at the tellers' windows.

Are all individual accounts covered separately by the FDIC? Up to how much? Most people know that the FDIC covers individual accounts up to $100,000. What they don't know is that an individual account is determined by adding up each account held under a common name or Social Security number.

Example: If a person has a savings account with $50,000 in it and a certificate of deposit for $60,000 at the same bank, $10,000 is uninsured.

Accounts set up under the Uniform Gifts to Minors Act are considered to be the child's account, even though the parent has control over it.

What about joint accounts? Are they fully protected? Joint accounts held by the same combination of persons at the same bank are only protected up to $100,000, regardless of whose Social Security number appears on them.

Example: A husband and wife with two joint accounts of $100,000 each are insured only up to $100,000, not $200,000.

Avoid this restriction by using both individual and joint accounts.

Example: If you have an individual savings account of $100,000 and a joint savings account with your spouse of $100,000 at the same bank, each account has full protection. Your spouse can have an individual savings account of $100,000 and receive full coverage on it as well.

Are all deposits covered by the FDIC? Mutual funds and other investments made through a bank are not protected. If you have any questions concerning FDIC insurance, call the FDIC at 800-934-3342.

Are trust accounts treated separately by the FDIC? Yes, but only if the trusts are for members of your immediate family—a spouse, child or grandchild. But, if you set up an account in trust for your father, for example, it is treated as part of your account.

Trust accounts for a spouse, child, or grandchild (including step and adopted children) enjoy separate coverage, even if you have both an individual and a joint account.

Example: If you have an individual account with $100,000, a joint account with your spouse of $100,000, and a trust account for your spouse of $100,000, the accounts are all fully insured.

Can an individual open accounts at several branches of the same bank and receive full protection for each? You cannot increase the limit of coverage by depositing funds in different branches of the same bank.

Self-defense: Diversify your funds among several banks.

Are IRAs and Keoghs fully protected? At the moment, each retirement account is treated separately from individual accounts and receives full coverage.

Example: If you have an individual account of $100,000, an IRA of $100,000 and a Keogh of $100,000 at the same bank, each account is fully insured.

Important: After December 19, 1993, IRA and Keogh accounts will be lumped together for purposes of coverage limits. But transitional rules afford some protection for existing accounts.

Self-defense: As IRA or Keogh CDs mature, roll over sufficient amounts to other institutions to maximize FDIC coverage.

Source: Cody Buck, a former executive of the FDIC and author of *The ABCs of FDIC: How to Save Your Assets From Liquidation.* CoStarr Publications, Box 2052, Coppell, Texas 75019. 800-925-3252.

ATM Self-Defense

Discarding your ATM receipt at the bank may help thieves loot your account, says bank expert Ed Mrkvicka. High-tech bandits are using video cameras to observe/record customers punching in ID numbers at teller machines. Then they match it to the account numbers on receipts left behind. Self-defense: Guard your PIN number...retain receipts to match up against monthly bank statements. If there's a withdrawal discrepancy, report it immediately to the bank.

Bank Credit Cards Are Not All Alike

Should you keep the bank credit card you have now, or apply for ones that offer greater advantages? One Visa card or MasterCard could be very different from another Visa or MasterCard.

The MasterCard and Visa organizations do not issue credit cards themselves. They provide a clearing system for charges and payments on the cards and license banks to use the Visa or MasterCard name. It is the issuing bank that determines the interest rates and fees.

A bank's name on a credit card does not necessarily mean that it is the bank actually issuing the card. Issuance of credit cards is a high-risk, low-profit business. Seldom does a small bank issue its own.

Generally, a small bank will act as an agent for an issuing bank. The agent bank puts its name on the card, but it is the issuing bank that actually extends any credit.

Aside from costs, this can be important if the cardholder encounters an error. The correction might have to be agreed upon, not by a friendly local banker, but by an unknown, larger institution, perhaps in a different state.

Visa, for example, has about 1,400 issuing banks in the US and about 10,500 agent banks.

Choosing which card to take is becoming more difficult, because some of the nation's largest banks have begun active solicitation of customers throughout the US. Individuals must be especially careful about accepting any offer that might come in the mail.

A recently discovered quirk in the federal law allows federally chartered out-of-state banks to ignore state usury laws that limit the amount of interest or fees that the issuing bank may charge on its credit cards. In Arkansas, for example, state usury laws prevent local banks from charging more than 10% interest on credit card balances. But a federally chartered out-of-state bank, in lending to Arkansas residents, may charge whatever its home state allows. Even within individual states, the terms on credit cards can vary widely.

Aside from the actual rates and fees, individuals must carefully check the fine print of their contracts. Most banks, for example, do not charge interest on balances stemming from purchases until the customer is billed for such purchases. If the bill on which the charges first appear is paid in full by the stated due date, there is no interest charge to the holder. But some banks, those in Texas, for example, begin charging interest as soon as they receive the charge slip and make payments to the merchant. Thus, interest begins accumulating even before the cardholder receives the bill. These interest charges continue until the bank receives payment from the customer.

Source: Robert A. Bennett, banking correspondent, *The New York Times*.

Unsolicited Credit Card Danger

Don't throw away a credit card you receive but didn't request. *Reason:* By not letting the issuer know that you don't want it, the card's credit line—which could be thousands of dollars—may appear on your credit report. This may prevent you from getting credit you do want in the future. *Better:* Cut up the card and return it to the issuer, along with a letter requesting that the account be closed. Send your letter by certified mail, return receipt requested, and ask for an acknowledgment from the issuer that the account has, in fact, been closed.

Source: *Everything You Need to Know About Credit* by Deborah McNaughton, founder of Professional Credit Counselors, Orange County, California. Thomas Nelson Publishers, Box 141000, Nashville 37214.

Bank Self-Defense

Not all financial products purchased from a bank are covered by the FDIC—Federal Deposit Insurance Corp.—even if the principal investment is less than $100,000. *Uninsured:* Annuities, mutual funds, insurance policies, stocks, bonds and money-market funds.

Source: Cody Buck, former FDIC executive and author of *The ABCs of FDIC: How to Save Your Assets From Liquidation*. CoStarr Publications, Box 2052, Coppell, Texas 75109.

How to Beat the Banks Before They Beat You

Since deregulation, banks vary widely in their services and in the costs of those services. In order to turn the best profit, banks depend on the fact that customers don't know what to ask for.

How you can get the most for your banking dollar:

• Deal with the smallest bank you can find. After deregulation, most large banks decided to get rid of smaller depositors. They find it cheaper to serve one corporate account than 10 individual accounts. Smaller banks, on the other hand, are more responsive to individual depositors because they need this business.

Ask about checking accounts:

• What is the minimum-balance requirement? How does the bank calculate it? Watch out for a minimum-balance calculation that uses the lowest balance for the month. A figure based on the average daily balance is best.

• Does the balance on other accounts count toward the checking-account minimum balance?

•What is the clearing policy for deposits? This is especially important if you have a NOW account.

•What is the overdraft charge? Often it is outrageous. In parts of the Midwest, for example, most banks charge $20.

•Don't buy loan insurance from the bank. Credit life or disability insurance is often routinely included on loan forms and added to the cost of your loan. Don't sign any such policy when you take out a loan. This insurance benefits the bank—not you. It covers the bank for the balance of your loan should you die or become disabled. You can get more coverage from an insurance agent for half (or even less) of what the bank charges.

•Avoid installment loans. These loans are front-end loaded: Even though your balance is declining, you're still paying interest on the original balance throughout the term of the loan. Ask for a single-payment note with simple interest and monthly payments. If you do have an installment loan, don't pay it off early—this actually adds to its real cost.

•Pay attention to interest computations. Most people compare rates and assume higher is better. Look for interest figured on a day-of-deposit-to-day-of-withdrawal basis compounded daily.

•Avoid cash machines. The farther bankers can keep you from their tellers and loan officers, the more money they'll make and the less responsive they'll be to your needs. Bankers like machines because people can't argue with them.

•Negotiate interest rates. This sounds simple, but it means combating banks' tendencies to lump loans in categories—commercial, mortgage, retail, etc. For example, banks offer a long-time depositor the same interest rate on a car loan as they do a complete newcomer. But often all it takes to get a better rate is to say, "I think my car loan should be 2% lower. I've been banking here for 15 years and I have $10,000 in my savings account."

•Forget FDIC security. Given the option of a higher interest rate investment with a secure major corporation that probably has more reserves than the FDIC, many people will still automatically opt for the bank investment because of FDIC insurance. But the FDIC has only $16 billion in reserves. That's a miniscule portion of the money it's insuring. Now that more and more banks are closing every year, the FDIC may soon find itself in big trouble.

•Ignore the banks amortization schedule for mortgages. When you make your monthly payment, especially in the early part of your mortgage, very little goes toward the principal. However, if you choose to pay a small amount extra every month, this will go toward the principal and save you an enormous amount of money.

•Don't put all your money in one certificate of deposit. Now that you can deposit as little as $1,000 for the money-market rate, split your deposits so that you get the same interest rate and more liquidity. If you put your money into a $10,000 or $20,000 CD and then find you need to take out $1,000 or $2,000, you will have to pay a horrendous penalty. Instead buy 10 or 20 $1,000 CDs.

Source: Edward F. Mrkvicka, Jr., a former bank president and author of *The Bank Book: How to Revoke Your Bank's License to Steal,* HarperCollins, New York.

Prime Rate Secret

Banks calculate their lending rate in arbitrary ways that differ from institution to institution. Your rate may be based on the prime rate set by large money center banks, but it will be calculated and applied by the bank's own formula, which will almost always be higher. *Self-protection:* Before taking out any loan, read and be sure you understand the fine print that spells out the interest rate adjustment formula. Then make comparisons from bank to bank.

Source: Edward F. Mrkvicka, Jr., president of Reliance Enterprises, a financial consulting company, Box 413, Marengo, IL 60152 and editor of *Money Insider,* a monthly newsletter.

Safe-Deposit Boxes

Guarantee that you will be able to locate all important documents quickly by renting a bank safe-deposit box. Fees are reasonable. Only two keys are made to fit the box, and you keep both of them. The box cannot be opened without your permission unless you die or you don't pay your rental fee for a whole year. In a non-payment situation, you will receive a certified or registered letter to give you one last chance to pay up. If you don't, the contents of the box will be removed in the presence of a bank official, inventoried, verified, and then stored in a safe place until you eventually claim them.

Keep in your safe-deposit box:

- Birth, marriage, and death certificates.
- Divorce or separation agreements.
- Adoption or custody papers.
- Title papers to real estate, car, etc.
- Mortgage papers.
- Contracts and legal agreements.
- Stock certificates.
- Military discharge papers.
- Copies of credit cards.
- Copies of passport (or the original and keep copies at home).
- Photographs of the inside and outside of a home to support insurance claims.

Do not put in a safe-deposit box:

- Your will. Keep it at your attorney's office, with only a copy in the safe-deposit box. *Reason:* Safe-deposit boxes are sealed at death until the IRS sees what's inside. This could prevent relatives from getting into the box right away to see if a will even exists.
- Money or other valuables on which income tax has not been paid. This is illegal and your heirs might be taxed on the money at your death anyway.

Source: Safe Deposit Department, Marine Midland Bank, NA, New York.

Protecting Your Credit Cards

- Don't be fooled by a "Good Samaritan" phone call that your stolen or lost cards have been found. It may be from a thief seeking time to run up charges. Carry cards separately from your wallet. Leave infrequently used cards at home. Make photo copies of each card you own, and keep these at home and at the office with a list of the issuers' toll-free numbers.

Source: Peter Herrick, president of the Bank of New York.

- When you check your statements each month, be on the lookout for hotels and restaurants that throw away the ticket you sign, substitute another one with inflated tips or other charges, and then forge your name on the inflated ticket. *Where it happens frequently:* Las Vegas.

Source: John Kaiser, marketing director, Summa Four Co., Merrimack, NH, quoted in *Teleconnect,* 205 W. 19 St., New York 10011.

Prevent Credit Card Rip-offs

Here's a simple trick: Pick a number and if possible—make sure that all your credit card charges end in that number. *For example:* Say you choose the number 8 and your dinner bill comes to $20.00. Instead of adding a $3.00 tip, add $3.08. When your bill comes at the end of the month, check to see if all the charges have 8 as the last digit. If they don't, compare them against your receipts and report discrepancies to the card issuer.

Beware of Low Credit Card Rates

In many cases, bank cards with the lowest rates (11%-14%) can cost much more than cards with traditional 18%-21% charges. *Reason:* A growing number of banks begin tacking on interest charges the minute a transaction is posted to their books. This interest charge accrues until the charge amount and the interest are paid in full. Even if you pay your charges off as soon as you receive the bill each month, you'll still have to pay an interest charge. *Solution:* If you pay in full whenever you use a credit card, choose a bank that charges interest only on balances that are still outstanding following the payment due date on the bill.

Source: *Money.*

How to Cut Auto Insurance

Cut auto insurance costs by:

- Raising deductibles from $100 to $500 or even $1,000. That saves 35%–60% on premiums.
- Dropping collision coverage on cars over five years old.
- Finding out whether the car qualifies for discounts on autos less likely to be stolen or less costly to repair.
- Discontinuing medical coverage if it's duplicated by your employer's health plan.
- Reconsidering extras such as coverage for towing or car rentals during repair.

Source: National Consumer Insurance Organization, as reported in *Money.*

Traps in Homeowner's Insurance

Many home buyers hastily purchase homeowner's insurance to qualify for their mortgage. *Problem:* They don't understand the choices involved in insuring a home.

Basic insurance: If a fire or other catastrophe destroys your home, you get the replacement cost, which is enough to rebuild the home to its original state, provided you carry at least 80% of the replacement cost. *What you don't get:* The market value of the home so that you can go out and buy a similar one. Land value and neighborhood are inherent in market value, yet unrelated to replacement cost.

Carry whatever percent of the home's replacement value the insurance company requires. If you don't, you will be penalized by the percentage you underinsure.

Example: You have a $100,000 house and carry only $60,000 on it. That is three-quarters of the $80,000 required. If you have $20,000 worth of damage from a fire, you will get only $15,000 or three-quarters of your damage. If you were insured for $80,000, you would get full coverage.

How to ascertain replacement cost...

Most insurance companies will inspect your house if it is worth over $100,000.

Your broker has a replacement-cost guide. This determines the cost of the average home by computing the number of rooms and square feet. It is an educated guess.

If your home was custom built, get an independent appraisal.

Replacement cost versus actual cash value: Replacement cost is only useful when you rebuild your house. If you decide to walk away and buy another house, you will only get actual cash value. *What it is:* Replacement value minus depreciation.

Example: You have a 50-year-old home worth $100,000 and $80,000 worth of insurance. You might get only $40,000 if you decide not to build, because depreciation could take away as much as 50% of the payment. (Depreciation computed by an insurance company is not related to depreciation for taxes. Depreciation is rarely in excess of 50% on a home.)

Inflation protection: Many insurance companies automatically increase coverage by whatever it costs to rebuild a home in your area under an inflation guard endorsement.

Check out: Whether inflation increases are granted annually, semiannually, or quarterly. *Problem:* If inflation is running 10%, and you have a disaster after six months, you may have insufficient coverage. *Best:* Ask for an endorsement that increases protection quarterly.

Some companies offer an endorsement which guarantees to pay the full replacement cost, even if it is higher than the amount of the policy, provided you insured to 100% of the agreed-upon replacement cost at the time the endorsement was issued and you increased coverage when required by company reevaluations, annual adjustments for inflation, or alterations to the building. Additionally, the replacement cost will be paid even if you elect not to rebuild.

Other homeowner's policy coverage...

•Contents (furniture, china, clothing, etc.): *Coverage:* 50% of the insured value of the house.

•The cost of staying in a hotel or renting a temporary apartment or house while your own home is repaired. *Coverage:* Up to 20% of insurance on the home's contents.

•Third-party liability: Protection in case anyone is injured on your property. *Or:* Someone is injured through some action of yours off your property.

•Appurtenant structures such as a garage or shed. *Coverage:* 10% of home coverage.

•Theft away from home: This covers a suitcase stolen from a hotel room. *Extended theft:* Theft from a boat or locked car. *Caution:* Coverages are limited or optional in some states.

Examine policies for restricted coverage on jewelry, furs, silverware, fine art, guns, money and securities. Schedule high-value items so that you and the insurer agree on value before there is a loss.

Seek the broadest coverage possible within your budget. Some homeowner's policies are little more than fire-insurance contracts. *Caution:* No homeowner's policy covers floods. Flood coverage must be obtained separately. The best policies, known as all-risk policies, cover nearly everything and take the burden of proof of coverage away from you. They make the insurance company prove it is excluded from the contract.

Example: A deer jumped through a picture window and destroyed the entire interior of the house. A standard policy would not cover this incident. Under an all-risk policy, the company must pay unless it can prove the incident falls within a specific exclusion.

Look for credits for higher deductibles, particularly percentage deductibles.

Example: You insure your house for $100,000. Instead of getting a $500 deductible, you can get a larger credit for a 1/2% deductible, even though it also equals $500. Realize that if the amount of the insurance is raised, your deductible will rise proportionately.

Source: Judith L. Robinson, CPCU, president of general insurance brokers H & R Phillips, 550 Fifth Ave., New York 10017.

How Much Fire Insurance Do You Need?

Most standard homeowners' policies will pay the full value of the policy only if that value is 80% or more of the replacement value of the house. If coverage is below 80%, the maximum payment is limited to the replacement value minus a depreciation charge (usually quite large) figured according to the age of the house. The burden of keeping coverage to at least 80% of replacement value rests with the homeowner. *Advice:* Increase coverage annually, to keep up with inflation.

The Most Frequently Asked Questions About Health Insurance And Life Insurance

The National Insurance Consumer Helpline (800-942-4242) operates from 8:00 a.m. to 8:00 p.m. Eastern time, Monday through Friday, as a toll-free source of answers to insurance questions.

Although people's insurance needs differ, some questions to the Helpline come up again and again.

Most frequently asked questions lately...

How do I figure out if an insurance company is reliable and solvent?

Many companies investigate and report on insurance firms' finances. The big four raters: A. M. Best (Oldwick, New Jersey)...Duff & Phelps (Chicago)... Moody's Investor Service and Standard & Poor's (both New York City). These companies' reports are available in many library reference sections.

Other information sources: Your state insurance department (it requires yearly financial reports from the companies it licenses—but it doesn't provide ratings)...the companies themselves (call or write to the home office for a copy of the most recent annual report).

Note: Since rapid changes in the economy can quickly render reports obsolete, the companies are updating them much more frequently than in the past.

What is COBRA?

COBRA is the federal continuation-of-benefits requirement for most organizations with 20 or more employees. It lets you keep group health insurance with your former company for up to 18 months (36 months for certain qualified dependents). You must pay the full price of the insurance.

Limitation: COBRA does not help if the company goes out of business, since COBRA ties you to the employer's group plan, not to a particular insurance company.

What do I do when my insurance company refuses to repay me because it says my doctor overcharged me?

Most coverage levels are based on what doctors in a particular geographic area charge for a service. Check with other doctors—if yours is out of line, ask for a fee reduction. But if other doctors also seem to charge more than the insurance company is willing to pay, appeal the reimbursement by writing a letter listing the doctors you contacted and the amounts they quoted to you.

Will I still get good medical care if my employer switches to a Health Maintenance Organization and requires me to see only HMO doctors?

HMOs help keep costs down by using internists, pediatricians and general practitioners as "gatekeepers" to determine whether or not you need to see a high-cost specialist. This does not keep you from top-quality medical care, but does represent a change in traditional ways of selecting doctors. *Advantages:* Lower out-of-pocket costs...no deductibles...no cost for regular checkups and other preventive care.

What is the basic difference among types of life insurance?

Term insurance simply protects your family for a specified—and finite—period of time. It only pays death benefits if you die during this period. At each renewal, the benefit remains the same...but your premium increases. *Whole life* insurance protects you as long as you live. Premiums do not increase year-to-year, but are averaged out over your lifetime. Whole life provides an investment—*cash value*—as well. You can cancel the policy and receive a lump-sum payment. You only pay taxes on this amount if the cash value—plus any dividends you received—exceeds the sum of premiums you have already paid.

In the past, *whole,* or *traditional,* life was the only type with a cash-value component. Today, there are others: *Modified life, limited payment life* and *single-premium* whole life. Other alternatives with cash value options: *Universal, variable* and *current assumption whole life.* An insurance agent can explain the detailed differences and help determine which type is best for you.

How do annuities work?

An annuity is basically the opposite of life insurance. Instead of being designed to pay when a covered person dies, an annuity is designed to pay benefits as long as a person *lives.* Annuities are usually set up as retirement plans. Depending on your contract, the insurance company provides you with a regular income (monthly checks) for as long as you live. Your choice would be either an *immediate annuity,* bought by retirees and payable starting now...or a deferred annuity, where you deposit money into an interest-bearing account, for your payments to start at some specified future date.

What are accelerated death benefits?

This new form of payout is already offered by more than 100 companies. It allows 25% to 100% of life-insurance benefits to be paid while the insured is still living. These *living benefits* are paid in connection with terminal or catastrophic illness or a need for long-term care or confinement to a nursing home. As living benefits are paid, however, the payments received upon the policyholder's death are correspondingly reduced.

Warning: Tax treatment of these benefits is unclear. Life insurance payments are generally not taxable, but the IRS has not yet ruled on benefits paid while the insured is still alive.

What if someone dies and their policy can't be found?

For missing policies, send a self-addressed, stamped envelope to the American Council of Life Insurance, 1001 Pennsylvania Ave. NW,

Washington, DC 20004, and ask for a *policy search form.* A search takes three months—or more—after you submit the form.

What if a policy was issued by a company that I cannot locate?

Simply call the toll-free National Insurance Consumer Helpline. Within a few weeks, you will receive a reply from the ACLI, which maintains a list of companies that have merged...changed names...or gone out of business.

Sources: Melanie K. Marsh, manager, consumer affairs, Health Insurance Association of America, and Arlene Lilly, manager, public information, American Council on Life Insurance, both in Washington, DC. The two organizations, with the Insurance Information Institute, are the principal sponsors of the National Insurance Consumer Helpline. 800-942-4242.

How to Get More Out of Your Life Insurance

• Pay your premium annually—not monthly or quarterly, no matter what type of policy you own.

Insurance premiums are always lowest when you pay in one lump sum, once a year, rather than spreading out the payments.

If you can pay the single premium, you will save between 6% and 20%, depending on the interest rate your insurer charges for the luxury of paying in installments.

• Drop unnecessary riders. Nearly every life insurance policy (including term policies and whole life policies) offers riders—extras that push up the cost of owning the policy—for which you may have signed up or aren't aware you own.

Call your insurer or agent for a list of the riders in your policy and an explanation of each one. Then determine which to keep and which to eliminate. *Two examples of riders that have little value and can be eliminated...*

• *Waiver of premium for disability.* If you're already receiving disability coverage at work or through a policy you bought on your own, coverage through your life insurance policy may be unnecessary.

Even if you don't have any type of disability coverage, you're better off eliminating this rider and using the extra money to help pay for a *high-quality* disability plan with better features.

Important: Be sure you qualify for a new personal disability policy *before* canceling the life insurance policy rider.

• *Accidental death coverage.* This rider doubles the amount of coverage a family receives if the policyholder's death comes as a result of an accident. Your family's protection needs don't depend on how you die, so this rider is for gambling, not for financial planning.

• Get higher policy dividends by switching to a variable interest rate on policy loans. If you own a cash-value policy, your insurer pays annual dividends on the cash portion you have invested.

If you bought your insurance policy in the 1970s or early 1980s, you probably are receiving a low dividend in exchange for the ability to borrow money from the insurer at a low fixed interest rate of 5% to 8%.

Helpful: If you own such an insurance policy, you may be able to make a one-time switch from a fixed rate to a variable rate, which will boost your dividends. Call your insurer or agent to determine if such a switch is possible and to ask about the benefits and the drawbacks.

Important: Avoid this strategy if you borrow regularly from your policy and prefer the low fixed rate...or expect to do so.

• Reduce your policy's face value to improve performance. Most people don't realize this option exists. *Here's when it makes sense...*

You now have a cash-value policy that pays you an attractive interest rate—but its internal costs are no longer competitive.

You can make the policy more attractive by reducing the face amount—and, therefore, the internal charges—and continue to enjoy the high interest rate. You may also want to reduce the face amount in order to cut the premium you need to pay.

• Convert existing policies to other types. You may need some help with this one from an independent insurance consultant or a financial planner.

Here's the basic premise...

An existing insurance policy is too costly to keep and impossible to alter using one of the strategies already mentioned.

By converting from one type of policy to another, you can still salvage some of the policy's underlying value.

Source: Glenn Daily, one of the country's most astute life insurance experts. He is a fee-only insurance consultant and author of *Life Insurance Sense and Nonsense*, which is available from the author.

How to Get Your HMO To Cover Alternative Treatment

All HMOs rely on primary care doctors to provide or approve most care for their members. They also tend to cover only "medically necessary" and "nonexperimental" treatments.

Therefore, HMOs may not be willing to reimburse members for alternative medical treatments, such as acupuncture, biofeedback, massage therapy and chiropractic care.

But such treatments are growing in popularity. More than one-third of all Americans have already tried at least one of them.

Here's how to get your HMO to pay for alternative approaches...

• Find out if the HMO must pay for the treatment in your state, and under what circumstances. Some states now require that health insurers pay for certain treatments—especially chiropractic care. Your state's insurance department can fill you in.

• Convince your primary care physician to recommend an alternative treatment. Explain how it will likely succeed in treating your medical problem. Some HMOs will pay for alternative treatments—if you get a referral from your HMO doctor. Call the HMO to find out its policy.

• Ask alternative treatment providers if they know of HMOs that cover their care. Ask if they will allow referrals for alternative treatments. There may be limits—for example, chiropractic treatment for lower back pain may be covered, while the use of alternative therapies for chronic illness may not be.

• Ask your employer to add alternative therapies to your benefits. Some HMOs offer riders that expand coverage to include nontraditional therapies. It will cost your employer more, so you will probably see somewhat higher premiums as a result. The larger the number of your fellow employees who want such a benefit, the more likely it is your request will be granted.

• If treatment is denied coverage, use tax-sheltered money. Many employers offer flexible spending accounts, which permit you to set aside pretax dollars to pay for uncovered medical expenses.

Acupuncture and chiropractic care qualify, since the IRS has ruled that both are tax-deductible medical expenses. The IRS hasn't ruled on other treatments, so check with your employer. Also find out if you need a medical doctor's referral before getting your treatment.

Be careful when you set aside money in a flexible spending account. If you don't use all the money that is set aside by the end of the year, you forfeit the remaining amount.

Source: Alan Raymond, vice president of public affairs for Harvard Pilgrim Heath Care, an HMO, Brookline, Massachusetts, and author of *The HMO Health Care Companion: A Consumer's Guide to Managed-Care Networks.* HarperPerennial.

16

The New Investor

How to Protect Yourself from Investment Frauds

As more and more people move out of relatively simple investments, such as bank CDs and money-market accounts, and into higher yielding and more complex securities, the opportunities for misunderstanding increase. And so do the opportunities for securities fraud and deception.

When they do you wrong...

Review the record of your investment to identify any evidence of...

• Unsuitable recommendations. Securities laws require brokers and salespeople to make only those recommendations that are in line with your experience as an investor and other securities that you own.

Example: If you were looking to invest money from a maturing CD and typically invested only in CDs or money-market funds, the salesperson probably should not have encouraged you to speculate on commodities or options. And the adviser should have exercised caution in having you consider a complex tax shelter or mortgage-backed security.

• Churning. Your account should not show an excessive number of securities purchases and sales—and heavy commissions. Excessive means that the size or frequency of the transactions is out of line with the depth of your financial resources and the character of your investments.

• Unauthorized trades. There should not be any purchases or sales of securities appearing on your account statement that you do not recall personally authorizing. You have only 30 days in which to make any corrections to your account.

Misstatements and omissions...

Deception can be far more subtle and indirect, however. *This includes...*

• Important information left unsaid and never put down in written form.

• Guarantees implied.

• Risks not made clear.

If you feel sure that misstatements or material omissions of fact were what led you to make the unfortunate investment, you still have protection under securities law.

Many investors who have put money in unfamiliar fixed-income securities in the past few years, for instance, feel they have been misled about yields. The problem is that most individuals purchase bonds on the basis of a phone conversation and, as a result, tend to ask few questions.

Key questions to ask yourself about an investment in bonds...

• Were you informed that the attractive, high-yielding bond you bought with a maturity date years away was subject to a call? Were you unpleasantly surprised when the bond issuer called the bond—paying you off at face value and cutting off your income stream long before you expected anything like that could happen?

• Was the yield information made clear in the phone conversation? You want to know the yield-to-call as well as the yield-to-maturity on the bond.

• Did you purchase a municipal bond with a surprisingly high yield only to discover that it was not "rated?" Always ask your broker if the bond is rated and what the rating is.

• Does the broker have information about anything that could affect the bond's rating?

Fighting back...

The statute of limitations for securities fraud is three years from the date of the transaction or one year from the date you can prove was the first time you could have detected the fraud, whichever is later. It's in your interest to bring up possible problems promptly.

• If you believe you spot an error, request in writing that the branch manager provide an explanation. Do not rely on a phone call to your broker to get action. Brokers are often reluctant to admit errors. If the branch manager's explanation doesn't satisfy you, write directly to the firm's office of supervisory jurisdiction. Send your letter by registered mail and get a receipt. Keep a copy of both.

• If you are not immediately satisfied by the response, make it very clear that you mean business. On any call you make after it becomes clear there is going to be a problem, tell the person that you are recording the call. (Telling them you are recording the call is really a signal that you are moving toward legal action. If you record without informing the other person, the tape cannot be used as evidence.) Most answering machines allow you to record calls. If brokerage executives won't talk with you under such circumstances, conduct everything by registered mail.

• Get the name and address of your state's securities commissioner. Call the secretary of state's office in your state capital for exact information. Get the official state securities complaint form. Fill it out and send it to the broker dealer as well as to the state authorities. Request restitution and an immediate response.

What to expect: Brokers are generally willing to settle small claims promptly to avoid further problems. The smaller the sum, the easier it is to recover.

Chances are that you agreed to arbitrate disputes when you opened your brokerage account. This can be an economical and effective way to handle disputes that involve $35,000 or less. For larger sums, you probably will need to engage a good securities lawyer.

Establish the claim...

If you are unable to recoup your losses from your broker or dealer, then, to establish a loss, you must sell the investment to prove how much less it was worth than your original investment. At a minimum, you can take a tax loss and collect 31 cents on the dollar as a deduction, or use the tax loss to offset capital gains elsewhere. If there are no capital gains, then the tax loss is subject to an annual $3,000 limit.

When you begin a suit to recover a loss, you and your lawyer will seek out the "deepest pockets" among the firms or individuals who can be considered liable for misrepresenting the investment.

The Civil Liabilities section of the 1934 Securities Act states that anybody mentioned in the transaction is liable, including lawyers, accountants, bankers, investment bankers, management, even real estate appraisers or public relations firms involved in the deal.

Sources: N. Richard Fox, Jr., a former senior manager of a national brokerage firm, and Vernon K. Jacobs, CPA, former vice president and controller of a major life-insurance firm. They are two of the founders of Heartland Management Co., a fee-only investment advisory firm, 6804 W. 107 St., Overland Park, Kansas 66212. Heartland also has an audiotape on how to get out of a bad investment.

Investment Lessons

There's no shortage of financial advice on Wall Street. The problem is that much of this financial advice is conflicting and leaves individuals confused or stuck in bad investments. So what's an investor to do?

To help individuals make better decisions, financial experts George Stasen and Robert Metz give us their basic lessons of investing...

Decisions/decisions...

• "Buy low and sell high" is sound financial advice—but there are actually four decisions to make. Stock-market experts like to say that timing is everything, and most investors strive to sell at the top of a market and buy at the bottom.

This strategy is also known as the "contrary opinion"—doing the opposite of what most other investors are doing at a given time.

But moving successfully against the crowd is very difficult.

Trap: Market cycles contain many small, deceptive movements—so the buy-sell phases aren't always clear. *Here are six decisions a contrarian investor must make...*

• When the market is approaching the bottom of a cycle, sellers no longer have the stomach to buy. This creates an opportunity for bargain hunters. To determine when the market has reached this point, you can evaluate stocks using historically low valuations of revenues, earnings, and dividends. Or you can wait for an uptrend before buying.

• After you buy, don't sell immediately after the bull trend becomes obvious to everyone. Let the crowd join you as the movement upward progresses.

• When serious overvaluation is reached, go against the majority and sell. Determine this moment by setting a price objective beforehand. Or base your timing on the heat of the market. Wait for the first sign of market weakness.

• As the downward cycle advances, resist the temptation to buy back your stock at a lower price. Wait until the market approaches the bottom again before buying.

• Don't confuse portfolio activity with progress toward investment goals. A common mistake made by many investors is rapid portfolio activity. They regard time as the enemy and believe that if they wait too long, that is an invitation for something to go wrong.

It's unrealistic, however, to expect that instant profits are easy to grab. When too much attention is focused on achieving short-term goals, the real opportunity—which is long-term—is forgotten. Think of time as an ally, not as an enemy.

• Beware of the company that offers creative excuses for underachievement. Some companies have a talent for making excuses for problems. Be especially wary of companies that wrap bad news in good news. *Danger signs:*

• When shortfalls and disappointments come with good-news announcements, such as the introduction of a new product or overhead-reduction programs.

• When you find your mailbox jammed with "We love you, shareholder" letters from the company.

• When bad news is accompanied by an announcement of a management shake-up. Did the company also say what took so long for them to clean up the problem? If not, incompetents may still be in charge.

Once credibility has been destroyed, it takes a long time for a company to win it back. When management repeatedly says, "Things will be better next year," it's time to sell.

• Focus on essentials...skip the merely interesting. Experienced investors are humble. They've learned that they can't possibly know everything. Less seasoned investors, on the other hand, may feel that if they had only a few more hours to do research, their investment returns would be considerably better. Usually this is hogwash.

Save time by not seeking out the opinions of yet another expert. Formulating intelligent questions that you then go out and seek to answer is much more valuable than collecting opinions.

Focus on an industry's prospects, the strength and track record of a company, and the long-term implications of a new development.

• Good corporate news can lead to a dangerous sense of euphoria. When there's good news, companies can't wait to circulate it. Many ladle it out in advance, tipping off key stock-market analysts. The result is that these stocks often rise before the news hits the media and afterward rise only slightly—or even fall.

Reasons: Many pros "sell on the news"—or take profits as the news becomes widely known and the price rises—and companies often use good news as an opportunity to seek more equity financing.

Similarly, beware of remarkably upbeat presentations at investment conferences. Instead, wait a few weeks or a month, and you'll almost always be able to buy the stock cheaper. *Opportunity:* Look at the volume in the weeks before an "announcement." If it's high, this tells you that you may be late in getting the word.

• Study the composition of a company's board of directors. The role of a company's board of directors is to represent the interests of all stockholders. One way to determine whether the directors are representing your interests is to look at the people who make up the board.

How to tell a good board from a bad one...

• Determine how many directors come from the company and how many are from the outside. If most are from the inside, the board may not be independent enough to resist undue pressure from top management.

• Examine the credentials of the outsiders. If they are not particularly distinguished, they may have been chosen as "good buddies."

• If the board is small—fewer than five members—it's likely that outside directors were chosen for their cooperative attitude toward management preferences.

On the other hand, a large board—more than 10—is probably too unwieldy to support much independence on the part of outside directors.

• The company's proxy statement will reveal the extent of each director's stock ownership and options and interest in the future of the company. Token holdings are danger signs.

• Learn to distinguish the truly underappreciated stock from the real losers. *Key questions:* Is the stock misunderstood by Wall Street or is it more likely that management misunderstands what's happened to its market?

Don't be fooled by a company's aura or unduly impressed by its past glories. "What have you done for me lately?" is a legitimate question to ask. "What do you plan to do tomorrow?" is an even better one.

Don't jettison a stock simply because it's the biggest loser in your portfolio. That's a short-term balm that usually turns into a long-term mistake.

Sources: George Stasen, a venture-capital expert and chief operating officer of Supra Medical Corp., and Robert Metz, a financial journalist. They are coauthors of *It's a Sure Thing: A Wry Look at Investing, Investors, and the World of Wall Street,* McGraw-Hill, 1221 Avenue of the Americas, New York 10020.

The Dumb Mistakes

• *Mistake:* Following every trend put forth by the press. Sure, serious investors are supposed to know better since they deal with financial matters daily. But big investors are just as insecure as small ones, and they often give in to the many opinions of the financial press. The problem is that the press and the pundits are wrong just as often as they are right.

Don't be distracted by what you read in the papers. Keep yourself focused on your personal financial goals, and don't join every prominent economist and fund manager in second-guessing the economy and companies that momentarily falter.

• *Mistake:* Taking high-rate-of-return risks. If a broker shows you an investment returning 15% a year when comparable investments are paying 3%, there's a reason for the difference. Be suspicious if an investment seems too good to be true. Even sophisticated folks' greed occasionally overtakes their common sense—and they wind up losing money.

• *Mistake:* Not protecting the assets you already have. This often occurs when you're holding a stock whose price has declined precipitously. Say you bought at $10 a share and it has fallen to $5 a share. A common reaction is to say you'll sell when the price recovers. What you're really saying is that you expect this stock, which has fallen by 50%, to rise by 100%.

If you are so convinced that the stock is a good prospect, you should invest more in the stock. When the rationale for holding onto the stock is expressed in these terms, most people back off. The point is, be realistic. When an investment fails, sell it, forget about it... and go on to better things.

• *Mistake:* Trying to time the market—predicting each upturn and downturn, and constantly shifting from one asset class to another, such as stocks to bonds, growth companies to value companies, and so on. Even the pros are unable to do this consistently.

The only person who gets rich with market timing is your broker—by raking in commissions. Successful investors use time and patience. They set their goals and stick with them —overrunning temporary market fluctuations.

• *Mistake:* Not monitoring your holdings. You may not be doing as well as you think. Once every six months, tally up your net worth—not counting your house. Over time, that number should be rising.

You should set a specific target for how much you expect your assets to grow over the next three years and the next five years. I aim for at least 10% average growth a year. At that rate, your assets will double every seven years.

• *Mistake:* Neglecting your greatest asset... you. The rate of return on your own labor is far greater than you can get on any other investment. Think of how much income you produced between last January 1 and the end of the year. Regardless of whether you made $20,000 or $200,000, you went from no earnings at all to your total annual salary or business income. Be sure to take good care of yourself. You want to safeguard your most valuable money-making machine—you.

It's also important to invest in yourself. If your company doesn't provide a car phone, but you know it can help you conduct business, buy one yourself. If your 10-year-old knows more about computers than you do, increase your knowledge by taking a course at night school. Continuously strive for excellence...it will pay off financially.

• *Mistake:* Being afraid to invade your principal. Only the super-wealthy can afford to live on their income alone. Sure, it's great to save for a comfortable retirement, but once you've stopped working, don't forget to use some of the money you've accumulated to improve your quality of life.

Example: A 60-year-old woman with a $10 million portfolio worries about the cost of nursing-home care—until she's told that, with her assets, she could afford to hire a staff of 50 for 24-hour care for the rest of her life.

If you are worried about outliving your principal, make sure your portfolio is not 100% in fixed-income investments. Historically, they have had a low rate of return. *Better:* Fashion a diversified portfolio of stocks and bonds, which will produce a higher rate of return. That way, you can systematically withdraw some of the "growth" by selling stocks.

Your real goal should be to accumulate enough money to support you and your life partner for the rest of your lives, not to make your kids wealthy after you die.

• *Mistake:* Being embarrassed to invest small amounts of money. What's important is to establish the habit of savings, even if you're investing only $5 or $10 a month. There are several mutual-fund families that have a low minimum initial-investment requirement, and no minimum-investment requirement after that.

They know that people who get hooked on the savings habit tend to be very loyal customers. So don't be embarrassed to earmark modest sums for your portfolio. And when larger sums become available—because of a tax refund or a bonus at work, for example—siphon off at least some of that money for investments.

• *Mistake:* Being too busy making money to become financially successful. Regardless of whether you make $50,000, $100,000, or $200,000, it's important to keep track of your spending. There's no doubt that spending all you make can give you the sensation of being wealthy. Yet it's not how much you spend but how much you save that matters. The old adage, "Pay yourself first" works only if you adopt a good method for paying yourself.

Solution: Once a month, when you write a check for your rent or mortgage, get in the habit of writing another check—say, for $50 or $100—for your investments.

Once you get in the saving habit, you won't even notice a dent in your spendable income.

Source: Lawrence A. Krause, chairman of Lawrence A. Krause & Associates, Inc., a San Francisco financial-planning firm. He is the author of *The Money-Go-Round: How You Got On and How to Get Off*, Simon & Schuster, 1230 Avenue of the Americas, New York 10020.

Broker Self-Defense

Check your broker's background. Toll-free hotline—800-289-9999—will advise about criminal indictments, civil judgments, pending disciplinary proceedings and securities-dispute arbitration decisions involving your broker. *Sponsor:* National Association of Securities Dealers, Monday to Friday, 9 a.m. to 5 p.m., Eastern Time. No charge for individuals.

Surviving the Over-the-Counter Stock Market

Over-the-counter stocks, being small and often not well followed by many brokers, are especially susceptible to rumors and false reports. Stockbrokers and underwriters flourish on heavy trading and are usually themselves the source of misleading reports.

Basic wisdom: When a company sounds too good—its product will replace toothpaste—watch out!

• *Rule of thumb:* If you don't know why you own a stock—or why you're buying—or why you're selling—then you're in someone else's hands. This makes you more vulnerable to the caprices of the market.

• OTC stocks, particularly new issues, are usually short-term plays. One should never buy without having a sell target in mind.

• If the selling price is reached, even within a week of buying, stick to the sell decision unless there is some major mitigating factor you hadn't considered before.

• About 80% of all new issues will be selling below their issue price within 18 months. *Reason:* Most new issues are overpriced in relation to existing companies. But they are all destined to become just another existing company within a year.

• In evaluating a new issue, find out who the people involved are. If the underwriter is or has been the target of the Securities and Exchange Commission's investigations, this is often mentioned in the prospectus. The SEC prints a manual of all past violators. Avoid underwriters that have had lots of SEC problems. The strong companies rarely use them to go public.

• Check out the auditors of a new-issue company. (They will be named in the prospectus.) If the auditor is not well-known or is in trouble with the SEC, question the numbers in the financial reports.

• A danger in over-the-counter stocks is a key market maker who crosses buy and sell orders among its own brokerage customers so that the market price is artificial. If such a broker collapses, so will its main stocks. This illustrates the danger of buying a stock dependent on only a single market maker. To avoid such a problem, invest in stocks quoted on NASDAQ, where by definition there are at least two strong market makers, and hopefully a lot more.

• Spot companies just before they decide to go onto NASDAQ. When they do, their price inevitably rises because of the increased attention. Very often the managements will simply tell you if they have NASDAQ plans or not. *Tip-off:* If they've just hired a new financial man, it's often a sign of a move to NASDAQ.

Source: Robert J. Flaherty, editor of *The OTC Review*, Oreland, PA.

Techniques for Evaluating Over-the-Counter Stocks

•Growth potential is the single most important consideration. Earnings increases should average 10% over the past six years when acquisitions and divestitures are factored out.

•Cash, investments, accounts receivable, materials, and inventories should be twice the size of financial claims due within the next year.

•Working capital per share should be greater than the market value of the stock (an $8 stock should be backed by $10 per share in working capital).

•Long-term debt should be covered by working capital, cash, or one year's income.

•The balance sheet should show no deferred operating expenses and no unreceived income.

The criteria for final selections include:

•Ownership by at least 10 institutions reported in Standard & Poor's Stock Guide.

•Public ownership of between 500,000 and one million shares, with no more than 10% controlled by a single institution.

•Continued price increases after a dividend or split.

•Strong likelihood of moving up to a major exchange. (A good sign is strong broker and institutional support.)

Avoid companies that are expanding into unrelated fields, where they lack the required management experience and depth, and have stock selling at prices far below recent highs. This sign of loss of investor support can take months to overcome.

Source: C. Colburn Hardy, *Physician's Management.*

How to Spot a Market Decline Before it Starts

Strong market moves frequently end in one- or two-day reversal spikes. Those spikes often provide advance warning of significant market turning points. *Checkpoints that show when a market decline may be coming:*

•The market will rise sharply in the morning on very high volume running at close to 15 million shares during the first hour of trading.

•From 10:30 a.m. (Eastern time) on, the market will make little or no progress despite heavy trading throughout the day.

•By the end of the first day, almost all the morning's gains will have been lost, with the market closing clearly toward the downside. Occasionally, this process will be spread over a two-day period.

•*Steps to take:* When you see the pattern, either sell immediately or await the retest of the highs that were reached during that first morning. Such a retest often takes place within a week or two, on much lower trading volume. This may prove to be the last opportunity to sell into strength.

How Bear Market Rallies Can Fool You

Bear market rallies are often sharp. They're fueled, in part, by short sellers rushing to cover shares. However, advances in issues sold short often lack durability once short covering is completed.

Here is what you need to know about bear market rallies:

•They tend to last for no more than five or six weeks.

•Advances often end rapidly—with relatively little warning. If you are trading during a bear market, you must be ready to sell at the first sign of weakness.

•The first strong advance during a bear market frequently lulls many analysts into a false sense of security, leading them to conclude that a new bull market is underway. The majority of bear markets don't end until pessimism is widespread and until the vast majority is convinced that prices are going to continue to decline indefinitely.

•Although the stock market can remain "overbought" for considerable periods of time during bull markets, bear market rallies generally end fairly rapidly, as the market enters into "overbought" conditions.

•Price/earnings multiples for the group soar far above historical norms.

•Heavy short selling appears. Early short sellers of the stocks are driven to cover by sharp rallies. Their covering of shorts adds fuel to late rallies within the group. (Short sellers who enter the picture later, however, are likely to be amply rewarded.)

Trading tactics that work for professionals:

•Exercise extreme caution, first and foremost.

•Place close stop orders on any long and/or short positions taken.

•Enter into short sales only after these issues have shown signs of fatigue and of topping out, and then only after recent support levels have been broken.

•Wait for a clear sign that the uptrend has ended before selling out.

Spotting the Bottom Of a Bear Market

Here's how sophisticated investors recognize that a bear market is near its last phase:

•Downside breadth increases. That is, market declines become broader, including even stocks that have been strong before. More issues are making new lows.

•"Oversold" conditions (periods in which the market seems to decline precipitously) extend for longer periods of time. Technical recoveries are relatively minor.

•Pessimism spreads, but analysts and bullish advisories still discuss "bargains" and "undervalued issues."

•Stocks continue to be very sensitive to bad news. The market becomes very unforgiving of poor earnings reports and monetary difficulties.

•Trading volume remains relatively dull. Prices seem to fall under their own weight, the result of a lack of bids rather than urgent selling.

Important: The bear market isn't likely to end until pessimism broadens into outright panic, and until public and institutional selling become urgent. One of the most reliable nontechnical signals that the bear market is over is when the mass media begin to headline the fact that the stock market is hitting its bottom.

How to Make Money In Market Declines

Mistake: Most investors tend to place capital into the stock market following important market advances. This increases your risks.

Instead:

•Adopt a planned strategy of making investments in phases as the market declines. Market declines of greater than 10% are relatively unusual during bull markets and investors should look upon them as an opportunity.

•Don't take quick profits early in intermediate advances and reinvest quickly into new stocks. You miss the really good moves and simply incur additional commission costs.

•Prepare for market advances during periods of market decline. Determine which groups are best resisting market decline, and plan to purchase into such groups upon a 10% market decline. Hold for a minimum of several weeks, preferably months.

•Don't chase stocks that have already risen sharply in price, particularly when the price rise has been based upon speculative expectation.

•Try to ferret out true value—stocks in companies that feature solid balance sheets, regular earnings growth, increasing dividend payout.

•Avoid stocks with institutional followings. They tend to underperform the market.

•Study the market on days when trading is quiet. If such days show positive closing action, you can presume that the professionals are positioning themselves for market advance.

Knowing When to Wait Before Buying

Investors often think they are buying stock at a bargain price, only to see it fall further because of an overall market falloff. *Signs that such a falloff is ahead:*

- Just before the decline, the market advance becomes very selective. Gains are recorded in just a few industry groups rather than across the board.
- Speculative interest runs high in the American Stock Exchange and over-the-counter markets.
- During the first phase of the decline, the stocks that failed to participate at the end of the previous advance show the most severe declines. The strongest industry groups tend to keep rising on short-term rallies. This pattern traps unwary traders who believe that stocks are at bargain levels.
- During the second phase of the decline, most groups participate, but the previously strong groups decline only slightly.
- During the final stages, even the once strong industry groups fall sharply. Odds are that the decline will soon come to an end. Wait for evidence that all segments of the market have declined before stepping in to buy.
- As a general rule, groups that were strongest during the previous rally will advance sharply when the market starts to recover, although they may not remain in the forefront throughout the next market cycle.
- Strong market rallies often take place at quarterly intervals.
- Leaders of one quarter often do not maintain leadership in the next upward cycle.

Questions to Ask Before Buying a Stock

You'll want a yes answer to just about every one of these questions before taking a long position in a stock.

- Is the price/earnings ratio of the stock (price divided by latest 12-month earnings) well below the price/earnings ratio of the average listed issue?
- Have earnings of the company been rising at a steady rate over a period of years, preferably at a rate exceeding the rate of inflation?
- Has the company had a recent history of steadily rising dividend payouts?
- Has the stock recently risen above a clearly defined trading range that lasted for at least five weeks?
- If not, has a recent sharp decline ended with the stock trading on extremely high volume for that issue, without the price falling further?
- Have insiders of the company purchased more shares of the company than they have sold?
- Has the company recently purchased its own shares on the open market?
- Has the stock remained relatively undiscovered by the advisory services and brokerage houses? (One sign that an issue is near the end of a rise is that many advisory services suddenly begin to recommend its purchase.)

Source: Gerald Appel, president, SignAlert Corporation, money managers, Great Neck, NY.

Stocks that Benefit When Oil Prices Fall

- Airlines. Fuel prices will be lower.
- Homebuilders. Interest rates fall because lower oil prices add liquidity to the system. Lower interest rates boost home-building activity.
- Restaurants. The nondiscretionary portion of the average paycheck is 86%. With more discretionary income, people will eat out more.
- Motel chains. There will be more auto travel.
- Automobiles. Lower gasoline prices.
- Retail industry. Another area buoyed by more discretionary spending.
- Brokerage industry. People may invest some of that extra money.
- Interest-rate-sensitive stocks. As rates fall, these companies benefit.

•Japan. The yen will rise and the Japanese economy becomes healthier due to lower oil prices.

Source: Barry Sahgal, managing director of research, Ladenburg Thalmann & Co., New York.

Wise Tactics for Picking a Mutual Fund

•Analyze the advertising the mutual fund runs in the financial press. Usually it gives an excellent performance record to lure new investors.

•Consider the time frame of the fund's performance. It may be a very select period, when the fund's performance was exceptional, or a time when everyone did well in the market. During a longer period the fund may have had just a so-so performance.

•Find out what happened to the fund in down markets.

•Avoid fad funds. You can learn about new funds from many financial periodicals, from reference books such as Wiesenberger's handbook on mutual funds, or from the no-load fund directories put out by a number of organizations. Too often, when a particular industry such as gold, high technology, or international stocks gets hot, the funds jump in to grab a piece of the action. But they don't have the ultimate ability to use the money they raise, because they have bought at the top of the elevator.

•Study the discipline of the funds that interest you. This is stated in the prospectus. Some funds have a mandate to be fully invested at all times. *Trap:* In a major market slide, such as the one from 1968 through 1974, full investment (even with the strictest discipline) will not bring about good performance. It is better to find a fund that can get in and out of cash instruments. *Alternative:* Switch in and out of various funds yourself, based on the signals of a competent timer.

•Identify the risk profile of the fund. Read the prospectus to learn the price/earnings ratio and dividend yield of the average stock the fund holds. Is the average stock selling at 27 times earnings (the high end of the spectrum)? Or is it at an average or below-market multiple, as usually befits a more conservative fund? Does the firm buy volatile stocks? Find out if the fund manager is a trader or a long-term investor. And then decide whether the profile conforms to your own investment style and needs.

•Don't sign up for a family of funds with the belief that, if the stock market sinks immediately, you can switch into a money-market fund. Most funds require that money be at the institution at least 30 days before a switch is allowed.

•Mutual funds aren't banks. Although many people are used to check-writing privileges on money-market funds, they should not view equity mutual funds the same way.

•Distinguish between an investment portfolio and transactions portfolio. Don't put rent money into an equity fund. Mutual funds fall in value at times. You don't want to be forced to liquidate at a loss.

How to Read a Mutual Fund Prospectus

A mutual fund prospectus is not easy reading. The way to pry out the information needed to make a good investment decision is to focus on the following questions:

• *Does the fund's portfolio mesh with your investment goals?* Some funds have highly volatile portfolios and employ leverage or margin selling to enhance return, but at greater risk.

• *What's the fund's performance record?* Select a fund that has matched or surpassed Standard & Poor's 500 during periods of both rising and falling markets. Most prospectuses include several years' performance data. Best performers are usually funds with less than $50 million in assets.

• *What are the minimum initial and subsequent investments?* The lower the better.

• *Is there a switch privilege?* It is highly desirable to pick a fund that allows investors to switch back and forth between a firm's equity and money-market funds by phone. (Some funds charge for switching, but the charges usually don't amount to much, except for the frequent trader.)

• *Are there fees for opening and closing an account?* There is no reason to pay such fees.

• *Is it a load (i.e., sales commission) fund or a no-load?* As a group, no-load funds, those without sales commissions, perform pretty much as well as those with fees.

• *What are the limitations on how the fund can invest money?* Some funds must diversify their portfolios, while others allow management to concentrate highly on one or more industry groups. As a general rule, diversification reduces risk.

• *Does the fund have a policy of moving into cash during bear markets?* While a fund can cut losses this way, it may also delay reinvestment in equities when the market starts to rise. Long-term holders often adopt the strategy of investing in funds that have a record of increasing cash positions by selling equities before bear markets or at least at their earliest stages.

Source: *Switch Fund Advisory*, MD.

Evaluating a Mutual Fund

Before taking a position in a mutual fund, answer these questions:

• *Does the fund suit your tolerance for risk?* Certain funds are extremely volatile in price action. They suit investors with risk capital better than those who cannot afford to run the risk of a sharp decline in their capital. Secure a price history on the fund, either from the fund itself or by visiting the public library of a financial publication. Analyze the fund's historical ups and downs.

• *Does the fund have a good track record during declining markets?* Does the management make an attempt to reduce portfolio exposure during down markets or does the fund generally stay fully invested? Don't expect helpful answers to questions like these from a commissioned salesperson for the fund.

• *Has the fund's management altered policies in the past counter to your own investment objectives?* Certain funds are steadily increasing redemption charges to discourage trading. Or they're imposing restrictions that may not suit your purposes. Verify the facts in the current prospectus. Inquire if any changes are contemplated.

Fitting Your Psychology To a Mutual Fund

Techniques useful to investors for evaluating performances:

For aggressive investors:

• Each week that the market rises, divide the closing price of the mutual fund at the end of the week by the closing level of either the Standard & Poor's 500 Stock Index or the NYSE Index. Plot the results on a graph for comparison. If the fund is indeed stronger than the average during a rising market, it will show up clearly, indicating that it is suitable for an aggressive investor.

• Remember that since such funds also frequently decline more sharply than the averages during falling market periods, they may be suitable only for investors with an accurate sense of market timing.

For safety-oriented investors:

• Each week the market declines, divide the closing price of the mutual fund at the end of the week by the closing level of one of the averages. If your fund resists the downtrend more than the average stock during a falling market, the plotted results will show the fund's line declining less than that of the average.

• Don't be disappointed when mutual funds advance less than more aggressive funds during rising market periods.

For investors who want to try to beat the averages:

• At the end of each week divide the price of the mutual fund (rising or falling) by the price of one of the broad market averages, and plot the results. The result will demonstrate the relative strength curve of the fund, indicating whether it is outperforming the broad market, regardless of the price trend.

•To protect yourself, as soon as your fund's relative strength curve begins to show weakness, consider switching your holdings to a better-performing vehicle.

Selecting a Full-Service Stockbroker

Be sure that you do the interviewing. Don't let the prospective broker turn the tables and interview you. If you are reluctant to ask all these questions, select at least some of them and have the answers supplemented with a resume.

•Where did he study? What?

•How long has he been with the brokerage firm? How long has he been in the securities industry?

•What was his prior employment? Why did he leave his last place of employment?

•From where does he get his investment recommendations? His firm's research department? Company contacts? Friends in the business? His own research? A combination?

•Can he supply a certified history of his firm's and his own research recommendations?

•Does he have any client references?

•What is his theory on giving sell advice and profit taking?

•How many clients does the account executive service? (You want your telephone calls to be answered promptly.)

•How diversified is the brokerage firm? Does it have, for example, a bond department? How about an economist? An in-house market technician (essential for timing)? Money-market experts? Commodity department? Option department? Tax shelter experts?

•How many industries does his firm's research department follow? How many companies? How many senior analysts does the firm have?

•Will you get weekly, monthly or only occasional printed research reports?

•What fees, if any, will be charged for such services as securities safekeeping?

•What is the firm's commission structure? What discounts is it willing to offer?

•Can the investor talk directly to the investment-research analyst to get firsthand clarifications and updates on research reports? Must everything be funneled through the account executive?

•What is the financial condition of the brokerage firm? (You want the latest annual and quarterly financial statements.)

•How many floor brokers does the firm have at the various stock exchanges? (You want prompt order execution.)

•Is the potential broker willing to meet personally on a regular basis (monthly or quarterly, depending on portfolio size and activity) to discuss progress?

•What kind of monthly customer statements are prepared? (More and more firms now offer tabulation of monthly dividend income, portfolio valuation and annual portfolio yield estimate.)

Using Discount Brokers

Discount brokers generally charge 35% to 85% less in commissions than full-service houses. Savings are particularly good on trades involving large numbers of shares, but discounters generally don't give investment advice. Otherwise, confirmations, monthly statements, and account insurance are generally the same for discounters as they are for full-service brokerage firms.

Investors who can benefit by using discounters:

•Investors liquidating market holdings.

•Investors buying on margin. Margin rates are generally better, but this matters only if you're borrowing a substantial amount.

•Beneficiaries of estates who are moving inheritance from stocks and bonds to other kinds of investments.

•Employees whose only holdings are stocks in the companies they work for, who sell these stocks occasionally.

•Lawyers, accountants, and other professionals who believe their personal contacts and own market analyses make for better guidance than what brokers are offering.

•Retired persons or other investors with free time to do their own market research.

Who should not use discounters?

•Investors interested in commodity trading. Discount houses handle stocks, bonds, and options only.

•Investors who need mortgages, tax shelters, special bonds.

•Those with less than $2,000 to invest. Savings on discount commissions at this level do not outweigh the plus of free advice from full-service houses.

•Individuals without stock market experience.

Source: J. Bud Feuchtwanger, financial consultant, NY.

How to Place Orders With a Stockbroker

Most investors are familiar with the basic forms of execution orders which they may give to their stockbrokers. The most common are limit orders (orders to buy and/or sell at the best available price), and stop loss orders (orders to buy and/or sell at the best available price if specified price levels are crossed).

Far fewer investors are familiar with other instructions:

•Fill or kill orders. These are either executed immediately or canceled. The investor wants to buy and/or sell immediately in light of current market conditions.

•Clean-up basis. Buy an amount of stock at the asked price only if the purchase "cleans up" all available stock at that price. If the order is executed, the investor has reasonable assurance that no other heavy seller exists at the price range at which he purchased the shares. So price is unlikely to drop rapidly.

•Not held. The investor provides the floor broker with full authority to use his judgment in the execution of the order, which may mean a more advantageous price. But if the floor broker makes an error in judgment, the investor has no recourse.

•All or none. When buying or selling multiple lots, the investor requests that his entire position or none be sold at a limit price. He can often save on commissions by trading in large lots.

•Short, short exempt. If the investor holds securities or bonds which may be converted into common stock, he can sell short the amount of stock into which these convertible issues may be converted without waiting for an uptick. To do this, he places a "short, short exempt" order. *Advantages:* The market for many convertible securities is thinner than the market for the underlying common. He will often get superior executions by selling the common short and then turning the convertible security into common, which is then employed to cover the short sale.

Source: Irving Waxman, R.F. Lafferty & Co., New York.

When Not to Listen To Your Broker

The few words the average investor finds hardest to say to his broker are, "Thanks for calling, but no thanks." There are times when it is in your own best interest to be able to reject a broker's blandishments.

•When the broker's hot tip is that a certain stock is supposed to go up because of impending good news—*ask yourself:* If the "news" is so super special, how come you (and/or your broker) have been able to learn about it in the nick of time? Often insiders have been buying long before you get the hot tip. After you buy, when the news does become "public," who'll be left to buy?

•When the market is sliding. When your broker asks, "How much lower can they go?" the temptation can be very great to try to snag a bargain. *But before you do, consider:* If the stock, at that price, is such a bargain, wouldn't some big mutual funds or pension funds be trying to buy up all they could? If that's the case, how come the stock has been going down?

•Don't fall for the notion that a stock is "averaging down." It's a mistake for the broker (or investor) to calculate that if he buys more "way down there," he can get out even. Stock market professionals average up, not down.

They buy stocks that are proving themselves strong, not ones that are clearly weak.

How to Protect Yourself In Disputes with Stockbrokers

•Keep a diary of all conversations with stockbrokers that involve placing of orders, purchase recommendations, and other important matters. A detailed record adds credibilty if the dispute goes to court, arbitration, or the broker's boss.

•Note the exact time of conversation, as well as the date. The brokerage firm is liable if it fails to place an order promptly and you lose money as a result of the delay.

•If necessary, complain to the head of the brokerage firm. That's sure to get attention.

•If that doesn't get results, write a complaint letter to the SEC, which regularly examines such letters.

•If none of these work, get a new broker.

Source: Nicholas Kelne, attorney, American Association of Individual Investors, Chicago.

When Not to Pay A Stockbroker's Commission

It's not necessary to use a broker and pay a commission to make a gift of stock. Or if a sale of stock is negotiated privately.

How to transfer stock ownership to another person:

•Enter the other person's name, address and Social Security number on the back of the certificate.

•Sign the back of the certificate and have the signature guaranteed by a commercial bank.

•Send it by registered mail to the transfer agent, whose name is on the certificate.

•Allow two to six weeks for the other person to receive the new certificate. There will be no charge, although in some states the seller, or donor, has to pay a small transfer tax.

Investing in Gold

Almost all the advisers who pushed gold several years ago continue to believe every portfolio should contain some gold as a protection against inflation or economic collapse. *Here are some shrewd ways to invest:*

•Stay away from the gold futures market. Diversify holdings among gold coins, bullion, and stocks of South African gold mines.

•Pick the mines with the most marginal, high-cost production. These companies are traded internationally, and their reserves are known. As the price of gold goes up, their production becomes economic and they offer very high yields.

•Keep in mind that, as a rule, the price of mining shares moves with the price of gold, although the swings are more exaggerated. Calling the turn in the gold market is difficult because gold is a very emotional investment. The political stability of gold-mining countries is a factor to consider.

•When buying or selling, remember that gold prices are generally strong on Fridays and lower on Mondays. This is because investors are reluctant to carry short positions over weekends, when central banks sometimes make announcements that affect prices.

•Prices are also stronger toward the end of the year and weaker in summer. The supply decreases toward the end of the year because laborers on short-term contracts to South African gold mines return home to harvest crops. Demand decreases in summer, when the European gold-jewelry industry closes.

How to Choose A Prime Growth Stock

Prime growth stocks should meet all or most of the following characteristics:

•A dominant position in a growth industry.

•A long record of rising earnings and high profit margins.

•Superb management.

•A commitment to innovation and a good research program.

•The ability to pass on cost increases to the consumer.

•A strong financial position.

•Ready marketability of the stock.

•Relative immunity to consumerism and government regulation.

Source: *Preserving Capital* by John Train, Clarkson N. Potter Publishers, New York.

Before Investing in Condos or Co-ops

Despite the recent drop in housing starts, many investors are turning again to condominium and cooperative apartment houses, especially in big cities. Smart investors today can profit from errors made in the last decade. Now they know that:

•It's best to avoid investing in the development of condos or co-ops that are surrounded by rental apartments. *Best investment:* Co-ops and condos that are next to single-family housing.

•People who buy individual apartment units like buildings where apartments cost less than comparable single-family housing nearby. *Rule of thumb:* Apartments should sell for 25% less than the lowest-priced houses in the area.

•Apartment buyers also avoid units in outlying areas. For psychological reasons, people don't mind commuting 20 to 30 miles to work from a suburban house, but many dislike an apartment in a remote area.

•It's easier to overbuild the apartment market than standard housing because the cost per unit is cheaper for apartments. When there's a housing glut, a co-op or condo can have high vacancy rates for many months or even years.

•Factors that make houses cheaper will almost always make apartments difficult to sell. *Examples:* Lower interest rates. Oversupply. Changes in zoning or building codes that favor house construction.

Source: Vincent Mooney, real estate consultant on condominium building and conversion and president of Condominium Home Realtors, Tulsa, OK, and author of *Condoeconomics*.

Cashing CDs Before Maturity

•Many investors don't realize that they can also buy bank CDs through Merrill Lynch and other brokers. *Benefit:* Merrill Lynch maintains a market in CDs, so it's possible to sell them back before maturity.

Comfortable Retirement: What it Takes

Comfortable retirement requires about 50%-75% of the final working year's income.

Source: *CPA Digest,* Milwaukee.

Making Voluntary Contributions to a Company Pension Plan

Making voluntary payments to your company's pension plan, in addition to the contributions your employer already makes for you, makes tax sense.

•Make sure you make the maximum contribution to your company's 401k savings plan. *Reason:* These additional contributions will reduce your taxable income. Also, the interest earned accumulates tax free until withdrawal.

•The maximum annual contribution limit is the lesser of $9240 or your company plan's lower limit. Check with your company's benefits coordinator for more information.

Source: Martin Fleisher, an attorney in private practice who specializes in employee benefits, Springfield, MA.

How to Get the Most Out of Your IRA

Your IRA may be your most important source of retirement income. You can contribute up to $2,000 a year, as long as you're working (until the year you reach age 70½). In addition, if you leave a job, you might be able to roll over your pension or profit-sharing distributions into your IRA. As the years go by, an IRA can grow into big money.

The pros and cons of the most common ways to invest IRA money:

Banks or savings & loans...

•Usually don't charge any fees.

•Your money is insured by the federal government up to $100,000. If your IRA grows larger than this, just open a second account at a different bank.

•*A psychological advantage:* Most people are familiar with local banks and trust them. But many taxpayers feel nervous about stocks, bonds and similar investments.

•Banks offer IRAs the same accounts (except checking) as any other depositors, including passbook savings accounts, money-market accounts and CDs of varying rates and lengths.

•Penalties are charged for early withdrawal of CDs (though some banks will waive the penalty for depositors at retirement age).

•*Essential:* Keep a detailed record of maturity dates of all CDs or time deposits, so you'll know when you can withdraw the funds or switch investments.

Insurance companies...

•Insurance companies sell retirement annuities. *Most common:* Traditional fixed-rate annuity, at a specified interest rate, which guarantees a specific amount at retirement for each $1,000 contributed.

•*Advantage of fixed annuity:* You know in advance how much you'll get. And you're guaranteed an income for your lifetime (and your spouse's, if the annuity is set up that way). You can't outlive your investment.

•*Big disadvantage of fixed annuity:* No protection against inflation.

•In recent years, many insurance companies have begun offering variable annuities, invested in money markets, stocks or other investments that rise and fall with the economy and the rate of inflation.

•*Advantage of variable annuity:* They've generally worked out much better in inflationary times.

•*Disadvantages of a variable annuity:* Less certain than fixed-rate annuities and involve some risk.

•Generally, insurance companies charge fees for setting up and maintaining an IRA. There also may be a charge on contributions and withdrawals.

•These fees are tax deductible to the extent allowed by law. Pay them separately from your IRA contributions...and deduct the amount as "IRA fees" as a miscellaneous deduction on your income tax return.

Mutual funds...

•*Advantages of mutual fund IRAs:* Flexibility and diversification. Most mutual fund companies operate several funds—money market, common stock, bond funds, etc. *Important:* You can usually move your money from one fund in the family of funds to another at will, usually for little or no charge.

•*Caution:* Some funds are more speculative than others. Some are growth funds and some are income funds. (And some funds charge sales commissions.)

Brokerage houses...

•The main attraction of a brokerage house as a trustee for an IRA account is for the taxpayer who wants to manage his own IRA by setting up a self-directed account. The brokerage house is still the trustee, but you make all investment decisions—what to buy, what to sell, etc.

•*Caution:* This kind of account is for the experienced investor, who is willing to take the responsibility—and the risk.

• Brokerage houses normally charge a fee for setting up and maintaining an IRA, as well as their normal commissions on any transactions.

• The fees (but not the commissions) are deductible if separately billed and paid.

Source: Peter I. Elinsky, tax partner, KPMG Peat Marwick, CPAs, Washington, DC.

Early IRA Withdrawals

Although the Tax Reform Act clobbered the IRA deduction for many taxpayers, it created a penalty-free way to withdraw money from the account before you reach age 59½.

• *Old law:* You had to pay an additional 10% penalty tax on distributions from IRA accounts before age 59½.

• *New Law:* You won't pay the extra 10% penalty tax if you convert the account to an annuity and receive the money in a scheduled series of substantially equal payments over your life or your life expectancy.

How to Read the Economic Indicators

We hear these terms on the news all the time —*Gross Domestic Product, Consumer Price Index, Consumer Confidence Index,* etc.—yet most of us have no idea what these indicators are or how they affect the financial markets.

Here are six of the most important economic indicators, when they are released and how to invest based on their results.

Federal Reserve Board's policy...

The Federal Reserve Board directs monetary policy, which is largely influenced by the chairman, currently Alan Greenspan. He has the power to control the markets by tightening the money supply or pumping more into the system. This affects the value of money directly. *What to do:*

...whenever the chairman makes a public statement, read the key sections and study the commentary of the professional Fed watchers. The chairman's viewpoint usually takes a while to work its way through the system—but eventually it has a considerable impact.

Interest rates...

Focus on long-term bond rates and the discount rate, which is the rate the Fed charges banks to borrow money. Long-term rates change continually. The discount rate only changes when the Fed wants to make a shift in monetary policy. *What to do:*

...don't dive into the market—or bail out—at the first change in the discount rate. That alone will not alter the overall direction of the market. You can lose money by reacting too early either way.

...two or three moves in the discount rate—in either direction—constitute an unmistakable trend, and the markets will react dramatically. Know in advance how you'll respond if that second move occurs. If you're going to act at all, act fast.

...if the interest rate trend is up, rethink the asset allocation in your portfolio. Cash will likely outperform stocks and bonds. In this environment, choose a fixed-rate mortgage over an adjustable-rate mortgage, since you'll want to lock in at the low rate.

...when the trend is down, you should be buying stocks and bonds.

Gross Domestic Product (GDP)...

The GDP is the dollar value of all goods and services produced in the US. It is announced at the end of March, June, September and December, and provides a snapshot of how fast the economy is expanding or contracting. The markets typically interpret GDP growth of between 0% and 3% as anemic...3% to 5% as robust and healthy...and more than 5% as frothy and probably unsustainable. When the GDP drops for two consecutive quarters, the economy is officially in a recession. A total of three consecutive quarters in which the GDP increases is considered a growth trend. *What to do:*

...if the GDP is growing at a slow pace following a steep decline, it's a good time to buy stock or real estate. The values of both will rise as the economy gets stronger.

...if the GDP is growing at a fast pace, quality growth stocks are good investments. Just

keep in mind that with expansion comes contraction and the growth environment will not last forever.

Warning sign: If growth is 5% or more for two consecutive quarters, the Federal Reserve, which regulates the flow of money into the economy, will probably raise short-term interest rates to slow borrowing and combat inflation. Consider selling some stocks and shifting the profits into long-term bonds.

...if the GDP growth rate is declining, review your stock portfolio. *My strategy:* Hold those blue chip issues that are solid, long-term investments...and sell the rest.

Producer Price Index (PPI)...

Released around the 15th of the month, the PPI measures the rate of change in wholesale prices according to commodity, industry sector and production stage—or what it costs to manufacture goods. PPI helps show the direction of inflation—I consider three consecutive months of movement up or down a trend. *What to do:*

...when the PPI is rising slowly—0.3% or less per month—inflation is under control. Combine that with a slowly rising GDP and investors have the best of all possible worlds. Be wary of a one-time jump in the PPI—either up or down. It won't move the markets significantly. Pay careful attention to how the PPI is interpreted by the media and analysts—not just what the number is.

...if the PPI advances sharply for two consecutive months at the equivalent of a 6% annual rate (about 0.5% per month), it's costing companies a great deal to make goods. *My strategy:* Sell your stocks and bonds before the market overheats. Also, purchase big-ticket items before those wholesale prices are passed along to consumers.

...if inflation is rising and the PPI rate of change starts to slow or declines, buy stocks and bonds. Companies will be earning higher profits as it costs them less to make goods, but they can still charge consumers higher prices.

Consumer Price Index (CPI)...

Often referred to as the cost of living, the CPI measures the change in consumer prices for goods and services bought by households. It is released in the middle of every month—always one day after the PPI. *What to do:*

...if the economy is expanding moderately (a GDP of 4% or under) and the CPI is also rising at a modest rate (annual rate of about 3%), consider buying stocks or real estate...and avoid bonds because interest rates are likely to rise.

...if the CPI moves up sharply for two months and the cause of the rise is not easily explained by the economists, avoid bonds. *Attractive:* Stocks that will either profit from inflation or not get clobbered in the recession that may be looming.

...if the CPI falls by 1% or more for two months —I like stocks that pay dividends. To lock in yields before they fall, add quality corporate bonds and Treasury bonds to your portfolio.

...if the CPI rises by 4% or more over four consecutive months, expect interest rates to rise. Buy short-term CDs.

Consumer Confidence Index (CCI)...

The CCI reflects consumers' attitudes toward the economy, the job market, their own financial situations and the future. The government releases the CCI during the first 10 days of each month.

When assessing the CCI, remember that consumers account for two-thirds of all US economic activity. So how we're all feeling matters. *What to do:*

...don't react to the month-to-month ups and downs of the CCI. Rather, value it as a big-picture forecaster.

...if inflation is high and consumer confidence falls below 80—20% lower than the index's benchmark of 100—prepare for a recession.

...if inflation is low and the CCI shows signs of reviving—lower unemployment and rising auto or home sales, for example—bet on a stronger economy. Big-ticket durable goods, such as autos and appliances, may soon do very well.

Source: Jay J. Pack, vice president of Burnham Securities, Inc., 1345 Avenue of the Americas, New York 10105, and member of the New York Society of Security Analysts. He is coauthor, with Nancy Dunnan, of *Market Movers: A Complete Guide to Economic Statistics, Trends, Forces, and News Events—and What They Mean to Your Investments,* Warner Books, 1271 Avenue of the Americas, New York 10020.

17

Taxes

How to Get More Time To File Your Return

If you need extra time to prepare your tax return, you can get it automatically: Just file Form 4868 with your local IRS Service Center by April 15. The deadline for filing your return will be pushed back four months to August 15. If you're self-employed, the extension gives you four more months in which to make contributions to a Keogh plan (if the plan was set up by December 31 of the preceding year).

Caution: A filing extension does not extend the time for estimating the tax you'll owe for the year. (You are no longer required to pay this tax, as was the IRS rule for many years.) The instructions on Form 4868 tell you how to estimate your tax.

Never simply file a late return without getting an extension. The penalty for filing late without an extension is 5% of the unpaid tax per month, up to a maximum penalty of 25%. There's also a minimum penalty for not getting your tax return in within 60 days of its due date—$100 or 100% of the tax due, whichever is less. You'll also be penalized for paying your taxes late, and you'll be charged interest on the late-paid tax.

Second extensions: It is possible to get a second filing extension from the IRS by filing Form 2688. But the second extension isn't automatic. You must have a valid reason for requesting it, such as a death in the family or loss of your records. A second extension, if granted, gives you an extra two months—until October 15—to file your return.

Checklist: Before Mailing Your Return

Check to make sure you've completed everything on this list. A slipup can cause delays and inconvenience. Moreover, every time you draw attention to your return, you increase the chance of an audit. *Checklist:*

•Do your name, address, and Social Security number appear on page 1? If you used the IRS address label, be sure you have made any necessary corrections.

•Have you put your Social Security number on every page, every document, and every check to be sent to the IRS?

•Are all Form W-2s attached?

•Are all other necessary forms and schedules attached?

•Have you checked and rechecked your arithmetic?

•Is the form signed and dated? Both husband and wife must sign a joint return.

•If you owe money, is your check or money order attached to the return? Have you written your Social Security number on the check? Have you written the year and "Form 1040" on it?

•Is the return addressed to the correct IRS office?

•Have you made a copy of the return for your own records?

Big Tax Refund? You've Done Something Wrong

If you got a fat tax refund this year, don't feel too happy about it. It means you overpaid your estimated taxes or had too much withheld from your salary. In effect, you made an interest-free loan to the government, when you could have been using the money for yourself—in an interest-paying bank account.

Trap: The IRS can withhold all or part of your refund to offset a tax liability, a debt to a government agency (for instance, a student loan), or unpaid child support.

What to do: File a new Form W-4 or W-4A to reduce the amount withheld from your salary. If you pay estimated tax, reduce your quarterly payments.

Caution: Don't overdo it. You can be hit with underpayment penalties unless withholding taxes plus estimated tax payments amount to at least 90% of your total tax bill.

Tax Refunds: The Second Time Around

It's not too late to get a cash refund for past years by filing a Form 1040X with the IRS. Take the time to review old tax returns to see if you overlooked anything that may lead to getting money back.

The time limit for amending your original tax return is three years from the date you filed the original return or two years from the date you actually paid the tax, whichever is later. Early filers are treated as though they had filed on the actual due date of the return.

Caution: Filing an amended return may invite the IRS to take a second look at your original return. If there's anything on it that you think may not pass this additional IRS scrutiny, you should be wary about amending. On the other hand, if you'll get back a significantly larger refund by amending, or you know the IRS can't challenge anything on the original return, it may be worth the risk.

What you can amend...

The most common oversights that eventually lead to an additional refund:

•Filing the wrong form. Short-form filers might well have been able to file a long form and get the benefit of a lower tax bill. But you're not stuck with your original choice. Perhaps you used the short form because you were in a last-minute rush to file the return, or you thought the long form was too difficult. If you file a long form this year but filed a short form for the past two years, check your earlier returns to see if you missed anything.

No matter what your original reason for filing the short form, it is worth taking the time now to see how much you would save by filing the long form.

•Overlooking deductions. As you fill out your return this year, perhaps you will remember deductions that you should have taken in the past. If you forgot to claim an item to which you were entitled, consider amending that year's return.

•Overlooking credits. Taxpayers often forget about or miscalculate certain tax credits. *Carefully review the following on your past returns:*

•Excess Social Security tax paid.

•Child care credit.

•Earned income credit.

•Using the wrong filing status. When a married couple files separately, the overall tax bill is usually larger. If you would have saved taxes by filing jointly, you are allowed to amend your return. However, it doesn't work the other way: Once you've filed a joint return and the due date of the return has passed, you can't change the filing status to married filing separately.

•Overlooking exemptions. If you were supporting a parent who didn't live with you during the year, you may have forgotten to claim him or her as an exemption on your return.

•Neglecting to do five- or 10-year averaging on lump-sum distributions. Many taxpayers forget this special tax saver when they receive a lump sum from their retirement plan and don't expect to roll it over into another plan. If you received such a distribution, make sure you compared your tax liability with five- or 10-year averaging and without it, to see which one produced the lower tax.

•Overpaying Social Security. If you worked for more than one employer in a single year, you may have paid too much Social Security tax. The maximum you must pay changes from year to year, but you can find out the amount by looking at your old returns.

•Neglecting to check for retroactive tax changes. Sometimes the IRS, Congress, and the courts make retroactive decisions that may allow you to take a deduction for something that was disallowed in the past. Keep informed about all tax changes to see if any of them affect your past returns.

Source: John L. Withers, special consultant for IRS regulations and procedures, Deloitte & Touche, Washington Service Center, 1900 M St. NW, Washington, DC 20036.

More Facts on Amended Returns

You can file an amended return or claim a refund on Form 1040X within three years after the original return was due or two years after you actually paid the tax, whichever is later.

The time limits are absolute. If you're even one day late, your claim must be disallowed. Use Form 1040X if you file early and discover an error before April 15. You'll get faster handling.

You can use Form 1045 for claims based on carrybacks (net operating losses, certain credits). This will get you a fast refund, as the IRS must act within 90 days. But the action isn't final. The claim can be disallowed later. Time limits on these claims are figured from the year the carryback arose.

Form 1040X has space to write your income, deductions, and credits as you reported them on your original return and the changes you want to make for those amounts. *Important:* Include explanations for the changes you are making and the year you are amending on page 2. You must calculate the new tax on the corrected amount, just as you would on your regular return.

State all possible grounds. If the matter ever reaches court, you may be limited to the exact claim stated on the form. If, for example, you're not sure whether an item should be claimed as a business loss, a casualty loss, or a bad debt, state all three grounds in the alternative. You can even assert inconsistent grounds.

Where to send it: Mail the amended return to the IRS Service Center where you now live. If you moved during the year, mail it to the Service Center at your new address. Be sure to complete the information on the front of the 1040X about where your original return was processed in order to expedite your return.

Caution: When you amend your federal tax return, your state tax liability from that year may be affected, too.

It's important to assess your audit risk before you amend your return. It depends on how much you'll get back by amending, why you're amending, and the safety of your original return.

Question: Is the amount that you are getting back worth the risk for what you might possibly lose?

Safer amendments:

•Changes of very small dollar amounts, especially where the amount on the original return is very small, too.

• Mathematical changes.

Not-so-safe amendments:

• Any change that has huge tax consequences on your return.

• Tax-shelter losses.

• Losses from business activity.

• Reclassifying ordinary income to capital gain.

How Long Should Tax File Documents Be Kept?

• Normally, tax returns and supporting documents should be kept for three years from date of filing.

• If income previously has been underreported by 25% or more: Six years.

• In cases of previous failure to file or serious suspicion of criminal fraud: Indefinitely.

Suggestion: Put canceled checks and supporting documents into a manila envelope, mark with the tax year and the discard date, and put it on the top shelf of your highest closet. You'll only need this material if you're audited. Returns should be kept in an accessible file drawer.

Source: Stephanie Winston, president of The Organizing Principle, 461 Park Ave. South, New York 10016, and the author of *The Organized Executive.* Warner Books.

Frequently Overlooked Deductions

"Points" paid for mortgage on purchase or improvement of principal residence.

State unemployment and disability taxes withheld.

Expenses related to seminars attended for business purposes. Deductible items include registration fees, travel, lodging and 50% of the cost of meals.

Investment-related expenses:

• Travel expenses to check on income-producing property.

• Cost of telephone, postage, office supplies and automobile operaton (trips to and from broker).

• Books, magazines and newsletters on investment, financial, or tax matters, including appropriate daily papers (e.g., *Wall Street Journal, New York Times*).

• Insurance and storage charges for merchandise held as a speculative investment.

Out-of-pocket expenses incurred in providing charitable services. May deduct actual cost of auto usage, tolls and parking.

Out-of-pocket expenses incurred in changing jobs. Include the cost of printing résumés or traveling to an interview.

A portion of health insurance for the self-employed.

Charitable contributions made through payroll withholdings (e.g., United Way).

Deductible items on December credit card statement, even if paid in the following year, including:

• Medical expenses.

• Charitable contributions.

• Miscellaneous business expenses.

Tax reform note: Employee business expenses and miscellaneous deductions are allowed only to the extent they exceed 2% of adjusted gross income.

Source: Barry Salzberg, CPA, partner in charge of Executive Financing Counseling services with the firm of Deloitte & Touche, 1 World Trade Center, New York 10048.

Tax Return Completion Checklist

In dealings with the IRS, no news is good news. More precisely, in this case, no mail is good news.

Every time the IRS sends a letter to a taxpayer, it means that someone within the service has taken another look at the return in question. Every look taken increases the chance that "problems" will come to light (if they haven't already).

There are a number of simple steps you can take to minimize the risk of ongoing activity with your tax return.

• Before filing, make sure your return is complete. Check to see that all necessary forms and schedules are present and accounted for. This includes any and all attachments (e.g., if you donate common stock to a charitable organization, you must attach a statement of certain information regarding the gift.) Staple your return together securely. Missing pages generate correspondence.

• *Make sure the return is accurate:* Check, double-check, and recheck all arithmetic.

• Make sure your reporting is consistent with the information the IRS receives.

For example, if you have invested in IBM and General Motors stock through XYZ Brokerage, your return should list dividends paid to you by XYZ, not IBM or GM, because the IRS will receive a 1099 form from XYZ.

• Double-check to see that the return is signed by all necessary parties.

• Finally, file your return on time. By all means request an extension if you need one, but mail your return well before the expiration date.

In the event you must file at the last minute, use registered mail in order to have evidence of timely filing.

Source: Ralph C. Ganswindt, partner specializing in closely held businesses, with Arthur Andersen & Company, 777 East Wisconsin Ave., Milwaukee, WI 53201.

Answering Unreported Income Notices

The IRS mails millions of computer generated notices to taxpayers whose returns did not show dividend or interest income as it was reported to the IRS by banks and financial institutions. The notice recalculated the tax due, added interest charges...and imposed a negligence penalty.

How should taxpayers handle such notices? What can they learn from these notices that will help in preparing future returns? Here's the procedure:

First step: Study the notice carefully and define the problem. Discover precisely which item, or items, of income the IRS says you did not report. You'll find this information on a separate page of the multipage notice.

Second step: Review your copy of the return and the 1099 forms you used to fill it out. Determine whether the IRS notice is right or wrong. Never automatically write out a check for the amount the IRS says you owe. The notice could be dead wrong—many are.

Third step: Answer the notice, in writing, within the time limit given—usually 30 days. Write to the IRS Service Center at the address given in the notice.

• If the IRS is right and you did accidentally fail to report an item of income: Pay the tax and interest but ask that the negligence penalty be waived.

Sample letter:

IRS Service Center
City, State

Re: John and Sally Connell
Social Security Nos...
Form 1040-1992

Gentlemen:

In response to your notice, a copy of which is attached, you will find enclosed a check payable to the IRS in the amount of $x, consisting of tax of $y and interest of $z.

The item in question was inadvertently omitted from our return as filed under the following circumstances: (Give the reason for the accidental omission of the income.) It is contended that this constitutes reasonable cause for the inadvertent omission of this item. It is respectfully requested that the negligence penalty assessed in your notice be abated.

Sincerely yours,
John & Sally Connell

• When you did report the income or the notice is otherwise wrong:

Review the notice and your return to discover the cause of the discrepancy. One of several things may have happened. The IRS may be working with an incorrect 1099. Or the 1099 may be right and you reported the income but not as you should have.

Sample letter:

Gentlemen:

In response to your notice, a copy of which is enclosed, I am submitting the following in explanation of the alleged omission. (Examples follow.)

1. The dividend of $1,200 reported on my return as being received from General Motors should have been reported as being received from Merrill Lynch as nominee. A copy of my Schedule B is enclosed. (Circle the item where it appears on your Schedule B to show that you reported it.)

Lesson: Report dividends from stock held in street name by your broker as dividends received from the broker as nominee and not from the company. That's the way the 1099 will show them.

2. Dividend of $400 from Dreyfus Liquid Assets Fund was reported as interest income of $400 from Dreyfus. A copy of my Schedule B is enclosed. (Circle the item.)

Lesson: Most money-market funds report their income as dividends and not as interest. Report the income as it is reported to the IRS on the fund's 1099.

3. Interest of $600 from Citibank was on an account owned jointly by myself and my brother. I reported only one half of the interest—$300. A copy of my Schedule B is enclosed.

Lesson: The correct way to report interest from a joint account would be: "Interest, Citibank, $600, less amount reported by others, $300. Net amount: $300."

4. Interest of $500 from Wells Fargo Bank was reported on my return as $100, per corrected Form 1099, a copy of which is enclosed.

Lesson: Review all 1099s when you receive them. Immediately request corrected copies of any that are wrong. Report the correct information on your return. If the IRS doesn't pick up the correction, you'll have it in your files should you need it.

5. Interest of $2,140 from American National Bank was nontaxable income distributed from my IRA account and immediately reinvested in another IRA. I enclose a copy of a corrected 1099 from American National showing $0 taxable interest in this account.

How to end the letter:

If there are any further questions, please contact me.

• If you get a second notice that seems to have ignored your letter:

Gentlemen:

In response to your notice dated March 28, I received a similar notice dated February 23. I answered the first notice with the enclosed letter. It would appear that my response was not received in time to prevent the second request for payment from being issued. (Enclose photocopies of both notices and a copy of your original letter.)

Sincerely yours,
John & Sally Connell

Some Excuses that Work And Some that Don't

Taxpayers who face penalties for misfiling returns or misreporting income will do the best they can to come up with a good explanation. Some excuses work—others don't.

Excuses that work...

• Reliance on bad IRS advice from an IRS employee or an IRS publication. If the advice came from an employee, you must show that it was his job to advise taxpayers and that you gave him all the facts.

• Bad advice from a tax professional can excuse a mistake if you fully disclosed the facts to the adviser. You must also show that he was a competent professional, experienced in federal tax matters.

• Lost or unavailable records will excuse a mistake if the loss wasn't the taxpayer's fault and he makes a genuine attempt to recover or reconstruct the records.

• Incapacity of a key person can be a legitimate excuse. *Examples:* Serious illness of the taxpayer or a death in his immediate family.

Excuses that don't work...

• Pleading ignorance or misunderstanding of the law generally does not excuse a mistake. *Exception:* Where a tax expert might have made the same mistake.

•Someone else slipped up. You are personally responsible for filing your tax return correctly. You can't delegate that responsibility to anyone else. If your accountant or lawyer files late, for example, you pay the penalty.

•Personal problems don't carry much weight with the IRS. For example, don't expect to avoid a penalty by pleading severe emotional strain brought on by a divorce.

How to Get What You Need from Your Accountant

The biggest mistake people make in dealing with the professionals they hire to work on their tax returns is to drop everything in the professional's lap and walk away. To get the most from your accountant, you must take an active role in the preparation of your returns...even if you pay hundreds of dollars in preparation fees to the most prestigious firm in town. Not only must you help your accountant find everything that will save you tax dollars, but you must also understand how every figure that's reported on the return was arrived at.

•Organize the information. This saves his time and your money.

•Bring to his attention any out-of-the-ordinary deductions...job-hunting expenses, child care or dependent care, unreimbursed business travel, etc.

•Be complete. The more last-minute changes you call in after your return has been prepared, the bigger your bill will be.

•Mention changes in essential personal and financial data. If, for example, you don't tell your accountant that you're supporting aged parents, he isn't likely to know about the dependency exemptions or possible medical deductions for them, or to recommend a multiple-support agreement with your brothers and sisters.

•Discuss your audit tolerance. If you want a return that will save you top tax dollars, you must take aggressive positions on your various financial dealings. The more aggressive you are, the more likely your return will be audited. If you want to cut your audit risk, you must take a more conservative approach to the way you handle your return. You can't have it both ways.

•Assume that your return will be audited. Using a tax professional doesn't lessen that likelihood. Your accountant isn't responsible to the IRS for your return. You are. The IRS auditor will ask you how your charitable contributions were calculated, how your interest was calculated, or when depreciable assets were purchased.

•Keep worksheets detailing the calculations for each figure on your tax return.

Source: Paul N. Strassels, a former IRS tax-law specialist.

Should You File a Joint Or Separate Tax Return?

The effect of a joint tax return is to treat a married couple as one taxpayer, no matter which spouse realized the income. Filing a joint return will usually result in tax savings because the joint return rates are generally more favorable than the rates for married persons filing separately.

•Credit for child care expenses is only available on a joint return.

•Keep in mind that when a couple files a joint return, both parties are liable for the full amount of tax due, regardless of who earned the income.

But there are some advantages to filing separately:

•In community property states, all community income and deductions are reported one-half on each return. This can result in lower tax-bracket filings.

•Some married couples file separate returns so they won't have to disclose to their spouse the source and extent of their earnings.

•Filing separate returns may make sense if one of the spouses has extraordinary medical expenses. These expenses are deductible only to the extent that they exceed 7½% of the combined income of both spouses. Therefore, the smaller income on a separate return might result in a deduction that would be reduced or eliminated on a joint return because of the larger combined income.

• In certain states, the income tax saving from filing separate returns can be greater than the federal tax saving from filing a joint return.

Source: *Tax Hotline,* 55 Railroad Ave., Greenwich, CT 06830.

Before Mailing in A Tax Return

Getting the details right the first time can save the time and trouble of dealing with the IRS later. *Checklist:*

• Sign the return.

• Did your preparer sign?

• Did you answer every question on the return?

• Put your Social Security number on every page and every attachment, including your check.

• Put your tax-shelter registration number on the return.

• Make copies of your return.

• Compare your return with last year's to make sure you didn't overlook anything.

• Put the return away for a few days or a week so that you can look at it with a fresh eye before mailing it.

• Send it by certified mail so there will be no question that your return was filed on time. Mailed on time is considered to be filed on time by the IRS.

• Use a separate envelope for each return.

• Put your children's returns or estimated payments in separate envelopes.

• Attach your W-2.

• Include your check if you owe money to the IRS.

• Include any receipts and forms required to prove your charitable contributions.

• Include a check for the tax you owe if you are filing an extension request.

Top Filing Mistakes... According to the IRS

• Miscalculating medical and dental expenses. This deduction is based on your adjusted gross income—AGI. Carefully complete up to the AGI line on your 1040 before attempting to figure your medical expenses.

• Taking the wrong amount of earned income credit. Use the worksheet in the instruction booklet to avoid mistakes.

• Entering the wrong amount of tax. Use the right tax tables.

• Confusion about income tax withheld. Don't confuse this with the Social Security tax that was withheld from your pay.

• Unemployment compensation errors. Use the special formula in the IRS instruction booklet to calculate the amount of taxable unemployment.

• Mistakes in calculating child and dependent care expenses. Use Form 2441 and double-check your math.

• Errors in tax due. Believe it or not, taxpayers often err in determining the bottom line of their tax return—are they entitled to a refund or do they owe the IRS? Carefully compare the tax you owe with the amount you have paid through withholding or estimated tax payments.

• Overlooking credits. Read all IRS instructions carefully.

• Adding income incorrectly. Mistakes are frequently made by taxpayers when adding the income section of Form 1040.

Source: *IRS Publication No. 910.*

Filing Late

Reasons for getting an extension:

• You don't have all the information you need to fill out the return.

• You need time to find the cash to make a contribution to your Keogh account. (Unlike IRAs, which must be made by April 15, Keogh contributions can be made up to the extended due date of your return—as late as October 15.)

• You have a complicated transaction that you need time to ponder.

Timetable:

• First extension. April 15 is the due date for tax returns. But you can get an automatic four-month extension by filing Form 4868 by April 15. If you pay late you'll owe late-payment penalties, plus interest on the tax paid late. *Trap:* You must make estimated tax payments on Form 1040-ES by April 15. You can't get an extension of time to make quarterly estimated payments.

• Second extension. It's possible to get a second filing extension of two months. But the second extension isn't automatic; you must have a valid reason for requesting it, such as a death in the family or loss of your records. *Loophole:* It has been my experience that the closer you file to October 15 (after August 15) the less chance there is that you'll be audited. A second extension may be the way to get off the audit treadmill if you've been audited every year for the last few years.

Source: Edward L. Mendlowitz, partner, Mendlowitz Weitsen, New York.

To Avoid Late-Filing Penalties

A person who files a late tax return without getting a prior extension faces stiff penalties. It's possible to avoid these penalties, but you must convince the IRS that you had a good excuse for filing late.

Situations in which the IRS has said it may accept a late return without penalty:

• The return was postmarked on time, even if it had insufficient postage.

• The return was filed on time but in the wrong IRS district or office.

• The return was filed late because of inaccurate information received from an IRS employee.

• A filing delay was caused by the destruction of the taxpayer's records in a fire, flood or other casualty.

• An individual couldn't get proper tax forms from the IRS, in spite of asking for them at a reasonable time.

• The filer was not able to get necessary information from an IRS official, despite a personal visit to an IRS office.

• The taxpayer died, was seriously injured or was forced to be away from home for a reason that was unexpected and beyond his or her control.

• The taxpayer was ignorant of the law, in that he or she never had to file a particular kind of form or return before.

• The death or illness of an immediate family member.

• Incapacitating illness of the taxpayer himself.

• A competent and informed tax adviser told the taxpayer that a tax return was not necessary.

How to proceed: Make your request for abatement of the penalty in writing to your local IRS Service Center. Give a detailed explanation of your reason for filing late. Use the term "reasonable cause" both at the beginning and the end of the letter. To speed up the process, attach your letter to the return you are filing late. Don't wait until you get a penalty notice—that could take months.

Not-So-Safe Amendments

Filing an amended return to take a deduction for the following may result in an audit because of the high susceptibility of these items to audit:

• Travel and entertainment expenses.

• Unreimbursed business expenses.

• Casualty losses.

• Transactions with relatives.

• Charitable donations of property.

• Home office deductions.

Audit Triggers

Red flags most likely to bring on an audit:

• Deductions that are excessively high in relation to your income. A return that shows $50,000 of income and $40,000 of itemized deductions is almost certain to be pulled for an audit. Keep your deductions reasonable. But don't cheat yourself just because you're afraid of an audit. Attach an explanation to your return for an item that you believe the IRS may question. When your return gets kicked out of the computer that screens all returns for possible audit, an IRS official will read your explanation. If he's satisfied, he will probably put the return back into the processing system without sending it on to be audited.

• Undocumented charitable gifts. Attach a statement to your return showing the date of all property contributions, the fair market value, and the name of the charity. If you don't automatically supply this statement, the IRS will pull your return to look for it—increasing your chance of audit. You must now attach an independent appraisal for charitable gifts of property worth more than $5,000.

• Overstated casualty losses. Many audits are triggered because taxpayers exceeded the legal limits on casualty-loss deductions. Use the IRS worksheet, Form 4684. You can deduct only the part of your loss that exceeds 10% of your adjusted gross income. And then you deduct only the lesser of what you paid for the item or the decrease in its value as a result of the casualty.

• Overstated medical deductions. To be deductible, medical expenses must exceed 7½% of your adjusted gross income.

• Tax shelters with very large losses. These almost always trigger an audit. Avoid tax shelters unless you get professional advice. Make sure it's a legitimate shelter.

• Inclusion of Schedule C. Self-employed individuals must file a Schedule C with their tax returns. It shows all business-related income and deductions. *Warning:* It is also a red flag for an audit. Prepare it carefully, and have the records to back it up.

• Home-office deductions. These must meet stringent IRS guidelines. The office must be used regularly and exclusively for business purposes. If your family watches television there when it's not in use as an office, you lose the deduction. The office must be your principal place of business. If you have an office at the company where you are employed, you can't deduct the home office. But if you freelance in a different business at night, the office is deductible.

• Overstated business expenses. The IRS will scrutinize these deductions. Keep your travel and entertainment deductions reasonable. (And be very careful to stay within the tax law's limits for deducting your business car and computer.)

• Sloppy returns. Simple errors cause many tax returns to be kicked out of the IRS computers This means the chances for audit are greater because the return is now in human hands. *Don't make these mistakes on your return:*

• Errors in simple mathematics.

• Failure to transfer totals correctly from one page to the next.

• Use of the wrong rate tables for your filing status (single, joint, head of household, etc.).

• Failure to follow IRS instructions.

• Failure to answer all questions. A blank space where there should be an answer will wake up the computer.

• Failure to attach W-2s or other required statements.

Source: Michael L. Borsuk, tax partner and managing partner of the Long Island office of Coopers & Lybrand, Melville, NY.

Most Frequently Overlooked Job-Related Deductions

• Moving expenses incurred to get a new job, including the cost of selling your residence and getting out of your lease.

• Job-hunting expenses, including the cost of typing or printing a résumé, employment agency fees, etc.

• Professional magazines related to your job.

• Work- or business-related educational expenses that don't qualify you for a new trade or business.

• Transportation necessary for medical care. You can deduct your actual expenses or a standard mileage rate of 10¢ per mile, plus parking fees and tolls in either case.

•Traveling expenses to a second job, if you go directly from the first job to the second.

•Business gifts up to $25.

How to Avoid the 2% Floor for Miscellaneous Deductions

Miscellaneous itemized deductions include expenses directly connected with the production of investment income, such as...

1. Fees for managing investment property.
2. Legal and professional fees.
3. Fees for tax preparation and advice, investment advice and financial planning.

Problem: Most taxpayers are unable to deduct any investment expenses on Schedule A because their total miscellaneous expenses don't exceed 2% of their adjusted gross income.

Solution: Put as many expenses as possible out of reach of the 2% floor by accounting for them elsewhere on your return. *Possibilities:*

•Schedule C. Report non-wage miscellaneous income such as that earned from consulting, lecturing, or speaking engagements, on Schedule C as business income, rather than as "other income" on the 1040. The expenses you incur in producing that income are deductible on Schedule C, where they are not subject to the 2% floor.

•Schedule E. Expenses of earning rent, royalties, or other income that is reportable on Schedule E are deductible on Schedule E, where they are not subject to the 2% floor.

•Adjust the cost of assets. Add the expenses of acquiring a capital asset to the asset's cost. This will reduce the amount of capital gain you must report when you eventually sell. While this approach doesn't give you a current deduction for the expense, it does reduce the tax you pay on the gain.

•Bunch payment of expenses so that you get two years' worth into one year and exceed the 2% floor in at least one year.

Source: Richard Lager, national director of tax practice, Grant Thornton, CPAs 1850 M St. NW, Washington, DC 20036.

Most Frequently Overlooked Real Estate Deductions

•Points, also called loan origination fees, paid for obtaining a mortgage on your principal residence. They must be a customary practice in your area.

•Mortgage prepayment penalties.

•Real estate taxes. If you sold your home during the year, don't forget the portion you paid while you still owned the house.

•Your proportion of co-op or condo real estate taxes.

If You Can't Pay Your Taxes

Most creditors must have a court order before they can seize your property. All that's required of the IRS is that it present you with a bill for unpaid tax and wait 10 days. After that, if you still haven't paid, it can seize your bank accounts, garnish your wages, and even sell your house. Fortunately, the IRS seizes property only as a last resort in the collection process. Before invoking its enforcement powers, the IRS generally gives financially strapped taxpayers a chance to try to work out a payment agreement.

Here's how to proceed when there's no cash to pay the bill:

•File a tax return. The worst thing you can do when you owe the IRS money is not file a tax return. Owing money to the IRS that you simply can't pay is not a crime. The IRS can't put you in jail for not having the money. But it is a crime not to file a tax return—a crime for which you can go to jail. By filing, you also avoid the big penalties for late filing. If you don't get your return in on time (or don't have a valid extension), you'll incur a late-filing penalty of 5% a month (or any fraction of a month), up to a maximum of 25% of the tax you owe.

•Pay what you can when you file your return. Keep to a minimum your penalties for late payment and interest on the tax you owe.

•Six to eight weeks after you've filed, you'll get a bill for the unpaid balance. The bill will include interest and penalties. Don't ignore it. If you're still short of money, arrange a meeting at your local IRS office to work out an installment-payment arrangement.

•Be prepared to submit a financial statement showing that you don't have assets that can be liquidated to pay your tax. Don't expect the IRS to give you extra time to pay if you have certificates of deposit in the bank that you simply don't want to cash in early.

•Go easy on the hard-luck stories when asking for an installment arrangement. The IRS has heard them all. Concentrate on negotiating, in a businesslike manner, a series of monthly payments that you'll be able to manage.

•When you give the IRS an analysis of your monthly income and expenses, show that there's money left over for tax payments. If you come up broke each month, the IRS will be less inclined to agree to installment payments. Where will you find the money to make the payments?

•The IRS likes to see a tax bill paid up in a year or less. If you can figure out a way to pay the debt in less than a year, you have a better shot at getting an installment agreement than if you say you need five years to pay.

•File all your delinquent tax returns before you negotiate an installment agreement. Establish all your tax liabilities, and have them all covered by the agreement. *Trap:* If you agree to a payment plan for one year and then get a bill for other years' back taxes, you'll be in default on the agreement. The IRS will then demand payment in full.

•Never miss a payment without first talking to a revenue officer. You're technically in default of the agreement when you miss just one payment. And when you're in default, you have to start over again, trying to negotiate a new agreement.

•If you can't make a payment: Meet with a revenue officer. Explain the unusual circumstances that make it impossible for you to pay and hope that the officer will alter the terms of your agreement.

Source: Randy Bruce Blaustein, Esq., partner, Blaustein & Greenberg, New York, and author of *How to Do Business With the IRS.* Prentice-Hall, Inc.

Negotiation Tactics

•Provide only the information requested. *For an office audit:* Take with you only the documentation relating to the requested items.

•If the agent requests support for other items, suggest, diplomatically, that since this would require yet another meeting, perhaps such information could be mailed in.

•Involve a supervisor only if necessary. If you've reached an impasse—because of an honest disagreement or a personality conflict—enlist the agent's help by asking, "Would you discuss this with your supervisor?" Communicate through—not around—the agent.

•Avoid a change of agents, if possible. You'll avoid the double audit that results from starting afresh.

•Know your appeal rights, and let the agent know that you do. Use this knowledge to achieve agreements. Agents like to close cases "agreed."

•Sign an agreement form only if you truly agree with all the proposed adjustments. Never allow yourself to cave in to pressure. If unsure, ask for time to consider and to consult your tax adviser.

Dealing Personally With the IRS

Taxpayers sometimes choose to deal personally with the IRS on routine matters. Here are some pointers to help you deal productively with the Service:

•Be prepared. It's to your advantage to organize and summarize all requested information. Have an adding machine tape to show how you calculated each questioned deduction. This will expedite the review and let the reviewer know you're in control.

• Be honest. Don't try to disguise a problem area, such as lack of certain types of documentation. Never risk arousing IRS suspicion. *Best:* Explain the problem in terms of what proof you have. If that's not sufficient, then ask if you can gather additional proof to satisfy the IRS.

• Be businesslike. Use good-sense rules of courtesy and tact in your dealings with the IRS.

• Be prudent. Limit your involvement to nontechnical, routine matters. Do only what, and as much as, you feel comfortable doing. *Alarm bells:* Uncertainty, anxiety, frustration and anger are the signs that professional help is needed.

• Office audits held at a local IRS office—are typically used to determine if income and deductions claimed are properly supported by documentation. They are usually limited to several items, and are not likely to involve technical or legal issues.

• Field audits—held at the taxpayer's business and/or residence are generally used to scrutinize a variety of IRS concerns—in many cases related to business returns—often involving technical or legal issues. Discuss how best to handle such an audit with your tax adviser. In most cases, it's wise to have your adviser represent you at the audit.

Source: Roy B. Harrill, tax partner in charge of firm-wide practice for IRS procedures and administration, Arthur Andersen & Co., Chicago.

Keeping It Simple

When you mail your tax return to the IRS each year, do not include any other tax filings that you may owe the IRS that are not directly related to your return. In one recent case, a taxpayer included an important nonreturn filing with his return to save postage—and the IRS said it never got it. A court eventually ruled for the taxpayer, after describing an IRS computer log of filed documents as an incomprehensible maze of figures without any legend. But it is much safer to keep things simple for the IRS by sending evey filing in a separate envelope, requesting a certified mail delivery receipt for each filing you send.

Filing Safety

When you mail your tax return to the IRS this April 15 be sure you correctly fill out the certified mail receipt you will keep as proof of filing. When a taxpayer miscopied two digits of an envelope number onto a receipt and the numbers didn't match, the court rejected the receipt as proof of filing.

More Time to Claim a Refund

When a tax is paid through several partial payments, the full amount of the tax is deemed paid when the very last payment is made, according to a recent court decision. This is especially important if you later decide you are entitled to a refund of the tax. *Why:* You can claim a refund of the full tax within a statute-of-limitations period computed from the date of the last payment—even if the limitations period has expired as to earlier installment payments.

Levy Lifted when Notice Mismailed

An individual argued that an IRS levy was invalid because the notice of levy had been sent to the wrong address. The IRS said that the notice had been properly sent to the address shown on the individual's tax return, but he objected that he had since moved. *Court:* The address on the tax return is the proper mailing address when it is the IRS's last known address for a taxpayer, even if the taxpayer has moved. But here the taxpayer had told the IRS of his move, and the IRS had sent letters on other matters to his new address. Thus, the notice hadn't been sent to the last known address, and was invalid.

Extension Save

Paul E. Harper requested a filing extension for his tax return. On it he estimated that he owed no further taxes for the year, and he made no payment when he filed it. When it turned out that he still owed more than $90,000 in taxes for the year, the IRS retroactively revoked the extension and imposed late filing penalties. *Court:* Mr. Harper had relied upon an accountant to prepare the extension, and the accountant had underestimated the tax still due because full business records for the year weren't yet available—which was why the extension had been requested. The extension had been filed in good faith, so it was valid.

Invalid Alterations

The IRS asked Joseph Monti for extra time to examine his return, so he proposed terms for an extension. The IRS changed the terms in its favor, then sent an extension to Mr. Monti with a cover letter saying it had been prepared as per your request. Mr. Monti signed the form and returned. The IRS then found a typographical error in the expiration date of the extension and corrected it, giving itself even more time for the audit. *Court:* The IRS's behavior in altering the extension without informing Mr. Monti was inexplicable. The extension was invalid and the audit deadline had passed, so Mr. Monti was free from the potential tax.

Measure Your Audit Risk

Divide the total amount of itemized deductions you claim on Line 28 of your Schedule A by your Adjusted Gross Income on Line 31 of your 1040 tax return. If the ratio is...

...*less than 0.35*, you are in the "safe" zone—your risk of an audit is only one in 10,000.

...*0.35 to 0.44*, you are in the "caution zone," at some increased risk.

...*more than 0.44*, you are a prime candidate for an audit—your risk is about one in 10.

If you file a Schedule C reporting self-employment income, divide your total expenses reported on Line 28 by your gross income reported on Line 7. A ratio of...

...*0.52 to 0.63* puts you in the caution zone.

...*more than 0.63* puts you in the high-risk group.

Insight: It is the *total amount* of your deductions, rather than the size of any particular deduction, that has the greatest impact on your audit risk.

Source: Amir Aczel, PhD, associate professor of statistics, Bently College, Waltham, Massachusetts, and author of *How to Beat the IRS at Its Own Game.* Four Walls Eight Windows.

Tax Break for Retiring Business Owners

When one of the owners of a private business decides to retire or leave the firm, he/she is likely to cash out some of his interest in the business through a stock redemption—by selling his stock back to the company.

Snag: Under general rules, partial redemptions are taxed as *dividends*—so capital gains treatment does *not* apply, and the proceeds of the redemption are taxed at ordinary rates as high as 39.6%.

To the rescue: It *is* possible to obtain capital gains treatment—and a top 28% tax rate—for the gain on the redemption. *How:* By selling the individual's *entire* interest in the business.

Caution: Special rules apply when the remaining shareholders are family members.

Best: Plan any stock redemption to take place as part of one's *full* retirement, in a clean break with the company. Tax savings can be significant.

Source: John N. Evans, tax partner in charge of the Enterprise Group, Arthur Andersen LLP, 1345 Avenue of the Americas, New York 10105.

18

Staying Healthy

About Your Immune System

The immune system can be compromised by many things—from an ordinary cold to deadly cancers. That's the bad news.

The good news is that your immune defenses regularly repair themselves, and there are simple measures you can take to assist them when they have been breached.

Basically, your immune system is a thriving swarm of billions of white blood cells, all with just two goals...

- Recognize germ invaders.
- Respond to the threat.

When bacteria enter your body—for instance, through that razor nick you got yesterday—specialized cells called neutrophils rush to the scene to virtually devour the marauders. Other cells soon come by to clean up any bacterial fragments.

Against viruses—which are more insidious than bacterial infections because they sneak into our cells and commandeer them for their own evil purposes—your immune system dispatches antibodies to tackle the attacking aliens.

More important, your immune system has memory cells that look at the viral perpetrators and remember those particular villains for the rest of your life. When antibodies recognize and defeat a virus, your system has established an immunity.

Vaccines and medications may be thought of, in a sense, as backups that assist a person when the immune system is overloaded.

There are a lot of microscopic threats out there. But, don't worry. We have plenty of memory cells—enough to recall every virus, bacteria, or toxin that is in existence.

Why it fails...

Without an immune system, even the mildest infection would be lethal. Under normal circumstances, our immune system serves us admirably. When it does malfunction, it is usually for one good reason or another...

•Stress. Chronic, unrelieved stress is probably the most severe threat to your immune system. Along with depression, grief, and anxiety, stress can trigger chemical changes, stimulating the release of neuropeptides, which adversely affect the operation of your immune system.

•Exertion extremes. Moderate exercise is necessary for basic health, of course, and that includes maintaining a healthy immune system. But, too much exertion—for instance, marathon running, mountain climbing in arctic conditions, or other such strenuous activities—has been shown to temporarily depress immune system functions.

•Malnutrition. The relationship between nutrition and the immune system is still a puzzle. We do know, though, that those with poor diets are more susceptible to illness and infections, increasing the burden on their immune systems.

•Rapid and excessive weight loss, through quirky diets or periods of starvation, also drastically reduces your immune system's effectiveness.

It is natural to want to keep your immune system operating at its peak efficiency. Remember, though, that it has gotten you this far without much attention. As with a smoothly running computer, tinkering with your immune system can do more harm than good.

Routine maintenance...

•Keep stress at a reasonable level. Stress reduction is critical for your immune system to function well. If you're not addressing this common problem, make it a health-care priority.

•Vaccinations. These are key to preventing "sneak attacks" on your immune system. Follow the vaccination schedule your child's pediatrician recommends. You may be due for a tetanus booster yourself. When traveling internationally, seek medical advice on specific vaccinations you may need.

•Follow a balanced diet. Sustaining a fit immune system is another good reason for healthy eating. But, avoid the temptation to "boost" immunity defenses through fad diets or the currently popular vitamin or mineral therapy. Such self-treatment can have serious consequences. Large doses of iron, for example, can cause dangerous digestive tract problems. And, while vitamin A is crucial to combat infections, massive supplemental doses can actually suppress vital immune functions.

•Follow your physician's advice exactly when you are ill. Take *all* medication prescribed, especially antibiotics, which we tend to discontinue using immediately after symptoms disappear.

Give your immune system time to fight your illness and recover afterward. Finally, realize that we often have unrealistic expectations for our health. A few colds a year is not a sign that something is wrong with your lifestyle. Being sick occasionally is just a part of being alive. Thanks to your immune system, so is getting well.

•Stay happy. Just as depression and anxiety can adversely affect all aspects of your health, a happy and optimistic outlook will contribute to a healthier immune system. Recent studies show that this may not be entirely psychological, but may have a neurological basis as well.

Source: David S. McKinsey, MD, codirector of epidemiology and infectious diseases at the Research Medical Center, 2316 E. Meyer, Kansas City, Missouri 64132.

Diseases Humans Get from Pets

The same household pets that raise our spirits can also transmit diseases—some serious and potentially deadly—to us. *The most common of these diseases are...*

•Cat-scratch fever. This usually mild infection—caused by a bacterium found on the claws of cats—produces swelling and inflammation in the area around the scratch. It usually goes away without treatment.

To avoid trouble: Clean cat scratches carefully. Your doctor will probably prescribe a course of antibiotics to clear up persistent symptoms.

•Lyme disease. This tick-borne bacterial infection can be carried by dogs, cats, horses, etc. and passed to their owners. It is easily cured with antibiotics—*if it's detected early.*

Late detection can result in severe—and permanent—neurological problems and arthritis.

To avoid trouble: Keep pet dogs and cats as tick-free as possible. Check your body for ticks after each venture into tick-infested areas. See a doctor immediately if you develop fever and a bull's-eye rash around a bite.

•Plague. Although this potentially deadly infection is rare, an Arizona man recently died of pneumonic plague. He caught it by breathing the same air of an infected cat that he pulled from a crawlspace.

There are actually three kinds of plague, depending on which part of the body is infected...*pneumonic plague* affects the lungs, *bubonic* the lymph nodes and *septicemic* the bloodstream. Bubonic plague and septicemic plague are usually spread by the bites of fleas from cats and rodents, but pneumonic plague is often spread through the air.

To avoid trouble: See a doctor at once if you develop a high and persistent fever in conjunction with badly swollen lymph glands—or with difficulties in breathing.

•Psittacosis. Caused by a bacterium found in the droppings of parrots, parakeets, pigeons and turkeys, this illness produces coughing, shortness of breath, fever, and other pneumonia-like symptoms.

To avoid trouble: Bird owners who develop these symptoms should see a doctor. Persistent symptoms can usually be cleared up with a course of antibiotics.

•Rabies. The disease remains a real threat. Rabies is frequently transmitted to humans when pets, bitten by infected wild animals, bite their owners.

To avoid trouble: Make sure your pet is fully immunized, especially if rabid wild animals have been spotted in your area. Alert your local health department of any domestic or wild animal that behaves oddly, attacks without provocation, or foams at the mouth.

Helpful: If a person is bitten by an animal not known to have been immunized against rabies, the animal must be captured and tested for rabies. Otherwise, the bite victim must undergo the standard four-shot series of immunizations.

•Rocky Mountain Spotted Fever. Like Lyme disease, this ailment is tick-borne and is easily cured with antibiotics. But Rocky Mountain Spotted Fever is sometimes fatal.

To avoid trouble: Again, keep dogs and cats tick-free, and check yourself after venturing into the outdoors. See a doctor immediately if you develop a fever and body rash in conjunction with headaches and muscle pain.

•Toxoplasmosis. Spread by microscopic parasites found in cat feces, this relatively uncommon disease produces, in most cases, a mild flu-like illness that clears up without treatment.

Exception: Toxoplasmosis that develops during pregnancy. It can cause *spontaneous* miscarriage or serious health problems in the newborn, including jaundice, seizures, high fevers—even birth defects and mental retardation.

For a safe pregnancy: Wash your hands carefully after handling cat litter. If swollen glands or a fever develops, see your doctor and have your blood tested for toxoplasmosis.

Source: Evan Bell, MD, an infectious disease specialist in private practice in New York City, where he is affiliated with Lenox Hill Hospital.

Genetic Predisposition to Heart Disease or Cancer

If there is a history of heart disease or cancer in your family, there's a straightforward way to cut your risk by up to 90%, no matter how strong your genetic predisposition to these killers.

Like many American families, my family was hard hit by heart disease.

My father was just 12 years old when his father died of a heart attack...and I was only 22 when the same fate befell my dad. By the time I reached my mid-30s, I too seemed headed for an early death. I was overweight, I had Type II diabetes and my cholesterol level was elevated. According to the statistics of the Framingham heart study, my risk of a heart attack was 175% of normal. ("Normal" in our society is a 75% chance of having a heart attack in one's lifetime.)

I decided to try to cut my disease risk by adopting the 30%-fat diet recommended by the American Heart Association. *Problem:* The diet had little effect on my excess weight, diabetes and cholesterol levels.

Reversing the inevitable...

At this point, I immersed myself in scientific literature and developed an alternative approach to this problem. I cut my fat intake all the way down to 10% of calories and adopted a program of regular exercise and stress control. In a few months I lost 45 pounds, my diabetes vanished and my cholesterol level fell so low that my risk of heart attack wasn't just normal, it was below that of someone with no family history of heart disease. My risk of heart disease fell 97%.

Bonus: I felt more relaxed and energetic than I had in years.

Here are the most common questions people ask me...

What exactly is involved with your "10% solution"? Several things. First, regular aerobic exercise. I recommend working out at least four times a week, for at least 45 minutes each time. Next, stress control. Learn to strike a balance between self, friends, family, and work. Stop smoking. Get plenty of sleep. *Note:* I don't mean to gloss over these nondietary recommendations because they're all-important. But the issue of fat intake is more critical—and more often misunderstood.

What's it like to eat a 10%-fat diet? Most people think it must be terribly Spartan. In fact, while you will have to eliminate certain foods from your diet, you can continue to enjoy many of the foods you currently eat. The key is learning the subtle art of food substitution.

Illustration: A meal of broiled chicken, peas in a cream sauce, baked potato with sour cream and a dish of ice cream contains a whopping 55 grams of fat. But a similar meal of baked skinless chicken, steamed peas, baked potato with nonfat sour cream, and a dish of nonfat frozen yogurt contains only nine grams. Once you get used to low-fat eating, this meal is just as satisfying—and much more healthful.

But I love fatty foods. I don't think I have the willpower to eat as you recommend. What can I do? Oddly enough, while it's quite hard to eat a little less fat, it's actually quite easy to eat a lot less.

Reason: If you cut back only to, say, 20% or 30% fat, your appetite for rich, fatty foods never goes away. Consequently, every meal becomes a test of your willpower. But after five to six weeks on a 10%-fat diet, your taste buds actually begin to change. Fatty foods you once enjoyed will begin to taste too greasy while foods that once seemed impossibly bland will become tastier. *Bonus:* Because you'll be eating so little fat, you'll easily lose excess weight—while never feeling hungry or deprived.

Are any foods prohibited? I divide foods into three categories—those to eat as often as you like, those to eat occasionally and those to avoid.

Emphasize...

- Breads made without oils, butter or margarine and any other whole grains or grain products.
- Pasta made without oil or eggs.
- Cereals free of fat, salt, or sugar.
- Fruits, fruit juices, and vegetables (except avocados and olives, which are too fatty).
- Peas, beans, lentils, and other legumes.
- Nonfat dairy products.
- Tofu and other soy products.
- Egg whites.
- Lean meats, preferably fish or fowl. Up to 4 ounces daily of fish, clams, oysters or mussels or white meat of chicken or turkey (without skin). If you want red meat, choose round steak, flank steak, or other lean cuts.

Eat occasionally...

- Sugar, sucrose, molasses, and other sweeteners.
- Breads and cereals made with added fat.
- Pastas made with eggs.
- Low-sodium soy sauce.
- Low-fat dairy products (one-percent fat).
- Olive or canola oil...use very sparingly.
- Caffeinated drinks...no more than two cups daily.
- Lobster, crab, and shrimp. They contain too much cholesterol to be eaten regularly.
- Smoked or charbroiled foods. They contain a potent carcinogen.

Never eat...

- Fatty meats, including organs, cold cuts, and most cuts of beef and pork. Poultry skin is pure fat.
- Meat fat, butter, hydrogenated vegetable oils, lard, and margarine.

• Nondairy creamers and other sources of tropical oils like palm or coconut.

• Mayonnaise.

• Polyunsaturated fat, including corn oil and most vegetable oils.

• Whole dairy products, including cream, whole milk, and sour cream.

• Nuts (except chestnuts, which may be eaten regularly).

• Salt or salty foods.

• Egg yolks.

• Fried foods.

How can I tell how much fat I'm getting? At first you'll need to keep a food diary. Jot down the calorie and fat content of each food you eat. At the end of each day, calculate the all-important fat percentage.

Procedure: Multiply your total daily intake of fat (in grams) by nine (the number of calories in each fat gram), then divide this number by your total daily calories. If this number is above 10%, you must find ways to cut out more fat. After several weeks, you'll be able to judge your fat intake without using the diary.

How about polyunsaturated fats? Margarine, corn oil, and other sources of polyunsaturated fat have long been touted as safe alternatives to saturated fats. In fact, they are far less healthful than once thought—and may be more harmful than saturated fats.

Recent finding: Polyunsaturated fat not only raises levels of LDL (bad) cholesterol, but also reduces levels of HDL (good) cholesterol. And now it looks as if polyunsaturated fat promotes the growth of cancer cells.

Cancer rates in the US began to rise just about the time polyunsaturated fats began to replace saturated fats in the American diet. *To be safe:* Limit your intake of all fats—saturated and polyunsaturated fats in particular.

Are there any immediate benefits to eating less fat? Absolutely. Each time you eat a fatty meal, your red blood cells become "sticky." They clump together, moving slowly through the circulatory system and clogging up capillaries. This deprives your brain of oxygen, resulting in grogginess. But when you stop eating such meals, your red cells return to normal, and your capillaries open up. *Result:* You feel calmer and more energetic, you sleep better and your complexion improves. And at the same time a subtler but even more important change is taking place within your body. The fatty plaques inside your arteries shrink and your immune system grows stronger.

Doesn't a vegetable-rich diet raise your intake of pesticide residues? No. The pesticide content of fruits and vegetables is well below that of meat—which comes from animals raised on pesticide-sprayed crops. But to minimize your intake of potential toxins, buy organic produce.

Source: Raymond Kurzweil, chairman of Kurzweil Applied Intelligence, a Waltham, Massachusetts–based computer manufacturer. He is the author of *The 10% Solution for a Healthy Life: How to Eliminate Virtually All Risk of Heart Disease and Cancer,* Crown Publishers, 201 E. 50 St., New York 10022.

What a Good Dermatologist Does

Dermatologic emergencies are rarer than other types of medical emergencies, but as anyone who's ever suffered a sudden rash or allergic reaction knows, they're not unheard of.

For this reason, a good dermatologist is accessible 24-hours-a-day, seven days a week—preferably via a professional answering service (answering machines are sometimes unreliable). *Rule:* After-hours calls should be returned within four hours.

Of course, accessibility isn't the only mark of a good dermatologist. *Other considerations:*

• Proper delegation of work. As a cost-cutting measure, some dermatologists are now leaving much of their routine office work to nurses or assistants. *Problem:* Assistants may lack the training to perform these procedures safely and effectively.

I believe nurses can safely take patient histories, check blood pressure, change dressings and perform the most basic procedures, such as opening pimples and administering ultraviolet treatments.

The bulk of work, however, including chemical peels and collagen injections, should be performed by the dermatologist. You're paying for a dermatologist's expertise...don't let yourself be exploited.

•Institutional affiliation. Besides being certified by the American Board of Dermatology, first-rate dermatologists are affiliated with a medical school or major hospital—or both. Such institutional affiliations confirm that the dermatologist is a skilled practitioner, up-to-date on the latest methods of diagnosis and treatment. It also indicates that he/she is in good standing within the medical community.

Bonus: If necessary, patients of a hospital-affiliated dermatologist can often get admitted to the hospital faster and with fewer headaches than patients of an unaffiliated practitioner.

•Medical philosophy. By the time certain forms of skin cancer are detected, it is often too late—they've spread and become fatal. Therefore, it's absolutely essential that dermatologists stress preventive care.

However, simply urging patients to wear sunscreen or avoid the sun is not enough. A top-notch dermatologist listens to patients' questions, then explains all aspects of prevention—how the sun damages the skin, for example, and how best to use protective clothing and sunscreen.

As an extra precaution, your dermatologist should offer a total surface examination of your skin. Such an exam, performed periodically, catches melanoma and other dangerous lesions in their earliest stages—when treatment is still effective.

Cost: $115 to $125 (often included in the price of a routine office visit). *Note:* Surface exams should be performed annually on adults with especially fair skin, every three years or so on those with darker skin. Your dermatologist should suggest what's most appropriate for you.

•Cost-consciousness. Like most doctors, dermatologists receive free drug samples from pharmaceutical salespeople. A thoughtful practitioner passes these samples along to patients, saving patients the needless expense and aggravation of filling their own prescriptions.

Source: Neal B. Schultz, MD, a dermatologist in private practice in New York City. Dr. Schultz is on staff at Mt. Sinai Hospital and Lenox Hill Hospital in New York City.

New and Healthier Way Of Looking at Life

Heart disease, cancer, AIDS, and other life-threatening illnesses bring pain and suffering, to be sure. But they can also serve as a "wake-up" call, bringing a new and healthier way of looking at life...of distinguishing that which truly matters in life from mere distractions.

Of course, it's best to learn these invaluable lessons before you're diagnosed with a life-threatening illness...

•Don't be afraid to show your vulnerabilities. Almost all of us were raised to be strong in the face of adversity, to put on a "brave front" no matter what. *Problem:* Acting one way when we're feeling another way saps our vitality, leaving us vulnerable to depression and illness and resentful of the world. We wind up with few friends and little support to help us through life's inevitable crises.

Better way: Admit your frailties. If you feel you need help, ask for it—and be willing to help others.

Exercise: Next time someone asks how you're doing, admit your true feelings. If you feel fine, say so. But if you feel lousy, admit it. Being honest might be hard at first, but it paves the way to honest, caring communication. That's essential for good health and happiness.

•Relinquish your need to be in control. As a young doctor, I thought the key to life was to get things done. My daily routine involved jotting down and then ticking off entries on "to-do" lists. When I failed to get everything done, I got nervous and frustrated.

As I grew older and got in closer touch with my feelings, I came to realize that life is inherently disorderly. Now I know that living well means forgetting about rigid schedules. It means learning to find happiness, fulfillment, and tranquility in the face of disorder.

Lesson: Stop trying to control all situations. Don't be a slave to your intellect. Make plans, but don't be upset by redirection. Something good may come of this redirection.

•Learn how to say "no." Our parents and teachers taught us that it's rude to say "no" to others. So when people ask for favors or tell us how to behave, we give in to their wishes.

Danger: Saying "yes" when you'd rather say "no" may be good manners, but it's destructive to our health. Doing so keeps us in unfulfilling jobs and makes us bitter. It leads us to do things we detest, and it distracts us from the things we cherish. We wind up resentful and possibly ill.

Better way: Stand up for yourself. If you don't want to mow the lawn, pursue a particular career, etc.—don't do it. I'm not asking you to be selfish or needlessly rude. I'm merely asking you to have enough self-esteem to stand up for yourself, to pursue life on your own terms, to realize that you can say "no" when someone asks you to change your plans.

• Confront your fears. People in crisis often seek peace of mind by burying or denying their fears. But real peace of mind comes only when we confront our fears head-on.

What to do: First, define exactly what it is you're afraid of. Don't say, "I'm afraid of dying." Be specific.

• Are you afraid of pain?

• Or what a medical treatment might do to you?

• Or that no one will take care of you?

Once you've pinned down your exact fear, find a metaphor for it. I tell patients to imagine their fear as a tiny baby crying in a crib. I tell them to pick up the baby, caress him/her and see what happens. This exercise shows people that they're distinct from their fears and suggests that they, and not their fears, are in control. Learning to control fear is very reassuring.

• Live in the moment. If you spend all your time ruing the past or fearing the future, you'll have a hard time deriving any pleasure from the present. To fight this tendency, remind yourself that death could come at any moment. Don't let that thought frighten you. Just try to assimilate it into your psyche. Once you do, you'll be freer to enjoy a blue sky or a poem or the presence of a loved one. *Ultimate goal:* To approach life with a childlike sense of awe and wonder.

• Identify your true feelings. Ask a child what he wants to do, and you'll get 40 answers.

Ask an adult, and the response will likely be, "I don't know. What do you want to do?" Adults have a hard time knowing what to do—for an afternoon or a lifetime—because they're so out of touch with their feelings that they've lost track of what really matters to them.

People without emotions live almost like automatons. Helen Keller used to ask, "If you had three days to see, what would you choose to see in those days? Your answer to this question will teach you about what you truly love in your life."

• Define pain and suffering in positive terms. When I ask my lecture audiences if they think life is fair, they usually answer with a resounding, "No!" But I believe that life is fair. All of us experience difficulties, problems, pain, and losses. But while some people give in to self-pity, others retain their vitality and optimism—even in the face of terminal illness.

Lesson: We should not only avoid suffering, we should respond to it in a constructive manner.

Strategy: Redefine whatever pain you're feeling as labor pains. Just as the anticipation and joy of bringing a new baby into the world can help to ease a mother's suffering during childbirth, other types of pain will seem less awful if you view them as integral to the process of birth you're undergoing.

Examples: The pain of chemotherapy leads to the birth of a person who is cancer-free... the pain of divorce leads to the birth of a happy single person.

• Refuse to be a victim. To some extent, we're all prisoners. Some of us are prisoners in the literal sense. Others, suffering from some debilitating ailment, are prisoners of our own bodies. Still others are imprisoned by emotional scars from a difficult childhood or a violent crime. No matter what form your prison takes, you don't have to feel or behave like a victim.

Example: Franklin Roosevelt could have pitied himself after polio left him wheelchair-bound. Instead, he became president of the United States.

Bottom line: No matter what befalls you, retain the ability to choose what sort of life to lead.

Source: Bernard S. Siegel, MD, a noted lecturer on healing and the founder of Exceptional Cancer Patients (ECaP), a nonprofit support group for people with cancer, AIDS, or other life-threatening illnesses. A retired surgeon formerly on the staff of Yale University School of Medicine, Dr. Siegel is the author of three books, including *How to Live Between Office Visits: A Guide to Life, Love, and Health*, HarperCollins, 10 E. 53 St., New York 10022.

Cholesterol Testing

Cholesterol testing can usually wait until men reach age 35 and women age 45. Adults found to have elevated cholesterol at younger ages will obtain almost all the benefits of cholesterol-lowering therapy by waiting until middle age to start treatment.

Earlier treatment could actually do harm if dietary control did not succeed and patients started lifelong regimens of medications that could have side effects.

Source: Research led by Stephen Hulley, MD, MPH, epidemiologist, University of California at San Francisco.

20 Simple Ways To Stay Healthy

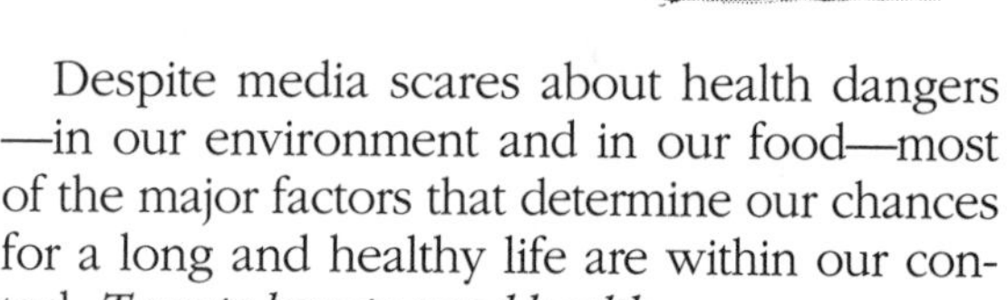

Despite media scares about health dangers —in our environment and in our food—most of the major factors that determine our chances for a long and healthy life are within our control. *Twenty keys to good health:*

1. Don't smoke. Cigarette smoking is the leading cause of premature disease and death in this country, causing nearly 500,000 deaths each year in the US.

2. Don't smoke. Ninety percent of cases of lung cancer—the number-one cause of cancer deaths in America—are caused by cigarette smoking.

3. Don't smoke. Cigarette smoking is the leading cause of *preventable* cases of cancer of the esophagus, pancreas, throat, bladder and cervix.

4. Don't smoke. Smoking is one of the top-three modifiable causes of heart disease. The other two are high blood pressure and elevated blood cholesterol.

5. Don't smoke. Cigarettes are the leading cause of emphysema and other chronic lung diseases.

6. Never drink and drive. Driving under the influence of alcohol is the top cause of traffic accidents. An estimated 25,000 Americans die each year from vehicular accidents related to alcohol. Don't drive under the influence...and don't ride in a car driven by someone who has been drinking.

7. If you drink, use alcohol responsibly. A large portion of *non-vehicular* accidents are also related to alcohol consumption. Drinking interferes with your ability to swim, ski, use power tools, drive a boat or perform other activities.

Long term excessive use of alcohol can cause serious health problems, including cirrhosis and other liver diseases, disorders of the heart and nervous system and throat cancer.

Complete abstinence from drinking isn't necessary for good health. The key is moderation.

8. Wear your seat belt every time you drive. The National Highway Safety Administration says conscientious use of seat belts could reduce traffic deaths by 50% and injuries by 65%. Other experts estimate even higher.

Air bags are no substitute for seat belt use. Seat belts protect you in all collisions...but air bags only work in frontal collisions—only 20% of all crashes.

9. Put a working battery in your smoke detector. Fires are the second most common cause of accidental death in the home, claiming more than 5,000 lives every year. If everyone used smoke detectors, the death toll would be reduced by 40% or more.

Following manufacturer's instructions, test your smoke detector regularly to make sure that it's working. Replace worn-out batteries promptly. And remember to put the batteries back in after you remove them for any reason—such as after setting off a false alarm while cooking.

10. Beware of the effects of too much sunlight. Overexposure to sunlight is the leading

cause of deadly melanoma as well as superficial skin cancer...not to mention premature wrinkling of the skin. If you're going to be in the sun, wear sunscreen with an SPF of at least 15 and reapply it every few hours. Try to stay out of the sun between 11:00 a.m. and 3:00 p.m., when it's strongest. And never, ever let yourself get sunburned.

11. Wear a helmet when you ride a bike—and make sure your child wears one too. Strapping a child into a carrier seat won't protect his/her head.

12. Practice safe sex. Safe sexual practices help you protect yourself against a variety of sexually transmitted diseases. *Best protection:* Abstain from sex outside a mutually faithful relationship with a partner whom you know is not infected.

13. Don't use cocaine. Cocaine use interferes with your ability to work and function, and can have deadly effects on the cardiovascular system. *Hidden danger:* You can't know the quality of what you're buying on the street, even from a trusted supplier. You risk your life with even one use.

14. Avoid obesity. Being more than 20% over your ideal weight increases the risk or severity of many medical problems...heart disease, high blood pressure, diabetes, arthritis, gallbladder disease, respiratory ailments, pregnancy problems, complications after surgery, etc.

15. Eat a variety of foods in moderation. Although obesity can be harmful, unwise dieting can also be dangerous. Some of the currently popular formula-based diets are safe, but others provide too few calories for good health. Many so-called diet aids—starch blokers, spirulina, glucomannan, body wraps, etc.—have never been shown to be of any benefit.

Losing weight and keeping it off requires you learn to live *with* food...not without it. Eat plenty of grains, fruits and vegetables, and cut way down on fats. Don't expect overnight results. And whether or not you're overweight, meet your nutritional needs by keeping in mind the guidelines: *Variety, moderation and balance.*

16. Exercise daily. Exercise reduces the risk of coronary disease, lessens tension...and helps control weight.

Important: If you have health problems, are at risk for heart disease, or aren't used to exercising regularly, consult a physician before beginning an exercise program. Avoid injury by starting slowly and increasing your activity level *gradually.*

17. Get your blood pressure and cholesterol checked regularly. High blood pressure and high cholesterol levels greatly increase your risk of heart disease, the number-one killer in this country. Have your blood pressure checked at least once a year, twice a year if you're over 40 and more often if you're at risk for heart disease. Have your blood cholesterol and lipoprotein levels (the so-called *good HDL* and *bad LDL)* checked at least once every five years. If your blood pressure, total cholesterol or cholesterol-to-HDL level is elevated, follow your doctor's advice about how to reduce it.

18. Have regular screening exams for cancer ...including a Pap test, breast examination, prostate exam and tests for colon cancer. Early detection frequently means the difference between beating cancer and dying from it.

19. Be skeptical of medical fads and scares. They often turn out to be groundless...and lead to *unhealthy,* or at the very least, irrational behavior.

Example: The panic over Alar. Two years ago, people were panicked by perfectly nutritious apples over an issue that turned out to have no basis in science.

Example II: The oat bran fad. Oat bran is wholesome, but it's no magic bullet. Expecting too much from it could cause you to eat an unbalanced diet—which would *not* be good for your health.

20. Pay attention to the real risks. Like everything else in life, good health involves setting priorities. We're surrounded by health information and can't humanly follow all the advice we read. There's much more to life than worrying about health. Learn to separate the real dangers from the hypothetical ones so you can avoid the major, proven risks...and still enjoy life.

Source: Elizabeth M. Whelan, ScD, MPH, president of the American Council on Science and Health, 1995 Broadway, New York 10023. Dr. Whelan is the author of 21 books on health-related subjects, including *Toxic Terror,* Jameson Books, 722 Columbus St., Ottawa, Illinois 61350.

Secret of Good Health: An Ongoing Relationship With Your Doctor

People who seek out a doctor only after a significant medical problem surfaces are missing a very important point about good medical care—that is, a congenial, ongoing relationship with your primary doctor affords several key benefits. *Most important...*

•Quick answers to medical questions. Such a relationship gives you someone to call in case of a medical emergency, or, important, too, if a simple problem or question arises. It's psychologically easier to call a doctor to discuss a problem if he/she already knows you. And a doctor familiar with your medical history gives sound medical advice—and gives it fast—with greater confidence than a doctor who comes to your case "cold."

•Individualized treatment. Any competent doctor knows the importance of taking a good medical history. But only a doctor familiar with your social and behavioral patterns as well as the specifics of your medical chart can individualize treatments for you. Individualized treatment means not only avoiding unpleasant or needlessly aggressive treatments, but also getting treatments that are more effective and convenient.

Example I: Because of the slight risk of barotrauma (pressure-related injury) to the ear, patients with ear congestion are usually told to avoid air travel. But a doctor familiar with a patient might be able to help a sufferer take the slight risk and take steps to enable him/her to fly, including possibly a short course of powerful anti-inflammatory steroids.

Example II: Some people with basically normal blood pressure are vulnerable to "white coat" hypertension. This condition, in which the anxiety of visiting the doctor causes a transient rise in blood pressure, is essentially harmless. A doctor who knows a particular patient is susceptible can easily make arrangements for testing to be done in a nonclinical setting. But a doctor unaware of this susceptibility might needlessly prescribe antihypertensive drugs.

•Reduced anxiety. One of the most important things that a doctor does for his/her patients is reassure them when medical problems strike. A doctor who has seen you through previous medical problems will be reassuring when new problems arise. Visiting a "new" doctor typically produces a great deal of anxiety—even in the absence of a serious medical problem.

•Fewer missed diagnoses. A doctor who has treated you for years is better able to spot subtle, yet often significant, changes in your appearance and health. What's appropriate for one patient might suggest a serious problem in another—even if these results fall within "normal" ranges.

Examples: A patient whose white blood cell count has for years hovered around 4,500 cells per deciliter suddenly turns up with a count of 9,000. Because 9,000 is within "normal" range, a doctor new to this patient might give a clean bill of health. But a doctor who knew the cell count was out of line with previous counts would suspect trouble—perhaps leukemia—and could order additional tests to find the problem. Conversely, a patient with a chronically enlarged pupil who suffers head trauma would quickly wind up getting a CAT scan or some other anxiety-provoking diagnostic test...unless the doctor knew the enlarged pupil was a preexisting and harmless condition.

•More effective counseling. A doctor who knows you is more effective at persuading you to make good decisions regarding your diet, use of alcohol, tobacco and other drugs, and ways to cope with anxiety. Also, such a doctor is more helpful in times of personal upheaval, such as the loss of a job or the dissolution of an important relationship.

•Earlier intervention. Many family physicians are now making available to their patients quick, convenient medical tests—blood-pressure tests, throat cultures, pap smears, mammography and screenings for colon and testicular cancer. Patients in close contact with a primary physician are more apt to have problems diagnosed—and treated—at the earliest possible moment.

Source: Bruce Yaffe, MD, an eminent internist and gastroenterologist in private practice in New York City.

The Language of Health

With medical costs rising astronomically and no relief in sight, it's increasingly important for Americans to reduce their dependence on outside experts—and take at least some control of their own health care.

One of the best tools for doing so is also one of the most basic—language.

The language of health...

There are many ways that language can be used to affect our health—both for good and bad. *Included:*

• Messages that we give ourselves. Whether we're aware of it or not, most of us talk to ourselves continuously.

Pessimistic, helpless messages *(I feel terrible, and there's not a thing I can do about it)* tell the body to give up.

Positive messages *(I can stand this discomfort, and I will feel good again)* help the body to fight illness.

• How we respond to others. Chronic exposure to hostility is a risk factor in many diseases—and the primary factor in heart disease.

We can't always avoid hostility and conflict, but we can learn to use language to deflect a verbal attack and spare ourselves mental and physical strain.

• Metaphors we use. Visualization can be an effective healing tool in dealing with illness.

Example: Patients are advised to imagine the disease as an army of enemy invaders, and the immune system as a good army destroying the invading forces.

But warlike images are only helpful to people comfortable with military themes. For others, violent imagery may work *against* healing by equating illness with violence and slaughter.

As an alternative, focus on *fixing* rather than killing.

Examples: Think of your immune system as a gardening crew pulling up weeds...or a road crew fixing potholes in the street...or a piano tuner restoring harmony to an out-of-tune instrument.

• Doctor/patient relationships. When doctors and patients don't communicate well with each other, patients wind up with poor health care.

A pain-phobic society...

What we tell ourselves about pain has a profound impact on our well-being. TV commercials bombard us with the notion that pain is terrible—that no one should ever hurt even a little. But pain is a normal part of life.

That doesn't mean that discomfort should be ignored. If running makes your shins hurt, *rest* ...don't push on for another mile.

Pain alerts us to our limitations, and chronic discomfort *may* be an indicator of a physical condition that requires medical attention.

People who panic every time they're in pain end up spending a lot of money needlessly on doctors and drugs, without appreciable benefits. In fact, their fears—and the drugs' side effects—may make them feel even worse.

Coping with pain...

If you're plagued with chronic or acute pain, instead of telling yourself, *I can't bear this,* substitute the thought, *I can stand this pain for 15 minutes.*

Then spend that 15 minutes doing something you enjoy—gardening, playing music, absorbing yourself in a challenging project at work. At the end of 15 minutes, you're likely to find that the pain is gone.

If not, say, *I can stand this pain for another 15 minutes.* You'll notice that the pain ebbs and flows. This attitude enables you to go on with your life, instead of focusing your life around the pain.

Another way to cope with pain is to keep a journal. Describe what the pain feels like and what sets it off. Give it a name. Compare it with something else that has a similar distinguishing feature.

Example: My pain is like an earthquake—sudden and unpredictable.

As you start to define your pain and give it boundaries, you will see it less as an overwhelming force that's controlling you, and more as an object...which you can control.

Deflecting attack...

We can relieve ourselves of a great deal of stress by learning not to get hooked into other people's hostility.

Verbal attacks aren't always easy to recognize. Someone can be smiling, or using words like *sweetheart* and *darling*, and still be sending a hostile message. *Key:* Verbal hostility has a characteristic melody in which many words are emphatically stressed.

Examples: "*Why* do you *always* think *only of yourself?*" Or, "I'm *only* thinking about what's *best for you.*"

There are several ways to deflect verbal hostility...

• Remember that nobody can fight alone. If you refuse to fight, even the most hostile verbal attacker will give up.

• When in doubt about how to handle an attack, try the boring baroque defense. Treat the attack as if it were a serious, rational question or statement, and talk the other person into a coma.

The idea is to answer in such excruciating detail that the attacker has no fun at all. *Example:*

Attacker: "*Why* can't you ever stick to your *diet?*"

Boring baroque defense: "You know, that's an interesting question. I think it has to do with when I was a kid in Wisconsin, and our family...no, maybe it was when we were living in Illinois. Yes, it must be Illinois, because that's when my uncle was working for the Post Office, and...."

This technique won't work if you let sarcasm creep into your voice. You must keep your tone serious.

How to talk to doctors...

It's easy to become resentful when dealing with doctors, especially if the doctor is brusque, uses jargon or acts condescending. Unfortunately, in our society, inequality is built into the doctor-patient relationship.

Acting resentful, however, will not help you achieve your health goals. The doctor is as trapped in the system as you are, and communicates in doctor-speak because he/she has been taught to.

Your doctor is a channel through which you get access to medicine, surgery and other treatments that affect your health. Annoying your doctor makes about as much sense as annoying your computer or arguing with a traffic light.

To get what you need, learn to interact with your doctor effectively...

• Before your appointment, make a list of things you want the doctor to know and any questions you need answered. Don't leave the meeting until those subjects have been covered to your satisfaction—even if you have to repeat your questions several times.

• Remember that a meeting with a doctor is not a social conversation. Don't worry about being entertaining or bouncing the conversational ball back and forth.

• Keep each question or statement to 18 seconds at most. Research shows that's the longest period of time doctors allow patients to talk before interrupting them.

• Don't try to talk like a doctor. If you've been feeling short of breath, say so—don't say you have *dyspnea.* Using medical jargon may be taken as a challenge—the doctor may try to top you by using even more technical language, and you won't get your questions answered.

Your goal isn't to impress the doctor, it's to get the information and care that you need.

Source: Linguist Suzette Haden Elgin, PhD, who teaches communications skills to health-care professionals nationwide. She is the author of a series of books on verbal self-defense, most recently *Staying Well with the Gentle Art of Verbal Self-Defense,* Prentice Hall Business and Professional Publishing, Route 9W, Englewood Cliffs, New Jersey 07632.

Women Should Go to the Bathroom More Often

There is no rule on how frequently a person should go to the bathroom. *What is important:* Following the calls of nature and going when you have to.

Unfortunately, many women *don't* listen when it comes to moving their bowels. *Trap:* Women—much more so than men—are uncomfortable in unfamiliar places, and suppress their body's signals.

If suppressed too often, the colon becomes less sensitive to stimulation and grows too full, making it difficult to expel. This is worsened by hard stools, caused by not drinking enough water, not eating enough fiber, being inactive ...and by one's natural cycle (women tend to be constipated premenstrually).

Common, unfounded fears: Too much water will make me gain weight...too much fiber will make me feel bloated.

Danger: Chronic constipation increases the risk of diverticulosis—small herniations in the colon that can cause bleeding from the rectum and may require surgery. This condition can lead to diverticulitis—inflammation of these herniations that can obstruct the colon or lead to serious abdominal infection. *Added danger:* Chronic laxative abuse impairs colon function. Avoid stimulant laxatives, including natural herb-types.

Bottom line: Eat a high-fiber diet, drink plenty of water, exercise and go when you have to. See your doctor if you notice an abrupt change in bowel habits to rule out other medical causes.

Source: Bruce Yaffe, MD, an internist who specializes in gastroenterology. Dr. Yaffe is in private practice at 121 E. 84 St., New York 10028.

Keep Your Own Medical Records

Keep your own medical records. *Reasons:* Few of us see only one doctor, so it is unlikely that anyone has your complete medical history ...most people change doctors several times—it may be difficult to obtain copies of your past doctors' records...doctors' records may be incomplete—they may have only scant detail on health problems, may not include drug reactions and probably don't include over-the-counter (OTC) treatments, vitamins or prescription refills. *Helpful:* Set up a notebook with sections for family medical history...personal medical history...doctor visits (including dental and eye care)...outpatient procedures...hospital records ...laboratory test results...prescription and OTC medication...immunizations.

Source: Charles B. Inlander, president of The People's Medical Society, 462 Walnut St., Allentown, Pennsylvania 18102. 800-624-8773. The organization publishes *Your Complete Medical Record*, a system for maintaining an individual's health history.

Dental Floss Update

There's a great new dental floss from the *Gore-tex* people. *Glide* floss is thinner than most flosses currently on the market...and much, much stronger than any of them. It really does glide over teeth—and doesn't shred, like other flosses. At $3.50 for a 15-meter package, it's about three times more expensive than others. But for people with "tight teeth," this floss is best.

Source: Alan Winter, DDS, periodontist in private practice, 30 E. 60 St., Suite 302, New York 10022.

Stroke Stoppers

Cut the risk of stroke by 30% or more by lowering blood pressure and stopping smoking. *Important:* Exercising regularly, even if only modestly, and treating any irregular heartbeat cuts risk.

Source: Roundup of medical experts, reported in *Men's Health*, 33 E. Minor St., Emmaus, Pennsylvania 18098.

Myopia Warning

Close-up visual activity—like playing video games or reading—can bring on *myopia*. Extensive reading and game-playing seem to make nearsightedness likelier. *Reason:* Unknown. *Likely:* Nearsightedness has a strong genetic component that may be triggered or worsened by close-up activity.

Source: Hilda Capó, MD, assistant professor of clinical ophthalmology, Bascom Palmer Eye Institute, University of Miami School of Medicine.

Aspirin Miracle

A remarkable, inexpensive key to better health is probably right in your medicine cabinet. It's called acetylsalicylic acid—better known as aspirin.

Research suggests that one aspirin tablet, taken every other day, helps reduce risk of heart attack, certain kinds of stroke, cancer of the gastrointestinal tract and possibly Alzheimer's disease, among other serious ailments. All this for $1.83 per year—less than a penny a day.

Caution: Aspirin is not a substitute for healthy habits like eating a balanced diet, exercising regularly or not smoking, nor should it be taken regularly without your doctor's approval.

About aspirin...

Aspirin's active ingredient, *salicin,* occurs naturally in the willow tree. Willow leaves and bark have been used to relieve pain and inflammation at least since the time of Hippocrates.

Aspirin was first made commercially in Germany at the turn of the century. If it had first been synthesized today instead of a century ago, odds are it would be available only by prescription. *Reason:* Aspirin is far more complex and powerful than many people realize.

Inexpensive generic aspirin is just as effective as more costly brands. In fact, there's less difference than you might imagine. Although there are many brand names of aspirin for sale in the US, all the salicin found in these aspirin formulations is made by just six companies.

How aspirin works...

No one knows exactly how aspirin works. It seems to interfere with the production of *prostaglandins,* hormones made by the body in response to injury. Aspirin seems to reduce the pain and swelling caused by prostaglandins.

Prostaglandins are also involved in blood-clotting. By blocking prostaglandin synthesis, aspirin acts as an anticoagulant. That probably accounts for its effectiveness against heart attack and stroke.

Aspirin also seems to prevent atherosclerosis, the buildup of fatty deposits in the arteries. However, it cannot *reverse* atherosclerosis.

Aspirin and heart attack...

In the 1950s, doctors first observed that patients who took aspirin for pain while recovering from a heart attack were less likely to have a second attack.

Supporting data on aspirin's preventive value come from the Physicians' Health Study, a five-year study of more than 22,000 male doctors between the ages of 40 and 84.

Half of the subjects took a standard five-grain aspirin tablet every other day. *Result:* Subjects older than 50 who took aspirin were 44% less likely to suffer a heart attack than were similar men given a placebo (sugar pill).

If the group who took aspirin had also been eating well and getting moderate exercise, even fewer might have had heart attacks.

Researchers looked only at men. However, a subsequent study of female nurses suggests that aspirin also helps prevent heart attacks in women.

Another study found that coronary care unit patients given aspirin immediately after a heart attack were about 25% more likely to survive the attack than patients who did not receive aspirin.

Evidence also suggests that an aspirin a day lowers the risk of a second attack.

And stroke...

Most strokes occur as a result of atherosclerosis. When arteries are narrowed, even a tiny blood clot can block blood flow to the brain, thereby depriving the tissue of oxygen.

Aspirin apparently fights stroke by preventing atherosclerosis and thinning the blood, which helps prevent blood clots.

One warning sign of impending stroke—sometimes the only warning—is a *transient ischemic attack* (TIA). This temporary deficiency of blood in the brain is caused by a blockage of blood flow or by a piece of arterial plaque or a blood clot that lodges in a blood vessel inside the brain. *Symptoms:* Weakness, numbness, dizziness, blurred vision, difficulty in speaking.

A study by Dr. James C. Grottar (published in the January 28, 1988, issue of the *New England Journal of Medicine*) showed that taking aspirin after a TIA cuts the risk of stroke by 25% to 30%. Although aspirin is often prescribed for TIA, it is not usually appropriate for anyone with high blood pressure or an increased risk of hemorrhage.

And colon cancer...

Cancers of the colon and rectum account for roughly one out of five cancer deaths in the US.

In 1991, the *Journal of the National Cancer Institute* reported that people who took aspirin or other nonsteroidal anti-inflammatory drugs at least four days a week for three months *halved* their risk of colorectal cancer. The results held for men and women across a broad range of ages.

A recent Emory University study suggested that taking one aspirin a week significantly reduces the risk of these cancers. Another study found a 50% reduction in the colon cancer death rate among daily aspirin takers.

But another study of older subjects (average age 73) showed that frequent aspirin users face a *heightened* risk of kidney and colon cancer, as well as of heart attack. More research is needed. But—at least for younger patients, the preliminary findings are promising.

And Alzheimer's disease...

A University of British Columbia scientist recently observed during autopsies of arthritis patients—who tend to take a great deal of aspirin—that their brains showed fewer than expected signs of Alzheimer's disease.

This observation certainly doesn't prove that aspirin prevents Alzheimer's. However, it does suggest an important avenue for future research.

And more...

Though aspirin isn't very helpful in relieving migraine pain, it may help prevent migraines. Preliminary research suggests that migraine sufferers who take aspirin regularly may be able to reduce their headaches by as much as 20%.

Aspirin seems to stimulate the production of *interferon* and *interleukin-2*—immunity-boosting proteins produced inside the body. This may explain why aspirin may prevent certain kinds of cancer...and suggests that it could be used in the fight against other immune disorders.

Finally, some evidence suggests that aspirin helps prevent cataracts, diabetes and gallstones. As with other possible uses of aspirin, these potential uses of aspirin require further study.

Aspirin precautions...

• *If you're thinking about starting an aspirin regimen, check with your doctor first.* This is especially important if you're taking anticoagulants...if you have diabetes, gout or arthritis... or if you are taking any other over-the-counter or prescription drug.

Caution: Aspirin should generally be avoided by anyone with asthma...ulcers or other chronic stomach problems...or an allergy to aspirin.

• *If you're pregnant or nursing an infant, take aspirin only with a doctor's consent. Danger:* Aspirin taken during the last three months of pregnancy can injure the fetus or cause birth complications.

• *If regular aspirin irritates your stomach, ask your doctor about buffered or coated aspirin.* Also, tell your doctor if you experience ringing in the ears or hearing loss while taking aspirin.

• Drink with caution when taking aspirin. Aspirin boosts the concentration of alcohol in the blood. If you want to drive safely after a party, for instance, you may need to drink even less or wait longer than you normally would.

• *Children should not be given aspirin without a doctor's approval. Reason:* Aspirin has been linked to Reye's syndrome, a rare but potentially fatal brain disorder.

Source: Robert S. Persky, coauthor of *Penny Wonder Drug: What the Label on Your Aspirin Bottle Doesn't Tell You,* The Consultant Press, Ltd., 163 Amsterdam Ave., #201, New York 10023.

Coffee Hazards

Although a cup or two of coffee a day is safe for most people, there are exceptions...

• People who have a genetic susceptibility to the effects of caffeine. *Example:* Some people experience heart palpitations after drinking only a single cup.

• People with high blood pressure or heart disease. Coffee exacerbates symptoms in these people.

• Women who are pregnant or trying to conceive. As little as one cup of coffee a day reduces a woman's ability to conceive by 50%, according to one recent study. Some studies suggest that women who drink coffee during pregnancy are more likely to have miscarriages and low-birth-weight babies, but this finding remains a topic of debate among researchers.

Trap: In men, coffee apparently boosts the mobility of sperm cells...although recent evidence suggests that it increases the incidence of abnormal sperm—which may lead to miscarriage.

Heavy consumption...

Drinking more than two cups a day can cause even more serious problems...

• Ovarian cancer. One study showed that it's twice as common among women who drink two or more cups of coffee a day as among women who drink only one cup a day.

• Digestive disorders. Nausea, bloating, gas, heartburn and ulcers have all been linked to excessive coffee drinking. The caffeine, oils and acids in coffee irritate the stomach lining. *Surprising:* Most of the irritants are formed during the roasting of the beans, so switching to decaf won't help.

Most troublesome: Drinking coffee on an empty stomach. In some people, the increase in stomach acid causes an almost immediate stomachache.

• Headaches. Heavy coffee consumption causes alternating constriction and dilation of blood vessels. This then leads to so-called "rebound" headaches that can occur on a daily basis.

• Breast cysts. Women who drink four or more cups a day are twice as likely to suffer from fibrocystic breasts as other women, one recent study found. Another study found that women whose daily consumption of tea is greater than four and one-half cups are 10 times more likely to suffer from premenstrual syndrome (PMS) than other women. (Tea has about half as much caffeine per cup as coffee.)

Helpful: Eliminating, or at least reducing, coffee intake a week or two before your period.

To cut back or quit...

Cutting coffee consumption all at once can lead to severe headaches and other symptoms of withdrawal. Try cutting back gradually...

• Switch to decaffeinated coffee for every other cup you drink. Gradually increase your consumption of decaf until your caffeine consumption is negligible. *Warning:* Conventional decaf is processed using the solvent methylene chloride—a known carcinogen. To protect yourself, choose water-processed (Swiss-process) decaf, which is made with a natural compound. Or choose another hot beverage, such as herbal tea or a grain-based coffee substitute.

• Cut back by one cup every three or four days—until you're drinking only the amount you want.

Life with less coffee...

Learn to live and enjoy life with less coffee. Exercise—a short run, yoga or stretching—can provide that burst of energy you used to get from coffee. And if you've been using coffee to relax, consider a massage, a hot bath or a stroll through your favorite park. They can be just as relaxing and more fun.

Source: Bonnie Edwards, RN, BSN (Bachelor of Science and Nursing), University of California, San Francisco. She is the author of *America's Favorite Drug: Coffee and Your Health,* Odonian Press, Box 7776, Berkeley, California 94707.

Women Get Less Preventive Care

Women get less preventive care than they should—often because doctors do not give them enough information, or because preventive exams are not covered by insurance. *Troubling survey:* In the past year, 35% of women surveyed had not had a Pap smear...33% had not had a clinical breast exam...36% had not had a pelvic exam...39% had not had a complete physical...44% of those 50 and older had not had a mammogram.

Source: Survey of 2,525 women by the marketing and research firm Louis Harris & Associates, 630 Fifth Ave., New York 10011.

The Yeast Trap

New evidence suggests that many puzzling, chronic health problems resistant to treatment —from infections and allergies to the aches and exhaustion of chronic fatigue syndrome—are yeast-related.

One type of yeast is regularly found on the body's mucous membranes, especially the intestinal tract and vagina. When we talk about this kind of yeast, we usually mean Candida albicans, by far the predominant type found in the body.

In a healthy man or woman, candida (pronounced *can-did-a*) is kept under control by so-called "friendly" bacteria living in the intestinal tract. But several factors can upset the yeast-to-bacteria balance—especially long-term use of broad-spectrum antibiotics. When this happens, yeasts grow out of control—leading to unpleasant symptoms.

Based on my critical review of continuing research, I believe there are three possible mechanisms for yeast's troublesome effects...

- Just as some people are allergic to pollens or mildew, some may be allergic to candida.
- Candida may produce certain toxins that are harmless in small amounts, but that in larger quantities weaken the immune system... leaving the body vulnerable to disease.
- Yeast overgrowth in the intestinal tract (candidiasis) may lead to changes in the intestine. In turn, these changes can cause the body to absorb and react to allergens in food.

The connection between yeast and health problems is highly controversial. Beginning with Dr. C. Orian Truss's article in the late '70s, a number of reports have linked yeast to illness, but the mainstream medical community remains skeptical.

Yet, my experience in treating hundreds of chronically ill patients, as well as similar experiences of a number of colleagues, suggests that a diet designed to curb yeast growth—along with certain antifungal medications—helps alleviate many symptoms that have proven resistant to other forms of treatment.

Do you have a yeast problem?

There is no simple diagnostic test for a yeast-related problem. For this reason, patients must undergo a thorough physical exam to rule out other possible causes of their symptoms. *Next step:* A complete medical history.

You may have a yeast problem if you...

...have used antibiotics repeatedly over a long period of time, such as for control of acne or recurrent infections.

...have taken corticosteroids. One known side effect of nasal cortisone spray is candidiasis of the nose.

...have used birth control pills. Women on the Pill are far more prone than others to vaginal yeast infection.

...eat a high-sugar diet. A recent study at St. Jude Research Hospital in Memphis found that mice eating large quantities of the sugar glucose had 200 times as much candida in their intestinal tracts as did other mice.

...experience frequent digestive problems, such as abdominal pain, bloating, constipation or diarrhea.

...have a history of vaginal or urinary infections. Women develop yeast-related health problems far more often than men for a number of reasons. These include anatomical differences and hormonal changes associated with the menstrual cycle that promote yeast growth.

...have symptoms involving many parts of the body—for which usual examinations have not found a cause.

Treating a suspected yeast problem...

The cornerstone of treatment is a sugar-free diet. Yeasts in the digestive tract feed on sugar —and multiply. Some patients show remarkable improvement from dietary changes alone. Others need additional help—in the form of over-the-counter anti-yeast preparations sold in health food stores...and, for more serious cases, from prescription antifungal medications.

The yeast control diet...

- Eliminate sugar and other simple carbohydrates, such as honey and corn syrup.
- Avoid foods containing yeast or molds, such as cheese, vinegar, wine, beer and other fermented beverages, and pickled or smoked meats. Although breads are probably safe, try eliminating yeast-leavened breads for a few weeks.

Note: Yeast-containing foods should be avoided not because intestinal yeast feeds on food yeast—it doesn't. But most people with candida related problems are sensitive to yeast in foods and can have negative physical reactions. As the candida problem improves, the sensitivity may subside...and yeast can again be included in your diet.

• Strengthen your immune system by boosting your intake of vegetables, minimally processed whole grains and other wholesome foods. Eat lean rather than fatty meats, and cut back on other sources of fat. Avoid potentially harmful additives, including artificial colors and flavors.

Some physicians recommend eliminating fruits from the diet, because fruits are quickly converted to simple sugars inside the body. I believe fruits are safe—unless your yeast-related symptoms are severe. However, I do recommend avoiding commercially prepared fruit juices, which may be contaminated with mold.

Follow this recommended diet for at least three weeks. If your symptoms subside, resume eating forbidden foods one by one. If your symptoms flare up again after you add one of the forbidden foods, stop eating that food for good.

Good news: After they show significant improvement, most people find that they can follow a less rigid diet—and can occasionally consume a bit of sugar.

Over-the-counter remedies...

Many preparations sold in health-food stores can be a useful adjunct to the yeast-control diet...

• *Citrus seed extract,* an antimicrobial substance made from tropical plants. Because the extract can irritate mucous membranes, it should be generously diluted with water before drinking.

• *Caprylic acid,* a saturated fatty acid available in tablet form. It helps keep yeast from reproducing.

Note: Some patients develop digestive problems or notice a slight worsening of yeast-related symptoms during the first week on this medication. If these don't go away within a few days, stop the medication and check with your doctor.

• *Lactobacillus acidophilus,* a friendly bacterium that helps restore the normal balance of intestinal flora. It is present in yogurt, especially homemade varieties. Store-bought yogurt that contains active cultures will be labeled to that effect. Be sure to buy only unsweetened varieties. Acidophilus is also available as a nutritional supplement.

• *Garlic.* This herb is known to stimulate the immune system...and at an international medical conference several years ago, researchers reported that garlic also seems to fight candida. Persons wary of the taste of cooked garlic—or its effect on the breath—should consider aged garlic extract (Kyolic), a deodorized supplement. It is widely available in local health food stores.

Antifungal medications...

When a yeast-related symptom fails to respond to diet or supplements, prescription medication often helps—although the drug may take up to a year to have any effect in severe cases. *Drug options:*

• Nystatin (Mycostatin or Nilstat). In more than 30 years of use, this oral medication has demonstrated no toxic side effects. It knocks out candida in the intestines. It is not absorbed by the bloodstream, however, so it is ineffective against particularly severe cases of candidiasis.

• Fluconazole (Diflucan). This safe, highly effective anti-yeast medication has been available in the US for about three years. Unlike nystatin, fluconazole is absorbed into the bloodstream.

• Itraconazole (Sporanox). This medication, a chemical "cousin" of fluconazole, was approved for use in the US earlier this year. Although it appears to be quite safe, a related drug, ketoconazole (Nizoral) has been linked to liver damage.

For more information on yeast-related health problems, send a self-addressed, business-sized envelope with 64 cents postage to the International Health Foundation, Inc., Box 3494-HC, Jackson, Tennessee 38303.

Source: William G. Crook, MD, a fellow of the American College of Allergy and Immunology, the American Academy of Environmental Medicine and the American Academy of Pediatrics. He is the author of *The Yeast Connection* and *Chronic Fatigue Syndrome and the Yeast Connection*, both published by Professional Books, Inc., Box 3246, Jackson, Tennessee 38303.

Depression— How to Spot It, How to Beat It

Many Americans share a tragic misconception about depression—that people who are depressed could "snap out of it," if they wanted to. As a result, more than 30 million Americans troubled by emotional illness never get the help they need.

The result is devastating. Sufferers feel hopeless, inadequate and unable to cope with daily life. Their self-esteem is shattered—and so are their ties with family and friends. What's more, depression is often lethal. Up to 30% of people with serious mood disorders kill themselves.

Feeling "blue" from time to time is a normal part of life—we all experience the sadness of failed relationships, the loss of loved ones, etc. Periods of sadness that are mild and short-lived do not require medical help.

Understanding...

But if enjoyable activities, the passing of time and confiding in friends, family or even psychotherapists fail to alleviate emotional pain, you may be suffering from a biological form of depression. Such disorders, triggered by chemical changes in the brain, call for medical treatment. They cannot be cured by talking to a therapist or reading a self-help book.

While the causes of depression are not fully understood, new technology has provided insight. Scientists believe that depressed people have decreased amounts of certain mood-regulating chemicals called neurotransmitters.

In most cases, depressive illness caused by such chemical imbalances is inherited. *Evidence:* Children of depressed parents have a 20% to 25% risk of having a mood disorder. Children of nondepressed parents have a 5% risk.

Warning signs of depression...

If you have felt sad or down in the dumps in recent weeks, or if you've lost interest in many or all of your normal activities, you may be suffering from depression. *Warning signs:*

- Poor appetite or overeating
- Insomnia
- Sleeping more than usual
- Chronic low energy or fatigue
- Restlessness, feeling less active or talkative than usual, feeling "slowed down"
- Avoidance of other people
- Reduced interest in sex and other pleasurable activities
- Inability to derive pleasure from presents, praise, job promotions, etc.
- Feelings of inadequacy, low self-esteem or an increased level of self-criticism
- Reduced levels of accomplishment at work, school or home
- Feeling less able to cope with routine responsibilities
- Poor concentration, having trouble making decisions

If you're experiencing four or more of these, consult a doctor immediately.

Kinds of emotional illness...

The most common type of depression is unipolar illness, in which the person's mood is either normal or depressed. *Other common types:*

- Dysthymia. This condition is marked by a chronic mild state of depression. Sufferers of dysthymia experience little pleasure and are chronically fatigued and unresponsive. Sadly, many people suffering from dysthymia mistake their illness for a low-key personality...and never get the help they need.
- Manic depression. Patients whose periods of depression alternate with periods of euphoria are suffering from manic depression (bipolar disorder). During the "high" periods, manic-depressives may also have an inflated sense of self-esteem...a decreased need to sleep...a tendency to monopolize conversations...the feeling that their thoughts are racing...increased activity...impulsive behavior (including buying sprees, promiscuity, rash business decisions).

Though manic episodes sometimes occur when a person has never been depressed, they are frequently followed by severe depression. *Danger:* Manic-depressives often do not realize that they're ill, even though the problem may be obvious to family and friends. As with all forms of biological depression, manic depression calls for immediate treatment.

•Cyclothymia. A variant of manic depression, this disorder is characterized by less pronounced ups and downs. Like manic-depressives, cyclothymics are often unaware of their problem and must be encouraged to seek help.

Diagnosis and treatment...

First, have a complete physical exam to rule out any medical disorders. Certain ailments including thyroid disease and anemia can produce various symptoms that mimic depression.

If the exam suggests no underlying medical problem, ask for a referral to a psychopharmacologist—a psychiatrist who is trained in biological psychiatry. *Caution:* Nonphysician therapists, such as psychologists and social workers, lack medical training and cannot prescribe medication...and may be less adept at distinguishing between *biological* and *psychological* forms of depression.

When a biological form of depression is diagnosed, antidepressants should almost always be used as the first line of treatment. They completely relieve or lessen symptoms in more than 80% of people with severe emotional illness... and they are not addictive, nor do they make people "high." Once medications have brought the depression under control, however, psychotherapy often proves helpful—especially to patients embarrassed or demoralized by their illness.

Antidepressants...

Among the oldest and most effective antidepressants are the so-called tricyclics and monoamine oxidase inhibitors (MAOIs). These drugs are often very effective, but they must be used with caution.

Tricyclics have a wide range of side effects, including dry mouth, constipation, blurred vision and sexual difficulties. MAOIs must never be taken in combination with foods containing high levels of tyramine—such as aged cheese. Doing so causes a potentially dangerous rise in blood pressure. Other side effects include low blood pressure, sleep disturbances, weight gain and sexual difficulties.

Although these medications are still valuable in the treatment of depression, newer classes of drugs, including fluoxetine (Prozac), sertraline (Zoloft) and paroxetine (Paxil), are often superior. These new medications have few side effects, although some people who take the drugs complain of drowsiness or anxiety. *Note:* Despite one recent report claiming that Prozac caused some patients to attempt suicide, follow-up studies have not confirmed this finding.

For manic depression, the clear treatment of choice is lithium. Common minor side effects include diarrhea, a metallic taste in the mouth, increased frequency of urination, hand tremor and weight gain.

For seriously depressed or suicidal patients who do not respond to antidepressants, electroconvulsive therapy (ECT) is often a lifesaver. In this procedure, electrical current is applied to the brain via electrodes.

Sad: Many patients who stand to benefit from ECT refuse it altogether—because they consider it a brutal form of treatment. Today, however, patients receive a general anesthetic and a muscle relaxant prior to the application of current, so there's no emotional or physical trauma. Side effects—including slight confusion for several hours after treatment and occasionally memory loss—generally fade with time.

How to find the right help...

If your family doctor cannot recommend a good psychiatrist, contact the nearest medical school or teaching hospital. Many have a special treatment clinic for depression. Local branches of the American Psychiatric Association will provide names of psychiatrists in your area, but they cannot evaluate the psychiatrist's training in biological psychiatry.

The National Foundation for Depressive Illness (800-248-4344) gives referrals to psychiatrists interested in pharmacological treatment of mood disorders. Finally, additional information can be obtained from the National Depressive and Manic-Depressive Association (312-642-0049).

Source: Donald F. Klein, MD, professor of psychiatry at the Columbia University College of Physicians and Surgeons and director of research at the New York State Psychiatric Institute, both in New York City. Dr. Klein is coauthor of *Understanding Depression: A Complete Guide to its Diagnosis and Treatment,* Oxford University Press, 200 Madison Ave., New York 10016. 800-451-7556.

Uncommon Advice for Avoiding Common Colds

As a healer and scientist, I've developed my own highly effective system for defending myself against the common cold. *Result:* I don't get colds anymore. And my students rarely do.

To avoid getting colds, I've figured out what I usually do just *before* I get one. I then avoid those situations—or take action as soon as possible to keep a cold from developing.

Common causes...

• Overwork...and other sources of stress. When things get tough, make an effort to take *extra* good care of yourself. Go to bed earlier than you usually do...take time out for a nap after you eat lunch...meditate, which calms the mind, lowers stress level and recharges your energy.

Helpful exercise: Sit or lie down, and slowly inhale. As you inhale, imagine your body filling with the color red...relax...breathe out.

Do this three times. Then repeat, in turn, with orange, yellow, green, indigo and white. These are the colors of the *chakras*—the energy centers in the body's *auric field.**

If you have trouble meditating, a good alternative is dancing to your favorite music...and it's wonderful exercise for your whole body.

• Poor diet. Eating a well-balanced diet is a simple—yet vital—way to keep the immune system strong. And take a daily multivitamin/mineral supplement. *Also:* Don't postpone meals—eat when it's time to eat.

If you slip, as we all do, and binge on high-fat, high-sugar foods, be sure to eat *very* well for the next few days. *Important:* Lightly cooked vegetables and salads, grains and low-fat proteins, especially fish.

• Exposure to somebody who has a cold. Go home and gargle with salt water. Take extra vitamin C. Wash your hands.

• Exposure to cold, damp weather. Many people fail to dress properly when the weather starts to turn chilly. *Be realistic.* Be more aware of the weather—dress appropriately. If you do get a chill, warm yourself immediately. *Helpful:* A hot bath.

*The auric field is the field of bioenergy that runs through and around the body. The more powerfully charged, balanced and clear it is, the stronger your immune system is and the less susceptible you are to illness.

More self-defense...

• Exercise. Regular physical exercise enhances the body's immune system tremendously.

• Don't work under fluorescent lights. They have a negative impact on the human energy field.

• Get sun for 10 to 20 minutes a day. The sun charges the auric field.

• Drink a gallon of clean water every day. It washes out waste material and toxins that are left in the system as a result of the healing process. Don't load up on fruit juice—it's full of sugar. If you want fruit, *eat* it.

• Avoid cold, dry air. This is especially damaging if you have a sore throat or laryngitis. Use a steam vaporizer at night.

• Eliminate negative thoughts. Negative thoughts create an imbalance in the auric field. If the imbalance lasts for a long enough period of time, you can become ill. To erase negative thoughts, figure out what's causing them...and take action to eliminate the problem. Don't just put the blame for your negative thoughts on others and attempt to live with the problem.

At the first sign of a cold...

• Stop eating all wheat and dairy foods. They generate mucus.

• Increase vitamin C intake. I take 2,000 mg of vitamin C every two hours, up to 10,000 mg a day, for two days. *Warning:* Too much vitamin C can cause pain in the joints...and diarrhea. Tolerance levels vary greatly by individual—fine-tune your intake to figure out exactly what yours is.

• Take deodorized garlic pills. It clears mucus out of the digestive tract amazingly fast...and, because it is deodorized, you won't taste or smell like garlic. Sold over-the-counter at drug and health food stores.

Source: Barbara Brennan, a faith healer, physicist and psychotherapist. The Barbara Brennan School of Healing trains people to become professional healers. She is author of *Hands of Light,* available from her school, Box 2005, East Hampton, New York 11937, 516-329-0951.

Staying Healthy

In recent years, most Americans have launched what amounts to a health revolution. *What we know now:* We have a great deal of control over our own health. There are steps we can take that will enhance the way we feel, both physically and emotionally.*

Studies have shown us that most medical problems are related to lifestyle. *As a result, we're:*

• Smoking less. There has been a significant drop in smoking among adults (although not among teens). *Reason:* Cigarettes have unequivocally been linked with lung cancer as well as heart disease (the country's number-one killer).

• Drinking less. There has been a dramatic decrease in the consumption of alcohol in recent years. We now know that alcohol, if it is consumed at all, should be drunk in moderation.

And even the *definition* of moderation has changed. Where it used to mean two drinks a day, we now recognize that the threshold may well be lower. Each person must determine on his/her own how drinking affects his health and appearance.

• Exercising more. More and more people have started a program of regular exercise. *Gained:* A decrease in the risk of heart disease and an increase in life expectancy.

• Eating well. Most Americans have made positive changes in their eating habits. We are limiting our intake of certain foods—especially fatty items—and *adding* certain foods—especially fruits and vegetables—to our diet to help prevent cancer and other diseases.

The next step...

Despite our new awareness, one very important health factor—*stress*—is still being overlooked by many people.

When we're alarmed or anxious, our heart speeds up and our cholesterol and sugar levels rise. *Possible results:* Heart attacks...backaches ...stomach problems...increased sensitivity to pain. Stress can also be a precursor to the abuse of alcohol and drugs...even food.

*This doesn't mean that it's your fault if you get sick. Taking things that far causes needless emotional damage. And it doesn't mean that people who become ill should ignore proven treatments and try to *will* themselves back to health. They can't.

Stress can be caused by everything from the loss of a job to traffic noise. Although you can't escape stress in today's world, you can learn how to handle it.

How to cope with stress...

Studies have shown conclusively that people who have socially involved lives have far fewer health problems and live longer than people who are isolated.

Note: This does *not* mean that single people are in trouble. It's not so much whether we live with others (although married couples usually report better health) as whether we interact with people regularly and feel like we belong.

The most helpful contacts are regular activities that occur at least once a week—church, club meetings, card games, discussion groups, etc. *Even better:* Volunteer work.

The Institute for the Advancement of Health recently conducted a study that found that people who volunteer regularly—at least once a week for two hours—are 10 times more likely to be in good health than people who don't. Benefits range from an increase in their overall sense of well-being to a decrease in stress-related problems.

The most important component in volunteering is getting involved with the people you're helping. Just writing a check is not enough.

Example: A woman with multiple sclerosis volunteered on a telephone hotline. Although she usually had problems just picking things up, she found that while she was counseling others she could drink a glass of water without much trouble. Volunteering obviously didn't cure her ...but it did help her feel and function better.

Although we don't know exactly why social contact is so beneficial, we suspect it may be due to a *buffering* effect. The support and concern of others helps to ease life's pressures. The old wisdom that sharing one's burdens helps to lighten them appears to hold true.

Volunteering links us to people in a very special way. It decreases our awareness of our problems. And, at the same time, it increases our sense of commitment, challenge, joy and self-esteem—positive emotions that help ward off stress.

Completing the cycle...

Up until now, the health revolution has been inwardly focused. But changing how we eat, drink, smoke and exercise is only part of the picture. It's time to focus outward as well. You can't stay well in a stressful world unless you're involved with people. And, although nothing can guarantee perfect health, helping others is a major step in the right direction.

Source: Allan Luks, executive director of Big Brothers/ Sisters of New York, 223 E. 30 St., New York 10016. He is the former executive director of the Institute for the Advancement of Health.

To Protect Your Immune System

Your immune system is made up of white blood cells. To give optimal protection, these cells should be working 24-hours-a-day. They're directly affected by the quality of food you eat,* the way you behave, and the nature of your thoughts.

Dangers to the immune system:

- Excessive sugar.
- Inadequate protein.
- Inadequate zinc, iron, or manganese.
- Inadequate Vitamin C or Vitamin E.
- Diet and psychology are intimately related. Be especially cautious during times of stress, bereavement, sorrow, and trauma. They often translate into suppression of the immune function.
- Monitor magnesium intake. Most people don't get enough magnesium in their diets. And a magnesium deficiency can create anxiety symptoms. The minimum amount necessary is usually 300 to 500 milligrams a day. Under conditions of high stress, you would need more magnesium (since it's utilized very rapidly at such times). *Best sources:* Green leafy vegetables, lean meat, whole grains.
- Exercise enhances the function of your immune system by reducing stress.

*The amount of nutrients you need is best determined on an individual basis. To find out how much you need, consult a physician who specializes in disease prevention. Also useful: *Nutrition Against Disease* by Dr. Roger Williams, Bantam Books, New York.

- Examine your expectations about health. Do you expect, and accept, a couple of bouts with colds or flu each year? Instead, focus on strengthening your immune system. Sickness a couple of times a year is inevitable only if your immune system has been compromised.

Source: Jeffrey Bland, Linus Pauling Institute of Science and Medicine, Palo Alto, CA and author of *Nutraerobics,* Harper & Row, New York.

Dr. Dean Ornish Clears Up the Confusion Over Cholesterol

Despite all that's been said and written about cholesterol in recent years, many Americans remain understandably confused on the topic. While most of us know that too much cholesterol in the bloodstream can cause heart disease, many people remain unclear on certain subtle but very important issues...

What's a healthy cholesterol level? For years, the American Heart Association and the National Institutes of Health have recommended an optimal total serum cholesterol level of less than 200 milligrams per deciliter.

But we now know that roughly one-third of all heart attacks occur in individuals with cholesterol readings between 150 and 200. In fact, only when cholesterol falls to 150 or lower does heart disease cease to be a meaningful risk.

Unfortunate: The average American has a cholesterol level around 220... and the average American develops heart disease.

What about "good" and "bad" cholesterol? Total serum cholesterol is made up of two different compounds—low-density lipoprotein (LDL) cholesterol...and high-density lipoprotein (HDL) cholesterol.

- LDL (bad) cholesterol forms fatty plaques inside your coronary arteries, which can lead to heart attack.
- HDL (good) cholesterol is what the body uses to remove excess LDL from the bloodstream.

Doctors sometimes use the ratio of total cholesterol to HDL as another means of gauging heart disease risk.

Example: Someone with a total cholesterol count of 200 and an HDL level of 50 has a ratio of 200/50 or 4:1. In general, a ratio of 3.5 (200/57 is 3.5:1) or lower puts you at minimal risk for heart disease. The lower the ratio, the lower the risk—at least for people eating a traditional fatty, cholesterol rich diet.

Exception: Vegetarians and others on a very low-fat, low-cholesterol diet with less than 10% fat and virtually no cholesterol. Because they consume less fat and cholesterol and thus have less LDL in their blood, their bodies don't need to make as much HDL. Consequently, they may have high ratios yet they have a reduced risk of heart disease.

What causes high cholesterol? The single biggest factor is simply eating too much saturated fat and cholesterol. In fact, in the traditional American diet, roughly 40% of calories come from fat...and foods rich in fat are often rich in cholesterol. In countries where people eat much less cholesterol and less fat and where cholesterol averages around 130, heart disease is very rare.

Eating too much fat causes not only heart disease, but also has been linked with cancers of the breast, prostate, and colon, as well as stroke, diabetes, osteoporosis and, of course, obesity.

There is a genetic variability in how efficiently or inefficiently your body can metabolize, or get rid of, dietary saturated fat and cholesterol. On one end of the spectrum, some people are so efficient that they can eat almost anything and not get heart disease. On the other end of the spectrum are people who may get heart disease no matter what they eat. Ninety-five percent of people are somewhere in the middle. If your cholesterol level is less than 150, then either you're not eating very much fat and cholesterol or your body is very efficient at getting rid of it. Either way, your risk is low.

If it's above 150, begin by moderately reducing the amount of fat and cholesterol in your diet. If that's enough to bring it down below 150, that may be all you need to do, at least as far as your heart is concerned. If not, then continue to reduce the fat and cholesterol in your diet until your cholesterol stays below 150...or you are following a low-fat vegetarian reversal diet.

Which foods contain cholesterol? All foods derived from animals, including meats, poultry, fish, and dairy products. Meat is also high in iron, which oxidizes cholesterol into a form that more quickly clogs arteries. Skim milk has almost no fat and virtually no cholesterol. "Low-fat" milk is not really very low in fat. Foods derived solely from plants contain no cholesterol.

Caution: Some plant foods, including avocados, nuts, seeds and oils, are rich in saturated fat.

Just because a food is "cholesterol-free" doesn't mean it's good for your heart. All oils are 100% fat, and all oils contain at least some saturated fat, which your liver converts into cholesterol.

How often should I have my cholesterol checked? About once every two years, starting as early as age two. *To insure a reliable reading:* Find a testing lab certified by the Lipid Research Clinics. Use the same laboratory each time. Be sure to fast for at least 12 hours prior to your test.

How can I get my cholesterol under control? Exercise—it raises HDL cholesterol.

Stress raises LDL cholesterol, as does eating a high-fat, cholesterol-rich diet.

So the best way to raise HDL and lower LDL is to get regular exercise, avoid smoking, practice meditation or other stress management techniques and eat a healthful diet.

If you have heart disease: Eliminate all animal products except egg whites and nonfat dairy products...and all high-fat vegetable products, including oils, nuts, seeds, avocados, chocolate and other cocoa products, olives and coconut. In most cases this "reversal" diet not only keeps heart disease from progressing, but also reverses its course.

Eat more vegetables, fish, and skinless chicken. Use skim milk instead of whole milk. Use as little cooking oil as possible. Avoid oil-based salad dressing. If after eight weeks your cholesterol remains high, go on the "reversal" diet.

What about cholesterol-lowering drugs? I prescribe cholesterol-lowering drugs for people with heart disease who make only moderate changes in diet and lifestyle. Why? Several studies have shown that people with heart disease who only follow the American Heart Association guidelines tend to show worsening of their disease. People who follow the reversal diet—or who take cholesterol-lowering drugs—often can stop or reverse heart disease. Diet is preferable, because you avoid the high costs and side effects (both known and unknown) of drugs.

Source: Dean Ornish, MD, assistant clinical professor of medicine and an attending physician at the School of Medicine, University of California, San Francisco and at California Pacific Medical Center. He is the author of *Dr. Dean Ornish's Program for Reversing Heart Disease.* Ballantine Books, 201 E. 50 St., New York 10022.

Eight Rules for Staying Healthy

Some people work too hard at making themselves healthy. Actually, the human body is an intricate organism with feedback mechanisms to maintain itself in a healthy state. *Eight ways to help your body do its best:*

- Eat a well-balanced diet. For most people, diet should be high in fiber content.
- Maintain a comfortable weight. Being too thin is not healthier than maintaining your normal weight.
- Do not take vitamin supplements if your diet is proper.
- Learn to cope with stress. The best ways to achieve this are through relaxation exercises, biofeedback courses or, if necessary, psychotherapy.
- Exercise all muscle groups daily without excessive strain.
- Avoid sleep medications. If anxiety or depression causes poor sleep patterns, come to grips with the underlying problems.
- Establish good rapport with a physician you can trust.
- Listen closely to your body. Good health is a combination of using common sense and allowing the body to heal itself. By avoiding all the good things in life, you will not live longer. It will only seem longer.

Source: Dr. Bruce Yaffe, fellow in gastroenterology and liver diseases, Lenox Hill Hospital, New York.

Health Hints

- Before buying vitamins: Check Vitamin A and D dosages. Safe limits are 10,000 International Units for A, 400 for D. Signs of overdosage: Irritability, fever, bone pain (Vitamin A); lethargy, loss of appetite, kidney stones, or kidney failure (Vitamin D).
- Don't take Vitamin C and aspirin together. Studies at Southern Illinois University indicate that combined heavy doses produce excessive stomach irritation which could lead to ulcers (especially for those with a history of stomach problems).
- Eye care: Use eyedrops sparingly, especially commercial brands. They relieve redness by constricting blood vessels so eyes will look whiter. If used frequently, varicose veins can develop and eyes will become permanently reddened.
- The best cold medicine may be no medicine at all. No capsule or pill can cure a cold or the flu and may actually prolong the discomfort and hinder the body's own inherent ability to fight off the virus. *Best advice:* Rest and drink fluids.

Source: *Harvard Medical Health Letter,* Cambridge, MA.

Making a Plan For Wellness

Passing an annual physical exam was once enough to satisfy most people about their health. But today an increasing number strive beyond that— for optimal health or the condition of "wellness." *How to set up a wellness plan for yourself:*

- Try to clarify your most important reasons for living and write them down in a clear and concise fashion.
- With these in mind, identify the health goals that bolster your chances of living longer and healthier. *Be specific:* Do not plan to lose weight but to lose 20 pounds in six months. *Other possible goals:* Lowering blood pressure by a specific amount, accomplishing a dramatic

feat, such as riding the Snake River rapids or completing a marathon.

• List supportive actions for each goal. *Example:* Joining a fitness club, training for long-distance running.

• Also identify the barriers to each goal and how they can be overcome.

• List the payoffs for each goal, whether they are new energy at the office or more fun at the beach.

• Before starting the program, list friends you can rely on for bicycle rides, tennis or other activities in the plan. Virtually no one can hope to stay on a wellness plan without support from friends.

• Once the plan is under way, set realistic quarterly benchmarks to track your achievements. A log or diary is usually helpful.

Source: *14 Days to a Wellness Lifestyle,* Donald B. Ardell, Whatever Publishing, Inc., Mill Valley, CA.

The Major Threats To Your Life

The biggest, most deadly risks today are smoking and drinking.

• Smoking's association with lung cancer is well-known, but perhaps more startling is the fact that the habit doubles your risk of death from coronary heart disease (which accounts for 40% of all deaths these days).

• The deleterious effects of alcohol are less well-known. Even though wine consumption lowers your risk of heart disease, the overall impact of drinking is that three drinks before dinner regularly doubles your risk of premature death. The major causes of alcohol-related deaths are auto accidents, cirrhosis, suicide, gastrointestinal diseases.

Source: John Irquhart, MD, a former professor of physiology and bioengineering and coauthor (with Klaus Heilman, MD) of *Risk Watch: The Odds of Life,* Facts on File Publications, New York.

Life's Real Risks

Although we live in an era of low risk, with people living longer and healthier lives than ever before, we nevertheless seem to feel more at risk than we used to. Not all of our fears are well founded.

Here are some common myths many of us believe—and the realities:

• *Myth:* People were healthier and life was safer in "the good old days." *Reality:* Your chance of premature death 50-75 years ago was much higher than it is today.

• *Myth:* Pollution is a serious risk that never existed in the past. *Reality:* Pollution has shown no statistical sign of being a serious risk. If pollution were a big risk, you might expect a rise in certain cancers in the general population, like cancer of the bladder, since many substances that go into the body come out in concentrated form in urine. This hasn't happened.

• *Myth:* Death or injury by criminal violence has increased greatly. *Reality:* Life in London in the 18th century, Tom Jones vintage, included cutthroats and cutpurses just like today. Although murder is on the rise in our cities today, much of it is confined either to people who know each other or to young males in the lower socio-economic brackets.

• Myth: We're having a cancer epidemic. *Reality:* The opposite is true. We're having an epidemic of one kind of cancer—lung cancer caused by cigarette smoking. If lung cancer is removed from the statistics, fewer people than ever are dying from cancer. The perception of an increase in cancer is due to the increased longevity of the population. Cancer is an age-related disease: The longer you live, the more likely you are to get it.

• *Myth:* The risk of dying in an auto accident is greater today than 50-75 years ago. *Reality:* In England, although there are 10 times as many cars on the road as 50 years ago, and 30% more people, the same number of people are killed in cars today as in the 1930s. US statistics are similar. This is because people drive better, roads are better, cars are safer and medical care is better.

• *Myth:* We shouldn't use nuclear energy to produce power because the risk of an accident is too great. *Reality:* More people die in mining accidents every year than in nuclear power plants. The actual problems of nuclear power are minimal compared with the environmental damage from fossil-fuel generation (including destruction of the land by strip mining, of the seashore by oil drilling and of the forests by acid rain).

Source: John Urquhart, MD, a former professor of physiology and bioengineering and coauthor (with Klaus Heilman, MD) of *Risk Watch: The Odds of Life,* Facts on File Publications, New York.

Building Your Stress Resistance

• Change your expectations. The difference between expectations and perception of reality is the measure of how much stress you will experience. *Example:* If you begin the day with an attitude of "the world is changing, finances are fluctuating, nothing stays the same," and you perceive that to be so, you'll experience very little stress. If, instead, you assume that tomorrow will be the same as today and that things will go as you planned, you'll experience a lot of stress if your expectations aren't met. Either the environment or your own performance will displease you. *Remedy:* Be more realistic about your expectations and pay attention to your perceptions of reality.

• You won't be able to deal with stress if you feel that your past performances have been inadequate. You'll just assume that you'll fail again. *Remedy:* Find out the average or expected performance for any given job and gear yourself to that. People under stress tend to feel extremely anxious and afraid. These feelings often come across to others as anger rather than fear. If people see you as hostile (even though it is not really so), it may adversely affect any evaluation of your performance.

• Seek a socially cohesive work situation. In England during World War II, there was less illness and higher performance among Londoners who weathered the bombings than before, or after, the war. Great social cohesiveness was provided by an external enemy. That same kind of cohesiveness occurs in any organization geared toward a strong goal.

• Do relaxation exercises. The purpose is to get the focus on a nonlogical part of the body. It's the constant logical planning and rumination that keep stress going. *Best:* Approaches that focus on breathing. Proper breathing triggers other parts of the body to relax. The body is born with the innate ability to counter stress. These exercises allow you to activate that mechanism, and eventually you'll be able to call upon it at will.

• Make time to do something relaxing. Take some time away from your desk to window-shop or do something "silly." Eat lunch out of the office. Plan something pleasurable each week, and then follow through. *Caution:* If you eat while under stress, you'll have a 50% higher cholesterol level after the meal than if you were relaxed.

• Physical exercise helps only if you do it right. For instance, if jogging is just another chore that you don't enjoy, but you squeeze it into a heavy schedule because you feel you should, it only puts an extra load on your heart. Exercise while under stress can be dangerous. But if you see the trees and smell the air and feel high and good after running, you're doing it right. Exercise that makes you feel good is as helpful as any relaxation technique.

Source: Dr. Kenneth Greenspan, psychiatrist and Director of the Center for Stress and Pain-related Disorders, Columbia Presbyterian Hospital, New York City.

Attitudes that Combat Stress

In today's fast-moving, success-oriented world, it seems as though one must be able to withstand a very high stress level in order to get ahead and stay ahead. Many ambitious people put themselves under a crushing stress burden for years, eventually paying the price in heart disease, ulcers and so on.

But there are busy, high-achieving people who are seemingly immune to stress.

You can be one of them:

• Seek out and enjoy change. See it as a challenge. This is extremely important. How we view a stressful event determines how our bodies and minds react. If an event is seen as a threat and we feel victimized, the actual physiology of the body changes to meet the threat. If we see change as a challenge, with potential for growth and excitement, the body's response is entirely different.

• Don't be overly self-critical. Perfectionists —a very stress-vulnerable group—are always condemning themselves for not having coped well enough in the past. When a new challenge comes along, they view it as just another threat to their self-esteem.

• Identify with your work. When your work seems an extension of your personality it ceases to be an alien threat. Work-related stress then becomes less dangerous because it's for something you've chosen.

• Have a sense of control over your life. If you participate in the planning of a project and handle your part in its execution you will have a sense of control and get a sense of completion when the job is complete. This is why top managers are under less stress than middle managers.

Source: Dr. Kenneth Greenspan, psychiatrist and Director of the Center for Stress and Pain-related Disorders, Columbia Presbyterian Hospital, New York City.

Executives' Ranking Sources of Stress

What bothers executives most:

• Failure of subordinates to accept or carry out responsibilities: 92% of those responding to a survey listed this as their most serious problem.

• Inability to get critical information: 78%.

• Firing someone: 48%.

• Incompetent coworkers: 47%.

• Owner or board of directors challenging recommendations: 33%.

• Subordinates who question decisions: 5%.

• Conducting performance reviews: 3%.

Source: The Atlanta Consulting Group, Atlanta, GA.

The Best Ways To Control Stress

• Work at something you enjoy (not always easy to do, but a goal to strive for).

• Express your feelings freely.

• Relax (another tough order for some people).

• Identify and prepare for events or situations likely to be stressful.

• Talk to relatives, close friends or others about personal matters. Don't be afraid to call on them for help.

• Participate in group activities (such as church and community organizations) or hobbies that you enjoy.

Source: National Health Information Clearinghouse, Washington, DC.

Thorough Check-Up For Men

A man's thorough physical includes these procedures:

• Blood pressure test (most important).

• Eye and eye pressure exam.

• Check of lymph nodes and thyroid for swelling.

• Stethoscopic exam of heart and lungs.

• Stress tests (particularly for vigorous exercisers).

• Examination of the aorta.

• Testicle examination.

• Reading of pulse in legs.

• Proctoscopic exam of rectum and lower large intestine.

• Prostate examination.

• Stool sample for blood.

• Superficial neurological exam (reflexes and muscle strength).

• Laboratory test: Blood sugar, cholesterol, uric acid, complete blood screening (every three years), triglyceride, kidney function and calcium.

Source: *M* magazine.

What to Ask Your Plastic Surgeon

No matter how many questions you have or how trivial you feel they are...ask!

• Realistically, what will be done? Not what can be done, or what you can hope for, but what you can expect.

• What will happen if you don't get the result the doctor promises? How will he remedy that situation? Will you have to pay for the unsatisfactory job? Will he do a corrective procedure at no cost? *Crucial:* Preoperative and postoperative pictures taken by the same photographer. Only with photos can you prove that you didn't get the promised result.

• What is the chance of real damage, and if it happens, what might the extent of it be? Plastic surgeons aren't gods. They are physicians who have had extensive training in delicate repair of skin—but nobody can break the integrity of normal skin without leaving a mark. If you have a big growth in the middle of your cheek, you can't expect the doctor to cut it out without leaving a mark. *Other areas of concern:* The chances of infection and other complications.

• Where will the surgery be done? Although many reputable plastic surgeons operate out of their own offices, surgery done in a hospital inevitably offers more quality control. There's much less room for nonprofessionalism in a hospital, where nurses and operating room teams are provided by the institution and there is peer review of a surgeon's work. *Generally safest bet:* A doctor who is university affiliated and teaches in a hospital or medical school.

• May I see your book of "before and after" pictures? You may want to speak to a surgeon's other patients, but since this might violate confidentiality, he may only be willing to show you before and after pictures. If he offers you a whole book of good results, you can feel confident.

• Can the surgery be done in stages? *Why that can be important:* A male model had facial moles treated with liquid nitrogen. His skin darkened, and there were brown spots and scars. The surgeon hadn't done a trial on one mole, but had treated them all at one session. *Suggestion:* If you have many of the same defects, have one corrected first to see if you like the result.

• Is there a less serious procedure that will produce a similar result? Collagen injections available today can sometimes eliminate both wrinkles and acne scars. Suction lipectomy can remove fat pockets. Look into such lesser procedures before undergoing full-scale surgery.

• How much will it cost?

• How much time will it take?

• How long will I be out of work or away from home?

What to Look for On Eye Checkups

You should have a professional eye examination by an ophthalmologist or optometrist every two years, even if there has been no noticeable change in your vision since your last visit.

The examination should include:

• Full medical history, including details on previous or existing eye disease or injury in yourself and your family (first visit).

• Measurement of visual acuity, with and without corrective lenses.

• Tests for color blindness and stereopsis (binocular vision).

• Examination of the eyes' ability to track a moving object (usually with a tiny flashlight).

• Examination of the pupils' ability to constrict and dilate in response to changes in illumination and viewing distance.

• Screening for defects in the visual field (peripheral vision). This important test could indicate the presence of tumors, brain damage or a detached retina.

•Microscopic examination of the external portions of the eye, as well as the lens, optic nerve, retina and other interior structures. (Your eyes will be dilated for this step.)

•Screening for glaucoma.

Source: Richard L. Abbott, MD, associate clinical professor, department of ophthalmology, Pacific Presbyterian Medical Center, San Francisco.

A Skilled Eye Examination Checks More than Vision

By looking carefully into the eyes, a skilled physician can detect clues to literally hundreds of different systemic illnesses. The eyes can act as an early warning system for diseases that may not otherwise be apparent:

•High blood pressure: Changes in the eyes can include blood vessel spasm or narrowing and microscopic hemorrhages within the retina. Swelling of the optic nerve in the back of the eye indicates severe high blood pressure that requires emergency treatment.

•Diabetes: A patient might experience blurriness of vision and sudden sightedness. This change occurs because high blood sugar affects the water content of the lenses, causing them to swell. Distance vision improves and near vision deteriorates. Once the sugar problem is corrected, vision often returns to normal. Examination of the retina can reveal vascular changes, some of which respond to laser therapy. This could prevent visual disability in the future.

•Heart valve infection: This is most characteristic in patients who have run a low-grade fever over a period of time and may have a history of childhood heart disease or rheumatic fever. *How it happens:* From a wound or infection somewhere else in the body, the bloodstream is temporarily seeded with certain bacteria that can settle on a heart valve, especially if it was previously damaged. The bacteria slowly grow like vegetation on the valve. The symptoms can be very subtle, including headaches, sweating and low-grade fever. Occasionally little infected blood clots with bacteria on them travel to the eyes. Called *Roth spots*, these might be the only clue to a heart-valve problem that could be cured with intensive antibiotic therapy.

•Strokes: Episodes of amaurosis fugax (temporary blindness) can be evidence of an impending stroke or an indication of atherosclerosis of the carotid artery (the large artery in the neck).

•Brain tumors and other neurological problems. Some can come to light as a result of vision problems, such as loss of peripheral vision.

•Thyroid disease. This can cause swelling and increased prominence of the eyes. Sometimes only one eye seems to bulge, or there may be a too-wide stare or an eyelid lag.

•Inflammatory diseases. Rheumatoid arthritis and certain back diseases occasionally cause the eyes to be red and very dry, sandy, and scratchy.

•Hereditary defects. On occasion, metabolic disorders can be seen in the eyes. It may be possible to examine an entire family to see who is at risk for a particular genetic disease.

•Infectious diseases. Long-term syphilis and other abnormalities in the bloodstream may affect the eyes.

•Don't be frightened if the ophthalmologist recommends a medical checkup. Very often there are minor or unimportant findings that require confirmation of your general health.

Source: B. David Gorman, MD, adjunct ophthalmologist and coordinator of resident education at Lenox Hill Hospital.

How to Buy Contact Lenses Wisely

As contact lenses become more sophisticated, the options for wearers seem endless and the differences confusing. Before buying lenses, take into account your budget, your lifestyle and the degree of vision correction you need.

Regardless of the type of lenses you end up with (hard, gas-permeable, soft, or extended-wear), follow these guidelines:

•Select a professional eye-care specialist you trust and who comes well recommended.

•Be wary of discount commercial eye-care establishments. They deal in quantity, not quality, and emphasize product, not service.

•Be aware that physical changes can take place in the eyes as a result of wearing contacts. Your eye-care professional should carefully monitor such changes and adjust for them, if necessary.

•Ask about a service (or insurance) contract that offers replacement lenses at reduced fees. This is usually worth the modest price, as you may well lose a lens every year or so.

•Follow the cleaning/disinfecting procedures recommended by your eye-care professional. If you take shortcuts, you could shorten the life of your lenses and/or damage your eyes.

•Although you may wear your lenses every day, keep an updated pair of glasses to wear in emergencies.

Source: Robert Snyder, OD, an optometrist in private practice, Beach Haven, NJ.

How to Take Your Temperature

•Take your temperature first thing in the morning for the most accurate reading.

•Wait 30 minutes after eating, drinking, smoking, or exercising so your mouth will be neither cooled down nor heated up.

•Shake down the thermometer to below normal—mercury rises from the last reading.

•Relax.

•Hold the thermometer under the back of your tongue for four minutes.

•Don't move your tongue, breathe through your mouth or talk.

•When using a rectal thermometer on an infant, lubricate it with water-soluble jelly and hold the baby's legs so a quick movement won't dislodge it or break the glass.

•Leave the thermometer in at least two minutes. Don't use the new disposable thermometers. They're not very accurate. *Better:* The old-fashioned kind.

Testicular Cancer

Without prompt treatment, 29% of men who have testicular cancer will die from it. But virtually all could be cured if treated within a month of the onset of symptoms. *To lower your chances of being a victim:*

•Give yourself a testicular self-exam once a month. The exam takes only three minutes. The best time to do this is after a warm bath or shower, when the scrotum is most relaxed.

•Technique: Examine the testicles separately, using fingers of both hands. Put your thumbs on top of the testicle and your index and middle fingers underneath. Roll the testicle gently. (If it hurts, you're applying too much pressure.)

•Be aware that a normal testicle is firm, oval and free of lumps; behind it you'll feel the epididymis (sperm storage duct), which is spongier.

•If you feel a small, hard, usually painless lump or swelling on the front or side of the testicle, you could have a problem. When in the slightest doubt, see a doctor.

Source: *Prevention,* Emmaus, PA.

Skin Cancer Alert

Malignant melanoma, a form of skin cancer, has doubled in incidence in the past 10 years. If the cancer is caught and excised in the earlier stages of development, the patient can be cured. But if the malignancy goes too deep, the cancer invades the body, and neither radiation treatment nor chemotherapy is effective.

•Malignant melanoma can develop independently as a dark tumor in the skin or it can come from a potentially malignant lesion, the "dysplastic atypical mole."

•People with dysplastic moles should be checked by a dermatologist at least every six months.

Characteristics of malignant melanoma and dysplastic moles:

•Bigger in size than a pencil-eraser head.

•A mixture of colors in the same mole.

•Asymmetrical shape.

•Bumpy texture.

• Irregular or notched borders.

• Development of malignant melanoma is directly related to the sun. It is more common in fair-skinned, blue-eyed people, who are more sensitive to the sun. Many victims of malignant melanoma had a severe, blistering sunburn in childhood or adolescence, and areas such as the back that get weekend sunburns are often affected. Malignant melanoma and dysplastic moles also tend to run in families.

• *Myth:* A mole that suffers trauma (such as a cut during shaving) or sprouts hair will become cancerous.

Source: Harold T. Eisenman, MD, a dermatologist and dermatopathologist in private practice in West Orange, NJ.

Adult Acne: Myths and Realities

Pimples, breakouts, blemishes, zits. There are almost as many words for acne as there are myths about it.

To promptly dispel one such myth—acne is *not* a problem only for teenagers. In fact, more and more adults are seeking help for this embarrassing skin condition.

More acne myths...

Myth: Acne is caused by poor hygiene. In fact, the process that leads to breakouts takes place well beneath the skin's surface. It has nothing to do with dirt.

Acne occurs when oil (sebum) from the skin's sebaceous glands mixes with dead cells and clogs ducts in hair follicles. These oily plugs —called *comedones*—are the whiteheads and blackheads that can lead to tender swellings called cysts deep within the skin.

Myth: Pimples are caused by chocolate or greasy food. There's no evidence that any particular food causes acne...nor that acne is caused by psychological stress or too much—or too little—sex.

In reality, we still don't have a very clear idea of what causes acne. We suspect, however, that several factors are involved...

• Heredity. Acne seems to be inherited. If one identical twin has acne, there's more than a 95% chance that the other twin will have it, too. Also, 80% of acne sufferers have siblings with acne...and 60% have at least one parent who had acne while growing up.

• Oily skin. Acne is most common in people with oily skin. However, it also occurs in those whose skin is normal or even dry...and some people with very oily skin have no acne.

• Hormones. The sebaceous glands of acne sufferers may be oversensitive to androgens (male hormones)—which are produced by both males and females. Female hormones (estrogens) decrease sebum production. But even small amounts of androgens can counteract large amounts of estrogen.

• Blocked follicles. In a person with normal skin, cells lining hair follicles flake off periodically and are carried to the surface of the skin by sebum. But in people with acne, these dead cells block the follicles and form comedones. *Result:* Stagnant sebum that accumulates beneath the comedones is metabolized by skin-dwelling bacteria, releasing substances that inflame the skin.

Myth: Scrubbing the skin helps get rid of acne. Vigorous cleansing with washcloths, soaps or cleansers can cause additional pimples by damaging already weakened follicles.

Better: Wash gently with soap and water. Pick a detergent (nonsoap) skin cleanser that's oil-free. (Oils can clog pores and promote comedones.) Or find a soap that contains the drying agent benzoyl peroxide. It kills acne-causing bacteria and dries oily, acne-prone skin.

Caution: Benzoyl peroxide can cause excessive dryness or peeling. About 3% of users develop an allergic rash.

Myth: Taking vitamin A or applying vitamin E to the skin helps acne. Vitamin A is useless against acne—because acne is not caused by a vitamin deficiency. In large doses, vitamin A is toxic. But some vitamin A-like drugs called *retinoids* (including tretinoin and isotretinoin) are helpful.

Since acne is often associated with oily skin, applying vitamin E or any other kind of oil is the last thing you want to do.

Many acne sufferers find that their skin improves when they bask in ultraviolet (UV) light from the sun or a sunlamp. *Problem:* Such exposure causes wrinkles, discoloration, benign skin growths and even skin cancer.

For this reason, dermatologists generally treat acne not with UV light but with drying agents, antibiotics and other drugs.

Myth: Squeezing blemishes is harmless. In fact, this can easily break the walls of affected follicles and spread inflammation. It may also cause permanent scarring.

Instead of performing this form of "self-surgery," keep your skin clean, apply warm compresses to large pimples or cysts and use appropriate medication prescribed by a dermatologist.

Prescription therapies...

Dermatologists have a variety of effective acne treatments to offer, including topical agents and antibiotics. *Most effective:*

• Tretinoin (Retin-A). For mild to moderately severe acne. Tretinoin dries the skin, clearing up existing blemishes and helping prevent new ones. Common side effects include skin irritation and increased sensitivity to sunlight.

To minimize these possible problems, ask your doctor about using lower-strength tretinoin ...and about limiting your exposure to sun and drying agents like benzoyl peroxide.

• Antibiotics. For mild to moderately severe acne. Topical antibiotics (lotions or creams) work by penetrating follicles to kill blemish-causing bacteria. Side effects include dryness, peeling and itching—but these are typically caused by alcohol in the lotion, not the antibiotics.

For deep pimples or cysts, antibiotic pills are often more effective. Side effects include stomach and intestinal upset.

Oral antibiotics sometimes cause vaginal yeast infections. *Reason:* Just as antibiotics kill bacteria on the skin, they kill vaginal bacteria. These are what normally keep yeast under control.

Self-defense: Ask your doctor about adjusting the dose of antibiotic or switching to another one. In some cases, eating yogurt containing *lactobacillus* bacteria helps keep yeast under control.

• Isotretinoin (Accutane). The strongest treatment available for severe cystic acne. Isotretinoin works by shrinking overactive oil glands. *Side effects:* Dry skin, chapped lips, dryness inside the nose and eye irritation. Some patients experience pain in their bones, muscles and joints.

Isotretinoin may also raise cholesterol levels and affect the liver. If taken during pregnancy, it can cause birth defects. For these reasons, isotretinoin is appropriate only for people with very severe acne that has not responded to other treatments. Patients must be closely monitored during isotretinoin therapy, which typically lasts 20 weeks.

• Hormone therapy. Because estrogen seems to help alleviate acne, women with severe acne are sometimes treated with birth-control pills, which contain estrogen. Side effects may include nausea, weight gain and breast tenderness.

• Acne surgery. Various surgical methods are used to remove blackheads and whiteheads and open up pimples and cysts.

Beware: To avoid scarring, only a doctor or a trained medical assistant should perform these removal procedures.

What to do about scars...

There is no perfect solution for acne scars. Before opting for any procedure, be sure you understand what results to expect, possible complications and cost...

• Dermabrasion. Best for soft, scooped-out scars, this technique removes the upper layers of skin with a rotating steel brush. Skin remains red and sensitive for several months. Antibiotic salves are often applied to prevent infection.

Complications may include blotchy skin, tiny white pimples called *milia*—and more scarring.

• Excision. There are several surgical techniques to improve "ice-pick" scars. These procedures result in new, less obvious types of scars. In some cases, skin discoloration occurs.

• Fillers. Some scars can be minimized via injections of collagen (a protein derived from cows) or of fibrin (a substance derived from human blood). Both substances may cause allergic reactions. Improvement lasts only about a year.

Silicone is a long-lasting filler, but it doesn't have FDA approval. Only a limited number of physicians can use it—on an experimental basis.

Acne rosacea...

People with acne rosacea have a defect in the small blood vessels. Initially, their skin may simply look ruddy instead of pimply.

But left untreated, rosacea causes visible veins, acne blemishes and thickening of the skin. The nose can become coarse and distorted by bumps.

Patients with rosacea must avoid aggravating factors like hot liquids, spicy foods and alcohol. Sunlight, extremes of temperature and stress also provoke the condition.

Treatments include topical antibiotics and corticosteroids. The newest medication is metronidazole gel, which decreases acne and improves the red rash.

Source: Richard A. Walzer, MD, special lecturer at Columbia University Medical School and consultant in dermatology at Columbia-Presbyterian Hospital, New York City. He is the author of *Treating Acne: A Guide for Teens and Adults*, Consumer Reports Books, 101 Truman Ave., Yonkers, NY 10703.

Dr. Andrew Weil on Cholesterol, Nutrition, Weight...and More

What is cholesterol—and what is the difference between "good" and "bad" cholesterol? Cholesterol is a waxlike substance that is needed for the body's normal metabolism. It travels through the blood system in little protein "packages" called lipoproteins.

One type of cholesterol is *low-density lipoprotein*—or LDL. It is commonly referred to as "bad" cholesterol because it damages the arterial walls. *High-density lipoprotein*—or HDL—is called "good" cholesterol because it appears to protect the arteries from damage.

Your body naturally produces all the cholesterol it needs. This is why you don't need any dietary cholesterol and should avoid foods that raise the cholesterol levels in your blood. If your cholesterol is too high, you are at greater risk of developing coronary artery disease.

What to do: Ask your doctor for your total cholesterol count and how it breaks down into LDL and HDL. Total cholesterol should be less than 180 milligrams per deciliter of blood—but a higher level may be fine if the ratio of HDL to LDL is high. If your total cholesterol level gets low enough—under 140, for example—you may not need to worry at all about the HDL/LDL level.

Exercise has been shown to boost HDL. Alcohol may also raise HDL, but since it has many adverse effects, I don't recommend you start drinking in order to boost your HDL level. If you do drink, opt for red wine and stick with one or two glasses per day.

How can I lower my level of bad cholesterol? Controlling cholesterol has more to do with what you *don't* eat than with what you *do* eat. While some foods help lower cholesterol, no one food will dramatically reduce cholesterol.

What to do: Cut back on saturated fats, which are found in meats, eggs, butter, whole milk and whole-milk products. They are also found in processed foods made with animal fats and in palm and coconut oils. The amount of saturated fat you consume has the most direct dietary influence on how much cholesterol circulates in your blood. Foods that contain cholesterol can boost your blood cholesterol level.

Don't assume that products labeled *cholesterol free* are harmless. They may contain saturated fats, so read package labels carefully.

How important is fiber...and how much do I need to eat? Fiber is a term for the *indigestible* components of the plant foods we eat. The intestines of people who eat a lot of fiber function better, since fiber increases the bulk and frequency of bowel movements. Constipation is often caused by a lack of fiber.

Studies have shown that adequate fiber intake may also lower the risk of colon cancer.

What to do: The average adult should eat 40 grams of fiber each day—about twice as much as most people consume. You can increase your fiber intake by eating cereals that contain bran. Read labels carefully to make sure the product contains between four and five grams of bran per one-ounce serving. You can also increase your fiber intake by including hearty amounts of fruits, vegetables and whole grains in your diet.

Source: Andrew Weil, MD, director of the Program of Integrative Medicine at the University of Arizona College of Medicine in Tucson and a leading expert on alternative medicine, mind/body interactions and medical botany.

19

Healthy Healing

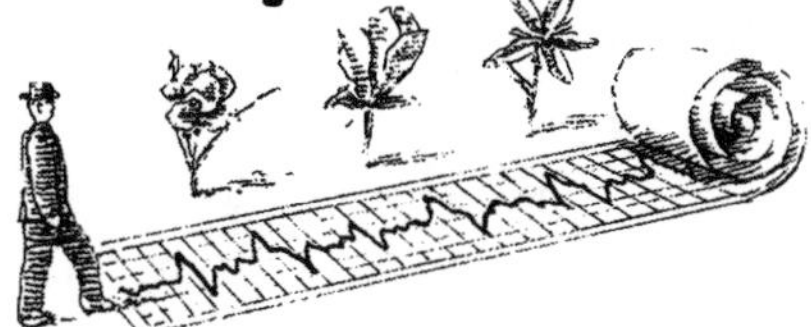

Faster Healing

Heal faster—by increasing your intake of zinc. Cuts, scrapes, blisters, and minor burns heal about one-third faster in those who take a minimum of 15 mg. of zinc daily. Fast healing decreases the chances of infection, scarring and stiffness. *Best:* A multiple vitamin-mineral supplement containing zinc rather than plain zinc tablets, which sometimes cause heartburn or indigestion.

Source: *Prime Time: A Doctor's Guide to Staying Younger Longer* by John E. Eichenlaub, MD. Prentice-Hall, Route 9W, Sylvan Ave., Englewood Cliffs, New Jersey 07632.

10 Common Health Problems

Many common diseases can be treated quite easily. Others take more effort. There are some we can't do anything about—but that go away by themselves. Even though doctors can't cure every disease, there's no harm in seeing a doctor when you aren't feeling right. At the very least, your physician can help you understand what's going on in your body, and advise you on relieving the discomforts.

Colds and flu...

These are caused by viruses, and nothing a doctor gives you will cure them. The infection will run its course by itself—usually within a few days though sometimes it takes several weeks.

Cold clues: If you have congestion, a cough and/or a sore throat, you probably have a cold.

Flu clues: If you have a fever and your muscles feel weak and tired, it's probably flu.

Antibiotics are completely ineffective against viral infections—though patients continue to demand them.

The best we can do is treat the symptoms. Aspirin, acetaminophen, or ibuprofen can relieve pain and fever. *For cough medicines, decon-*

gestants, and throat treatments: Those containing dextromethorphan are most effective.

Bed rest will not make the cold go away any faster, but it might make you feel better in the meantime.

Bladder infections...

Bladder infections affect far more women than men. Because the urethra is shorter in women than in men, germs that live around the anus and vaginal area can travel up to the bladder fairly easily.

Antibiotics generally clear up most bladder infections within a week.

Some people believe baths encourage the spread of germs into the bladder. This has never been proven, but it can't hurt to take showers instead of baths until the infection clears up.

Cranberry juice is a popular folk remedy. It makes the urine more acidic—a hostile environment for germs. But, you have to drink a large amount of juice (a quart or two a day) for it to be effective.

It's hard to find pure cranberry juice—look for it in health food stores. The kind you buy at the supermarket is mostly water and sugar and won't do a thing.

Irritable bowel syndrome...

Irritable bowel syndrome (IBS) is considered the most common digestive complaint. When the intestinal muscles don't function as smoothly as they should, patients may experience constipation, diarrhea, cramps, and bloating, or some combination of the above.

No one really knows what causes IBS...and there's no sure cure. *Helpful:*

- Adding fiber to the diet can be beneficial. Eat lots of fruits and vegetables.
- If you know you're sensitive to certain foods—such as caffeine, other acidic foods, seeds, etc.—avoid them.
- Get plenty of exercise.

Also helpful: Low doses of antidepressants. We're not sure why—it may be that they alter nerves in the brain that regulate muscle function.

Lower back pain...

The back is very poorly designed for walking upright. The muscles are too small and weak to support the weight of the upper body, and the disks are easily injured. Ordinary wear-and-tear makes a certain amount of back pain almost inevitable with age.

If you experience acute pain, rest the back as you would any injured area. Applying heat and taking ibuprofen usually helps ease the pain. Most acute backaches subside within a few weeks.

If your problem is chronic, be aggressive. Most doctors don't know much about back pain, so look for one who specializes in backs—and who *doesn't* rush to recommend surgery. Minor complaints can often be helped by exercise programs and physical therapy to strengthen the back.

Psoriasis...

Psoriasis is a condition in which the skin grows more rapidly than normal, causing patches to turn red and flake off.

We don't know what causes psoriasis. Once the condition has erupted, however, any injury or irritation to the skin is likely to result in an outbreak. So psoriasis sufferers should avoid getting sunburned, and wear gloves when doing the dishes or if working with harsh chemicals.

Doctors commonly prescribe cortisone creams, which work by discouraging skin cells from multiplying. But long-term use of cortisone is a bad idea—it will make the skin thin and delicate.

Exposure to ultraviolet light is another fairly common treatment, but it increases the risk of skin cancer.

Best treatment: Tar, applied topically. Tar is a very old remedy. The current bottled solutions are not nearly as messy or smelly as the older kind of solutions. If the sufferer's doctor doesn't know about tar treatment, find a doctor who does.

Panic attacks...

It's very common for patients to complain of pounding heart, dry mouth, sweating, difficulty breathing, and feelings of intense anxiety or fright—for no obvious reason.

Some people are awakened in the night by these attacks—others may experience them in the middle of a meeting. They seem to be most common among young adults.

We don't understand much about panic attacks, except that they're usually harmless.

Symptoms are caused by the release of adrenaline, and they subside when the body runs out of adrenaline...usually after 20 or 30 minutes. They're generally not a sign of heart disease. And they don't usually occur often. If the attacks are chronic and interfere with everyday functioning, several medications can help. Check with your doctor.

Impotence...

Not so long ago, impotence was thought to be a psychological problem, and patients were sent to psychiatrists for long, expensive treatments. Now we know that there are many physical causes as well—and that most cases respond to treatment fairly quickly.

Drugs are a common physical cause. Marijuana, alcohol, even smoking can interfere with sexual performance.

Impotence is also a frequent side effect of high blood pressure medication. If you take drugs for high blood pressure, ask your doctor about adjusting the dosage. There are so many different medications that you should be able to find one that doesn't cause this side effect.

Impotence is also associated with diabetes—but only as a long-term complication associated with damage to nerves or arteries.

Psychological causes include boredom, depression and anxiety.

It's rarely necessary to embark on a long, involved course of psychotherapy in order to cure impotence. Often, just understanding that these emotions can contribute to the condition —and that it's temporary—is enough to provide relief. For stubborn cases, sex therapy may be helpful.

Migraine headaches...

Unlike some other kinds of headaches, migraines are *vascular.* Blood vessels in the scalp become highly sensitive, and heartbeats stretch the arterial walls, creating a throbbing pain.

Migraine attacks tend to start during the teen years and decrease as a person gets older. They usually disappear by middle age.

Unless your symptoms are truly peculiar, don't invest a lot of time and money in tests—they probably won't show anything. Fortunately, migraines are treatable. Several drug families—including antidepressants and antihistamines—can be helpful.

Helpful: Standard pain medications, such as acetaminophen or Darvon, will relieve mild pain.

Better: Drugs that stiffen the arteries. Caffeine does this—a few cups of coffee for a minor attack may be effective.

For severe migraine, ergotamine is effective and prescribed by many doctors to be taken at the first sign of a migraine. It can be taken as a pill, suppository, or inhalant, and is sometimes combined with caffeine.

Nausea is a common side effect, so if the pill form makes you nauseous, ask your doctor about experimenting with the other forms.

Insomnia...

The best treatment for insomnia may be to put it in perspective. Very few insomniacs spend a lot of time feeling sleepy during the day. They may be sluggish in the morning, but once they get going they don't feel too bad.

Upsetting: Lying awake in the middle of the night, trying to sleep and feeling frustrated because you can't.

Sleeping pills don't cure insomnia—they just induce poor-quality sleep. And they can be addictive.

Try to view insomnia as simply irritating—not dangerous. If you can't sleep, don't drive yourself crazy about it. Turn on the light and read.

Note: Insomnia can be a symptom of depression. If that's the case, then the underlying problem should be addressed.

Warts...

Warts are viral and contagious—you can catch them from going barefoot in a public place, using someone else's comb or from scratching and spreading your own warts. However, they may not appear until up to a year after exposure.

Though unattractive, warts are not dangerous. They're more common in children than adults—it's possible that we build up resistance as we age.

The vast majority of warts go away by themselves within a year or two. Treatments include freezing with liquid nitrogen, corroding with acid, and burning or electrocoagulation. I prefer liquid nitrogen—it's simple, effective and not very painful.

Source: Family practitioner Michael Oppenheim, MD, who practices in Los Angeles. He is the author of *A Doctor's Guide to the Best Medical Care* and *The Complete Book of Better Digestion*, both published by Rodale Press, 33 E. Minor St., Emmaus, Pennsylvania 18098.

Natural Remedies For a Stuffy Nose

Chinese ephedra—Ephedra sinica—is an ancient medicinal herb used as a bronchodilator and a stimulant. The source of ephedrine—predecessor of pseudoephedrine, the active ingredient in Sudafed—this dried herb comes in pill form, or works well when you drink it as tea. *Caution:* No more than one cup every four hours. *Also helpful:* Bioflavonoids—available at vitamin and health food stores. Take one or two capsules...stuffiness should clear up in about 20 minutes.

Important: Check with your doctor before using. Ephedra is not for use by those with hyperthyroidism or prostate disease.

Source: Marvin Schweitzer, ND, is a naturopath with the Center for Healing Arts, in Orange, Connecticut.

Music Can Help Heal the Brain

A prescription for music therapy is becoming more common as scientists prove how combinations of sounds affect brain and body.

Humans have long used the rhythm and tempo of music to make repetitive tasks easier. Stanford University experimenters recorded electrical patterns from the elbows of women 18 to 35-years-old performing tasks. They found music really did improve synchronization of nerves and muscle signals.

Music is being studied intensively today for its physiological effects. It has been shown to be beneficial for muscular development, physical coordination, a sense of timing, mental concentration, memory skills, visual and hearing development, and stress control. The cerebellum, at the base of the brain, is devoted to the regulation of the sort of movement we use when playing an instrument or dancing to music. Current research suggests one of the cerebellum's fundamental functions may be to help us learn and remember movements.

Dr. Jon Eisenson, a Stanford University Medical Center professor emeritus of hearing and speech science, has long advocated music for stroke and brain-trauma patients unable to speak.

Many beneficial physical effects can be derived from listening and moving to music. In fact, merely listening to music has been found to lower blood pressure and reduce sweating and respiratory rates.

Music can also change moods. Just think of how rock concert patrons behave—or how you feel when you hear a song associated with a past love.

Source: Arthur Winter, MD, FICS, director of The New Jersey Neurological Institute. He is a coauthor, with his wife, Ruth Winter, of *Build Your Brain Power*, St. Martin's Press, 175 Fifth Ave., New York 10010.

Healthier Blood Pressure Levels

Blood pressure is more likely to remain at healthy levels in people who eat a diet that is rich in beans, rice and other sources of vegetable protein...higher than usual in polyunsaturated fat...and low in saturated fat and cholesterol.

Source: Kiang Liu, PhD, professor of preventive medicine, Northwestern University Medical School, Chicago. His study of more than 1,800 men, ages 40 to 55, was reported in *Internal Medicine News and Cardiology News*, 12230 Wilkins Ave., Rockville, Maryland 20852.

Drill-less Dentistry

Drill-less dentistry is now offered by some dentists. A new process called *kinetic cavity preparation* "sandblasts" away decay with a high-speed stream of tiny particles. *Eliminated:* Heat, vibration, noise, smell and friction—and 80% of pain. There's less need for anesthesia. This new process can be faster, too.

Source: Ronald Goldstein, DDS, clinical professor, school of dentistry, Medical College of Georgia, Augusta. He maintains a private practice in Atlanta.

Your Dentist and Your Medical History

Your medical history should be known by your dentist as well as your doctor. Without this knowledge, dentists may fail to take the precautions necessary to prevent complications in treating "medically compromised" persons—those with heart trouble, infectious disease or certain other medical problems. *Also:* A dentist who knows your medical history will be better able to treat and/or arrange for medical care in case of an emergency.

Source: Barbara J. Steinberg, DDS, professor of medicine and assistant director of the division of dental medicine, Medical College of Pennsylvania, Philadelphia. Her recommendation appeared in the *Journal of the American Dental Association,* 211 E. Chicago Ave., Chicago 60611.

Best Cold Medicines

For teens/adults: Combination antihistamine decongestants. They reduce nasal congestion, postnasal drip, coughing—and also reduce cold symptoms involving the ears. These medicines don't appear to be helpful for young children.

Source: William Feldman, MD, head of division of general pediatrics, Hospital for Sick Children, Toronto. His study, which reviewed 106 studies on colds, was published in the *Journal of the American Medical Association,* 515 N. State St., Chicago 60610.

How to Warm Cold Hands Caused by Stress

Cold hands are often a sign of stress if you are indoors and there is no reason for them to be chilled. Biofeedback research indicates that techniques to warm hands can also reduce the stress load. *What works:*

• Close your eyes and imagine yourself holding and playing with something soft and warm.

• Touch your cheeks, which are usually warm, and imagine the warmth flowing into your fingers.

• Interlock fingers, squeeze gently for one second, release for one second.

Repeat sequence several times.

Source: Robert Hall, president, Futurehealth, Inc., Bensalem, PA.

Headache Relief Without Drugs

Relief from incapacitating tension, vascular and migraine headaches is possible without drugs, using a self-administered form of acupuncture know as acupressure.

The technique:

• Exert very heavy thumbnail pressure (painful pressure) successively on nerves lying just below the surface of the skin at key points in the hands and wrists. As with acupuncture, no one's sure why it works.

Pressure points to try:

• The triangle of flesh between the thumb and index finger on the back of your hands (thumb side of bone, near middle of the second metacarpal in the index finger).

• Just above the protruding bone on the thumb side of your wrist.

How to Treat Fever

•Take aspirin or acetaminophen only when your temperature is over 102° and you're uncomfortable.

•Dress lightly enough so that body heat can escape.

•Sponge with tepid water, not alcohol (the vapors can be dangerous).

•Take a bath and wash your hair if you feel like it—the evaporating water may lower your temperature.

•Drink eight to twelve glasses of liquid a day to avoid dehydration.

Fever: When to Call the Doctor

Call the doctor for a fever when:

•A child's temperature goes above 102° or an adult's over 101°.

•The fever persists for more than 24 hours with no obvious cause.

•The fever lasts for more than 72 hours, even if there's an obvious cause.

•An infant under three months old has any temperature elevation.

•There is a serious disease involved.

•In short, call the doctor when you feel really sick (even if you haven't got a fever).

What to Do About Colds

Doctors cannot cure a cold. But sufferers can help themselves by keeping in mind what is known about the ailment. *Essentials:*

•Chills don't cause colds, but they encourage existing viruses to multiply.

•Colds spread most effectively by direct contact and are most contagious in their early stages before the symptoms are even noticeable.

•The body's process of curing a cold requires about the same energy as hard physical labor. Keep vigorous exercise to a minimum so your energy goes toward fighting the cold.

•Taking vitamin C may help. Advocates suggest one to three grams a day at the outset of a cold and 500 milligrams daily throughout its duration.

•Avoid stress during a cold. It reduces antibody production in the nose and mouth.

•Don't numb pain by drinking alcohol.

Source: *Executive Fitness Newsletter,* Emmaus, PA.

The Office Cold is a Myth

People pick up relatively few cold viruses from their associates at work. An office may have many people nursing colds, but chances are few of them have the same virus strain. The majority of colds are caught at home. And the main carriers are children, who are exposed to the most viruses through close association and direct physical contact with their playmates. Parents then catch the cold from the sick child.

•Shaking hands with someone who has a cold and then rubbing your eyes can be riskier than standing directly in front of a sneezing person. Current research indicates that most colds are probably spread by direct physical contact. The viruses grow in the nose and eyes (but not the mouth). When infected people wipe or blow their noses sloppily, some of the cold virus can get onto their hands. Outside the body, the virus can survive as long as a day. *Result:* Unless washed off, it spreads to toys, furniture, drinking cups and other people's hands.

Colds are contagious, beginning with the onset of symptoms until the symptoms vanish. *Worst period:* The first two to three days.

•Use a tissue or handkerchief when covering coughs and sneezes. Bare hands pick up the virus and spread the cold.

•Wash your hands frequently when around people who have colds, especially after touching things they have handled.

•Keep hands away from nose and eyes immediately after contact with a person with cold symptoms.

•Do not rely on household sprays to disinfect objects. Their value is unproven.

Source: Jack Gwaltney, Jr., MD, professor of internal medicine, University of Virginia Medical School.

A Cough: Getting Rid of it the Old-Fashioned Way

Skeptics of cough medications say home remedies may be more effective and less risky. *Try these:*

•Chicken soup.

•Fruit juices.

•Vaporizers and humidifiers.

•A drop of honey on the back of the tongue.

Sources: Dr. Sidney Wolfe, MD, and others, quoted in *Executive.*

Back Strain and Driving

The probability of spinal disk problems is three times greater for those who spend a big part of their work lives driving. *To reduce the strain on your back:*

•Keep your head and shoulders erect while driving. Place a 1½-inch-thick pillow, or a wicker back support, at the small of the back. Keep the back pressed against it.

•Change driving position often.

Take frequent breaks to stretch your legs and do one or two of these exercises:

•Grab your wrists, and raise your arms to shoulder height. Try to pull your arms apart for a count of six. Repeat three times.

•Hold your forehead, then push your head against your hand. Repeat for each side of the head. Do slowly three times.

•Lace your fingers behind your head and press back against them. Do slowly three times.

•Using the car to steady you, do at least four deep-knee bends when you stop for a rest.

Source: Shirley Linde, author of *How to Beat a Bad Back,* Rawson, Wade Publishers, New York.

Using Your Mind To Fight Cancer

Your beliefs can be powerful allies against cancer. The body produces billions of cells and routinely identifies and kills cancerous ones. Once the major cancer-removal job is done by surgery and chemotherapy, your body can take over. But you must free up energy to mobilize your body to fight cancer.

•Express your feelings. Patients who express anger and sadness survive the longest. Expressing your feelings reduces stress and releases energy. Suppressing feelings uses up valuable energy that should be mobilized to fight the cancer. *Example:* In a study at Johns Hopkins, patients with metastatic breast cancer who survived more than a year were those who expressed their depression, anxiety, and sense of alienation. They were also judged by their doctors as being poorly adjusted to the disease and as having negative attitudes toward their doctors.

•Avoid blame, guilt, and self-criticism. You are not being punished for wrongdoing. The question *Why me?* should be replaced with *What can I do about it now?*

•Seek support. Discuss your situation with a therapist, family member, or support group. *Important:* Talk with a former cancer patient who has been pronounced cured or has survived for years with the disease. This can be a powerful combatant of negative feelings.

•Take positive steps to help yourself. Recognize that your life has changed, probably forever, and that your old ways of coping are no longer viable and may even be implicated in your illness. *What must change:* Gratification from compulsive goal-seeking. The cancer patient must start to develop a sense of self-worth that comes from within rather than from outside goals such as success, money, or sexual conquests.

•Learn to say no. Every moment is precious. Why waste it on trivia or worrying about whether an extra phone call will bother your doctor.

•Speak the unspeakable. The relatives and friends of cancer patients often feel certain subjects are taboo. This leads patients to suppress their feelings in order to protect their loved ones. But when patients and the people they're close to talk openly about their feelings, it can be an enormous relief and source of strength.

•Participate in choosing your treatment to reduce the stress of feeling like a passive victim. You may feel emotionally and physically debilitated by the side effects of chemotherapy and slip into thinking that you have to take these drugs for your doctor. Remind yourself that you are taking the drugs because they are powerful allies of your body.

•You must choose a doctor you feel has some concern for you as a human being and who takes your values and life goals into consideration when medical decisions are made. Your doctor should give you information about treatment plans and alternatives and be open to negotiating alternatives with you rather than assuming a "take it or leave it" attitude.

Source: Neil A. Fiore, PhD, a psychologist who works for the University of California and has a private practice in Berkeley. He has worked with many cancer patients, and is the author of *The Road Back to Health: Coping With the Emotional Side of Cancer,* Bantam Books, New York.

Antibiotics: Handle with Care

Say you have a scratchy throat, aching muscles and a mild headache. If you're like millions of Americans, you'll reach for an antibiotic in your medicine cabinet or ask your doctor to prescribe one.

Better think again. Overused and vastly misunderstood, these so-called miracle drugs may do you more harm than good, especially if taken when they are not needed.

Antibiotics are designed to fight *bacterial* infections. But too often, we take them casually and for the wrong reasons—for *viral* infections such as a cold or flu.

Sometimes we use antibiotics prescribed for a previous illness to treat a current one...or we may even take antibiotics prescribed for a friend.

Or we may discontinue antibiotics too soon, before they've had a chance to do their job. Unfortunately, such careless, naive and inappropriate use not only is ineffective but also can pave the way for more serious illnesses later on.

Breeding trouble...

Even when taken under the *best* of conditions—when we have a clearly identified bacterial infection and use a drug designed to fight it —antibiotics don't always work.

Reason: Some bacteria manage to survive despite the antibiotic. With the more vulnerable bacteria knocked out, *drug-resistant* survivors are free to multiply and cause a new infection that cannot be cured by the antibiotic.

To make matters worse, some bacteria defend themselves by *developing* resistance to antibiotics after repeated exposure. This renders the same antibiotic far less potent the next time around.

Indeed, bacteria have evolved many ingenious—and very tricky—ways to elude the effects of antibiotics.

Some simply expel any antibiotic that gets inside their cell membrane. Some destroy or chemically alter the antibiotic so that it is no longer active. Others mutate to become less sensitive to the effects of the drug.

Bottom line: Using antibiotics too often or for prolonged periods of time promotes buildup of drug-resistant bacteria among the protective bacteria colonizing our skin and intestinal tract. If we should someday need an antibiotic to fight a truly serious infection, it may be far less effective in doing its job, leaving us possibly without effective treatment when we really need it.

Unfortunately, turning to another antibiotic may not help. Bacteria resistant to one drug are often resistant to other drugs—a property known as "multiple drug resistance."

Classic case: A South American businessman who had been using antibiotics for sore throats, colds and other minor viral complaints developed acute leukemia along with a serious intestinal infection. The doctors successfully treated his leukemia. Ironically, however, the common *E. coli* bacteria causing his infection proved resistant to *eight* different antibiotics. The bacteria spread to several of his internal organs. He died several weeks later.

Because of his abuse of antibiotics, this man had transformed ordinarily harmless bacteria into bacteria that were resistant to several drugs ...and which eventually killed him.

Deadlier diseases...

Paradoxically, taking too little of an antibiotic can be just as hazardous as taking too much. Consider tuberculosis, for example, a bacterial disease that was once all but eradicated—but which recently has been making a major comeback throughout urban America.

One reason TB has returned is that many TB patients take their medication sporadically—or stop taking it too soon. Such erratic habits spawn drug-resistant strains of TB bacilli. Then these haphazardly treated and still-infected individuals spread the same drug-resistant bacteria to others.

Result: What was once an easily curable disease has become a formidable—and growing—threat to public health. Antibiotic misuse has also brought about new, drug-resistant strains of gonorrhea, strep throat, urinary tract infections, childhood ear infections, pneumonia, meningitis and salmonella.

Getting to the source...

Doctors also play a part in the widespread mishandling of antibiotics and the consequent emergence of drug-resistant bacteria.

Patients typically demand antibiotics, thinking they will relieve the symptoms of a cold or flu or other viral conditions invulnerable to antibiotics. And some doctors give in to these demands—even though they may be well aware that prescribing antibiotics in such cases is useless. Some prescribe antibiotics too freely without clear evidence of a bacterial infection.

Often it is relatively easy to distinguish a viral from a bacterial infection—just by the symptoms on physical examination. The definitive way to tell the difference is to perform tests, called bacterial cultures, of the affected body site, such as the throat. Using this information, the doctor can determine the likelihood of a bacterial infection and the need for an antibiotic.

Another problem: Too many times doctors rely on "broad-spectrum" antibiotics to hit every possible cause of the infection. Unfortunately, such antibiotics generate more bacterial resistance than the narrow-spectrum drugs.

Other drawbacks...

Antibiotics can cause gastrointestinal problems and allergic reactions. Prolonged use can lead to yeast infections and to toxicity in critical internal organs.

Another common side effect of antibiotics is the overgrowth of certain undesirable bacterial flora, including those that produce dangerous toxins.

Example: Diarrhea caused by excessive growth of intestinal bacteria may follow treatment with certain broad-spectrum antibiotics. Candida and other yeasts are resistant to antibiotics. If present, they can easily overgrow an area where the protective bacteria have been eliminated by antibiotics.

Being safe and smart...

Used prudently and with caution, of course, antibiotics play a critical and often life-saving therapeutic role. They can even help *prevent* infections under certain vulnerable conditions.

Example: For surgical patients and individuals with diseased heart valves or heart murmurs, antibiotics are highly effective at preventing potentially life-threatening bacterial infections.

To use antibiotics wisely and well:

- Be discriminating before taking antibiotics. Do not demand that your doctor prescribe them.
- Take an antibiotic only after your doctor has prescribed one for your current condition.
- Follow directions carefully. Take antibiotics only at the correct dosage and for the prescribed time period.
- Never take an antibiotic prescribed for someone else.
- Never save antibiotics for future use or give them to others. Discard unused prescriptions. *Caution:* Antibiotics tend to lose their potency over time, so old pills may be medically useless ...and possibly dangerous.

Example: The popular antibiotic tetracycline undergoes a chemical change that renders it toxic to the liver.

Source: Stuart B. Levy, MD, professor of medicine and molecular biology/microbiology, Tufts University School of Medicine, Boston. He is the author of *The Antibiotic Paradox: How Miracle Drugs Are Destroying the Miracle*, Plenum Publishing, 233 Spring St., New York 10013.

Self-Hypnosis for Your Health

No one knows exactly how self-hypnosis works, but it seems to suppress the "I can't do it" mentality that keeps us bogged down with bad habits.

It helps relax the conscious, logical, self-doubting part of your mind while activating the subconscious, creative, self-empowering part.

Entering a hypnotic trance lets you create problem-solving strategies called *posthypnotic suggestions* that you can put into action afterward.

The basic method...

Anyone—even a confirmed skeptic—can learn to hypnotize himself. There is no single technique that works for everyone, but some variant of the following technique should prove helpful. You will most likely have to do a little experimentation.

Step 1: Find a quiet, comfortable place—one where you won't be disturbed. Make sure it's not *too* comfortable, or you'll fall asleep. If your household is particularly chaotic, you might try sitting in your parked car.

Step 2: Close your eyes, and breathe deeply from your belly. With each exhalation, think about ridding yourself of any pain or tension. Zero in on any area of tension.

If you become aware of a tense spot, touch it with your hand. Say aloud (or to yourself), "Please relax."

Step 3: Recall a past experience that made you feel successful, alive, aware and really "at peace." Don't just *think* about the experience. Relive it—noticing all the sights, sounds, smells and how great you felt. Be sure to keep your eyes closed.

This experience is your "gateway" to the hypnotic state. Each time you want to go into a trance, recalling it should get you there quickly and easily.

As soon as you reach that point, nod or lift your index finger as a signal to yourself.

Step 4: Count backward from 20 to zero. As you do, imagine walking down a staircase. When you reach the bottom, ask yourself, "How relaxed can I feel right now?"

Repeat this question five, 10, even 20 times—until you're fully relaxed. Then signal yourself with another nod or lift of a finger.

Step 5: Imagine that the staircase has led you to a hillside. Gazing down into the valley, you can clearly see, feel and even hear the things going on in your life right now. From this vantage point, you can be objective about your problems—and creative about solving them.

This is the point at which you can give yourself one or more posthypnotic suggestions.

The more specific your suggestions are, the better. If you want to curb overeating, for example, you might tell yourself, "I'll observe. While I'm observing, I'll ask myself what I really want." Ninety percent of the time, it's something other than food.

Step 6: Give yourself a signal, then start back up the staircase. Count each step from zero to 20. When you reach the top, you'll come out of the trance.

Source: Brian M. Alman, PhD, a psychotherapist in private practice in Leucadia, CA. He is coauthor of *Self-Hypnosis: The Complete Manual for Health and Self-Change.* Brunner/Mazel.

20

Nutrition

Food Oddities/ Food Realities

While there's little doubt that a diet that's high in fat and cholesterol is linked to heart disease, such a diet is by no means the sole culprit. In fact, it's quite clear that the primary causes of heart disease are your genes, obesity, smoking, uncontrolled high blood pressure or diabetes, and a sedentary lifestyle. Yet many Americans are now adopting extreme diets in a misguided attempt to protect their health. Extreme diets not only fail to eliminate risk, but in some cases they can raise the risk—of heart disease and of several other ailments. *Here's why...*

Case study #1...

A middle-aged man's triglyceride and cholesterol levels remained high even though he had been on a radical low-fat/low-cholesterol diet for eight years. He was worried—and rightly so—that unless his levels were brought under control, he would eventually suffer a fatal heart attack, like several other members of his family.

A battery of tests revealed that this man's ultra-low-fat diet had thrown his metabolism completely out of whack. In fact, he was eating so little fat that his body was behaving as if it were starving. *Result:* His liver was producing more, rather than less, bad cholesterol, and his triglycerides were out of control.

To reverse the problem, I recommended that this man—who had been living mostly on steamed vegetables and skinless chicken—eat more fat. He did so reluctantly, but eventually it brought the fat in his diet from roughly 10% of his total calories to 25%. His triglyceride and bad-cholesterol levels fell to a much safer level. His risk of heart disease is now dramatically reduced—all as a result of raising his fat intake.

While adding fat to the diet is not the answer for everyone, it can help those whose fat intake is dangerously low.

Case study #2...

A woman in her thirties was experiencing many vague, troubling symptoms, including anxiety, dizziness and a feeling of pressure inside her chest. Her previous doctor had prescribed nitroglycerine for her chest pressure, and—believing her other symptoms to be psychosomatic—had given her sedatives. He also had recommended psychiatric care.

That doctor's diagnosis was incorrect. I traced this woman's emotional problems to a bad case of hypoglycemia, caused by a poor diet, and to multiple allergies, including severe reactions to mold, pollen and certain foods. Once these allergies were treated, her symptoms disappeared. She is now full of energy, anxiety-free, and the chest pressure has vanished and she no longer feels the need to carry nitroglycerine pills.

Allergies can produce all sorts of symptoms beyond a runny nose, itching, hives, etc. Mysterious symptoms call for thorough allergy testing by an experienced allergist.

Case study #3...

A middle-aged business executive came in to see me after his boss told him he needed help controlling his extreme emotional volatility.

Even though he had a history of severe allergies, he did not suspect that allergies were to blame for his emotional problems. He thought he might need to see a psychotherapist. Yet, as it turned out, he was allergic to food additives and to a mold found in certain foods.

Once he changed his diet and began regular allergy treatments, his emotional explosions disappeared.

He got a promotion, his marriage improved ...and he stopped coming to see me. Two years later he called to say that he was again having emotional problems. When I asked how his allergy treatments were going, he confessed that he had stopped them. He resumed treatment, and his symptoms again disappeared.

Case study #4...

A nine-year-old boy was suffering from severe Attention Deficit Disorder (ADD), plus some apparently unrelated symptoms including a skin rash and indigestion.

His ADD was so severe that he was scheduled to be transferred from his regular class to a special-education class—and his parents were distraught at the prospect. I discovered that his "mental" problem was actually the result of a hypersensitivity to sugar. Once sugar was eliminated from his diet, he calmed down immediately. Not only was he able to stay in his regular class, but he is also now an outstanding student.

Self-defense...

Though the specifics of these cases vary widely, I recommend for all my patients the same basic medical advice for preventing illness. *Key points:*

• Maintain your total fat intake to roughly 25% of calories. That's leaner than the traditional American diet, which is roughly 40% fat, but more fatty than the 10%-to-15%-fat diet recommended by many health gurus. Avoid fried foods and fatty cuts of meat—hamburger, sausage, etc. Limit your intake of both saturated fats (butter, tallow, lard and tropical oils) and polyunsaturated fats (corn oil, safflower oil, margarine, etc.). Concentrate on monounsaturated fats such as olive oil and canola (rapeseed) oil. They're far less likely to act as oxidants in the body, and thus are less likely to promote formation of atherosclerosis and heart disease.

• Exercise regularly. Twenty to 30 minutes at least three times a week is ideal.

Caution: Working out at extremely high intensity promotes formation of free radicals, substances that promote oxidation in the body and thus lead to premature aging and heart disease.

• Don't smoke. Period.

• Drink alcohol sparingly, *if at all.* Consume at least six eight-ounce glasses of water a day.

• Take supplemental vitamins and minerals. For maximum protection against oxidants, take vitamin E (400 international units a day), vitamin C (1,000 milligrams, twice daily) and beta-carotene (25,000 international units daily) ...but check with your doctor first.

• Consume 1,500 mg. of calcium a day to help ward off osteoporosis and colon cancer. A cup of low-fat yogurt contains roughly 400 mg...a cup of whole milk/291 mg...a cup of skim milk/302 mg.

Source: Thomas Brunoski, MD, a physician in private practice in Westport, Connecticut. Dr. Brunoski specializes in the treatment of medical problems with nutritional and allergy therapy rather than medication.

Food Danger

The bacteria that cause food poisoning are frequently tasteless, colorless, and odorless. *Self-defense:* Keep refrigerator temperature at 40°F and freezer at 0°F. *Also:* Don't eat foods you feel might be unsafe. Refrigerator life for raw fish is, at most, two days...fruit/one week...leftovers/three to four days...raw meat and poultry/two to three days.

Source: *American Institute for Cancer Research Newsletter,* 1759 R St. NW, Washington, DC 20069. Four issues/year.

Breakfast Cereal Trap

Most people buy dry cereal because it's convenient...but prices keep going up and a large family can finish a $4 box in one sitting. *Better:* Buy only if the price is less than eight cents per ounce (it can run as high as 20 cents per ounce —that's 40 cents per serving). Low-cost options (five to eight cents per serving): Cooked oatmeal...cornmeal mush...cooked rice (serve like oatmeal—with milk and sugar)...homemade pancakes, waffles, granola, muffins... eggs and toast.

Source: Amy Dacyczyn, editor of *The Tightwad Gazette,* RR 1, Box 3570, Leeds, Maine 04263.

How to Protect Yourself When Buying Seafood/ When Eating Seafood

Seafood and fish are an excellent protein source that is low in saturated fat, light on calories, and high in vitamins, minerals, and the omega-3 fatty acids that help reduce the risk of heart disease.

But there *are* risks. More than 80% of the seafood eaten in the US has not been inspected for chemical or microbial contaminants. Fortunately, there are things that you can do to enjoy maximum health and minimum risk...

• Avoid chemical contaminants. When you buy fish, choose younger, smaller ones, since they've accumulated fewer contaminants. Low-fat, offshore species like cod, haddock, and pollack are especially good choices. Always trim the skin, belly flap, and dark meat along the top or center, especially when it comes to fatty fish such as bluefish. Don't use the fatty parts to make sauce. Don't eat the green "tomalley" in lobsters or the "mustard" in crabs.

• Avoid natural toxins. When traveling in tropical climates, avoid reef fish such as amberjack, grouper, goatfish, or barracuda, which are more likely to be contaminated. Buy only seafood that has been kept continuously chilled, especially mahi-mahi, tuna, and bluefish, which produce an odorless toxin when they spoil.

• Avoid disease-causing microbes. Bite for bite, raw or undercooked shellfish is the *riskiest* food you can eat.

Self-defense: Don't eat shellfish whose shells remain closed after cooking. Do not eat raw fish or shellfish if you are over 60, HIV-positive, pregnant, have cancer or liver disease, or are vulnerable to infection. Cook all fish and shellfish thoroughly. Raw clams, oysters, and mussels should be steamed for six minutes.

• Don't buy fresh fish that has dull, sunken eyes, or fish that smells "fishy." Do not buy ready-to-eat seafood that is displayed too close to raw seafood.

Source: Lisa Y. Lefferts, an environmental health consultant in Hyattsville, Maryland, who specializes in food-safety, environmental policy and risk-assessment.

Nutritional Supplements

Over-the-counter nutritional supplements—popular among bodybuilders and fitness buffs —often contain ingredients whose effects on the human body are poorly understood...and they may be toxic. *Particularly suspect:* Supplements containing ingredients derived from the testicles, hypothalamus glands, adrenal glands or pituitary glands of animals. However, because different supplement manufacturers use different names for the same ingredient, and because Food and Drug Administration regulations allow supplements to contain untested ingredients, it's often hard to tell what's safe and what's potentially dangerous. *Generally safe in moderation—with doctor's OK:* Conventional vitamin and mineral tablets.

Source: Rossanne M. Philen, MD, a medical epidemiologist at the Centers for Disease Control and Prevention in Atlanta.

Margarine Health Risks

Women who eat the equivalent of four or more teaspoons a day have a 50% increased risk of developing heart disease. And women eating other forms of solid and semisolid vegetable fat—equal to six or more spoons of margarine daily—have a 70% increased risk. These types of vegetable fats are found in cookies, cakes and fried fast-foods.

Source: Eight-year study of more than 88,000 women, aged 34 to 59, led by Walter Willett, DrPH, professor and chairman, department of nutrition, Harvard School of Public Health, Boston.

Odor and Weight Loss

Sniffing your favorite food odors helps weight loss. In a recent study, dieting patients inhaled a common food additive that smells like corn chips whenever they felt hungry. They had 10 times the weight-loss of those who didn't. *Reason:* The olfactory bulb, the part of the brain that processes aromas, is linked directly to the part of the brain that controls hunger. Strong odors of any favored food may diminish hunger. *Dieting strategy:* Sniff food deeply before eating...eat hot food (smells are enhanced by heat)...chew thoroughly to get more aroma molecules to the olfactory bulb.

Source: Alan R. Hirsch, MD, neurological director for the Smell and Taste Treatment and Research Foundation, Chicago. 800-458-2783.

Fat Facts

Some poultry is fattier than others—and some parts are fattier than some cuts of beef. If you are on a low-fat diet, you should know...

- Chicken has 1½ times the fat of turkey.
- Skinless chicken thighs have almost twice the fat of skinless drumsticks.
- A 4-oz. skinless chicken thigh has more saturated fat than 4 oz. of thoroughly trimmed, select-grade round steak, sirloin—or even pork tenderloin.
- Chicken wings are fattier than drumsticks—backs are even fattier than thighs.

Self-defense: Stick to breast (white) meat... eat ground chicken and turkey only if made from breast meat—with no skin. Beware the "other white meat"—pork. Typical trimmed cuts of pork are one-third fattier than skinless chicken—and twice as fatty as skinless turkey.

Source: Bonnie Liebman, director of nutrition, Center for Science in the Public Interest, 1875 Connecticut Ave. NW, Washington, DC 20009.

Muffin Madness

The average muffin contains 800 to 900 calories—which can be 50% *or more* of the required daily caloric intake. *Problem:* Most muffins—even bran and sugar-free ones—*aren't good for you.* Breakfast should be 300 to 400 calories. Replacing a muffin with a low-fat option—even with no other dietary changes—can help you lose weight. *Weight-loss guidelines:* A man needs 12 calories per pound of body weight to sustain his daily needs (*Example:* 2,160 calories for a 180-pound man)...a woman needs 11 calories per pound. To lose weight, eat less than that number by making low-calorie substitutions for high-calorie foods and begin an exercise program. *Important:* Check with your doctor before beginning any weight-loss program.

Source: Jeffrey Fisher, MD, a cardiologist in private practice, 311 E. 72 St., New York 10021, and clinical associate professor of medicine, New York Hospital-Cornell Medical Center.

The Truth About Chinese Food

Chinese food can contain surprisingly high amounts of fat. One dinner-size take-out order of kung pao chicken (chicken and peanuts in hot pepper sauce) has 76 grams of fat—more than the 60 or so grams the average person should eat in an entire day. *Self-defense:* Order steamed or stir-fried vegetables or Szechuan shrimp—they contain one-fourth the fat of kung pao chicken. Eat a cup of rice for each cup of entrée...mix entrées with steamed vegetables...before eating, lift individual food pieces onto the rice, leaving behind excess sauce, egg and nuts. Then eat directly from the rice bowl.

Source: Jayne Hurley, RD, associate nutritionist, Center for Science in the Public Interest, Washington, DC. She is coauthor of a study of Chinese food published in *Nutrition Action Healthletter,* 1875 Connecticut Ave. NW, Washington, DC 20009.

Your Grandmother Was Right

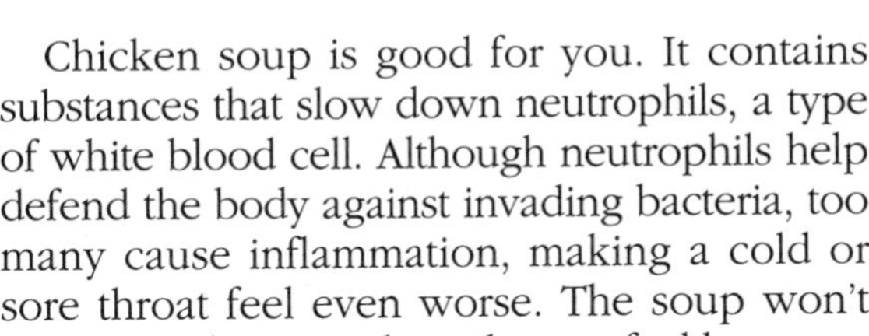

Chicken soup is good for you. It contains substances that slow down neutrophils, a type of white blood cell. Although neutrophils help defend the body against invading bacteria, too many cause inflammation, making a cold or sore throat feel even worse. The soup won't cure you—but it might make you feel better.

Source: Stephen Rennard, MD, chief of pulmonary and critical-care medicine, University of Nebraska Medical Center, Omaha. His study of chicken soup was presented at a meeting of the American Thoracic Society and reported in *New Choices,* 28 W. 23 St., New York 10010.

How to De-Fat Your Favorite Recipes

Choosing low-fat prepared foods in the supermarket is as easy as reading labels. Preparing a heart healthy meal from scratch, however, is an entirely different matter.

If you'd like to reduce the fat content of your favorite recipes, remember the three r's—reduce, remove and replace.

- Reduce fat by spraying pots with a thin film of cooking oil instead of dumping in a tablespoon of oil...or use nonstick cookware, for which no oil is needed.
- Remove skin from poultry and all visible fat from meat.
- Replace...

...whole milk or cream with skim milk, evaporated skim milk, low-fat yogurt or homemade mock sour cream (made with eight parts cottage cheese, one part skim milk and lemon juice to taste).

...regular cream cheese with light cream cheese or homemade mock cream cheese (made with two parts each of ricotta cheese and dry-curd cottage cheese and one part low-fat yogurt).

...high-fat cheeses with skim, reduced-fat or light varieties of American, Swiss, mozzarella or Monterey Jack cheese.

...bacon with Canadian bacon or lean ham.

...one whole egg with two egg whites...or ¼ cup egg substitute...or one egg white combined with one teaspoon of vegetable oil.

...one ounce of baking chocolate with a mixture of three tablespoons of powdered cocoa and one tablespoon of vegetable oil.

...sour cream with plain low-fat yogurt or reduced-fat sour cream.

...oil for sautéing or in sauces with beef, chicken or vegetable broth.

Source: Linda Hachfeld, MPH, RD, a registered dietitian in Mankato, Minnesota. She is the author of *Cooking a la Heart,* Appletree Press, 151 Good Counsel Dr., Suite 125, Mankato, Minnesota 56001.

Sweets Trap

Candy, soda and other sweets, if consumed in large quantities over time, can contribute to high triglyceride levels, a risk factor for heart disease. *Problem:* Most sweet snacks contain large amounts of sucrose, a simple sugar that is converted to triglyceride in the blood. In an average daily diet of 2,000 calories, no more than 200 should come from simple sugars. In a typical chocolate bar, 108 of the 254 calories are from simple sugar. Normal triglyceride levels run from 40 to 250 milligrams per deciliter of blood. Levels above 500 are considered high. Consult your physician if you are unsure of your triglyceride level.

Source: Steven Zeisel, MD, PhD, chairman, nutrition department, University of North Carolina, Chapel Hill.

Lean Cuisines

You can stay on your diet even while dining at your favorite restaurants. *Here's how to order to avoid excess fat, sugar, cholesterol or salt:*

•Italian: Pasta dishes with marinara (meatless) sauce. Baked or broiled chicken or veal. Pizza with mushrooms, bell peppers, and tomatoes (but ask them to go light on the cheese). Minestrone.

•French: Grilled swordfish. Chicken breast with wild mushrooms. Steamed vegetable plate. Salade nicoise (with dressing on the side). Poached salmon. Raspberries.

•Mexican: Chicken taco in a steamed corn tortilla. Tostadas (light on the avocado, sour cream on the side). Red snapper Vera Cruz. Avoid fried rice or beans.

•Chinese: Broccoli, scallops, and mushrooms sautéed with ginger and garlic. Stir-fried bean curd or chicken. Steamed fish and rice. Ask for preparation without MSG or soy sauce.

Source: Dr. Cleaves Bennett, author of *Control Your High Blood Pressure Without Drugs,* and Chris Newport, a Paris-trained nutritionist and chef, cited in *Los Angeles.*

The Healthy Gourmet

•Cut fat in your favorite recipes by 25% to 50%. *Example:* If the recipe suggests one cup of oil, try ¾ cup. If that works, try ⅔ cup the next time. In many casseroles and soups try eliminating butter or margarine completely.

•Instead of sautéing vegetables in oil or butter, add several tablespoonfuls of water or broth and steam them in a covered pot.

•Compensate for lost fat flavor by adding spices and herbs.

•Use skim or low-fat milk instead of whole milk...evaporated skim milk instead of cream.

•In sauces that call for cheese, stick to grated Parmesan or Romano (about 25 calories per tablespoonful).

•Rather than starting sauces with a fatty "roux," add cold milk or fruit juice to the flour or cornstarch.

•Substitute veal, skinless poultry, or flank or round steak for fat-marbled cuts of beef.

•Slice meats thinly and add more vegetables to the meal.

Source: *Tufts University Diet & Nutrition Letter,* NY.

How to Reduce the Fat in Your Food

•Sauté vegetables in a few tablespoonfuls of soup stock rather than in fat.

•Sauté and fry foods less often. Steam, broil, bake, and poach instead.

•For salads and cooking, use corn, safflower or olive oil—sparingly.

•Substitute egg whites or tofu for egg yolks.

•Use low-fat yogurt instead of sour cream or mayonnaise.

•Try low-fat cheeses such as part-skim mozzarella in recipes.

•Use ground turkey or crumbled tofu in place of ground beef.

•Thicken cream-style corn with a mashed potato or uncooked oatmeal.

•Replace nut butters with bean spread for sandwiches and snack dips.

Source: *Medical Self-Care,* Inverness, CA.

All Calories Aren't Equal

Dieters myth: A calorie is a calorie is a calorie. *Reality:* Fat calories are more fattening than carbohydrate calories. A single fat calorie has a greater chance of being converted into body fat than a single carbohydrate calorie.

• *Reason:* The body burns up 25 of every 100 carbohydrate calories converting them into fat—net gain, 75 calories. But it burns up only 3 calories of every 100 fat calories—net gain, 97 calories.

Source: Dr. Jean-Pierre Flatt, of the University of Massachusetts Medical School.

How to Read Nutrition Labels

Cutting down on cholesterol, sugar and salt requires a close reading of nutritional labels.

A simplified guide to understanding the fine print:

• *Ingredients:* They are listed in descending order, according to their weight.

• *Sugar:* Whether it's called sugar, dextrose, sucrose, corn sweetener, corn syrup, invert sugar, honey, or molasses, the food has little nutritive value if it's among the first three ingredients. When listed as a minor ingredient, a combination of two or more sugars may mean a hefty sugar count.

• *Cholesterol:* Avoid coconut and palm oil. They are more saturated than animal fats. Nonspecified vegetable oils frequently mean palm or coconut. When purchasing margarine, choose the brand with liquid vegetable oil as the primary ingredient. It contains less saturated fat.

• *Salt:* While sodium levels are not shown on many ingredient lists, look for brands that list sodium by milligrams. *Rule of thumb:* No one should consume much over 4,000 milligrams of sodium daily. Those on restricted diets should have considerably less than that amount.

8 Ounces of Milk

Types of milk vary in taste, fat content and nutritional value. *Here's the breakdown:*

• *Buttermilk:* 90 calories, two grams of fat. Easily digested, since active bacteria break down the milk sugars.

• *Dry nonfat milk:* 80 calories, less than one gram of fat. As nutritious as whole milk, but with a flat taste.

• *Low-fat (2%) milk:* 120 to 140 calories, five grams of fat. A good choice when fat restriction is important but calories are secondary.

• *Skim (nonfat) milk:* 80 calories, less than one gram of fat. Best for dieters and those on a strict low-fat diet.

• *Whole milk:* 150 to 180 calories, eight grams of fat. Best only for children under two years old.

Source: *Berkeley Wellness Letter,* published by the University of California, Des Moines, IA.

How to Get Along Without Cream And Mayonnaise

Fat is the enemy of both the heart and the waistline. Learn to substitute yogurt and other low-fat milk products. They are tasty as well as healthy.

Yogurt...

• Thicken commercial yogurt. Line a sieve with a paper coffee filter and place it over a bowl. Pour in the yogurt and let it drain until it is the consistency you want...that of light, heavy or sour cream.

• Use the drained yogurt as a base for any dip that originally called for sour cream. (If the yogurt seems too thick, beat a little of the drained whey back into it.)

• In cooking or baking, replace each cup of cream or sour cream with ¾ cup of drained yogurt mixed with 1 tablespoonful of cornstarch. The yogurt should be at room temperature.

•In dishes such as beef Stroganoff, where the yogurt-cornstarch mixture replaces sour cream, fold it gently into the beef at the last minute...and let it just heat through.

Basic Recipes...

•*Light mayonnaise:* Mix ⅓ cup thickened yogurt into ⅔ cup mayonnaise.

•*Light salad dressing:* Mix ⅔ cup slightly thickened yogurt into ⅓ cup mayonnaise.

•*Mock sour cream dressing*:* Mix 1 cup drained low-fat yogurt with 2 tablespoonfuls of wine vinegar. Add a dash of sugar (or substitute), a bit of garlic powder, and ¼ cup vegetable oil. Mix and chill.

Other good substitutions...

•Replace the cream in cream soups with buttermilk, which is satisfyingly rich, yet low in calories. To eliminate any hint of buttermilk's slightly acidic taste, add a liberal amount of mild curry powder.

•Mix 1 cup skim milk with ½ cup dry skim milk. Add to soup to thicken it. This works with all cream soups, including vichyssoise.

**The Low-Cholesterol Food Processor Cookbook* by Suzanne S. Jones, Doubleday, Garden City, NY.

Just When You Thought It Was Safe to Eat Salt...

The vast majority of foods sold in stores are laden with salt. Since we've eaten these foods for most of our lives, we're conditioned to expect the taste of heavily salted foods.

To cut down on salt intake:

•Reduce salt gradually. When people are abruptly placed on a very low-sodium diet, they develop cravings for salt that cause them to revert to their former eating habits. But a gradual reduction of salt will change your taste for salt...so much so that food salted to its previous level will taste unpleasant. *Time:* Allow up to three months to adjust to a salt-free diet.

•Keep daily records of the amount of sodium you eat. This is now relatively easy because federal law requires most grocery store foods to be labeled for sodium content. A pocket calculator is sometimes useful as you shop, but don't think you'll have to keep count for the rest of your life. After a couple of months, separating high- from low-sodium foods will be almost automatic.

•Substitute other flavor enhancers, especially herbs and spices.

•If you have children, start now to condition their taste by not feeding them salty foods. For the first time, low-sodium baby food is now on the market.

Source: Dr. Cleaves M. Bennett, clinical professor, University of California at Los Angeles, and author of *Control Your High Blood Pressure Without Drugs,* Doubleday, New York.

Tasty, Low-Salt, Low-Fat Cooking

If your doctor puts you on a no-salt, modified fat, cholesterol and sugar diet, with limited alcohol consumption, you might feel as though you're in a gastronomic straitjacket. However, the benefits are enormous—no more edema, a reduction in blood pressure, considerable weight loss and a feeling of well-being—and you can increase your food intake without increasing your weight.

Basics of the diet...

Do use:

•Low-sodium cheeses.

•Seltzer.

•Trimmed meat.

•Stews and pan drippings skimmed of all fat.

•Fish, poultry without skin, veal and lamb.

Don't use:

•Eggs, except those used in food preparation.

•Sugar. Drinks made with sweet liqueurs. Soft drinks.

•Canned or packaged foods.

•Sodas with high salt content.

•Rich and/or salty products—bacon, gravies, shellfish, organ meats, most desserts except fruit and fruit ices.

Tricks to fool the taste...

•The sweet-and-sour principle. A touch (sometimes as little as half a teaspoonful) of sugar and a dash of vinegar can add the sweet-and-sour flavor needed to fool the palate.

•Garlic. Essential in salad dressings and tomato sauces. Use it with rosemary to transform broiled chicken, broiled fish or roast lamb.

•Fine or coarse black pepper. When broiling and roasting meats and chicken, use as much as a tablespoonful for a welcome flavor. Use a moderate amount in soups, stews and casseroles (the pungent nature of pepper will not diminish in these as it will with broiling and roasting).

•Crushed hot red pepper flakes. A good flavor distraction or flavor addition. Not for every palate.

•Curry powder. Use judiciously and without a large number of other spices. Combine it only with a bay leaf, green pepper, garlic or black pepper. Add smaller amounts for rice, more for poultry or meat.

•Chili powder. Similar to curry, but you might want to add more cumin, oregano or garlic. Also try paprika, ground coriander, ground hot chilis. They're good with almost any dish made with tomatoes.

•Homemade hot-mustard paste. Dry mustard and water does wonders for salad dressing and grilled foods.

•Freshly grated horseradish. Goes well with fish or plain yogurt.

•Bottled green peppercorns. A welcome touch for bland foods.

•Plain boiled or steamed rice, cold yogurt relish, chutneys and other sweet relishes are a good foil for spicy dishes.

Cooking techniques...

•Charcoal broiling helps compensate for lack of salt.

•Steaming is preferable for fish and better than boiling for vegetables.

•No-salt soups are difficult to make palatable. *Solution:* A stockpot going on the back of the stove, to which you add bones, cooking liquid, vegetables. The more concentrated the broth, the greater the depth of flavor. Use only the freshest, ripest vegetables.

Source: Craig Claiborne, food critic.

"Good" Foods that Can Be Bad for You

•Blood-sugar-sensitive types who experience a temporary lift from sugar followed by fatigue should be cautious about fruit juice intake. Six ounces of apple juice contain the equivalent of more than five teaspoonfuls of sugar—40% more sugar than a chocolate bar. *Recommended:* Eat a whole apple or orange instead of drinking juice. The fiber dilutes the sugar impact. *Alternative:* Eat cheese, nuts or other protein with juice.

•Nondairy cream substitutes, often used by those on low-fat diets, usually contain coconut oil, which has a higher fat content than most dairy products.

•Decaffeinated coffee can lead to significant stomach acid secretion, causing heartburn and indigestion in many persons. Caffeine was assumed to be the culprit. A new study shows that decaffeinated coffee is even worse. The effect is seen in doses as small as a half cup of decaffeinated coffee. People experiencing ulcer symptoms, heartburn and dyspepsia should avoid decaffeinated as well as regular coffee.

•Most commercial products billed as alternatives to salt are based on potassium chloride. *Problem:* Although potassium chloride does enhance flavor, it leaves a slightly bitter or metallic taste. And excessive potassium may be as bad for your health as too much salt. *Alternatives to the alternatives:* Mrs. Dash, a commercial blend of 14 herbs and spices; Lite Salt, a half-sodium, half-potassium blend. Or try adding parsley.

•One of the few proven substances that can bring on flare-ups of acne is iodine. Excessive, long-term intake of iodine (a natural ingredient of many foods) can bring on acne in anyone, but for people who are already prone to the condition, iodine is especially damaging. Excess is excreted through the oil glands of the skin, a process that irritates the pores and causes eruptions and inflammation. *Major sources of iodine in the diet:* Iodized table salt, kelp, beef liver, asparagus, turkey, and vitamin and mineral supplements.

•Chronic diarrhea, gas and other stomach complaints are often linked to lactose intolerance, the inability to digest milk. One of every four adults suffers from this problem. Their bodies don't make enough lactase, the enzyme that breaks down milk sugar in the intestinal tract. *Among the offending foods:* Milk, ice cream, chocolate, soft cheese, some yogurts, and sherbet. Lactose is also used as a filler in gum, candies and many canned goods.

•People on low-sodium diets should check out tap water as a source of salt intake. Some local water systems have eight times the amount of sodium (20 milligrams per quart) that people with heart problems or hypertension should use.

•Health-food candy is really no better for you than traditional sweets. *Comparison:* Health-food candy often contains about the same number of calories. The fat content is often as high or higher. Bars made of carob are caffeine free, but the amount of caffeine in chocolate is negligible. And the natural sugars in health bars have no nutritional advantage over refined sugars.

Sources: *Journal of the American Medical Association,* Chicago; *Dr. Fulton's Step-By-Step Program for Clearing Acne,* by J. E. Fulton, Jr., MD, and E. Black, Harper & Row, New York; *The Sodium Content of Your Food,* Consumer Information Center, Co.

Best Whole-Grain Breakfast Cereals

Whole-grained breakfast cereals are a rich source of protein, vitamins, minerals and fiber. *Bonus:* They have relatively low percentages of cholesterol, fat and calories. *Added bonus:* Often the cheapest cereals are the best nutritionally.

What to look for:

•Cereals in which the first listed ingredient is a whole grain—whole-grain wheat, oats (rolled or flour), whole corn kernels or bran.

•Cereals with three or more grams of protein per serving.

•Avoid cereals with sugar or other sweeteners (honey, corn syrup, fructose) as a main ingredient. *Guide:* Four grams of sugar equals one teaspoonful.

•*Also avoid:* Cereals with dried fruits. They are concentrated sources of sugar. *Better:* Add your own fruits.

Drugs vs. Nutrition

Don't overlook the interaction of medication and nutrition.

•Chronic aspirin users can suffer microscopic bleeding of the gastrointestinal tract, a condition that also causes loss of iron. Aspirin can also increase requirements for vitamin C and folic acid.

•Laxatives may deplete vitamin D.

•Antacids can lead to a phosphate deficiency.

•Diuretics prescribed for hypertension can promote the loss of potassium.

•In all these cases, vitamin and mineral supplements may be the solution.

Avoiding the Lure Of Megavitamins

When it comes to vitamins, the old advice is still the best: There is no reason to take more than the recommended dietary allowance (RDA) of any vitamin, except for relatively rare individuals who cannot absorb or utilize vitamins adequately. If you want nutrition "insurance," take a regular multivitamin capsule containing only the RDA of vitamins.

A megadose is 10 or more times the RDA. This is the level at which toxic effects begin to show up in adults.

Some of the medical problems adults may experience as a result of prolonged, excessive intake are:

•Vitamin A. Dry, cracked skin. Severe headaches. Severe loss of appetite. Irritability. Bone and joint pains. Menstrual difficulties. Enlarged liver and spleen.

•Vitamin D. Loss of appetite. Excessive urination. Nausea and weakness. Weight loss. Hypertension. Anemia. Irreversible kidney failure that can lead to death.

•Vitamin E. Research on E's toxic effects is sketchy, but the findings suggest some problems: Headaches, nausea, fatigue and giddiness, blurred vision, chapped lips and mouth inflammation, low blood sugar, increased tendency to bleed, and reduced sexual function. Ironically, one of the claims of vitamin E proponents is that it heightens sexual potency.

•The B vitamins. Each B has its own characteristics and problems. Too much B-6 can lead to liver damage. Too much B-1 can destroy B-12.

•Vitamin C. Kidney problems and diarrhea. Adverse effects on growing bones. Rebound scurvy (a condition that can occur when a person taking large doses suddenly stops). Symptoms are swollen, bleeding gums, loosening of teeth, roughening of skin, muscle pain.

Vitamin C is the vitamin most often used to excess. Some of the symptoms of toxic effect from Vitamin C megadoses:

•Menstrual bleeding in pregnant women and various problems for their newborn infants.

•Destruction of Vitamin B-12, to the point that B-12 deficiency may become a problem.

•False negative test for blood in stool, which can prevent diagnosis of colon cancer.

•False urine test for sugar, which can spell trouble for diabetics.

•An increase in the uric acid level and the precipitation of gout in individuals predisposed to the ailment.

Source: Dr. Victor Herbert, author of *Nutrition Cultism: Facts and Fictions,* George F. Stickley Co., Philadelphia.

Candy Bar Myth

Many people think that candy bars are a good "quick energy" source. Not true, in reality, the high amount of fat in chocolate slows absorption of the candy bar. The tired person looking for a pick-me-up should opt for fruit or a bagel.

Source: Bonnie Liebman, director of nutrition, Center for Science in the Public Interest, Washington, DC.

Foods that Can Give You a Headache

MSG is not the only culprit. Look out for tyramine-containing foods like:

•Aged cheese.
•Chicken livers.
•Chocolate.
•Pickled herring.
•Beer.
•Champagne.
•Red wine.
•Sherry.

•Ice cream. A brief, but intense pain in the throat, head or face sometimes results from biting into ice cream. The pain is a physiological response of the warm tissues of the mouth to the sudden cold. The pain is sometimes felt throughout the head because cranial nerve branches in the area spread the pain impulse along a broad path. *Prevention:* Allow small amounts of ice cream to melt in the mouth before eating successive large bites.

Sources: Joel R. Saper, MD, and Kenneth R. Magee MD, coauthors of *Freedom from Headaches.*

Lower Cholesterol Naturally

Corn bran lowers cholesterol naturally. Men with high cholesterol who supplemented their low-fat diet with 20 grams of corn per day bran saw sharp decreases in their levels of total cholesterol, triglycerides and very low-density lipoproteins (VLDL). Levels of LDL and HDL did not change significantly.

Source: Jan M. Shane, PhD, RD, associate professor of human nutrition, Illinois State University, Normal.

Nondairy Creamer Warning

Nondairy creamers are often made of coconut or palm oil, which are high in saturated fat. They contain at least as many calories as light cream. *Better choice:* Milk with 1% or 0.5% fat. It has a similar consistency and flavor as half-and-half...but only a fraction of the fat.

Source: Kim Galeaz, RD, American Dietetic Association, 216 W. Jackson Blvd., Suite 800, Chicago 60606.

The Truth About Carnitine Supplements

Carnitine supplements marketed as "fat burners" and "energy enhancers" do *not* enhance athletic performance. These amino acid supplements—increasingly popular in recent years—had been thought to boost stamina and promote weight loss. *Reality:* A recent study found that even high doses of the supplements had no effect on performance.

Source: Matthew Vukovich, PhD, assistant professor of exercise science, Wichita State University, Wichita, KS.

Nutritional Supplements... What You Really Need

• *Folic acid.* This B vitamin (also called *folate*) reduces blood levels of *homocysteine.* Recent research has linked high levels of this amino acid (a byproduct of cell metabolism) to both heart attack and stroke.

Folic acid also guards against colon cancer and birth defects. Since these defects occur in the first two months of pregnancy, any woman who even *thinks* she might become pregnant should take a daily supplement containing 400 micrograms (mcg) of folate.

Sources: Green leafy vegetables, whole-wheat bread, nuts, peas and beans. *RDA:* 400 mcg.

• *Vitamin B-6.* This vitamin works with folic acid to break down homocysteine. If all Americans upped their daily intake of folic acid and B-6, 50,000 fewer people would die annually of heart attack and stroke.

Sources: Meat, poultry, fish, liver, whole-grain products, most fruits and vegetables. *RDA:* 2 mg.

• *Vitamin D.* This vitamin facilitates the body's absorption of dietary calcium. It's essential for healthy bones.

Sources: Fortified dairy products, fortified cereals and breads, liver, eggs and cod liver oil. Also synthesized in the skin during exposure to sunlight. *RDA:* 400 international units (IU).

• *Vitamin E.* Along with vitamin C and beta-carotene, vitamin E is a potent antioxidant. It neutralizes "free radicals," cell-damaging molecular fragments that circulate through the body.

Unfortunately, it's hard to get sufficient vitamin E from a healthful low-fat diet—so supplements are necessary.

Sources: Vegetable oil, wheat germ and nuts. *RDA:* 30 IU.

• *Beta-carotene.* More than 200 studies have shown that this antioxidant plays a key role in preventing cancer.

Sources: Broccoli, cantaloupe, carrots. *RDA:* There is no RDA for beta-carotene.

• *Selenium* is another cancer-fighting antioxidant. A recent study in China involving 30,000 people found a dramatically reduced risk of cancer among individuals who took supplemental vitamin E, beta-carotene and selenium.

Sources: Fish, shellfish, meat, whole-grain cereals, dairy products. *RDA:* There is no RDA for selenium.

• *Vitamin C.* Studies have linked this antioxidant to reduced risk of lung, colon and gastrointestinal cancers. It may also help prevent heart and eye disease.

The typical American diet provides 120 mg a day of vitamin C. That's twice the RDA, but a recent National Institutes of Health study suggested that the RDA is *too low.* A daily intake of 250 mg is better.

Sources: Citrus fruits, green peppers, broccoli, cabbage, cauliflower, potatoes, tomatoes. *RDA:* 60 mg.

• *Calcium.* This mineral is crucial for preventing osteoporosis—and it's *not* just for older women. A high calcium intake—along with sufficient vitamin D—is important for all ages, to build bone tissue and retain it.

Adults need 1,200 to 1,500 mg of calcium a day. To get this much from food, you'd need to drink about five glasses of milk...or eat several servings of yogurt, cheese or broccoli. For most people, it's easier to take a daily calcium supplement.

Sources: Dairy products, green leafy vegetables and beans. *RDA:* 800 mg.

Source: Jeffrey Blumberg, PhD, professor of nutrition at Tufts University and chief of the Tufts University Antioxidants Research Laboratory, both in Boston.

21

Fitness

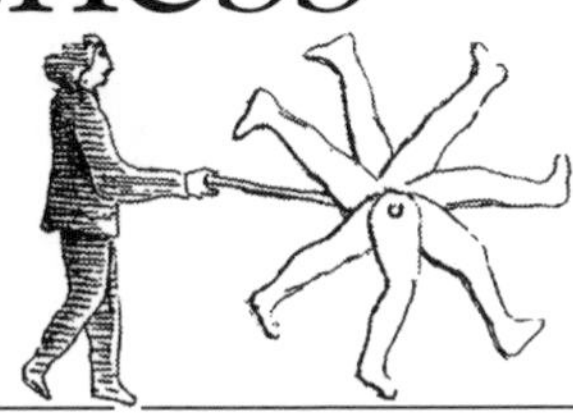

Vitamins and Workouts

Supplements of vitamins C and E significantly reduce muscle damage that can occur during heavy physical training.

Result: Athletes taking vitamin supplements can potentially train longer and harder—and recover faster—than athletes who do not use the supplements. *Unexpected bonus:* The vitamin supplements also helped keep male athletes' testosterone levels—and sex drives—at normal levels.

Source: Research led by Ian Gilliam, lecturer, Phillip Institute of Technology, Canberra, Australia, reported in *The Medical Post*, 777 Bay St., Toronto, Ontario M5W 1A7.

Headphones and Jogging Danger

Noise triggers a release of adrenaline, which constricts the blood supply to the ears and diverts it to the arms, legs, and heart. Aerobic exercise also diverts blood from the ears to those muscles. *Result:* The one-two punch of loud music and less blood destroys cilia in the ear canal...doubling risk of hearing loss.

Source: Audiologist Richard Navarro, PhD, quoted in *Men's Health Advisor 1992*, edited by Michael Lafavore, editor, *Men's Health* magazine, 33 E. Minor St., Emmaus, Pennsylvania 18098.

Walking vs. Running

Running and walking are equally effective forms of exercise. Both improve your muscle tone and cardiovascular system...and help you burn calories. *Advantages of walking:* Easier on joints...better for those starting a fitness program—especially older or overweight people.

Advantage of running: Provides a better cardiovascular workout for those already fit.

Caution: If you have a family history of heart disease or have been inactive, ask your doctor before starting to run.

Source: Mark Anderson, PhD, PT, ATC, professor of physical therapy at the University of Oklahoma Health Sciences Center.

Benefits of Exercise

Once-a-week exercise lowers the risk of adult-onset (type II) diabetes by as much as 23%. *Furthermore:* Vigorous exercise from two to four times a week reduces a person's risk of developing diabetes by 38%...at five times or more per week, the risk is cut by 42%.

Danger of inactivity: Lack of exercise contributes to as many as one of four cases of type II diabetes.

Source: Study of more than 21,000 male physicians, aged 40 to 84, reported in *The Johns Hopkins Medical Letter, Health After 50,* 5 Water Oak, Fernandina Beach, Florida 32034.

Better Jogging

Rest one or two days a week for a balanced training program. The body must have time to replenish the *glycogen* (blood sugar) lost during training. Weak muscles—drained of energy—are more prone to injuries. If trained hard without resting, the body cannot regenerate the muscle filaments, which can cause damage in the long term.

Source: David L. Costill, PhD, director, Human Performance Laboratory, Ball State University, Muncie, Indiana, writing in *Runner's World,* 33 E. Minor St., Emmaus, Pennsylvania 18098.

Healthy Walking

Brisk walks strengthen your immune system—but too-strenuous workouts can lower immunity to colds and flu. Exercising near your maximum capacity for just 45 minutes—or more—produces a six-hour "window" of vulnerability afterward. *Better:* Exercise at a moderate level—the equivalent of a brisk walk —if not training for competition.

Source: David Nieman, DrPH, professor of health, department of health and exercise science, Appalachian State University, Boone, North Carolina.

The Best Exercise Videos

Exercise videotapes are not all alike. A videotape that one person finds highly motivating may prove discouraging—even dangerous—to another.

For a safe and satisfying workout, match the tape to your specific needs*...

- Best for beginning exercisers: *Jingo,* by Debbie and Carlos Rosas. This easy-to-follow video blends non-impact aerobics—no jumping—with elements drawn from dance and martial arts. 60 minutes.

Available from Niawave, Box 712, Portland, Oregon 97207.

- Best for dancers: *The Hip Hop Solution,* by Victoria Jackson. This innovative video affords a good workout and teaches dance steps made famous by pop musicians. 30 minutes.
- Best for "step" enthusiasts: *Step Aerobic and Abdominal Workout,* by Jane Fonda. By far, the best video for users of the popular "step" apparatus. No tricky choreography, just a high-intensity workout. 57 minutes.
- Best for die-hard exercisers: *Firm Arms and Abs* and *Lean Legs and Buns,* both by Karen Voight. Demanding videos for already-fit people who want to boost muscle tone. Users must provide their own dumbbells, ankle weights and weight-lifting bench. 47 minutes/51 minutes.
- Best for stress relief: *Yogarobics,* by Larry Lane. Blends gentle exercise with soothing relaxation techniques. 53 minutes.
- Best for overweight people: *Sweatin' to the Oldies,* by Richard Simmons. The first of a four-tape series, this is a fast-paced, effective weight-

*Unless otherwise noted, all videotapes are available through videotape stores. A good mail-order source for exercise tapes is Collage Video Specialties, 5390 Main St. NE, Minneapolis 55421. 800-433-6769.

loss program presented with humor, compassion and—most important—a high-energy band playing hit songs. 43 minutes.

•Best for pregnant women: *Pregnancy Program*, by Kathy Smith. Safe workouts for all stages of pregnancy and the postpartum period. Mixes low-impact aerobics with exercises for flexibility and good posture. 95 minutes.

•Best for kids: *Hip Hop Animal Rock*, by Gilda Marx. Uses animated animals to teach kids proper exercise techniques. Suitable for ages five through 12. 30 minutes.

•Best for persons over age 50: *Positive Moves*, by Angela Lansbury. Great motivation plus gentle strength and stretching exercises from the famous actress. Also includes general tips for active living and recipes. 46 minutes.

•Best for back pain sufferers: *Back Health*, by Joanie Greggains. Pain-free routine for toning muscles in the back, buttocks and legs. Includes tips on pain prevention. 38 minutes.

•Best for disabled people: Exercise tapes for paraplegics, quadriplegics, amputees and persons with cerebral palsy are available from Disabled Sports USA, Rockville, Maryland. 301-217-0960. 30 minutes each.

Source: Peg Jordan, RN, author of several books on fitness and editor-in-chief of *American Fitness*, 15250 Ventura Blvd., Sherman Oaks, California 91403.

Mistakes Hikers Make And How to Avoid Them

When it's done right, hiking is a serene, soul-warming pursuit—an opportunity to see nature with fresh eyes and to rediscover the joy of one's own company.

When it's done wrong, however, hiking can be miserable, frustrating, painful...even injurious.

What makes the difference is preparation, equipment, trail smarts and common sense.

You don't need a vast amount of technical knowledge, equipment or experience to enjoy hiking. *But you do need to avoid these common errors:*

•*Mistake:* Buying equipment without doing your homework. Not all packs, sleeping bags, boots, tents and stoves are created equal. For reliable product reviews, check the annual spring ratings issue of *Backpacker* magazine.

•*Mistake:* Hitting the trail without a dress rehearsal. Lace up and load up before you take your first hike.

Load your pack, then adjust the straps and belts for a comfortable fit. Find uneven terrain where you can test your pack and boots. A paved road, no matter how steeply inclined, will not tell you what you need to know.

•*Mistake:* Buying unsuitable boots. For most beginners, lightweight fabric boots are preferable to leather ones.

The fabric boots (which are comparable to tough nylon sneakers) are more comfortable, and don't require a break-in period. They also have less negative impact on the trail, since they don't drag so much soil.

Leather boots, however, are more durable and provide more support, and are more sensible for cold-weather hiking.

To buy the right size: Try the boots on while you are wearing two thick pairs of socks. *Reason:* When hiking, your feet will swell by a half-size...and the extra pair of socks simulates that.

•*Mistake:* Using inadequate blister prevention. Hikers are most likely to develop blisters from boot-rub on their heels.

Prevention: If you are prone to getting blisters on a specific part of your foot, put a piece of moleskin on it prior to hiking. Carry some moleskin with you.

•*Mistake:* Carrying too much weight. Beginners should limit themselves to a maximum of 25% of their body weight. That means a 160-pound hiker should pack no more than 40 pounds.

To lighten your load: Buy a nylon mummy sleeping bag, rather than a heavier cotton bag. Carry food that is boxed or bagged rather than canned.

•*Mistake:* Packing unnecessary items. You won't have any need for a hatchet or bowie knife (a pocket knife will serve as well)...an oversized, high-powered flashlight (keep it small)

...or several changes of clothes (one change should suffice for any hike up to 10 days).

• *Mistake:* Hiking in too large a group. Large groups damage the trail ecologically. *Best:* No more than eight people.

• *Mistake:* Backtracking needlessly. Many hikers dislike covering the same ground twice to get back to their car.

Solution: Split your group into two parties. Drop one party off at one end of the hike, then park the car at the other end. The car key is exchanged when the two parties pass on the trail. *Note:* This method also works with two cars...the parties trade keys when they pass.

• *Mistake:* Failing to limber up. By investing a few minutes in stretching your hamstrings, calves, feet, shoulders and back muscles, you can do much to avoid muscle strains down the trail.

• *Mistake:* Moving too fast. Most hikers will be comfortable with an average pace of two miles per hour.

At three miles per hour (the pace favored by some hiking clubs), many hikers will experience premature fatigue. They will also risk a wide range of injuries, from blisters and sore feet to knee problems and sprained ankles.

• *Mistake:* Competing within your group. A hike should be a cooperative venture. To keep the group together, set the pace by your slowest member. You may also need to shift some heavy gear from someone who's lagging to someone who's shooting far ahead.

• *Mistake:* Forgetting to rest enough. I recommend a 10-minute rest every hour, and a break of 30 to 60 minutes every three hours. There is no absolute formula...when you are tired, stop.

• *Mistake:* Being inflexible. Always consider the possibility that you may not reach your goals. Someone in your party might get hurt...bad weather might slow you down. Plan a bail-out route or a shorter schedule—just in case.

Source: Cindy Ross, a contributing editor to *Backpacker* magazine, and the author of *A Woman's Journey on the Appalachian Trail,* Appalachian Trail Conference, Box 807, Harper's Ferry, West Virginia 25425, and *Journey on the Crest: Walking 2600 Miles from Mexico to Canada,* The Mountaineers, 306 Second Ave. W., Seattle 98119.

Better Pre-Race Warm-Up

Arrive early enough to prepare yourself mentally for the task ahead...jog easily for about a half hour or so, using visual imagery to picture yourself running the race you've planned... leave time to stretch and make one last bathroom stop...stay active after your warm-up jog to keep your heart rate up...about five minutes before the gun, take six to eight short runs of about 100 yards each, gradually working your way up to just under race pace.

Source: *Running & FitNews,* 4405 East-West Hwy., Suite 405, Bethesda, Maryland 20814.

Bike Smarts

Maintain the right tire pressure...lubricate the chain frequently...rotate tires every 1,000 miles ...always carry a spare tube when planning to ride in the rain—flats happen more often in bad weather, when patches are hard to apply. *Useful:* Write your name, address and phone number on a piece of masking tape, and stick it to the fork's steerer tube—so that if the bike is stolen, you have a better chance of getting it back.

Source: *600 Tips for Better Bicycling,* by the editors of *Bicycling.* Rodale Press, 33 E. Minor St., Emmaus, Pennsylvania 18098.

High-Top Hoopla

High-top athletic shoes offer no more protection against ankle sprains than low-tops. *Survey:* 600 college basketball players were given either low-tops, standard high-tops or high-tops with inflatable air chambers. Of the 15 sprains that occurred during one season, seven were in players wearing standard high-tops, four in players wearing low-tops and four in players wearing inflatable high-tops.

Source: Jeffrey L. Tanji, MD, family physician and a researcher at the University of California, Davis, School of Medicine. His survey was published in the *American Journal of Sports Medicine,* 230 Calvary St., Waltham, Massachusetts 02154.

Safer Hiking

Hiking fans—take along a first-aid kit containing topical antibiotics and 1% hydrocortisone cream...bandages, gauze dressing and athletic tape...saline eye irrigators...sunblock for skin and lips...pain reliever...decongestant...antacid ...diarrhea medication. *Recent survey:* Illness or injury affected 82% of people who backpacked along the Appalachian Trail.

Source: David Josephs, MD, practicing physician, Indian Health Service, Crownpoint, New Mexico. His study of 180 backpackers was published in *The Journal of Family Practice,* 25 Van Zant St., Norwalk, Connecticut 06856.

How to Stay Fit While You Sit

Exercises to do at your desk to keep mentally alert, tone sagging muscles and relieve muscle strain:

• Tummy slimmer. Sit erect, hands on knees. Exhale, pulling abdominal muscles in as far as possible. Relax. Inhale. Exhale as you draw in stomach again. Repeat 10 to 20 times.

• Head circles. Drop head forward, chin on chest, shoulders relaxed. Slowly move head in large circle. Reverse direction. Do 5 to 6 times each side.

• Torso twist. Raise elbows to shoulder level. Slowly twist around as far right as possible, then reverse. Do 10 to 12 turns each way.

• Heel and toe lift. Lean forward, hands on knees. Lift both heels off floor, strongly contracting calf muscles. Lower heels, lift toes high toward shins. Do 10 to 15 complete movements.

Source: Doug MacLennon, The Fitness Institute, Willowdale, Ontario.

Exercising When You Don't Have Time

• While you talk on the phone, do leg raises, arm exercises or isometrics.

• Park your car far from the building and walk.

• Do things the hard way (walk the long way to the office, take six trips carrying things upstairs instead of saving items for one trip, shovel snow instead of using the snow blower).

• Exercise while watching TV (run in place, skip rope, use an exercise machine or do yoga, isometrics or toe-touching).

Source: Stephanie Bernardo, author of *The Ultimate Checklist,* Doubleday, New York.

Moving Gradually into A Fitness Program

• Before launching any fitness program, have a complete physical examination, including an electrocardiogram. Your doctor should schedule a stress test to check on the heart's capacity.

• Don't let your new enthusiasm for getting fit make you too competitive. If you try to get back to the level of achievement you reached as a college athlete, you risk severe injury to ankles, knees, and hips.

• Don't jump into a racquet sport or a basketball league. Instead, prepare your body with a six-month program of walking, stretching and perhaps light jogging and weight training.

• Choose a sport you like as a primary activity and a complementary activity to go along with it. A swimmer might walk or jog two days a week. A runner could work with weights.

Source: Everett L. Smith, director of the Biogerontology Laboratory, Department of Preventive Medicine, University of Wisconsin, Madison.

Working Up to Rigorous Exercise

It takes middle-aged men and women six months of regular exercise (fast walking, light jogging, weight training, etc.) to work up to rigorous exercise. Even then, they should move gradually into each workout. *The steps to follow:*

• Walk or jog in place for two or three minutes.

• Do 10 minutes of stretching.

• When you move into your sport, take the first five minutes at a slow pace (a relaxed volley in tennis, for example) until you break into a light sweat.

• For the first few months, aim for 40% to 60% of your maximum heart rate. After six months, go for 70%. After nine months, shoot for 85%.*

• Take 10 minutes to cool down with slow jogging and more stretching.

• Recognize when you've done too much (if it aches to take a step the next day).

*To calculate these goals, subtract your resting heart rate from your maximum rate—220 minus your age—and multiply by the desired percentage. Then add your resting rate to get your goal. *Example:* A 45-year-old man has a maximum heart rate of 175 and a resting rate of 60. To perform at 70% of maximum, he should reach a rate of 140.

Source: Everett L. Smith, director of the Biogerontology Laboratory, Department of Preventive Medicine, University of Wisconsin, Madison.

Swimming: The Best Exercise of All

Swimming helps the entire musculature of the body, particularly the upper torso. It tones muscles (but does not build them). *Greatest benefit:* To the cardiovascular system.

• *Best strokes for a workout:* Crawl, butterfly, and back strokes are the most strenuous.

• *Less taxing:* The side, breast, and elementary breast strokes.

• The elementary back stroke is best for survival. The face is clear of the water for easy breathing, and the limited muscle use saves energy.

• The side stroke is traditional for lifesaving. It can be performed with one arm, which leaves the other free to tow someone. It is very relaxing—and effective.

• *To build up the legs:* Hold a kickboard while swimming. This forces propulsion by the legs alone. Or swim with the flippers favored by divers. Their surface increases the resistance to the water, making the legs work harder.

Source: James Steen, swimming coach at Kenyon College, Gambier, OH.

Aerobic Ratings of Sports

• *Best for cardiovascular fitness:* Stationary bicycling, uphill hiking, ice hockey, rope jumping, rowing, running, and cross-country skiing.

• *Moderately effective:* Basketball, outdoor bicycling, calisthenics, handball, field hockey, racquetball, downhill skiing, soccer, squash, swimming, singles tennis, and walking.

• *Nonaerobic:* Baseball, bowling, football, golf, softball, volleyball.

Source: Dr. Franklin Payne, Jr., Medical College of Georgia, Augusta, GA.

Walk for Good Health

Exercise doesn't have to be strenuous or punishing to be effective. Despite its economy of muscle use, walking is considered by most experts to be one of the best exercises. *Benefits:*

• Preventative and remedy for respiratory, heart, and circulation disorders.

• Weight control. Walking won't take off pounds, but it keeps weight at a desirable level. (Particularly effective in keeping excess pounds from coming back, once they have been dieted off.)

• Aids digestion, elimination, and sleep.

• Antidote to physical and psychological tensions.

Best daily routine:

• Time. Whenever it can be fitted into daily routine. (A mile takes only 20 minutes.) People doing sedentary office work usually average a mile and a half in a normal day. Stretch that by choosing to walk down the hall to a colleague instead of picking up the interoffice phone.

• Place. Wherever it's pleasant and convenient to daily tasks. Walk at least part way to work. If a commuter, walk to the train. Walk, not to the nearest, but to the second or third bus or subway stop from the house. Get off a stop or two from the usual one. Park the car 10 blocks farther away. Walk 10 blocks to and from lunch. Walk after dinner, before sitting down to a book, TV or work.

•Clothes. Comfortable and seasonal, light rather than heavy. Avoid thin-soled shoes when walking city pavements. It may be desirable to use metatarsal pads or cushioned soles. (The impact on concrete weakens metatarsal arches and causes callouses.)

•Length. Walk modest distances at first. In the city, the number of streets tells you how far you've gone. But in the country, you can walk farther than you realize. *Consequences:* Fatigue on the return trip. *Instead:* Use a good pedometer.

•Walking for exercise should feel different from other kinds of walking. Set out at a good pace. Use the longest stride that's comfortable. Let arms swing and muscles stretch. Strike a rhythm and keep to it.

•Don't saunter. It's tiring. Walking at a good pace allows the momentum of each stride to carry over into the next.

•Lengthen the customary stride by swinging the foot a little farther ahead than usual. Lengthening the stride speeds the walking pace and also loosens tense muscles, puts other neglected muscles to work and provides continuous momentum that puts less weight on feet.

•Most comfortable pace: Three miles per hour. It generally suits the average male and is the US Army pace for long hikes. With the right shoes and unconfining clothes, most women will be comfortable at that pace, too.

Source: Aaron Sussman and Ruth Goode, authors of *The Magic of Walking,* Simon and Schuster, New York.

Easy Exercises to Strengthen Your Back

Strengthening the back and stomach muscles is the best protection against a back injury. If you have back trouble, consult your doctor before starting this, or any, exercise program.

•Flexed-knee sit-ups. Lie on your back, with knees bent and arms at your side. Sit up slowly by rolling forward, starting with the head.

•Bent-knee leg lifts. In the same position as the sit-ups, bring one knee as close as you can to your chest, while extending the other leg. Alternate the legs.

•Knee-chest leg lifts. Work from the bent-knee sit-up position, but put a small pillow under your head. Use your hands to bring both knees up to the chest, tighten the stomach muscles and hold that position for a count of 10.

•Back flattening. Lie on your back, flex the knees, and put your arms above your head. Tighten your stomach and buttock muscles and press the lower back hard against the floor. Hold this position for a count of 10, relax and repeat.

•Don't overdo the exercises. Soreness is a sign to cut back.

•Never do these exercises with the legs straight.

Source: *American Journal of Nursing,* New York.

Realities of Exercise Equipment

The sophisticated machinery that has turned old-fashioned gyms into today's health clubs is designed to offer continuous resistance during each of the movement exercises you use it for.

•Using machines is a much faster, more efficient way to build muscle strength than using weights.

•Doing all the exercises for all the muscle groups on a regular basis does not make you perfectly fit.

Strength and fitness are not equivalent. Although muscle strength is a component of fitness, you also need flexibility and heart-lung capacity. Stretching exercises make you flexible, and aerobic exercises such as running and bike riding build up your heart muscle and your lung capacity.

•Strengthening exercises do not turn fat into muscle. It doesn't work that way. People who are overweight need to follow a calorie-restricted diet and do aerobic exercises, which trigger the body to use up fat. Working out on machines only builds up muscle under the fat layer. However, combining a weight-loss program with strengthening exercises can improve body tone as the weight comes off.

• The machines are safe if you learn the proper technique for using each machine, including proper breathing, before you are allowed on the equipment alone. On the Nautilus, for example, all the straps must be secured before you start. If one is broken or missing, don't use the machine. Poor form on the machines can lead to serious injuries. So can using the wrong weight settings.

• *Good rule of thumb:* Use a weight setting that lets you do 8–12 repetitions comfortably. If you must struggle to get beyond five, the setting is too heavy. If you complete 10 without feeling any fatigue at all, it is too light. You will have to experiment with each machine to get the right setting. Then, from time to time, you can adjust the weights upward. But be cautious. Pushing yourself too hard not only invites injury, it also discourages you from sticking to the program on a regular basis.

How to Pick a Stationary Bicycle

A good in-home stationary bicycle should be made from sturdy steel (not lightweight aluminum).

Check that it has:

• A comfortable, adjustable-height seat.

• Smoothly rotating pedals.

• A selector for several degrees of pedal speed and resistance (simulated "uphill" pedaling that makes your heart work harder).

• A heavyweight flywheel, which creates a smoother and more durable drive system.

Sophisticated electronic gadgets, such as "calories-burned" or "workload" meters are frills.

To choose the right cycle: Visit a large sporting goods store and try a variety of models. The one that works you hard and still feels comfortable is right for you.

Source: Eastside Sports Medicine Center, New York.

How to Use a Stationary Bicycle

To ride without pain or injury:

• Check with your doctor, especially if you have any heart, knee, or leg problems.

• Raise the seat on your cycle high enough so that in the downward position your foot just reaches the pedal with your knee slightly bent. This is the proper mechanical position for cycling.

• Always warm up and cool down with your bicycle set on a low resistance level. After a three- to five-minute warmup, set a constant pedal speed and increase the resistance to the level of difficulty at which you want to work. Cool down with a lower resistance setting, again for three to five minutes.

• When you begin a stationary bicycle program, work at 60% of your predicted maximum heart rate. If your heart is beating faster, then you are overdoing it. As you become more fit, you can work at up to 80% of your predicted maximum heart rate. But remember to keep the increase slow and gradual.

• Start cycling in 10-minute sessions. Then increase to 15, then 20, and then 25 or more minutes per session. Gradual increases over a period of weeks help prevent injury to muscles and joints. Once you build up your physical strength, pedal for as long as you feel comfortable.

Source: Eastside Sports Medicine Center, New York.

To Get into Shape For Skiing

Being physically fit makes skiing more fun and helps prevent soreness and injuries. *What to focus on:*

• Muscle tone and flexibility. Stretching exercises keep your muscles long and pliable. They also warm muscles up for strenuous sports and help relax them afterward. Always stretch slowly. Hold the extended position for 20 to 30 seconds. Don't bounce.

• Do sit-ups with your knees bent to strengthen abdominal muscles (they can take stress off the back).

•Practice any active sport, from swimming to tennis, for three one-hour sessions a week.

•Jogging builds up the muscles of the lower torso and legs. Running downhill strengthens the front thigh muscles, essential to skiing. Running on uneven terrain promotes strong and flexible ankles. Biking builds strong legs and improves balance.

How to Improve Your Tennis

Here are some secrets that help tennis pros on the court:

•Psych yourself up for a big point by triggering the adrenaline response. *Here's how:* Open your eyes wide and fix them on a nearby object. Breathe deeply and forcefully. Think of yourself as a powerful, aggressive individual. Exhort yourself with phrases like "Fight!" Try to raise goose bumps on your skin—they signal a high point.

•To switch from one type of playing surface to another, practice easing the transition. If you're moving to fast cement from slow clay, for example, practice charging the net before the switch. If it's the other way around, spend extra time on your groundstrokes.

To play well against a superior player:

•Suspend all expectations. Avoid thinking about the situation. Watch the ball, not the opponent.

•Play your game. Don't try to impress your opponent with difficult shots you normally never try.

•Hit the ball deep and down the middle. The more chances for your opponent to return your shot, the more chances for him to err.

•Concentrate on your serve. No matter how outgunned you may be, you can stay in the match if you hold your serve.

Source: *Tennis* and *World Tennis.*

Martial Arts Schools Teach More than Martial Arts

The martial arts offer more than a simple exercise program. They build both physical and mental strengths. Students learn the skills to extricate themselves from dangerous situations and, if necessary, to defend themselves.

Styles and systems...

•Tai Chi Chuan uses slow, graceful movements.

•Karate employs powerful, focused techniques.

•Judo and aikido make use of joint locks and throws.

Finding the right school...

•To get a list of schools, talk with friends and check out the ads in your local Yellow Pages.

•Visit the schools to observe a few classes before you sign up.

•Clarify your goals before you make a choice —do you want mainly a physical fitness and self-defense program, or are you interested in the mental/spiritual aspects?

What to consider...

•A balanced approach to both the mental aspects (such as concentration and focus) and the physical aspects of the particular martial art.

•The temper of the fighting classes, if the school has them. Make certain that care is taken to minimize injuries. Fighting is a part of most martial arts, and you should be comfortable with the school's fighting program.

•Thoughtful answers to your questions. If the school is evasive in its explanations, it is probably not a good bet.

•Instructors create the training environment of the school. Make certain they suit you. Some people like a "marine sergeant," while others might prefer a more temperate teacher.

•Students should be brought into the regimen slowly in a progressive process. Only as a student gets used to one style should new techniques be added to his repertory.

•Make sure the school accommodates different levels of athletic ability and different ages. Inflexible standards may only frustrate you.

•Attitudes of students. Do they encourage and help each other? Or are they bullying? The attitude of the instructor is passed on to his students.

•Facilities. Is there room to practice in between classes? Does the school have exercise equipment such as weights and jump ropes? Are the locker rooms big enough for the number of students? Are there showers?

•Schedule. If you will have a hard time getting to the workouts, you probably won't go often enough.

Source: Ken Glickman, third degree black belt and coordinator of Educational Services, Greenwich Institute for American Education, Greenwich, CT.

Exercises that Can Harm You

The most important benefit of exercise is that, properly done, it increases longevity. But exercises that promote a single aspect of the body, such as form, stamina, coordination, speed, or strength, generally have a negative impact. *Especially dangerous are:*

•Muscle-building exercises. They can harm joints and connective tissues. Weight lifters are not known for longevity.

•Skill-producing activities. Ballet, handball, and squash require arduous training and stop-start patterns. Both are negatives for long life.

•Marathon sports. Jogging, swimming, cycling, and strenuous walking can work the body to the point of exhaustion. This is dangerous because stress and injury occur more easily during body fatigue.

•Speed-oriented activities. Those that require lots of oxygen, such as sprinting or speed swimming, can be fatal, especially for those who have not trained extensively for them.

Source: Dan Georgakas, author of *The Methuselah Factors: The Secrets of the World's Longest-Lived Peoples,* Simon & Schuster, New York.

Fitness Facts

•*Easy fitness plan:* Walk at least one mile a day at three miles per hour. Your body will thrive—and without the injury risk of running, the knee strain of bicycling, or the inconvenience of swimming. *Optimal plan:* Walk a mile twice a day at four-miles-per-hour.

Source: Dr. Henry A. Solomon, a New York cardiologist, in *Signature.*

•For every week you've laid off because of illness or vacation, allow one week to return to your full exercise program.

Source: Michael L. Pollock, director of cardiac rehabilitation and sports medicine, Universal Services Rehabilitation and Development, Inc., Houston, TX, in *Mademoiselle.*

Unexpected Health Club Hazard

Number and motility of sperm cells are decreased for up to six weeks after a dip in a hot tub.

•*Shocking:* Only one hour of soaking in water 102.4 degrees or hotter (most health clubs keep tubs at 104 degrees) causes immediate harm to sperm.

•*Fertility low point:* Four weeks after bath, when sperm that were immature upon bathing mature.

•*Remedy:* Patience...sperm life span is 75 days, so all damaged sperm are replaced within that time frame.

Source: Dr. Richard Paulson of the University of Southern California School of Medicine.

Winter Sports Pointers

•Ice skating is an underrated exercise that works all your muscles. It's also easy to learn ...most people can glide around the rink after three or four sessions.

•*Skier's hazard:* Sunburned corneas, caused by the sun's ultraviolet rays. (Snow reflects 85% of those rays, compared with 10% from water and 5% from grass.) *Helpful:* Goggles or wrap-around glasses made of impact-resistant polycarbonate.

Source: Dr. Paul Vinger, a Boston ophthalmologist and eye/medical consultant to the US Olympic Committee, in *Executive Fitness Newsletter.*

Home Exercise Machine Dos and Don'ts

- Treadmill. *Don't* grip or lean on handrails ...*do* keep arms moving while walking...*don't* lean too far forward while walking up an incline...*do* maintain good posture.
- Stairmaster. *Don't* lean all your weight on the handrails...*do* rest your hands on top of the machine for stability...*don't* let pedals hit the top or bottom of the machine's range... *don't* take "baby steps," using only a small portion of your own natural range of motion.
- Stationary bicycle. *Don't* hyperextend your legs on the downstroke...*do* adjust the seat so you maintain a slight bend at the knee.
- Rowing machine. *Don't* pull by lifting with your back...*do* use your legs to push your body away from your feet.
- Cross-country ski machine. *Don't* let your feet slide in front of the stomach pad...*do* lift your heels on the back stroke...*do* always keep knees slightly bent.

Source: Chris Vincent, MA, fitness consultant at the Athletic Club Illinois Center, Chicago.

Few Teenage Girls Exercise

Only 25% of female high school students exercise vigorously on a regular basis—compared with 50% of boys the same age.

Source: Gregg Health, Dsc, MPh, division of surveillance and epidemiology, Centers for Disease Control and Prevention, Atlanta.

Swimming Pool Danger

Lap swimmers might be inhaling high doses of chloroform, a carcinogen formed when chlorine reacts with water pollutants. *Evidence:* In a study conducted recently in an indoor swimming pool in Quebec, breath samples taken from men before, during and after an hour-long daily swim showed that chloroform concentrations rose from 52.6 parts per billion (ppb) before the swim to 100 to 1,093 ppb afterward. Researchers are now assessing the possible health risks associated with chloroform inhalation. It may be necessary to modify current water treatment practices in swimming pools.

Source: Benoît Lévesque, MD, medical adviser in environmental health, Centre de Santé Publique de Quebec, Ste.-Foy, Canada. His study was published in *Environmental Health Perspectives,* US Department of Health & Human Services, 1233 Research Triangle Park, North Carolina 27709.

A Stitch in Time...

To relieve a stitch—a cramp in the side—that occurs while running, try grunting loudly as each foot strikes the ground. A forceful grunt relaxes the diaphragm, relieving the muscle tension that may be causing the pain.

Source: Owen Anderson, PhD, editor, *Running Research News,* Box 27041, Lansing, Michigan 48909.

High Humidity Dangers

High humidity can lead to heat exhaustion or other serious problems even if it's not particularly hot. *Self-defense:* Drink six to eight ounces of water every 15 to 30 minutes—more if you are working hard or exercising vigorously. Do not take salt tablets. *Also:* Use oil-free sunscreens. Oil-based sunscreens can clog pores, slowing perspiration even further.

Source: *University of Texas Lifetime Health Letter,* 7000 Fannin, Houston 77030.

For a Perfect Abdomen*

Torso twists...

Stand with feet slightly more than shoulder-width apart, holding a broomstick behind your neck. Twist from side to side, keeping your hips facing forward. Start with 10 repetitions. Go up to 25 reps as you grow fitter. Or, time yourself as you do twists for one to three minutes.

Knee-to-elbow...

Stand with your hands behind your neck. Lower your left elbow to your right knee as you bring the knee up toward the elbow.

Return to starting position, then repeat with your right elbow and left knee. Move as fluidly as possible. Alternate sides till you've done 10 to 25 reps per side.

Side bends...

Holding a five- to 10-pound dumbbell in your left hand, stand with knees slightly bent, feet apart and your right arm behind your neck. Bend to the right, bringing your right elbow toward the floor.

Return to your starting position. Then switch the dumbbell to your right hand and repeat, bending to the left. Alternate sides till you've done 10 to 25 reps on each side.

Sit-ups...

Lie on your back with knees bent and feet flat on the floor. Sit up slowly, bringing first your head, then your neck and then each vertebra off the floor. Imagine that you're "peeling" your back off the floor, like a piece of tape.

As you reach a sitting position, bring both arms forward, stretching them past your shins.

Reverse the process, slowly lowering yourself to the floor. Do 10 to 25 reps.

Caution: Do not do sit-ups if you have back trouble.

Crunches...

Lie on your back with knees bent and feet flat on the floor. Place both hands behind your head, elbows out. Press your lower back against the floor by tightening your abdominals and curling your pelvis toward the ceiling.

Keeping your lower back against the floor, lift your head and shoulders about three inches off the floor. Keep your eyes focused on the ceiling and your elbows back. Then lower to the starting position. Repeat 25 times.

Kneeling arm and leg lifts...

Kneel with your head held so that your neck is aligned with your spine. Lift your right arm and extend it in front of you, as you lift your left leg and extend it behind you.

Tighten your abdominals. Hold this position for a count of three, lifting your leg and arm as high as you can without arching your back. Return to the kneeling position. Repeat on the opposite side. Alternate till you've done 10 to 25 reps on each side.

Sitting "v" hold...

Sit comfortably on the floor with your torso erect, shoulders relaxed and arms straight out to either side. Keeping your knees slightly bent, lift both knees as high as you can. Hold for 10 to 20 seconds. (Put your hands on the floor behind you for support, if necessary.)

As you become fitter, try this exercise with your legs held straight.

Jackknives...

Lie on your back with arms at your sides, hands clenched. Bend your knees slightly, keeping your feet together and your heels touching the floor.

Slowly sit up, bringing your knees to your chest. Let your arms extend as far forward as necessary.

Return slowly to starting position, keeping your abdominals contracted. Do 10 to 25 reps.

Caution: Avoid this exercise if you have back trouble.

Arm and leg lifts...

Lie on your stomach with legs straight and arms extended overhead.

Raise your right leg and left arm off the floor at the same time, then lower them.

Do 10 to 25 reps with the same leg and arm. Then switch sides and repeat with your left leg and right arm.

Caution: Avoid this exercise if you have back trouble.

Source: Radu Teodorescu, founder of Radu's Physical Culture, an exercise studio based in New York City and East Hampton, NY.

*Do not undertake any new exercise regimen without first consulting your doctor.

22

Better Sleep

The Straight Story On Sleep

•There's nothing particularly natural or inevitable about daytime sleepiness. Americans have developed an unhealthy tolerance of daytime sleepiness and fatigue.

•Both drowsiness and fatigue during the daytime hours are usually the result of sleep disorders of which sufferers often aren't aware. There are also chronic sleep disturbances of which the sleeper may not be aware. *Example:* Loud noises from aircraft or a nearby highway that disturb sleep regularly even though people don't always waken.

•Contrary to common notions, the inability to get a refreshing night's sleep is rarely caused by stress or anxiety. For people younger than 15 or older than 50, the main cause is usually a physical one. In older people, the most common problem is apnea, a disorder that causes them to stop breathing periodically during sleep. *Other frequent problems:* Asthma and chronic disease.

•A cool bedroom is not necessarily better for sleeping than a warm one. No temperature (within a normal range) has been proved better than another for sleep.

•Some people who have insomnia do sleep, and much more than they think they do. *The real test of sleeping well:* Whether you feel fully alert the next day, not the number of hours you've slept. If you sleep just five hours and you don't feel tired the next day, you don't have a sleep disorder.

•Heavy snoring followed by daytime sleepiness is virtually a sure sign of apnea. In this condition, episodes of impaired breathing or failure to breathe at all causes the apnea sufferer to wake up many times a night. *Most vulnerable to sleep apnea:* Middle-aged males (particularly those who are overweight) and people with large adenoids, a deviated septum or polyps. Some apnea sufferers are so used to their condition that they're not aware of their wakening, only of their daytime fatigue.

•A cigarette before bedtime is likely to keep you awake (in addition to creating a fire hazard). Nicotine is a stimulant to the central nervous system.

•The position in which you lie when going to sleep is not important. *Fact:* Everybody moves around many times during sleep.

•A couple of stiff drinks every night will not help you sleep. Stiff drinks before bedtime will more likely cause you to wake up in the middle of the night, when they wear off. Small quantities of alcohol (one drink) may help on a particularly difficult night, however.

•Drink a glass of milk and eat a light snack before going to bed. *Reason:* Hunger can disturb sleep. Avoid rich or spicy foods or stimulants such as coffee, tea, cola, drinks, or sweets. (Sugar is a stimulant.) Eating the wrong foods before bedtime may not actually keep you from falling asleep, but it will often wake you within a few hours.

•Check to see if there are noises that may be disturbing your sleep without your being aware of them. Mute the sounds by putting up heavy curtains or by using earplugs.

•Avoid too much mental stimulation in the period before you go to sleep. Don't discuss family problems or finances, and don't take up unfinished work problems before bedtime. *Instead:* Do some light reading or watch a television show that relaxes you.

•If you wake up in the middle of the night and can't get back to sleep right away, don't lie there. Get up, put the light on and use the time, perhaps to read. Lying in bed and trying to sleep without success only makes you more tense.

•Avoid strenuous physical exercise within a few hours of bedtime. It can cause excessive stimulation and stress, which can disturb sleep. Exercise can benefit sleep if taken in the afternoon or early evening. Morning exercise is of no great help in inducing a good night's sleep.

Source: Dr. William C. Dement, director, Sleep Disorders Center, Stanford University School of Medicine.

Good Sleep Demystified

People spend almost one third of their lives asleep. The primary sleep disorder is insomnia. That's difficulty falling asleep, trouble remaining asleep or early-morning awakening. *Causes:*

•Depression is often the cause of early awakening.

•Sexual stresses lead to nighttime insomnia.

•Boredom.

•Some medications, such as drugs for asthma and heart and blood-pressure pills, cause poor sleep.

•More than moderate alcohol intake usually disturbs the sleep cycle.

Ways to promote better sleep:

•Follow a good physical fitness program.

•Sleep in a quiet, dark, well-humidified room and in a comfortable bed.

•Avoid late-night physical or mental stress, snacks, coffee, cola, or drug stimulants.

•Do relaxing exercises or biofeedback exercises.

•Don't take sleeping pills.

Source: Dr. Bruce Yaffe, fellow in gastroenterology and liver disease, Lenox Hill Hospital, New York.

Improve the Quality Of Your Sleep

•Researchers cannot easily determine how much sleep is optimum for a specific person. They have determined that, on average, people need seven or eight hours of sleep a day.

•Keep a diary of sleeping patterns for at least 10-14 days. If you feel productive and alert, the average sleep time during that period is probably the amount you need.

•Establish a regular bedtime and wakeup schedule. Stick to it, even on weekends and holidays.

•Avoid trying to make up for loss of sleep one night by sleeping more the next. Sleep deprivation of two to four hours does not severely affect performance. Having the normal amount of sleep the next night compensates for the loss without changing the regular sleep pattern. And that has long-term benefits.

•Relax before bedtime. *Good ways to unwind:* Take a bath, read, have a weak nightcap or snack (milk is ideal for many people), engage in sex. Avoid late-night exercise, work, arguments and activities that cause tension.

•Knowing the reason for insomnia is the only way to start overcoming it. If the cause is not quickly obvious, see a doctor. Many emotional and physical disorders express themselves as sleep disturbances.

•Avoid sleeping pills. On a long-term basis, they are useless and sometimes dangerous. And when taken infrequently, they may produce a drug hangover the next day.

•Avoid naps in the middle of the day to compensate for lack of sleep the previous night. Take them only if you do it regularly and feel refreshed, instead of groggy, after a nap. *Test:* If you dream during a catnap, it is likely to delay sleep that evening or to cause insomnia.

•Don't attempt to reduce the total amount of sleep you need. Carefully researched evidence from monitoring subjects in sleep laboratories indicates these schemes are not only ineffective but unhealthful. The daily biological cycle cannot be changed by gradually cutting back sleep over a period of months. Older persons apparently need slightly less sleep, but even here the exact difference is not yet known.

Source: Dr. Charles P. Pollak, codirector, Sleep/Wake Disorders Center, Montefiore Hospital, New York.

Insomnia Trap

Many drugs can interfere with your sleep, including nasal decongestants, diuretics, cancer and blood pressure medications, some gastric ulcer drugs, such as Tagamet and Zantac, and several antidepressants—Marplan, Nardil, Parnate, Prozac and Wellbutrin. *Helpful:* If you suspect one of these drugs is interfering with your sleep, ask your doctor about changing medications or doses...and about taking the drug early in the day.

Source: Philip M. Becker, MD, director, Sleep/Wake Disorders Center, Dallas.

How to Become An Ex-Insomniac

•Condition your sleep environment. Learn to associate your bed and your bedroom with sleep.

•Pay attention to bedroom conditions, such as light, heat, noise. Shut off telephones if necessary. Keep temperature cool (around 68°). Make sure your mattress and your sleep clothing are comfortable.

•If you don't fall asleep right away, get up, leave the bedroom, and go do something else. Don't lie awake thinking about it or you'll begin to associate your bed and your bedroom with trying to get to sleep.

•Stick to a regular bedtime schedule. Go to bed at the same time every night—weekdays and weekends. Don't expect to catch up on missed sleep on the weekends. You can't do it. Trying simply disrupts your biological rhythms.

•Exercise early in the day. Late in the evening it's too stimulating.

•Sexual activity, within a comfortable relationship where no tension or anxiety exists, is helpful in inducing sleep.

•If you think widely advertised insomnia cures like vibrating beds, prerecorded cassette tapes, and sleep masks will relax you, try them.

•Don't take nonprescription, over-the-counter sleeping pills. Studies have shown "sugar pills" to be just as effective.

•If you have a particular emotional or physical upset, see your doctor.

•If sedatives are prescribed, use for no more than a week or two. Expect that the first night or two after stopping the pills will be very disturbed sleep. That's perfectly normal.

Source: Dr. Frank Zorick, clinical director of the sleep disorder center at Cincinnati Veterans Administration Hospital and the University of Cincinnati.

Sleep Can Be Disturbed By...

Only about one third of people wake up refreshed. While many sleep problems for the other two thirds are caused by anxiety, these factors can also reduce the quality of sleep:

•Alcohol. Can affect both dream and deepest-sleep stage. *Best:* Make your drink with dinner the last of the evening.

•Room temperature. A cold room does not make you sleep better. *Ideal:* 60–65°.

•Exercise. Aches and pains from strenuous exercise can keep you awake.

•Sex. Unless it is both physically and mentally rewarding, it can inhibit sleep.

•Caffeine. Effects linger 6 to 7 hours.

•Smoking. Nicotine is a strong central-nervous-system stimulant. Heavy smokers who quit usually sleep dramatically better within days.

•Irregular schedule. The body functions on a regular rhythm.

Source: *Executive Fitness Newsletter,* Emmaus, PA.

How to Fall Back Asleep

Agony: Awakening in the middle of the night and not being able to fall back to sleep. *Prime cause:* Advancing age. People over 50 tend to middle-of-the-night insomnia. Those under 50 often have difficulty falling asleep.

How to cope:

•Don't become angry when you find yourself awake at 3 a.m. Anger only excites you, preventing sleep. Fix your mind on a single relaxing image. *Example:* Visualize a flickering candle.

•If you are still awake after 30 minutes, go to another room. Watch an old movie on TV, or read a book or magazine.

•When you feel sleepy, return to bed. If sleep still eludes you, go back to the other room and read some more.

Preventive steps:

•Eliminate daytime naps if they have been a habit.

•Do not go to bed too early. This only increases the chances of middle-of-the-night insomnia.

•Set your alarm an hour earlier than usual. This makes you more tired for the following night. Advance the alarm by 15-minute increments until you are sleeping through the night. Then slowly extend your sleep period until you are back on a normal schedule.

Source: *A Good Night's Sleep* by Jerrold S. Maxmen, Contemporary Books, Chicago.

How to Stop Snoring

•Put a brick or two under the legs at the head of your bed. Elevating your head will keep the airway open.

•Don't use extra pillows. They'll only kink the airway.

•Avoid all depressants a few hours before bed. Take no alcohol, tranquilizers, sleeping pills or antihistamines late in the day.

•Lose weight. Three of four snorers are at least 20% over their ideal weight.

•Wear a cervical collar. It keeps the chin up and the windpipe open.

•Wear a "snore ball." Cut a small, solid-rubber ball in half. Using two patches of Velcro, attach the flat side of the half-sphere to the back of your pajama top. If done right, it should keep you off your back—the position for virtually all snoring.

Source: *Prevention,* Emmaus, PA.

To Eliminate Fatigue

•Analyze your lifestyle. Write down what you do every day. Be sure to include the amount of physical exercise you get and the kinds of demands (emotional and otherwise) that are made on you. Include your time with people and your time working alone. Document the times when you feel fatigued. Is it at work or at home? Is it better or worse around other people? Correlate your fatigue diary with your activity record, and look for patterns.

•Try some small changes in your work style. If your job puts you under constant pressure, take minibreaks to do some gentle stretches. If you spend a lot of time with other people, make some private time for yourself. If you do paperwork alone, schedule some social breaks.

•Pay attention to diet, and eat regularly. A breakfast of complex carbohydrates such as whole-grained toast and protein will keep you going until lunch. People who skip meals or have an erratic eating pattern are more fatigue prone.

•Stick to a regular, moderate exercise regimen—not weekend overexertion. The best exercise is walking. Besides being healthful and safe, it also gives you time alone to notice the outside world and reflect on your inner life. Aerobic exercise stimulates the brain to produce endorphins, the body's natural painkillers and antidepressants.

•Look within yourself. Do you like your job, friends, home life? Could you admit it to yourself if you didn't? If for the next two weeks you could do anything you wanted, what would it be? Is there a way of incorporating that fantasy into real life? What's the biggest price you have to pay for your current lifestyle?

•Once you identify problems, see what you can do about them. For example, if you like your job but hate the long commute, maybe you can stagger your hours to work fewer days a week—or move closer to the office.

•Get a physical checkup. Although there is no physical basis for fatigue in 99% of the people who visit doctors complaining of it, occasionally a health problem is a factor. The most common medical cause of fatigue is mild low thyroid, which occurs more commonly in women.

Source: Mary E. Wheat, MD, an internist at Mt. Zion Hospital and Medical Center, San Francisco.

How to Buy a Mattress

The quality of sleep makes the quantity less important. To enable you to relax, your mattress must provide proper support for your body, yet be resilient enough for comfort.

Basic considerations:

•Mattress prices. Depend on the materials, quality of construction, size, number of layers of upholstery and the store's markup. (May be lower in small neighborhood stores.) Queen-size innerspring sets cost $325–$800, sometimes discounted to $225–$500. A high-density queen-size foam mattress costs about $300.

•Construction. Innerspring or foam rubber are the basic types. Top-quality innerspring mattresses have covered metal coils, cushioning material and an insulator between the coils to prevent them from protruding. Foam mattresses are made of a solid block of urethane, high-resiliency foam or laminated layers of varying density sandwiched together (preferably 5–6 inches thick).

How to shop for a mattress:

•Sit on the edge of the bed. The mattress should support you without feeling flimsy, and it should spring back into shape when you get up. A reinforced border increases durability.

•Lie down. (If the bed is to be used by a couple, both partners should test it lying down.) Check several different firmnesses to choose the one you're most comfortable with.

•Roll from side to side and then to the center. The mattress should not sway, jiggle or sag in the middle. If you hear creaking springs, don't buy it.

•Examine the covering. The best is sturdy ticking with a pattern woven in, not printed on.

•Check for handles on the sides for easy turning, small metal vents to disperse heat and allow air to circulate inside, and plastic corner guards.

•Don't forget about the boxspring which bears up to 80% of the sleeper's weight. When you need a new mattress, both the mattress and spring should be replaced to ensure that the support system is specifically designed for the mattress.

Buy a sleep set made by a manufacturer with a good reputation and sold by a reputable dealer. Be very wary of advertised bargains.

Drug-Free Remedy For Insomnia

An epsom salt bath relaxes the muscles and calms the mind. Use two to three cups of Epsom salt, and make sure the bath water is as close to skin temperature as possible. *Also helpful:* Light a candle, burn some incense or play soft music to enhance the feeling of relaxation. Be sure to go straight to bed once the bath is over.

Source: Jane Guiltinan, ND, a naturopath and chief medical officer at Bastyr University Natural Health Clinic, Seattle.

Surgery for Sleep Apnea

Surgery for sleep apnea is usually unnecessary...and may be falsely reassuring. More than four of every five people who suffer from apnea (repeated interruptions of breathing, often caused by excessively lax tissue in the throat) can be helped by *continuous positive airway pressure* (CPAP). *How it works:* A CPAP mask, attached to a fan-driven pressure generator, blows air through the nose into the sleeper's throat, preventing the airway from collapsing. CPAP is only for apnea—not for simple snoring. *Apnea symptoms:* Daytime sleepiness...nighttime heartburn...frequent nighttime awakening.

Source: Daniel Wagner, MD, neurologist, Sleep-Wake Disorder Center, New York Hospital-Cornell University Medical Center, New York City.

Sleep Apnea and Driving

Sleep apnea can make you a bad driver. Individuals whose sleep is disrupted by this common nighttime breathing disorder are often very drowsy during daytime. In a recent study involving a driving simulator, performance in men with apnea was much worse than in men without apnea—including subjects who were intoxicated. If you suspect that you suffer from apnea, see a doctor...or contact the American Sleep Disorders Association, 1610 14 St. NW, Ste. 300, Rochester, Minnesota 55901.

Source: Charles F. P. George, MD, director, sleep lab, Victoria Hospital, London, Ontario. His study of 42 men was published in the *American Journal of Respiratory and Critical Care Medicine*, 1740 Broadway, New York 10019.

Exercise vs. Insomnia

Exercise can help beat insomnia. Exercise *well before* bedtime. Later, as you cool down, you will begin to relax and be ready for sleep.

Exercise too near bedtime is stimulating, causing increased alertness that can interfere with falling asleep.

Caution: If an exercise routine helps you sleep better, keep it up. If you stop, insomnia may return in a few days.

Source: Peter Tanzer, MD, in private practice in Pittsburgh, clinical assistant professor of medicine, University of Pittsburgh School of Medicine, and author of *The Doctor's Guide for Sleep Without Pills.* Tresco Publishers.

Insomnia and Painkillers

Insomnia can be caused by over-the-counter painkillers that contain caffeine. *Examples:* Aspirin-free Excedrin and Anacin. In a recent study of 2,885 patients, those who took caffeinated formulations of aspirin and acetaminophen were nearly twice as likely to report sleep problems as those taking similar noncaffeinated analgesics.

Source: S. Lori Brown, PhD, MPH, research scientist officer, Food and Drug Administration, Rockville, MD.

How to Stop Nightmares

Stop recurrent nightmares by changing them after you wake up. *How:* Recall the nightmare in the fullest detail possible...change a significant element in it—like transforming a tiger into a pussycat...replay the entire nightmare in your mind with the new scenario. If the nightmare continues, keep changing elements until the fear disappears.

Source: *The Owner's Manual for the Brain* by Pierce Howard, PhD, director, Center for Applied Cognitive Studies, Charlotte, NC. Bard Press.

23

Coping with Emergencies

It Pays to Prepare For Emergencies

Emergencies, of course, come without warning. But that doesn't mean you can't be prepared when they do arrive. *Steps to take now:*

• Familiarize yourself with the emergency rooms in your area. Look into freestanding urgent-care clinics as well as hospital emergency rooms. Ask your doctor which facility is best for which type of emergency—and chart his/her recommendations on a family bulletin board.

Know where the entrance and parking area are for each emergency facility recommended by your doctor. Go for a visit. Park in a visitor's space and go in and look around. If the admissions clerk is not busy, ask how things work in an emergency.

Call your county health department. Find out the rating of each local emergency room. Level 1 facilities offer only basic emergency care... Level 2 offer more advanced care...and Level 3 are comprehensive trauma centers capable of handling the most severe, life-threatening emergencies. *Caution:* If you go to a Level 3 center for a minor cut, you may have to wait in line behind people with more serious injuries.

• *Always carry in your wallet...*

• Health insurance card.

• Insurance company phone number.

• Your blood type, although it will be tested for verification anyway.

• A list of all medications you take regularly.

• Your doctor's name, address and phone number.

• A brief description—written and signed by your doctor—of any health condition that might affect emergency care.

• The name and phone number of any pharmacy where your medication history is on file—ideally one that is open 24-hours-a-day.

• *Keep handy in your home—and tell everyone the location of...*

• A comprehensive first-aid manual, such as the one published by the Red Cross and sold in bookstores. Be sure that it's up-to-date.

•Instructions for doing the Heimlich maneuver.

•A blood pressure cuff.

•Literature on emergency treatment for any disease or condition relevant to anyone who lives or works regularly in your house—heart disease, epilepsy, asthma, etc.

•*Always wear a bracelet or pendant describing any serious medical condition...Examples:* Diabetes or severe allergies.

•*Learn...*

•Basic first aid.

•Cardiopulmonary resuscitation (CPR) for adults and children—especially if you have a pool.

•The Heimlich maneuver.

•How to take blood pressure—even if no one in your family is hypertensive.

•*Tape to your telephones the numbers for...*

•Your family doctor and any medical specialists used by your family. List the specialty beside the name and number, just in case the caller doesn't know, for example, that Dr. Jones is a cardiologist.

•Family dentist, orthodontist, endodontist, periodontist, etc.

•Police and ambulance. Call ahead to inquire about the normal response time for each.

•Private ambulance.

•Fire department—for first aid as well as fires, in case neither your doctor nor your first-aid squad can be reached.

•Poison-control center. Ask your hospital about the location of the nearest one.

•Emergency room.

•Family veterinarian and animal hospital.

•Neighbors who could be called at any hour, especially those who have a car.

•*Read...*

•All parts of your health insurance policy pertaining to emergency care. Make sure you know how soon after an emergency you must notify the insurance company...and whether your policy offers better coverage at certain hospitals.

•Your first-aid manual.

•*For an elderly or infirm person...*

•Sign him/her up with an emergency response system.

•Provide him with a portable telephone. Make sure he keeps the telephone charged and nearby at all times—especially if he is wheelchair-bound.

•Arrange with someone—neighbor, friend or commercial elder-care service representative—to check on the person each day.

Source: Neil Shulman, MD, associate professor of medicine, Emory University School of Medicine, Atlanta. He is the publisher of *Better Health Care for Less*, 2272 Vistamount Dr., Decatur, GA 30333. Dr. Shulman is coauthor of *Better Health Care for Less*, Hippocrene Books, 171 Madison Ave., New York 10016. He also wrote the novel *Doc Hollywood*, which was made into a movie.

Dealing with a Medical Emergency

In a medical emergency, emotions can run high. Knowing how to get someone to the hospital quickly and efficiently can not only calm the patient, it may even save his life.

Call your local municipal emergency number for a public ambulance. The response time is usually quicker than for a private ambulance.

•Answer all the dispatcher's questions as completely as possible. The answers determine the priority of your call. A broken leg, for example, may not get assistance as quickly as a heart attack.

•Tell the dispatcher exactly what condition the patient is in, as clearly and calmly as possible. Simply saying "I think he is having a heart attack" is not enough. Try to be specific about all the symptoms you have observed.

•Don't hang up until the dispatcher does. Let him decide when he has enough information.

•Give the dispatcher your phone number even if he doesn't ask for it. If something happens to delay the ambulance, he may need to reach you.

•Give careful directions that include your street address, prominent landmarks and any other information that will help the ambulance crew find your location quickly.

•Tell the dispatcher that you will have someone wait outside, put the porch light on, or hang a bed sheet out the window so the driver can see where you are right away.

•Stay with the victim or at least keep him in sight.

•Gather all relevant information, such as insurance numbers, medical history, medications currently being taken (the actual bottle of pills is even better) and anything else that concerns the patient's condition.

•You can usually ride in the ambulance with the patient, unless the patient needs emergency procedures en route.

•In that case, get the name and address of the hospital and the care unit where the patient will be admitted, to go there on your own. (Don't speed or run lights.)

•At the hospital, find out who is caring for the patient. Let the floor nurse know that you are there. Offer to expedite the admitting office paperwork.

Source: Brian Maguire, director of training, BRAVO (Bay Ridge Ambulance Volunteer Organization), NY.

The Well-Stocked Medicine Cabinet

What you *shouldn't* have in your medicine cabinet is as important as what you put in it.

General guideline: Check with your doctor before purchasing any over-the-counter medication...or if your symptoms persist longer than a few days.

What to include...

•Pain, fever and anti-inflammatory medicines. *Examples:* Acetaminophen (Tylenol, Datril and Panadol). It reduces pain and fever without damaging the intestinal tract. However, it is not an anti-inflammatory—it will not reduce swelling.

Aspirin and ibuprofen (Advil, Nuprin and Medipren) relieve pain and inflammation... aspirin also relieves fever. *Warning:* At high doses, both can lead to internal bleeding and wearing away of the stomach lining. *At greatest risk:* The elderly.

Aspirin is also associated with ulcers and *tinnitus* (ringing in the ears)...ibuprofen with kidney toxicity. *Self-defense:* Always take aspirin or ibuprofen with food or liquid antacids, and never exceed the recommended dosage—no more than eight regular-strength tablets a day.

•*First-aid materials:* Hydrogen peroxide for cleaning wounds (*not* alcohol, which is drying and more irritating), antibiotic creams, cotton swabs, gauze pads, surgical tape, adhesive bandages, blunt scissors and tweezers.

•*Skin protectors:* Petroleum jelly or mild moisturizers for dry skin...over-the-counter vaginal cream for mild yeast infections...hydrocortisone cream (no more than 0.5% strength) for poison ivy or other rashes.

Caution: Do not use hydrocortisone on face or genitals without consulting a doctor. And don't use it on fungal infections, such as athlete's foot or jock itch—it will make the problem worse.

•Syrup of ipecac...to induce vomiting after ingesting a poison.

Caution: Call a poison control center before administering—vomiting makes certain kinds of toxins more destructive.

What to use less of...

•Over-the-counter cold remedies. These fight symptoms but don't cure colds. And by drying out mucous membranes, they can hamper the body's natural defenses, slowing recovery.

Antihistamines can be sedating—don't drive or operate machinery while using them.

Decongestants can constrict blood vessels and increase heart rate, making them dangerous for people with heart problems or hypertension. Talk to your doctor before taking them.

Cough medicines may contain alcohol, as well as added decongestants and antibiotics. Read the label carefully and don't exceed recommended dosages.

What to leave out...

•Diet pills. These are completely ineffective over the long-term—they work only as long as you take them. They can be addictive. And they are very, very dangerous for people with heart problems—especially *undiagnosed* heart problems—or high blood pressure.

•Decongestant nose drops. These create a rebound effect—when you stop using them, you become as congested as before...if not more. *Better:* Steroid nasal sprays, available by prescription only.

Source: Robert L. Perkel, MD, clinical associate professor of family medicine at Thomas Jefferson University, Philadelphia 19107.

Car Emergency Equipment

- Flashlight with fresh batteries.
- Flares or warning reflectors.
- Extra washer fluid.
- First aid kit.
- Drinking water and high-energy food.
- Booster cables.
- Extra fan belt and alternator belt.
- Fully inflated spare tire.
- Tool kit (including jack, lug wrench, screwdrivers, pliers, adjustable wrench and electrical tape).

Extras for winter driving:

- Tire chains and traction mats.
- Ice scraper.
- Warm clothing or blankets.
- Square-bladed shovel.
- Extra antifreeze.

When to Go to the Emergency Room

A hospital is advisable when *any* of these symptoms are present—and you can't see your doctor:

- Suspicious abdominal pain. Most pain in this area stems from a temporary digestive problem and will subside by itself. But if the pain is accompanied by fever, extreme tenderness or sensitivity to jarring (it hurts more when you hop), emergency treatment is called for. The same advice holds for any extreme, writhing pain.
- Visible blood in vomit or the stool. These symptoms generally point to a dangerous condition.
- Any condition that steadily becomes worse.
- Respiratory symptoms that suggest pneumonia. Although most pneumonias are caused by viruses and are self-limiting, the bacterial varieties can progress rapidly and are life-threatening. *Danger signs:* Difficulty breathing or shortness of breath, yellow-green sputum and a high fever—more than 102°F—with shaking and chills.

Your best guide in self-diagnosis is common sense. It can also be helpful to ask the opinion of a family member or friend.

Source: Mickey Eisenberg, MD, director of emergency medical services at the University of Washington Medical Center, Emergency Department, 1959 NE Pacific St., Seattle 98195.

How to Beat Hospital Emergency Room Traffic Jams

The first rule for coping with the crowded, and often chaotic, conditions prevailing at many hospital emergency rooms is to seek treatment elsewhere whenever appropriate.

Severe chest or head pain, uncontrolled bleeding, loss of consciousness or breathing difficulties do call for a visit to the ER.

However, many cuts and other seemingly serious problems can often be treated safely—and with far less delay—right in a doctor's private office.

Smart strategy: Discuss with your physician before an emergency arises precisely which emergencies he/she can treat...and which call for the services of an emergency room.

Important: Know whom to contact if your physician is out of town when trouble strikes.

Key emergency room strategies...

- Know the emergency rooms in your area. Some ERs offer only "plain vanilla" service—suturing cuts, setting fractures, treating heart attacks and the like.

Others, such as trauma centers, burn centers and head treatment centers, have the specialized staff and equipment required to treat more difficult cases.

You won't always be able to pick your emergency room—there may be only one in your community, for instance, or you might be away from home when illness or injury strikes.

For times when there is a choice, however, try to pinpoint in advance the one, or ones, best suited to meet the special needs of your family members. If you have children, for instance, pick an emergency room that is capable of dealing with pediatric cases. If a family member is mentally ill, find an emergency room that has psychiatric backup. Discuss local emergency rooms with your family doctor, and with friends and family members. Do your own research, too—phone the various emergency rooms directly. In most cases, a staff doctor or nurse will discuss with you the specifics of the facility.

• Know how to call an ambulance. Although dialing 911 now works in most areas, some communities still require patients to direct-dial the ambulance dispatcher. If you're unfamiliar with the procedure in your area, consult with your family doctor—and the emergency rooms of your choice. Knowing the exact procedure often saves precious minutes that spell the difference between life and death. *Note:* Public ambulance services seldom let patients choose which hospital they'll be taken to. However, it's usually no problem to be transferred—by private ambulance, if necessary—to the emergency room of your choice after you've gotten initial treatment at the first emergency room and if you are not critically ill or unstable.

• Know your medical history. Unlike your family doctor, who is well acquainted with your medical history, emergency room personnel have only a few minutes—if that—to find out all they need to know regarding your health. Any difficulty in taking your history delays your treatment and opens the door to potentially deadly mistakes—such as giving penicillin to someone allergic to it.

To be safe: Prepare a list detailing your allergies, chronic ailments and what medications you take, as well as the name and phone number of your family doctor and the particulars of your health insurance policy. Take this list along with you, if possible, when you head for the emergency room. If you can, also bring along recent electrocardiograms, medical test results, etc. *Alternative:* A medical information card or—better because it is more obvious to rushed emergency room personnel—a Medic-Alert medical information bracelet. The bracelet contains all vital information and allows emergency room physicians to obtain much more medical information by calling into a computer bank that stores that information. For information on purchasing a bracelet, call 800-ID-ALERT.

• Alert your family doctor as soon as possible after an emergency. If you don't have time to phone before leaving for the hospital, phone as soon as possible after you arrive. Whether your physician comes to the emergency room and speaks to the staff in person or communicates with them by phone or fax, your doctor's guidance will greatly facilitate your treatment.

• Bring along a friend or family member. Having someone to talk to while you await treatment not only comforts you and helps you pass the time in the emergency room, but also gives you an "advocate" to press for better or more prompt treatment. An advocate also helps convey to emergency room personnel important information regarding your condition.

• Stand up for yourself when necessary. Emergency room patients often are troubled because they have to wait so long before being treated. Emergency rooms do not operate upon a first-come, first-served basis. Instead, all patients are evaluated using a rigid triage process —those judged sickest or most gravely injured are treated before those whose illnesses or injuries are less severe regardless of who arrived first. Attempting to "jump ahead" of others awaiting treatment is futile. Of course, triage nurses do sometimes make mistakes—serious ones. If you feel that you need immediate attention—or if your condition significantly worsens as you await treatment—speak up...fast!

Source: Stephan G. Lynn, MD, FACEP, director, department of emergency medicine, St. Luke's/Roosevelt Hospital Center, New York.

Heart Attack Self-Defense

Before using CPR, call 911—if an adult is having a heart attack. Doctors used to recommend that trained rescuers give one minute of cardiopulmonary resuscitation before calling the emergency number. *New finding:* Survival and recovery rates are better if 911 is called first. *Important exception:* For children under age eight, a trained rescuer should use proper techniques *before* calling 911. All untrained rescuers should call 911 immediately.

Source: Emergency Cardiac Care Committee and subcommittee, American Heart Association, guidelines for cardiopulmonary resuscitation and emergency cardiac care, reported in *Journal of American Medical Association*, 515 N. State St., Chicago 60610.

If You're All Alone And Choking

A choking person can save himself by falling so that a table or chair hits his diaphragm, thrusting it up against the lungs. It is the forced expulsion of air from the lungs that blows out the obstruction.

Source: Henry J. Heimlich, MD, originator of the "Heimlich maneuver" (whereby a second person saves the choker).

Home Emergencies

Vital information about the house should be known by everyone in the family in case of emergency. *Key items:*

• The location of the fuse box or circuit-breaker panel.

• Placement of the main shutoff valves for the water and gas lines.

• The location of the septic tank or the line to the main sewer.

• Records of the brands, ages and model numbers of the stove, refrigerator, freezer, dishwasher, furnace, washer and dryer.

Source: *Woman's Day*, New York.

Frostbite Remedies

If you can't get indoors, breathe warm air onto the affected area or get it near warm skin. *Example:* Keep frostbitten hands under clothing and under the armpits. *Important:* Do not massage frostbitten skin. Rubbing can worsen skin damage even in mild cases of frostbite.

Source: *Johns Hopkins Health After 50*, 550 North Broadway, Suite 1100, Johns Hopkins, Baltimore, MD 21205.

Poison First Aid Basics

This year alone, three million people in the US will be the victims of accidental poisoning. More than 400,000 will become ill...and more than 500 will die.

Depending on the amount taken, many medicines—prescribed or over-the-counter—can be toxic. And accidental poisoning can occur anywhere—at home, on the job, etc.

If you suspect that someone has been poisoned...

• Check the person's physical appearance. If he/she shows signs of illness, call 911 or your local emergency number immediately.

If he is not breathing, administer rescue breathing and, if necessary, cardiopulmonary resuscitation (CPR). If you do not know these procedures, find someone who does...or follow the phone directions of trained medical personnel.

• Try to determine what substance the person has ingested and in what amount. This will help medical personnel to determine the appropriate course of treatment, if necessary.

• Contact your regional poison-control center. The number can be found on the inside cover of your phone book.

Using information that you provide, the poison center will determine the danger posed to the patient and tell you what to do.

Warning: Do not administer an antidote unless directed to by a poison center or a physician. Administered in incorrect dosages, some antidotes can have serious side effects.

Source: Scott Phillips, MD, an expert in clinical toxicology at Rocky Mountain Poison Center, Denver.

How to Treat a Cut

When you first cut yourself, decide quickly if you need to see a doctor.

You do need medical help if...

• The cut is deep—or bleeds a lot.

• You've cut an artery. You'll know because bright red blood will spurt out.

First aid: Apply pressure on the side of the wound nearer the heart.

• You've cut a large vein—at the wrist or higher and at the ankle or higher. (A toe or finger is not critical.) *Dark* blood flows steadily from a vein.

First aid: Apply pressure on the side of the wound away from the heart.

When in doubt about what you have cut...

Apply pressure directly on the wound—*and seek medical attention promptly.*

• You've cut yourself on something dirty. If you have not had a booster within the last year, a tetanus shot is advisable.

• You've cut a hand or foot and can't move your fingers or toes.

• You've sliced off a finger, toe or even a flap of skin. These can often be reattached. Wash and transport the piece in anything that's clean. A handkerchief that has been ironed is always good to use.

For less serious cuts...

• Clean the cut. Use an antiseptic, such as peroxide, or tap water.

• Cover it with a clean bandage—and remove bandage when a scab forms.

• Replace soggy dressings.

• Avoid picking scabs.

• Monitor the healing process. Watch for signs of infection. *See a doctor if:*

A cut that hurt at first, stops hurting and then becomes painful again...Streaky red lines arise, leading away from the wound...You feel tender lumps either near or far away from the cut—your lymph nodes may be swelling...A pus-filled abscess forms...A fever develops.

Source: Jack Rudick, MD, professor of surgery, Mount Sinai School of Medicine, New York.

Better Burn Advice

Nothing hurts quite the same way that a burn does. Even the smallest of burns—from a spatter of grease or the touch of a hot iron—can smart for hours or even days. Although millions of Americans suffer burns each year, most burns (more than 90%) are relatively minor...

• *First-degree burns* affect the skin's top layer, causing redness, pain but *no* blistering. They can be treated at home and heal within hours.

• *Second-degree burns* also affect some underlying skin and can cause redness, blistering, sensitivity to air and more severe pain that may not subside for several days (many sunburns are classified as second-degree burns). These burns frequently require a visit to a hospital for treatment.

Most minor burns are caused by grabbing hot objects without realizing how hot they are or spilling hot drinks or boiling water.

And most of these burns involve the hand.

Important: Hand burns must be treated more aggressively than burns on most other parts of the body. *Reason:* The hands contain many delicate muscles and tendons in a relatively small area. If not treated quickly, permanent damage can result.

Treating minor burns...

• *Run cool water over the burn.* This will ease the pain and even reverse some damage.

• *Apply salves liberally.* Several over-the-counter products, including petroleum jelly, shark-liver oil and aloe vera gel can be used to temporarily ease the stinging.

• *Monitor the burn very closely.* If it shows any signs of infection, be sure to see your doctor immediately. *Caution:* Burns are very susceptible to secondary infections. *Helpful:* Over-the-counter antibiotic products.

Things to avoid...

• Ice. Although ice can make a burn feel better, a burn packed in ice or immersed in ice water can make the injury worse. *Warning:* You can get a burn from grabbing very *cold* as well as very hot objects.

• Butter. The salt in the butter will aggravate a burn.

Second-degree burns...

Second-degree burns should be treated by a doctor...who will:

• *Cleanse and treat the burn.* It will be washed in soapy water and then rinsed with a saline solution. Fluid may be removed from unbroken blisters, and the skin left in place to provide a natural cover.

Many emergency departments use drugs containing 0.5% silver nitrate solution or a 1% silver sufadiazine cream. They may also be prescribed for home use. These thick creams and gels are applied over the burn, which is then wrapped in a sterile dressing.

New: Duoderm (Squibb), a sterile air-tight dressing, is used for several weeks until the body begins to generate new skin.

• *Help you cope with the pain.* Analgesics may be prescribed.

• *Know your tetanus status.* People who suffer second-degree burns require current tetanus immunization. If you haven't had a tetanus shot in five years, you will be given one.

Severe burns...

Immediate hospitalization in a facility with a burn-care unit is needed to treat severe burns.

• *Third-degree burns* adversely affect the skin's full thickness. The burned area has a white leathery appearance. Although you may not suffer from blisters or even pain (because of destroyed nerve endings), these burns are actually very dangerous.

• *Fourth-degree burns* affect the skin's full thickness *and* underlying tissues, including muscles, tendons and bones. The burned area has a blackened appearance.

Treating severe burns...

Skin-grafting procedures may be necessary. Such procedures are performed by a surgeon or plastic surgeon or burn-care specialist who takes live skin from one part of the body and moves it to another part to replace cells that have been destroyed and won't regenerate. In cases where large amounts of skin are needed, it may be removed from a donor's cadaver.

Note: A great deal of promising research is now being conducted in the area of skin-grafting. *Artificial skin,* for instance, may soon be put to use in the treatment of severe burns and minimize disfigurement.

Source: Steven Chernow, MD, medical director of the emergency department of University Hospital of Boston University.

First Aid for Chemical Burns

Chemical burns to the eye usually don't cause permanent damage if rinsing starts within 15 seconds. After that, chances of recovery decline rapidly. Any innocuous water fluid can be used. Continue flushing for at least 20 minutes.

Source: John Paul Wohlen, Bradley Corp., Menomonee Falls, WI, writing in *Plant Engineering.*

Summer Safety Advice

Warm weather brings a variety of fun-filled activities including family cookouts and visits to the beach...but it also brings a range of potential health hazards...

• Animal bites. Observe extreme caution when approaching unfamiliar animals and insist that your children do likewise. Use cold water to separate fighting dogs or cats—never your hands.

Bite treatment: Superficial bites from a pet call only for washing with hot, soapy water. Pet bites that draw blood, however, as well as any bite from a wild animal, require immediate medical attention—you may need antibiotics to prevent infection.

Rabies defense: Capture or kill the biting animal, if possible, and have the local health department check it for rabies. If the animal proves rabid, or if for some reason the animal cannot be tested, you must undergo a course of rabies prophylaxis—a series of five shots administered over a one-month period. Contrary to popular belief, these shots are given in the arm, not the abdomen.

Good news: Rabies is extremely rare among cats, dogs, squirrels and rodents—although skunks, bats, raccoons, foxes and cattle are sometimes infected.

•Bee stings. Avoid bright colors, perfumes, soft drinks and sugary foods while in bee territory. Instead, douse yourself with bug repellent and don white or khaki clothing, long sleeves and pants, sturdy shoes and insect netting.

Persons allergic to bee venom should carry an epinephrine injector while outdoors...and should avoid lawn-mowing, flower-picking and other activities that are likely to put them in proximity to bees.

If you're bitten: Gently remove the stinger from your skin. Use ice packs and cold compresses to minimize swelling.

•Drowning. The third-leading cause of accidental death in the United States, drowning claims more than 4,500 victims a year.

To reduce risk: Swim, snorkel and scuba dive only with a partner...wear a Coast Guard approved life preserver whenever you're on a dock or aboard a boat...never dive into water of unknown depth.

If you become fatigued while swimming, float face-down—lifting your head only to breathe—until your strength returns or help arrives. Most people can float quite easily simply by filling their lungs with air.

•Head injuries. Motorcyclists, bicyclists, skateboarders and roller skaters should at all times wear helmets approved by the Snell Memorial Foundation. Skateboard only on driveways, empty lots, parks and other traffic-free areas. Roller skate on public roads in light traffic only if you are sufficiently skilled to move smoothly and predictably.

•Heat exhaustion and heat stroke. Strenuous exercise in hot, humid weather can cause fatigue, confusion, unconsciousness and even death.

At greatest risk: Athletes, laborers, children, the elderly and persons taking antihypertensives, antipsychotics, antidepressants and certain other prescription drugs.

To avoid trouble: Consume plenty of water or electrolyte drinks (such as Gatorade), and take frequent breaks. If you begin to experience symptoms, get out of the heat immediately. Remove all clothing, then apply cool water or ice to the skin. If symptoms persist, go immediately to the emergency room. If you are with someone who has lost consciousness, call an ambulance or get that person to an emergency room.

•Lawn mower accidents. There are more than 60,000 lawn mower accidents a year.

Self-defense: Protect yourself and your family by clearing away rocks, branches and other obstacles before mowing...wearing protective glasses, sturdy shoes and earplugs...and keeping small children indoors. Never give children mower rides—the risk of falling under the blades is too great.

•Lightning. Each year, lightning causes more than 100 deaths.

To avoid being struck: During rainstorms, avoid golf courses and other large, open areas ...isolated trees, towers and other tall structures ...wading in puddles or swimming...and holding or touching anything metallic. Quickly get inside or into a car. If nearby shelter is unavailable, head for a heavily forested area.

Last resort: Crouch.

If you are struck, seek immediate medical attention. If someone nearby has been struck, immediately call for emergency medical help. Lightning causes not only severe burns, but also cataracts and potentially fatal electrical disturbances in the heart.

•Playground injuries. Last year alone, more than 250,000 children sustained playground injuries. Inspect playground facilities carefully beforehand. *Common dangers:*

•Swing sets.

•Monkey bars and other equipment situated less than six feet from fences and other obstructions.

•Equipment loosely anchored in the ground.

•Equipment not surrounded by rubber mats, wood chips, sand or other energy-absorbing materials.

•Improper spacing of rungs and steps. (Less than nine inches separation, and children's heads can be trapped.)

•Swing seats made of wood or metal rather than rubber, canvas or another soft material.

•Fine, chalky sand found in some sandboxes. It may contain asbestos-like fibers that some believe cause respiratory problems. Children should play only in sandboxes containing coarse sand.

•Sunburn. Red, blistered skin is only one result. Less conspicuous but far more ominous is the fact that even one severe sunburn boosts your lifetime risk of melanoma and other forms of skin cancer by 10%. Gradual tanning is safer, but it too can lead to cancer—and should be avoided.

Sun-taming tools: Broad-brimmed hats, UV-absorptive sunglasses and sunscreen rated at least SPF 15. Stay out of the sun between 11 a.m. and 3 p.m., the hours of greatest sunlight intensity. *Note:* The effects of sunburn cannot be undone. However, cold compresses combined with aspirin or ibuprofen will ease discomfort as your skin recovers.

•Tick bites. Insect repellent is one obvious precaution, but it also makes sense to wear light-colored clothing (dark colors hide ticks), a long sleeved shirt and long pants tucked into your socks.

Upon returning indoors, conduct a thorough head-to-toe body search. If you find a tick, gently pull it off using your fingers or tweezers. Removing a tick using a hot match or nail polish only boosts the odds that the tick's head will be left in your skin, where it can cause infection.

Warning: Anyone bitten by a tick should be extremely wary of Lyme disease and Rocky Mountain spotted fever, two serious tick-borne illnesses. See a doctor at the earliest hint of telltale symptoms—fever, headache, muscular aches or a skin rash (especially a circular rash around the bite). Both illnesses are curable if caught early. Left untreated, however, they lead to several potentially lasting ailments, including double vision, arthritis, irregular heartbeat—even death.

Source: Kelley Hails, MD, former clinical instructor of medicine, Michigan State University College of Human Medicine, East Lansing. Dr. Hails specializes in emergency medicine.

What to Do If Someone Faints

Old-time fainting remedies are dangerous. Placing a fainter's head between his legs could cause brain damage. Most smelling salts contain ammonium hydroxide, which can cause chemical burns of the nose and lungs. *Better:* Lay the fainter on his back. Then raise his legs. Gently massage the calves to return blood to central circulation. Wait about 20 minutes and then raise the person in stages.

Source: *RN.*

Taking a Spill

Relax and give in to your fall. Try to slide as you touch the ground. Drop any packages right away. If you tumble forward, put open hands out to break the impact and protect your face. When falling backward, try to sit as you go down, to protect your spine. If you catch a foot in a hole, drop to the side that's caught.

After the fall: Breathe deeply and get up very slowly—so you won't get dizzy and fall again.

Source: *Woman's Day*, New York.

First Aid: Diabetic Coma

Thousands of people die each year because they fall into diabetic comas and do not get the right treatment promptly.

Trap: Most diabetics' family members, friends and coworkers do not know how to properly react during such a crisis.

What to watch for: Just as there are two types of diabetes, there are two types of diabetic comas:

Hyperglycemic coma...

Patients lack enough insulin to digest sugar. *Result:* They become hyperglycemic (have excess blood sugar).

Warning sign: The inability to keep down fluids.

Times of greatest risk: When diabetics are ill, their insulin requirements rise.

Timing: These comas come on gradually over anywhere from several hours to several days.

What to do: Rush the person to the emergency room. Only professionals can administer the intravenous fluids, insulin and salts needed to correct the problem.

Hypoglycemic coma...

Patients produce excess insulin and digest sugar too fast. *Result:* They become hypoglycemic (have low blood sugar).

Warning signs: Fight or flight symptoms—anxiety, tremors and agitation. People entering these comas may act inappropriately, as if drunk.

Times of greatest risk: When patients take too much insulin...or take the right amount but miss a meal...or exercise too hard.

Timing: These comas can occur very quickly, without warning. *Note:* If your child is diabetic, be sure his teachers know that comas like this may arise.

What to do: If the person is still alert and conscious, feed him carbohydrates or protein. *Best:* Six ounces of juice or skim milk. Avoid giving the person extra table sugar or excess concentrated sweets—they force blood sugar too high. This treatment can be repeated in 20 minutes if the person fails to respond adequately.

If the person cannot ingest food, get immediate medical help. If this is not possible give him a glucagon injection. All families of insulin-dependent diabetic patients should have a glucagon kit and know how to use it.

Source: James R. Gavin III, MD, PhD, William K. Warren Professor for Diabetes Studies, department of medicine, Oklahoma University Health Sciences Center, St. Francis Medical Research Institute, Oklahoma City, OK 73104.

Dental Emergencies

Toothaches, broken or knocked-out teeth, fractured jaws and other dental emergencies require immediate attention.

How to minimize pain and maximize treatment until you reach the dentist...

• Bleeding. Slight bleeding is common following a tooth extraction. If the bleeding persists longer than an hour, try pressing gauze or an ice cube against the area for 20 minutes. If that fails to stanch the flow, apply a wet tea bag. *Note:* Profuse bleeding typically requires sutures.

• Broken tooth, filling or crown. Control pain with an over-the-counter analgesic—then get to the dentist as soon as possible. Be sure to take along the piece of tooth, filling or crown.

• Gum boils. These painful, pimple-like swellings form when pus from an abscess works its way to the surface. Since they are usually a sign of a serious infection or gum disease, always consult your dentist promptly if one appears. *Helpful:* Rinse your mouth with warm salt water to keep the pus draining.

• Knocked-out (avulsed) tooth. Often these can be successfully reimplanted—if you get to the dentist promptly and if the tooth is handled delicately. *What to do:* Gently rinse the tooth in water or milk, taking care not to detach any attached soft tissue. Place the tooth in water or milk, and take it with you to the dentist or the nearest emergency room.

• Mouth sores. To reduce discomfort, apply a paste of baking soda. *Also helpful:* Over-the-counter analgesics and topical anesthetics (Anbesol, Orajel, Campho-Phenique, etc.).

• Toothache. Most toothaches result from an inflamed or dying nerve, and invariably get worse until the tooth has been treated. Take an over-the-counter analgesic, and treat the inflamed area with a few drops of oil of clove. *Avoid:* Aspirin and hot packs applied directly to the gum.

Source: Jack Klatell, DDS, chairman of the department of dentistry, Mount Sinai School of Medicine, New York. Dr. Klatell is coauthor of *The Mount Sinai Medical Center Family Guide to Dental Health.* Macmillan Publishing Co.

Big Help in Little Emergencies

• To remove a sticky bandage without pain, first soak a cotton ball in baby oil and douse the bandage with it. The oil significantly reduces the bandage's adhesion.

Source: *Parents,* New York.

• A quick, handy ice pack in an emergency is a bag of frozen vegetables (like peas or corn niblets). The bag is clean, water-tight and pliable enough to fit almost any part of the body. (It is, of course, only a stopgap substitution.)

Source: *Harvard Medical School Health Letter,* Cambridge, MA.

• To remove a ring from a swollen finger, use a few feet of string. Slip a few inches under and through the ring toward the wrist. Then wind the long end of the string tightly down the finger toward the tip, with the loops touching one another. (In most cases this will not be painful.) Finally, take the short end of the string and pull on it toward the fingertip. As the coil unwinds, the ring is pulled along until it falls off.

Source: *Emergency Medicine,* New York.

• Muscle trick to relieve cramps and spasms: Contract the muscles in the muscle group opposite the one that is cramped. This confuses the troubled muscle, making it relax. (*Example:* If your calf cramps, tighten the muscles in the front of your lower leg to relieve the discomfort.)

Source: *American Health.*

• Treating burns with butter or greasy ointments is dangerous. Neither is sterile and either can make subsequent treatment by a doctor more difficult. *Better:* Flush a burn with cold water or immerse it in cold water for up to 30 minutes. *Alternative:* Apply cold compresses. Cover with clean bandages. Never puncture a blister. For serious burns, seek a doctor at once.

Source: Gustavo Colon, MD, associate professor of plastic surgery, Tulane University Medical School, quoted in *Vogue,* New York.

Poison Control

Any home where youngsters live or visit should have an ample supply of ipecac—to induce vomiting in case of accidental poisoning.

Suggested: One bottle for each child under 12.

Source: Chris Keyes, MD, director, North Texas Poison Center, The University of Texas Southwestern Medical Center at Dallas.

Bee Sting First Aid

Remove the stinger if it is visible by scraping gently with a butter knife or credit card. Do not squeeze the area and pull with tweezers or fingers—that can release more venom.

After removing the stinger, wash the area with soap and water and apply a cold pack to reduce pain and swelling.

Though rare, serious allergic reactions to bee stings occur within minutes. If the person who has been stung collapses, develops hives or swollen lips or eyes or has trouble breathing, call 911 immediately.

Source: Recommendations from the American Academy of Allergy, Asthma and Immunology, 611 E. Wells, Milwaukee 53202.

911 and CPR

Rescuers should start CPR *before* calling 911 when trying to resuscitate a child or a young adult. Clear the airway, do one minute of breaths/chest compressions, *then* call 911. With individuals over age 30, call 911 first. *Reason:* An older person whose heart stops is probably experiencing *ventricular fibrillation.* This heart condition requires prompt treatment by emergency personnel. But a young person whose heart stops usually has only an obstructed airway—which can be cleared by anyone with minimal training. If you lack CPR training, call 911 first, then return to the victim and try to help.

Source: Richard O. Cummins, MD, professor of medicine, University of Washington, Seattle.

24

Self-Defense

How to Tell When Someone is Lying

Detecting a lie isn't easy…even for experienced law-enforcement professionals. They spend many hours studying videotapes to understand the psychology of liars as well as the physical and emotional signs that give them away.

My research, however, has uncovered a variety of telltale clues that often can help you determine when someone is trying to deceive you.

What is a lie?

It's important to remember that not every untrue statement is necessarily a lie. Some are innocent mistakes, some are attempts to be polite…and some are purposeful and to be expected.

Example: At a magic show, the audience knows the magician is trying to fool them. The magician knows that they know it, so his/her untrue statements are not lies.

When I use the word "lie," I mean a deliberate attempt to mislead someone without making that person aware of it.

Lies are also usually at the other person's expense. They may be outright false statements…or a concealment of something the liar is obligated to tell.

Example: A job applicant who omits information that he is required to disclose, such as a previous job.

Why we believe lies…

Sometimes people deliberately overlook obvious lies because they want to believe what they're being told. This is especially true when the misinformation confirms the listener's way of doing things.

Straining to accept a lie may be a short-term way to avoid admitting that you have been fooled, but you may not be able to avoid the truth in the long term. So it is important to know when you're being told a lie—and how to overcome the psychological factors that cause you to accept the misinformation.

How to spot a liar...

A person who is lying is likely to give himself away through a variety of clues related to one or more of the emotional effects that lying produces.

• Fear of being caught. A liar who is afraid of being caught may signal that fear verbally and/or physically. Watch out for words that are evasive, indirect and halting—and a voice that is strained and/or higher pitched than normal.

These signs are not definite proof of lying. They are best when you can compare the "suspicious" indicator with what is normal behavior for the suspected liar.

• Unconscious gestures. Psychologists recognize three kinds of gestures that change in different ways when someone is nervous...as a liar often is. But detecting them is not easy. I have found that it takes at least eight solid hours of training exercises with videotapes for the average person to acquire the necessary sensitivity. The basic clues...

• Emblems. These are deliberate gestures whose meanings everyone understands, such as shrugging your shoulders to show you don't know. Someone telling a lie may give it away by unconsciously signaling via an incomplete emblem...like shrugging only one shoulder. Not everyone makes these slips. They are subtle—therefore, hard to notice.

• Illustrators are body movements that accompany speech...like the way people move their hands when asked to describe a spiral staircase.

Lies are likely to be accompanied by fewer than normal illustrators because the liar has to think more about his invented story than someone who is telling the truth.

• Manipulators are fidgeting gestures—like scratching or twisting hair—that become more common when someone is nervous. But everyone is aware of the stereotype that guilty people look nervous, so any liar with normal intelligence will try not to fidget. Therefore, fidgeting is usually not a very good indicator of lying.

• Facial clues. A lie-catcher needs to become sensitive to the two messages sent by the face —the false expression that the person wants to give...and the true expression that he cannot hide.

• Squelched impressions, when his concealed emotion starts to emerge and he quickly covers it with a false smile.

• Micro-expressions, when the true feeling flashes on his/her face for an instant. While micro-expressions are easy to miss, you can train yourself to catch them.

• Inability to control muscles. This occurs when certain facial muscles used in natural expressions of emotion cannot be controlled because the emotion is not felt. That is why a genuine smile, not a fake one, crinkles the eyes.

Caution: Truly skilled liars—or those who have come to believe their own lies—may not give any of these clues because, like actors, they are able to truly feel the emotion they are trying to express to you.

Bottom line...

There is no infallible way to detect lies, because all liars are different.

Source: Paul Ekman, PhD, professor of psychology at the University of California, San Francisco. He is the author of *Telling Lies: Clues to Deceit in the Marketplace, Politics and Marriage*, W.W. Norton and Company, 500 Fifth Ave., New York 10110.

What to Do if There's a Burglar in the House

Outdoor lighting, alarm systems, timers that automatically turn on and off household lights, and other precautions all help protect your home from burglary.

Just as important as taking steps to keep burglars outside is planning what to do if someone makes it inside. *Most important:*

• Create a "safe haven." Inside every home should be a specially equipped room where occupants can retreat in case of an attack or intrusion. This room—ideally a bathroom or bedroom—should have a window or some other means of escape...a solid-core door with a one-inch deadbolt that latches from the inside...a telephone...and a list of emergency phone numbers. If your home is equipped with an alarm system, install a panic button inside your safe room.

•Develop an escape plan. Know the fastest way out of your house from every room. Periodically rehearse your escape. Make sure windows, doors, and other escape routes can quickly be opened from the inside.

•Don't go to investigate. Confronting a burglar face-to-face can turn a simple burglary into an assault or even murder.

More prudent: Leave the investigation to the police. If you arrive home and find evidence of a break-in, *don't go inside.* The intruder might still be there. Leave the premises immediately and call the police.

If the burglary takes place while you're inside, lock a door between yourself and the intruder—ideally that of your safe haven—and telephone the police. If you cannot reach a phone, open a window and yell for help.

If it's possible to escape without risking an encounter with the burglar, then do so. Call the police from a neighbor's house.

•Remain calm. If you come face-to-face with an intruder inside your home, try not to panic. The more level-headed you are, the more likely you'll be able to think of a way to defuse the situation...and the less threatening you'll appear to the burglar.

If you don't provoke him, odds are he/she won't harm you. Most burglars just want to get out of the house once they've been detected. Don't attack or attempt to hold him until the police arrive. Just give him a wide berth so he can escape.

Most important: Fight only if attacked. Then use any weapon at hand—a knife, scissors, a heavy object, a canister of irritating chemical spray, etc. A gun is useful only if you know how—and are willing—to fire it at the intruder. If you wield a gun tentatively, he might take it away and use it against *you.*

Source: Richard L. Bloom, founder of the Crime Deterrent Institute, Houston. A frequent lecturer on crime prevention and victims' rights, Bloom is the author of *Victims: A Survival Guide for the Age of Crime,* Guardian Press, 10924 Grant Rd. #225, Houston 77070. 800-771-8191.

Antacid Warning

Eating too many calcium-containing antacid tablets can damage the brain and the heart. A 53-year-old man with mild kidney trouble who consumed 20 to 25 antacid tablets a day suffered both a stroke and a heart attack. *Cause:* Too much calcium in his blood from the antacids. *Self-defense:* Get dosage instructions from your doctor before taking antacid tablets.

Source: Jeffrey Frank, MD, director of neuromedical/neurosurgical intensive care, The Cleveland Clinic Foundation.

How to Avoid Becoming a Victim Of a Violent Crime

From purse-snatching and car-jacking to assaults, rapes, and kidnappings, violent crime has become a frightening fact of everyday life. While there's little you can do to control the rise of these crimes, there are ways to limit your chances of becoming a victim.

In your car...

•Car-jacking self-defense. Unlike professional car thieves, who have no wish to encounter car owners, car-jackers are out for a thrill—and violence for them is thrilling. Tell yourself *now* that if someone tries to pull you from your car or demands your keys, you will behave passively and give them the car. When the event occurs, you should instinctively give up the vehicle rather than panic and fight back.

•Keep doors locked while driving. Close windows in slow traffic and at red lights. When coming to a stop, leave enough room between you and the car in front. This will allow you to maneuver around the vehicle if necessary.

•Pay attention to your surroundings. Car-jackers almost always approach on foot. Avoid self-absorbed distractions, such as combing your hair, fumbling with cassette tapes, etc.

•Park under a street light or as close as possible to the mall or well-lit buildings and stores.

Avoid parking next to potential hiding places, such as dumpsters, woods, etc.

• Scan parking lots before approaching your car. Try to walk with other people, or ask a doorman or security guard for an escort.

• Have your key ready in your hand as you approach your vehicle. Look inside the car and around the outside before getting in. *Caution:* On some new cars, all doors will unlock when the driver's door is unlocked—a dangerous feature if someone is hiding outside the passenger door. If you do sense danger, retreat to a place of safety and call the police immediately. Do not confront an intruder.

On the street...

• Carry purses and briefcases close to the body—but be able to release them if necessary. *Avoid:* Shoulder straps across the body, straps wrapped around the wrist. People have been dragged by the straps and injured in purse-snatchings. If someone tries to take your wallet or purse, let it go. *Useful:* "Fanny pack" belts and pouches seem to be an unattractive target for street thieves.

• On the bus or subway, do not sit next to an exit door or place briefcases or purchases on an empty seat. Robbers tend to grab valuables as they are leaving and while doors are closing.

• If you are held up, do not resist. Most armed robbers only want your money. *Problem:* Many will turn to violence if they are alarmed or disobeyed. Surrender your valuables quickly.

At home...

• Keep doors and windows locked, especially after you turn in for the night. Keep curtains drawn after dark. Most home intruders are opportunists.

• Install deadbolt locks with reinforced strike plates on front and back doors. A few dollars will purchase a reinforced strike plate that secures the door frame to the first wall stud. Locks like these are also deterrents.

• Secure sliding glass doors by placing a broomstick or piece of wood along the interior track and by blocking the dead space in the upper channel that allows the door to be lifted off the track.

• Consider installing an alarm system. Ground-floor windows can be equipped with an alarmed jamming stick for $30 to $40.

• Never confront a burglar. If you come home to a door that's ajar or has been tampered with, leave the scene immediately and call the police. If you wake up to find an intruder in your bedroom, pretend to be asleep until he leaves.

• Don't depend on your dog to alert you. Most people command their dogs to *stop* barking when a stranger arrives. Many a dog has slept through a burglary or been seduced by a doggie treat.

• Do not open the door to strangers. If you have to hire an unfamiliar repairman, ask someone to be with you at home or plan to be on the phone when he arrives...or pretend there is someone else at home. If a repairman or stranger arrives at your door unannounced, do not let him/her in. Lock the door and call his office for verification.

• If you think you hear a prowler, call the police. Don't assume it's just the wind, that the police are too busy, or that they might get mad if no one is there. It is always better to feel foolish than to be a victim.

• Unless you are well-trained, do not keep a gun in the house. People who are untrained with firearms are more likely to have them stolen or taken away from them by intruders, who may have arrived unarmed. If you do keep a gun in the house, the gun and ammunition should be stored separately.

Caution: According to law, in order to shoot an intruder on your property, you must be "in fear for your life." This does not mean in fear of losing your TV and jewelry.

• Know your neighbors. Neighborhood watch programs and "telephone trees" to alert neighbors of strangers in the area are very effective.

At work...

• Know your neighbors. Set up a building-wide security policy to identify visitors. "Business watch" programs for merchants in shopping areas are highly effective, too.

• Team up in pairs to use public rest rooms or locked rest rooms located in public hallways. Avoid using remote stairwells alone.

•Keep the office's doors locked when working late, on weekends, or early in the morning.

•Do not get on an elevator with someone who makes you feel uncomfortable or unsafe.

•When traveling on business, ask a bellhop to accompany you to your hotel room and to check it before you enter. Avoid ground-floor rooms. Make sure that the phone is working and that security numbers are provided. Never open the door to someone you're not expecting. If someone knocks unannounced, call the lobby for verification.

At play...

•Exercise with a partner, or take along a dog or stick while jogging. Avoid isolated parks and paths. Wear glasses if you normally need them, and do not use a stereo headset. Avoid loose clothes that are easy to grab.

•At parks, beaches, or other recreation areas, know where the ranger or lifeguard stations are located. Leave expensive cameras, jewelry, and credit cards at home or locked in the trunk of the car. Do not use recreation areas after hours.

In all situations...

•Make direct eye contact with people around you. This sends a message of confidence, an effective deterrent to violent crime. Criminals seek passive, distracted victims, who make easy targets.

•Trust your instincts. Humans are extremely instinctive. *Important:* Tune into the messages. Some of the most common statements police officers hear following a crime are, "I had a feeling I shouldn't have walked to my car," "The guy gave me the creeps, but..."

Bottom line: If a situation makes you nervous, avoid it. Learn to respect your instincts and act on them.

Source: Patricia Harman, a crime-prevention officer with the Prince William County, Virginia, police force. Harman, who conducts lectures nationally on personal safety, is the author of *The Danger Zone: How You Can Protect Yourself from Rape, Robbery, and Assault,* Parkside Publishing, 205 W. Touhy Ave., Park Ridge, IL 60068. 800-221-6364.

The Most Commonly Asked Legal Questions

Sooner or later, you'll probably need the advice of a lawyer. What are you most likely to ask about and how can these legal problems be resolved? Here are the top eight...

When and how can I use small claims court? This is a quick, inexpensive way to solve minor legal problems (typically around $1,000). You don't even need a lawyer.

Step 1: Look in your local telephone directory under "Courts," "City of..." for Small Claims Court, Justice Court, Magistrate's Court, or Court of Common Appeals. You must sue in the county where the defendant lives or conducts business. Check the county clerk to make sure it's the right court, and to get the proper legal name for the company you're suing.

Step 2: When you arrive at court for the first time, a clerk will give you a complaint form to fill out. *Cost:* Between $2 and $10. It asks for your name and address, the defendant's name and address, a brief description of why you're suing and the damages claimed. *Note:* Small claims courts only award money. They cannot order actions.

Step 3: The clerk will assign you a hearing date (usually in about two weeks) and notify the defendant by mail. Often the sessions are held in the early evening.

Step 4: Before your hearing, gather evidence—contracts, photographs, accident reports, witnesses—and organize how you will present your case. A written outline helps. Be sure to get to court on time.

Step 5: If the judge is overloaded, you may be asked to submit your dispute to arbitration—to an impartial third party...often an attorney. That may make sense, but you should know that an arbitrator's decision is final. You won't be able to appeal it to a judge or a higher court. If the defendant fails to appear, you will be sent before an arbitrator who will listen to your testimony and award you appropriate damages (usually including repayment of your filing fee and interest). If the defendant, after being notified by mail, fails to pay up, call the court clerk and ask how to use law-enforcement personnel to collect your judgment.

Is there a statute of limitations on medical malpractice? Yes. As with other causes of action, claims of medical malpractice must be initiated within a given period of time, which differs from state to state. In New York, in the absence of qualifying circumstances, a medical malpractice suit must be initiated within 30 months of the act. However, New York and most other states grant children under age 18 who are the victims of malpractice an extension of time within which to sue. Ask your local bar association for the name of an attorney who can tell you exactly what the law is in your state given your particular circumstances.

What can I do if my landlord refuses to make repairs...or paint? A lease is a contract entitling the landlord to receive rent if he/she provides you with certain guarantees, including a "warranty of habitability" that the place is safe and livable. This means the plumbing should work, etc. Repairs must be made within a "reasonable" period of time, which, of course, varies depending on whether it's a dangerous gas leak or merely a broken dishwasher.

Recourse: Most towns have special housing courts where tenants can file complaints without a lawyer. You could also send the landlord a letter by certified mail warning him that if repairs are not made immediately you will hire a contractor yourself and deduct the cost from your monthly rent.

Under very damning circumstances—if, for example, he has a policy of refusing repairs in order to drive tenants out—you could withhold rent. However, this carries with it the risk of eviction. Don't do it without first consulting a lawyer.

The terms for painting are usually specified in the lease. If the landlord stalls, you can go to the special housing court or to small claims court to have your rent reduced or to get the money needed to hire a painter yourself.

Do I need a lawyer when I'm buying a house? Yes. Buying a house is an extremely complex undertaking and you should be represented by counsel who will look out for your best interests. Is the title good? Does the seller have a faulty deed? Are there any outstanding claims against the property? Does the house satisfy zoning ordinances? Many of these questions are matters of subtle legal interpretation, and you will want written guarantees that fully protect you.

What happens if my credit card or ATM card is stolen? Under the Consumer Credit Protection Act consumers are liable for only $50 if a credit card is stolen, and even that may be waived under some circumstances. However, a different standard applies to automated teller machine cards. Under the federal Electronic Fund Transfer Act, your liability is limited to $50 if you notify the bank within two business days. Thereafter, your liability jumps to $500.

If an unauthorized transfer appears on your bank statement and you don't report it within 60 days of the mailing date you risk losing everything in your account plus any credit line. Report any lost or stolen card to the bank immediately by phone and in writing.

Protection: Don't carry your ATM password in your wallet, and avoid obvious numbers like your birth date and the first four digits of your Social Security number.

Am I legally entitled to see my personnel file at work? You might be, depending on the kind of job you have and the state in which you work. Virtually all employees of the federal government have access, and union contracts provide this same privilege to many workers in the private sector.

Otherwise, your rights depend on the laws of the state where you work. California's Labor Code mandates access to all records "which are used or have been used to determine that employee's qualifications for employment, promotion, additional compensation, termination, or other disciplinary action." Letters of reference and records relating to the investigation of possible criminal offenses are exempt.

Many states have similar statutes, and Oregon requires employers to keep personnel records available to employees for at least 60 days after termination of employment. Contact your State Department of Labor to find out what the law allows.

What can I do about a noisy neighbor? Depending on the specific complaint, your neighbor's actions may constitute a violation of civil or criminal law. Playing loud music late at night amounts to disorderly conduct, for which you can call the police. Civil steps can also be taken under the "nuisance" law, which provides that people have the right to reasonable comfort in their homes. Acts that might be perfectly proper under some circumstances become unlawful if they interfere with your enjoyment of this right.

Example: Your neighbor can use a chain saw, but not at midnight. He has the right to mow his lawn, but maybe not at 6 a.m. on a Sunday morning since he could do it at another time that wouldn't interfere with others' one day to sleep in late.

Do I have a case when I wait for a delivery person who never comes? Yes. This is a breach of contract. If you take a half day off work, for example, and the couch isn't delivered as promised, the store has violated its part of the contract. Call and ask for a new delivery time at your convenience. Most stores can deliver at night, for example, although they don't advertise that. Failing satisfaction, demand that the cost of additional time off from work be deducted from your bill. If all else fails, take the case to small claims court.

Source: Thomas Hauser, lawyer and author of *The Family Legal Companion.* Allworth Press

Crime Victims

Crime victims who remain calm stay safer. If you are calm, an enraged assailant is more likely to calm down too, and you can prevent any undue harm. *To keep yourself calm:* Breathe slowly and deeply...say the word "relax" over and over in your head...view the mugger as a person instead of an evil criminal—this image is much less intimidating. *To keep the assailant calm:* Be respectful—listen closely to what he says...never argue...give up any possessions he asks for.

Source: Arnold Howard, a black belt in karate in Mesquite, Texas, teaches self-defense nationwide.

Fabric Danger

Formaldehyde resin used to keep no-iron linens, permanent-press clothing, and polyester/cotton fabrics wrinkle-free emits formaldehyde fumes for the life of the fabric—which could be years. *Symptoms of formaldehyde vapor inhalation:* Tiredness, headaches, coughing, watery eyes, respiratory problems. *Self-defense:* Buy only natural fibers, which are generally not treated with formaldehyde. *Also:* Avoid fabrics with labels reading "easy care 100% cotton" or "no-iron cotton," which could mean formaldehyde finishes.

Source: *The Nontoxic Home and Office: Protecting Yourself and Your Family from Everyday Toxics and Health Hazards* by consumer advocate Debra Lynn Dadd, Jeremy P. Tarcher, Inc., Los Angeles.

Beware of Telemarketers

Beware of telemarketers who ask for your checking account number rather than your credit card number. With a checking account number, they can print a "demand draft," which permits them to withdraw your money. Your bank probably won't notice that your signature is missing because drafts look like checks and are processed quickly.

Source: Gerri Detweiler, a consumer credit consultant in Arlington, Virginia. She is author of *The Ultimate Credit Handbook.* Good Advice Press.

How to Get Rid Of Nightmares

A nightmare, technically, is a frightening dream that wakes you up. If you don't wake up, it's a bad dream. Nightmares' contents are no different than the contents of normal dreams, according to my research. *What is different:* How you react to your dreams.

How we respond to our dreams is affected in great part by how we feel both physically and emotionally. You can get rid of your nightmares by getting rid of things that can cause you to react badly to your dreams. *These include:*

• *Medications.* Certain drugs can increase the incidence of nightmares. Beta blockers (for hypertension and irregular heartbeat), tricyclic antidepressants, sleeping pills, nasal sprays.

Solution: Ask your doctor about changing prescribed medications.

• *Stress.* Feeling on edge increases your susceptibility to nightmares.

Solution: Use stress-reduction and relaxation techniques...and exercise.

• *Illnesses.* Any illness can make you feel bad. And feeling bad can cause nightmares. Sometimes, a nightmare can warn you of a medical problem that hasn't even been diagnosed yet.

Solution: For minor illnesses, the nightmares will go away as you get better. If other nightmare-causing factors are ruled out, see your doctor for evaluation.

• *Miscellaneous problems.* For many, nightmares have no obvious cause.

Solution: Figure out what's causing the nightmares by making a connection between the nightmare and real life. *To make the connection:* Think metaphorically.

Example: A nightmare about being assaulted may be a metaphor for feeling threatened or intimidated by your boss, or a friend or relative.

Alternate solution: Confront a recurrent nightmare by imagining how you want it resolved before you go to sleep.

Examples: A person who dreams that he's being followed by a stranger can imagine that the person is simply a friend who wants to say hello...a child who dreams that a monster is chasing him can imagine turning to the monster and saying, "You can't scare me anymore. Go away."

Source: Milton Kramer, MD, director, Sleep Disorder Center, Bethesda Oak Hospital, Cincinnati.

Lead Poisoning From Pewter

Eating or drinking from pewter can cause lead poisoning. Even though pewter sold in the United States is supposed to be safe, don't bet your life on it. Although the US has regulated lead content in pewter manufacturing since 1867, it is difficult to establish an item's age or country of origin.

And pewter products that contain no lead may be soldered with it. *Bottom line:* Any pewter should remain suspect until it has been tested for lead leaching. *Home test:* The Frandon Red Alert Kit, 800-332-7723.

Source: Richard Wedeen, MD, nephrologist and author of *Poison in the Pot: The Legacy of Lead.*

Computer News That You Can Use

Protect computer systems by using modems that will connect with an outside call only if the call comes from an authorized phone number. A hacker trying to gain access to the system won't be at such a number, and so won't be able to succeed.

Source: Eric Paulak, editor, *411,* 11300 Rockville Pike, Rockville, MD 20852.

How to Prevent Cellular Phone Fraud

Even companies that make minimal use of cellular phones are vulnerable to being ripped off by the growing number of cellular hackers.

Achilles' heel: The phone's electronic serial number (ESN)—embedded on a computer chip inside the phone...and its mobile ID number (MIN)—the telephone number assigned by the cellular phone company.

These numbers can be detected and decoded by criminals equipped with special devices that pick up cellular phone signals and record the two key numbers. These can then be used for illegal cellular service, ending up on the company's bill. They can also be picked up from office files or computers. *Self-defense:*

- Instruct the cellular carrier to block all international calls—unless you absolutely must use your cellular phone for overseas calling.
- Keep all cellular phone records locked.
- Don't keep ESNs and associated MINs on a computer. If a hacker wants your numbers, chances are he'll know his way around computer files as well as he does around the cellular airwaves.
- Don't divulge ESNs and associated MINs to anyone except the person responsible for dealing with the cellular company. The numbers should be in as few hands as possible to maintain maximum security.
- Ask for the most detailed form of billing available from the carrier—so you can carefully scrutinize calling records.

Source: Dick Sharman, The Guidry Group, telecommunications consultants, 1400 Woodloch Forest Dr., Woodlands, Texas 77380, quoted in *411*, 11300 Rockville Pike, Rockville, MD 20852.

Diamond Savvy

Beware of a diamond that has been set so that the pavilion (bottom) of the stone is blocked from view or enclosed in metal. A closed back is often a sign that something is being hidden. *Examples:* The stone may be a rhinestone (glass with a foil back)...a lower quality diamond with a coating to improve its color...a single-cut diamond made to appear like an expensive brilliant-cut diamond.

Source: *The Diamond Ring Buying Guide* by Renée Newman, International Jewelry Publications, Box 13334, Los Angeles 90013.

New Gold Card Scam

A caller says you have been pre-approved for a gold card and he/she just needs a little information to send the card to you. He asks for Social Security, checking account and credit card numbers and your mother's birth name. You never get the card. The caller gets information to tap into your bank accounts and credit lines. *Self-defense:* By law, credit card issuers must have your written approval to send you a card. Tell any caller to send you an application by mail. Or just hang up.

Source: John Barker, National Consumers League, 815 15 St. NW, Washington, DC 20005. 202-639-8140.

The Angry Victim Syndrome

Some victims are strong-willed people who get angry when they can't control others.

These people, whom I call *angry victims,* want others to live up to their often unreasonable expectations...and then feel angry when people inevitably disappoint them.

In order to change, angry victims have to realize that the problem lies within themselves, and that controlling others is not the solution.

Who's an angry victim...

Angry victims, most of whom are women, swing between two poles—the desire to control...and the desire to please.

Example: When Laura disagreed with her husband, she would first suppress her anger in order to please him. Eventually, however, she would swing to the control pole and fly into a rage. But then, she would start to worry about losing him ...and backpedal, apologizing profusely for getting so angry. *Result:* He became confused and the relationship ultimately suffered.

Angry victims constantly flip back and forth in their emotions because they're not comfortable in either mode. They're afraid that if they exert too much control, people will become distant and angry with them.

At the same time, they're afraid that if they try too hard to please, people will take advantage of them.

Whichever pole they gravitate to, they're *afraid* of something...and sure to lose no matter what they do. *Result:* Angry victims live in a state of constant fear.

Since pain hurts more if you're already fearful and tense, angry victims are often stunned by the depth of the feelings generated by a minor disappointment. A normal domestic problem can seem like a tragedy.

Example: Len's wife, Nora, got tied up at the office one night. She came home late and forgot to call. Len felt rejected and flew into a rage.

Although angry victims expect a lot from their friends and loved ones, most have a limited tolerance for the expectations and desires of others. This allows them to blame others for their problems.

Example: Sue, who hadn't had a serious relationship in years, finally met a man who appeared to be perfect for her...but two months later, she was complaining about him. For one thing, he dropped in whenever he wanted to, which she thought was rude and demanding. After some counseling, Sue realized that she hadn't had a relationship for so long because she didn't want to put up with anyone else's schedules. The problem was hers, not his.

Are you an angry victim?

There are three aspects to the angry victim syndrome:

- Fear of abandonment.
- Fear of engulfment.
- Need to control.

If you suspect you're an angry victim, give yourself these tests:

- Abandonment test. Fantasize that everyone in your life calls you on the same day and says they never want to talk to you again. How much rejection would it take—one person, two people, 10 people—for you to feel devastated?

If even one rejection would be extremely hurtful, you're probably trying too hard to please people.

- Engulfment test. Fantasize that everyone in your life calls you on the same day and invites you out to dinner. How many offers would it take to make you uncomfortable?

Again, the fewer people it would take, the more likely it is that you're afraid of being overwhelmed with a lot of love and attention.

- Control test. Think back to minor disappointments, when people who you depended on did something that you thought was wrong. What was your reaction to those incidents? Did you laugh or cry or get angry?

If you got angry or frustrated, you probably have a control problem. And the sooner you felt that way, the bigger the problem.

How to stop being an angry victim...

If the above test shows that you could be an angry victim, follow these steps:

- Go easy on yourself. Most angry victims are extremely self-critical. Don't beat yourself up because you've discovered the problem—understanding that you have a problem should be the first step toward overcoming it.
- Realize that your expectations are not unnatural. They come from our bedrock fears about the world—that we're not going to be loved and cared for...that we can't control what happens to us.

Instead of rejecting these fears, be aware of them and be honest about them...with other people as well as with yourself.

- Let others know how you feel. Talking things over with people you're close to is the best way to work out your angry-victim problems.

Example: Jody was upset because her friend Tina never seemed to have enough time for her. She fought the desire to get angry and told Tina how she felt. Tina explained that her idea of friendship was having a lot of casual friends to see occasionally for lunch. Although the two couldn't be close friends, the conversation helped Jody break out of her angry-victim cycle.

- Recognize when you're out of balance. Work to stay in the *golden zone*—where you feel adequately loved yet adequately free to do what you want and reasonably in control of your life.

This is a very hard balance to maintain, and you won't get there by pushing yourself. *Better:* Respect and acknowledge your needs for love, freedom and control.

Source: Martin G. Groder, MD, a psychiatrist and business consultant in Chapel Hill, NC. His book, *Business Games: How to Recognize the Players and Deal With Them,* is available from Boardroom Classics, 55 Railroad Ave., Greenwich, CT 06830.

Better than an Unlisted Number

Have the phone company publish the number under your wife's maiden name...or your dog's name...or some other easily remembered "made-up" name. This will also keep strangers from getting your phone number, and it costs you nothing. Unlisting costs a few dollars a month. *Added benefit:* You'll be able to identify some sales calls immediately ("Hello, Mr. Fido...").

Source: Herbert J. Teison, publisher, *Travel Smart,* 40 Beechdale Rd., Dobbs Ferry, NY 10522.

High-Heel Danger

High-heeled shoes shift most of the wearer's weight to the front of the foot. *Result:* Calluses ...hammertoes...blisters...Achilles' tendinitis... Morton's neuroma (an inflammation of the nerve between the third and fourth toes). Shoes with narrow, pointed toes can cause ingrown toenails ...corns...bunions.

Help for feet: If you must wear high heels—elevate tired feet...soak them in a warm water bath...massage them gently.

Source: *University of Texas Lifetime Health Letter,* 7000 Fannin St., Houston 77030.

Instant Revenge Against Obscene Phone Caller

Electronic voice boxes are available with a preprogrammed joke script by comics such as Henny Youngman and Jackie Mason. Hold it up to the phone, press a button and have the last laugh.

Warning Signs Burglars Fear

If a burglar sees warning signs, no matter how outlandish, on your house, he will think twice before breaking in. These signs should be handwritten, in large, clear print, on six-inch by eight-inch cards posted above each doorknob. Don't put them on the street or in your yard where passersby can see them. You don't want to give a burglar a reason to case your place and find out they are not true. Make up your own wording. Just be sure the signs look fresh and new. *Some suggestions:*

- "Danger: Extremely vicious, barkless German Dobermans." In his nervous frame of mind, a burglar probably isn't going to wonder if there is such a thing. He won't want to take the chance.
- "Knock all you want. We don't answer the door." Most burglars check to see if anyone's home before breaking in. About 95% of those questioned said they'd pass up a house with that sign.
- "Carpenter: Please do not enter through this door. My son's three rattlesnakes have gotten out of the cage, and we've closed them off in this room until he returns. Sorry for this inconvenience."
- "Attack dogs trained and sold here." Again, 95% of those questioned said they'd pass up a house with that sign. Have one engraved, and post it on your front door (so it can't be seen from the street).
- Leave extremely large bones and two-foot wide dog dishes near all entrances. A person up to no good will think a very large dog lives there.

How Burglars Say They Break In

Some burglar-survey results:

- 75% were more likely to go through windows than doors. (Sliding glass doors are easier to open than wooden ones.) *Remedy:* Storm windows. No one surveyed would bother with them at all.

•85% cased out a house before hitting it. *Important:* If you see a stranger hanging around, call the police.

•Only 20% picked locks or tried to pick them. It takes too much skill. There are so many faster ways into a house.

•63% cut the phone lines before entering. *Remedy:* A sign saying that the police will be notified automatically if the phone lines are cut.

•65% said that a large, unfriendly dog would scare them away. *Most frightening:* Dobermans.

•80% looked in garage windows to see if a homeowner's car was there. *Remedy:* Cover your garage windows.

•50% said that neighborhood security guards didn't deter them.

•72% made their entrance from the back.

•56% continued to burglarize if they were already inside when they realized people were home sleeping.

Choosing the Right Lock

There are two major components to a truly thief-resistant lock system: Strong, tamper-proof basic hardware and a key that is impossible to duplicate without your knowledge and permission.

Assuming that the main access door to your house or apartment is structurally sound and hinged on the outside, the standard mechanism for keeping it securely closed is an interlocking deadbolt latch. What makes the latch burglar-proof is the outside lock that controls it and the plate that protects the lock.

• *Current best cylinder and plate:* The Abloy disklock. Instead of pins, which can be picked, it has rotating disks like the tumblers on a bank vault door.

• *Next best locks:* The Fichet, Medeco, Bodyguard and Miwa systems.

Add-on security devices:

Steel gates for windows near fire escapes or at ground level (gates must be approved by the fire department).

Source: Neal Geffner, vice president, Abbey Locksmiths, New York.

Choosing a Locksmith

•Go to the locksmiths' shops to size them up.

•Make sure the store is devoted exclusively to the locksmith business and isn't just doing locksmithing on the side.

•Ask to see the locksmith's license if it's not displayed. There are a lot of unlicensed people doing business illegally.

• *Best:* Locksmiths who belong to an association. They are keeping up with the latest developments. Look for a sticker in the window indicating membership in a local or national locksmiths' association.

A Secure Door

•If you're buying a door, buy a metal flush door without panels and get an equally strong frame to match it. *Cost:* About $500. *What makes a good frame:* A hollow metal construction, same as the door.

•On a metal door, use a Segal lock on the inside and a Medeco on the outside with a Medeco Bodyguard cylinder guard plate. If it's a tubular lock, get Medeco's D-11. It gives you the option of a key on the inside, and you don't need a guard plate.

•If your door has panels on it, put a piece of sheet steel on it. If the panels are glass, replace them with Lexon, an unbreakable plastic.

•If you have a wooden door, get what the industry calls a police lock. This is a brace lock with a bar that goes from the lock into the floor about 30 inches away from the base of the door. Also, get a police lock if your door frame is weak. It keeps the door from giving because of the brace in the floor. Even the best regular locks won't protect you if the whole frame gives.

•Jimmy bars: Don't bother with them. They're psychological protection only. If you have a metal door, a good lock is sufficient protection. Use a jimmy bar on a metal door only if the door has been damaged through a forcible break-in and is separated from the frame. The bar will straighten out the door and hide some of the light shining through. On a wooden door, a jimmy bar can actually help a burglar by giving him leverage. He can put a crowbar up against it, dig into the wood and break through the door.

•If your door opens out instead of in, get a double bar lock—one that extends horizontally on each side. With a door that opens out, the hinges are often exposed on the outside, allowing a burglar to remove the door from its hinges. With a double bar lock, he can't pull the door out.

Source: Sal Schillizzi of All-Over Locksmiths, Inc., New York, a national safecracking champion.

Buying a Burglar Alarm

Home alarm systems, once mainly for the rich, are coming into widespread use because locks aren't deterring burglars. Recent FBI figures show that 82% of the time, illegal entry is gained through home doors, most often the front door.

Burglars just break open the door with their shoulders. Faced with a deadbolt or double lock, the burglar will use a heavy tool to take out the frame.

•What to look for in an alarm: One that sounds off (not a silent alarm), so that the burglar is aware of it and alarm central (a security company office or the local police) is alerted.

•Select a system with sensors on vulnerable doors and windows. Good systems need a complex electrical tie-in in the basement, as well as a control panel installed away from prying eyes and little children. Good systems can also switch on lights and TV sets and alert alarm central by automatic telephone dialing or a radio signal.

•Have a secondary line of defense. This can be a few thin electronic pressure pads under rugs in high traffic areas or strategically placed photoelectric cells.

•Choose a reputable, well-tested system. The brand names are American District Telegraph (ADT), Honeywell, Silent Knight and ADEMCO.

•Be aware of the danger of continual false alarms. The police may ticket you if the family is to blame.

•Don't forget to test your alarm system regularly.

•Don't be lulled into a false sense of security.

•Continue to take all necessary precautions with locks and garage doors.

Best Places in Your House to Hide Valuables

Even if you have a safe, you still need a good hiding place for the safe key or combination. It should not be hidden anywhere near the safe. And, if you don't have a safe, you should hide your jewelry and other valuables where they won't be found.

•Don't hide things in any piece of furniture with drawers. Drawers are the first place burglars ransack.

•Don't hide anything in the bedroom. Thieves tend to be most thorough in checking out bedrooms. Find hiding places in the attic, basement or kitchen. In 90% of burglaries, the kitchen is untouched.

•Don't be paranoid. If you have thought up a good location, relax. A burglar can't read your mind.

Try hiding things in the following spots:

•Inside the phony wall switches and generic label cans sold by mail-order houses.

•In a book, if you have a large book collection. So you don't forget which book you chose, use the title to remind you (for example, *The Golden Treasury of Science Fiction*). Or, buy a hollowed-out book for this purpose.

• Inside zippered couch cushions.

• In the back of a console TV or stereo speakers (thieves usually steal only receivers, not speakers) or in the type of speakers that look like books.

• Under the dirt in a plant. Put non-paper valuables in a plastic bag and bury them.

• Under the carpet (for small, flat things).

• In between stacks of pots in the kitchen, or wrapped up and labeled as food in the refrigerator or freezer.

• Inside an old, out-of-order appliance in the basement.

• In a pile of scrap wood beneath the workbench.

• In the middle of a sack of grass seed.

Source: Linda Cain, author of *How to Hide Your Valuables,* Beehive Communications, Medfield, MA.

What to Do if You Come Home During a Burglary

• If you walk in on a burglar by accident, ask an innocent question.

Example: "Oh, you're the guy who's supposed to pick up the package, aren't you?" If, at this point, the burglar tries to run away, it's smart to step aside.

• Resist the temptation to yell or otherwise bring on a confrontation. Go as quickly and quietly as possible to a neighbor's and call the police from there.

• Avoid walking into your home while a thief is there by leaving a $20 bill conspicuously placed, near the door. If the bill is gone when you return home, someone else may be there. Leave at once and call the police.

Source: Margaret Kenda, *Crime Prevention For Business Owners,* AMACOM, NY and *How to Protect Yourself From Crime,* Avon Books, NY.

Safe Food Storage

• Yellow bananas can be held at the just-ripe stage in the refrigerator for up to six days. Although the peel might discolor slightly, the fruit retains both its flavor and nutrition. Ripen green bananas at room temperature first. Mashed banana pulp can be frozen.

• Nuts in the shell keep at room temperature for only a short time. Put them in a cool, dry place for prolonged storage. Shelled nuts remain fresh for several months when sealed in containers and refrigerated. For storage of up to a year, place either shelled or unshelled nuts in a tightly closed container in the freezer.

Storage times for frozen meats vary significantly. *Recommended holding time in months:*

• Beef roast or steak, 12.

• Ground beef, 6.

• Lamb, 12.

• Pork roasts and chops, 8-12.

• Bacon and ham, 1-2.

• Veal cutlets and chops, 6.

• Veal roasts, 8-10.

• Chicken and turkey, 12.

• Duck and goose, 6.

• Shellfish, not over 6.

• Cooked meat and poultry, 1.

Keep an accurate thermometer in your refrigerator or freezer. *Optimal refrigerator temperature:* 40°F for food to be kept more than three or four days. *For the freezer:* 0° is necessary for long-term storage. *Note:* Some parts of the freezer may be colder than other parts. Use the thermometer to determine which areas are safe for keeping foods long-term.

Freezing leftovers:

• Raw egg whites: Freeze them in ice cube trays.

• Hard cheeses: Grate them first.

• Soup stock: Divide it into portions.

• Stale bread: Turn it into crumbs in the blender.

• Pancakes, french toast and waffles: Freeze and reheat in the toaster oven at 375°.

• Whipped cream: Drop into small mounds on a cookie sheet to freeze and then store the mounds in a plastic bag.

• Citrus juices: Freeze in an ice cube tray.

•Freezing fish: Make a protective dip by stirring one tablespoonful of unflavored gelatin into ¼ cup lemon juice and 1¾ cups cold water. Heat over a low flame, stirring constantly, until gelatin dissolves and mixture is clear. Cool to room temperature. Dip the fish into this solution and drain. Wrap individual fish pieces in heavy-duty freezer wrap. Then place them in heavy-duty freezer bags. Use within two months.

•If you do your own food canning, preserve only enough food to eat within one year. After that time, quality deteriorates.

Sources: Tom Grady and Amy Rood, coauthors, *The Household Handbook,* Meadowbrook Press, Deephaven, MN, and Joan Cone, author of *Fish and Game Cooking,* EPM Publications, McLean, VA.

Keeping Food from Becoming Tainted

When in doubt, throw it out. This is the general rule concerning food you think may have become spoiled. This includes frozen food that has thawed too long or dishes that haven't been properly handled. *Example:* Cheesecake left on a counter to cool overnight can easily go bad.

Other tips for storing and handling food:

•Keep food at temperatures below 45°F or above 160°F.

•Always keep in mind that food left away from heat or cold for two to three hours is probably unsuitable for eating. This is particularly true of foods that are moist, high in protein and low in acid.

•Refrigerate leftovers as soon as possible. Don't let them sit at room temperature for more than two hours.

•Reheat food in wide, shallow pans rather than deep, narrow ones. Place foods in a preheated oven, not one that's warming up.

•When refrigerating large quantities of dishes such as stews, spaghetti sauce or chili, pour them into large, shallow containers. The point is to expose the greatest mass to the preserving effects of the cold refrigerator.

•If possible, thaw frozen foods by placing them in the refrigerator. If thawing must be done quickly, immerse the food in cold water or use a microwave oven.

To Avoid Food Poisoning

•Never let food cool to room temperature before putting it in the refrigerator. Slow cooling encourages the growth of bacteria.

•Do not thaw frozen foods for hours at room temperature. Allow them to thaw slowly in the refrigerator, or, wrap them in plastic and soak in cold water.

•Bacteria in raw poultry, fish or meat could contaminate your cutting board. Scrub the board after each use.

•Do not use cans that bulge or that contain off-color or unusual-smelling food. *Dangerous:* Tasting the contents to see whether they are bad.

•Lead poisoning can result from storing food in open cans. The solder that seals the tinned-steel can leaches into the contents. *Most hazardous:* Acidic foods, especially juices. They interact quickly with metal.

•Although cooking spoiled food destroys bacteria, it does not remove the poisons the bacteria produced.

Source: *Modern Maturity.*

What to Do If You're Mugged

Getting mugged these days is a real and personal threat, not something that happens just to other people. Fortunately, most muggings are simple robberies in which neither the criminal nor the victim is hurt. However, the possibility of violence is always there.

Suggestions:

•Cooperate. Assume the mugger is armed. No matter how strong or fit you are, you are no match for a gun or knife. Remember that your personal safety is far more important than your valuables or your pride.

•Follow the mugger's instructions to the letter. Try not to move too quickly or too slowly—either could upset him.

•Stay as calm as possible, and encourage companions to do the same.

•Give the mugger whatever he asks for. Don't argue. But if something is of great sentimental value to you, give it to him, and only then say, "This watch was given to me by my grandfather. It means a lot to me. I'd be very grateful if you'd let me keep it."

•When he has all he wants of your valuables, ask him what he wants you to do while he gets away—stay where you are, lie face down, whatever. If he dismisses you, leave the scene immediately, and don't look back. Don't call the police until you are in a safe place.

Some important don'ts:

•Don't reach for your wallet in a back pocket without explaining first what you plan to do. The mugger might think you are reaching for a gun.

•Don't give him dirty looks or make judgmental remarks.

•Don't threaten him with hostile comments.

•Don't be a wiseguy or a joker. Even smiling is a dangerous idea. He may think you are laughing at him.

•Don't try any tricks like carrying a second empty wallet to give to a mugger. This could make him angry. Some experts even recommend that you carry at least $50 with you at all times to keep from upsetting a mugger.

Source: Ken Glickman, third degree black belt and coordinator of Educational Services, Greenwich Institute for American Education, Greenwich, CT.

Toilet Seat Danger

You can catch diarrhea, intestinal bugs, and hepatitis from toilet seats. *Trap:* When toilets are flushed, a fine mist of water that could contain contagious fecal bacteria rises and lands on toilet seats and flush handles. *Best defense:* Clean your toilet three times a week with disinfectant...avoid using public rest rooms—especially the most popular middle stall... stand before flushing.

Source: Dr. Charles Gerba, University of Arizona.

Wash Away Poison Ivy

Poison ivy can be nipped in the bud if you wash the resin off your skin within 10 minutes of exposure.

Source: *The Pharmacist's Prescription: Your Complete Guide to the Over-the-Counter Remedies That Work Best* by F. James Grogan, Pharm. D., Rawson Associates, New York.

Tap Water Danger Signals

Check the color of your water to find clues to its quality.

Green stains in your sink or toilet are a sign of higher-than-normal levels of copper which may cause kidney problems. Brown stains may mean that there are high levels of iron in your water.

25

Breaking Bad Habits

Smoking: The Sobering Facts

By now, most Americans are well aware that smoking causes lung cancer.

But tobacco is a far bigger villain than most of us could ever imagine. Cigarettes, pipes, cigars, snuff, and chewing tobacco kill more than 434,000 Americans each year—accounting for almost one out of five premature deaths in this country.

Lung cancer is just the first in a long and harrowing litany of tobacco-related problems.

Other tobacco dangers...

• Addictiveness. While some people have likened the addictive potential of nicotine to that of heroin, the good news is that tens of millions of people have been *trying* to quit smoking.

• Back pain. Smoking is probably a major risk factor in recovery from back pain (the leading cause of worker disability in the US) because poor oxygen levels of those who smoke prevent lumbar disks from being adequately oxygenated.

• Bladder cancer. Smoking causes 40% of all cases of bladder cancer, accounting for more than 4,000 new cases annually.

• Breast cancer. Women who smoke are 75% more likely to develop breast cancer than are nonsmoking women.

• Cervical cancer. Up to one-third of all cases of cervical cancer—7,000 new cases a year—are directly attributable to smoking. Women who smoke are four times more likely to develop the disease than are nonsmoking women.

• Childhood respiratory ailments. Youngsters exposed to parents' tobacco smoke have six times as many respiratory infections as kids of nonsmoking parents. Smokers' children also face an increased risk of cough, chronic bronchitis, and pneumonia.

• Diabetes. Smoking decreases the body's absorption of insulin. *Also:* Smoking exacerbates the damage of small blood vessels in the eyes, ears, and feet of diabetics.

•Drug interactions. Smokers need higher than normal dosages of certain drugs, including theophylline (asthma medication), heparin (used to prevent blood clotting), propranolol (used for angina and high blood pressure), and medications for depression and anxiety.

•Ear infections. Children of smokers face an increased risk of otitis media (middle ear infection).

•Emphysema. Smoking accounts for up to 85% of all deaths attributable to emphysema (chronic obstructive pulmonary disease).

•Esophageal cancer. Smoking accounts for 80% of all cases of esophageal cancer, which each year kills 15,000 Americans.

•Fires. Smoking is the leading cause of fires in homes, hotels and hospitals. The toll is astronomical in terms of suffering and of economic loss.

•Gastrointestinal cancer. Preliminary research indicates that smoking at least doubles the risk of cancer of the stomach and duodenum—the portion of the small intestine just downstream from the stomach.

•Heart disease. Smokers are up to four times more likely to develop cardiovascular disease than nonsmokers. *Mechanism:* Carbon monoxide and other poison gases in tobacco smoke replace oxygen in the blood cells, promote coronary spasm and cause accumulation of clot-producing platelets.

•Infertility. Couples in which at least one member smokes are more than three times more likely to have trouble conceiving than nonsmoking couples.

Explanation: Tobacco smoke interferes with the implantation of a fertilized egg within the uterus. It reduces the number and quality of sperm cells in a man's ejaculate and raises the number of abnormal sperm cells...and increases a man's risk of penile cancer. Women who smoke are more likely to miscarry or deliver prematurely than nonsmoking women. Some scientists now theorize that toxins in the bloodstream of pregnant smokers pass through the placenta to the fetus, sowing the seeds for future cancers.

•Kidney cancer. Smoking causes 40% of all cases of kidney cancer.

•Laryngeal cancer. Smokers who smoke more than 25 cigarettes a day are 25 to 30 times more likely to develop cancer of the larynx than nonsmokers.

•Leukemia. In addition to tobacco smoke condensate, better known as tar, tobacco smoke contains several powerful carcinogens, including the organic chemical benzene and a radioactive form of the element polonium, both of which are known to cause leukemia.

•Low birth weight. Women who smoke as few as five cigarettes daily during pregnancy face a significantly greater risk of giving birth to an unnaturally small, lightweight infant.

•Mouth cancer. Tobacco causes the vast majority of all cancers of the mouth, lips, cheek, tongue, salivary glands and even tonsils. Men who smoke, dip snuff or chew tobacco face a 27-fold risk of these cancers. Women smokers —because they have tended to use less tobacco—face a six-fold risk.

•Nutrition. People who smoke tend to have poorer nutrition than do nonsmokers. People who smoke also have lower levels of HDL (good cholesterol).

•Occupational lung cancer. Although a nonsmoker's risk of lung cancer increases six times due to prolonged occupational exposure to asbestos, that risk jumps to 92 times in an asbestos worker who smokes.

•Osteoporosis. Women who smoke experience menopause on an average of five to 10 years earlier than nonsmokers, causing a decline in estrogen production—and thinning bones—at an earlier age.

•Pharyngeal (throat) cancer. Last year cancer of the pharynx killed 3,650 Americans—and the vast majority of these deaths resulted directly from smoking.

•Premature aging. Constant exposure to tobacco smoke prematurely wrinkles the facial skin and yellows the teeth and fingernails.

•Recovery from injury or surgery. Smokers have delayed wound and bone healing. They also have a greater risk of complications from surgery, including pneumonia (due to weaker lungs) as well as a longer hospital stay.

•Stroke. Smoking doubles the risk of stroke among men and women. *Special danger:* In women who smoke and use oral contraceptives, the risk of stroke is 10-fold.

•Tooth loss. Use of snuff or chewing tobacco causes gum recession and tooth abrasion, two frequent contributors to tooth loss.

Source: Alan Blum, MD, family physician, department of family medicine, Baylor College of Medicine, Houston. Dr. Blum is the founder and president of Doctors Ought to Care (DOC), c/o department of family medicine, Baylor College of Medicine, 5510 Greenbriar, Houston 77005, an anti-smoking group long-recognized for its service to public health.

Kicking the Cigarette Habit

Tactics for giving up cigarettes vary according to the underlying motivation for smoking. *Keys to the right strategy:*

•Habitual smokers reach for a cigarette in response to such cues as talking on the phone or drinking. *First step:* Make the cigarettes difficult to reach, or put them in a hard-to-open package.

•Positive-effect smokers actually enjoy smoking. *First step:* Find an equally enjoyable activity that can't be done while smoking.

•Negative-effect smokers smoke because of nervousness or depression. *First step:* Professional advice on the basic problem.

•Physically addicted smokers should quit cold turkey. The reactions to quitting are always unpleasant. But the worst of them will be over in a week.

Source: *Executive Fitness Newsletter,* Emmaus, PA.

Learning Not to Smoke

Will-power has less to do with kicking the cigarette habit than acquiring the skills to stop smoking. One widely successful treatment uses a gradual, self-directed learning program.

First, plan to stop smoking during a relatively stable period in your work and social life. Understand your smoking habits by keeping a simple diary that records how many cigarettes you smoke daily and how badly you want each one. Score the craving on a scale of one (automatic, boredom) to four (powerful desire). Firm up your commitment by enlisting a nonsmoking buddy to call up and encourage you several times a week.

Phase out the cigarettes in three stages...

1. *Taper.* Heavy smokers should reduce to 12 to 15 cigarettes daily. If that's your present level, then reduce to eight or nine a day. Use a smoke suppression drill, a mental learning process, each time you have an urge to smoke. Begin by focusing on the craving; then immediately associate it with a negative effect of smoking, such as filthy lung passages, clogged, fatty arteries, or skin wrinkled and aged by carbon monoxide and nicotine. *Next:* Relax and imagine a peaceful scene. Follow up with a pleasant image associated with nonsmoking (smooth skin or greater vitality).

2. *How to withdraw.* One week before your scheduled quitting date, smoke only four cigarettes a day. Smoke two cigarettes in a 15-minute period. Wait at least an hour, and then smoke the other two. While gulping down the cigarettes, concentrate on the negative sensations: Scratchy throat and lungs, foul breath. Keep up negative thoughts for at least five minutes after finishing the last cigarette.

3. *Quit.* When a smoking urge arises, conjure up the negative image, relax, and follow it with a pleasing fantasy. Also, call your non-smoking buddy for moral support.

Note: Never label yourself a failure. If you have a relapse, return to the tapering phase, and try the procedure again.

Source: *The American Way of Life Need Not Be Hazardous to Your Health* by John Farquhar, MD, W.W. Norton & Co., New York.

Prescription Drug Addiction

For every person addicted to heroin in the US, there are 10 hooked on prescription drugs. And withdrawal can be as painful as from any in the illicit-drug world.

Why addiction happens: The doctor prescribes a psychoactive drug (one that affects the mind or behavior) to relieve a physical ailment. By altering your moods, psychoactive drugs can affect your ability to make judgments and decisions. Some drugs mask the symptoms of serious ailments or can impair your physical activity. These drugs have their place among useful medications (generally for short-term relief), but they do not cure physical ailments.

Most commonly abused psychoactive drugs: Codeine, Valium, Librium, Demerol, Dalmane, and Nembutol. *Worse:* Mixing drugs or combining a drug with alcohol.

•If your physician is reluctant to make a specific diagnosis or refuses to explain the effects of drugs, find another doctor.

•Question every prescription you're given: Will it cure the ailment or will it just relieve the symptoms?

Source: *Executive Fitness Newsletter,* Emmaus, PA.

Ex-Smoker Alert

Former smokers should not fall prey to long-term use of nicotine gum, available over the counter. *Nicorette* is to help smokers quit...not provide a long-term smoke-free source of nicotine—one of the most addictive drugs around. And don't expect that chewing this gum is enough to quit. *Most important:* Making a commitment to quit...combined with as many other strategies as possible, including group therapy, visualization exercises and support of family, friends and doctors. *Note:* While there are some risks associated with nicotine gum, the risks from smoking are far greater.

Source: Harlan Krumholz, MD, is assistant professor of cardiology at Yale University School of Medicine, New Haven, CT, and author of *No If's, And's or Butts: The Smoker's Guide to Quitting.* Avery Publishing Group.

If You're Having a Hard Time Quitting...

Try smoking only at scheduled times—such as 9 a.m., noon and 3 p.m. Forty-four percent of smokers who adhered to this schedule during a nine-week smoking-cessation program were smoke-free a year later. That compares with 22% who quit "cold turkey," or 18% who quit by cutting back without following a schedule. *Theory:* By *forcing* you to smoke at specific times—whether or not you really want a cigarette—this regimen breaks the associations between smoking and stress, fatigue and other events that trigger the urge to light up.

Source: Paul M. Cinciripini, PhD, associate professor of behavioral science, University of Texas M.D. Anderson Cancer Center, Houston.

Allergy Attacks Are Often Food-Related

In a survey of 266 cases of the life-threatening allergic response *anaphylaxis,* 34% were caused by food, spices or food additives. *Usual culprits:* Shellfish and peanuts. Aspirin and non-steroidal anti-inflammatory drugs caused the most drug-related attacks. Anyone at risk for anaphylaxis should keep the drug *epinephrine* on hand.

Source: Stephen F. Kemp, MD, advanced subspecialty resident, clinical and laboratory immunology, University of South Florida College of Medicine, Tampa.

To Get Through to An Alcoholic

To get through to an alcoholic and help him/ her confront the addiction, educate yourself about the disease. Wait for a time when he is sober—and you are both calm. Then discuss the facts—focusing on his behavior, not on moralizing or possible motives. Keep a journal of incidents to back up what you say. Explain how his addiction hurts you, but do not ask him to end it for your sake—people end dependency only for themselves. Have a plan of action. Propose a written or verbal contract to make sure it is followed. Steer the alcoholic toward professional help.

Source: David Smith, president, American Society of Addiction Medicine, Chevy Chase, MD.

26

Psychology

The Power of Positive Relationships

People who build constructive relationships with their personal friends and family members gain important benefits...

- They are healthier.
- They live longer.
- They succeed in most of their activities.

A Duke University study of 1,300 patients who had suffered coronary attacks showed that those patients who were socially isolated ...unmarried, with no confidants...had a death rate three times as high as those with stronger social ties. *How positive relationships help...*

- Sociable people take better care of themselves. People who value their friendships with others are more likely to stop smoking...continue to take required medications...go to the doctor more often when they're ill. That's because even when they are tempted to let things slide, their friends get after them.

Example: In a support group for women with breast cancer observed by Dr. David Spiegel of Stanford University, when one woman mentioned new pains, the other women in the group convinced her to report it immediately to the doctor even though she was inclined to wait until her next appointment.

- Sociable people are physically healthier. Researchers have found that social ties have physiological effects that make people healthier. Sociable people feel less depressed...notice fewer aches and pains...have lower levels of stress-related hormones.

Psychologist James Pennebaker found that when people discussed stressful events with others, even with strangers, their blood pressure declined.

Building better relationships...

Obviously, it's in everyone's self-interest to build good relationships with others...and fortunately it's a skill that can be learned even if it doesn't come naturally.

If you want to form more positive relationships but have always found it difficult because of your personality, your best strategy is to begin by changing your behavior, not your attitudes. *Strategies that can help you improve your relationships...*

• Practice listening. At least once a day, when someone is talking to you, force yourself to let that person finish what he/she is saying. Even if you find it hard to pay attention, don't interrupt or disconnect...at least look attentive.

It may be difficult at first, but gradually you will learn that other people may have something worthwhile to say, you can learn something from them...and when you show them that you recognize that, you'll get through to them better, as well.

You will gradually come to appreciate where other people are coming from, become *more tolerant,* and find relationships with others easier to make and more enjoyable.

• Get involved with community affairs or volunteer work. If you don't already have satisfying personal relationships, one good way to make connections is to participate in community-service activities. Research studies have found that men who volunteered had greater longevity and reported better health than their non-volunteer counterparts.

Volunteering to help other individuals or groups is not only an excellent way to learn specific caring behaviors, it also enlarges your capacity for empathy with others and helps reduce your social isolation.

Helpful...

Seek out opportunities for about two hours a week of one-on-one helping...try to help strangers...look for problem areas where you can feel empathy with those you are helping...look for a supportive formal organization so you can feel part of a team...find a service that uses a skill you possess...and when you are volunteering, forget about the benefits you are giving or receiving—concentrate on enjoying the feeling of closeness with the person you're helping.

• Have a confidant. The best source of personal support is an intimate relationship with at least one person. A spouse or best friend with whom you share your inner life can help you carry out your duties...act as a sounding board to help you make important decisions...and comfort you when you are feeling down.

If you already have a confidant, cultivate the relationship to forge even closer ties. If you don't, try to find someone suitable.

• Get a pet. If you're initially uncomfortable with people...or live in socially isolated circumstances...positive relationships with animals can produce dramatic health benefits. A University of Maryland study of coronary patients showed that only 6% of the pet owners died within a year...compared with 28% of those without pets.

Source: Redford Williams, MD, director of behavioral research at Duke University. He is coauthor of *Anger Kills: Seventeen Strategies for Controlling the Hostility that Can Harm Your Health,* Times Books, 20 E. 50 St., New York 10022.

Secrets of Stress-Resistant People

Most people in America live incredibly hectic lives. We push ourselves to manage successful careers, families and relationships.

We're constantly pushing for more...and more...and more.

Result: Most of us are up to our necks in stress—and that stress is climbing.

Raymond B. Flannery, Jr., PhD, tells us more about stress and how to better cope with it...

What exactly is stress?

Stress is the physical and psychological distress that we experience when our day-to-day problems exceed our abilities to solve them.

While most of us think of stress in emotional terms, it also causes dramatic physiological changes. It floods the body with adrenaline, speeds up the heartbeat, deactivates the immune system and focuses our thinking.

When we are in genuine danger—facing an automobile accident or being attacked by a vicious dog, for instance—stress-induced physiological changes can be lifesavers.

But when stress becomes chronic, persisting even without the threat of physical danger, it serves only to damage our physical and emotional health.

Stress forces the body to go into overdrive, sapping our energies, making our lives joyless and sending us to early graves.

Is life more stressful today than in years past?

Probably so. Life was hard prior to 1900, but stress as we know it did not become a particular problem until the past few decades.

In fact, stress wasn't a problem for earlier generations precisely because life was so hard. Our ancestors worked long hours at hard physical labor just so that they could procure adequate food and shelter. They were physically exhausted at day's end.

Now, thanks to the ready availability of most consumer goods and the proliferation of telephones, TVs and countless other labor-saving devices, we can choose to work fewer hours and have more leisure time. Yet today's faster pace of life leaves us frantic.

Result: We've stopped focusing on the truly important things in life—good relationships with the people that we love, for example—and stress ourselves trying to acquire and make use of everything that's in sight.

It's ironic that although America has the greatest array of consumer goods in the history of the world, instead of making our lives easier, these goods have imprisoned us.

How do labor-saving devices cause stress?

These devices encourage us to think we can and should do more, to cram more living and greater productivity into each day.

The telephone affords us instant access to people all over the world. TV distributes vast amounts of information at the speed of light. Computers let one person do the work of many.

Although these breakthroughs can be helpful, they may actually increase our stress levels. *Reasons:*

- We have to work hard to earn the money to buy such devices, and more work means more stress.
- Once we own these devices, we feel we must put them to best use. As a result, we spend time using them even when we don't really need to.
- Such devices have to be maintained, and that takes even more time and money.

Lesson: Before you buy anything new, make sure it really will make your life better.

What are the signs of excessive stress?

The earliest signs include a loss of a sense of well-being—malaise, boredom, reluctance to get up each morning and face another day.

Next come emotional problems, including anxiety, depression, edginess and aggression. Some people experience a decline in the libido.

Eventually, physical symptoms emerge. These include headaches, ulcers and cardiovascular disease.

People under severe stress try to do several things at once. They go through life running when they should be walking. *Result:* Many of these people wind up in the hospital with injuries sustained in easily avoidable accidents.

What is the primary cause of stress?

The pervasive cultural misconception is that it is possible for a person to *have it all*—a happy family, a high-paying job, a nice home, good vacations, etc.—*all at the same time.*

In fact, there's no way for any of us to have everything, at least not all at once. Getting what you want in one aspect of life necessitates sacrifices in others.

Bottom line: Each of us must learn what is truly important to us, and devote less energy worrying about or striving for trivial things.

Are you talking about materialism?

I'm talking about *excessive* materialism. Although there's nothing wrong with hard work, we should also make it a point not to work or think about work when we're not on the job.

Just look at the way Americans relax. We listen to the radio, watch television, cook food in the microwave, ride the exercise bike and more—*all at the same time.*

We no longer know how to relax. As a result, we're sleeping less and exercising less than we should, eating the wrong foods and hurting ourselves in various other ways. Sometimes it's okay to do nothing.

But can people really be happy in our society now without having it all?

Yes. Most people think that they know what they need to be happy, and they spend their whole lives going after it. In fact, it's a rare person who really does know.

Many people who attain the material success that they've been striving for soon become disillusioned with its trappings. Often they go back to school or start a new career. That makes sense.

That's something that all of us should remember.

What should I focus on if having it all may be harmful?

Try to obey the central tenet of most religions —*concern for other people.* This not only helps them, it also gives you a better perspective on your problems.

Life is short. Day-to-day snafus that drive us crazy are meaningless if you consider the plight of others. One hundred years from now, who will care if you were stuck in traffic?

How can I become stress-resistant?

I advise several things. *Included:*

- Assume control of your life. Learn to distinguish avoidable sources of stress from unavoidable ones...and focus only on what you can avoid.

If something is a continual source of stress in your life, try to resolve it. If doing something is impossible, accept it.

- Make a long-term commitment to something or someone. Long-term goals make short-term problems and sacrifices easier to bear.

Bonus: People with something to live for are happier and healthier, whether the commitment is to raise good children, get a college degree or write a book.

- Take better care of yourself physically. Cut your intake of caffeine, nicotine and other stimulants, but do so gradually to avoid headaches and other withdrawal symptoms.

Devote time each day to meditation or some other form of genuine relaxation. Do aerobic exercise at least three times a week. *Caution:* If you're 35 or older, consult a doctor before beginning a rigorous exercise program.

- Develop an extended network of friends and family. The more people you know and care for, the greater your resources of emotional and financial support in times of trouble.

Just how effective are these steps?

Very effective.

The notion of becoming stress-resistant is not nonsense. The process takes several months, but it really does work.

I have successfully taught these skills to business and professional men and women, and their health and well-being have improved remarkably.

What mistakes do people make in trying to reduce stress?

The biggest problem is failing to identify the real source of the stress. There's no way to reduce your stress level if you're trying to solve the wrong problem.

Example: An administrative assistant in a law firm got into intense arguments almost every day with her boss. One night, she came home especially jittery, and burned dinner. When her husband asked if he could help, she lashed out at him and went to the bedroom to sulk. Although this vented her anger, it didn't address the real problem—her stressful work situation. Only after she recognized the true source of her stress was she able to learn how to control it.

Is it possible to have too little stress?

Yes. Each of us operates best with a specific level of visual and auditory stimulation. Too much stimulation, and we become cranky and hostile. Too little, and we get bored.

Important: Determine just how much stress you need to be happy and productive, then strive to attain that amount—no more and no less.

Source: Raymond B. Flannery, Jr., PhD, assistant professor of psychology, department of psychiatry, Harvard Medical School, Cambridge Hospital, 1493 Cambridge St., Cambridge, MA 02139. He is the author of *Becoming Stress-Resistant,* Continuum, 370 Lexington Ave., New York 10017.

How to Get Over Shyness

Most people think of shyness as a minor problem...but many people are so shy that they don't fully live their lives. By hiding from interactions that make them uncomfortable, they become increasingly lonely and unhappy.

People who are shy suffer from low self-esteem. Because they have no reserve of self-confidence, they see any rejection or social slip —no matter how small—as an indictment of their worth as a person. Over time, these rejections set the stage for a lifetime of shyness.

The truth about shyness...

•*Myth:* That far more women than men are shy. *Truth:* At least as many men—possibly more—say they are shy.

•*Myth:* That shy people are born shy. *Truth:* Many shy people report they weren't shy at all until adolescence. At that point, they became self-conscious—often about their looks—and had problems establishing their identity.

•*Myth:* That shy people are aloof and unfriendly. *Truth:* Most actually crave companionship.

•*Myth:* That loners are shy. *Truth:* People can be reclusive without being shy. They simply choose to be alone.

How to overcome shyness...

•Make a list of social interactions that are difficult for you. Start with the easiest.

Example: Asking a clerk at the store if there is a shirt in your size.

Continue working on your list until you come to the interaction that you find most difficult.

Example: Going to a business party where you don't know anyone.

•Take small steps to overcome the problems on your list. Start with the first—the easiest.

Example: If you're shy with store clerks, practice going into stores and asking simple questions—*What time do you close...does this come in red...is this item on sale?*

Concentrate on short interactions. That way, if you're overcome by shyness, you can back off quickly...and try again and again.

Goal: After repeated practice, you will be able to perform this interaction without feeling shy.

•Move on to the next challenge. Achieving each step will build self-confidence. Don't push yourself. If you try to take on too much too soon, you risk negative reinforcement.

Example: A person tries to overcome his/her shyness by forcing himself to go to a party...has a horrible time...and is very reluctant to try again.

Also helpful...

•Join a therapy group for shy people. This is one of the best treatments because you get the support of others and have a laboratory in which you can take risks in a supportive environment.

•Make a list of major accomplishments. Pull it out and review it just before you go into a social situation. This will defuse your shyness by reminding you of the things you are good at.

•Give yourself permission to be shy in some situations. By accepting your shyness under some circumstances, you decrease your anxiety and you're more likely to enjoy yourself.

Helpful self-statement: I'm going to be shy at dinner tonight...and it's okay.

•Don't assume that others are judging you. Tell yourself that you refuse to give them the power to do so.

Helpful self-statement: I'm going to be myself, no matter what.

•Focus on others. Listen carefully and intently to what they're saying. It's impossible to be self-conscious while you're concentrating on someone else.

Source: Psychologist Christopher J. McCullough, PhD, author of *Managing Your Anxiety,* Jeremy P. Tarcher, Inc., 5858 Wilshire Blvd., Los Angeles 90036.

How to Make It in the Needy...Numbing 1990s

Almost 20 years ago, I wrote that anyone who wanted to succeed could do so. That remains true today...but it is both more difficult and more important to succeed now than it was then.

Today, management at all levels is less tolerant of those who fail to produce...and less generous to those who are merely competent. Corporations are eager to trim workers who do not excel, and company loyalty is not enough to ensure survival.

Even if you do your job well, success is not an automatic consequence. It results from a systematic approach that makes sure you get things done and that others see you as successful. To achieve these two results, you must cultivate a number of specific qualities—energy, competitiveness, realism, memory and communication.

Energy...

Success requires a great deal of energy. This does not mean a capacity for long hours of hard work. It means enthusiasm to get things done—combined with the ability to do them right.

•Structuring your time. If you are not a hard worker by nature, structure your time to encourage achievement by following two rules:

•Break up your workload into small, manageable parts.

•Reward yourself as you complete each task.

As you reach each goal, you will develop a sense of accomplishment that will encourage you to continue.

Example: My energy level used to dissipate within two hours of my arrival at the office each morning. I found myself trying to deal with a deluge of phone calls, letters to answer and people waiting to see me.

Solution: I decided to spend my first hour each morning doing nothing but answering mail. By completing this limited but essential chore, I was able to start my day with an "achieving" frame of mind. Then, I rewarded myself with a short coffee break and was ready to go on to successfully tackle the more ambitious tasks of the day.

•Focus on the important tasks. You won't get very far if you stick to small tasks, but it is tempting to put off an important job that will take a few hours or days of hard work.

A simple trick to tackling large projects: Promise yourself a period of relaxation after you complete the necessary hard work. That will help you put in the extra effort to finish the job as quickly as possible and show how much you can accomplish when you work at a high level of efficiency.

•Eat and sleep well. You won't have much energy in the afternoon if you have a heavy midday meal, so stick to a light lunch. If you get drowsy in the middle of the afternoon, don't be embarrassed to take a short nap...as long as everyone is aware of how busy you were in the morning and how energetic you are after your nap.

•Look energetic. Promote an image of success, both to others and yourself, by always appearing energetic. Always move briskly... don't slouch—stand straight, with head up, stomach in, chest out...and never keep your hands in your pockets.

Competitiveness...

To get ahead, you must be willing to compete with others and eager to accept responsibility.

Sometimes, competition leads to direct confrontation. Make sure that it is no more brutal than it has to be and that you keep the advantage. *Rules of direct confrontation:*

•Don't sit opposite your opponent—it sharpens the conflict. Try to sit side-by-side. To keep your resolve, look at his/her mouth, not eyes.

•Strike the first blow...capture the advantage by stating your case rapidly and terminate the initial confrontation as soon as possible.

•Take responsibility for your position. Otherwise, you will get bogged down in a pointless discussion of your personal opinion. Successful people carry out decisions after they have been made...they don't agonize after the fact.

You also must accept responsibility without being asked. This means taking on vital tasks that others avoid because the tasks are perceived to be too trivial or tedious. Within a short time, you will acquire knowledge and skills that nobody else has, and more important responsibilities will begin flowing to you.

Hint: Pay careful attention to routine memos that everyone else ignores. You will find many problems as you search for solutions. If you suggest and volunteer to implement improvements, your reputation for success will grow.

Realism...

To succeed, you must see the world as it is ...not as you think it should be. *Some important examples:*

•Be realistic about other people. You can't trust everyone, and those whom you can trust may not always perform the way you want them to.

•Be realistic about yourself. Recognize your good points...but be aware of your faults.

•Study your past failures. You may find a way to transform them into successes.

Important: Realism must be balanced by an ability to fantasize. Dreams of success will motivate you to achieve them in reality.

Memory...

You are unlikely to succeed unless you can remember what you have to do and who you should know.

•Use the best memory aid. *Lists.* Don't try to memorize every fact you need to know—simply write them down.

•Remember people's names. Get them correct from the start. When you are introduced to someone, repeat his name several times during the first conversation and make sure of the spelling. At the earliest opportunity, write down the name together with other useful memory-jogging information, such as the person's occupation and where you met.

Hint: If you run into someone whose name escapes you, a graceful solution is to announce your own name. The other person will usually reciprocate.

Communication...

Successful people know how to let others know who they are and what they want. Good verbal communication requires you to speak and write clearly in positive terms.

Hint: Try to postpone areas of disagreement until you have demonstrated how much agreement you share.

Use body language to get attention.

Example: At meetings, don't sit forward with your elbows on the table. Sit back to listen. When ready to speak, straighten out, move forward and put your arms on the table. You will get everyone's attention.

•Speak in public successfully. Speak in short sentences...touch on a variety of points...be unambiguous...summarize at the end. And always finish sooner than the audience expects.

Source: Michael Korda, editor-in-chief of Simon & Schuster. He is author of four nonfiction best-sellers, including *Success! How Every Man and Woman Can Achieve It,* Ballantine, 201 E. 50 St., New York 10022, and five novels, including *The Immortals,* Simon & Schuster, 1230 Avenue of the Americas, New York 10020.

How to Handle The Bullies in Our Lives

Bullies are those who, by using threats of physical or emotional force, try to get others to follow their will. *There are two types...*

Malignant bullies are the worst. Fortunately, they are less-often encountered. These tyrants deliberately aim to cause harm and should be avoided if possible.

Nonmalignant bullies are much more frequently part of our lives. At one time, all of us have had to deal with a boss, a spouse, a parent, a child, a relative, a friend, etc., who acts in a bullying way.

It is unpleasant to deal with these bullies, but it is possible to defuse the encounters if you understand the psychology that motivates them and use your understanding to counter their tactics.

Bullies are anxious people...

Bullies act the way they do in order to relieve their own anxieties. When faced with problems that they perceive as urgent, bullies use threats and bluster to transfer their anxieties to someone whom they hope will handle the problem.

Nonmalignant bullies do not care if their tactics harm their chosen victims. Causing harm is incidental to their main objective—relieving their own anxieties. To make these bullies change their tactics, you must adopt a strategy that will...

•Convince them that their bullying will not succeed, and...

•Demonstrate a better way to deal with the underlying anxieties.

Two unsuccessful strategies...

Many fail to deal well with bullies because their self-defense strategies don't meet *both* objectives. Common approaches that fail are love and power. *Reasons...*

Love. The victim recognizes that the bully is motivated by anxiety and tries to relieve that anxiety by being kind, helpful and caring. *Result:* The bully's anxiety is relieved...but he/she has found a willing partner who can be victimized every time a new problem arises.

Example: When a wife caters to a domineering husband's unreasonable demands, she is responding with love to bullying. But the bully —her husband—is accepting her behavior as tribute, not love.

Power. The bully's chosen victim refuses to submit and replies in kind. *Result:* A continuing power struggle. The bully will change his tactics after a while. But with his anxiety unresolved or even increased, he will seek revenge in indirect ways.

How to handle bullies...

Achieving the two objectives of a successful anti-bullying strategy requires *detachment,* so you can analyze the source of the bully's anxiety, and *calm confrontation,* so that the bully realizes you will not submit to threats but are willing to negotiate.

Example: Clerks who work at department store complaint desks deal every day with irate customers who often threaten them. The clerks are trained not to take the situations personally. They understand that the customers are trying to bully them because of their own anxieties that the store will not exchange the unwanted items or give refunds. The complaint desk clerks explain the store policy and make it clear that threats will not help.

Result: The threatening customer may still be angry, but he calms down and discusses his claim rationally...or goes away.

The same combination of detachment and calm confrontation is the way to deal with the bullies you know personally.

Exception: Bullies who won't go away. If detachment, constraint and calm confrontation have no effect, confront the pattern when the bully is not anxious. Discuss and support new ways to plan, budget and anticipate in order to reduce anxiety.

If that is not enough, consider the ultimate confrontation: *I do not want to be bullied again. Please stop it. If you won't or can't, then I would like to realign our relationship.*

Bullying at work...

Example: Your boss repeatedly seeks to humiliate you publicly and threatens to fire you whenever he/she is anxious about a project on which you are working.

One day your boss starts screaming at you in the hall about the progress report you handed in last week. It set a revised project-completion date two weeks later than you had estimated earlier. He calls you an incompetent idiot who may not be with the company much longer if you can't meet the original deadline. *Wrong reactions:*

- Thinking of your financial position, you cringe and tell your boss that it might be possible to finish the project sooner than you thought.
- You decide this marks the day you have taken enough abuse and announce in colorful terms in front of the whole office that the delay is due to the blustering bully's typical failure to provide the additional worker he had promised.

Neither of these emotional reactions to your boss's unreasonable threats will serve you well. Whenever you are faced with a bully, you have to determine the framework.

Strategy: Tell your boss calmly, but firmly, that you are willing to discuss the project with him but in a more private setting.

When you meet for the discussion, apologize for any actual errors that you have made... but not for the failure to achieve an impossibly perfect level of performance. State realistically what you think can be done to meet his goals ...and if he continues to threaten you, call his bluff.

Firmly but politely, tell your boss, "If you really want to fire me, that's your choice. But if you want me to help on this project, we have to get down to business immediately."

Bullying in family situations...

- Within the family, bullying in place of negotiation or calm discussion often stems from a lack of understanding of normal development patterns. Parents and teenagers...adult children and older parents...husbands and wives...do not understand each others' needs, and they often resort to threats to try to get what they want.

Example: A teenager who is anxious because his/her parents won't give him something that he wants may try to bully them emotionally. He may threaten to drop out of school...to take drugs...even to run away.

Strategy: Be tough, but reasonable. Ask him, "Do you want to talk over what is bothering you, or are you just going to bluster? If you don't want to talk now, go away for a while and come back whenever you're ready to discuss your problem."

Example: An aged parent, unable to take adequate care of him/herself, may not consider entering a nursing home because of his anxiety about the physical, emotional or financial aspects of the new accommodations. He uses emotional bullying tactics against well-intentioned adult children who suggest the idea.

Strategy: The adult children should defer making any choices until they have discussed the situation with professionals and explored all possible living arrangements.

If it is clear that the parent's current living arrangement poses serious risks to his life or health, the children should state their case firmly but politely...and take the appropriate action, difficult as it may be.

• Husbands/wives in roughly equal power relationships often end up in situations in which they bully each other.

Example: George and Mary are a middle-aged couple with one late-born young child, George, Jr. Both have many independent interests that they want to pursue outside the house in their limited spare time. Each one feels the other should stay home to watch Junior. Their constant arguments on the subject often end when one says, "I'm leaving now," and goes out. That is bullying...because one party insists on an outcome to which the other has not agreed.

Strategy: Next time this situation occurs, the victim of the bullying should state calmly, "You are welcome to leave now...but when you come back we are going to discuss this problem and determine a mutually agreeable solution."

George and Mary have to budget their free time until they agree on how to divide responsibility for Junior. Neither will find the result to his/her complete liking, but it will have been achieved by mutual thinking—the opposite of bullying.

Source: Martin G. Groder, MD, a psychiatrist in private practice and a business consultant, 104 S. Estes Dr., Suite 304, Chapel Hill, NC 27514. His book, *Business Games*, is available from Boardroom Classics, 55 Railroad Ave., Greenwich, CT 06830.

Hints for a Happier Life

Give yourself permission to be happy...act on a spontaneous impulse now and then, and do something fun...pick one or two things you want to accomplish each day and then celebrate those accomplishments...learn to think like a child—inquisitive, curious, flexible... choose to forgive those who have hurt you in the past...each day, make a difference in one person's life by being encouraging, uplifting and inspiring.

Source: *Downscaling: Simplify and Enrich Your Lifestyle* by Dave and Kathy Babbit, publishers of *Downscaling 46510*, Moody Press, 150 W. Chicago Ave., Chicago 60610.

Stress Reducers

Put troubles into a broader perspective. Step outside yourself, and ask who will know or care about the problem in five years—or even 50 years. Use delays creatively—in a waiting room or on a delayed train or plane, read, write or reflect on your life. Practice gratitude—and spend a day being thankful for your life.

Source: *Kicking Your Stress Habits: A Do-it-Yourself Guide for Coping with Stress* by Donald Tubesing, PhD, psychologist, Duluth, MN. Whole Person Assoc. Inc., Box 3151, Duluth 55803.

Simple Secrets of Being Healthier and Happier

Did you know that loosening your necktie or collar will improve your vision?

Indeed, according to Cornell University researchers, tightly knotted ties interfere with blood flow to the brain and eyes. So, computer operators, pilots, surgeons and other professionals who must pay close attention to visual detail should avoid confining neckwear. If you must wear a tie, make sure your shirt has plenty of neck room and leave the top button on your collar unfastened. Make the knot loose enough that you can slip a finger between your collar and neck.

Other ways to feel healthier, smarter and safer...

• Exercise in the morning. A recent study showed that 75% of morning exercisers were likely to still be at it one year later, compared with 50% of those who worked out at midday and 25% of the evening exercisers.

Explanation: As the day progresses, people are more apt to think of excuses for avoiding exercise.

• Minimize your exposure to pesticides. They have been linked to birth defects, nerve damage and cancer...yet pesticide use has doubled over the last 20 years. *Self-defense:* Wash fruits and vegetables in hot, soapy water —and rinse thoroughly. Buy US-grown produce whenever possible—imported produce is more apt to contain pesticide residues. Be especially careful when cleaning strawberries, peaches, cherries and apples.

• If you eat bacon, cook it in a microwave. Bacon cooked in a microwave contains lower levels of cancer-causing compounds called nitrites than bacon that is pan-fried or baked. Drain away as much fat as possible—bacon drippings contain twice the level of nitrites as the meat itself.

Vitamin C helps counter the cancer-causing effect of nitrosamines (which are formed when nitrites combine with amino acids in the stomach). People who eat bacon, ham, pepperoni, bologna or other nitrite-preserved meats should be sure to include oranges, tomatoes and other vitamin C-rich foods in their diet.

• Cure hiccups with sugar. Swallowing a teaspoon of sugar almost always does the trick. In a recent study published in the *New England Journal of Medicine,* sugar worked in 19 out of 20 people—some of whom had been hiccuping for as long as six weeks!

Other effective remedies: Grasping your tongue with your thumb and index finger and gently pulling it forward...swallowing a small amount of cracked ice...massaging the back of the roof of the mouth with a cotton swab...and eating dry bread slowly.

Caution: Hiccups that recur frequently or persist for more than a few minutes may be a tip-off to other health problems, including heart disease. Consult a doctor for such hiccups.

• Don't suppress a cough. Coughing is the body's way of clearing mucus and other debris from the lungs.

• To avoid motion sickness, close your eyes. Motion sickness occurs when your eyes and the motion-sensing system of the inner ear receive conflicting signals—the inner ear says you're moving in one direction while your eyes say you're going in another. Keeping eyes closed helps reduce the conflict.

If you're prone to motion sickness in cars, offer to drive. Like closing your eyes, keeping your eyes focused straight ahead on the road helps reduce queasiness. *Also helpful:* Air from the air conditioner or an open window directed toward your face.

• Don't aggravate a strained back. Many people use heat immediately after a minor back injury. But heat increases circulation to the area, causing increased swelling and inflammation. *Better:* To reduce swelling and pain in the first few days following a back strain, use cold compresses made of crushed ice wrapped in a towel. Keep the pack on for 20 minutes, then leave it off for 20. Repeat this cycle for two to three hours a day for three to four days. Only after this interval should heat be applied.

Caution: For severe or persistent back pain, consult a doctor.

• Eat fresh fruit. Fruit juice doesn't give you as much fiber—or vitamins and minerals—as whole fruit. Dietary fiber promotes regularity and helps regulate digestion of carbohydrates. The sugar in fruit is absorbed more slowly than the same sugar in fruit juice. The longer absorption time makes fruit more filling, a boon if you're watching your weight. This keeps your blood sugar levels stable, leaving you feeling more energetic.

• Don't drink tea if your blood is iron-poor. Tea contains tannins, compounds that inhibit iron absorption. (Herbal tea is okay.) *To raise iron levels:* Eat more green, leafy vegetables, lean red meat, poultry, fish, wheat germ, oysters, fruit and iron-fortified cereal. Foods rich in vitamin C help your body absorb iron from other foods.

• Stop snoring—with a tennis ball. Sewn into the back of your (or your mate's) pajama top, it discourages sleeping on the back, a major trigger of snoring. *Also helpful:* Using blocks to raise the head of your bed...or using pillows to elevate the snorer's head.

• Use a cookie jar to lose weight. But—instead of cookies, fill the jar with slips of paper reminding you to do some calorie-burning activity, like going for a walk or gardening.

•Make exercise a game. If you're a swimmer, for example, see how long it takes you to "swim the English Channel." If you swim in a standard 75-foot pool, you'll have to do 1,478 laps to go the 21 miles from Dover to Calais. For stair-climbers, reaching the 29,028-foot summit of Mt. Everest takes 49,762 stairs. Be creative in whatever form of exercise you pursue, and you'll be more apt to stick with it.

•Be careful when shoveling snow. To avoid back injury or heart attack, keep knees bent and both feet firmly planted...push the snow aside instead of lifting it up...protect head and hands from the cold and avoid caffeine or alcohol before going outdoors.

•Develop a "cancer-resistant" personality. Although this finding remains controversial, cancer seems to be more prevalent among people who take a hopeless, helpless view of life, suppress their feelings, allow anger to build and have long-standing unresolved conflicts with loved ones.

A lifetime of built-up emotions may cause a release of hormones that interferes with the body's natural defenses against disease. To reduce the risk, actively try to solve problems within your control. Don't hold grudges.

Researchers have found that people who survive cancer or live longer with the disease tend to be feisty, demanding and emotionally expressive.

Source: Don R. Powell, PhD, president and founder of the American Institute for Preventive Medicine, Farmington Hills, Michigan. A licensed psychologist, he is the winner of numerous awards for his work in the health field and is the author of *365 Health Hints*, Simon & Schuster, 1230 Avenue of the Americas, New York 10020. The book was written in consultation with physicians, dietitians, exercise physiologists and other health-care professionals.

How to Fight the Blahs

•Count your blessings.

•See a funny movie or TV show.

•Read a joke book.

•Go for a long, brisk walk.

•Spend a weekend in a deluxe hotel with breakfast in bed.

•Listen to beautiful music.

•Read a very good and engrossing novel.

•Exercise a lot.

•Rent a convertible and ride with the wind around you.

•Go to the airport and watch the planes land and take off.

•Buy a new and exciting game for your video machine.

•Look at old family albums.

•Sing songs around the piano with friends.

•Get a haircut.

•Go for a swim.

•Buy a dog or cat to keep you company.

•Get some new tapes or records.

•Buy something you have always wanted.

•Fix up your house.

•Go to an art museum.

•Meditate.

•Clean out your closets or bureau drawers.

•List your assets and accomplishments.

•Call a special friend who always makes you feel happy.

•Take a deep, warm, bubbly bath.

•Eat a large piece of chocolate cake.

•Blast the stereo and sing along at the top of your lungs.

•Spend some time at a religious retreat.

Fighting Holiday Blues

Visits to psychiatrists and physicians jump 25% or more during the holiday season that lasts from Thanksgiving to New Year's. *The most common underlying causes of distress:* Holiday depression, boredom and burnout. *Specifically:*

•A longing for happier holidays (real or imagined) in days past.

•Loneliness. This is especially true for those in a new location or those who have recently lost a loved one or gone through a divorce.

•The feeling that holidays should be a happy time, that family life should be perfect, and that presents will bring your heart's desires.

•For those whose health is frail, a primitive fear of not getting through the cold, dark winter.

The best ways to combat the blues:

•Don't expect too much. Unrealistic anticipation only breeds disappointment. As expectations are reduced, every pleasant surprise becomes a bonus.

•Be selective about the festivities you attend. Enjoy the fellowship more than the alcohol.

•Try not to be alone. But spend your time with people who are comfortable and easy to be around.

•When the holidays seem too grim, take a trip or try some totally new experience. Perhaps volunteer work in a hospital, where the emphasis will be on bringing cheer to others.

•Skip those Christmas-shopping crowds by ordering your gifts by mail and visiting small, local shops or those in out-of-the-way places.

•Keep holiday entertaining simple. If traditions become too much of a burden, try something offbeat (for example, decorating with cut flowers instead of ornate evergreens). Or, go out. Above all, don't try to give huge, exhausting affairs.

•Unless you love to receive cards from others, save the bother and expense of sending them yourself.

The Simple Secret of Sabotaging Self-Sabotage

If we routinely fall short of our goals... and/or make decisions that interfere with our personal, professional or financial growth... and/or feel inadequate to meet the challenges in our daily lives—we may be victims of our own *self-defeating behaviors.*

Self-defeating behaviors are responses that originally protected us and helped us to cope with life...but which now work against us.

Example: A child who is subjected to excessive criticism learns to keep a low profile—to avoid notice or possible derision. Such a child is apt to mature into a painfully shy adult, incapable of making friends or achieving career goals.

By coming to understand these negative patterns and the purposes they once served, we can learn to replace our destructive behaviors with constructive ones.

Variety of self-defeating behaviors...

The average person in our culture regularly indulges in a dozen or so self-defeating behaviors.

These range from serious threats to health, such as smoking or drug abuse...to more subtle forms of self-sabotage like perfectionism, procrastination, hostility, compulsive worry or shyness.

Displaying a self-defeating behavior does not mean you're "sick." It simply means that you're still being controlled by negative external forces that have been *internalized*—family members, church, school, etc. These institutions are too often sources of criticism, prejudice, unrealistically high expectations and even abuse.

We may have been victims of these environmental influences earlier in our lives. But as adults, we victimize *ourselves*—by continuing to behave in ways that are no longer helpful.

Dangerous patterns...

Because these destructive patterns are learned and reinforced *unconsciously,* it's sometimes hard to spot the danger they pose. Two powerful forces keep these destructive patterns alive...

•A promise of protection. For example, you might think to yourself, *If I worry all the time, I'll be prepared when disaster strikes.*

•Fear. This is often expressed as an almost superstitious thought—*If I stop worrying, disaster will surely strike.*

Unfortunately, the behavior doesn't deliver on the promise...and people wind up being ruled by the fear.

Example: Chronic worry undermines both your health and your enjoyment of life. When bad things do happen, you're too tied up in knots to deal with them effectively.

Five steps for changing self-defeating behavior...

Step 1: Identify the behavior. We'll continue to use the example of compulsive worry.

Step 2: Identify the situations that trigger the behavior. You may feel as if you fret *constantly.* But give the matter some thought and you may notice that you worry only under certain circumstances—for example, when you're trying to fall asleep...when your child comes home late from school...when a major project is due at work.

Step 3: Observe how you build the behavior. Self-defeating behaviors aren't floating around in space waiting to attack us. We create them by following a specific pattern of thoughts and behaviors. Breaking down the parts of this sequence can help us to regain control.

There's always a split-second between the triggering situation and the moment we begin to construct the behavior.

In this instant we *choose* to think a self-defeating thought...focus on that thought...and begin behaving so as to reinforce the thought.

Example: You come home early from work and are enjoying the afternoon paper. *Trigger:* You glance up at the clock and notice that your 13-year-old daughter is 15 minutes late. A split second later you think that something terrible may have happened to her.

You may also hear an inner voice saying, *If I continue to enjoy myself, and something awful does happen to her, it will be my fault.*

Panic sets in, and you imagine all of the horrible possibilities—*What if she's been mugged ...kidnapped...hit by a car?*

Finally, you cement the behavior by *disowning* it—you find a way to shift the responsibility for your reaction to a source outside yourself. *If only she would call when she's going to be late, I wouldn't feel this way.*

It's nearly impossible to change this pattern once it's been set in motion—one step follows automatically on the heels of another. But—by repeatedly observing the sequence of mental events, you can learn to break this pattern of behavior in the future.

What once happened automatically will gradually become a conscious process—and will therefore lose much of its power.

Key: In the split second before you build the self-defeating behavior, you'll begin to ask yourself, *What can I do instead?*

Step 4: Find a healthy replacement behavior. Simply trying to stop the self-defeating behavior is a recipe for certain failure—you cannot replace something with nothing. Instead, you must *substitute* another, more constructive action. *Examples:*

- Engage in gardening, weight-lifting or another physical activity that leaves you no mental energy for worrying.
- Force yourself to repeat to yourself reassuring, rather than catastrophic, statements.
- Calm yourself with deep breathing exercises.
- Call an upbeat friend.
- Organize a messy drawer.
- Read.
- Take a nap.
- Plan your weekend.

Where to find replacement behaviors:

- Your past. What did you do before negative experiences led you to create the self-defeating behavior?
- Role models. What would one of your "heroes" do in a similar situation?
- Your body. What would feel good physically in this situation?
- Your wiser self. Often, we already have the answers we need—if we can only trust ourselves.
- Feedback from others. Ask friends and other people you trust for suggestions.

Step 5: Practice replacing the old behavior with the new, healthier one. At first you'll need to be vigilant. It will feel unnatural not to slip into the old pattern.

But if you persist, you'll reprogram your unconscious mind...and the new, self-enhancing behavior will become as automatic as the self-defeating behavior once was.

Source: Robert E. Hardy, EdD, a licensed psychologist affiliated with Personnel Decisions, Inc., a Minneapolis-based international consulting firm that applies the principles of behavioral science to building successful organizations. He is coauthor, with Milton R. Cudney, of *Self-Defeating Behaviors,* Harper/San Francisco, 10 E. 53 St., New York 10022.

Traumatic Events Don't Have to Be Traumatic

Sooner or later we all suffer a traumatic life event—the death of a loved one, a divorce, a job loss, a serious illness. When it happens, the rules for staying healthy and happy all change. People who suffer a trauma have to replace the resources—both internal and external—that they have lost. They must reinvent their lives.

What is traumatic...

Trauma is often caused by the loss of anyone who is very important to us—a spouse, a parent, a friend, etc.

Although the loss of a relationship is the most common cause of trauma, it can also result from a loss of *productivity*...whether it's a job or an endeavor—raising children, volunteering, following creative interests, etc.

The loss of a productive outlet causes a change in our identity or role. And this makes us question who we are.

Many people think trauma is something that strikes from the outside. But traumatic problems—midlife depression, for instance—can arise from within, as well.

How not to cope...

Most people who experience a trauma feel out of control. They think their whole world is falling apart and they don't know what to do about it. It's like having a nervous breakdown. *Common no-win reaction:*

• Feeling like a victim. Victims sit back and say, *Look at what life has done to me.* They blame their problems on other people or organizations, and then expect to be rescued. Victims don't want to take responsibility for recovering.

• Becoming aggressive. You can sue the company that fired you or the hospital where a relative died. But in the end you'll get little satisfaction, and you're doing nothing to rebuild your life. Aggressors think they're acting in their own best interest. But once again, they're focusing on external forces.

Better ways...

The best way to recover is to focus internally. You need to concentrate on yourself for a while. A major life crisis is a time to turn inward and challenge yourself to recover. Appraise your situation realistically. Face the fact that you are in trouble and look for ways to make even this experience useful.

Example: A man who is in the midst of a painful divorce should ask himself what he can do to develop new relationships and be a better partner.

Different kinds of trauma require different kinds of action...

• Death of a loved one. When someone close to us dies, we confront our own mortality. We wonder why we are alive.

Helpful: Use this as an opportunity to evaluate what you are contributing to society. Look for ways to make your life better and more productive.

• Major illness. Although cancer and other illnesses are terrible traumas, there is much we can learn from them.

Helpful: Realize that this illness may even help you in some ways.

Example: People who have had heart attacks often start eating right and exercising for the first time in their lives. *Result:* They wind up healthier than ever.

• Breakup of a relationship. Although it's difficult to do, we all have to admit that there is no one relationship that can take care of us forever ...we can't rely on any other person to do the things we need to do for ourselves.

Helpful: Ask yourself how you contributed to the problem—perhaps you were too needy. Look for ways you can act differently in the future. *Important:* Many people who make a healthy adjustment after a relationship fails start loving themselves for the first time.

• Job loss. People who lose a job immediately start redoing their résumés, reading the classified ads, networking, etc. But your first task should be to get over the trauma by taking care of yourself—eat well, exercise, get enough rest.

Helpful: Realize that it may take a year or more to find the right job and rebuild your life. Nothing good is going to happen in a hurry. See the job loss as an opportunity to get out of a rut and do something different—something you've always dreamed of doing.

Source: Kathryn D. Cramer, PhD, president of Heath Psychology Consultants, 206A N. Clay St., St. Louis 63122. She is the author of *Staying on Top When Your World Turns Upside Down,* Viking Press, 375 Hudson St., New York 10014.

How to Cope with This Age of Diminished Expectations

With all the talk about excessive taxes and budget deficits, people in the US have come to accept a faltering economy as almost inevitable.

Result: We have greatly diminished expectations for the future of our economy...and our own standard of living.

Where people used to expect a robust economy with steady economic growth, nowadays we're satisfied just to keep our heads above water.

If this current economic drift continues, the US is destined to become a second-rate economic power by 2000. *Precedent:* Great Britain, once the world's mightiest empire, has seen its power, its wealth and its citizens' relative standard of living suffer steep and apparently permanent declines.

Meet the enemy...

Many people think there is something fundamentally wrong with our government—with politicians, in particular. I disagree. Politicians are not a special breed of people, greedy and dishonest. They're just caught between what they think is right and what will play well in the hometown newspaper.

The real problem is not with the politicians, but with the voters. Most people in the US are unwilling to suffer the kinds of changes that need to be made to save our economy.

Example: Some of our cities and even some states are facing bankruptcy because the voters refuse to accept new taxes. Yet they expect government services to continue at the same level.

Imaginary problems...

Many people spend much too much time worrying about things that do not matter. *Examples:*

- Inflation. Although rising prices cannot be ignored, at its current level, inflation has no impact on the growth of the economy. Pushing for zero inflation is dangerous. It's an impossible, inappropriate goal.
- The trade deficit. Our foreign debt is increasing at a rate so slow that it will not cause any significant problem for our economy in the foreseeable future.
- The budget deficit. Although the deficit was a problem a couple of years ago, recent legislation has dramatically cut government spending. In fact, the automatic spending limitations imposed by the Gramm-Rudman Act are so severe that they are now wreaking havoc on public services.
- Excessive taxes. Many people blame our declining standard of living on a too-high tax burden. Not so.
- Tax rates in the US are lower than those in other developed countries. The real problem is unfair distribution of the tax burden.

Incomes exploded during the 1980s, but only for people at the top of the economic ladder. Those lower rungs saw a decline in their standard of living because the income tax burden is unfairly shouldered by those in the lower brackets. I don't advocate soaking the rich, but the well-to-do could easily survive higher tax rates.

- Bloated bureaucracy? Many people think their tax dollars are wasted on an army of unproductive bureaucrats who do little but shuffle paper. This is a misconception. *Reality:* The federal bureaucracy is not bloated. In fact, the combined salaries of all non-military federal employees amount to no more than 5% of the US budget.

What's really wrong...

While most people are worrying about the imaginary problems, the real problems are being ignored. *Included:*

- Our crumbling educational system. At one time our kids were the best educated. Now they're among the worst. We've obviously fallen behind Germany and Japan, and also behind Spain and other nations of comparatively modest means.

Poor education produces poor workers... which means reduced productivity, which translates into less money to spend on education—a vicious cycle.

Self-defense: Agitating for better education is the single most powerful weapon against a faltering economy.

•Our crumbling infrastructure. Visitors from abroad have asked me, *If the US is such a great country, why are the roads and cities in such terrible shape?* And they're right to question.

Roads, bridges, communications networks, railroads and other systems essential to fast, efficient movement of goods and information—the national infrastructure—are in a sorry state. And they're getting worse. The decline of our nation's infrastructure is the most obvious damage done to our economy by the tax cuts of the 1980s.

Self-defense: Support higher taxes. A nation that's unwilling to pay for the maintenance of its infrastructure cannot grow and prosper.

Source: Paul Krugman, PhD, professor of economics, Massachusetts Institute of Technology. A former consultant for the International Monetary Fund, the World Bank, the United Nations and the State Department, Dr. Krugman is the author of several books, including *The Age of Diminished Expectations: US Economic Policy in the 1990s,* MIT Press, 55 S. Hayward St., Cambridge, MA 02142.

How to Survive Turmoil

Our response to a disaster is highly correlated to the way we handle life issues in general. Some of us deal with them well, while others get depressed and self-blaming.

The best response is what I call *reasonable vigilance,* a recognition and acceptance of the randomness of events. This attitude is one we should all try to adopt, since disasters of all sizes are an inevitable part of life.

Typical responses...

Self-blame is probably the single most virulent and negative psychological response to disasters. Some people blame themselves even when their home is destroyed by a runaway truck. *Trap:* A refusal to accept the senselessness of events. We personalize disaster—so no matter how unpredictable the occurrence, we think it's somehow connected to us.

Example: The Wall Street executives, traders and brokers that I work with responded to the 1987 stock market crash with crushing guilt. They felt terrible that they hadn't sold before the crash. They thought they had let their clients down. Many had information that they should have told, information that they didn't act on. This intensified their guilt.

A loss of trust in the system can also result. Some traders and investors who lost a lot of money began to think that the system was unreliable, and they were terrified to trade. This can generalize to other people or systems until the person develops a pervasive lack of trust. Relationships with others can be seriously affected.

Example: A trader who lost several hundred thousand dollars became highly irritable, fearful, depressed and mistrustful—and his sex life died.

The adaptive response...

An adaptive response means understanding that the world is basically unfair and metes out bad and good luck independently of what you hope and pray for, dream of or desire. It means living your life with reasonable vigilance—*not* with constant caution. Reasonable vigilance includes accepting a certain amount of risk as part of being human.

People need to review the demands, shoulds and ought-tos by which they live. These always surface when disaster strikes and make recovery more lengthy and painful.

Typical: I should have made better financial decisions. I shouldn't have built my house on a hill that might have a mud slide. *What people forget:* When they made the original decision, they probably had all the data available at the time. It's not that the decision was foolhardy or reached prematurely.

Helpful: When disaster strikes, take an inventory of how you made the decision that got you into trouble—buying an unstable stock or building a house in a dangerous location. It will lower your anxiety to realize you couldn't have anticipated the disaster.

Key: Reasonable judgment. If you built a house along a shore that is flooded every year, or refused to set a bail-out figure on an investment, you may be riding more on ego than on good sense. You may not be able to acknowledge that you're human—fallible—and that there's a time to admit your mistakes and get out.

To bounce back...

Draw a time line from the time you were one-year-old until the present, dividing it into years and months. Then plot disasters you've experienced and the residue from them. *What you'll see:* Each disaster is an infinitesimal pimple on your lifeline. Even a real tragedy, such as a premature death in the family, still dominates only a certain part of your life, not all of it.

Try projection imagery. Imagine yourself a year down the road being free of guilt, shame or depression. See yourself being able to talk and even joke about the disaster. Projection imagery will give you a sense of hope.

Remind yourself that time *does* heal all wounds. Don't expect things to right themselves immediately. Depression, fear and guilt are all appropriate and typical responses to disaster. You have to work through these feelings before you can accept and reconstruct your life.

Don't get down on yourself for feeling bad. It's natural to be upset when something terrible happens. And don't let others try to talk you out of it.

Example: A woman bought a car that turned out to be a lemon. Although others tried to minimize her loss because she had not lost a fortune, she had only a small income and had used *all* her savings for the car.

If your disaster is economic, recognize that there are Indians living along the Amazon who are probably happier than the richest man in the world. Some people are so ego-driven that they'll run back into a fire to snatch their favorite antique, or commit suicide over a lost fortune.

Most important element: Perspective. As long as no one close to you has been seriously hurt or died, you really haven't lost much at all.

Source: Psychologist Barry Lubetkin, PhD, director of the Institute for Behavior Therapy, 137 E. 36 St., New York 10016.

How to Forgive And Forget

To forgive another is the greatest favor you can do—for yourself. It's the only way to release yourself from the clutches of an unfair past. Beyond that, it opens the possibility of reconciliation, often a gift in itself.

What to do:

• Take the initiative. Don't wait for the other person to apologize. (That cedes control to the one who hurt you in the first place.)

• If the forgiven person wants to re-enter your life, it is fair to demand truthfulness. He or she should be made to understand, to feel the hurt you've felt. Then you should expect a sincere promise that you won't be hurt that way again.

• Be patient. If the hurt is deep, you can't forgive in a single instant.

• Forgive "retail," not "wholesale." It is almost impossible to forgive someone for being a bad person. Instead, focus on the particular act that hurt you. (It might help to write it down.)

• Don't expect too much. To forgive doesn't mean you must renew a once close relationship.

• Discard your self-righteousness. A victim is not a saint. You, too, will need forgiveness some day.

• Separate anger from hate. *To dissolve your hate:* Face your emotion and accept it as natural. Then discuss it, either with the object of your hatred (if you can do so without escalating the hatred) or with a trusted third party.

• Forgive yourself. This may be the hardest act of all. Candor is critical. Admit your fault. Relax your struggle to be perfect. Then be concrete and specific about what is bothering you. Your deed was evil. You are not.

• *To make self-forgiveness easier:* Prime the pump of self-love. Do something unexpected (possibly unappreciated) for a person you care about. By acting freely, you'll find it easier to think freely.

Source: Lewis B. Smedes, author of *Forgive & Forget,* HarperCollins, New York.

Disarming Difficult People

To deal with infuriating people, what counts is your response, not what they do. If you don't confront them, you end up making a negative judgment on yourself. *Familiar types:*

- The person who keeps repeating negative remarks about you made by others.
- The person who keeps referring to everything he has done for you.
- Those who insist you act in a certain way: "Isn't my daughter Frannie wonderful?" (demanding applause). Or, those who tell a joke or story and wait for you to laugh on cue.

How to handle such people:

- Avoid recriminations.
- Don't attribute bad motives or bad character.
- But make the point that you have as much right to your response—or lack of response—as the speaker does to his. You'll put a stop to the annoyance, and in most cases you'll also improve the friendship.
- Understand that if this doesn't work and you lose a friend, that's better than to be in a state of constant, impotent fury.

Source: Dr. George Weinberg, author of *Self Creation,* Avon Books, New York.

Stop Driving Yourself Crazy

Driving can make your pulse race and your blood pressure soar. About 40% of Connecticut's one million commuters, for instance, are troubled by stress while on the road, according to a recent survey by that state's Department of Transportation. Although you can't do anything about the traffic, you can keep it from getting to you.

Self-defense...

- Join a car pool or take public transportation to work. The conversation and companionship will take your mind off the commute, even when it's your turn to drive. When you're a passenger, you have the freedom to work, read —or sleep.
- When you drive alone, visualize your car as a refuge, not a battleground. Use this as getaway time to recharge your batteries and relieve the pressures of the day.
- Listen to soothing music. Play your favorite tapes. If you listen to the radio, do so without constantly switching stations. If you don't want to hear a particular song or commercial, just lower the volume.
- Buckle up. Somewhere in your subconscious you know it's safer—and therefore less stressful—when you drive with a seat belt. *Also:* Be a safe driver. Don't tailgate, make quick lane changes, run yellow and red lights, etc. You'll not only feel safer, you'll *be* safer.
- Give yourself extra time to reach your destination. Eliminate the need to rush. And remember, everyone is sometimes late...people will understand.
- Don't be a traffic judge and jury. If another driver does something stupid, stay calm. *Don't let it bother you.*
- Don't fight the traffic. Give in. Go with the flow. You can't prevent the flooding or the jackknifed tractor-trailer and anxiety about it isn't worth it.
- Believe that you are the master of your own behavior. *Exercises:* Drive using your brakes as infrequently as possible. Keep several car lengths between you and the car in front of you.
- Know when *not* to drive. Never, ever drive after drinking alcohol or taking antihistamines or other drugs that can impair your performance.

Source: Psychiatrist Martin Brenner, MD, an authority on driver stress and freeway violence and a recovering Road Warrior. His *Stress Care Driving Program* was developed for the Connecticut Department of Transportation.

How Not to Be a Victim of Negativity

We've all had the experience of feeling uneasy or uncomfortable in certain places or with certain people, often without knowing why.

Although we usually blame these feelings on ourselves, much of the time they are being transmitted to us by others.

What this means: Knowing how to defend yourself against invisible emotional assaults is even more important than knowing how to defend yourself physically.

Negative emotions...

It's a difficult concept for many westerners to grasp...but everything in the world is made up of energy, even our emotions. And because most of us aren't aware of this, many people become psychic sponges for the negative emotional energy of others.

Example: You have lunch with a friend who's getting divorced and is very depressed. Although you feel great when you sit down, by the time the check arrives you're in a funk that lasts the rest of the afternoon. *What happened:* You absorbed some of your friend's negative energy.

Some people find it impossible to defend themselves against emotional energy. These very sensitive people never develop strong egos or boundaries. Not knowing where they end and others begin, they indiscriminately absorb whatever's around them.

Babies aren't born with any defenses, physical or emotional. They must develop over time. *Result:* We all take on the family neurosis—self-denial, not expressing your feelings, internalizing your anger, etc.—at a very early age.

Enlist your psychic defenses...*

• Identify your area of vulnerability. Most people are especially susceptible to at least one kind of negative emotional energy—anger, sadness, fear or physical illness. *Ask yourself:* Which of those emotions brings back a strong reaction that I remember from childhood?

Example: I grew up in a family where every single person was physically ill in one way or another. That's probably why I became a healer. *Trap:* If I'm not careful, I pick up the pains of my clients.

• Set up your defenses. This involves developing your psychic sight, learning to see clearly everything that is around you.

Example: Keep your psychic antennae up at work instead of shutting them down. Try to figure out who's feeling good and who isn't. See what kind of energy—good or bad—is coming from your boss.

*Psychic self-defense does *not* mean shutting off your emotions and becoming invulnerable. *Goal:* To keep your heart open from a position of strength. People who try to close themselves off emotionally draw negativity to them like a magnet.

• Protect yourself from encountering negative energy. Before you go to work, for instance, visualize your office filled with blue light. Blue is the color of peace and is a potent pain reliever.

Example: I know a nurse who performs this exercise every morning before going to work in a ward for premature infants. *Result:* When she gets to work, all the babies are calm. On mornings when she forgets to do this exercise, she finds chaos. She says it never fails.

You can use this technique for any event that's making you anxious.

• Release negative energy that you've picked up from others. Close your eyes and take a couple of deep breaths. Clear your mind and relax each part of your body as much as you can. Look inside yourself to see if you can find where that person's negativity has affected you. Then eliminate that negativity.

Example: If you had a fight with your boss, visualize him yelling at you. Notice what happens in your body—see where you feel tense, angry or frightened—and relax each part of your body where you feel that negativity. Then imagine a circle of light around you that acts as a shield. See your boss's anger bouncing off of it. *Say to yourself:* "This anger isn't mine. I let it go. I can protect myself and take a stand in the face of anyone's anger."

• Repair the energy of the environment. If, for instance, you want to repair the energy in your office after a scene with the boss, open a window and literally air the place out. Visualize the fresh air and sunlight coming in and cleaning the environment of angry feelings.

• Forgive. Forgiving people who have hurt or frightened you releases their power over you. *Reason:* When you feel anger and hatred towards someone, you—not they—get stuck with all the negativity.

This doesn't mean condoning something terrible that someone has done. It means saying, *I can let this go...I'm not going to let you harm me further.*

More psychic self-defense...

• Pay attention to your intuition. Ignoring it is an easy way to get into trouble.

Example: One afternoon, I had a strong feeling that I should move my car to a different parking area. I was in a rush and ignored my feelings—and when I got back to the car, I found it had been broken into.

•Take a healing break. After an upsetting emotional encounter where you've absorbed a lot of negativity, spend a few minutes in the sun. The sun is a great healer. At the end of the day, take a shower. Water is a cleanser and gives off healthy negative ions.

Exercising is another wonderful way to help heal yourself. Going to the gym, taking a shower and then putting on clean clothes makes you feel refreshed because you've counteracted all the day's negative energy.

•Be aware of what you eat. Food is a balancer of energy.

People who overeat are often tremendous psychic sponges who are trying to protect themselves by making themselves numb. Because food closes down the psychic channels, eating builds a boundary between them and the world.

Source: Elizabeth K. Stratton, MS, who has a private practice as a counselor and healer in New York and teaches workshops in psychic self-defense and holistic healing techniques around the country. She's on the faculty of the Esalen Institute, the New York Open Center and Omega Institute.

The Mind-Body Relationship

•Mental abilities don't deteriorate with age, contrary to popular belief. Wisdom—the ability to use past experience to judge a problem for which there is no correct answer—grows at least through a person's sixties. And the ability to grasp new relationships slows down, but can remain strong. *Helpful mental exercise:* Challenging reading, adult education courses, games.

Source: *University of California Wellness Letter.*

An understimulated brain will often attempt to counter boredom by causing back pain, obesity, hypertension and even cancer. *Most susceptible:* Once-active people who feel they've seen it all. *Helpful:* Seek out the new and fresh in the ordinary—even a new way to brush your teeth.

Source: Dr. Augustin de la Pena, University of Texas Medical School, in *New Age Journal.*

•An energy slump (postprandial dip) affects many people between 2 p.m. and 4 p.m. Although it often follows lunch, it doesn't seem to be caused by eating or digesting. *To combat the dip:* Run a physical errand, rather than doing purely mental work.

Convert Worry Into Productivity

Reduce worrying by disassociating it from common worry-inducing situations. Techniques from Penn State psychology researcher Thomas Borkovec:

•Set aside a half-hour worry period each day.

•When you start to worry, put it off until the worry period.

•Replace worrisome thoughts with task-oriented thoughts.

•Use the worry period to think intensively about current concerns.

All About Happiness

Sometimes happiness seems like a terribly elusive goal. We tend to forget that it doesn't come as a result of getting something we don't have, but rather of recognizing and appreciating what we do have. *Some steps on the pathway to happiness:*

•When you think about time, keep to the present. Those who are excessively future-oriented often score very high in despair, anxiety, helplessness and unhappiness. As much as practical, focus on the here and now.

•Don't dwell on past injustices. You'll be unpopular company. No one wants to hear about how you got a raw deal in your divorce or how your boss doesn't appreciate you.

• Develop the habit of noticing things. An active mind is never bored. Make a resolution to notice new things each day—about nature, people, or anything else that interests you. Ask questions. Don't assume you know all the answers or that showing curiosity will be considered prying. Most people love to talk about themselves or their interests.

• Don't wear too many hats. Focus on one thing at a time. Set time aside for your family, yourself, your golf game, etc.—for having fun.

• Drop your bucket where you are. Take advantage of what you already have. There are already interesting, stimulating adventures waiting in your own backyard. Get to know your own children, for example.

Source: Dr. Frederick Koenig, professor of social psychology, Tulane University, New Orleans.

Benefits of a Personal Philosophy

Developing a personal philosophy of life is crucial for meeting crises to be faced day by day. (And those crises can get more complicated as one grows older.) *The virtues are:*

• It provides a guideline for living.

• It sounds an alarm when one's behavior is inconsistent with one's beliefs.

• It supports the ability to make a rational explanation of life's events, including the most disruptive or seemingly senseless ones.

What's required in a personal philosophy:

• It must be comprehensive. Ideally, it will provide an ability to meet all life's normal crises in a balanced way.

• It requires one's full commitment. Personal philosophy can't be taken on and off like a coat. It has to provide a sense of worth.

Meeting the Challenge Of Personal Growth

• Personal growth is a positive commitment that is aided by in-depth reading and conversations with those who have done it. Search out people who are skilled in a field in which you wish to advance. Learn about the dedication required and the attitudes that will help to make your effort fruitful.

• Never forget the level of application demanded. *Depressing cycle:* Beginners start out wildly enthusiastic, eager to master a chosen endeavor, such as playing the violin or unraveling the secrets of Zen. But they have been oversold on self-development without effort, and they quickly become discouraged at the first patch of difficulty. Do experimental trials before making the total commitment. Try a class, session, interview, or book. Be certain you are ready to give yourself to the project.

• Persevere when the spirit is weak. Many creative people develop mental blocks from the fear of defeat or failure. The term "writer's block," for example, describes a creative person who has temporarily lost the courage to take the risks that writing entails. A negative attitude is a defense employed by people hoping to avoid the pain of failure by rejecting their chances of success.

• You are more likely to be courageous when you have a positive mind-set. And, it will be easier to find purpose and the strength to accomplish the objective.

• Knowing your limits and accepting yourself. That is also part of realizing your potential.

Source: Martin G. Groder, MD, a practicing psychiatrist, business consultant and author of *Business Games: How to Recognize the Players and Deal with Them,* Boardroom Books, 55 Railroad Ave., Greenwich, CT 06830.

Becoming a More Complete Person

Many executives neglect personal growth in favor of career.

Penalties for failing to develop other interests:

• Produces a feeling that life has gone stale.

• Lowers the ability to love or take interest in family and community.

• Leads to despair. You pretend that you don't mind being so job-oriented, but you do.

Rewards of extending your interests:

•You drop some psychological defenses and use that energy to enjoy life more fully.

•You lose the anxiety, confusion, and identity crises of youth. You appreciate the joys that being older brings.

Source: Richard C. Hodgson, in *Business Quarterly,* published by the School of Business Administration, University of Western Ontario, London, Ontario.

How to Enjoy Yourself By Yourself

The problem most people have with doing things by themselves is a holdover from when they were teenagers—being alone meant nobody loved you. Remember that being alone doesn't mean rejection. A lot of people who are with someone would rather be alone.

To avoid loneliness or boredom when you're alone, try these activities:

•Go out to eat. Make a reservation at a nice restaurant, dress well and tell yourself: "I'm going to ask for a good table and enjoy myself!" Once you get there, you might ask another interesting-looking person eating alone to join you.

•Go to the movies. Many people avoid going to the movies alone when they're in their hometown. One advantage is that no one is constantly whispering comments to you, asking questions about the movie or stealing your popcorn.

•Look in stores. Shopping just for the fun of it is another thing busy people don't often do. Look around. There's always something to learn about products and merchandising.

•Take a tour. Pretend you're a tourist, and see your town through others' eyes. *Best:* Walking tours. You see a lot and get exercise.

•Meander by yourself. Discovering an unfamiliar place is fun. And doing it at your own pace is wonderfully relaxing.

Growing-Up Realities

•Negative events in infancy do not irreversibly damage the mental health of the adult. Some repair is possible if the environment becomes more benevolent.

•The behavior of an infant does not provide a good preview of the young adult. A one-year-old's tantrums don't foreshadow teenage delinquency, for example. Many infantile qualities disappear as their usefulness is outgrown. Adult behavior becomes more predictable after the age of five than it was before.

•Human beings are not saddled with a fixed "intelligence" or "temperament" in every situation. These qualities are related to context and can vary in different circumstances.

•A biological mother's physical affection is not basic to a child's healthy emotional growth. More important is consistent nurturing from primary caregivers, related or not, female or male. The key is a child's belief in his own value in the eyes of the caregivers.

Source: Dr. Jerome Kagan.

Stopping Unwanted Thoughts

The average person has more than 200 negative thoughts a day—worries, jealousies, insecurities, cravings for forbidden things, etc. (Depressed people have as many as 600.) You can't eliminate all the troublesome things that go through your mind, but you can certainly reduce the number of negative thoughts. *Here's how:*

•When a negative thought begins to surface in your mind, pause. Just stop what you are doing for a few seconds. Don't say anything—talk reinforces the bad feeling.

•Take five deep, slow breaths. By taking in more oxygen, you flush out your system and lower your level of anxiety. If you do this correctly, you will approach a meditative state.

•Concentrate on a pleasant, relaxing scene —a walk on a breezy beach, for example. Take two to three minutes for a minor trouble, up to 10 minutes for a serious upset.

•Use this technique continuously until the upsetting thoughts begin to decrease. Then practice it intermittently.

Source: Elior Kinarthy, PhD, professor of psychology, Rio Hondo College, Whittier, CA.

The Tough Job Of Setting Your Personal Priorities

How you already allocate your own time is the best indicator of what's important to you. It tells you what your priorities really are. Anxiety about personal time management comes from confronting what you are doing with what you think you should be doing.

•Confront your real needs and time values and be honest about what you see.

•Resist the temptation to be sucked into other people's needs. Face the risks inherent in not answering some phone calls, not answering certain letters, not jumping when someone asks you to do something.

•Beware of the open door policy at the office. People who report to you need something more important than ready access.

•Be honest about how you feel about meetings. Many executives complain about them as time-wasters but actually call many meetings themselves because they enjoy chairing them, being the center of attention and putting other people's ideas down.

•Consider cutting down on dictated formal letters. Dictation is inefficient but ego-satisfying. Most memos and letters can be answered by a handwritten note or comment across the original. And people appreciate the quick turnaround much more than the perfectly typed memo or letter.

Source: Charles E. Dwyer, Wharton School, University of Pennsylvania, Philadelphia.

Fitting Priorities Into Categories

Even some of the most efficient managers sometimes lose ground because they don't accurately weigh the relative importance of their activities. To prevent this problem in your life, categorize activities carefully according to priority, and revise the categories daily.

•Category A. Important and urgent.

•Category B. Important but not urgent.

•Category C. Urgent but not important work. This category is usually the big trap because the crisis nature of the activity makes it seem more important than it is.

•Category D. Neither urgent nor important. For example, cleaning drawers, straightening files.

•Activities will vary in urgency as time passes, so it is important to revise the priority list each day.

•Tackle the A and B priorities, and then the C tasks, if you have the time. If you never get to the D jobs, what has been lost?

Source: Milton R. Stohl, president, Milton R. Stohl Associates, Farmington Woods, CT.

Selfishness is Not Necessarily a Sin

The whole notion of sacrificial relationships is wrong, whether you are sacrificing yourself to other people or vice versa. What's essential to relationships is exchange.

Selfishness, or honoring the self, means:

•Be aware of yourself and the world.

•Think independently and have the courage of your own perceptions.

•Know what you feel and accept your right to experience such feelings...fear, anger or other emotions we often consider negative.

•Accept who you are, without self-castigation or pretense.

•Speak and act from your innermost convictions and feelings.

•Refuse to accept unearned guilt. Attempt to correct the guilt that you have earned.

•Commit yourself to your right to exist. Acknowledge that your life does not belong to others and that you were not put on earth to live up to someone else's expectations.

•Be in love with your own life and with your own possibilities for growth, joy and the process of discovering your human potential.

Source: Dr. Nathaniel Branden, a Los Angeles psychologist and author of *Honoring the Self,* Jeremy P. Tarcher, Inc., Los Angeles.

Avoiding Needless Personal Sacrifices

A fair number of men and women remain workhorses for their entire lives to avoid the stigma of selfishness. *Example:* A middle-aged man who is bored with his career may want to switch to another career that will give him personal fulfillment. If the change involves a drop in family income, he is often accused of being "selfish."

The steps to change involve having the courage to face up to the following:

•Human relationships should be based on an exchange of values, not of sacrifices. Here a market analogy is apt (without implying that human relationships are meant to be materialistic):

If you want something someone else has, you must offer value in exchange that will be perceived as roughly equal, appealing to the self-interest of whomever you wish to trade with. *Formula for respect:* Never ask anyone to act against his or her self-interest.

•Other human beings are not put on earth to satisfy your needs, wishes or expectations. You are not put on earth to live up to someone else's needs, wishes or expectations.

•What we call our fear of being selfish is really our fear of disapproval or our fear of being condemned for perfectly honest and legitimate forms of self-assertion.

•When we do sacrifice ourselves to others, we hate them for it and make them pay for it in all sorts of indirect and underhanded ways.

Source: Dr. Nathaniel Branden, a Los Angeles psychologist and author of *Honoring the Self,* Jeremy P. Tarcher, Inc., Los Angeles.

How to Get Out of a Rut

No matter how old you are or what kind of rut you're in, there is a way out.

•Accept that no one is going to do anything for you. It is your responsibility, and yours alone, to change your own life.

•Start thinking constructively about what you want rather than moaning about what you don't have.

•*If you're upset about your career, stop complaining and ask yourself:* What do I really want to do? Where do I want to do it? With whom? Under what circumstances? What are my skills? (Include not only business experience but also hobbies, interpersonal skills and non-job-related skills.)

•*Ask yourself:* What are my short-term goals? Long-term goals? Think long and hard and in great detail about what would make you happy. Don't be afraid to fantasize or hatch grandiose schemes. You may be able to make at least parts of your fantasy come true.

•Give yourself an imaginary $10 million and think about what you would do with it. Be specific. Then use your brain to see how much of your fantasy you can turn into reality. *Sample fantasy:* To live on a South Sea island and spend all my time sunbathing, fishing and picking coconuts. It may not be possible to move to the South Seas and loll about all day, but if you're living in a cold climate and really love the tropics, you might be able to get a job in Florida and spend all the spare time that you choose sunbathing and fishing.

•Change your job without leaving the company. Negotiate a move to another state. Redesign your job so you can focus on your strengths and hand over other tasks.

Source: The late John C. Crystal, founder of John C. Crystal Center, New York, which offers intensive courses in creative life/career planning.

Breaking an Undesirable Habit

•Before trying to break a habit, take at least a few days to observe it in action.

•Then try to stop completely instead of tapering off. Performing the act reinforces it, while abstaining strengthens the habit of not doing it.

•Don't fret over lapses. It takes time to establish new patterns.

•Be aware that you cannot change just any habit. Work hardest to change those that both annoy others and violate your own standards. You can improve yourself only if the changes sought are in accord with your own moral and ethical standards.

Source: Dr. George Weinberg, author of *Self Creation,* Avon Books, New York.

Rid Yourself of Nervous Gestures

Audio-video cameras are an excellent way to check yourself for nervous physical gestures that can interfere with your ability to communicate effectively. Record a conversation with another person or the draft of a talk you are about to deliver. *Look for:*

•Repetitive phrases such as "you know."

•Cracking your knuckles.

•Rubbing your nose.

•Pulling your ear.

•Adjusting your glasses.

•Stroking a mustache.

•Jingling change in a pocket.

•Leaning too heavily on the lectern.

•Pacing back and forth all the time.

•Shifting weight from one foot to the other.

•Using a chart pointer excessively.

Source: James K. Van Fleet, author of *Lifetime Conversation Guide,* published by Prentice-Hall, Inc., Englewood Cliffs, NJ.

If You Want a Drastic Change in Your Life

•Start your own business. This does not have to be a total gamble. *Overlooked clue to success:* Research not only your venture but yourself. Too many people go into businesses they are personally unsuited for. *Example:* The couple who dreams of running a little hotel in the mountains won't make a go of it if they're shy, retiring types.

•Start communicating openly with your family. This hardly sounds like a prescription for drastic change. However, lack of communication is the primary reason for a marital rut. It can be an exciting, startling and totally new experience to find out what your spouse and children really think.

•Consider going to a weekend marriage workshop, sometimes called a "marriage encounter." This is a group of couples with an experienced leader. Spouses are taught how to be open with each other. It can be more effective than marriage counseling, which is often the last stop before the divorce.

Source: The late John C. Crystal, founder of the John C. Crystal Center, NY. The Center offers intensive courses in creative life/career planning.

How to Plan a Major Change in Your Life

The change that's needed to execute any major personal plan: Willingness to accept less than 100% perfection. *Set the parameters of performance:* The ideal level and the acceptable level. Then aim for performance within that range. That's easier said than done.

Between the recognition of what has to be done and the courage to change, you must do some hard work.

•Sit down with an accounting spread sheet and, on the vertical axis, write down all the things you want to do in your personal life. On a separate list, write down all the things you want to do in the business.

•Spend two to three days working out this list.

•Think audaciously, creatively, freely. *For instance:* I want 2,000 people working for me. *Or:* I want to run a $1 billion company. *Or:* I want to be married to Michelle Pfeiffer.

•After the list is made, mark the items, A, B or C, using this ranking:

A: Top priority—the things that need to be done tomorrow (or at least sometime in the future).

B: The things impacting today.

C: Lowest priority—the things that I should have done yesterday, but didn't.

•*Rationale:* You have to change the tempo of what you do. And you must do it on paper. You can't change what happened yesterday—so it gets lowest priority. The only thing you can really affect is what happens tomorrow. That's where to put all the energy and skill.

•Ask yourself, of everything listed, what tasks can be done by someone else.

•On the horizontal axis, assign the tasks.

•Work out some sensible (not grandiose) time schedule for meeting all the goals you really plan to meet.

How to Push for Change

To improve the likelihood that a recommendation for a change will be accepted:

•Demonstrate a thorough knowledge of the status quo, including essential figures.

•Make claims for improvement absolutely accurate. Quantify them whenever possible.

•Do not play down the real costs of change.

•Investigate the less obvious effects a change could have in some areas, in order to head off a quick rejection because of the side effects.

•Find someone to play devil's advocate and test the validity of the proposal before presenting it.

•Bring copies of supporting data to the proposal meeting.

Source: *Purchasing,* Boston, MA.

Focusing on Your Strengths

Some evening at home, go into your bedroom and close the door. Tell the family you need some time alone.

•Take off your clothes and stand in front of the mirror. You'll feel absurd. Everyone does.

•Talk to yourself. You'll feel even more absurd. Everyone does.

•Ask yourself what you like about what you see. Most people are very hard on themselves. I'm too fat. Too gray. Too many wrinkles. You have to get over that—and you only can do that if you stick to it. *Keep talking:* My arms are strong. My legs aren't too bad. My back is straight.

•The lesson, both personal and professional: Don't focus on improving the flaws. Accept the flaws and identify the strengths that you have to work with.

•In business, too, achieving the goals you want to achieve is a process. The process is using the company's strength—and your own.

Coping with Disappointment

We have become addicted to the notion that personal change is a simple, painless matter. TV and the movies always present a dramatic crisis and then a resolution. Advertising tries to convince us that this car or that perfume will make us powerful or sexy. Even psychology has contributed by spreading the fiction that a book or weekend seminar will profoundly and quickly transform our lives. But true change doesn't happen overnight. It takes time, commitment, energy, and courage.

Disappointment styles...

There are four basic disappointment styles. Once you identify your patterns, you can start to deal with the problems they cause you.

•Acquiescent. She (it's most often a she) responds not from her inner needs but from a desire to please. Disappointment results from the impossible attempt to meet all the demands, real or imagined, of others.

•Deprived. This type was deeply disappointed in early life and has developed a defensive posture based on always expecting the worst. *Typical premises:* "Life is pain" and "You never get what you want."

•Romantic. This is a variation of deprived. Romantics were emotionally deprived in childhood and so became attached to unrealistic fantasies of being rescued by love. But since they feel undeserving of intimacy, they sabotage relationships and then cling to the anguish long after a relationship has ended. They are constantly disappointed as each successive lover ultimately fails to fulfill their ultra-romantic expectations.

•Self-important. These individuals view themselves as special and therefore different from others. They expect the world to recognize their superiority and to treat them accordingly. Having been raised by families that convinced them they were favored beings, they are disappointed when the rest of the world doesn't treat them the same way.

To prevent disappointment...

•Maintain flexible expectations. Flexibility allows you to plan for the future in a realistic manner while maintaining your excitement and enthusiasm. *The key:* When you find your expectations aren't being met, change them.

•Put more into "assessment" and less into "wish." Every expectation is a combination of an assessment (what you've determined will probably happen) and a wish (what you want to happen). Often our wishes exceed our assessments, and our expectations are therefore unrealistic. But you can change your attitudes to avoid future disappointment. *How to go about it:* Know what you expect from your family, job, friendships, etc. Then make sure your expectations are realistic. *Ask yourself:* Has this expectation ever been met before? What were the conditions under which it was met? Do I have control over those conditions?

•Have fewer expectations. The ability to live in the present without preconceived notions of how life should be is a great gift. If you can accept life in the here and now, enjoying whatever comes your way, you'll experience much less disappointment and much more fulfillment.

Source: David Brandt, PhD, a clinical psychologist and author of *Is That All There Is? Overcoming Disappointment in an Age of Diminished Expectations,* Pocket Books, NY.

Recovering from a Disappointment

Some steps that will help you to recover from disappointment:

Acknowledge the pain and allow yourself feelings of loss and dispossession.

•Take a step back to gain perspective. No single hoped for event is necessary to your survival. Remember some of your past disappointments and realize that life went on—that you achieved satisfaction without fulfillment of those particular expectations.

•See the positive side. Disappointment is a lesson in reality. It tells us what's possible and what isn't. It may tell you to give up a certain set of expectations or to change your behavior in order to make what you expect actually happen.

Coping with a Major Loss

The death of a loved one, the loss of a job, separation or divorce, all involve change and loss. A sense of loss accompanies all major changes in life, even when the change is positive, such as a job promotion, marriage or a job transfer.

Stages by which people respond to a major loss:

•Shock or denial.

•Fear and paralysis.

•Anger, at others or at oneself.

•Sadness and depression.

•Acceptance and reformulation of goals.

All the stages are important to the process of adaptation:

•The omission of any single stage can result in depression or incomplete adjustment because the energy needed to cope with the present remains bound up in the past.

•The longer people have to rehearse a new situation and work through feelings about it, the less stress there will be and the less time it will take to adapt. For example, research among widows shows that those whose husbands died after a long illness, such as cancer, had a much less difficult time making the transition to widowhood than those whose husbands died unexpectedly, in a car crash, for example.

Learning from Failure

Sooner or later, everyone who is ambitious will experience a failure. Many don't recognize, however, that failure is necessary. You can't succeed without struggle. But if you're able to learn from what went wrong, you can do it right the next time.

•Evaluate honestly what stands between you and success, both in the outside world and within yourself.

•Find a mentor who will be open with you about his or her own struggles with such blind spots.

•Read biographies of people who overcame their own fears to become successful.

Taking Criticism

•Don't read more into the criticism than the speaker intends.

•Don't be deaf to positive comments.

•Separate legitimate from inaccurate criticism.

•Don't argue about the critic's feelings rather than the facts of the situation.

•Delay a direct response until you have figured out whether the critic is trying to come off better by putting you down.

•Make sure the critic knows enough to make an intelligent observation about the subject. Then, pick your response to fit the circumstances.

Source: Dr. Jack E. Hulbert, North Carolina Agricultural and Technical State University, Greensboro, NC, and Dr. Barbara Pletcher, director, National Association for Professional Saleswomen.

How to Save Face While Encouraging Criticism

While most people agree that dissent and discussion are vital, many bristle when their own ideas are challenged or criticized. How to be open and avoid ego damage:

•Ask for specific ways to strengthen or improve an idea rather than for a general opinion.

•Meet in individual sessions rather than in a group. Opposition is easier in private.

•Solicit reactions to only one part of the proposal at a time.

•Ask for written criticism. It can be less traumatic and can be put aside for a calmer moment.

Source: *Personal Report for the Executive,* Research Institute of America, New York.

How to Profit From Criticism

You can improve yourself by encouraging friends to criticize you, and learning how to take criticism. Your critics may not always be right. But if you don't get the truth from others, you may never find out.

•Let your critic finish what he has to say before you answer.

•Don't go into the reasons for your actions or behavior. This is really just a way of excusing them.

•Don't jest. It is insulting to the critic.

•Show that you have understood (whether or not you agree) by briefly repeating the criticism in your own words.

•Let your critic know that you understand how your behavior has caused inconvenience or made him feel.

•Don't open yourself to criticism for what you are—only for what you do. You are not responsible for anything but your actions. It is by changing these that you can change yourself.

Source: Dr. George Weinberg, author of *Self Creation,* Avon Books, New York.

Big Drains on Personal Energy

Unwillingness to face up to emotions leads to fatigue. Normal energies are expended in the effort to repress sadness or anger. *Some common instances:*

•Grieving that hasn't been attended to. Surprising, but typical examples, are getting a new job and moving to a new city. The event can be exhilarating. But, the new situation still implies some loss. This holds true for promotions or getting married—which mean saying goodbye to certain freedoms, contacts, options. People who don't deal with the negative aspects of even the most positive changes are vulnerable to psychological fatigue. Some of their energies remain bound up in the past.

•Situations of acknowledged loss, i.e., the death of a loved one or the fact that the children have grown up and left home, or having to face the fact of limited potential (executive's sudden realization that he'll never fulfill career objectives).

Recognizing Psychological Fatigue

As a rule, if a person has been overworking for some time and then takes three or four days off and sleeps adequately, he should be refreshed.

But often rest is not the answer. People whose tiredness is psychological need stimulation. The more rest such a person gets, the more tired he becomes.

Who's prone to psychological fatigue:

•People who are unwilling to ask for what they want or who keep waiting for people to guess.

•People who refuse to say what they don't want. Nothing saps energy and produces fatigue as much as unacknowledged resentment.

•If chronic tiredness persists and the doctor says there's no physical cause, acknowledge the problem is a psychological one.

•Explore the feelings engendered by work or by important relationships.

•Figure out what unmet needs and wants you have in these areas.

•Determine which expectations are realistic and which aren't, and how to go about resolving that draining aspect of your life.

Source: Gisele Richardson, management consultant, Richardson Management Associates, Montreal.

Tension-Reducing Techniques

Basic rules for tense individuals:

•Wake up early to avoid hurrying and getting keyed up before leaving the house.

•Take a short walk after lunch. Do it any time that tension is high. (Just say, "I'll be back in five minutes," and go.)

•Have a daily quiet hour. No phone calls or visitors.

•Plan social engagements to allow for a short relaxation period between the end of the business day and the start of the evening's activities.

•Always be prepared for those tense moments during the day and, when they come, concentrate on breathing slowly and deeply.

Source: *Personal Health.*

Reducing Pain-Producing Jaw Tension

Five exercises to ease discomfort:

•Start by opening the mouth wide, then closing it. Do this repeatedly and as rapidly as possible.

•Continue the same motions, but now place the palm of your hand beneath the chin when opening the mouth, and above it when closing. This offers a slight resistance.

• Repeat the same two steps with a sideways motion of the lower jaw, first doing it freely and then doing it against the resistance of the palm of the hand.

• Go through the same steps with a motion that protrudes the jaw.

• Chew a piece of gum alternately on each side of the mouth, then in the center of the mouth. Do each exercise for three to five minutes.

Source: Patricia Brown, RN, *American Journal of Nursing,* New York.

How Nine Celebrities Handle Anxiety

Many successful people have developed their own special ways of dealing with anxiety with a significant emphasis on physical activity. Their approaches may be worth a try for you.

• Yogi Berra, baseball great:

"I spend lots of time on the golf course, often with my son, who is also a ball player. And I like to play racquetball."

• Jane Brody, *New York Times* science writer and author of the bestselling *Jane Brody's Nutrition Book* and *New York Times Guide to Personal Health:*

"I find the best way to avoid anxiety is to exercise. I drop everything and do something physical—jog, swim, whatever. I clear the slate and calm down. When I come back, things don't seem so bad. Another thing—I keep a continuing calendar and try not to let too many things pile up at once. And I have also learned the fine art of saying "No."

• Joyce Brothers, psychologist and TV personality:

"Whenever I get anxious, I swim. (Studies indicate that 15 minutes of strenuous exercise have a more tranquilizing effect than strong drugs.) Another good way to fight stress and anxiety is take a long, brisk walk."

• Dr. Frank Field, CBS science editor:

"The key word, for me, is 'awareness.' Once I am aware of my anxiety, I stand back and look at it. If someone tells me that I am shouting, I try to do something about it—not just deny it. I get swept up with so many things that often I am unaware that I am becoming anxious. So then I take control of myself."

• Eileen Ford, Ford Model agency:

"I do yoga deep breathing. The tension just flows from my body."

• Roger Horchow, founder of The Horchow Collection:

"I don't have much anxiety in my life. When I do, I guess it is when I eat too much. But mostly, I try to work harder to eliminate what is bothering me...try to accomplish more and deal with the source."

• Reggie Jackson, baseball great:

"My best cure for anxiety is working on my collection of old cars. I also enjoy building cars, and I find that doing physical work can relieve stress for me. Reading the Bible also puts my mind at ease and gives me spiritual comfort."

• Ann Landers, syndicated columnist:

"My work is not anxiety-producing, but occasionally, if there is a hitch, I get into a hot bath, take the phone off the hook and count my blessings. I have a great deal to be thankful for, and I know it."

• Dr. Ruth Westheimer, prominent sexologist:

"When I get anxious, I say, 'Ruth Westheimer, get hold of yourself.' The important thing is to recognize your anxiety. Sometimes this makes it go away. If it were a really serious anxiety, I would go for professional help."

Depression Myths And Realities

Common as it is, depression is shrouded in popular misconceptions. Whether short-term and mild or more serious and longer-lasting, those feelings of low self-esteem, aimlessness and purposelessness afflict many people periodically. You'll be able to cope with depression better if you understand the major fallacies about it.

•If you're feeling depressed, the cause must be psychological. *Fact:* Not necessarily. Many psychiatrists consider much emotional distress to be caused by genetically inherited body chemistry. Also, a variety of physical illnesses, such as viral infections, can cause low psychological moods.

•People who lack ego strength and character are more likely to get depressed than those with strong personalities. *Fact:* If anything, it's the strongest characters who are most subject to feelings of depression and low periods. Strong personalities have very high standards of success and morality and suffer most from a loss of self-esteem.

•Men and women are equally susceptible to depression. *Fact:* Women are more likely, by a ratio of two to one, to develop feelings of depression. On the other hand, men tend to have more serious depressions and a higher rate of suicide.

•Depression will affect you psychologically but not physically. *Fact:* Prolonged and serious periods of depression can result in weight loss, sleeplessness and other stress that can make the sufferer vulnerable to serious physical problems, such as heart attack and multiple sclerosis.

•Falling in love will lift you out of depression. *Fact:* People who are feeling low and emotionally distressed are too internally preoccupied to be either very interested or successful in handling relationships. Feelings of depression also cause a decrease in the sexual impulse.

•Help for depression can come only from long-term psychotherapy. *Fact:* There are ways of combating depression effectively that don't require long-term therapy. Antidepressant drug therapy may help in several weeks. People who are having a mild, short-term depression may profit from seeing a therapist or a counselor several times. However, serious and disabling depression that lasts for months does call for continuing professional treatment.

•Tranquilizers will help you combat feelings of depression. *Fact:* Valium and alcohol are both depressants themselves, as are all tranquilizers. The only medications that work are antidepressant drugs, which must be carefully prescribed.

•The cause of your depression is usually obvious. *Fact:* The cause that seems most obvious is most often not the real one. *Reason:* Depression has to do with unconscious conflict. For example, one of the frequent causes of depression is repressed hostility. When that hostility is acknowledged, the depression usually lifts.

•You always know when you are depressed. *Fact:* There are common forms of depression in which people do not know how they feel. Such people express their depression in other ways. Obese people and alcoholics often may not feel depressed, but their obesity or drinking are the equivalent. People who feel their depression have an advantage because they, at least, have a chance to do something about it.

•There are usually some after-effects from depression. *Fact:* It's possible, after a period of feeling depressed, to jump right back to where you were with no residuals. Depression does not change the psyche.

Source: Michael Levy, MD, psychiatrist, New York.

How to Cope With Depression

•Avoid isolation. Talk with someone who can provide counsel.

•If a period of depression lasts for more than a few weeks, or if your ability to function is impaired, more professional help is needed.

•Recognize that your outlook during a low period is going to be pessimistic and distorted. In such a period, your judgments of yourself, of your situation and of other people are not based on reality.

•Difficult as it may be, try to be active, do things and see people. People who are most successful at coping with feelings of depression are those who fight them.

Source: Michael Levy, MD, psychiatrist, New York.

How to Treat Compulsive Shopping

Compulsive shopping that cannot be controlled with the help of psychotherapy and/or support groups can usually be controlled with antidepressant drugs, including *fluoxetine* (Prozac) and *fluvoxamine* (Luvox). In a recent study, compulsive shoppers given fluvoxamine experienced a marked decrease in their urge to shop and in their time spent shopping.

Source: Donald Black, MD, associate professor of psychiatry, University of Iowa College of Medicine, Iowa City. For information on support groups in your area, contact Debtors Anonymous, Box 400, Grand Central Station, New York 10063.

New Treatment for Manic-Depression

Two drugs long used to treat epilepsy—*divalproex sodium* (Depakote) and *carbamazepine* (Tegretol)—control manic episodes without the weight gain, grogginess and memory impairment often caused by lithium, the standard treatment. New treatments for manic-depression are needed because about one-third of individuals with manic-depression fail to respond to lithium...and 60% who take it regularly will have another manic episode.

Source: Charles L. Bowden, MD, professor of psychiatry, University of Texas, San Antonio. His three-week study of Depakote use in 179 manic patients was published in the *Journal of the American Medical Association*, 515 N. State St., Chicago 60610.

Help for PMS Sufferers

Premenstrual depression can be controlled with *sertraline* (Zoloft). *Recent study:* More than 200 women with a history of premenstrual depression were given sertraline. Six out of 10 reported feeling less depressed. They were better able to function both at work and at home.

Source: Kimberly A. Yonkers, MD, assistant professor of psychiatry, University of Texas Southwestern Medical Center, Dallas.

Let Go of Bad Feelings

Children naturally tend to want to forget problems and move on to new things. Parents tend to dwell on trouble, trying to make sure children learn lessons from difficulties. But everyone in the family will benefit from chalking up some troubles to experience and then getting on with life.

Helpful: Agree as a family that when someone gets upset, he/she will use a key word such as *quicksand* to convey the frustration of how it feels to be stuck with negative emotions...instead of blowing up. Then tell someone how you feel, take deep breaths...and go for a walk—to defuse inner tension.

Source: Sheldon Lewis, a New York-based journalist specializing in psychological aspects of health and illness. He is coauthor of *Stress-Proofing Your Child: Mind-Body Exercises to Enhance Your Child's Health*. Bantam Books.

Negative Listening Undermines Communication

Negative listening is waiting for the other person to stop speaking so you can say what you wish...or providing an answer without knowing the question...or finishing someone else's sentences out loud. *Much more effective:* Ask questions to find out someone's wants and concerns ...then listen carefully to his/her answers. True communication—shared meaning and understanding—requires asking questions and absorbing the answers.

Source: *The Master Motivator: Secrets of Inspiring Leadership* by Joe Batten, consultant on leadership and motivation, Des Moines. Health Communications.

27

Very Personal

Surprising Cause Of Impotence

Impotence is caused in 10% to 15% of all cases by injury during intercourse. Weight-induced pressure or abnormal bending of the erection can cause chronic impotence by damaging the lining of the erection chamber. The most common situation in which such injuries occur is when the female is on top.

Source: Research led by Irwin Goldstein, MD, Boston University Medical Center.

PID Danger

Bacterial vaginosis (BV), which affects up to one in four women, raises a woman's risk for pelvic inflammatory disease (PID) and infertility. *Problem:* BV is frequently misdiagnosed as yeast infection—and the two conditions require different treatments. *BV symptoms:* A foul or "fishy" vaginal odor and a milky discharge that can stain undergarments. Your doctor can administer a vaginal pH test and a microscopic examination for "clue" cells.

Source: James McGregor, MD, professor of obstetrics and gynecology at the University of Colorado.

Unreliable Birth Control

Breast-feeding is unreliable as a means of birth control, even though the ovaries do remain unresponsive to fertility-stimulating hormones for some time after the birth of a child. *Recent finding:* Nursing mothers do take longer to resume normal ovulation after childbirth than do mothers who bottle-feed, but the effectiveness and duration of this contraceptive effect vary greatly. Some women become fertile again in as little as 90 days after childbirth, while others remain infertile for as long as a year. *Rule of thumb:* The effect lasts longest when a nursing mother continues to nurse her baby at night as well as during the day...and when she delays the introduction of solid foods in her baby's diet. But because of the risk of unwanted pregnancy, it's safer to rely on other methods of birth control. *Flip side:* Breast-feeding mothers who do want to conceive may experience problems doing so.

Sources: Susan K. Schulman, MD, a pediatrician in private practice in New York City, and Audrey Rosner, CPNP, coauthors of a report on post-partum fertility.

All About the Virtues of Being Open...Very Open

True intimacy is the key to personal, emotional, and physical health and interpersonal fulfillment.

True intimacy is achieved when two people travel beyond conventional romance and explore each other's emotions, experiencing the deepest level of trust, openness, and sharing. They feel a flame in their spirits, a celebration of self and each other, a movement toward wholeness, and a lust for life.

Genetic predisposition and cultural norms do play a role in how close we allow ourselves to get to others. It starts at the beginning of life, in the bond that unites mother and child and serves as a model of giving and receiving care.

Everyone can experience true intimacy—if they're able to overcome the barriers that prevent them from freely expressing themselves.

The basics of intimacy...

True intimacy is a two-way street. It requires that two people be able to express the following:

•Trust. You must be able to rely on the other person to live up to his/her word so you can be open without the fear of being betrayed.

•Empathy. This requires putting yourself in someone else's shoes, to know and anticipate what the other person is feeling.

•Enthusiasm and courage. Both are needed to shatter illusions, strip defenses, break through stereotypes, confront fears, and explore emotional boundaries together until our insides "touch."

•Sharing each other's worlds. You must be able to maintain a solid sense of self. While you are fully engaged with the other person, you do not give up your separate life.

Sex and intimacy...

The spiritual connectedness and awakenings triggered by true intimacy can be achieved in a relationship without sex—between friends and family members. But sex within an intimate relationship can unite mind, spirit, and body to an explosive energy release. When no limits are placed on the physical interactions, touch and nonverbal communication can express deep levels of pleasure and intimacy.

The goal is to be with someone who expresses an equal interest and commitment to the journey toward true intimacy. Most people, however, are not so fortunate. Types of people who fight true intimacy...

•The macho but insecure man who tells a woman he loves her in order to seduce her into a sexual relationship.

•The workaholic who says he/she wants to be in love but constantly breaks dates to work.

•The martyr who appears to fall madly in love but constantly with "the wrong people." People who profess they want but cannot find anyone capable of true intimacy have an intimacy problem themselves.

•The avoiders, or those who engage in transitory relationships or make superficial commitments. They do not seek or encourage strong emotional ties. These include loners, control freaks, abusers, misanthropes, self-absorbed narcissists, and romanticists endlessly seeking the perfect romance.

•Intimacy junkies, who are so concerned about being emotionally close to others that it interferes with their ability to accomplish responsibilities. When deprived of the "rush" of such closeness, they get depressed and are further unable to function.

This problem can lead to an endless cycle of starting and ending relationships, an inability to make commitments, chronic infidelity, and destructively inappropriate choices of partners.

Fears...and realities...

The goal to achieving true intimacy is to acknowledge your fears...and analyze your misperceptions. See your fears as repressed excitement, and mobilize this energy to be intimate. Make an effort to get over the most common fears...

- Fear of being judged.
- Fear of abandonment, rejection, or loss.
- Fear of conflict.
- Fear of being hurt.

At the same time, you must also move beyond the common misperceptions about intimacy...

- *Misperception:* A long-term relationship with true intimacy gets boring. *Truth:* It is quite the opposite. There is no limit to learning about oneself and each other. Face guilt, shame, laziness, and other feelings underlying boredom. Keep digging deeper into each other's archeology of self. See boredom as an opportunity into which risk, engagement, action, and communion can enter.
- *Misperception:* Intimacy is a loss of freedom. *Truth:* Fear of intimacy is a prison of the self where no one can touch you. More intense intimacy frees you to discover yourself.
- *Misperception:* People who resist intimacy are tough. *Truth:* These people are missing joy and deep down can be very lonely, disengaged, and alienated.

Overcoming the hurdles...

- Explore and self-analyze your feelings. The deeper you know and feel for yourself, the deeper you are able to enter the lives of others. Understand the past that defines present patterns of intimacy.

Example: The woman who witnessed her father's constant betrayal of her mother grows up mistrusting all men.

- Be open and honest. Disappointment over past relationships and other issues cause you to close up emotionally.

Example: A 40-year-old man in danger of losing his job and being unable to send his child to college becomes fearful of sharing his concerns with his wife, so he shuts her out.

- Develop self-esteem and independence. In order to feel confident about sharing oneself, and prevent being either suffocating or suffocated in a relationship, one must develop a secure sense of self. Repeat affirmations and focus on successes.
- Unfreeze your emotions. The deeper you feel, the more you can enter another's life.

Exercise: Imagine lying on a rug before a fire with your partner. He/she whispers "I love you" in your ear. Feel the tenderness flowing.

- Recover your "personal mythology." Identify the negative stereotypes that you grew up with...and recognize the truth about who you are and what relationships and life are all about. Identify these stories so that you can recognize the difference between living a lie and experiencing a more honest and fulfilling relationship.

Limits to intimacy...

It's important to remember that in real life, the perfect balance needed for true intimacy is difficult to achieve—or sustain. Each person can be rocked anywhere along the way by insecurities, illness, distractions, stress, etc. In addition, people can naturally have different goals, careers, or levels of sophistication, maturity, or commitment. Frequently, there is discouragement or depression over these barriers to true intimacy.

Solution: Appreciate and adjust to differences as best as possible, but expect fluctuations in intimacy levels. Work toward the greatest potential of sharing, but allow for supplemental relationships with friends.

Source: Sam Keen, PhD, author and philosopher who practices in northern California. Keen is the author of several books, including the best-selling *Fire in the Belly and Inward Bound: Exploring the Geography of Your Emotions*, Bantam Books, 1540 Broadway, New York 10036.

Is it Possible for Men To Get Breast Cancer?

Men can get breast cancer—although the disease is far more common in women. About one out of nine women develop breast cancer, compared with about one out of 1,000 men. *At highest risk:* Men who have male or female blood relatives with the disease.

Source: A study led by Karin Rosenblatt, University of Washington School of Public Health and Community Medicine, Seattle.

Old Condom Danger

Old condoms rupture far more frequently than new ones. *Study:* 262 couples were asked to test about 5,000 condoms over a four-month period. *Result:* Less than 5% of brand-new condoms ruptured during intercourse. But condoms a year or two old broke about 10% of the time... and seven-year-old condoms broke about 19% of the time.

Source: Research by Markus Steiner, BA, contraceptive use and epidemiology division, Family Health International, Research Triangle Park, North Carolina.

College Students' Hepatitis B Problem

Incidence of this sexually transmitted disease has increased 77% in the past 10 years among college-aged adults. It is 100 times more contagious than the human immunodeficiency virus (HIV), which causes AIDS. Symptoms range from mild nausea and vomiting... to more dangerous liver disease and death. *Important:* Hepatitis B vaccinations for all college students—especially those who have had more than one sex partner in six months... engage in unprotected sex...or have had other sexually transmitted diseases.

Source: MarJeanne Collins, MD, chair, American College Health Association's Vaccine Preventable Diseases Task Force, Baltimore.

Cycling and Sex

Male bicyclists who ride up to 100 miles a week may become impotent. Repeated thrusting down on the pedals pounds the groin against the seat, damaging the critical arteries and nerves. *Initial symptoms:* Buttock numbness and difficulty getting an erection for a day or two. *Trap:* Damage may be irreversible and may not be apparent for years. *Self-defense:* Padded bike seat and shorts...rise off the seat occasionally, especially when sprinting...a correct size bike—you shouldn't have to shift your body on the downstroke.

Source: Harin Padma-Nathan, assistant professor of urology, University of South Carolina School of Medicine, quoted in *American Health,* 80 Fifth Ave., New York 10011.

Most Preferred Time for Sex

The most preferred time for sex is between the hours of 8 p.m. and midnight. *Second favorite time:* Before breakfast on the weekends.

Source: Survey of 3,144 men and women, reported in *New Woman,* 215 Lexington Ave., New York 10016.

Decreased Sperm Count Can Be Reversible

Decreased sperm count and motility—common in heavy smokers—may be reversible. *Key:* Vitamin C. Male smokers who received 200 or 1,000 milligrams of ascorbic acid daily for four weeks produced more healthy sperm than did heavy smokers who did not take the supplements. The larger dose produced a greater improvement.

Source: Earl Dawson, PhD, associate professor of obstetrics and gynecology, University of Texas Medical Branch, Galveston. His study of 75 male smokers was published in *Fertility and Sterility,* 1209 Montgomery Highway, Birmingham, AL 35216.

Women and HIV

HIV infection is often overlooked in women who visit hospital emergency rooms for routine care. *Recent study:* Only 18% of HIV-infected women were diagnosed as having the virus (compared with 40% of men).

Source: Ellie E. Schoenbaum, MD, department of epidemiology and social medicine, Montefiore Medical Center, Bronx, New York. Her study of more than 850 men and women treated in a New York City emergency room was published in the *American Journal of Public Health*, 1015 15 St. NW, Washington, DC 20005.

More Men Declining Sex

More men are declining sex. Men see sex as another area in which to perform, while women see it as a form of relaxation. *Other reasons:* Preoccupation with work or school...fatigue...stress...illness...depression...anxiety...fear of pregnancy...dislike of birth control...lack of exercise or too much exercise. *Self-defense:* Better communication...women's willingness to be sympathetic to partners' problems.

Source: Janet Wolfe, PhD, New York City psychologist and author of *What to Do When He Has a Headache*, Penguin Books, 375 Hudson St., New York 10014.

Why People Have Extramarital Affairs

Common hidden motives for having an affair:

• Unwillingness to confront the possibility of a breakup. Outside excitement takes the partner's mind off the real problem, which may be a lack of intimacy, respect, or sexual satisfaction in the marriage.

• Need for emotional support and courage to break up a weak marriage. Rather than risk being left alone emotionally, the partner looks for a new attachment in the form of an extramarital affair before walking out on the old one.

• Fear of intimacy. Some people find that commitment and intimacy provoke anxiety. The only way they believe they can tolerate marriage bonds is by savoring the feeling of freedom that affairs give them.

• Need to show resentment or anger toward the spouse indirectly.

Source: The late Dr. Helen Singer Kaplan, psychiatrist, head of the Human Sexuality Teaching Program, New York Hospital–The Cornell University Medical College, New York.

Sex Therapy

It isn't easy for couples who have sexual problems to seek professional help. *The most common problems:* Lack of interest. Trouble with erections and orgasms. Pain, real or imaginary.

When to consider therapy:

• When the problem becomes so great it jeopardizes the relationship.

• When preoccupation with the problem becomes so overwhelming that work suffers and enjoyment of life wanes.

• Especially dangerous: Trying to avoid the problem by drinking, abstaining from sex or turning to extramarital partners.

To find a reputable therapist:

• Ask your physician or county medical society for a recommendation.

• Review the directory of The American Association of Sex Educators, Counselors and Therapists. It sets education and training standards.

• Look for a therapist with degrees in a behavioral science (psychology, psychiatry) as well as training in sex therapy. Although sex therapy focuses primarily on sexual problems, a knowledge of psychology is essential because sexuality is so connected with total personality and life events.

• If a sex therapist doesn't ask at the first visit if you've had a medical exam, or refer you for one, find another therapist.

Most Common Sexual Concerns

Among men:

• Premature ejaculation. It is easier than you think to control the timing of ejaculation. You have to find the point at which you can no longer stop yourself from ejaculating. During masturbation, practice ways in which you can decrease or increase feelings of arousal. Discover which fantasies or behavior triggers your excitement and what diminishes it, and learn how to focus on the latter, in order to postpone ejaculation. But don't use the old-fashioned trick of thinking about baseball scores or work, which can be destructive to sexuality. Instead, focus on any minimally sensual thought, which at least keeps you in the realm of being sensual (but not at the peak of excitement).

• Sexual deviations and fetishes. Men are very much concerned with what they consider unnatural desires, such as the wish to be spanked by women or to wear women's clothes. These desires arise from deep psychological needs, such as the need to be punished for feeling sexual or a wish to be "close to Mommy" by dressing like her. If these kinds of problems are causing disruptions in your life, seek professional counseling.

• A desire for more sexual aggressiveness from female partners. A great many men wish that their wives or lovers would take the sexual initiative and behave less passively.

Unusual Infertility Cure

Weight gain may cure infertility in some women. Women below their medically ideal weight may experience reproductive-cycle shutdowns which make pregnancy less likely or impossible. Eighty-five percent of women studied who had been unable to conceive for four years became pregnant after gaining an average of eight pounds through a well-balanced diet—and without the use of hormones, drugs or surgery.

Source: G. William Bates, MD, professor of obstetrics and gynecology, Medical University of South Carolina, Charleston.

The Physical and Psychological Roots Of Impotence

Many factors can cause impotence. Contrary to the opinion that has prevailed since Masters and Johnson did their research, not all impotence is caused by psychological problems. New research shows that a variety of physical problems can cause impotence and that these are treatable. Included are hormonal problems and vascular and neurological conditions.

Impotence may be caused by medical or organic factors if:

• Medications are being taken to lower blood pressure, or if antidepressants, tranquilizers, antihistamines, or decongestants are being taken.

• A man drinks heavily. Alcohol has very strong negative effects on sexual function, including possible long-term problems such as reduced production of the male hormone, decreased sperm production, and reduced sex drive.

• There is a major illness, especially diabetes, thyroid disease, or arteriosclerosis. Illness doesn't dictate erection problems but should be considered as a possible cause.

• The man has lost sexual desire (as well as capacity).

Impotence is likely caused by psychological factors if:

• A man has firm erections under some circumstances (waking at night or in the morning, during masturbation, etc.). This indicates that the physical mechanism is in good working order and that the difficulty probably stems from emotional factors.

• Firm erections are lost just before or after entry. The odds here greatly favor an emotional cause.

• The problem started suddenly, over a period of a month or less. Most likely this is an emotionally caused impotence, since physical problems affect sexual function more gradually. There are exceptions, however. Emotional causes are not always sudden in their effect. And medical causes can surface quickly, especially if a drug is prescribed.

•The problem started after a very stressful emotional experience (the death of a spouse, the loss of a job, a divorce, rejection by a partner).

•Penis size. A very common concern, disguised with euphemisms such as "I have a handicap." (*Translation:* I think my penis is too small.) The solution is to understand that psychologically the small penis is not a deterrent to sexual pleasure. It is important to find out what penis size means to you or your partner and the ways it affects your desire and pleasure.

Among women...

•Not having orgasms. The first part of the solution is to learn not to focus on the missing orgasm—if it is missing. Studies show that at least half the women who think they don't have orgasms in fact do have them, but they're looking for some ideal of an orgasm that they've heard about. Genuinely nonorgasmic women can often overcome this problem by learning to achieve orgasm via masturbation. After acquiring the capacity to accept the sexual pleasure she has learned to give herself, a woman can usually go on to the next step, the pleasure of orgasm with a male partner.

•Conflict over the way they're treated in relationships with men. Men are much more concerned with sexual performance and physical fears than are women. Women care far more about the psychological and emotional aspects of relationships than do men. Many women still settle for "half a loaf" in a relationship. The first step out of this trap is to reject the false security of relationships that offer very little satisfaction.

•Problems integrating the role of parent and lover. It isn't only men who suffer from the madonna-prostitute complex (separating women into categories such as the "pure madonna" and the "sexy enticer"). Women also suffer from this syndrome. The most common example is the woman who has a child and thus comes to feel she isn't sexy and shouldn't feel sexy because she is now a mother. She may avoid sex on the grounds of fatigue, a problem with the baby or concern over money.

Among both sexes...

•Whether it's healthy to get involved in a sexual relationship with someone much older or much younger. There usually isn't a great deal wrong with this sort of thing, even though such pairings are often a holdover from incestuous childhood desires. When such desires are acted out by two adults, it can be taken as psychological information, but nothing else.

Sources: Dr. Judith Kuriansky, clinical psychologist and sex therapist, New York; Saul H. Rosenthal, MD, editor of *Sex Over Forty.*

Intimate Relations

•Couples rate talking to each other about their own relationship as the #1 topic to avoid ...especially couples in the "romantic potential" stage (in between a platonic friendship and an intimate relationship).

•Most couples are afraid of revealing their differing levels of involvement. The partner who is more committed fears scaring the other away, while the less committed may fear hurting the other person.

Sources: Study by Leslie Baxter, Lewis and Clark College, and William Wilmot, University of Montana.

•Affection expressed physically but not necessarily sexually is important to a love relationship. Nonsexual physical affection nurtures feelings of caring and tenderness and opens new avenues of communication. The newfound closeness can give your sex life, as well as your relationship, new vigor.

Source: Dr. Bernard Zilbergeld, clinical psychologist and coauthor of *Male Sexuality,* Bantam Books, New York.

•Men today welcome a woman's sexual initiative, contrary to the macho myths of the past that have put men in charge of initiating sex. Most men prefer to take turns taking the lead because they enjoy feeling desirable and giving sexual decision-making power over to their partners at least some of the time.

Source: Donald L. Mosher, PhD, professor of psychology, University of Connecticut, Hartford.

•Foreplay works best if a woman takes more responsibility for her own arousal. *Problem:* Many women believe it's the man's duty to arouse them. *What works:* Being honest about needs and desires...not worrying about the kids, jobs, etc...being specific about technique.

Source: Judith E. Steinhart, sex therapist, in *Medical Aspects of Human Sexuality,* Secaucus, NJ.

Sexual Side Effects of Mood Altering Drugs

• Librium and Valium have quite opposite effects on different individuals. For some, these drugs reduce inhibitions and increase sexual desire. In other cases, they decrease libido.

• Depression itself often causes a lack of interest in sex. Antidepressant drugs sometimes increase libido and sometimes decrease it. Other sexual side effects vary widely and are not well recorded. Possible problems include impotence, testicular swelling, breast enlargement and milk secretion, impaired ejaculation in men and delayed orgasm in women.

• Many medications used to treat psychosis have adverse sexual side effects that have not been fully documented. Among the symptoms are impotence, difficulty in ejaculation, irregular menstruation, abnormal lactation, increased and decreased sexual desire and even false positive pregnancy tests.

• Sleeping pills reduce the desire for sex. As administered in therapy, barbiturates often diminish sexual inhibitions, which raises sexual enjoyment. But chronic use of sleeping pills causes difficulty in reaching orgasm. *More dangers:* Men can become impotent, and women may suffer menstrual problems.

Sources: Joe Graedon, pharmacologist and author of *The People's Pharmacy* and *The People's Pharmacy-2* (Avon Books) and Dorothy DeMoya, RN, and Dr. Armando DeMoya, MD, both of Georgetown University, writing in *RN,* Oradell, NJ.

Some Antidepressants Are Better for Your Libido

Ask your doctor about switching to *nefazodone* (Serzone). In a recent study of 160 patients, 89% of men reported sexual satisfaction while on this antidepressant...compared with 50% on the more popular drug *sertraline* (Zoloft). Women on nefazodone reported a greater ability to achieve orgasm. The drugs were equally effective against depression.

Source: Alan Feiger, MD, a psychiatrist in private practice in Wheat Ridge, CO. His study was published in the *Journal of Clinical Psychiatry,* Box 752870, Memphis 38175.

Drug Holidays Help Sex Life

About 40% of people taking antidepressants lose interest in sex or find they cannot reach orgasm. Many have found they can reverse the effect for the weekend by discontinuing their medication after taking it Thursday morning, and resuming doses at noon Sunday. Ask your doctor if this drug-holiday approach might work for you.

Source: Anthony Rothschild, MD, psychiatrist, McLean Hospital, Belmont, MA 02178.

Incontinence Self-Defense

Give yourself plenty of time to empty your bladder completely...limit fluid intake, particularly alcohol and coffee, for a few hours before bedtime...help stretch your bladder by increasing the intervals between urination... strengthen the muscles that squeeze the bladder outlet shut by practicing Kegel exercises. *How:* Contract the pelvic floor muscles for five seconds. Repeat 12 contractions eight times a day. For women with "stress incontinence" (incontinence triggered by coughing, sneezing, straining or even simply standing up), try Kegel exercises with specially designed vaginal weights and cross your legs before coughing or sneezing.

Source: Kristene E. Whitmore, MD, clinical associate professor of urology, University of Pennsylvania, Philadelphia.

28

The Savvy Consumer

How to Make the Most Of Coupon Clipping

By clipping coupons and mailing in hundreds of rebates, Sue Diffily has saved $3,700 on her supermarket bill during the past three years. *Her cost-cutting, income-stretching secrets...*

Setting aside time...

At my clipping peak five years ago, when all of my three children were still at home and my food bill was $500 a month, I saved $75 every two weeks by using coupons and rebates. While today my food bill is lower, I still devote 17 hours each month to coupon clipping and rebates:

•Three hours for coupon clipping and sale hunting.

•Eight hours for filing the coupons.

•Four hours filling out paperwork on rebate offers.

•Two hours meeting with my coupon club, where I swap coupons and rebates.

This tally excludes the eight hours a month I spend shopping, since I would do that anyway.

Payoff: About $9 an hour in income, after taxes and expenses. It's a job for which I make my own hours and answer only to myself.

Rating the sources...

•Supermarket flyers are a great source of store coupons and company rebate forms. They are distributed through the mail or at the stores themselves. You can also find valuable rebates in the flyers of supermarkets at which you don't ordinarily shop. Many contain rebate offers from national companies—such as Pillsbury or General Mills—which are valid regardless of where you purchase the items.

•Daily newspapers—especially Wednesday and Sunday supplements—and women's and parenting magazines, such as *Parents, Good Housekeeping, McCall's, Ladies' Home Journal,* etc., often have coupon sections.

•Coupon club. Although it's not essential to join a club to profit from coupon clipping, it can't hurt. I joined one about 10 years ago by responding to an ad in my local supermarket. Today, six of us meet for two hours once a month to pool nearly 1,000 unwanted coupons and rebate offers. Anyone in the club is welcome to take as many coupons as he/she would like. But a simple rule applies to the rebate forms—which may be worth several dollars apiece or much more—when you take one, you replace it with another.

• Family and friends. They can be a great resource. If you put the word out, you'll be deluged with coupons they've clipped for you.

Organizing your files...

• Coupons. I keep my coupons in an expandable, accordion folder. Some people file them alphabetically by brand. This is great if you can keep track of every brand. However, I find this too difficult.

I prefer to organize my coupons by product category—breakfast products, meat and poultry, dairy and oils, beverages, desserts, cleaning products—which is how I shop.

Every two weeks, before I go shopping, I comb my file and pull out any coupons that are due to expire that month as well as any others I think I'll use. I also check the newspapers to see which products are on sale at my favorite supermarket. When I shop, I take along a shoe box filled with coupons.

• Rebates. Until recently, most rebate offers required that you mail a box top or side in with the rebate form. To save these items required a fair amount of space—for me, that meant three boxes, each of which was 1-foot-by-2-feet-by-1½-feet deep.

But lately, companies ask only for the product's bar code or proof-of-purchase seal, which is much less bulky. For every product I buy, I simply tear off the front of the product package, put it in a large resealable bag, and slip in the proofs-of-purchase and bar codes as I accumulate them. This helps me know immediately which products they're for, in case a rebate is offered.

To keep track of my rebates, I keep a notebook. I divide the pages into columns for the company, the particular item, the date I mailed the form, the amount of the offer, and the date I received the rebate. It usually takes between one and three months to receive a rebate.

In the event of a long delay, I call the company's 800 number. In most cases, the rebate check arrives soon after my call—often with some free coupons thrown in.

Some people spend their rebates as soon as they get them. To stay motivated, I have set up a separate bank account. Whenever I've collected $10, I make a deposit.

Saving more...

I don't clip every coupon—and I don't use every coupon I clip. I only purchase items that I know my family will use. If I overbought just to cash in my coupons, I'd be losing money on the deal. My other strategies...

• Watch for sales. By waiting until prices are marked down, you effectively increase the value of a coupon.

• Don't get locked into brand loyalty. I'll buy a store brand if the price is right and I have a good coupon. Often, one brand turns out to be just as good as any other brand, and if I don't like the store brand, I avoid it in the future.

• When you find a good deal, stock up. My family used to laugh when I'd come home with 20 bars of soap or a dozen bottles of cooking oil that I bought on sale with a coupon for each. But I knew we would use them eventually. In the long run, these big purchases make great financial sense.

• Look for "double plays" and "triple plays." These can save you two or three times what you would have saved with just a coupon.

Double play: This purchase involves a combination of a sale and a coupon or rebate.

Example: While I like a particular brand of lipstick, it normally costs about $6, which I feel is a bit steep. But when the company ran a "buy-one-get-one-free" sale, I got four for a total of $12. With a rebate form I obtained at my local beauty aids store, I got back $2.50 per stick. *My net cost:* 50 cents per stick.

Triple play: This is a purchase involving a sale, a coupon and a rebate. By capitalizing on all three, you could wind up paying virtually nothing for an item.

Example: My favorite detergent normally costs $3.99 for a 64-ounce box. I'll accumulate a number of $1 coupons for that brand—and then use them all when it goes on sale for $1.99. *My net cost:* 99 cents per box. But if I then use a typical rebate—$2 back for two proofs-of-purchase—I get the detergent free.

Triple plays and organization are the keys to couponing and refunding.

Source: Sue Diffily, a homemaker and former second-grade teacher who lives in Smithtown, New York. She lectures locally on coupon clipping.

Appliances: Repair or Replace?

Appliance repair people are becoming scarcer by the year, and the cost of service calls has gone through the roof. Consumers face a difficult decision over whether to repair appliances or opt for new ones. A survey of appliance marketers and repair people disclosed what life expectancy appliances have and how to determine whether they are worth fixing.

• Televisions. The big, old American sets (like Zenith and RCA) frequently lasted ten years. Today, most sets last from five to eight years.

After that, the set will start needing a new high-voltage transformer, a new picture tube, and a new tuner. It's best to replace the television at that point.

Television repair. It costs from $250 to $300 to repair or replace the picture tube of a color television (including parts and labor). It costs more to replace the tube of a 13-inch or 19-inch color television than of a 23-inch set.

Reason: Most color replacement tubes are rebuilt from old tubes. And there are more 23-inch tubes around to salvage because that size used to be more popular.

The most expensive television set to repair is the Sony. Repair people find it the most difficult to work on, and its parts are hard to get. Picture tube replacement can cost $400.

• Air conditioners. They should have a life expectancy of ten to twelve years.

Two problems may arise at that time: The compressor fails or the Freon leaks. If Freon leaks, don't expect a repair person to fix it permanently.

• Refrigerators. They have the same time span and problems as air conditioners.

• Dishwashers and washing machines. They last ten to twelve years.

Longest-lasting items: Stoves, vacuum cleaners.

Rule of thumb...

When repairs cost 50% of the price of a replacement, it's time to get rid of the appliance.

If you are going to repair...

Try to deal with authorized service centers. They have a better knowledge of individual brands. Furthermore, you can be sure with an authorized service center that you are getting the right parts.

When buying a new unit...

The best buys on appliances can usually be had at discount appliance stores or through buying co-ops. The discount stores advertise loss leaders to get you into the store. Go with the advertised special.

Alternative...

Rebuilt appliances. They come with complete warranties and are generally below the discount house's prices.

Better Shopping

Department store fluorescent lighting often distorts colors. *Result:* You may not be able to tell the true color of clothing, lipstick or other merchandise you've purchased until you get it home. *Self-defense:* If what you buy doesn't live up to your expectations, take it back and demand a refund—the store's poor lighting isn't your fault.

Source: *Live Better for Less*, 21 E. Chestnut St., Chicago, IL 60611.

How Amy Dacyczyn Avoids Overspending At the Supermarket

Although most people go to the supermarket with a budget in mind, they usually spend much more money than they had planned to spend. But by using a variety of strategies, I spend only $180 a month to feed our family of eight.

The first step to saving money at the supermarket is to overcome your most common excuses for why your bill is so high...

The big myths...

• *Myth:* Never shop with your kids. *Reality:* If you can't say no to your children, you have a parenting problem, not a shopping problem.

• *Myth:* Shop the aisles in reverse order to avoid temptation. *Reality:* If you can't resist temptation, you have a problem with self-discipline, not budgeting.

• *Myth:* Menus must be planned in advance to save at the supermarket. *Reality:* Don't plan meals more than one day in advance, or you're likely to spend more at the supermarket.

Example: If you scheduled pork chops and they're too expensive, you'll probably buy them anyway. *Better:* Stock up on foods that are purchased at a good price. Then prepare meals with the foods you have already bought. There should be pork chops that you bought on sale in your freezer.

Supermarket strategies...

Once you've overcome the myths, you're ready to put serious money-saving strategies into place. *My favorites...*

• Work on your attitude. Saving money on groceries depends on a consistent attitude toward shopping—every time you shop. It is essential that you enter the supermarket fully conscious and determined about what you will—or will not—buy.

If you are prone to impulse shopping, you must decide to take control of your shopping habits.

Helpful: Practice. Try the strategies listed below, and learn more about what it costs for your family to eat the food you normally buy. Before you know it, nothing on earth could induce you to spend your hard-earned cash on a hamburger mix or sugar-coated cereal.

• Shop with a list. Make a list of specific groceries that you will buy at certain prices...but be flexible. What's on your list may not be on sale, but you may find a great deal on something that's not on your list.

Key: Be steadfast about what you will not buy. Certain products, such as toaster pastries, are too expensive at any price.

• Keep a price book. This strategy helps to save me more time and money than anything else I do.

In fact, comparison shopping is essential, since most people's memory for prices is not as good as they think it is. It's easy to figure out the cheapest can of green beans in one store, but most of us shop at more than one location—supermarkets, wholesale clubs, farmers' markets, natural food stores, discount stores—and foods come in different-sized packages.

To keep track of prices, I carry a small loose-leaf notebook that fits in my purse. On each page, I have listed the prices I've encountered for a specific product, with abbreviations for the store name, brand, item size, price and unit price. The pages are arranged alphabetically by product for easy reference.

Try shopping at a different good value store each week, so that you visit them all within a month. You will soon find patterns emerging.

Example: Cheese is usually a good buy at the wholesale club and seldom on sale at the supermarket.

Added benefit: You'll soon find that not every advertised sale is really a sale. Prices at the same store for the same item may vary from week to week by as much as a third.

Rule of thumb: The items at the front and back of the sale flyers are usually the best deals, though there may be a few on the inside pages.

•Buy groceries in bulk. This does not necessarily mean you have to buy huge quantities. It simply means you must buy enough of each item at its lowest price to provide for your family from sale to sale—or to last until your next trip to the wholesale club. Buying in bulk can save the average family at least $50 a month.

Helpful: Not all food has to be stored in the kitchen. If you were offered $50 a month to rent the space under your bed, would you do it? Use a closet or a shelf in the garage for that bargain case of peanut butter.

For maximum savings: Invest in an extra freezer. For example, the largest Sears model costs less than $6 a month to run. Even apartment dwellers can often arrange to keep locked freezers in the basements of their buildings.

•Determine which products are the least expensive, and how to buy them as inexpensively as possible.

Examples: I calculate which meats are the least expensive based on portion size, and I watch for sales. I generally choose from the lower end of cuts—with occasional treats. I also calculate the cost per gallon of fruit juice, whether it is frozen, bottled or canned.

My family drinks apple, orange or grape juice ...or lemonade made from sugar, water and lemon juice concentrate. We don't buy processed blends of fruit juices, which are always more expensive than other juices. We do buy store brands.

Stay away from: Single serving packages, snack packs, lunch sizes...almost anything disposable, except toilet paper and tissues.

Examples: Diapers, paper plates, napkins, tablecloths.

•Set limits on what you are willing to pay for staple food items. Gradually, you will determine realistic upper limits for the items you routinely buy. Stick to your limits.

Example: In my area of the country, I will pay no more than 69 cents a pound for meat on the bone—or $1.20 a pound or less for boneless.

•Buy food in its "original" form. Avoid convenience and processed foods. Pop your own popcorn. Make your own breading for chicken and pork. Buy regular oatmeal rather than processed cereal or "instant" oatmeal.

Source: Amy Dacyczyn, author of *The Tightwad Gazette,* Villard Books, a book of cost-cutting strategies that have appeared in her newsletter of the same name. Rural Route 1, Box 3570, Leeds, ME 04263.

To Make Wool Garments Last Longer...

Brush wool clothes frequently...rest wool for at least 24 hours before wearing again... refresh it by hanging in a steamy bathroom... use sturdy hangers. Remove spots and stains promptly. *To remove:*

...alcohol or food—place a towel under the area. Sprinkle soda water over it and rub gently toward the center of the spot.

...coffee or tea—sponge with glycerine. If none is available, use warm water.

...grease—sponge with dry-cleaning solvent or spot cleaner.

...ink—immerse in cold water.

...mud—once dry, brush and sponge from back of the garment with soapy water.

...lipstick—rub white bread over the area with a firm, gentle motion.

Source: The Wool Bureau, Inc., 330 Madison Ave., New York 10017.

Supersavers

•When food shopping, weigh produce priced by the bunch, such as carrots, celery, broccoli, onions, and fruit. Buy the heaviest and get extra pounds free.

•Drink water. It takes 15,000 eight-ounce glasses of tap water to equal the cost of a six-pack of soda.

•Freeze your credit card—literally. Freeze in a plastic bag partially filled with water (it will not damage the magnetic strip). In an emergency, thaw.

• Furnish a college student's dorm or apartment with "finds" from garage sales.

• If you have a chronic illness, schedule telephone home visits with your doctor in place of regular office visits. This is a new option you should explore with your doctor.

• Veterans and senior citizens can qualify for an exemption on property taxes. Your local tax office has information on the amount to which you are entitled.

• Make your own stationery. Press small flowers and leaves in a thick phone book. Later glue the dried flowers on paper for an elegant look.

• Enlist your children's help to lower the utility bill. Post last month's bill and let them share any money saved in the future.

• Put summer grass clippings, autumn leaves, and vegetable scraps in a "compost pile." Next spring there will be free mulch and fertilizer for the garden.

• Get a shoe "tune-up." Have the uppers conditioned, attach neoprene protective soles, and apply a sealant to uppers that allows wear in any kind of weather with minimal damage.

• When the supermarket sells out of the loss-leader items, always ask for rain checks and buy at rock-bottom prices when items are back in stock.

• Do your own wallpapering after viewing a do-it-yourself video. Purchase wallpaper at a discount store for additional savings.

• Save on your food budget. Contact the County Cooperative Extension Agent and receive information on gardening in your locale.

Source: Jackie Iglehart, editor of *The Penny Pincher*, 2 Hilltop Rd., Medham, NJ 07945.

Beware of Paying Full Price

Never pay full price unless you are sure you have exhausted all other options. Decide if you must have something new, or can buy it used. If you need an item urgently, improvise—try borrowing it instead of rushing out to buy it.

Source: *The Tightwad Gazette: Promoting Thrift as a Viable Alternative Lifestyle* by Amy Dacyczyn, founder, *The Tightwad Gazette* newsletter, Villard Books, 201 E. 50 St., New York 10022.

Limited-Edition Collectibles Trap

Very few coins, plates, and artworks touted as rarities make good investments. They are manufactured on assembly lines and sold at high prices by professional direct-marketing firms. Within a couple of years, you can find these items at secondhand stores for a fraction of their original prices.

Source: *Scrooge Investing* by Mark Skousen, PhD, adjunct professor of economics, Dearborn Financial Publishing, Inc., 520 N. Dearborn St., Chicago 60610.

Filing Savvy

File all receipts for returned merchandise with receipts. When you get your credit card statement, make sure you were credited for the returned item. *If no credit appears:* Contact your credit card company at the 800 number on your bill.

Source: *How to Return Just About Anything* by Patricia Forst, Longwood, Florida-based lecturer on consumer satisfaction, Thomas Nelson Publishers, Box 141000, Nashville, TN 37214.

Avoid Service Contracts

Manufacturers' service contracts are almost never a good buy. Salespeople push them because they carry high sales commissions. But the contracts very rarely pay back their costs—and are usually not renewable when a product has reached the end of its typical useful life—when it might start to need major repairs. *Better than a service contract:* Pre-purchase research to find reliable, high-quality products.

Source: *100 Ways to Avoid Common Legal Pitfalls Without a Lawyer* by Stephen Christianson, Esq., a Virginia-based lawyer specializing in civil litigation, Citadel Press, 600 Madison Ave., New York 10022.

Better Clothes Buying

To gauge the true cost of a piece of clothing, calculate the price-per-wear. *Example:* A $200 pair of shoes, worn twice a week for a year, costs about $2 per wear. But a $25 pair, worn for only two special occasions, costs $12.50 per wear—not a bargain. An item's versatility and durability can be more important than its purchase price.

Source: *Out of the Rat Race,* Gregory Communications Group, Box 95341, Seattle 98145.

Pay Special Attention at The Checkout Counter

Group special sale items together when unloading the grocery cart, along with anything missing a price tag or a tag that may be wrong. Pay special attention when these items are rung up—they are the most likely to be rung incorrectly, even in stores using scanners. *Self-defense:* Watch closely as all items are rung up—and check your receipt at home.

Source: *Money,* Rockefeller Center, New York 10020.

Lightbulb Savvy

Compact fluorescent bulbs screw into standard lightbulb sockets and give off light that looks like that from incandescent bulbs...but last more than 10 times as long and use only one-quarter the energy. *Cost per 60-watt bulb:* About $20, plus $10 of electricity over its lifetime. Ten traditional bulbs would cost less (about $10) but use $45 of electricity. *Best places to use:* Where lights are left on at least two hours per day. *Caution:* The fluorescent bulbs won't fit all lamps or covered fixtures.

Source: *You Can Change America* by The Earth Works Group, dedicated to facilitating change at a grassroots level, Earthworks Press, 1400 Shattuck Ave., Box 25, Berkeley, CA 94709.

Better Shopping

Plan ahead. Do extensive research to find out just what you need. Plan finances so you can pay as much cash as possible.

Source: *The Tightwad Gazette: Promoting Thrift as a Viable Alternative Lifestyle* by Amy Dacyczyn, founder, *The Tightwad Gazette* newsletter, Villard Books, 201 E. 50 St., New York 10022.

Better Lawn Mowers

Cordless, rechargeable electrics need no oil, gas, starter ropes or tune-ups—and are much quieter than gas-powered mowers. Electrics use far less energy—around $5.50 a year, about the same amount as a toaster. And they generate practically no pollution. Using a gas mower for one hour creates as much pollution as driving a car 50 miles. *Cost:* $350 to $550—about the same as high-end gas mowers.

Source: Joel Makower, editor, *The Green Consumer Letter,* 1526 Connecticut Ave. NW, Washington, DC 20036.

No-Haggle Trap

Car buyers who shop at one-price "no-haggle" dealerships to avoid the discomfort of negotiating may pay as much as $1,000 more for the convenience. *Reason:* Prices at no-haggle dealerships are inflexible and typically higher than those that consumers could negotiate for themselves at traditional showrooms.

Source: W. James Bragg, author of *In the Driver's Seat: The New Car Buyer's Negotiating Bible,* Random House, 201 E. 50 St., New York 10022.

Generic Drug Savings

To save money on drugs, ask your doctor for a generic version of the prescription (at a savings of up to 70%)...comparison shop at pharmacies ...consider mail-order (for discounts of up to 40%). *Major mail-order pharmacies:* Action Mail Order/800-452-1976...Family Pharmaceuticals (Medi-Mail)/800-922-3444...Medi-Mail/800-331-1458.

Source: *Money,* Rockefeller Center, New York 10020.

Multiple-Deposit Leases

When leasing a car, ask the finance company for a "multiple-deposit lease." It will allow you to leave a larger deposit in exchange for a lower interest rate. *Result:* Reduced expenses over time. *Example:* You're told that the minimum deposit for a three-year lease on a $30,000 car is $500, and your monthly payments will be $520. If you leave $4,000 instead, your payments would be $460—or a total savings of $2,160. That's more than 54% return on your investment, since the $4,000 deposit is returned to you at the end of the lease.

Source: Art Spinella, vice president and general manager of CNW Marketing/Research, a Bandon, Oregon firm that tracks car-leasing trends.

Supersavers #2

•Prolong the life of shoes by using an unfinished cedar shoe tree ($10 to $20 per pair). Cedar slowly withdraws moisture from leather, leaving the shoes pliant and looking like new.

•Use a clothesline or drying rack instead of a dryer and save $0.50 to $1 on each load of laundry.

•Water lawns and gardens in the early morning to reduce evaporation and prevent fungus. Just before sunrise is best.

•Shop "high-and-low" at the supermarket. The most expensive items are stocked at eye level. Bend over—or stand on tiptoe—to reach for cheaper items.

•Make your own baby food. Puree home-cooked foods in a food processor, and freeze individual portions in an ice tray. Store food cubes in a plastic bag.

•Buy ready-to-use pizza dough from a pizza shop, add your own toppings and bake at 450 degrees for about 20 minutes.

•Rotate and keep tires properly inflated. Everyone knows tires last longer that way—and you get better gas mileage—but only a small percentage of people follow through.

•Save energy by using a toaster oven for small items. It heats the house less in summer and doesn't need to preheat.

•Decrease excessive use of water and prevent septic system overflow by installing an ultra-low flush toilet, which will cut indoor water usage by 25%. Toilets are the biggest indoor water-wasters.

•Grow your own fruit and save space by planting dwarf fruit trees, which grow to one-third the size of regular fruit trees and produce two-thirds the amount of fruit.

•Assemble a 72-hour emergency kit. Be prepared for hurricanes, earthquakes, tornadoes, etc. A good source for these items is Emergency Essentials, a mail-order company in Orem, Utah. For a free catalog, call 800-999-1863.

•Grow a variety of vegetables in a small space by interplanting—planting seeds of one type of vegetable in between seeds of another. A few good combinations are tomatoes/basil, beans/corn/squash/carrots, and peppers/carrots/onions. For a free list of these combinations, send a self-addressed, stamped, business-sized envelope to *The Penny Pincher.*

Source: Jackie Iglehart, editor of *The Penny Pincher,* 2 Hilltop Rd., Medham, NJ 07945.

How to Be a Bargain Shopper

The biggest problem most shoppers have with bargaining is a feeling that nice people don't do it. Before you can negotiate, you have to get over this attitude. Some ammunition:

•Bargaining will not turn you into a social outcast. All a shopkeeper sees when you walk in is dollar signs. If you are willing to spend, he will probably be willing to make a deal.

•Bargaining is a business transaction. You are not trying to cheat the merchant or get something for nothing. You are trying to agree on a fair price. You expect to negotiate for a house or a car—why not for a refrigerator or a winter coat?

•You have a right to bargain, particularly in small stores that don't discount. Department stores, which won't bargain as a rule, mark up prices 100%-150% to cover high overhead costs. Small stores should charge lower prices because their costs are less.

The savvy approach:

•Set yourself a price limit for a particular item before you approach the storekeeper.

•Be prepared to walk out if he doesn't meet your limit. (You can always change your mind later.)

•Make him believe you really won't buy unless he comes down.

•Be discreet in your negotiations. If other customers can overhear your dickering, the shop owner must stay firm.

•Be respectful of the merchandise. Don't manhandle the goods that you inspect.

•Address the salesperson in a polite, friendly manner. Assume that he will want to do his best for you because he is such a nice, helpful person.

•Shop at off hours. You will have more luck if business is slow.

•Look for unmarked merchandise. If there is no price tag, you are invited to bargain.

Tactics that work:

•Negotiate with cash. In a store that takes credit cards, request a discount for paying in cash. (Charging entails overhead costs that the store must absorb.)

•Buy in quantity. A customer who is committed to a number of purchases has more bargaining power. When everything is picked out, approach the owner and suggest a total price about 20% less than the actual total.

•If you are buying more than one of an item, offer to pay full price on the first one if the owner will give you a break on the other. Or, ask to have an extra, probably small-ticket, item thrown in.

•Look for flawed merchandise. This is the only acceptable bargaining point in department stores, but it also can save you money in small shops. If there's a spot, a split seam or a missing button, estimate what it would cost to have the garment fixed commercially, and ask for a discount based on that figure.

•Adapt your haggling to the realities of the situation. A true discount house has a low profit margin and depends on volume to make its money. Don't ask for more than 5% off in such a store. A boutique that charges what the traffic will bear has more leeway. Start by asking for 25% off, and dicker from there.

•Buy at the end of the season, when new stock is being put out. Offer to buy older goods —at a discount.

•*Neighborhood stores:* Push the local television or appliance dealer to give you a break so you can keep your service business in the community.

Source: Sharon Dunn Greene, coauthor of *The Lower East Side Shopping Guide,* Brooklyn, NY.

What Goes on Sale When

A month-by-month schedule for dedicated bargain hunters:

January...

- After-Christmas sales.
- Appliances.
- Baby carriages.
- Books.
- Carpets and rugs.
- China and glassware.
- Christmas cards.
- Costume jewelry.
- Furniture.
- Furs.
- Lingerie.
- Men's overcoats.
- Pocketbooks.

- Preinventory sales.
- Shoes.
- Toys.
- White goods (sheets, towels, etc.).

February...

- Air conditioners.
- Art supplies.
- Bedding.
- Cars (used).
- Curtains.
- Furniture.
- Glassware and china.
- Housewares.
- Lamps.
- Men's apparel.
- Radios, TV sets and CD players.
- Silverware.
- Sportswear and equipment.
- Storm windows.
- Toys.

March...

- Boys' and girls' shoes.
- Garden supplies.
- Housewares.
- Ice skates.
- Infants' clothing.
- Laundry equipment.
- Luggage.
- Ski equipment.

April...

- Fabrics.
- Hosiery.
- Lingerie.
- Painting supplies.
- Women's shoes.

May...

- Handbags.
- Housecoats.
- Household linens.
- Jewelry.
- Luggage.
- Mothers' Day specials.
- Outdoor furniture.
- Rugs.
- Shoes.
- Sportswear.
- Tires and auto accessories.
- TV sets.

June...

- Bedding.
- Boys' clothing.
- Fabrics.
- Fathers' Day specials.
- Floor coverings.
- Lingerie, sleepwear and hosiery.
- Men's clothing.
- Women's shoes.

July...

- Air conditioners and other appliances.
- Bathing suits.
- Children's clothes.
- Electronic equipment.
- Fuel.
- Furniture.
- Handbags.
- Lingerie and sleepwear.
- Luggage.
- Men's shirts.
- Men's shoes.
- Rugs.
- Sportswear.
- Summer clothes.
- Summer sports equipment.

August...

- Back-to-school specials.
- Bathing suits.
- Carpeting.
- Cosmetics.
- Curtains and drapes.
- Electric fans and air conditioners.
- Furniture.
- Furs.
- Men's coats.
- Silver.
- Tires.
- White goods.
- Women's coats.

September...

- Bicycles.
- Cars (outgoing models).
- China and glassware.
- Fabrics.
- Fall fashions.
- Garden equipment.
- Hardware.
- Lamps.
- Paints.

October...

- Cars (outgoing models).
- China and glassware.
- Fall/winter clothing.
- Fishing equipment.
- Furniture.
- Lingerie and hosiery.
- Major appliances.
- School supplies.
- Silver.
- Storewide clearances.
- Women's coats.

November...

- Blankets and quilts.
- Boys' suits and coats.
- Cars (used).
- Lingerie.
- Major appliances.
- Men's suits and coats.
- Shoes.
- White goods.
- Winter clothing.

December...

- After-Christmas cards, gifts, toys.
- Blankets and quilts.
- Cars (used).
- Children's clothes.
- Christmas promotions.
- Coats and hats.
- Men's furnishings.
- Resort and cruise wear.
- Shoes.

How to Choose the Right Checkout Line

Successful people play to win. They know the rules, devise plans of attack and follow their plans with discipline, whether it's on the job, in the stock market—or just doing the grocery shopping. *To spend less time in the supermarket...*

•Look for the fastest cashier. Individual speeds can vary by hundreds of rings per hour.

•Look for a line with a bagger. A checker/bagger team will move a line up to 100% faster than a checker working alone. When the supermarket uses optical scanning equipment, the bagger increases line speed by more than 100%. *Note:* Two baggers in the same line are barely more helpful than one.

•Count the shopping carts in each line. If all else were equal, the line with the fewest carts would be the quickest. But...there are other factors to consider. *Look for...*

A) Carts that contain many identical items. Two dozen cans of dog food can be checked out faster than a dozen different items. They don't have to be individually scanned or rung into the register.

B) Carts that contain a lot of items. Because each new customer requires a basic amount of set-up time, it's better to stand behind one customer who has 50 items than behind two customers who have 10 items each.

C) Carts that contain a lot of produce. Each item has to be weighed.

D) People with bottles to return. This can take a lot of time.

E) People who look like they're going to cash a check. This too can take a lot of time. *Most likely check-cashers:* Women who clutch a purse.

Source: David Feldman, author of *How to Win at Just About Everything,* Morrow Quill, William Morrow & Co., 105 Madison Ave., New York 10016.

A Good Desk Chair

A good desk chair can add as much as 40 minutes to your workday because you won't develop fatigue-induced problems...back strain, leg cramps, etc. *Important:* Don't sit for longer than 60 minutes at a time or you will tire your body.

What to look for in a chair:

•*Seat:* Made of porous material to let body heat dissipate. Opt for a hard one, slightly contoured to the buttocks (soft cushions roll up around and put pressure on joints).

•*Front of seat:* Rounded or padded so it doesn't cut off circulation in your legs.

•*Backrest:* Extends the width of the chair. Conforms to your spine, and supports the lower and middle back. Straight at the shoulder level to prevent neck strain. Small of the back should fit snugly into the chair back.

• *Height:* Your feet should rest flat on the floor. Otherwise circulation to your feet is slowed. This also takes some of your body weight off your lower back. Be sure height is adjustable.

• *Arm supports:* Firm, softly padded, at least two inches wide.

• *Swivel ability:* This enables you to face your work at all times. You'll avoid eyestrain from moving your eyes back and forth.

• Look for back- and position-adjustable chairs that let you move forward, tilt backward, sit upright for posture changes that rest and relax you if you're sitting for hours at a time.

Source: *Do it at Your Desk: An Office Worker's Guide to Fitness and Health,* Tilden Press, Washington, DC.

Recognizing Quality In Clothes

To take advantage of sales, discount designer stores or consignment shops, look for the details that signal first-class workmanship, label or no label.

• Stripes and plaids that are carefully matched at the seams.

• Finished seam edges on fabrics that fray easily (linen, etc.).

• Generous seams of one-half inch or more.

• Buttons made of mother-of-pearl, wood or brass.

• Neat, well-spaced buttonholes that fit the buttons tightly.

• Felt backing on wool collars to retain the shape.

• Ample, even hems.

• Straight, even stitching in colors that match the fabric.

• Good-quality linings that are not attached all around. (Loose linings wear better.)

Source: Viki Audette, author of *Dress Better for Less,* Meadowbrook Press, Deephaven, MI.

How to Care for Leather Clothes

Leather and suede garments need the same careful treatment as furs. Otherwise, you may lose them.

• Buy leather garments a little bigger than you need, because they can never be enlarged. This is particularly important in women's trousers.

• Be aware that leather and suede may shrink in cleaning.

• Avoid wearing your leather garment in the rain. If the garment does become wet, dry it away from heat.

• Use a dry sponge on leather occasionally to remove the surface dust.

• Wear a scarf inside your neck to prevent oil stains from your skin.

• Don't store the garment in a plastic bag. Put dust covers over the shoulders.

• Never put perfume on a suede or leather garment. Even putting it on the lining is risky.

• Don't pin jewelry or flowers on leather garments. Pinholes do not come out.

• Store leathers as you do furs, in a cool spot. Better yet, store your leathers at the same time you store your furs.

Source: Ralph Sherman, president of Leathercraft Process, New York.

What Dry Cleaners Don't Tell You

The dry cleaning process is not mysterious but it is highly technical. After marking and sorting your clothes on the basis of color and material type, the cleaner puts them into a dry cleaning machine. This operates like a washing machine except that it uses special solvents instead of water. After the clothes have gone through the dryer, the operator removes stains from them.

A good dry cleaner will use just the right chemical to remove a stain without damaging the fabric. Pressing correctly is next—also a matter of skill. With some fabrics, the garment is put on a form and steamed from the inside to preserve the finish. After pressing, the clothing is bagged.

What to look for:

• Suits should be put on shoulder shapers.

• Fancy dresses and gowns should be on torso dummies.

• Blouses and shirts should be stuffed with tissue paper at the shoulders.

• Except for pants and plain skirts, each piece should be bagged separately.

Taking precautions:

• Examine your clothes before leaving them with the cleaner. Point out stains and ask whether or not you can expect their removal. For best results, tell the cleaner what caused the stain.

• Don't try to remove stains yourself. You may only make them worse. Bring stained clothing to the cleaner as soon as possible. Old stains are harder to remove.

• Bring in together all parts of a suit to be cleaned. Colors may undergo subtle change in the dry cleaning process.

• Check all pockets and remove everything. A pen left in a pocket can ruin the garment.

• Read care labels carefully. Many clothes cannot be dry cleaned at all. Do not dry clean clothing with printed lettering or with rubber, nylon or plastic parts. If in doubt, ask your dry cleaner.

• Make sure your dry cleaner is insured if you intend to store a large amount of clothing during the winter or summer months.

• Don't wash clothes and then bring them to the cleaner's for pressing. The saving is minimal.

• Ask if the dry cleaner will make minor repairs as part of the cleaning cost. Many cleaners offer such service free.

• Don't request same-day service unless absolutely necessary. Rushed cleaners do a sloppy job.

• "French cleaning" means special handling for a fragile garment. The term used to be applied to all dry cleaning, since the process originated in France. Now it indicates shorter dry-cleaning cycles or even hand cleaning. *Best:* Alert your dry cleaner to the term "French cleaning" on the label.

How to Buy Sunglasses

• Be sure they are large enough.

• Make sure no light enters around the edges.

• For best performance, select frames that curve back toward the temple.

• If you choose plastic lenses, remember that they scratch easily. So clean them with a soft cloth, not a silicone tissue.

• If your main concern is preventing glare, buy greenish grays, neutral grays and browns.

• Avoid other colors, which absorb wavelengths and can upset color balance.

• Always try on sunglasses before buying. The world should appear in true colors, but not as bright.

• If you plan to wear sunglasses near water much of the time, get polarized lenses, which block glare reflected off the water. You can have an old pair of prescription lenses tinted to a desired polarized density.

• *Best all-round sunglass choice:* Sunsensor lenses that adjust from dark to light.

Picking the Right Running Shoes

Running shoes do not need to be broken in. They should feel good the moment you try them on. *Look for:*

• A heel counter that holds your heel in place and keeps it from rolling in and out.

• Flexibility in the forefoot area so the shoe bends easily with your foot. (If the shoe is stiff, your leg and foot muscles will have to work too hard.)

• An arch support to keep the foot stable and minimize rolling inside.

• A fairly wide base for stability and balance. The bottom of the heel, for example, should be as wide as the top of the shoe.

• Cushioning that compresses easily. (Several different materials are used now.) The midsole area absorbs the most shock and should have the greatest amount of padding. However, the heel (which, particularly for women, should be three-quarters of an inch higher than the sole) needs padding, too. Too much causes fatigue, and too little causes bruising.

• Start with the manufacturers' least costly shoes first. Try them on. Then keep trying up the price range until you find the one that feels best. Try on running shoes with the same kind of thick socks you will be wearing with them.

• Adequate toe room (at least one-half inch of clearance). Running shoes, particularly in women's sizes, run small, and women often need a half-size or whole-size larger running shoe than street shoe.

Source: Gary Muhrcke, proprietor of the Super Runner's Shop, New York.

How to Buy Ski Boots

First rule: If a boot is not comfortable in the store, it will be worse on the slopes.

• Toes should be able to wiggle while the heel, instep and ball of the foot are effectively, but not painfully, immobilized.

• Buy in a shop with an experienced shop technician who can expand the shell and modify the footbed and heel wedge.

• Check forward flex. When you bend your foot, you should feel no pressure points on your shin or upper ankle.

• Look for a high boot with a soft forward flex. Low, stiff boots concentrate loads just above the ankle, which can be painful for the occasional skier.

Choosing a Long-Distance Telephone Service

Guidelines to help make the decision easier:

• Choose a service that offers the cheapest rates for your calling pattern. (Analyze your last year's telephone bills to see where you called, when you called, and how long you talked to each location.) If you are a heavy long-distance phoner, a company's minimum monthly charge won't hurt you. If you make few long-distance calls, however, the minimum charge might be more than your average telephone bill.

• Some companies also have minimum monthly usage requirements and/or volume discounts. Again, choose according to your needs. If you make only a few short calls a month you'll be hard pressed to justify the minimum. If you have high long-distance bills, a volume discount may offer big savings.

• Consider whether a company charges by distance or according to its service abilities in the areas you call most frequently. If you tend to call distant or hard-to-reach places, a "cheap" service with fewer connections may end up costing you more.

• Rounding off the number of minutes per call can add as much as 10% to your phone bill, especially if you make a lot of shorter calls. Check to see if the company you are considering rounds to the minute or to the tenth of a minute.

• Test each long-distance carrier that you consider for line clarity and ease of connection. There is still a big difference among services.

Source: Robert Krughoff, author of *The Complete Guide to Lower Phone Costs,* Consumers' Checkbook, Washington, DC.

How to Change Your Mind After Buying from Door-to-Door Salespeople

Impulse buys made from door-to-door salespeople or at houseware parties need not be binding. Under Federal Trade Commission rules, you have three business days to reconsider at-home purchases of $25 or more.

What to do:

• When you buy something from a door-to-door salesperson, always ask for two copies of a dated cancellation form that shows the date of sale and a dated contract with the seller's name and address. The contract should specify your right to cancel.

•If you wish to cancel, sign and date one copy of the cancellation form and keep the second copy. Send the cancellation to the company by registered mail (receipt requested).

•You can expect sellers to act within 10 days. *Their obligations:* To return any signed papers, down payment and trade-in. To arrange for pickup or shipping of any goods. (Sellers pay shipping.)

•You must make the merchandise available for pickup. If no pickup is made within 20 days of your dated cancellation notice, the goods are yours.

•If you agree to ship the goods back and then fail to do so, or if you fail to make the goods available for pickup, you may be held to the original contract.

•Be aware that the same rules apply at a hotel, restaurant or any other location off the seller's normal business premises. They do not apply to sales by mail or phone, or sales of real estate, insurance, securities or emergency home repairs.

How to Buy a Good Man's Shirt

When choosing a man's shirt, look for these signs of quality:

•Soft tissue-paper packaging (no cardboard).

•A well-set collar finished with small, flat stitches.

•16-18 threads per inch in a moderately priced shirt and 22-26 threads per inch in a very good shirt.

•Cross-stitched pearl or bone buttons.

•Smooth, supple collar fusing (proving that it has not been glued to the material inside and will not flop after laundering.

•Removable collar tabs.

Source: *Personal Style* by James Wagenvoord, Holt, Rinehart & Winston, New York.

Buying a Cellular Phone

Before you buy a cellular phone, be aware that:

•They are now connected to brain cancer in some studies.

•Phone bills are expensive because you're billed for incoming as well as outgoing calls. And—an access charge is tacked on to your monthly bill.

•Insurance costs may go up because few basic auto policies now cover the theft of cellular phones from cars. Figure on $50 a year per vehicle for additional insurance.

•Some equipment is being marketed by companies that may not be in business in the future as the competition gets tougher.

•The phone is worth the expense whenever (1) Making calls from your car actually frees you for more productive activities at the office, or (2) You can prove that the calls really result in an increase in company business.

What to look for today when you buy a cellular phone:

•A speaker-phone model so you can talk without holding the handset, a valuable feature because it lets you keep both hands on the wheel except when you're dialing.

•A system that hooks into the company switchboard. Then office calls can be forwarded directly to you by the switchboard operator.

•An electronic lock that lets you dial a code number to stop calls from being made to or from the phone.

•A switch that enables you to talk on both frequencies that cellular transmitters use in cities when they're available. Phones with only one frequency occasionally lose quality when the car passes through an area where there's interference with the radio waves that carry the conversation.

•A manufacturer that's been in existence for several years and isn't known to have financial problems.

Source: Fritz Ringling, vice president of communications research, Gartner Group, Stamford, CT.

Supersavers #3

•Wax-paper liners from cereal boxes can be saved. They are high quality and perfect for placing between meats before freezing, lining cake pans or rolling out pie dough.

•Lipsticks. Rather than discarding them when the tips flatten, extend their use by applying with small paint brushes.

•Prepared foods at the supermarket are more costly than buying raw ingredients and cooking them yourself, but they can be a less-costly alternative to eating out.

•Phone services. Cancel any add-on services that you don't use, such as call-forwarding, call-waiting, speed-dialing, etc.

•Permanent flowers. Don't replace dusty silk-flower arrangements. Clean them by washing under running water. They dry beautifully and look like new.

•Cloth napkins, which you can launder, are much cheaper to use than paper ones. *Save more:* Buy no-iron tablecloths at garage sales, cut into 18-inch squares and hem the edges.

•Nonfat dry milk is an effective substitute for pricey coffee creamers.

•Hospitalized friends. When mailing a card to a friend in the hospital, use his/her home address for the return address. If he has left the hospital when the card arrives, it will be "returned" to him. You will save a stamp, and he will be sure to receive your card or note.

•Plastic hangers that come with socks can be used as hangers for doll clothes.

•Make your own brown sugar. Mix one cup of white sugar with one tablespoon of molasses (two tablespoons for dark brown sugar). Store in a jar or plastic bag.

•A narrated videotaped record of your home and furnishings can be made in case your home or property suffers damage. Update the video every two years—or when changes are made. Keep the tape in a safe place, and keep a second copy off the premises—in a safe-deposit box, or with a friend or with family.

•Don't cover presentable floors with wall-to-wall carpeting. Save by buying a remnant and having the edges bound. Leave 12" to 18" of floor exposed. For a room that is 12' x 14', go with a remnant that is 10' x 12' or 9' x 11'. When the remnant begins to wear, turn it 180 degrees. Get twice the life at less than half the price.

Source: Jackie Iglehart, editor of *The Penny Pincher*, 2 Hilltop Rd., Medham, NJ 07945.

How to Buy Shoes That Really Fit

Shoes should provide a lot of cushioning. The running shoe is the most physiologic shoe made. Soft and malleable, it provides cushioning and a little bit of support.

•If you're a woman and you wear a high-heeled, thin-soled shoe, have a thin rubber sole cemented onto the bottom to cushion the ball of the foot.

•Fit shoes with your hands, not with your feet. There should be an index finger's breadth between the tip of the toes and the front of the shoe.

•Tell the salesperson to start with a half-size larger than you usually wear and work down. The shoe shouldn't be pushed out of shape when you stand. The leather should not be drawn taut.

•An ideal heel height for a woman is 1½-2 inches. This is not a magic number, simply the most comfortable. If a man wore a 1½–inch heel, he'd be more comfortable than in the traditional ¾–inch heel.

•If you have flat feet, look for low-heeled shoes that feel balanced. They should not throw your weight forward on the balls of your feet or gap at the arches.

•Buy shoes in the late afternoon when your feet have had a full day's workout and are slightly spread. Shoes that you try on first thing in the morning may be too tight by evening and uncomfortable for all-day wear.

Source: John F. Waller, Jr., MD, chief of the foot and ankle section, Lenox Hill Hospital, New York.

29

Funtime

Have More Fun At Disney World

•Plan what you want to do before you go. The less time you spend waiting in lines and the more you are able to see, the more value you get for your money. Call in advance to see if any rides are closed for repair.

Also...

•Get going early. The theme parks open about one-half hour earlier than the "official" opening time. The same four rides you can enjoy in one hour early in the day could take up to three hours after 11:30 a.m. *Recommended:* Arrive 50 minutes before the official opening time, an hour and a half on major holidays.

•Avoid major holidays. Disney World is busiest from Christmas Day through New Year's Day, the week of Washington's Birthday and during spring break and Easter weeks.

Least busy times: After Thanksgiving weekend until Christmas, September until the weekend before Thanksgiving, January 4th through the first half of February, the week after Easter until early June.

Lightest days: Friday, Sunday.

•Buy tickets in advance by mail from Disney World or a Disney store. Do not buy tickets at non-Disney hotels, because you'll have to pay up to 10% more.

*Admissions options:** 1 Park/1 Day, about $40 for an adult. 4-Day Value Pass, about $132. 4-Day Park Hopper, about $146. 5-Day Pass, about $198. Annual Passport, $243. Florida-resident Pass, $222.

Best bets: For one- or two-day visits, one day tickets. For longer visits, the 4- and 5-Day Passes. If you do not plan to visit the smaller attractions, don't pay for the Super Pass.

•Save the Magic Kingdom for last, especially if you are traveling with children who may not appreciate the more serious parks. Its rides and attractions are highly rewarding for kids and

*Admission prices are subject to change without notice. For more information, call 407-824-4321.

adults. *Recommended:* See EPCOT first, then MGM, then the Magic Kingdom. Allow a full day for each park.

•Consider a non-Disney World hotel. Some hotels near the Main Gate entrance on US 192 are closer to MGM and the Magic Kingdom than many on-site hotels. Staying off-site can cut your lodging costs by 40% to 60%. Savings on food off-site, especially breakfast and lunch, can be tremendous.

Trade-off: Luxury, convenience. The Disney hotels are much nicer than off-site hotels, and provide certain advantages.

Examples: Child-care options, preferential treatment at the theme parks, transportation independence for teenage children. Most of the expensive Disney hotels provide transportation to the various Disney parks. You do not need a car unless you want to visit attractions outside of Disney.

Best bets: Stay on-site during busy seasons. Join the Magic Kingdom Club ($65 for two years) for Disney hotel and admissions discounts. During the off-season, there is little impact on convenience staying off-site, and off-site may be more convenient if you plan to visit Universal Studios or other area attractions.

•Evaluate travel packages carefully. Choose a package with features you'll use. Compare package prices with what you would pay booking the trip yourself. If you don't intend to rent a car, choose a package that includes transportation from the airport. Cab fare to Disney World can run up to $42 one way.

•Limit on-site snacks. It is easy to spend $40 a day on popcorn, ice cream, etc. *Helpful:* Bring snacks, and set an itinerary before entering the park: *We're going to go like crazy until 11:30, have a snack break, then go to a show and then sit down and have lunch.*

•Watch out for souvenir-madness. Even the most jaded visitors to Disney World find themselves wanting a Mickey T-shirt. Prepare your kids to stay within a budget and set limits for yourself, too.

•Remember that you will be in Florida. Bring sunscreen, sunglasses, hats, cool, comfortable shoes, aspirin, etc. Drink plenty of fluids. If you suffer from motion sickness, stay off the wilder rides.

Source: Bob Sehlinger, author of *The Unofficial Guide to Walt Disney World & EPCOT,* Prentice-Hall Travel, New York.

Cut Costs in Las Vegas And Atlantic City

You don't have to be a high roller to enjoy free meals, rooms and drinks in Las Vegas or Atlantic City. *Here's how:*

•Garage parking. Available to even non-gamblers. Have the parking ticket validated at the casino cage.

•Drinks. Served to anyone at a table or slot machine. Most hotels will also buy a round when you finish playing. Order from a casino waitress or ask the pit boss for a "chit" to be used at any hotel bar.

•*Breakfast or coffee-shop lunch:* Bet $5 to $10 per hand for one hour. Ask the dealer or pit boss for a "meal ticket."

See the pit boss for the following...

•*Line pass:* $5 to $10 per hand for an hour. Allows entrance to the casino show via the shorter VIP line.

•*Free show pass:* $50 to $200 per hand (depending on the performer) for four hours.

•*Room discounts:* $25 per hand for four hours. The "casino rate" averages 50% and ranges up to 100% off the regular room rate.

•*Room, food, drinks and a show:* $100 per hand for four hours per day, for three days.

•*Airfare, mini-suite, food, drinks:* $200 per hand, four hours per day, for three days.

•*First-class airfare, suite, food, drinks:* $500 to $1,000 per hand, at least four hours a day for three days.

Other ways to cut corners...

Join a casino slot club. Members earn points equal to about 1% of what they wager in the slot machines. Points can be redeemed for cash or room and food credits. *Membership:* Free.

Have your play "rated"—or tracked—by the casino. Up to 40% of what rated players are expected to lose (even if they don't) is rebated in room, food and beverage credits. Contact the pit boss.

Sit down at a game just before a table is scheduled to close, usually between 2:00 and 4:00 a.m. The pit boss will be generous with comps to get you to leave.

Source: Max Rubin, author of *Comp City: A Guide to Free Las Vegas Vacations*, Huntington Press, Las Vegas, NV.

Videotaping Basics

To hold the camera as steady as possible, keep your feet apart with your weight evenly distributed between them...tuck elbows into your body for support...for a smooth, side-to-side pan, keep the bottom half of your body still and pivot the upper half, "rolling" your body over a solid support, such as a wall...in windy conditions, find a firm support—wall, railing, car trunk—to lean against.

Source: *John Hedgecoe's Complete Guide to Video* by John Hedgecoe, professor of photography, Royal College of Art, London, Sterling Publishing Co., New York.

Rules to Keep a Friendly Poker Game Friendly

Neighborhood poker—exemplified by the guys on *The Odd Couple*—is more than just a game. It's a friendship around a table. And friendship thrives in a comfortable atmosphere where friends show each other consideration. *Bottom line:* Poker should be fun. To set the scene:

Make it comfortable...

•The room. It should be big enough for a table and at least seven chairs, with plenty of room to get up and leave the table without bumping other players. *Important:* A window that opens at the top...if there's cigarette and cigar smoke, it has to go somewhere. Provide large ashtrays or your floor will suffer.

•TV. Good for players who drop out of the game...and for everyone when there's a major sports event. It doesn't matter where the TV sits, but keep the sound low—it can be turned up for the exciting moments.

•Music. It's up to the individual group whether to have music...and what kind of music. Play the radio, so that no one has to hop up to change tapes, etc.

•Table. A round table is preferred, but any shape will do. Use a tablecloth to make a smooth, cushioned surface. Chips bounce when tossed on a bare table top.

•Chairs. Use strong, metal folding chairs... wood is not strong enough. Comfort is not a concern in poker games. If you're winning, you'll be very comfortable.

•Cards. Use high-quality cards. Cheap cards crease and bend easily—a card with a folded corner will be a marked card for the rest of the evening.

Use two decks at a time, each with a different color backing. While one deck is being dealt, the other can be reshuffled by the player who dealt the previous hand. Hold on to decks from previous weeks in case you need an emergency replacement deck.

•Chips. Have at least three colors—one for each of the minimum and maximum bets, and one for double the maximum. Clay chips handle better than plastic. They're available from gambling supply houses—check your *Yellow Pages*.

•Food. Chips, pretzels, popcorn and nuts are the old standbys. Select food that can be eaten with one hand, leaving the other free to hold cards.

Later in the evening something more substantial will be necessary. Cold cuts or pizza work well. Both can sit for a while and remain edible, require few utensils and don't make a mess. Use paper plates, and keep plastic bags handy for garbage. *Mistake:* Chinese food. It's too messy.

Food should be supplied by the host...but paid for by all. Arrive at a set donation or take a cut from each pot.

•Disaster control. Keep plenty of paper towels and a portable vacuum cleaner handy.

•Clean-up philosophy. Nobody leaves until the garbage is bagged, ashtrays are emptied and the immediate area is made neat.

Playing etiquette...

•Know what you are going to deal when the deck comes to you. Poker has a rhythm. Being indecisive breaks it.

•Turn all your cards face down to indicate you're out of a hand. Or toss them to the dealer or into the pot so they're out of the way. Take care that no one sees your cards. What one player knows, all should know.

•Clean up condensation from beverage bottles and cans. Wet cards ruin the game.

•Be honest. You only have to be caught once to be marked forever.

•Bring enough money to play for at least half the night. The worst thing you can do is quit early and leave only four players. *Rule of thumb:* Bring enough money to buy three full stacks of chips.

•If you must leave early, make it known in advance. This gives the other players a chance to find someone else.

•If you drink beer...bring beer. Once it comes into the house, though, it's community property. *Note:* If you want to drink or eat something different than what is being served, bring it.

•Keep your up cards fully exposed in a stud game so everyone can see them. Players who try to cover up their cards in a stud game are not trusted.

•Announce your ante. Say something like "I'm in" loud enough so that others hear you. Then, if the pot comes up short, you'll have witnesses.

Don't give another player advice on betting, even if asked. Your advice could sabotage a bluffer, or simply be bad advice.

•Once you've dropped out, don't look at another player's hand without permission. And don't react to what you've seen.

•Don't look at another player's hand if you've seen someone else's. Your expression could give something away. *Worse:* Giving advice to either of the player's whose cards you've seen. Your advice would be based on knowledge of two or three hands (including your own)—knowledge not available to other players.

•Don't call out what cards or possibilities another player has showing. Only the dealer has this right. This is all the more true when you've dropped out.

•Never help another player figure out what he/she has. A player must call his own hand.

•Don't feel sorry for a loser and hold the bet down. It's humiliating for the loser. Play to win big. It's not malicious—it's the game.

•Don't feel sorry for a novice. It's sink or swim. And you could find yourself in the position of carrying a bad player.

•Don't show your complete winning hand if you win the pot by default. You may have been bluffing and that's information no one paid to see...and you don't want anyone to know. Only by calling your final bet do players pay for the privilege of seeing your hand.

•Never play poker with someone whose nickname is a city. If he's good enough to be the best in town, he's good enough to beat anyone in your neighborhood.

Source: Stewart Wolpin, author of *The Rules of Neighborhood Poker According to Hoyle*, New Chapter Press, 381 Park Ave. South, New York 10016.

Dog-Training Basics

•Keep lessons short. Four half-hour lessons will be more productive than one full hour.

•Give lessons at the same time and place each day, in an area where there are no distractions.

•Don't attempt to teach just after the dog has eaten a full meal.

•Keep lessons consistent and interesting.

•Make sure you've got the dog's attention before giving a command.

•Limit commands to one or two words. Use the same tone of voice all the time.

•Praise or blame the dog during an act, not afterward, so it knows what it has done right—or wrong.

•Wait until the dog learns one lesson before moving on.

•Command with firmness and authority, yet with kindness and patience. Do not show displeasure if the dog makes a mistake—stop if you find yourself losing patience.

•Always finish with a game.

Source: *The Howell Book of Dog Care* by Tim Hawcroft, veterinary surgeon in private practice in Sydney, Australia. Howell Book House, 866 Third Ave., New York 10022. 800-257-5755.

Better Kitten Buying

Buy from a busy household with children. *Less desirable:* Kittens from pet stores or rescue shelters, where infectious diseases are common. *Traits to look for:* Interest when you play with a moving object...a glossy coat...clean, dry eyes and ears. *Minimum age:* eight to 10 weeks. *Warning signs:* Nasal discharge or sneezing...diarrhea...black dust in the coat (a sign of fleas).

Source: *A Miscellany of Cat Owners' Wisdom* by Kay White, Running Press, 125 S. 22 St., Philadelphia 19103.

Mistakes People Make Training Their Dogs

Dogs that misbehave are usually not to blame ...their owners are. With the proper training, almost any dog will be obedient. *Common dog-owner mistakes:*

•*Mistake:* Choosing the wrong breed in the first place. Different breeds have vastly different temperaments. Make sure to match the breed with your family's needs and situation.

Examples: Border collies, English setters and most other English breeds are usually easygoing, making them appropriate for families with children. Pit bulls, rottweilers and Middle European breeds, such as dobermans, are usually aggressive and not appropriate for families and children.

•*Mistake:* Start training too late. Dog owners often wait until a puppy is six months old to start obedience training—far too late. Bad habits learned during the first months of a dog's life are hard to break later on.

The best time to start training is as soon as the puppy leaves the litter—at 49 days (seven weeks). Between 7 and 13 weeks, the training should be very low-key. Put the puppy on a light leash or string. Show it how to sit, stay and come. But do not reprimand the puppy if it fails. *Note:* If you can teach your dog the sit, stay, come commands, you can teach it anything within the realm of its learning.

After 13 weeks, training can begin in earnest, with firm-voiced reprimands for incorrect behavior.

•*Mistake:* Failing to socialize the dog. Dogs should be introduced to everything they will normally encounter in their lifetimes as soon as possible—start at no later than eight weeks of age. They need to learn how to react to other dogs, cats, adults, children, noises, cars, etc.

Owners who fail to socialize their dogs early on often wind up with overly aggressive or overly timid animals. Dogs that fail to get socialization training by 11 weeks often prove difficult to train later on. Those that make it to 13 weeks with no socialization are impossible to train.

•*Mistake:* Being inconsistent. Dogs don't understand spoken language as humans do. They merely learn to associate a specific command—a particular word, whistle or some other signal—with a particular response.

Spoken commands should be short and must always be given in precisely the same manner. Inconsistent commands confuse dogs.

Example: A dog who learns to respond to the command *Sit,* cannot be expected to respond to *Come on, boy, sit down. I said sit.*

•*Mistake:* Failing to reprimand effectively or to consider the dog's age. Dog owners often scold their puppies for misbehavior. But puppies—unlike older dogs—really don't understand scoldings. They must be reprimanded in a different manner.

Be patient when you train a small puppy—it's only in kindergarten. If it does something wrong, patiently start the lesson over with encouraging words.

Then later loom over the adult dog to make it feel threatened. This makes you the dominant animal—the leader of the pack.

• *Mistake:* Using corporal punishment incorrectly. Never strike a dog with your hand—it makes it fear your hand—or with a newspaper. And never hit a dog in the face.

Using a strap or a leash, strike the dog lightly, a few times on the flank. Don't hurt your dog—just help it to understand that its behavior displeases you and show it in your voice. After the dog encounters the strap the first time, chances are it will respond merely to the threat.

• *Mistake:* Using food as a reward. Giving dogs treats is fine, but never train a dog using food as a reward. Doing so exercises its stomach ...not its brain.

Reward good behavior during training with a friendly word or a good pat. Save treats until after the training is completed for the day.

• *Mistake:* Overestimating a dog's attention span. Puppies 8 to 12 weeks of age learn fastest when given repeated, but short, training sessions—two minutes of training three times a day.

Don't continue a session if the dog is uninterested or fatigued. *Clue:* Watch the dog's tail. When it stops wagging...stop training.

Source: Dog expert Richard A. Wolters. He has published nine books about dogs, including *Family Dog*, Dutton, New York.

Stereo Savvy

When placing all components of a stereo system in a single cabinet, put the amplifier on the top shelf. That's because the amplifier produces heat that will rise and could damage the other components if allowed to build up in a confined space. Be sure there are at least two inches of space between the top of the amplifier and the top of the cabinet. Consider drilling a few small holes in the back of the cabinet and leaving the front doors open to assure adequate air circulation while the equipment is in use.

Source: Joseph Giovanelli, contributing editor, *Audio* magazine, New York.

Gambling Odds

No betting system will change the house odds at games that consist of "independent plays," such as craps, roulette and slots. The fact that 10 straight passes have been made at the craps table has no impact on the odds that another pass will be made. The length of time since a slot machine last paid off has no impact on when it will next pay off. Odds change in a game with "memory," such as blackjack, in which the cards that have already been dealt limit the cards that remain. Sports betting has independent plays, but the odds are different on each event.

Source: Wally DeShield, PhD in mathematics, writing in *Blackjack Confidential*, 513 Salsbury Road, Cherry Hill, NJ 08034.

Top 10 Skiing Resorts

What makes one ski resort more exciting than all the rest? According to our insider, it's the destination's diversity...thrilling trails, cushy lodges and lots of after-ski activities. *The following are his North American favorites...*

• Lake Louise, Alberta. Wilderness views of the Canadian Rockies. Fifty-two trails, a beautiful 515-room chateau abutting an alpine lake.

• Snowbird, Utah. One hour from Salt Lake City. Forty feet of snow each winter, plenty of difficult trails and a first-class spa.

• Snowmass, Colorado. Wide-open cruising terrain. Sixteen lifts (five of them high speed), 72 trails. Lodge lets you ski from your room to the lift.

Bonus: Trendy Aspen is only 10 minutes away by frequent, free shuttle bus.

• Steamboat, Colorado. Located above a quaint Western town, great mix of tree skiing and wide-open cruising trails. Has 108 trails and 20 lifts. Hot-springs-fed pools for bathing, horse-drawn sleigh rides.

• Stowe, Vermont. New England's tallest peak. Forty-five trails, modern lifts, improved snowmaking, great food and views. Cross-country skiing and night skiing. Twelve lifts (two high speed) and 90 trails.

•Sunday River, Maine. Super-efficient lifts, snowmaking and grooming, plus all-ability terrain and lodging that allows you to ski to and from your door.

•Taos, New Mexico. One of the finest ski schools. Seventy-two trails, 10 lifts, abundant powder and sun 300 days a year.

•Telluride, Colorado. An expert's paradise, located above an old silver-mining town nestled in a spectacular canyon. A modern ski lodging development.

•Vail, Colorado. Largest single ski mountain in the US. Twenty-five lifts (eight of them high speed), 4,014 acres of terrain, 121 trails, and lots of powder, thanks to the high altitude. And, there are horse-drawn sleigh rides—including evening trips to local restaurants.

•Whistler/Blackcomb, British Columbia. Two mountains, 28 lifts, 6,900 acres of terrain, a mile of vertical descent that allows skiers to take their time winding down their choice of 200 trails. Has an enchanting base village with more than 100 shops.

Source: An industry insider who has visited more than 120 North American ski centers during the past 22 years.

How to Choose a Kennel

When you need to board your pet for any length of time, visit the kennel with your dog a week or two before you leave him there. *Plan to spend some real time looking for:*

•Operators who own the kennel. They will have a real stake in your satisfaction.

•A staff that shows sincere concern for the pet's welfare, not willingness to do whatever you tell them.

•Kennels and runs that are well designed. A combination of two feet of concrete with four feet of fencing above it is desirable so that timid dogs can hide from their neighbors. *More important:* No dog can urinate into another dog's run. (Urine and feces spread disease.)

•A security fence around the entire establishment (in case a dog escapes from its run).

•Kennels that are neat and clean. Kennel helpers are picking up waste, hosing down runs, exercising the dogs, etc.

•Beds that will not harbor parasites. Fiberglass is good. Wood is bad. Dogs with parasites should be dip-treated before boarding.

•A requirement of confirmation of your dog's shots, either by a recent inoculation certificate or contact with your veterinarian.

Questions you should ask...

•What is the kennel owner's background? Ask about his/her experience in breeding and handling. Such experience helps the kennel owner notice when an animal is not feeling or moving well.

•What kind of food is used? A good kennel is flexible and serves nearly anything. Some even cook to order.

•What will you do if my pet won't eat? If a dog does not eat for two days, the kennel should try a variety of foods until it finds one that works.

•What kind of medical and behavioral history is taken? A thorough history includes more than a record of shots and your vet's name and phone number. You should be asked about your pet's temperament, behavior, sociability, likes and dislikes.

•Who will administer my dog's medication? Only the owner or the kennel manager should administer medicine, and careful records should be kept.

•What happens if my dog gets sick or there's a medical emergency? The kennel owners should call your veterinarian first, then bring your dog to your vet—or, if that's not possible, to a local veterinarian. If it's an emergency, your pet should be taken immediately to the kennel's attending veterinarian. Check the professional credentials of the kennel's attending veterinarian with your own vet.

•How often will my dog be walked? Dogs should be walked at least twice a day, in addition to exercising in their kennel runs.

Will my dog be played with, and how often? Your pet should be played with and petted at least twice a day. Some toys should be allowed.

Source: Michael and Phyllis Scharf, owners and operators of Pomona Park Kennels, Pomona, NY.

Planning Your Leisure Time

If you're like most people, there are lots of activities you'd like to do in your leisure time, but you never seem to get around to them. The solution is to plan—not so much that you feel like you're "on the job," but not so little that you fail to accomplish whatever is important to you, whether that means learning French or going dancing. *Recommended:*

•Create a "to do" list for your spare time just as you might for your workday. You probably don't want every hour accounted for, but you should at least list what you most want to do with each leisure evening or weekend.

•Allot some specific times on a regular basis when you will pursue the leisure activities that are most important to you. A scheduled time will help ensure the successful fulfillment of your plan.

•If it's culture you're after, consider getting at least one subscription series to eliminate some of the paperwork and phone calling that often accompany even leisure-time plans. (You will also avoid wasting time in line!)

•Set up regular social contacts, like monthly Saturday dinner with specific friends, so you spend less time coordinating your meetings and more time enjoying them.

•If you use too much of your recreation time for household chores, try delegating those tasks to professional help or family members. Or do it more efficiently and less frequently.

•If you often work in your leisure hours, consider that you may be more efficient if you plan, and carry out, pleasurable activities that energize you (and prevent work burnout).

•To keep your leisure-time plans active (not reactive to other people's demands on you), make appointments with yourself. You will be less inclined to give up your plans if someone else asks you to do something, since you have a previous commitment to yourself.

•Just as a "quiet hour" of uninterrupted time at the office increases your work efficiency, a "quiet" leisure hour enhances your nonwork time. On a fixed schedule, if possible, take some time each evening and weekend to meditate, listen to music, reflect, or just plain old "unwind."

•How can you find more hours for recreation? By setting your alarm clock only half an hour earlier on weekends you'll gain four hours a month. Become more efficient at work, so you can leave earlier (and not have to take work home as often). To find the time to read that mystery novel, try switching from showers to baths, and read in the tub.

Source: J. L. Barkas, PhD, author of *Creative Time Management,* Prentice-Hall, Englewood Cliffs, NJ.

47 Inexpensive Ways To Have a Good Time

Having fun can't be calculated in dollars and cents. Sometimes the less money you spend, the more you enjoy yourself. *Here are some inexpensive ways to have fun:*

•Explore the beach and collect seashells.

•Visit the zoo and feed the monkeys.

•Go to a free concert in the park.

•Pack a picnic and drive to an attractive spot for lunch.

•Go skiing at your local park or a nearby mountain.

•Window-shop at your favorite stores.

•Eat early-bird-special dinners at local restaurants. Then go home and see a movie on TV.

•Hug each other more.

•Dress up with your favorite person and enjoy a formal dinner at home with fine food and wine.

•Go camping or backpacking.

•Go gallery-hopping. See the latest art exhibits.

•Enjoy your public library. Go to the reading room and catch up on the new magazines.

•Go for a drive on the back roads to just enjoy the scenery.

•Visit friends in a nearby city. (Arrive around lunchtime.)

•Eat dinner at home. Then go out for dessert and coffee.

•Instead of eating dinner out, eat lunch out over the weekends. It's less expensive.

•Seek out discount tickets and twofers for local entertainment.

•Take in the local museum's cultural events, including low-priced lectures and concerts.

•Invite friends in for drinks when a good movie is on TV.

•Take an afternoon walk in the park.

•Row a boat on the lake.

•Have a beer-and-pizza party for friends.

•Go back to the old family board games.

•Raise exotic plants or unusual herbs in a window box.

•Learn to paint or sculpt.

•Learn calligraphy.

•Take a long-distance bus ride.

•Go out to the airport and watch the planes.

•Visit the local amusement park and try the rides.

•Have friends over for a bring-your-own-specialty dinner.

•Become a do-it-yourselfer.

•Take an aerobic exercise course.

•Join a local political club.

•Go shopping for something really extravagant. Keep the sales slip and return the item the next day.

•Play cards for pennies, not dollars.

•Go to the races and place $2 bets.

•Explore your own city as a tourist would.

•Learn to be a gourmet cook.

•Treat yourself to breakfast in bed.

•Hold a family reunion.

•Attend religious services.

•Learn a foreign language.

•Join a local chorale or dramatic club.

•Watch local sports teams practice.

•Play golf or tennis at local parks or courses.

•Read everything in your area of interest at the library.

•Buy books. Get many hours of pleasure (and useful information) for still relatively few dollars.

To Celebrate a Really Special Occasion

•Take over a whole performance of a play or concert for your special guests. During the course of the event, have a prominent individual step out of character and tell the audience about you and your special day.

•Have a song written especially for the occasion.

•Run a tennis or golf party, with a name professional hired to give lessons to all.

•Hire a boat and bring along a large group for a cruise and buffet supper.

•Arrange a block party.

•Rent a hay wagon and a big barn for a square dance.

•Hire the museum or the lobby of a key office building in the downtown area for a huge buffet supper and dance.

•Hire a well-known singer to entertain at a party.

•Have a cookout on the beach, with the guests digging for related buried treasures.

•Take over a country inn for a day, and run a big house party.

•Fly a group of friends to a special place for a holiday.

The Six Best Champagnes

•Taittinger Comtes de Champagne—vintage only. A rosé champagne that should go far to overcome Americans' prejudice toward this celestial brew. Taittinger also makes a fine blanc de blancs and a nonvintage brut.

•Dom Perignon—vintage only. Probably the most widely acclaimed champagne and deservedly so. Elegant and light, with delicate bubbles. The producer also makes, under its Moet et Chandon name, a vintage rosé champagne, a vintage champagne, a nonvintage champagne, and a nonvintage brut.

•Perrier-Jouet Fleur de Champagne—vintage only. This house produces champagne of the highest quality in a particularly popular style. The wine is austere, yet tasteful. It is also extremely dry without being harsh or acidic. Perrier-Jouet is introducing a rosé champagne.

•Louis Roederer Cristal—vintage only. Cristal's magic lies in its plays with opposites: Elegant yet robust, rich taste without weightiness. Roederer also produces a sparkling rosé, a vintage champagne, and a nonvintage brut.

•Bollinger Vieilles Vignes—vintage only. This is the rarest of all fancy champagnes. Its vines have existed since before phylloxera (a plant louse) killed most French grapevines in the middle 1800s. The wine is robust and rich flavored. Bollinger also makes a vintage champagne and a nonvintage brut.

•Dom Ruinart Blanc de Blancs—vintage only. Produced by Dom Perignon in Reims rather than in Epernay, it is a sleeper. It is held in low profile so as not to compete strongly with its illustrious co-product but is every bit as good. The wine is light (not thin), complex, very alive, yet velvety.

Source: Grace M. Scotto, veteran of the wine business and former owner, D. Scotto Wines, Brooklyn, NY.

Networking: Constructive, Fun Get-Togethers

Do you often wonder how to get to know someone you've met in passing without seeming too pushy? Would you be interested in finding out about current issues from people who are actually involved in them? It is possible to do all of the above, and in addition expand your business and social contacts and have a great time, without spending a lot of money. *Here are some suggestions from three veteran networkers:*

Networking dinners...

•Have dinners for 13 to 15 people on Tuesday, Wednesday or Thursday at 6:30 so people can come straight from work and leave at a reasonable hour.

•Don't worry about the mix. There's a surprising commonality that develops among people of all ages and professions. Avoid inviting co-workers, couples or business partners. Candor diminishes when a guest comes with someone he sees all the time. Guests who spark conversation especially well: Journalists, headhunters, celebrities.

•Use a modest typewritten or telephoned invitation. Send the invitations at least two weeks in advance.

•It's up to you, as the host or hostess, to get conversation started. Give informative introductions for each guest, mentioning at least three things people can ask questions about.

•A cozy, circular table keeps one conversation rolling rather than several private ones.

•The food needn't be fancy—only good, and plentiful, with lots of wine so tongues loosen. Chinese food works well because everyone seems to like it.

•Don't worry about inviting equal numbers of men and women. People are being matched for dinner, not for life.

Networking salons...

•Encourage guests to drop off their business cards as they enter. This serves as a conversation-opener and theme. Since business networking is the purpose, it is socially acceptable to go up to someone and ask, "What do you do?"

•People should be encouraged to exchange business cards. The cards you collect may become one basis for invitation lists.

•Hold salons on a regular basis, from 6 p.m. to 9 p.m. on Wednesday or Thursday. For example, every week it becomes a different, exciting mini-event with new people.

•People, not food, are the focus. You might have a simple but beautiful vegetable spread. The wine might be donated as a promotion.

Issue discussion groups...

•Finding people to invite is not hard. And it gets easier as time goes on.

•Send out a list of topics six months in advance to those who've come to previous groups, and they often recommend others. At this point, many people know about the groups and call to ask about upcoming evenings.

•The key to success is active participation. Encourage guests to do homework, read relevant articles and bring copies with them.

•To begin, each person introduces himself or herself briefly, explaining why he's interested in the topic, and then presents an interesting fact unrelated to the main topic for a 15-second presentation.

•The groups should be held after dinner hour. Each guest might bring something for dessert. Eat after the discussion to give people an opportunity to socialize.

•Get ideas for topics from articles that you file based on what you predict will be newsworthy in six months. Try to plan evenings around upcoming events. Topics tend to grow out of each other.

Source: Machlowitz, Rubin & Yaffe.

How to Taste a Wine

Careful tasting allows you to evaluate and appreciate a wine's quality and value. It also helps you identify the components that make a wine pleasurable to you.

Proper wine tasting is performed in systematic steps that involve three senses...sight, smell, and taste.

Sight:

•Study the wine's color by tilting a glass of it away from yourself and toward a white surface. The color is your first indication of its quality. Be aware that a white wine gets darker and richer in color as it ages, while a red wine becomes lighter. So a lighter-colored red is older and presumably better than a very dark one.

Smell:

•Swirl the wine in your glass by moving the stem while leaving the base of the glass on the table. This lets the wine's esters accumulate in your glass.

•As soon as you stop swirling the wine, bring the glass to your nose (actually put your nose into the glass) and inhale. What does the wine smell like? Fruity? Woody? Your sense of smell affects your taste buds, giving them a hint of what is to come.

Taste:

•Sip the wine, being conscious of three stages in the tasting process:

The attack is the dominant taste in the wine, the one your taste buds respond to first. (If a wine is very sweet, for example, that will be the first taste impression.)

The evolution involves the other taste components that you become aware of after the attack. Notice the more subtle flavors such as bitterness and acidity.

For the finish, evaluate how long the flavor remains in your mouth after you swallow. What is the aftertaste? Is the wine memorable? And do you like it?

Source: Mary Ewing Mulligan, director of education, International Wine Center, New York.

Naming Your Poison: The Hangover Potential Of Various Alcohols

Part of the reason you may feel bad after drinking stems from the congener content of the booze you consume. Congeners are toxic chemicals formed during fermentation. The higher their content in the beverages you drink, the worse you will feel.

Here's how various types of alcohol stack up:

• *Vodka:* Lowest congener content.

• *Gin:* Next lowest.

•*Blended scotch:* Four times the congener content of gin.

•*Brandy, rum and pure malt scotch:* Six times as much as blended scotch.

•*Bourbon:* Eight times as much as blended scotch.

How to Reduce Hangover Discomfort

•Retard the absorption of alcohol by eating before and during drinking, especially foods containing fatty proteins, such as cheeses and milk.

•Use water as a mixer. Carbonation speeds the absorption of alcohol.

•If you get a hangover anyway, remember that the only known cure is rest, aspirin and time. The endless list of other remedies—ranging from cucumber juice and salt to a Bloody Mary—have more to do with drinking mythology than with medical fact.

•Despite the preceding caveat, believe in a cure if you want to. Psychologists have found that believing something helps may actually do so.

Alternatives to Alcohol

Fruit juices for adults come in wine-type bottles, are alcohol- and caffeine-free, and cost relatively little. Essentially sophisticated ciders and grape juices, these grown-up drinks come in sparkling and plain versions that range in taste from crisp to sweet.

Sparkling juices...

- Grand Cru Cider
- Martinelli's Gold Medal Sparkling Cider.
- Challand French Sparkling Apple Juice.
- Ecusson Sparkling White Cider.
- Ecusson Sparkling Red Grape Juice.
- Meiers Sparkling Catawba.
- Meiers Pink Sparkling Catawba.
- Meiers Cold Duck.

Still juices...

- Grapillon French Grape Juice (white or red).
- Meiers Pink Catawba Grape Juice.
- Meiers Catawba Grape Juice.
- Lehr's Black Currant Beverage.
- Lehr's Pure White Grape Juice.
- Lehr's Pure Red Grape Juice.

Surviving Weekend Guests

Weekend guests can be a drag. They leave the lights on, show up late for breakfast and expect to be waited on. This is a checklist for the clever host or hostess who graciously but firmly takes charge and doesn't let guests become a nuisance.

•Be a benevolent dictator. The host or hostess has the right not to be put upon. If someone is cadging an invitation when you'd rather be alone, suggest another time. Set the dinner hour at a time that's most convenient for you.

•If you live without servants, tell guests what you want them to do—pack the picnic lunch, bring in firewood. You'll resent them if they're having fun and you're not.

•Don't let food preparation become a chore. Plan ahead to have options if you decide to spend the afternoon on the boat instead of in the kitchen. Have a dish you can pull out of the freezer, or a fish or chicken that will cook by itself in the oven or crockpot and maybe yield leftovers for other meals.

•Involve guests in preparation and cleanup. If guests volunteer to bring a house gift, ask for food. If guests have special diets that vary radically from your own, give them the responsibility for supplying and preparing their own food.

•Give guests a kitchen tour and coffee-making instructions so they can fend for themselves when they wake up.

•Present your own fixed responsibilities and activities. Don't be embarrassed to do something without your guests.

•Present optional activities for everyone. Mention anything you expect them to participate in. Discuss availability of transportation facilities and other amenities.

•Set up a way to communicate changes in schedules and important information (a corkboard for messages, an answering machine, etc.).

•Encourage independence. Supply maps, guidebooks, extra keys. And provide alarm clocks, local newspapers, extra bicycles.

Putting Off Unwanted Guests

Favorite ploys of city dwellers who don't want to put up all the out-of-town relatives and friends who invite themselves: "We'd love to have you, but..."

•The apartment is being painted.

•We will be out of town ourselves.

•The house is full of flu.

•My mother-in-law is visiting.

•The elevator is out of order.

•The furnace is broken and we have no heat or hot water (winter version).

•The air conditioning is out, and you know how hot and humid it gets here (summer version).

How to Make a Party A Work of Art

•Serve only one kind of hors d'oeuvre on each serving tray. Guests shouldn't have to stop their conversations to make decisions about food.

•Don't overload hors d'oeuvres on your trays. Space them elegantly, and garnish the trays with attractive combinations of flowers, vegetables, greenery, or laces and ribbons.

•Small bouquets of flowers and greenery tied with a satin ribbon make a convenient decoration that can easily be removed and replaced in the kitchen as trays are returned to be refilled.

•A layer of curly green parsley makes a good bed for hors d'oeuvres such as stuffed grape leaves, which have a hard time standing up by themselves. Parsley also makes a good bed for somewhat greasy hors d'oeuvres.

•Don't limit yourself to conventional equipment. Woven baskets, wood trays, colored glassware, lacquered trays, an unusual set of pudding molds—anything beautiful can be put to use for serving hors d'oeuvres.

•Heavy glassware is a good idea at an outdoor party. Unusual glasses (such as colored Depression glass) make drinks interesting, as do offbeat combinations of glassware and drinks (using long-stemmed wine glasses for mixed drinks, for instance).

•Lights should be soft but not dim. Abundant candlelight or tiny electric spots can be very effective.

Surviving the Cocktail Party Game

You can't avoid cocktail parties? How can you survive them? *Five tips:*

•If possible, attend with someone sociable and loquacious who will stand at your side and banter with passers-by as you think about tomorrow's headlines.

•Pick one interesting person, someone who seems to be eyeing the clock as longingly as you, and spend the next half hour getting to know that person as though you two were alone in the world. If you choose well, time will fly.

•Act as you would if the party were in your honor. Introduce yourself to everyone, and ask them about themselves head-on. People will be profoundly grateful for your initiative. They don't call you overbearing—they call you charming.

•Tell the host you have an injured leg. Then commandeer a comfortable chair and let people come to you. (They'll be glad for an excuse to sit down.) If no one does, find an oversized art book to browse through, or indulge in a few fantasies.

•Help the host. You'd be amazed at how overwhelmed a party giver can be and how many small tasks need doing—even with hired help. You can pass the hors d'oeuvres, hang up coats, refresh the ice buckets and generally free the host for socializing. What's in it for you? A chance to move around (some call it "working the room"), the gratitude of your host and a nice feeling of usefulness.

Source: Letty Cottin Pogrebin, writer and editor.

Hot Tub Etiquette

•Take a towel.

•If it's daytime and the tub is outdoors, you might want sunglasses.

•If you're ambivalent about dress (or undress), take your cue from the host or hostess. It's like avoiding the awkwardness of using the wrong fork at a dinner party. Nudity works best with everyone doing the same thing, too.

•Nonchalance is absolutely de rigueur—a combination of Japanese politeness and California cool is recommended.

•Sustain the mood by maintaining eye contact with members of the opposite sex, especially when they are getting in and out of the tub.

•If you think it's getting too hot, speak up. Better still, get out.

Great Party Themes

•A Raj ball with decor, food, music, and costumes out of India.

•A Venetian masked ball, where the guests dress formally and vie for the best and most elaborate masks.

•A night in Montmartre, with red, white and French blue decorations, wine, can-can dancers, and costumes from the Paris Left Bank.

•A Sunset Boulevard party: Decor and costumes are Hollywood, 1930s and 1940s vintage.

•A Kentucky Derby party around a TV set, with mint juleps and a betting pool.

•A speakeasy party: A password gets you in, the men wear wing collars, the liquor is drunk from cups, and hoods carry violin cases.

•A Wild West party: Dress is cowboys and cowgirls, and the room looks like an old saloon.

•An Old Customs House party: The invitations are in the form of passports, and guests wear costumes from their country of origin.

•A patriotic party: Guests wear red, white and blue, and there must be fireworks.

•A Mexican party with strolling musicians, waterfalls and Mexican food and drink.

•A Moroccan dinner where guests sit on low pillows, eat roast lamb and couscous with their fingers and watch belly dancers.

•A bal blanc with balalaikas for music, an ice-palace decor, Russian food and vodka.

•A New Orleans jazz party with hot music and Creole food.

•A Viennese waltz party: The music reflects the theme and guests dress appropriately.

•A physical-fitness party: Hold it in a health club, and let guests work out, then eat a healthful meal.

•Celebrity look-alike party: Guests dress as famous people from the past or present and try to guess each other's identities.

Source: Sheelagh Dunn, associate, Gustavus Ober Associates, New York 10021, a public relations firm that specializes in business parties.

Parties on Cruise Ships

If you want to impress your friends, invite them to the ship for a bon voyage party. It can be quite elegant but remain inexpensive.

•Make all the arrangements through the shipping company.

•The ship will usually supply setups, soda and hors d'oeuvres at a very modest price.

•Expect to bring your own liquor when the ship is in port, but you can easily buy a few bottles from a local liquor store and take them aboard.

•The steward can serve drinks and other items to your guests in your cabin.

•If your crowd is large enough, ask for a section of one of the public rooms.

•Play expansive host by holding nightly parties while cruising, and it won't be too costly. The ship's staff will help you with parties in your room or in a public room at a fraction of the cost of a party in a hotel ashore. You also usually get the service of waiters and bartenders at no cost (but you provide the tips).

Overcoming Dinner Party Jitters

•Define the goals of this dinner party. The main purpose may be to establish a professional connection or to bring together two people likely to be attracted to each other.

•Eliminate anxieties by verbalizing them. Ask your spouse or a close friend to listen while you describe your worst fears. Once verbalized, the actual possibilities will appear less of a problem than when they were vague apprehensions.

•Specify that the invitation is for dinner. It's not enough to say that you are having a get-together at 7:30.

•Let people know about dress—casual, nice but not formal, formal but not black tie.

•While phoning, mention one or two of the other guests, what they do and, if possible, what they are interested in. If a guest is bringing a friend, don't hesitate to ask something about the friend.

•Do not serve a dish you have never prepared before. Guests will enjoy what you prepare best.

•Have everything ready at least an hour before the party. Take a relaxing warm bath or shower. Allow extra time to dress and make up, and give yourself an additional 20 minutes to sit quietly.

•Arrange to be free from the kitchen when the first two or three guests arrive. They need the host's help to start up conversation.

• *For the single host:* Reduce last-minute anxieties by inviting a close friend to come over early, test the food and look over the arrangements.

Source: *Situational Anxiety* by Herbert J. Freudenberger and Gail North, coauthors, Anchor Press, Doubleday & Co., Garden City, NY.

Party Size

The kind of entertaining you do depends on the length of your guest list and the dimensions of your house.

•For 10 or fewer people, a sit-down dinner is appropriate.

•For 25, a buffet is usually better.

•An open house—usually 1-4 p.m. or 3-6 p.m.—can accommodate more people. If your rooms for entertaining hold 90 to 100 people for a party, you can invite as many as 250 to an open house. *Trick:* Stagger the hours you put on the invitations.

•To entertain several disparate groups—family, business associates and/or social friends—consider giving separate parties on succeeding nights. It takes stamina, but it does save effort and expense. You buy one order of flowers and greens for decorating the house. You assemble serving dishes and extra glasses (borrowed or rented) just once. You arrange furniture one time only. And you can consolidate food, ice, and liquor orders, which, in bulk, can save money. Extra food from the first party can be served at the second.

•Remove some furniture—occasional chairs and large tables—to give you space and keep guests moving. Clear out a den or downstairs bedroom, and set up a food table or bar to attract guests to that room, too. If you have a pair of sofas facing each other in front of a fireplace, open them out so guests can easily walk around them. Use a bedroom or other out-of-the-way place for coats. (You can rent collapsible coat racks, hangers included.)

•Set up different foods at different parts of the party area. If you have open bars, put different drink makings at each set-up. A group drinking a variety of cocktails will not be able to congregate for refills in the same place.

•To avoid bottlenecks: Don't put a bar or buffet table in a narrow hall, for example, or at the back of a tiny room.

•To make the most of a small space, have waiters to take drink orders and a bartender to fill the orders in the kitchen or pantry. Waiters can also pass the hors d'oeuvres in tight quarters, saving the clustering at a food table.

•Count on seven hors d'oeuvres or canapes per person. Stick to finger foods. You'll want a variety of 8 to 10 canapes, but pass each separately, starting with the cold foods and bringing out the hot dishes later.

•For long parties where a turnover of guests is likely, arrange two cycles of passing food, so the later guests get the same fresh selections as the earlier guests.

•Figure that a 40-pound bag of ice will provide enough cubes for 50 people. Get more if you are also chilling wine.

•Use a bathtub to keep the ice in. (No matter what kind of holder you devise for ice, the container will sweat and you'll have a puddle.)

A bathtub full of ice and chilling champagne can be a festive sight by itself. Or, you can decant from the tub to smaller ice chests for each bar. If the nearest bathtub is too far from the party area, buy a plastic garbage can to hold the major supply.

Source: John Clancy, chef, teacher, restaurateur and author of several cookbooks.

Hiring Help for a Party

•The ideal ratio is one tray carrier for every 10 guests.

•Two or three extra kitchen workers are sufficient.

•One extra person can tend bar for up to 30 to 40 guests.

•In the kitchen, set out a prototype of each hors d'oeuvre, and expect your helpers to make exact replicas.

•Servers should be neat and pleasant and should avoid conversing with guests.

•Serving people are responsible for maintenance—keeping the party attractive. Provide lots of ashtrays (if you permit smoking), and make sure servers are told to empty them frequently.

•Avoid hors d'oeuvres that lead to messy leftovers (for example, shrimp tails or skewered foods) if you don't have enough people to clean up after your guests.

•If you expect a caterer, empty the refrigerator and clear all kitchen surfaces. In an office, make sure all desks are cleared. Food should be prepared well in advance and, when possible, frozen.

•Stock wine and liquor a day or two ahead of time.

•Flowers and decorations should be in place two hours before the party.

Source: Martha Stewart, the coauthor of *Entertaining* and author of *Quick Cook* and *Martha Stewart's Hors d'Oeuvres*, all published by Clarkson-Potter, a division of Crown Books, New York.

How to Enjoy Holiday Entertaining

Although everyone is supposed to look forward to the holidays, they can be a season of great strain, especially for those who are entertaining. *To minimize the strain:*

•Include nonfamily in your invitations. *Reason:* Everyone is then on "party manners." Snide comments, teasing or rivalries are held back. This is not the time for letting it all hang out.

•Accept help. Encourage your family and friends not only to make their favorite or best dish but to be totally responsible for it—heating or freezing or unmolding and serving. Meals then become a participatory event, rather than one or two people doing all the work and the rest feeling guilty or, worse still, awkwardly attempting to help. (The one who hates to cook can supply the wine or champagne.)

•Let the table itself set a mood of fun, not formality. Use place cards wisely and make them amusing with motifs appropriate for each guest, rather than names. Or, let one of the younger children make them with a sketch of each guest or hand lettering. Set them out with forethought. Make sure a particularly squirmy youngster is nowhere near an aunt known for her fussy table manners. If there are to be helpers, seat them so they can get up and down with ease. Put the famous spiller where the disaster can be readily cleaned up. If the light is uneven, seat the older people in the brightest section.

•Put everyone around a table. It creates a warmer, more shared meal than does a buffet, and it's amazing how tables can expand. *Hint:* Use desk or rental chairs, which are much slimmer than dining chairs. (Avoid benches for older folks.)

•Borrowing and lending furniture, such as tables, can help you to find room for everyone. It doesn't matter if the setup is not symmetrical or everything doesn't match. A ping-pong table covered with pretty new sheets can provide plenty of room, or you can have tables jutting into hallways or living rooms.

•Have some after-dinner games ready. Ping-pong, backgammon, chess and cards are among the favorites. You may want to buy the latest "in" game or a new word game.

•Bringing out old family albums can be fun.

•Gift exchanging is really a potential hazard. Children, especially, can grump all day if something they expected hasn't been forthcoming. Grandparents often ask what is wanted, but they may be unable to do the actual buying. Do it for them. A check is not a fun package to open. If you want to be sure no one overspends, set a limit. Or set a theme. Or rule out gifts altogether, except for the children.

Source: Florence Janovic, writer and marketing consultant.

Planning a Big Family Reunion

Because a reunion brings together people of all ages, it presents special challenges. *To make your party more enjoyable for everyone:*

•Infants and toddlers. Parents will appreciate a place to change diapers and a quiet room for naps and nursing. Let them know if you can provide high chairs, cribs, safety gates or playpens. *Toys:* A box of safe kitchen equipment. *Food suggestions:* Mild cheese, bananas, crackers, fresh bread or rolls.

•Preschool children. Set aside a playroom. *Best toys:* Balloons, bubbles and crayons. Pay an older cousin or neighborhood teen to baby-sit.

•School-age children. A den or basement room and board games, felt pens and coloring books will keep them happy. Put them in charge of setting and decorating a children's dining table.

•Teenagers. Most teenagers find family reunions boring. For those who have to come, provide a room with a stereo, video games, and radio. Teenagers may be shy around relatives they don't know. When they come out of hiding, give them tasks that encourage their involvement with others, such as helping out grandparents.

•Older folks. They need comfortable chairs where they can hear and see what's going on without being in the way. Some may also need easy access to a bathroom and a place to rest or go to bed early. *Food considerations:* Ask if anyone needs a low-salt, low-cholesterol or special diabetic diet. Spicy foods are probably out.

•Make travel arrangements for those who can't drive so they don't worry about inconveniencing others.

•Now that you've seen to individual needs, how do you bring everyone together? *Common denominator:* Family ties. Make an updated family tree and display it in a prominent place. If you have an instant camera, take pictures as people arrive and mount them on the appropriate branch of the tree. *Special:* Ask everyone to bring contributions to a family museum. *Suitable objects:* Old photographs, family letters, heirlooms, written family histories, old family recipes. After dinner, gather around the fire and exchange family anecdotes. You may wish to record them.

Source: *Unplug the Christmas Machine: How to Give Your Family the Simple Joys of Christmas* by Jo Robinson and Jean Staeheli, co-authors, Morrow, New York.

Self-Indulgent Ideas For New Year's Eve

•Get away to a country inn and enjoy a peaceful respite away from home with your spouse.

•Have a white-tie party in your home, complete with champagne, caviar, an elegant menu, your stored wedding-present silver serving dishes and crystal and your fanciest table linens.

•Rent a batch of old movies for good friends to share throughout the night. Serve beer, popcorn and pretzels.

•Plan a dinner for people you haven't seen in at least five years and catch up on old times.

•Charter a yacht for a lavish but intimate supper-dance.

•Hire an artist to document your New Year's party with sketches.

•Run an ethnic party—French, Italian, etc.—with appropriate food, wine, music, and dress.

•Go to a ski resort for the weekend to enjoy the bracing air, good athletic activities and grog.

•Run a masked ball, complete with fancy dress costumes and prizes for the best. Have plenty of room for dancing and include at least one waltz.

•Have a wine-tasting party for a group of appreciative friends. Or, design a meal around special vintages from your own cellar that you want to share with some fellow wine lovers.

•Have a country party with a caller and musicians for square-dancing.

•Take a group to Atlantic City or Las Vegas and gamble the evening away.

•Organize a literary evening. Let each person recite or read from his or her favorite works. Or pick a favorite play and do a reading, with each guest taking a role.

•Invite close business associates for dinner to discuss the coming trends for the next 12 months—in business and in national and international politics.

Holiday Shopping

Those wonderful but tiring gift-buying chores can be relatively painless with organization.

•Know what you're looking for. Browse through mail-order catalogs and department store catalogs before you go out.

•Shop during the early morning or at dinnertime, when stores are least crowded.

•Shop by yourself. One person travels more efficiently than two.

•Wear comfortable shoes.

•If it will be a long tour with lengthy stops at several stores, leave your heavy winter coat in the car.

•Write the names of recipients on the sales slips and save them. They may come in handy for exchanges.

•Keep a list of what you give to whom, so you won't buy duplicate presents next year.

Guidelines for Christmas Tipping

•Newspaper deliverer: $5 to $10.

•Garbagemen: $5 to $10 each if it is legal in your community; a bottle of liquor or fancy foodstuffs are an alternative.

•Mailmen: While it is technically illegal to tip the postman, many people give $5 to $10 to their regular carrier.

•Deliverymen: $10 per person for those who come regularly to your house, like the dry cleaner, the milkman or even your United Parcel Service man, if you get a lot of packages.

•Baby-sitter: A record or a book for a regular teenage sitter; a bottle of perfume or $10 to $15 for an adult.

*For apartment dwellers:**

•Superintendent: $25 to $50.

•Doorman: $15 to $25.

•Elevator operator: $15 to $25.

•Concierge: $20 to $25.

•Handyman: $20.

•Porter: $15.

•Garage attendant: $15 to $20.

Outside the home:

•Restaurants where you are a regular customer: Maitre d', $20 to $40. Bartender, $10 to $15. Captain, waiter, busboy: Divide the average cost of a meal among the three of them.

•Beauty salon or barber shop: Give the owner-operator a bottle of wine or a basket of fruit. For employees who regularly attend you, $15 to $25.

•Butcher: $10 to $15 for regular good service.

•Tailor or seamstress: $10 or wine or perfume.

*If your building establishes a pool for tips that is divided among employees, you need only give an additional amount to those service people who have gone way beyond the call of duty for you this year.

How to Get Attention For Your Favorite Charity Event

•Hire skywriters to spread the message.

•Take a full-page advertisement in the local newspaper or advertise over a local cable TV station.

•Commission an artist to design a lithograph for the event.

•Have the mayor declare a special day and read a message from City Hall.

•Get a letter of congratulations from the President of the United States...or from the Governor of your state...or Senator...or Congressman.

•Run a special supplement of the event in your local Sunday newspaper.

•Videotape the event as news and offer it to your local TV station.

•Have special funny money printed with your face and message on it to give out as a token of the special event.

•Hire a marching band and have a parade.

•Arrange for displays of the event in the windows of local stores.

•Have cases of wine imprinted with a private label to mark the event.

•Have a special sandwich or dish named in honor of the event on the menu at a major restaurant.

•Have an automobile or train named in honor of the event.

•Hire the huge local stadium or concert hall.

•Have a street renamed for the day.

•Float specially designed and painted balloons all over town with the message you want to relay.

•Underwrite a special event—tennis, golf, marathon, polo, etc.

•Have the post office issue a stamp in your name. If this is not possible, print stamps designed by a major artist and have them affixed to all correspondence.

•Have a race horse named in honor of the event.

How to Really Appreciate Movies

If you really want to appreciate movies, stray a little from the heavily beaten track. There are a number of good critics in small or specialized magazines who can alert you to fine—and unusual—new films, as well as notable revivals.

Movie buffs typically go through three stages in their appreciation of films:

•First, they find movies awe-inspiring magic.

•Second, they begin to realize those are actors up there and that all kinds of technology are involved. In this stage, which some people never leave, they become "fans." Many fans don't care about movies—they're just interested in following their favorite actors.

•Third, they realize movies aren't magic, that it may be a miracle they ever get made, but that they're a human achievement that also happens to be marvelous. At this stage they can start to look at movies critically.

To get the maximum enjoyment from movies:

•Watch a lot of them. Make a special effort to see foreign films. You'll begin to see what's original and fresh and what's stereotyped.

•Learn about movie forms and genres and the unique visual language of cinema.

•Read, follow other art forms. Read about psychology, politics, history and other branches of knowledge.

•Avoid the rush. Don't dash off to see the latest blockbuster. It'll be around a while. See a film more likely to close soon, even though it was well-reviewed.

•Watch movies on cable TV and on cassettes. Both these forms have done a lot to make film scholarship possible and good movies accessible.

•Go to foreign films. More than a few are worth seeing, but most people aren't interested in them anymore. In the past, the "ooh-la-la" factor drew viewers. But now that American films are no longer censored, foreign films have lost their cachet.

Source: Andrew Sarris, film critic for New York's *Village Voice*, a professor of cinema at Columbia University, and author of *The American Cinema: Directors and Directions*, Octagon Press, New York, and *Politics and Cinema*, Columbia University Press, Irvington, NY.

Traps in Casino Gambling

Casino gambling can be high-risk entertainment, if you're not careful. *Avoid these common casino mistakes:*

•Making "flat bets"—wagering the same amount each time. Since the odds are against you, your progress will soon resemble a sales chart in a recession...peaks and valleys, but down in the long run.

•Trying to get even by chasing losses with meal money...or the next month's rent. It's a big mistake to dig into your pocket after your stake is gone. You can't outspend the casinos.

•Flitting from craps to baccarat to the slots. It's better to stick with one game until you're comfortable.

•Taking too many long-shot bets (such as "proposition" bets in craps). They generally offer the worst odds.

•Staying at a "cold" table too long. If a new dealer is giving you terrible cards, or there's a loudmouth across the table, or you don't like the smell of your neighbor's cigar, move on. The problem may be purely psychological, but it can throw off your game nonetheless.

•Accepting complimentary alcohol. When you drink too much you start making irrational "hunch" bets, and you get frivolous with your money.

•Playing when tired. The casino may stay open till 4 a.m., but you don't have to close the casino. Stick to your normal weekend hours.

•Getting caught up in the casino mentality. When everyone refers to $5 as a "nickel" and $25 as a "quarter," it's easy to treat money like plastic. Never forget that it's real money. Stick to your basic units and progressions.

•Viewing the dealer as a shark who's out to get you. At worst, the dealer is a mechanical device. At best, he can be your ally. *Example:* In a hot craps game, he may remind you when to take a bet down. To keep him on your side, don't forget to tip. (Dealers make two thirds of their income from tips.) *Tactic:* It's more effective to bet $1 for the dealer (giving him a stake in your game) than to give him $10 when you leave.

•Celebrating prematurely. Be happy when you win, but don't brag about it. You don't want to advertise that you're carrying a lot of money. And...don't play with a huge pile of chips in front of you. If you hit it big, convert to larger denominations, and put them in your pocket. (For safety, use the casino's valet parking. With a validated ticket it will cost you only a tip, and it's far better than walking three blocks to your car.)

•Forgetting what you came for. Take in a floor show and enjoy a good meal. If you lose at the tables, write it off as entertainment. If you're not a professional, that's the whole point of visiting a casino...to have a good time.

Source: Lee Pantano, a professional gambler, teacher, consultant, and editor of *Gamblegram*, Atlantic Highlands, NJ.

Winning at Poker

Not so many years ago, every poker book told you the same thing: Play tight (fold bad hands). This is still good advice, as far as it goes. *But there are other tactics to keep in mind:*

•Be selective but aggressive. Ideally, you should end a hand by either folding or raising. Avoid calling bets with vulnerable hands, such as two pair.

•To own the table psychologically, so that other players are glancing at you every time they make a bet, be friendly, but at the same time confusing and unpredictable.

•Never gloat. You want your opponents to enjoy trying to beat you.

•In a low-to-moderate-limit game, you can win without mathematical genius or brilliant originality. Most of your profit will come from your opponents' mistakes. *Their chief error:* Calling for too many pots with mediocre hands.

•Bluffing is a poor strategy in a low-stakes game. Unsophisticated opponents won't even understand your intended deception. Second, they're likely to call you anyway, a habit you want to encourage. Try a strategic bluff just once, early in the session, as an "advertisement."

•Discipline is especially crucial in a low-limit game, when you need more hands to make up losses.

•Decide in advance how you will react in each of various situations. Never play a hand out of impatience or on a "hunch." Play it for a good reason.

•Monitor yourself carefully. If you make a mistake, admit it to yourself and get back on track. Don't let one bad play erode your entire system.

•Don't look for immediate revenge after an opponent burns you on a big pot. If you force the action, you're apt to get burned again.

•Stay later when you're ahead and leave early when behind. When you're losing, you lose psychological control of the game, too. Opponents try to bluff you out of pots and are less likely to call your good hands.

•Watch for and learn to read opponents' "tells"—the mannerisms they fall into that tend to give away whether their hands are good or bad. *In general, follow the rule of opposites:* Players usually act weak when their hands are strong, and they commonly act strong when their hands are weak.

•Look for reasons to fold just as eagerly as you look for reasons to call.

Source: Mike Caro, a gambling teacher and columnist for *Gambling Times* and, according to world poker champion Doyle Brunson, the best draw poker player alive. He is also the author of *Caro on Gambling*, published by Gambling Times, Hollywood, CA.

Successful Poker: Reading Your Opponents

Bluffers generally:

•Breathe shallowly or hold their breath.

•Stare at their hands—or at you as you prepare to bet.

•Reach for chips out of turn.

•Bet with an authoritative pronouncement.

•Fling chips into the pot with an outstretched forearm.

•Show unusual friendliness toward opponents.

Players with powerful hands:

•Share a hand with a bystander (especially a spouse).

•Shake noticeably while making a bet. (This reflects a release of tension. Most players show obvious outward nervousness only when they feel they're in little danger.)

•Talk easily and naturally.

•Behave in an unusually gruff manner toward opponents.

•Lean forward in their seat.

•Bet with a sigh, shrug, or negative tone of voice.

•Ask, "How much is it to me?" or request another clarification.

•Glance quickly at the player's chips after receiving a (good) card.

Source: Mike Caro, author of *Mike Caro's Book of Tells—The Body Language of Poker*, published by Gambling Times, Hollywood, CA.

Darts: Tips from a Champ

•Start off with a set of three brass darts with a one-piece plastic shaft and flight. Brass darts are big and easy to handle. They're also the most durable. As you throw more, the dart will feel lighter.

•As your game improves, you'll want to buy tungsten darts. The darts are heavier, narrower, and a little harder to control.

•Buy a pressed bristle board. When you remove a dart from this material, it doesn't leave an indentation. Cork or wood boards are cheaper, but they'll disintegrate with heavy play.

•To play well, you need eye-hand coordination, good concentration and good balance. Keep your head still so that your eyes stay on the target.

•When throwing darts, use your forearm, not your entire body. (It's like hammering a nail.)

•Stay loose and fluid on the follow-through movement after the dart leaves your hand. If you jerk your arm back, the dart won't reach the board.

•Most newcomers to the game overthrow to the left of the target. You can start by aiming a little to the right, but that's not a long-term cure. You must see the pattern of your throw and move accordingly on the toe line.

• *Strategy:* The two most important targets are the triple 20 and the outer double ring.

• *Basic courtesy:* Shake hands before and after play.

• Take your darts out of the board promptly.

• Be quiet when someone else is shooting.

Source: Nick Marzigliano, singles champion of the Brooklyn (NY) Dart League.

Contest Winners: Secrets of Success

Cash, vacations, houses, cars, electronic equipment, cameras and much, much more are the dream prizes that keep millions of Americans doggedly filling out entry blanks for contests. More than $100 million worth of prize money and goods are dispensed annually through an estimated 500 promotional competitions and drawings.

Dedicated hobbyists know that there is an advantage of a planned approach to overcome the heavy odds against each entrant.

Here are some winning strategies:

• Use your talents. If you can write, cook or take photographs, put your energy into entering contests rather than sweepstakes. Contests take skill, so fewer people are likely to compete...improving your chances. Photography contests have the fewest average entries.

• Follow the rules precisely. If the instructions say to print your name, don't write it in longhand. If a three-inch by five-inch piece of paper is called for, measure your entry exactly. The slightest variation can disqualify you.

• Enter often. Always be on the lookout for new sweepstakes and contests to enter. *Sources:* Magazines, newspapers, radio, television, store shelves and bulletin boards, product packaging.

• Make multiple entries. The more entries you send in, the more you tip the odds in your favor.

• *For large sweepstakes:* Spread out your entries over the length of the contest—one a week for five weeks, for example. When the volume of entries is big enough, they will be delivered to the judges in a number of different sacks. The theory is that judges will pick from each sack, and your chances go up if you have an entry in each of several different mailbags.

• Keep informed. Join a local contest club or subscribe to a contest newsletter. Either source will help you to learn contest traps and problems—and solutions. They'll alert you, too, to new competitions.

• Be selective. You must pay taxes on items that you win, so be sure the prizes are appropriate for you. If you don't live near the water, winning an expensive boat could be a headache. (Some contests offer cash equivalents, but not all do.)

• If you do win, check with your CPA or tax lawyer immediately. You must report the fair market value of items that you win, whether you keep them, sell them or give them away. This can be tricky. Also, if you win, you can deduct the expenses of postage, stationery, etc. that you have used to enter this and other sweepstakes and contests in the same year. These costs are not deductible if you don't win.

• Most contests and sweepstakes ask you to enclose some proof of purchase or a plain piece of paper with a product name or number written on it. Many people assume that a real proof of purchase will improve their chances of winning. *Fact:* In a recent survey, more than half the winners of major prizes reported that they had not bought the sponsor's product.

Source: Roger Tyndall, coeditor with his wife, Carolyn, of the newsletter *Contest Newsletter*, Fern Beach, FL.

Reluctant Vacationers

Not everyone loves to get away from it all on a vacation. Some people really prefer to work. But families need vacations, and so do workaholics occasionally.

How to take yourself away from the office successfully:

• Make vacations somewhat similar to your year-round life, so that they offer continuity as well as contrast. If you enjoy a daily swim at the gym, be sure to pick a vacation stop with a pool. If you never step into art museums at home, don't feel you have to drag yourself to them when you're away.

•Leave your calculator, beeper, dictating device and briefcase at home.

•Avoid finishing lots of work at the last minute. It can leave you feeling frantic.

•Don't drive your staff crazy by leaving lots of lists and memos or calling continually. Limit yourself to two calls the first day and one a day thereafter.

•Take enough time off to recharge your energy. Two weeks may feel too long, but three days is too short.

Source: Dr. Marilyn Machlowitz, a New York organizational psychologist and consultant.

Don't Let Your Vacation Home Cut into Your Leisure Time

The most desirable thing to look for in a weekend house is ease of maintenance.

•Get rid of rugs in the summer.

•Ask the landlord to remove his accumulations of dustcatching peacock feathers and other decorator touches.

Keep your own importations to a minimum.

•Cut down on weekend cleaning chores and outdoor work with hired help.

•Consider expanding leisure time by commuting with the laundry. That's cumbersome, but better than hours in a laundromat on a sunny afternoon.

•Cultivate the fine art of list-making. Shopping and menu planning can be almost painless if the list is done right.

•If you're planning a Saturday dinner party, don't rely on the local supermarket for the perfect roast unless you've ordered (and confirmed) in advance. The accompanying wines might be better purchased at home, too, unless you're sure of your local supplier.

•Don't forget to take the same precautions as you would for a trip—extra reading glasses and copies of prescriptions might save you an unwanted journey home.

Fishing a New Lake

If you know where to start looking, you can fish any lake successfully.

Where bass congregate:

•Near trees that have recently fallen into the water.

•*In hot weather:* Under lily pads, especially in the only shallow spots around.

•*In consistently mild weather:* In backwater ponds and coves off the main lake. *Best:* Good weed or brush cover, with a creek running in.

•*Any time at all:* In sunken moss beds near the shore.

Source: *Outdoor Life.*

Portrait Photography Secrets

People are the most popular subject for photography. There are ways to turn snapshots of family and friends into memorable portraits. *Techniques:*

•Get close. Too much landscape overwhelms the subject.

•Keep the head high in the frame as you compose the shot. Particularly from a distance, centering the head leaves too much blank background and cuts off the body arbitrarily.

•Avoid straight rows of heads in group shots. It's better to have some subjects stand and others sit in a two-level setting.

•Pose subjects in natural situations, doing what they like to do—petting the cat, playing the piano, etc.

•Simplify backgrounds. Try using a large aperture (small f-stop number) to throw the background out of focus and highlight the subject.

•Beware of harsh shadows. The human eye accommodates greater contrast of light to dark than does a photographic system. Either shadows or highlights will be lost in the picture, usually the shadowed area.

For outdoor portraits:

•Avoid the midday sun. This light produces harsh shadows and makes people squint. Hazy sun, often found in the morning, is good. Cloudy days give a lovely, soft effect.

•Use fill light to cut shadows. A flash can be used outdoors, but it is hard to compute correctly. *Best fill-light method:* Ask someone to hold a large white card or white cloth near the subject to bounce the natural light into the shadowed area.

•Use backlight. When the sun is behind the subject (but out of the picture), the face receives a soft light. With a simple camera, the cloudy setting is correct. If your camera has a light meter, take a reading close to the subject or, from a distance, increase the exposure one or two stops from what the meter indicates.

•Beware of dappled shade. The effect created in the photograph will be disturbing.

For indoor portraits:

•Use window light. A bright window out of direct sun is a good choice. However, if there is high contrast between the window light and the rest of the room, use filter-light techniques to diminish the shadow.

•Use flashbulbs. A unit with a tilting head lets you light the subject by bouncing the flash off the ceiling, creating a wonderful diffuse top lighting. (This won't work with high, dark or colored ceilings.)

•Mix direct light and bounce flash. An easy way to put twinkle in the eyes and lighten shadows when using bounce light is to add a little direct light. With the flash head pointed up, a small white card attached to the back of the flash will send light straight on to the subject.

•Keep a group an even distance from the flash. Otherwise, the people in the back row will be dim, while those in front may even be over exposed.

Making New Year's Eve A Family or Neighborhood Affair

•Invite close relatives to spend the evening reminiscing and becoming a family again. Organize a slide show of old family photographs or show home movies to break the ice.

•If you are a runner, do an evening five miles with running friends and then see the new year in with a pasta feast. (New Yorkers can run in or watch a mini-marathon in Central Park, with fireworks at the finish line at midnight. Check for similar events in other cities.)

•Rent the local high-school auditorium and sponsor a band concert for the community. Or organize your own band with fellow musicians.

•Have a bake-in in your kitchen, with prizes for the best chocolate desserts.

•Have a multigenerational party for your whole family and friends of all ages.

•Spend New Year's Eve taking down holiday decorations, finishing your thank-you notes for holiday gifts, and otherwise cleaning the slate for the coming year.

•With your mate, make a list of do's and don'ts and resolutions for the new year.

•Organize a neighborhood "progressive dinner" with a different course in each house. Watch the time so you get to the last stop and the champagne by midnight.

•Rent a skating rink—ice or roller—for a big, many-family party with an instructor or two to get the fainthearted going smoothly.

How to Solve Caterer Problems Before They Arise

•The ideal way to select a caterer is to attend one of his or her parties.

•If that's not possible, ask for recommendations from your most trusted and sophisticated friends and acquaintances.

•Another source of information is gourmet magazines. Local publications often write articles about caterers, too.

•Many caterers provide pamphlets or sample menus, but these are a poor substitute for a solid personal recommendation.

•Try, if at all possible, to sample the food each caterer offers. Keep in mind, however, the kind of party you are planning. Someone who prepares exquisite nouvelle cuisine may not be the best person to cater a large outdoor barbecue.

• When you have the names of a few reputable caterers, meet with each, preferably where the party will take place. Many hosts are distressed by caterers' tendency to "take over" —to dictate all arrangements and ignore the host's concerns. Know your own feelings about this and try to gauge the caterer's willingness to accommodate you.

• Never hire anyone who has a specific number of parties in her repertory and simply "does" party number six at your home. Even if the caterer is to take total control, you want her to approach your party as a unique situation.

• Ask at the beginning of the discussion whether the caterer herself will be present at the actual function. If she plans to send an assistant, meet that person and make sure you have confidence in her abilities.

• Be sure also to discuss clean-up arrangements with the caterer.

• Although most caterers actually only prepare the food and hire the service themselves, they can certainly make arrangements (and take responsibility for them) with liquor stores, florists, musicians, etc. They can also recommend people whom you can contact directly (possibly helping you to cut corners economically). Or, you can come up with your own choices.

• Never hire independent help to serve your caterer's food. After the quality of the food itself, service is probably the most important ingredient in a successful party. Your caterer should work with people she knows and trusts.

• The caterer should draw up a contract that spells out every cost and makes the caterer's list of duties clear.

• You will probably be asked to make a down payment for up to half the total cost.

• The caterer's price is all-inclusive; you are free to tip the staff if you should wish to, but you need not feel obliged to do so.

• The caterer will expect to find the scene of the party clean and ready for her to get started. Your equipment (serving trays, etc.) should be at its sparkling best.

• Now you should stand back and let her do her job. Don't make any last minute additions to the menu or suddenly rearrange the floor plan.

Source: Germaine and Marcel Chandelier, owners and managers of Germaine's, Long Island City, NY.

How to Make Slot Machines Pay Off

• *Key to successful play:* A basic understanding of slot mechanics. In Las Vegas, dollar slot machines return on average 88¢–98¢ per dollar invested. (At the high end, they compare favorably with the odds offered by craps, roulette or any other game.)

These are long-term returns over six hours or six months...depending on the machine. The short-term return for a given player will vary tremendously—but not randomly. Every machine has a pay cycle and a down cycle. During its pay cycle, the machine will give back far more than you put in. It might stay "hot" for a hundred pulls or more, spilling out jackpot after jackpot. (At one machine, I hit a triple-bar jackpot—a $150 to $1 payoff—three times in a row.) But during a machine's cold cycle, you can easily drop $100 in less than an hour.

Finding pay-cycle machines...

• Observe before you play. If you see a player empty $100 or more into a machine (whether or not he hits a few small jackpots along the way) and walk away with nothing, step up and try your luck. There's a good chance the machine is near the end of a down cycle and entering a pay cycle.

• If you play a machine "blind," without prior observation, feel the coins in the tray after your first win. If the money is warm, it's probably been sitting in the machine for a time without a jackpot. *Point:* A down cycle may be ending. If the money is cool, move on.

• Ask a change clerk to steer you to a hot machine...with the unwritten understanding that you'll tip him/her 10% of your winnings on that machine. (Casinos tolerate this because it doesn't affect their overall take.)

•Play machines near casino entrances and exits. The house programs these slots to pay off the best, because their jackpots will attract the most attention. *Also hot:* Any machines near blackjack or other gaming tables. The casino hopes to lure to these machines wives who are watching their husbands play the other games. *Colder:* Machines isolated against the rear wall (and especially in the corners), where jackpots have less advertising value.

•Watch for empty coin racks—coin holders next to each machine used by players to stack coins for play or to hold winnings—and play the machine immediately to the left of one. An empty rack means the previous player busted. (When a player hits a jackpot, the rack is used to cart away the coins.) The more empty racks near a machine, the closer it is to a pay cycle.

•After I gave an extravagant tip, a casino mechanic once told me to look for three-reel machines with a cherry sitting in the middle reel. While worthless in itself, he said, the cherry was a sign that better times were coming. Since then, I've found that 75% of middle cherry machines return at least a small jackpot within five to six pulls. They're also good bets for a pay cycle.

•Your odds are best on single-line, dollar slots. Multiple-line machines offer a greater chance of hitting any jackpot, but the payoffs are much smaller. *Also:* For top value, play the maximum number of coins for each pull.

•"Progressive" slots, where the jackpot can build to $1 million or more, can be wildly profitable, but only if they're within their programmed payoff range.

Example: At the Sands in Las Vegas, a clerk told me (after a big tip) that one progressive machine always paid off when the jackpot reached between $48,000 and $64,000. I found it one night at $59,000 and pumped in $300 before I had to leave town. The next morning, the clerk called to tell me that the machine had been hit at 10 a.m., when its jackpot reached $62,000.

•If you ever see a new machine being uncrated, jump on it. Play it until it bursts. Casinos program new slots to pay particularly well for the first two days so they'll draw more business later.

Source: Dick Phillips, author of *Winning Systems on Slots,* Box 12336, Beaumont, TX 77706.

Secrets of Doing Crossword Puzzles Much Faster

In order to successfully complete a crossword puzzle, follow these helpful hints...

•Start with the fill-in-the-blank clues. These are usually the easiest and the least ambiguous.

•Next, try to fill in an across answer in the top row or a down answer on the left side. You can then proceed to answers that start with a known letter...and they're always easier to solve than answers where the known letter is in the middle.

•In a thematic puzzle, the longest blanks on the grid always relate to the theme.

•When the clue is expressed in the plural, the answer is probably plural. Most clues that are expressed in the past have answers ending in -ed. Most clues that are expressed in the superlative have answers ending in -est.

•Remember that e and s are the most popular word-ending letters. Also, puzzles use a disproportionate number of common letters and very few rare letters, such as q, z, x, j, etc.

•When you are missing one or two letters in a word, scan the alphabet. Plug in all possible letters or combinations...one is bound to work.

Source: David Feldman, author of *How to Win at Just About Everything,* Morrow Quill, William Morrow & Co., 105 Madison Ave., New York 10016.

The Pleasures of Organic Gardening

There really is no need to use chemicals and gasoline-powered machines when gardening or tending to your lawn. Organic methods are just as successful and use only fertilizers and pest controls found in nature. *Advantages:*

• Creates a healthier environment by rebuilding the top soil, protecting ground water and using less energy.

• Produces homegrown, organic (chemical-free) vegetables—fresher and cheaper than the ones you can buy in natural-foods stores or supermarkets.

Organic fertilizers...

While synthetic fertilizers feed the crop, they deplete the soil, then make future crops dependent on continued applications. Organic fertilizers feed the plants and nourish the soil.

All plants need...

• Nitrogen for lush foliage.

Best organic sources: Homemade or bagged compost—decomposed plants or animal wastes rich in nitrogen and other trace minerals. Add up to two inches to each garden bed yearly. *For fast results:* Use blood meal and dried blood (by-products of slaughterhouses), or cottonseed meal (ground from seeds of the cotton plant).

• Phosphorus for flower and seed production.

Best organic source: Colloidal phosphate, a rock powder, also rich in lime and trace minerals. *For fast results:* Try bone meal—it's effective, but more expensive.

• Potash (Potassium) for strong roots and solid branches.

Best organic sources: Granite dust (a rock powder) and greensand (a mineral-rich deep sea deposit). *For fast results:* Try wood ashes left from a wood stove or fireplace.

Important: Soil conditions in your garden—and the specific needs of plants you want to grow—should determine your choice of fertilizer. Your local garden center or the US Department of Agriculture's cooperative extension service can test your soil and recommend the best organic fertilizer for your needs.

Organic pest and weed control...

• *Insecticidal soaps:* Spray every three to five days for about three weeks to eliminate most pests on specific plants or plant groupings.

• *Fabric coverings:* Sheets of very thin-woven polyester or thin-spun polypropylene, sold as "floating" row covers or super-light insect barriers. Use only for vegetable gardens—not for ornamental plants...make sure plants have enough water—high temperatures under the fabric can make them dry...and remove covers over squashes, melons and cucumbers when the flowers start to bloom—in time for pollination.

• *Beneficial insects:* Bugs that kill harmful insects that eat your vegetables or plants. They can be purchased at local garden centers or by mail order.*

• *Mulching:* Cover the earth around each plant or row to deter weeds and conserve water with shredded bark mulch, wood chips, cocoa or buckwheat hulls. (Also use straw and shredded leaves for vegetable plants—but not for ornamentals.) Old mulch decomposes and can be worked into the soil. New mulch is spread after planting.

*Mail-order companies that sell these insects include: Gardens Alive!, 5100 Schenley Pl., Lawrenceburg, IN 47025, 812-537-8650...Gardener's Supply Co., 128 Intervale Rd., Burlington, VT 05401, 802-863-1700.

Source: Bonnie Wodin, Golden Yarrow Landscaping, Heath, Massachusetts 01346, designs custom gardens and landscapes. She also lectures frequently on horticulture and landscaping.

For Very Special Occasions

Here are some very classy, exclusive hotels frequented by those who know the right places to stay when they travel. Make reservations a few months in advance.

• *Malliouhana Hotel in Anguilla, the Caribbean.* On a small little-known island with few tourists. This new hotel is the ultimate in luxury. Suites and private villas are available, some the size of private homes. Tennis courts, boating and all water sports, including scuba instruction, attracts a jet-set crowd of all ages.

• *Baden-Baden in Schwarzwald, Germany.* In the elegant style of a 19th-century spa. Extensive grounds, impeccable service, an excellent restaurant and hot springs where you can "take the waters." Attracts an old world, conservative crowd.

• *Hotel Los Monteros in Marbella, Spain.* On one of the Mediterranean coast's most fashionable stretches. Wide range of sports, spacious rooms and tropical gardens. Has a 1920s charm reminiscent of the Gatsby era. Ask for a room with an ocean view. Attracts all types, from young families to older couples.

• *Hotel San Pietro in Positano, Italy.* Picturesquely perched on top of a cliff, with all 55 double rooms overlooking rocky coast and sea. Scenic beaches. Secluded and elegant, it attracts a young to middle-aged highly sophisticated crowd. Open March 14 through November 3.

• *Mount Kenya Safari Club in Nairobi, Kenya.* A distinguished private retreat located halfway up Mt. Kenya. 100 acres of rolling lawns, waterfalls, gardens, a heated pool, sauna, three dining rooms, and safari excursions for both photography and hunting. Special events such as African barbecues and tribal dances. Dress is formal, with jacket and tie required for dinner. Guests tend to be families, couples and ultra-exclusive tours and groups.

• *Lake Palace in Udaipur, India.* Originally an 18th-century royal residence. Located on an island in the Middle of Lake Pichola, it has air-conditioned rooms, exotic suites, water sports, a marble-inlaid pool, and a restaurant serving Continental and Indian cuisine. Guests are all ages but tend to be very sophisticated.

• *Hotel de Paris in Monaco.* A superior hotel. Has an underground passage to the Casino and Le Club. Palatial rooms and facilities. Spa, sauna, two restaurants and a cabaret. Old money stays here. Frank Sinatra is a regular, and the Prince of Monaco often comes for tea.

• *Voile d'Or Hotel in St-Jean-Cap-Ferrat, France.* Overlooks the harbor. Its spacious, French provincial-style rooms all have balconies and marble baths. A favorite honeymoon spot, the atmosphere breathes intimate elegance. Gourmet cuisine. Open February to October.

• *Splendido Hotel in Portofino, Italy.* A super-deluxe classic hotel on high ground overlooking the sea. Charming rooms, suites, gardens, a seawater pool, sauna and health spa. Attracts all types and ages, including many business-people. Open March 29 to October 29.

Source: Francesca Baldeschi, manager, Ports of Call Travel Consultants, Inc., New York.

Plan for Very Special Trips

If you're the type who finds the sameness of Holiday Inns comforting or prefers to have dinner at McDonald's—in Paris—this checklist isn't for you. But if you love country inns, a pot of coffee brewing in your room, four-poster beds, claw-legged bathtubs, lunch beside a swan pond, discovering the best wine cellar in Vermont or the trail that isn't on a map, then you might want to plan your vacations differently.

• Consult the guidebooks and travel agent last.

• Year round, collect information on all kinds of interesting vacation possibilities.

• Keep geographical files labeled Caribbean, West Coast, The South, New England, Europe, Israel, Japan, and Exotic Places, for example. You can make your own headings and add new folders when the catch-all category gets too full to be manageable.

• Subdivide your files into subject files labeled Ski Vacations, Tennis Vacations, Club Med Locations, Charming Inns/Elegant Small Hotels, Houses for Rent or Exchange and Great Restaurants in Other Places (to distinguish it from your home town restaurant file).

• File articles from airline magazines, newsletters and the travel section of your newspaper.

• Interview friends: When you agree with your friends' taste in food, furnishings, theater or painting, chances are you can trust their vacation advice.

• Talk with neighbors, clients, friends at work.

• Think of exchanging visits with friends you meet on vacation.

• Save picture postcards from active travelers.

• Eavesdrop in an airport or restaurant, on the bus or train to work. If you hear a total stranger describe a perfect meal she had in Kansas City, or a rustic lodge in the Adirondacks with a gorgeous view of the sunset, jot it down. Check out the details later. (That's where guidebooks and travel agents come in handy.)

• Books, movies, magazines. In vacation terms, life can imitate art. You'll want to visit Big Sur if you've read Henry Miller.

Best Uncrowded Resorts In Mexico

For the cheapest prices and probably the most exciting vacations, stay away from well-known, overcrowded resorts like Acapulco and Taxco.

Travelers who know Mexico well say they especially like:

• *Ixtapa,* 150 miles north of Acapulco on the Pacific. Warm, dry and uncrowded, the resort has one of the most luxurious hotels in Mexico, the Ixtapa Camino Real.

• *Merida,* the capital of Yucatan, is old, exotic and cheap. The elegant Montejo Palace costs much more than other hotels. Merida is the takeoff point for excursions to nearby Mayan ruins, where hotels are similarly priced.

• *Oaxaca* is near the site of some of the most beautiful pre-Columbian ruins. A 16th-century convent has been converted into El Presidente hotel.

• *Vera Cruz,* not touted by Mexico's tourist officials, is a picturesque old city on the Gulf of Mexico with some of the best food in the country. The six-hour drive from 7,200-foot-high Mexico City to sea-level Vera Cruz is spectacular. The beachside Mocambo Hotel is reasonably priced.

Offbeat Three-Day Weekends

For an extra-long weekend you will never forget:

• Ballooning. A great way to see the countryside. In most of the US, ballooning trips are available within 100 miles of major cities. You can also take a trip that includes gourmet picnics in France and Austria or wild-game-watching in Kenya.

• Spas. Most spa resorts include massage, aerobics, swimming and succulent diet cuisine, and many feature beauty facilities for facials, pedicures, etc. Spas can be found in Florida, California, Arizona, Texas, New York, New Jersey and Illinois. *A favorite:* World of Palmaire, Pompano Beach, Florida.

• Iceland. Not too far a flight from most northeastern cities, Iceland offers swimming in naturally heated bubbling springs and quick flights to the smaller islands (which the US astronauts used to simulate the lunar surface). Reykjavik, the capital, features great Scandinavian restaurants and shops.

• Tennis ranches. Besides excellent tennis facilities, these ranches usually provide horseback riding and swimming.

• Snowmobiling. Many national parks have snowmobile trails and rental arrangements and lodging is available in cabins or lodges at low, off-season rates.

• Cruise to nowhere. Going (or actually not going) from various East and West Coast cities on a cruise ship can be great fun. All normal shipboard cruise facilities are available for a luxurious weekend.

• Dude ranches. Most prevalent in the West and Southwest. Smaller private ranches and farms that take in guests are homier than the bigger ones. Families are especially welcome. An inexpensive get-away-from-it-all including riding lessons and home cooking.

• Biking tours. You can travel in the Berkshires, the Smokies, or any beautiful countryside.

Source: Carole M. Phillips, CTC, of Certified Travel Consultants, New York.

How to Select A Puppy

The main thing is to buy from a breeder rather than a pet shop. Don't buy a puppy on impulse. *Consider the following points:*

• It's best to see both the pup's parents or their photographs at the breeder (chief reason to buy there rather than at pet store). Not only will you see what the puppy will look like as an adult, you will also be able to judge its genetic inheritance by the health of its parents.

•Buy a puppy at 6 to 12 weeks of age. That's when they make the best adjustment to a new home.

Try these quick and easy visual tests:

•Shine a pocket flashlight at the pup.

•Show it a mirror.

•Roll a ball toward it.

•Wave a sheet of white paper.

•Drag an object along on a string.

Similarly, here are some hearing tests (to be done out of the puppy's sight):

•Blow a police whistle.

•Honk a car horn.

•Clap hands.

•Blow a kazoo or noisemaker.

•Body sensitivity is important in training. Gently pinch the puppy's ear between the ball of the thumb and the forefinger. Then push down its hindquarters, forcing it to sit. A puppy that doesn't react has little body sensitivity and won't feel corrections. A puppy that whines, cowers or runs away is so sensitive that it will fear corrections and be difficult to train.

•Temperament can be tested by seeing the puppy's attitude toward strangers. Jump right in front of the puppy. It should show neither fear nor anger. Surprise followed by friendliness is a good reaction.

Training Your Puppy

Some suggestions:

•Don't encourage a puppy to chew on facsimiles of valued objects. You can't expect it to tell an old shoe from a new one.

•Never place your hand or finger in a puppy's mouth when playing. That biting might seem cute today, but you won't enjoy it a year from now.

•Allow the puppy to climb and jump on you only when you're seated on the floor. If you let it jump on you when you're in a chair, you're teaching it to sit on furniture.

•Never encourage a puppy to bark on command. This can lead to excessive barking and a dog that "talks back."

•Puppies become bored and anxious easily. If you leave your puppy alone too long and too often, you must expect destructive behavior.

•Praise the puppy when it's good. Treat bad behavior with a stern *No* and a shaking or a harsh noisemaker. Physical abuse will teach a dog only fear.

What to Feed Your Dog

Commercial dog foods usually contain parts of an animal that a dog would never eat in the wild. Sometimes these foods include diseased animal parts rejected for human consumption. *To provide your pet a good diet:*

•Feed it table scraps, including meat, vegetables, grains, fruit and even salad.

•Avoid sugars and other sweets, except as treats.

•For variety, mix scraps with a little commercial food. (Buy only products that contain no additives.)

•Give your dog trimmings, tripe, spleen, kidney or liver served raw or partially cooked. (The entrails of a freshly killed animal are the first thing a wild dog eats.)

•Always supplement the diet with minerals and multivitamins, especially vitamins C and E.

Source: Wendell O. Belfield, DVM, author of *How to Have a Healthier Dog,* Doubleday, New York.

Appreciating Autumn

The fall is a season of holidays and rituals. In addition to the harvest, we celebrate Hallowe'en and Thanksgiving. And several religions also celebrate their New Year at this time of year.

Many of our celebrations have ancient roots. Merlin Stone, an historian who specializes in ancient religions, has this to say...

What makes autumn such a special time?

Although autumn is joyous because of the harvest, Hallowe'en and Thanksgiving, it can also be somewhat sad because of the approach of winter. Many people start to feel melancholy as the days grow shorter.

In many religions, fall is a time of judgment. For instance, the Jewish holiday of Yom Kippur is a day of atonement and judgment. The Jewish New Year, Rosh Hashana, also arrives in the fall.

Isn't it unusual, having a new year in the fall?

Although the Jewish New Year is now one of the few that comes in the fall, it wasn't always so.

The pagan new year was once in the fall. The Akkadians, an ancient Semitic people, also celebrated their new year in the fall.

Are there any other similarities between these holidays?

In the Sumerian religion, the new year marked the annual judgment of the people according to the laws of the goddess Nanshe, who dates back at least 5,000 years.

Although we think of pagan religions as being without ethics or morals, Nanshe raised very tough questions on judgment day. She stood in front of the people and asked: *Did you comfort the orphans? Care for the elderly and ill? Give shelter to the homeless? Give food to the hungry?*

Many of these ethical precepts were absorbed into Jewish law and Christianity. *Similar:* The Christian notion of St. Peter standing at the pearly gates looking in his book to see what kind of lives people led before he lets them enter heaven.

Also related to autumn being the time of judgment is the Greek goddess of justice, Themis. She is depicted with the scales of justice in her hand, the astrological sign of Libra, which occurs in late September and early October.

How does our holiday of Thanksgiving relate to ancient celebrations?

All over the world, whenever the harvest is brought in, it's a time of dancing, feasting and general joy to celebrate the abundance of food.

Even the ancient Greeks celebrated this event. Thesmophoria, the Greek harvest festival, and the rituals at Eleusis are in the ancient Greek month of Boedromion, in the fall.

The Greeks, in fact, had a wonderful myth that explained the seasons...

Demeter, the goddess of grain and the inventor of agriculture, had a little girl, Persephone, who one fall day was kidnapped by Hades, the god of the underworld. Persephone protested by refusing to eat while in captivity, but she accidentally ate four pomegranate seeds.

Demeter was furious at Zeus for allowing his brother Hades to kidnap her daughter. She refused to let anything grow until Persephone was returned. Persephone was held underground for the entire winter, and was returned to her mother in spring.

Every year, however, she has to go back to the underworld for at least four months because she ate the four pomegranate seeds. This is why we have at least four months of the year when nothing grows.

Where did Hallowe'en originate?

Hallowe'en comes after the harvest, when the earth is quiet. It's a time when pagan cultures believed the veil between life and death was the thinnest, allowing the living to communicate with the dead. The story of Persephone being taken to the underworld may also be related to this theme.

Today, Christians celebrate All Souls Day on the first day of November with prayers for those who have passed on.

The Jewish New Year celebration includes lighting candles for and remembering the dead. And many other cultures have or had similar observances.

In Scandinavia they used to celebrate the Alfablot, or elfblood, a rite where the goddess Hel raised the souls of the dead.

The Celts celebrated Samhain, which was basically the same as our Hallowe'en, as the start of the New Year. It is still celebrated by some people.

The Mexican Day of the Dead comes around the same time. Traditions include picnics in the cemeteries, lighting skull-shaped candles and leaving food for the dead.

Our non-religious Hallowe'en rituals—trick-or-treating, trying to frighten each other and dressing in scary costumes—are also quite ancient. The tradition of skeletons and ghosts on Hallowe'en comes from the sense that this is the best time of year to communicate with the dead.

How do you think we should celebrate the fall today?

Fall is a good time to remember the past and those who have gone before us. It's a great time to make resolutions. I suspect it was when our ancestors resolved to do things differently.

And fall is for making up for wrongs. During the Jewish New Year, people are supposed to think about whom they've wronged during the year and make amends. This can fend off fall depression and help you feel better about your relationships and yourself.

Go out and see the leaves change. Although green leaves are around all summer, the colored leaves fall quickly, reminding us of the temporary nature of beauty and of our own mortality.

I like to read O. Henry's short story *The Last Leaf.* Although it's basically melancholy, it also provides a bright ray of hope.

The story is about a little girl who becomes ill in the fall, and grows obsessed with the notion that she will die when the last leaf falls from the tree by her window. But a friend, an artist who visits her regularly, secretly paints a golden leaf on the wall behind the tree. It stays there all winter...and the little girl does not die.

Source: Merlin Stone, author of *When God Was a Woman,* Harcourt Brace Jovanovich, Orlando, FL.

You Can Communicate With Your Cat

We all know people who treat their pets as if they were human. Silly as it may seem, scientific research has proven time and again that animals and humans really *can* communicate.

With dogs, it's easy. They're social animals who are eager to communicate with just about anyone.

Cats, however, are another story. To communicate with a cat, you have to show respect and speak to him/her *on his own terms.* Only then will your cat open up to you.

A cat's-eye view of the world...

The first step in talking to your cat is to see the world as your cat sees it.

As far as your cat is concerned, he is an independent, solitary creature who sets his own rules. He has no owner. If anything, your cat thinks of you as his property. If you do something your cat likes, he will reward you. On the other hand, if you do something to upset him, *you* will be reprimanded.

How to talk to your cat...

- Observe your cat's behavior patterns. Cats tend to sit in certain places to sun or rest. To talk to your cat, you want to meet him on his own terms while he's relaxing.
- Let your cat rub against you when you enter the room. This is how he claims you. If you don't let your cat do this, he may become angry. He certainly won't talk to you.
- Rub your head against your cat's head. This is the way cats greet each other—they understand it quite well.
- Bring a gift. Cats love toys that move...or you can drag a stuffed toy mouse across the floor. If you really want to get in good with your cat, give him a paper bag or box to climb in.
- Speak softly and warmly. If your cat does not appear to be listening, establish eye contact. But don't stare too intently—that's considered aggressive.

If your cat still ignores you, and you really want him to listen, imitate the harsh, hissing sound cats make when they fight. This will get any cat's attention immediately.

How to listen to your cat...

- Listen to your cat's meows. Each type of meow has a different meaning. You don't have to meow back, but it will help the two of you to bond. Watch what your cat is doing at the time of his meow to help you figure out what it means.

Example: If your cat meows at the door, he obviously wants to go out. If he meows when you're eating, he wants to be fed.

Consider yourself on good terms with your cat when he purrs. Purring is the cat equivalent of a human smile. Your cat is pleased with you and with what's going on around him.

- Watch your cat's tail and eyes. Cats show their feelings by moving their tails in different ways and by the size of their pupils.

A tail straight up is the sign of a happy cat. A slightly bent tail means your actions are in question—he's not so sure about you. A lowered, swishing tail in a standing or crouching cat means you're going to get swatted if you don't stop what you're doing.

In the absence of extreme lighting conditions, large pupils indicate pleasure...narrow pupils, anger.

• Watch your cat's ears. Ears that are back mean displeasure, while ears that are up mean everything is fine and your cat is relaxed.

Source: Jean Craighead George, author of *How to Talk to Your Cat*, Warner Books, 666 Fifth Ave., New York 10103. She has been "owned by" approximately 172 cats of all ages over a 12-year period. She is also a nature writer who has written more than 56 books, many of them for children.

Family Vacations In the Caribbean

Antigua...

• *The Falmouth Harbour Beach Apartments* are near historic Nelson's Dockyard and overlook the harbor. The complex is within walking distance of the beach and a variety of attractions, including the restored Dockyard shopping area. All apartments have kitchens—a great money-saver. Extra roll-away beds and/or a crib can be added. 800-223-5695.

Curacao...

• *Princess Beach Resort and Casino,* a Crowne Plaza Resort. Windsurfing is the specialty here. Instruction is available. There's also a superb beach, two pools, a 12.5-mile protected coral reef for snorkelers—the underwater trail begins right off the resort's beach—and an aquarium nearby. 341 rooms. The all-day children's program includes swimming and other activities. 800-327-3286.

Dominica...

• *The Papillote Wilderness Retreat and Nature Sanctuary* is in a small rain forest. It is a superb base for exploring the Morne Trois Pitons National Park. There's also good diving, snorkeling, river swimming and hot-springs bathing nearby. 809-448-2287.

Grand Cayman...

• *The Cayman Islander* is across the street from Seven-Mile Beach, a spectacular stretch of sand. It's cheaper than most of the beachfront hotels because it's across the main street. Rooms are simple and large. There's a small playground, pool and café. Restaurants and shops are a short walk away. 800-962-2028.

St. Croix...

• *Chenay Bay Beach Resort* is ideal for families that want a secluded setting. There are 50 one-bedroom cottages on 30 acres, and all the rooms have air conditioning. The long, shallow beach nearby is perfect for kids, and there's a windsurfing school, swimming pool and restaurant on the premises. 800-548-4457.

Virgin Gorda, British Virgin Islands...

• *Guavaberry Spring Bay Vacation Homes* is a good deal on an expensive island. There are 16 one- and two-bedroom cottages with a view of Sir Francis Drake's Channel. A popular natural wonder, the Baths, is a short walk, and the beach is just down the hill. The small homes come with kitchens, linens and housekeeping. One-bedroom homes accommodate two...two-bedroom/two-bath units accommodate four. 809-495-5227.

Source: Laura Sutherland, author of *Great Caribbean Family Vacations.* St. Martin's Press.

Movies that Parents and Preteens Can Enjoy Together

In this age of dysfunctional families, functional families don't seem to get much attention. Here are some offbeat videos with resolutions of perplexing family problems.

• *Billie* (1965). The key relationship here is between a mother played by Jane Greer and a daughter played by Patty Duke. *Problem:* Tomboyish daughter wants to join the boys' track team. *Solution:* Mother is more amused than alarmed.

• *Curse of the Cat People* (1944). The "curse" is not a curse at all, but a fantasy benediction for a lonely child, Elizabeth Russell, who finds an imaginary playmate (Simone Simon) in the ethereal form of her father's mysterious first wife. The father (Kent Smith) and the mother (Jane Randolph) eventually come to terms with their child's fantasy, and the friendly spirit departs.

• *Goodbye, My Lady* (1956). A small boy (Brandon de Wilde) and an elderly man (Walter Brennan) form a surrogate family to care for a dog that brings joy to their humble rural lives.

• *Honey, I Shrunk the Kids* (1989). Rick Moranis holds this fragile conceit together with his comic gifts as an embattled nerdy scientist who accidentally reduces his children to tiny figures lost in the domestic landscape. All ends well after many laughs.

• *The Journey of Natty Gann* (1985). Meredith Salenger plays the title role of a young girl who rides the rails during the darkest and most desperate days of the Great Depression in search of her work-seeking father. Along the way, she picks up a life-saving companion, a loyal wolf who protects her from all the human refuse on the open road.

• *Paper Moon* (1973). Ryan O'Neal and his real-life daughter, Tatum O'Neal, make an unlikely father-daughter team when they meet for the first time at the grave of the little girl's mother. Their relationship blossoms despite many obstacles along the way.

• *Searching for Bobby Fischer* (1993). A seven-year-old child chess prodigy (Max Pomeranc) is thrust into competitive chess tournaments by his father (Joe Mantegna) against the wishes of his mother (Joan Allen). Ben Kingsley and Laurence Fishburne play chess "fathers" who pull this way and that on the child's psyche. Based on Fred Waitzkin's book about his son, a prodigy.

Source: Andrew Sarris is professor of film at the School of the Arts at Columbia University, New York, and a film critic for *The New York Observer.*

Wed Romantically Abroad

It's not difficult to arrange a romantic marriage ceremony—or renew your marriage vows—and full reception in Paris or Rome, in the European countryside or in a medieval castle or church. A US firm, Grand Luxe International, will handle the details for you—arranging for everything from flowers and a photographer on up. *Cost:* From $2,900, depending on the services you require. *Contact:* Grand Luxe International, 165 Chestnut St., Allendale, New Jersey 07401.

30

Travel Smarts

Health Hazards of Flying

Although crashing is the most obvious and dramatic threat faced by airline passengers, the risk of going down is so small as to be almost negligible. *More realistic threats:*

• Dry/oxygen-deficient air. Air inside an airliner cabin contains only 2% to 20% of normal relative humidity—and about 25% less oxygen —than air on the ground. Cabin air is about as thin as the air atop a peak 6,000 to 8,000 feet high.

For most passengers, dry, oxygen-poor air presents no particular problems beyond dry skin and thirst. But for those afflicted with certain chronic cardiovascular and respiratory ailments—especially heart disease, asthma and bronchitis—cabin air can be life-threatening. *To avoid trouble...*

• Drink at least one glass of bottled water for each hour you're aloft.

• Avoid alcohol, coffee, tea, colas and other beverages with a diuretic effect.

• Sit with your legs elevated to prevent blood clots in your lower legs—a real possibility if flight-induced dehydration is severe enough to cause your blood to pool and thicken.

• If you begin to feel breathless or faint while flying, ask a flight attendant for oxygen. Federal law requires airliners to keep oxygen tanks on board for just such an emergency. If your breathing difficulty persists, ask if there's a doctor on board.

• Reduced air pressure. As an airliner climbs to its cruising altitude, air pressure inside the cabin falls. Most passengers recognize this phenomenon by the familiar "popping" effect that occurs when air that's inside the ears is squeezed out. Unfortunately, not all the effects of reduced air pressure are as benign. *Dangers:*

• Severe intestinal gas, toothache and—far worse—sudden hemorrhaging of stomach ulcers, ovarian cysts, or surgical incisions.

• Reduced air pressure can also cause the bends in scuba divers who fly too soon after diving. And, a boy wearing a plaster cast developed gangrene when air trapped beneath the cast expanded and cut off circulation in his arm.

To avoid trouble: Wear loose-fitting pants while flying, and avoid beans and other gas-producing foods for several hours before take-off. If you suspect you have any loose fillings, have them repaired before your departure. If you've been diagnosed with ulcers or ovarian cysts, or if you've recently had surgery, consult a doctor before flying.

Do not fly with a plaster cast. Never fly within 12 hours of scuba diving (24 hours if you've dived below 30 feet or have been diving for several days).

• Contaminated air. Long notorious for poor ventilation and stale air, airline cabins have gotten even stuffier in recent years.

In the interest of cost-cutting, cabin air on most flights is now being recirculated for 12 minutes at a time.

In the past, cabin air was recirculated for only three minutes at a time before fresh air was pumped in.

Result: Cabin air is depleted of oxygen and laden with disease-causing germs, carbon dioxide, carbon monoxide and other contaminants—especially on flights where smoking is permitted.

Stale, contaminated air can cause coughing, shortness of breath and headaches, as well as eye infections, colds, the flu and even lung cancer.

To avoid trouble: Use a saline nasal spray to keep your nostrils clean and moist (the greater the moisture in your nostrils, the more effective they are at filtering contaminants from the air). On smoking flights, sit as far as possible from smokers.

• Radiation. Modern airliners fly in the upper reaches of the atmosphere, where cosmic and solar radiation are particularly intense. The longer and more frequent your flights, the greater your exposure. In most cases, this extra exposure causes no apparent problems. Under certain conditions, however, it can cause birth defects, infertility, and cancer.

To play it safe: Pregnant women should avoid flying during the first trimester, when rapidly dividing cells in the fetus are especially vulnerable to radiation.

Persons who spend more than 11 hours a week on an airplane should monitor their radiation exposure with a radiation film badge (dosimeter) worn at all times while aloft.

Frequent flyers should have regular check-ups by a doctor who specializes in aviation medicine.

For a list of flight doctors in your area, contact the Aerospace Medical Association at 703-739-2240 in Arlington, Virginia.

Source: Farrol S. Kahn, founder of the Aviation Health Institute in Oxford, England, and author of *Why Flying Endangers Your Health: Hidden Health Hazards of Air Travel*, Aurora Press, Box 573, Santa Fe, NM 87504.

Better Car-Rental Rates

Quote the advertised discount directly from the company's ad when calling the reservation number. *Problem:* Reservation agents often will not volunteer the best available price up front. *Helpful:* Mention the promotion's discount code, usually listed in small print beneath the boldly displayed rate, or in the description of the terms and conditions of the rental.

Source: Ed Perkins, editor, *Consumer Reports Travel Letter*, 101 Truman Ave., Yonkers, NY 10703.

Airfare-Bargain Traps

Airfare "bargains" are often not what they seem. *Example:* One airline recently offered a discount on companion tickets, but the base fare rate was higher than normal. *Self-defense:* Find a smart travel agent with access to reservation computers that can track prices...and delay buying a ticket until 14 days before your flight, *except during holiday periods*. For holiday travel, book early to be sure of getting a seat. Insist that your travel agent continue to inform you about all deals that become available to your destination.

Source: Herbert J. Teison, editor, *Travel Smart*, 40 Beechdale Rd., Dobbs Ferry, NY 10522.

Cheaper Travel

Ask about visitor transit-system passes. Many public transit systems in major cities sell passes that permit unlimited or extensive travel on buses, subways, trains and trolleys. Some are issued by the day, others cover multiple days or a week.

The price is more than one daily round-trip but can add up to significant savings—and you won't have to fumble for exact change each time you ride. For information, write, call, or visit the city tourist-information office.

Source: *Consumer Reports Travel Letter*, 101 Truman Ave., Yonkers, NY 10703.

Secrets of a Much More Comfortable Flight

Airline travel may be fast, but it is not always comfortable. Too often, travelers, especially those seated in coach, are crammed into confining seats, fed factory-produced meals and confronted with delays or lost luggage. Flights can be made more bearable, however, if you know how to work the system.

Getting a good seat...

Most travelers don't want to sit in the middle seat of a row. But if you're late checking in for a crowded flight, you're almost certain of getting one. *Problem:* Airlines automatically assign aisle and window seats first, even if the two passengers in a row are traveling together.

You can improve your chances of getting an end seat by asking the agent at the check-in counter to search the passenger list for two travelers with the same last name in the same row. Request the middle seat in that row. Chances are the other two passengers are related and will want to sit together, leaving you either the window or aisle seat.

Storing luggage...

Finding room for your carry-on luggage is always challenging. It is best, however, not to wait until you arrive at your seat to store your bags. Instead, put them in the first overhead compartment after you pass through the first-class cabin.

These compartments will likely be empty, since they are for the last passengers that board. In addition, you won't have to carry your bags to your seat as you enter or to the front as you exit the plane.

Better baggage handling...

Bags that have first-class or priority tags attached are usually first to come off the plane into the baggage claim area. Even if you're traveling in coach, you can benefit from this quick service by getting one of these tags.

Sometimes the airlines will give you a first-class tag if you ask for it. If not, try to find an old one from any airline. You can even make one up in advance by having a brightly colored card stamped with the word "priority" and laminated at a local printer. This will attract the attention of the baggage handlers.

Getting an upgrade...

Just because you have enough frequent-flier miles to qualify for a better seat doesn't always mean you'll get one, especially if the flight is crowded.

In fact, you may actually stand a better chance of getting one if the flight is overbooked. In this situation, airlines commonly offer free tickets to passengers turning in their tickets. If you hear this announced, immediately notify the check-in personnel that you're still interested in upgrading.

Reason: A surprising number of first-class travelers give up their seats for free tickets, opening up space in the forward cabin.

A more comfortable flight...

Strong sunlight is a common problem that travelers face when flying during the day. It often forces you to travel with the shade down. To avoid the sunny side when traveling eastbound, request an A, B, or C seat. When traveling westbound, request a seat on the other side of the cabin.

Source: Randy Petersen, who travels up to 400,000 miles a year and is editor of *InsideFlier*, a magazine for frequent fliers, 4715-C Town Center Dr., Colorado Springs 80916.

Developing Film

When having film developed, attach a label with your name and address to the container itself in case the envelope is lost.

Source: Professional photofinishers quoted in *The New York Times.*

Cutting Costs When Traveling to Europe

The costs of traveling to Europe can be cut without sacrificing comfort. All it takes is a willingness to ask questions and a basic knowledge of how the travel industry works. Using this strategy, which for example might involve traveling off-season, can trim 25% to 50% off the price of hotels, airfares, and car rentals.

Airfares...

There are big advantages to going through a strong travel agent. Many have tremendous buying power that allows them to pass along cut rates to their regular clients.

Or, consider a tour package. It is a great way to trim 25% or more off the cost of hotels and airfares.

Or, check for deals on airfares in your Sunday paper. Important: Don't bother calling on Monday. The deals are probably already booked up by then. *Better:* Call past fare promoters on Thursday before they send in their ads to the Sunday papers.

Hotels...

•Stay away from the center of town. Hotels away from the tourist centers are 15% to 40% cheaper than downtown hotels. Most major cities offer great public transportation so it isn't difficult to get around. Consider staying in small towns surrounding major cities. These usually have easy, inexpensive access to the more expensive tourist centers.

•Negotiate. Americans usually aren't comfortable bargaining about price. But it is a way of life in Europe. Most hotels, in fact, are willing to negotiate their rates, especially if you're planning to stay for at least three days. So long as there isn't a convention in town, you might get a break of 20% to 50%.

•Ask for the corporate rate. Virtually all hotels cut prices by at least 20% for business travelers.

Transportation...

Europe's special railway passes generally pay off if you're traveling far or at a fast pace. Buying individual tickets may be best for intercity or side trips.

Train travel may be best for a side trip. In most cases, purchase a second-class ticket. The cost is about a third less than first-class and the ride is still comfortable. Only in Italy, Spain, and Portugal, where second-class coaches get crowded, is it worth paying the premium.

Car rentals in Europe are always expensive. High local taxes is one reason. Some countries, however, traditionally offer lower rates. Good deals are usually found in Spain, Luxembourg, Ireland, and England. Also, check local rental companies. Sometimes they offer better rates than the big international firms. And always try to rent for a week on an unlimited mileage basis. The per-day charge is generally exorbitantly higher.

More money-savers...

•Entry fees for museums can be pretty high. Many major cities, such as Paris, sell museum cards that offer unlimited entry into its major museums for one low price. Some museums also set aside one day a week when admission is free.

•Tax refunds. European countries charge a value added tax of about 15% for most items. Visitors can get this back. The quickest way is to use a credit card. Ask for payment and VAT refund slips at the same time. If the store refuses, ask for specific details on VAT refunds for the country.

•Theater. In London, the discount ticket booth in Leicester Square sells tickets when available at half price. Many theater box offices also sell tickets at a discount that have been returned just before show time.

Source: John Whitman, who has logged more than two million miles exploring how to travel on a budget. He is the author of *The Best European Travel Tips,* published by Meadowbrook Press, available from the author, Box 202, Long Lake, MN 55356.

Jet Lag Smarts

To minimize jet lag, schedule important activities for when you will likely have the most energy. *High-energy times:* Evenings after jetting east...the next morning after jetting west.

Source: *Jet Smart* by Diana Fairchild, former flight attendant, Flyana Rhyme, Inc., Box 300, Makawao, Maui, HI 96768.

Traffic Tickets

1. Keep talking. The longer an officer chats with you before writing a ticket, the better your chances of getting off with only a warning. To buy yourself as much time as possible, pull your car off the shoulder as far as you can so the officer can talk to you without fear of becoming roadkill.

2. Know his place. Using a policeman's correct rank will make it seem that you're somehow involved with law enforcement or the military. Check his sleeve; if it has three or more stripes, call him "Sergeant" or "Sarge." If it has one or two stripes, call him "Corporal." If you see no stripes and he's a state cop, call him "Trooper." If he has no stripes and he's driving a county sheriff car, call him "Deputy." If you're not sure, call him "Officer."

3. Don't make a scene. The less an officer remembers about you and the stop, the better your lawyer's chances of getting you off the hook. Most tickets get reduced, or won by the defendant in court, because the cop doesn't remember the specifics of the stop.

Source: Sgt. James M. Eagan, retired New York State Trooper, author, *A Speeder's Guide to Avoiding Tickets.*

Nonsmoking Seats

Nonsmoking seats are *not guaranteed* on overseas flights on non-US airlines. US carriers must provide a nonsmoking seat to every passenger who asks for one, except standbys. International carriers usually set aside a limited number of nonsmoking seats on a first-come, first-serve basis. Policies keep changing—ask your travel agent before booking.

Source: *Condé Nast Traveler,* 360 Madison Ave., New York 10017.

Headphones In-Flight

Wear headphones in-flight—even if you're not listening to music. With headphones on, you're less likely to be disturbed by a talkative seatmate.

Source: *Office On the Go: Tools, Tips and Techniques for Every Business Traveler* by Scottsdale, Arizona computer consultant Kim Baker, Prentice-Hall, Route 9W, Englewood Cliffs, NJ 07632.

Easier Air Travel

A single airline flight number does not mean it is a nonstop flight—or even that you won't have to change planes to get to your destination. Airlines often label connecting flights as if they were on a single plane. Changing planes entails hassle and increases the risk of lost or delayed luggage. *Self-defense:* When making reservations, ask the agent if the flight requires you to change planes—most will not volunteer such information. If it does, ask if there's another, equally convenient flight available that lets you stay on the same plane throughout.

Source: *Consumer Reports Travel Letter,* 101 Truman Ave., Yonkers, NY 10703.

Flying Comfort

Door rows: Most wide-body jets have mid-cabin doors, and the seats right behind them have extra leg room due to the aisle to the door. *Exit rows:* Most narrow-body jets have mid-body emergency exits—with aisles that provide extra leg room. *Bulkhead rows:* If you have a seat right next to a cabin divider, nobody in front of you will be able to recline a seat into you.

Source: Ed Perkins, editor, *Consumer Reports Travel Letter*, 101 Truman Ave., Yonkers, NY 10703.

Safety Away from Home

Bring a smoke detector when you travel. This will protect against any hotel that—in violation of state laws—does not have smoke detectors in rooms...or has smoke detectors that have dead batteries. *Also helpful:* A portable burglar alarm that trips when someone tries to enter your room.

Source: *Office on the Go: Tools, Tips and Techniques for Every Business Traveler* by Kim Baker, Scottsdale, Arizona computer expert and consultant. Prentice-Hall, Route 9W, Sylvan Ave., Englewood Cliffs, NJ 07632.

Travel Advisories

Travel warnings from the State Department advise travelers about countries that are dangerous for Americans to visit. A warning means conditions are potentially threatening to American travelers—and the US cannot help them in emergencies. Warnings are updated every six months—but more often if events warrant. *For copies of warnings:* Send a self-addressed, stamped, business-sized envelope to Bureau of Consular Affairs, Room 4811 NS, Department of State, Washington, DC 20520. To check on a specific country: Call 202-647-5225, Monday through Friday, 9 a.m. to 5 p.m., Eastern Time.

Always Carry Your License

Always carry your driver's license when driving a car. *Risky:* Assuming that you have 24 hours to produce your driver's license after you are stopped for a driving violation. *Problem:* If you don't have your driver's license, you probably don't have any other identification either ...so you could be brought to jail. There's more flexibility with car registrations. It's generally OK to have a *photocopy* of your registration in your car and keep the original at home—or in your wallet. Most states accept a photocopy to prove ownership—call your state motor vehicle department to be sure. If your car is stolen and the thief is stopped by the police, the police will be suspicious when the name on the registration is different from that of the driver.

Source: Jim Eagan is a retired New York State police supervisor and author of *A Speeder's Guide to Avoiding Tickets,* Avon Books, 1350 Avenue of the Americas, New York 10019.

How to Get More Out Of Your Travel

- Take along a small tape recorder when you travel. This is easier than jotting notes or trying to find the time to keep a diary.
- Interview people you meet along the way. Ask them all about their lives, occupations and backgrounds. This will preserve the facts and actual voices of interesting people you meet.
- Tape guided tours. Guides give out lots of information that is forgotten during the excitement of a tour but can be enjoyed later.

How to Make the Most Of Your Time in Unfamiliar Towns

- Be a part-time tourist. An hour or two between appointments gives you enough time to check out the local aquarium, museum, library, antique district, park or waterfront. Major tourist attractions are often located near enough to a city's business district for you to mix meetings with pleasure conveniently.
- Have a great meal. Do some advance research, and equip yourself with a list of the best restaurants in each city on your itinerary. Then, when your free time coincides with a mealtime,

invest instead in a delightful hour of gourmet adventure.

•Look up old friends. Perhaps you can share that gourmet meal with a college friend you haven't seen in years, or surprise an uncle or cousin with a call or visit.

•Take pictures. If you're into photography, you know that a new environment frequently yields new visions and special scenes and subjects. Keep your eyes open and your camera ready.

•Go gift shopping. On autumn trips, carry a list of holiday gift ideas for friends and family. Use even a spare 15 minutes to pop in on the local boutiques and specialty shops. Charge and send your purchases, and when you get home they'll be there, all ready for your December giving.

•Bring busywork. When you're too tired to kill time on the move—or it's raining or the neighborhood is threatening or everything is closed—you should have something to do in your hotel room other than watch TV and order room service. Try catching up on a pile of periodicals or going through seed catalogues.

Source: Letty Cottin Pogrebin, author of five books including *Family Politics,* McGraw-Hill, New York.

Making the Most Of Travel Time

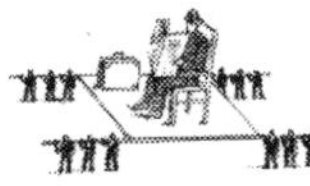

Some people claim that they can work on airplanes, trains or boats, but you may not be one of them. If you, too, are unable to concentrate while traveling:

•Go to sleep. Traveling is a natural soporific. Catching up on your sleep will give you an edge when you arrive.

•Find someone to talk with. Walk around and see if anyone who looks interesting has a copy of the Official Airlines Guide (which frequent travelers carry) or other travel guides. Start talking about travel, and you'll learn a few things.

•Clean out your wallet or briefcase. This is something you always mean to do but never get around to.

•Write letters. They don't take much concentration.

Killing Time Creatively At Airports

•Make phone calls. Check into your office, pick up a dozen phone messages and return eight calls before being driven from the public phone by the furious stares of others waiting to use it.

•Write letters or pay bills. Bring notepaper, envelopes, bills and your checkbook. Use your briefcase as a desk.

•Shop for the unexpected. Airport gift shops are notoriously glitzy. And at first glance, the merchandise in every gift shop looks alike except for the city etched into the beer mugs. But you may well find a Pierre Cardin belt at a bargain price in Cleveland, live lobsters in Boston and sourdough bread in San Francisco.

•Read indulgently. Buy a spy novel if you usually lean toward business books. Pick up a foreign magazine and test your French. Indulge in a crossword puzzle magazine or cartoon book. Read the local papers.

•Get a haircut or shoeshine. Men have the edge here. Although airport barber shops sometimes advertise "unisex," I've never seen a woman in any of them. Bootblacks will gladly shine a woman's shoes.

•Jog. With throngs of people running to catch their planes, no one will know you are just jogging along the concourses to kill time. Leave your coat and carry-on bag under someone's watchful eye while you run.

•People-watch. This is a surprisingly diverting pastime, especially for hyperactive types who don't often stop to observe the world around them.

•Eavesdrop. Airports are great places to tune in on some fascinating conversations—one as melodramatic as a soap opera dialogue, another as funny as a Mel Brooks sketch.

•Think. If you're uninspired by the above alternatives, you can simply stare out at the landing field, letting your mind go blank. Or you can give yourself a specific problem to mull over. Sometimes the brain does a better job of thinking at rest than it does under pressure.

Source: Letty Cottin Pogrebin, author of five books including *Family Politics,* McGraw-Hill, New York.

Saving Time and Money at Hotels

• When you arrive at a hotel, check your bags. Then go to the pay telephone in the lobby and call the hotel. Ask to have your reservation confirmed, give them your charge card number and go on your way. You'll sidestep convention check-in lines.

• To avoid the long check-out line after the convention, go down to the desk very early in the morning, before official checkout time, and check out. You won't have to turn in your room key, and you can still use your room until official checkout time (usually around 1 p.m.).

• Don't stay glued to your hotel room if you're waiting for a call. If you ask, the hotel operator will transfer your calls to another room, interrupt the call you're on for a more important one or hold any calls while you run out for a soda.

• Save money by not paying for things you didn't order. Don't charge anything to your hotel room. It's too confusing when you're checking out to verify the list of room charges. And it's only too easy for the hotel to make a mistake. If you don't charge anything at all, you'll know that extra items on your bill can't be yours. How to do it: Use your telephone credit card for calls, and pay cash for room service, laundry, etc. Use your credit card for food.

• Don't depend only on the hotel for services such as typing, film developing, etc. Call the local convention bureau. It's specifically set up to help out-of-town businesspeople, and every city has one.

Source: Dr. Barbara A. Pletcher, executive director of the National Association for Professional Saleswomen, is author of *Travel Sense,* Ace Books, New York.

Don't Be a Victim of Hotel Overbooking

It's not always the hotel's fault. Sometimes guests overstay. (Hawaii is the only state that allows hotels to compel guests to leave on time.) But hotels generally accept more reservations than they have rooms, betting that some reservation-holders won't show. Sometimes they bet wrong.

To keep from being a loser:

• Plan trips sufficiently in advance to get written confirmation of reservations. That gives you something extra to argue with should you need it. If there's no time for a written confirmation, try to get a confirmation number when the reservation is made.

• Get "guaranteed" reservations with a credit card. This does obligate you to pay for the room even if you can't make it. However, it reduces the incentive a hotel clerk has to sell your room to somebody else. American Express has an "assured reservations" program. Under it, the hotel that "walks" you has to pay for the first night's lodging in a comparable hotel room nearby, for a long-distance call to inform the office or family where you will be, and for transportation to the substitute hotel. Several chains have a similar policy.

• Arrive early in the afternoon, when last night's guests have checked out, but before the bulk of new arrivals.

• Take your case to a higher-up—probably the assistant manager on duty—since it's unlikely that the desk clerk will find a room after telling you he has none. The assistant manager might be persuaded to "find" one of the rooms that inevitably are set aside by luxury hotels for emergencies such as the arrival of a VIP. Make a loud fuss, some people suggest. This often works, since hotels try to avoid drawing public attention to their overbooking practices.

• If neither raving and ranting nor quiet persuasion moves the assistant manager, insist that he call other comparable hotels to get you a room, and at the same or lower price. The better hotels will usually do their best.

How to Save on Air Travel

•Fly between 9 p.m. and 7 p.m. Most airlines have cheaper night flights, especially on long distances.

•Plan business trips so that the schedule qualifies the business traveler for vacation excursion fares (discounts up to 50%).

•Fly out-of-the-way carriers looking for new business.

•Make sales or service trips, or tours of branch offices, using the unlimited mileage tickets offered by some airlines.

Source: Harold Seligman, president, Management Alternatives, Stamford, CT.

Getting a Good Airplane Seat

Getting the seat you prefer on an airplane has become an increasing problem.

•If you're assigned to a seat you don't like, go back to the desk when all the prereserved seats are released (usually about 15 minutes before flight time). Prime seats for passengers who didn't show up are available then.

•If you discover on the plane that you don't like your seat, don't wait until the plane takes off to find a better one. Look around the plane, and the second before they close the door, head for the empty seat of your choice. Don't wait until the seat-belt sign goes on.

•Prereserve a single seat on a nonjumbo where the seats are three across and you'll increase the odds of getting an empty seat next to you.

•Ask for a window or aisle seat in a row where the window or aisle is already reserved by a single. The middle seat between two singles is least likely to fill up.

Know When Not to Fly

Avoid flying if you have had:
•A heart attack within four weeks of takeoff.
•Surgery within two weeks.
•A deep-diving session within 24 hours.
Don't fly at all if you have:
•Severe lung problems.
•Uncontrolled hypertension.
•Epilepsy not well controlled.
•Severe anemia.
•A pregnancy beyond 240 days or threatened by miscarriage.

Source: *Pocket Flight Guide/Frequent Flyer Package.*

Your Ears and Air Travel

•Avoid flying with a cold or other respiratory infection. A cold greatly increases the chances of your suffering discomfort, additional fluid buildup, severe pain or even rupture.

•Take decongestants. If you must fly with a cold, or if you regularly suffer discomfort or pain on descent, decongestants can give real relief. For maximum effect, time them to coincide with the descent (which begins half an hour to an hour before landing). Use both oral decongestants and a spray for best results. *Suggested timing:* Take quick-acting oral decongestants two to three hours before landing or slow-release tablets six to eight hours in advance. Use nasal spray one hour before landing. *Caution:* If you have hypertension or a heart condition, check with your cardiologist about taking decongestants.

•Don't smoke or drink. Smoking irritates the nasal area, and alcohol dilates the blood vessels, causing the tissues to swell.

•Try the Valsalva maneuver. While holding your nose closed, try to blow through it as though you were blowing your nose. This will blow air through the ears. Do this gently and repeatedly as the plane descends. *Warning:* Don't use this method if you have a cold, as you'll be blowing infection back into the middle ear. Use the tried-and-true routines of yawning and swallowing instead. They can be quite effective if the problem is not too severe. Chew gum and suck candy. *Aim:* To activate the swallowing mechanism in order to open the eustachian tubes.

•If your ears are stuffed after landing, follow the same routine. Keep on with decongestants and gentle Valsalvas. Temporary hearing loss and stuffiness may persist for three to four weeks. If the symptoms are really annoying, a doctor can lance the drum to drain the fluid. If pain persists for more than a day, see a doctor.

•See a doctor before flying if you have a bad cold, especially if you have a history of ear pain when flying. If you absolutely must fly, the doctor can open the eardrum and insert a small ventilation tube that will allow the pressure to equalize. The tube should eject by itself in a few weeks...or you can go back to your doctor.

Source: Neville W. Carmical, MD, attending otolaryngologist, St.Luke's-Roosevelt Hospital Center, New York.

Coping with High Altitudes

One out of three travelers at altitudes of 7,000 feet above sea level (Vail, Colorado, for example) experiences some symptoms of altitude sickness. By 10,000 feet (Breckenridge, Colorado), everyone is affected. *Common complaints:* Headaches, nausea, weakness, lack of coordination and insomnia.

To minimize the effects:

•Take it easy the first two or three days. Get plenty of rest and don't schedule vigorous activities.

•Eat a little less than usual. Avoid hard-to-digest foods such as red meat and fats. Carbohydrates are good.

•Drink more liquids than usual. (Breathing harder in dry air causes you to lose water vapor.)

•Avoid alcohol, smoking and tranquilizers. Their effects are compounded at high altitudes.

Flyer's Health Secrets

•Taking your mind off the motion can help your body restore equilibrium without drugs. *How to do it:* Close your eyes, or concentrate on a spot in front of you, and hold your head as steady as possible. Then focus your attention on your breathing or on alternately tensing and relaxing your muscles. Continue to concentrate until the nausea has vanished.

•The low air pressure in an airplane's interior can aggravate some medical problems unless precautions are taken. Gas trapped in the colon can expand, causing severe discomfort or cramps. People with heart or lung diseases should check with their doctor in advance to discuss requesting supplemental oxygen.

•Don't fly with a serious sinus problem. If a sinus is blocked, the trapped air inside expands and can lead to serious infection. Improve drainage prior to ascent and descent with decongestants or nose drops.

•The arid atmosphere of pressurized cabins encourages evaporation from the skin's surface, drying the skin. *Remedies:* Avoid beverages that contain alcohol or caffeine (they both have a diuretic action). Drink plenty of water during the trip and afterward.

Getting to and from the airport:

•Arrive early to avoid stress.

•Schedule an appointment at the airport. If you're in a strange city, try to get your last appointment of the day to meet you there a few hours before your plane leaves. Why should you be the one to do all the running?

•Join an airport club. Most airlines have them. Choose the one that belongs to the principal carrier flying from your city. Then you can relax in comfort while you wait for your flight. *Benefits:* Special services to members, such as a separate check-in desk.

Source: *Healthwise* and Commission on Emergency Medical Services, American Medical Association, Chicago.

Car Rental Tips

Car-rental competition is hotter than ever, especially among the small intracity and intrastate firms. *What to keep tabs on:*

•Does the price include fuel? Very few still do. Dry rate means the customer buys the gas. Find out where gas is cheapest. Fill up there, too, before dropping the car off.

•Special restrictions or charges for one-way rentals.

•Special weekend or weekly rates.

•When luggage space is important, make sure you're getting a large enough vehicle. (A compact or intermediate model may still be suitable.)

•Extra charge if a larger car is substituted. There shouldn't be one if the rental firm does the switching.

•Special corporate discount. Comparison shopping on this could hold surprises.

•Special fly/drive packages offered by airlines.

•The rental firm's policy in case of car trouble.

•In case of an accident, does the contract include primary liability coverage? (In California and Florida, only secondary coverage is required.)

Source: *Medical Economics,* Oradell, NJ.

How to Avoid Vacation Time-Sharing Traps

Some owners of time-shares in beach-and ski-area condominiums are becoming disenchanted. *Reasons:* They find that committing themselves to the same dates at the same resort every year is too restricting. Or they find they overpaid.

To avoid problems:

•Locate one of the companies that act as brokers for swapping time-shares for owners of resort properties in different areas.

•Don't pay more than 10 times the going rate for a good hotel or apartment rental in the same area at the same time of year.

•Get in early on a new complex. Builders usually sell the first few apartments for less.

•Choose a one- or two-bedroom unit. Smaller or larger ones are harder to swap or sell.

•Deal with experienced developers who have already worked out maintenance and management problems.

•Pick a time in the peak season. It will be more negotiable.

•Look for properties that are protected by zoning or geography. Vail, Colorado, for example, has a moratorium on further time-share development.

•Beware of resorts that are hard to reach or are too far off the beaten track. Your time-shares will be harder to rent, swap or sell.

If Your Tour is a Disappointment

To get your money back:

•Go back to the travel agency or sponsor who promoted it with your evidence of a breach of contract.

•Keep all brochures or detailed itinerary that constitutes your contract.

•Keep evidence that the promises were not kept. *Example:* Out-of-pocket receipts, pictures you took of your hotel or room, etc.

•If you come to an impasse on the terms of the tour agreement, check with the American Society of Travel Agents in New York, for an explanation of standardized industry terms (first class, deluxe, etc.).

•*Last resort:* File a complaint with either small claims court or civil court. *Advantage with either:* You don't have to retain a lawyer. Judgments are made quickly.

•*Final action:* Class-action suits have been successful in cases where it's unclear who is at fault. Sometimes it's your only hope for recovering anything from wholesalers and suppliers that are hard to reach.

• *Warning:* If your complaint is with a travel agency that went out of business while you were on tour (such things do happen), your recovery chances are virtually nil against that business, no matter how far you take your case.

Source: Patricia Simko, Assistant Attorney General, New York State Bureau of Consumer Frauds, New York.

How to Get a Passport Faster

If you seek a passport at the height of the tourist season, you'll inevitably face a long wait. But whenever you go for your passport, you can ease the delay by doing the following:

•Go to the passport office in person.

•*Bring:* Your airline ticket, two passport pictures, proof of citizenship (an old passport, voter registration or birth certificate), a piece of identification with your photo on it and the fee.

•Give the passport office a good reason why you are rushed.

If your passport is lost or stolen when you're traveling abroad, here's what to do:

•Immediately notify the local police and the US embassy or consulate. An overnight replacement is sometimes possible in an emergency.

•To hasten this process, know your passport number.

•*Next best:* Have a valid identification document with you. A photostat of your passport is best.

Source: *Travel Smart.*

If You Lose Your Passport Or Credit Cards Overseas

•If your passport is lost or stolen, contact the nearest US embassy or consulate immediately. A consul will interview you.

•If he is satisfied of your US citizenship and identity, a new passport can be quickly issued. Most Americans are able to satisfy the consular officer on the basis of a personal interview and presentation of identification that was not stolen or lost with the passport.

•In some cases, the consul may find it necessary to wire the Department of State to verify that you had been issued a previous passport.

•The consul will be able to refer you to local offices of the major credit cards and travelers checks to report losses.

•If you lose all your money, the embassy will assist you in having funds transferred from a friend or relative in the US through State Department channels.

•The embassy will *not* lend you money.

Currency-Exchange Strategies

Even though the dollar has been strong, a sudden drop could leave you vulnerable while overseas. *To protect yourself:*

•Take about 40% of your travelers checks in commission-free foreign currency and the rest in dollars.

•Prepay your foreign hotel in its own currency to lock in the current rate.

•If you fly first class, business class, or on the Concorde, find out if you can pay for the return trip in foreign currency.

•When shopping overseas, ask for prices in the local currency. Then request a discount if you intend to pay that way.

What to Do If You're Arrested Overseas

In a sample year, 3,000 Americans were arrested in 97 foreign countries for offenses ranging from narcotics and disorderly conduct to murder. *If arrested, here's what you should do:*

•Don't panic. Keep your wits about you.

•Ask to contact the US embassy. Be polite but persistent in making this request.

When a consular officer comes to see you in jail, here's what he or she can do for you:

•Provide you with a list of local attorneys.

•Call an attorney for you if you are unable to make a call.

•Notify relatives or friends at home.

•Make sure your basic health and safety needs are being met.

•Make sure you're not being discriminated against because you're an American.

•Do not expect the embassy to get you out of jail. You are subject to the laws of the country you're visiting.

Source: John P. Caulfield, Bureau of Consular Affairs, US Department of State, Washington, DC.

Index

B

C

D

E

F

G

H

I

J

K

L

M

N

O

P

Q

R

S

T

U

V

W

Y

Z